The Taming of Free Speech

LAURA WEINRIB

The Taming of Free Speech

America's Civil Liberties Compromise

Harvard University Press

Cambridge, Massachusetts, and London, England

2016

First printing

Library of Congress Cataloging-in-Publication Data

Names: Weinrib, Laura M., author.
Title: The taming of free speech : America's civil liberties compromise /
    Laura Weinrib.
Description: Cambridge, Massachusetts : Harvard University Press, 2016. |
    Includes bibliographical references and index.
Identifiers: LCCN 2016010531 | ISBN 9780674545717 (alk. paper)
Subjects: LCSH: Freedom of speech—United States—History—20th century. |
    Employee rights—United States—History—20th century. | Civil rights—United
    States—History—20th century. | Labor movement—United States—History—
    20th century. | American Civil Liberties Union.
Classification: LCC KF4772 .W44 2016 | DDC 342.7308/53—dc23 LC record available at
    https://lccn.loc.gov/2016010531

For my parents, Estee and Richard Weinrib

Contents

The Taming of Free Speech

Introduction

CIVIL LIBERTIES once were radical. In the early decades of the twentieth century, labor partisans linked them to a *right of agitation:* a right of workers who were vulnerable in isolation to band together for a common goal. Civil liberties, they insisted, entitled workers to cease their work and to urge their fellow workers to follow them. In a legal culture dense with rules and regulations to protect private property and promote individual autonomy, the architects of the modern civil liberties movement claimed a right "prior to and independent of constitutions," secured without recourse to law.[1]

This book is the story of how the radical vision of civil liberties was born and how, very quickly, it transformed. At its center is the American Civil Liberties Union (ACLU), which framed popular and judicial understandings of civil liberties during the interwar period and after. When the ACLU was founded in the aftermath of the First World War, it declared itself an adjunct of the radical labor movement. Its defense of free speech was motivated by a deep-seated distrust of state institutions stemming from decades of hostile treatment of unions in the courts as well as the political branches; the rights it championed were the rights to picket, boycott, and strike. The ACLU's great achievement over the interwar years was to connect those rights to the American constitutional tradition. At first, conservatives complained that the fight for free speech was "just a camouflage to put over the radical movement." But their criticisms soon subsided. As labor militancy succumbed to state suppression and economic prosperity, the ACLU's leaders reoriented their agenda around the importance of personal freedom

1

and the value of democratic debate. In the process, they unhooked their redistributive aspirations from the freedom to espouse them. In the ACLU's mature approach, only the latter fell within the proper ambit of civil liberties advocacy.[2]

The new platform found eager adherents across the ideological spectrum. During the 1930s, business groups, the organized bar, and government officials all rallied around expressive freedom. They celebrated a concept of civil liberties grounded in the Constitution and enforced by the courts. And as the New Deal drew to a close, the United States Supreme Court inscribed their convictions into constitutional law.

The judiciary's embrace of the modern civil liberties program was a crucial moment in American history, but it was not a straightforward victory for progressive ideals. The ACLU had refashioned free speech as a neutral precept instead of a cover for particular economic aims. In so doing, it had produced a potent tool for the Right. Civil liberties protected conservatives as well as radicals, industry as well as labor. There was power in speech, and all insisted on their chance to seize its reins.

✦ ✦ ✦

By the end of the 1930s, the term *civil liberties* in the ACLU's title meant very nearly what it does today. Although it lacked "technical legal" significance, it was a "phrase of popular currency" that extended to freedom of speech and religion, the procedural rights of criminal defendants, and perhaps reproductive autonomy. The rights it encompassed were conventionally, albeit contentiously, described as *negative* rather than *positive*. In other words, civil liberties were asserted to block state power.[3]

Civil liberties were not always understood in that way. In fact, for the first half of the nation's history—until the institutional precursor to the ACLU introduced it into common usage during the First World War—barely anyone used the term at all. In its singular form, *civil liberty* had a long and storied history. For the great nineteenth-century jurist Francis Lieber, who linked it to "man's twofold character, as an individual and social being," civil liberty required "checks against undue interference, whether this be from individuals, from masses, or from government." That is, if civil liberty was a restraint on popular will, it was also a restraint on unbridled personal freedom. By the same token, *Black's Law Dictionary* opened its entry on civil liberty with a citation to the distinguished English jurist William Blackstone, who had explained in his *Commentaries* that the law, "though it diminishes the natural, increases the civil liberty of mankind." Civil liberty was more than a shield against the state. It required the exercise of state authority to rectify legal harms, whether by legislation or by common law. That duality was appealing to Progressive Era thinkers sympathetic to state power. Champions of civil liberty sometimes decried "excessive individualism" in "ownership," as well as licentious speech. Still, there was little to bind the historical notion of civil liberty to the right of agitation or its liberal successor. In its application, it was closely connected to the very traditions that later civil liberties advocates abjured. As the esteemed legal scholar Ernst Freund observed in his treatise on the police power, "Civil liberty is the chief means of acquiring property."[4]

The interwar activists and theorists who imagined civil liberties as vehicles to advance personal freedoms worked to ground their demands, if not their vocabulary, in historical understanding. In tracing the lineage of the rights they promoted, they often began with John Milton's *Areopagitica,* a tract against licensing and censorship that has made its way into some of the Supreme Court's canonical endorsements of free speech. They continued on to Montesquieu, who proclaimed that "words do not constitute an overt act," and (crossing the Atlantic) the celebrated 1735 trial of John Peter Zenger, which fostered a truth defense to charges of seditious libel. They pointed to early state constitutions that safeguarded expressive and religious freedom, and to the foundational amendments to the United States Constitution, which would someday be called the Bill of Rights. Throughout the nineteenth century, scholars and statesmen hailed the constitutional commitment to personal freedom as fundamental to American democracy. In his eminent treatise *Constitutional Limitations*, Thomas Cooley wrote that the "repression of full and free discussion is dangerous in any government resting upon the will of the people." Even Herbert Spencer's *Social Statics*—made an emblem of laissez-faire constitutionalism in Justice Oliver Wendell Holmes Jr.'s dissent in *Lochner v. New York*—contained a sweeping defense of free speech.[5]

In practice, however, personal freedoms were always subject to significant limitations. The infamous 1798 Alien and Sedition Acts authorized the suppression of much anti-government speech. Southern states targeted abolitionist literature, and President Abraham Lincoln was complicit in the arrest of political dissidents. While the worst repression came in wartime, the regulation of expression was a routine affair in nineteenth-century America. Periodically, courts considered whether crimes and torts that targeted expression exceeded statutory authority or transgressed constitutional rights. On all but a few occasions they rejected such claims out of hand. Many judges accepted the Blackstonian notion that freedom of press "consists in laying no previous restraints upon publications, and not in freedom from censure for criminal matter when published." A handful of lawyers defended radical expression in a language that mobilized the Constitution, but their efforts made little headway in the courts.[6]

As a rule, there was little tolerance in America for speech that threatened polite society, let alone the security of the state. Whatever the framers of the First Amendment to the United States Constitution intended to accomplish when they forbade Congress from "abridging the freedom of speech, or of the press; or the right of the people peaceably to assemble," the judiciary declined aggressive enforcement of personal rights. Until the interwar period, when the Supreme Court "incorporated" the provisions of the First Amendment into the Fourteenth Amendment and made them binding on state actors, expressive freedom was largely a matter of local preference, left to state constitutional safeguards. This contrasted sharply with the vigorous enforcement of liberty of contract, allegedly enshrined within the due process clauses of the Fifth and Fourteenth Amendments. Nonetheless, constitutional commentators accepted the situation as inevitable, even desirable. In assessing unpopular expression they habitually distinguished between *liberty* and *license,* inviting regulation of the latter. "Religion and speech and press are primarily free," Freund maintained, "but that does not prevent them from being subjected to restraints in the interest of good order or morality." There was no need, as there is today, for government actors to demonstrate that their interference with private expression was narrowly tailored to serve a compelling state interest. For most Americans, the right to speak freely was conditioned on the speaker's civilized conduct and compliance with social norms. "Everybody says they are in favor of free speech," an astute editorialist observed, "but not everyone agrees as to how free 'free speech' should be."[7]

In the conventional understanding, it was the First World War that awakened Americans to the civil liberties cause. The unprecedented scale of wartime repression engendered a new alliance between progressives and liberal lawyers on behalf of expressive freedom. Although their defense of free speech produced few immediate gains, it laid the groundwork for the emergence of a genuine civil liberties commitment after the Armistice. Disillusioned by the failure of the war to make the world safe for democracy and distressed by the pervasiveness of the postwar hysteria, this coalition reinvented free speech as a means of advancing the public interest and defusing social conflict. The Supreme Court interpreted the First Amendment as a constraint on government efforts to censor unpopular ideas. It overturned convictions for subversive speech, and eventually, it invalidated legislative efforts to suppress undesirable expression. For the first time, the argument goes, judges, academics, and public officials conceded that free speech served the public good, and that "the best test of truth is the power of the thought to get itself accepted in the competition of the market."[8]

This standard account captures only part of the story. True, demands for free speech intensified in the wake of the Armistice. On the whole, however, they retained an earlier emphasis on prudent policy and government forbearance, not countermajoritarian constitutionalism. As before the war, the progressive predilection for centralized state authority overlapped with conservative deference to law and order, and First Amendment challenges consistently lost in court. Beginning in the 1920s, civil liberties were gradually redefined as judicial checks on government abuses, but it would take over a decade for the new conception to take hold. Scholars have typically assumed that the same concerns that motivated the wartime progressives eventually persuaded a majority on the Supreme Court: that the groundbreaking dissents by Justices Holmes and Louis D. Brandeis—justifying free speech as a probe of truth and a prerequisite of democratic governance—prevailed at last in the marketplace of ideas. In fact, the impetus for transformation was not, at least not chiefly, the excesses of wartime patriotism. Rather, the new vision grew out of a state-skeptical brand of labor radicalism, grafted onto a conservative legal tradition of individual rights.

✦ ✦ ✦

The history of civil liberties presented in this book is an unfamiliar one. Although historians and legal scholars have richly documented the wartime suppression of dissenting speech, contestation over the definition and enforcement of civil liberties between the world wars has received insufficient attention. In particular, existing accounts have neglected the interwar struggle over labor's rights that helped to produce America's court-centered and constitutional vision of civil liberties.

There are three principal reasons why that is so. First, the study of civil liberties has been closely tied to constitutional scholarship, and for many decades, its history was pursued primarily in judicial decisions, influential law review articles and legal treatises, and the personal papers of judges and justices. Second, the vision of civil liberties that prevailed by the Second World War was so successful as to become controlling. The novelty and ambiguity of the label *civil liberties* enabled its wide dissemination during the 1920s and 1930s. In that period, a range of private actors and government officials endorsed such disparate ambitions as economic redistribution, federal prosecution of antilabor vigilantes, and enhanced protection for property. That all proceeded under the banner of civil liberties has obscured counterintuitive attitudes toward the linkage between civil liberties and judicial power, as well as concrete differences in the bundles of rights that competing claimants demanded. Finally, the labor partisans who built the civil liberties coalition of the interwar period were astute tacticians. They sought to soften the subversive potential of their program by divorcing their defense of expressive freedom from the underlying ambitions of the speakers they represented. To subsequent generations, even more than contemporaries, their protestations rang true. Reflecting backward, the interwar campaign for economic reordering appeared naive, its adherents incapable of achieving results. As the radical vision of labor power faded into fantasy, it was easy to believe that free speech and its champions were tame from the start.

To be sure, historians have long recognized the central role of anti-Red repression in the early annals of free speech, and they have underscored the labor leanings of early civil liberties advocates. Yet most have treated such connections as incidental to, even incongruous with, the underlying civil liberties project. With the modern First Amendment as their benchmark, they have regarded the radicalism of the civil liberties leadership as an impetus for attacking sedition laws or a precursor to a principled speech-protective position: a galvanizing source of outrage over viewpoint discrimination and selective enforcement, but ultimately a bias to be expunged, not an independent motivating vision. Perhaps as a consequence, the dominant literature on the interwar ascendance of expressive freedom has not adequately explained why or how the modern understanding of civil liberties triumphed.[9]

In the early twentieth century, civil liberties were not merely instruments for the downtrodden and disenfranchised to vent their grievances and preach revolution. Yes, the labor partisans who popularized the term demanded freedom for soapbox speakers to propagate their views, in the way that is familiar today. But they also meant something much more fundamental: more than rational persuasion, more than emotional exhortation. They sought to counter the consolidation of capital with organized power of their own. And to advance that broader project, they crafted a conception of civil liberties that extended to concerted economic activity as well as expression. In so doing, labor radicals and their civil liberties supporters declined to distinguish labor activity from other exercises of expression, as generations of lawyers, judges, and academics have done. They rejected the principle that picketing and boycotts were "verbal acts" susceptible of injunction when they unlawfully restrained commerce or caused irreparable damage to employer interests. A core contingent within the interwar civil liberties coalition believed that every exertion of economic pressure short of physical violence should be immune from legal regulation. The degree to which that position dropped out of legal argument after the Second World War, just as constitutional protection for controversial ideas became routine, has masked the extent to which it drove the interwar agenda. Such far-reaching aspirations never swayed the foundational free-speech theorists in the academy, and subsequent scholars, when they have noticed them at all, have typically dismissed them as fanciful, marginal, or insincere. In fact, the right of agitation was the conceptual ground in which modern civil liberties were rooted.[10]

In seeking to recover a fuller history of civil liberties, *The Taming of Free Speech* looks to the advocates and activists who shaped, sometimes unwittingly, the modern understanding. Occasionally they clashed in the courts, and their arguments are preserved in briefs and refracted through judicial opinions. More often, they promoted their views in organizational bulletins, private letters, and public addresses. Over time, proponents of civil liberties accommodated their ideological commitments to organizational needs, from fund raising to membership drives. To cultivate mainstream support, they publicized their victories in such comparatively uncontroversial areas as academic freedom and sex education. To deflect allegations of bias, they defended the speech of racists and fascists. They reacted to government accusations of radicalism and Soviet collaboration, the success of rights-based litigation and the corresponding failure both of direct action and of legislative and regulatory efforts, and the professionalization of civil liberties advocacy. They responded to the rise of dictatorships abroad as well as evolving domestic developments, including economic depression, partisan politics, and expanding administrative power. Along the way, they began to articulate distinctions between civil liberties and other causes, like civil rights and labor rights. By teasing out their many early approaches, this book emphasizes the accidents, inconsistencies, and idiosyncrasies through which the contending meanings of civil liberties were winnowed out.[11]

The leaders of the interwar civil liberties campaign argued over what civil liberties entailed and how they should be enforced. Even when they agreed on the content of the category, they often differed wildly as to why. For progressives, civil liberties served to legitimate the necessary and desirable exercise of state power in the social and economic realm. For conservatives, they promised to restore judicial credibility and shield individual rights. And for labor radicals, they opened space for a robust right of agitation. During the 1920s, when there was no realistic possibility of state protection for labor's rights, these various factions could all sit comfortably in the same civil liberties tent. In the 1930s, the prospect of state-centered reform forced them to take sides. Progressive reformers and organized labor went one way; conservative legalists the other. The ACLU's core leadership—still hostile to the capitalist system and still fearful of government power—was reluctant to choose. Progressives dismissed what philosopher John Dewey derisively called "the individualist and laissez-faire conception of civil liberties." But the champions of the right of agitation were uncertain. Their belief that civil liberties were checks on a coercive state was not so different from the Right's—a kinship that their critics within the New Deal and the labor movement were quick to point out.[12]

Although for a time they remained fellow travelers, the ACLU's leaders began to clash with their radical allies. Eventually, the organization accepted and even celebrated New Deal labor legislation. It also acknowledged a role for government in promoting public debate and in ensuring that the channels of communication would remain open. But it steadfastly opposed government meddling with the message—even when muting privileged voices or amplifying those of the disenfranchised promised to serve the interests of organized labor.

For their part, conservative groups proved just as adaptable as the early ACLU. Over the course of two decades, the ACLU had helped to move the courts from the defense of property to the defense of personal rights. Its lawyers cast free speech as a right against excessive administrative intrusion into private behavior and choices—a framing that was compatible with conservative reliance on individual rights and well suited to judicial enforcement. During the New Deal, conservatives confronted intrusive investigations of their political spending and administrative restrictions on their antiunion expression. And so, feeling the sting of government regulation, they embraced the Bill of Rights. Like its labor counterpart, the conservative role in crafting the civil liberties settlement has largely gone unnoticed. Through the lens of the Cold War, it is hard to imagine a world in which the "rights denied [and] the privacy invaded were those of the business corporation." Nonetheless, in the 1930s, many conservatives alleged just that. When *Lochner*-era legalism failed them, corporate lawyers exchanged its discredited rhetoric of economic liberty for the civil liberties language the ACLU supplied.[13]

The signal accomplishment of the interwar ACLU, from the perspective of the organization's founders, was to embed the right of agitation within a neutral right of expressive freedom, enforced by the judiciary and encompassed by the Bill of Rights. Its foremost failure was the alacrity with which the right of agitation was contained. By the end of the Second World War, free speech was firmly ensconced as a constitutional value, and the radical roots of civil liberties were practically forgotten.

✦ ✦ ✦

Between the world wars, no organization or individual was as instrumental in shaping contemporary understandings of civil liberties as the ACLU. But this book is not a history of the ACLU; it is a history through the ACLU. The organization was deeply connected to the foundational social movements of the interwar period, and it was involved in virtually every important free speech case in the federal courts between its founding in 1920 and the Second World War. The ACLU's governing bodies during those years were a who's who list of influential public figures. They included labor activists (Andrew Furuseth, William Z. Foster, Rose Schneiderman), civil rights leaders (James Weldon Johnson, Charles Hamilton Houston), celebrated social reformers (Jane Addams, Helen Keller), high-level government officials (Frank P. Walsh, Lloyd K. Garrison, Harold L. Ickes), prominent writers and intellectuals (Pearl Buck, John Dos Passos, Upton Sinclair), and future justices of the United States Supreme Court (Thurgood Marshall, Felix Frankfurter). Moreover, many of the most important legal and political theorists who wrote about civil liberties and their relationship to American democracy were tied to the organization, including Ernst Freund, John Dewey, Harold Laski, Zechariah Chafee Jr., and Alexander Meiklejohn.[14]

As broad as the ACLU membership was, its external network was even wider. The ACLU regularly collaborated with organizations on issues that implicated the interests of their particular constituencies. Its frequent partners—which also populate the pages of this book—included labor defense groups, especially the General Defense Committee of the Industrial Workers of the World (IWW) and the Communist-affiliated International Labor Defense (ILD); the National Association for the Advancement of Colored People (NAACP); the American Association of University Professors (AAUP); and eventually the American Bar Association (ABA). It also cooperated with government agencies, including Robert M. La Follette Jr.'s Senate Civil Liberties Committee and the Civil Liberties Unit of the Department of Justice. Through its sweeping approach to civil liberties claims, the ACLU occupied the field. In fact, when the bar sought to reclaim a role as the "enlightened guardians" of civil liberties in the late 1930s, commentators attributed conservative inattention to the cause over the previous decades to the dominance of the ACLU.[15]

And yet, for all its influence, the ACLU's early approach to civil liberties now seems strangely remote. Today, the ACLU's Web page recounts that "the ACLU was founded to defend and secure [constitutional] rights and to extend them to people who have been excluded from their protection—Native Americans and other people of color; lesbians, gay men, bisexuals and transgender people; women; mental patients; prisoners; people with disabilities; and the poor." Sure enough, the ACLU's interwar records teem with disempowered voices. But in their conversations with and on behalf of the ACLU, they did not advocate for their rights as individuals, or even (at first) as minorities. William Pickens's statement on lynching, prepared for the ACLU a year after its founding, exemplified the prevailing perspective: "Only by frankly recognizing the economic basis of lynching can we even begin to solve the problem," wrote the NAACP field secretary who was born to former slaves and famously fought for racial justice. "Its solution is obviously bound up with the cause of exploited labor—white and black alike. And that solution will become possible only as the black and white workers of the South both achieve the right to meet, speak freely, organize and strike." ACLU cofounder and longtime leader Roger Baldwin put the same point more succinctly: "The race issue at bottom is the labor issue," he wrote, "and the master class of the south knows it."[16]

During the 1920s and 1930s, the ACLU fought the deportation of aliens and the suppression of religious fringe groups. It defended the advocacy of birth control and of racially integrated public schools. But its overarching goal was to secure labor's rights. The organization's leadership regarded free speech as an implement of working-class power and a gateway to the general strike. It brought that framework to the seminal civil liberties cases of the 1920s—not only such obvious candidates as *Gitlow v. New York* and *Whitney v. California,* which involved radical defendants, but also controversies over compulsory public schooling and evolution, including *Pierce v. Society of Sisters* and *Scopes v. Tennessee.* Indeed, stripped of their labor context, these and other iconic cases of the early twentieth century have been incompletely understood. Labor radicalism guided the ACLU's approach to litigation and its connection with the progressive and legal establishments through which the values of civil liberties were promoted and institutionalized.[17]

That single-minded focus on labor presents a puzzle for the history of civil liberties. It is well documented that the American labor movement harbored a deeply rooted hostility toward the judiciary. For decades, labor organizers had been subject to prosecution for criminal conspiracy and for violations of public assembly and vagrancy laws. Efforts to improve working conditions through statutory reform were invalidated for infringing on employers' property rights and the contractual freedom of nonunion workers. Worst of all, the courts had issued injunctions against strikes, boycotts, and organizing efforts based on ex parte testimony by employers, and workers who failed to comply with their terms were subject to fines and criminal penalties for contempt. Almost always, it seemed, the courts had ruled against them. At a profound level, the labor partisans at the helm of the interwar civil liberties movement were disinclined to entrust the judiciary with enforcement of their cause.[18]

This is also a book, then, about how and why a pioneering social movement turned to litigation, and the stakes of its decision to do so. The ACLU's early program, modeled on the direct action espoused by the IWW, disavowed law of all kinds: legislative and administrative as well as judge-made.

Still, however much they willed it, the ACLU's leaders could not escape law's pull. On the contrary, they found themselves constantly called to press their cause in court. Sometimes, their lawyers raised claims they expected to lose, for the express purpose of revealing judicial hypocrisy. Other times, they sought to carve out space for labor agitation incrementally, by obscuring the radicalism of their goals. They pursued victories in areas less charged than labor and hoped the precedents would carry over, or they defended labor organizers by reference to procedural justice and rule of law. To their surprise, they won. And as they changed the law, the law changed them.

Ironically, their experiments helped to preserve liberal legalism at the very time it proved most vulnerable. In the 1930s, New Dealers launched a frontal assault on the federal courts. Advocates and politicians maneuvered to limit judicial power through legislation, constitutional amendment, and changes in personnel. To deflect such measures, conservatives appropriated the ACLU's sporadic legal victories of the previous years as evidence of the benefits of judicial review. Despite their efforts, the beleaguered Supreme Court abandoned its attachment to liberty of contract and acceded to state regulation of the economy. By the end of the decade, Americans trusted their state and federal governments to establish a minimum wage, ensure compensation for workplace injuries, and provide basic benefits in old age. In all this, they knew, the federal courts would not intervene. And yet, in areas as far ranging as evolution and modernist literature, judges were declaring controversial ideas to be none of government's concern. They accepted the administrative authority of the National Labor Relations Board (NLRB) to force employers to the bargaining table even as they invalidated antipicketing laws for infringing the First Amendment.

By conventional accounts, the "preferred position" of personal rights originated in the Supreme Court's fourth footnote of *United States v. Carolene Products Company,* which promised heightened judicial scrutiny of laws inhibiting the political process or targeting disfavored minorities. This book is unabashedly teleological in constructing an alternative historical path. It suggests that the theory of government embedded in footnote four was not a spontaneous solution by federal judges struggling to balance political will against minority rights. Nor was it, as some have proposed, primarily a response to fears stemming from the rise of totalitarianism in Europe. Rather, it was the product of two decades of social movement activism. In short, this book argues that the ACLU—guided by the lessons and ambitions, if not always the tenets, of the radical labor movement—was an unsung engineer of the post–New Deal constitutional order. A movement founded on antipathy to the judiciary helped to rescue judicial review.[19]

The emergence of civil liberties from the wreckage of New Deal constitutionalism has long been regarded as a triumph for the Left, the logical culmination of the New Deal's constitutional revolution. The new arrangement—judicial deference to state economic policy coupled with strong safeguards against government interference with civil liberties and civil rights—would become a pillar of postwar legal liberalism. Free speech was the linchpin of a new and distinctively American style of participatory governance. Adherents insisted that robust public debate would ensure both the integrity of democratic processes and the legitimacy of their outcomes.

To its instigators, however, the modern concept of civil liberties was a calculated bargain that backfired. Less than one year after the Supreme Court wrote workers' right to picket into the First Amendment, it began to write it back out. The constitutional revolution was beset by constitutional compromise.

The labor radicals at the heart of this history understood the risks of the regime they helped to create. They recognized that unrestrained expression could swamp the marketplace of ideas. Above all, they knew how often courts had blocked the way to democratic change. Even so, they hoped that a neutral vision of civil liberties would usher in a new and better world. On the eve of the Second World War, the radicals who launched the modern civil liberties movement disclaimed their early ambitions, but they did not abandon them. We are still living with the legacy of the deal they struck.

1

Freedom of Speech in Class War Time

D URING the tumultuous years of the 1910s, as Europe reverberated with the clamor of artillery fire, American democracy was reportedly under siege. The identity of the assailant was a matter of perspective. To organized labor, and to the social reformers who sometimes supported its cause, the antagonist was a judiciary that catered to corporate demands and thwarted every effort, whether by legislation or economic self-help, to mitigate the hardships of industrial capitalism. To conservative lawyers and their industrial clients, the problem was precisely the opposite. Independent courts were the greatest bulwark of personal liberty as well as property rights. The progressive campaign to curtail judicial power threatened the very foundation of rule of law.[1]

In the conflict over American governance, civil liberties were powerful weapons. Eventually, each side deployed them and claimed them as their own. At the height of the New Deal, when the judiciary was most vulnerable, contestation over the meaning and scope of civil liberties would prove to be decisive. And yet, before the 1910s, few considered them central to the struggle.

Scholars, judges, and advocates have long traced the emergence of a robust civil liberties commitment in the United States to the First World War. Blinkered by the post–New Deal equation of civil liberties with judicial enforcement of the Bill of Rights, they have searched court decisions for early celebrations of First Amendment freedoms. They have found them in the rare acquittals and dissents from convictions of antiwar

14

protesters and in the urgent exhortations of Zechariah Chafee Jr.'s classic disquisition, "Freedom of Speech in War Time."[2]

Broadening the lens beyond the First Amendment, however, the new visibility of civil liberties predated American engagement in Europe. In a decade marked by revolution and unprecedented destruction abroad, the true impetus for rethinking the American civil liberties tradition was not total war, but class war. After all, it was class war that shook the foundations of American institutions at the dawn of the new decade, and it was class war that made civil liberties the subject of sustained public debate and federal inquiry for the first time.[3]

To be sure, there was nothing new about violence in labor relations. In the half century since the Civil War, the United States had transitioned from a largely agrarian society to a sprawling industrial economy dominated by massive corporations. Skilled artisanal craftwork yielded to mechanization; immigrants and freed slaves flooded the factories. At the turn of the century, when President William McKinley died of bullet wounds inflicted by a former steel worker turned anarchist extremist, the notion that workers could parlay their surplus wages into independent capitalist ventures was hopelessly anachronistic. In short, the free labor ideology that had dominated American political thought for much of the nineteenth century was broken, and bloodshed occasionally resulted.

The labor movement that confronted the new economy encompassed an amalgamation of organizations with competing objectives and commitments. Some workers aspired to revolutionize the relationship between labor and capital through the collective cessation of production or by voting with their class. Others, content or constrained to work within the capitalist system, prioritized such "bread and butter" goals as higher wages and improved working conditions. Meanwhile, sympathetic reformers devised state-centered solutions to temper inequality and restore faith in democratic methods.[4]

These early responses to rising wealth inequality ran afoul of a judicial philosophy that critics described as a structural preference for property over persons. By the 1910s, even noncombatants in the class war questioned the judicial entrenchment of existing conditions, which industry so fiercely defended. Some conceptualized labor's tools—including the rights to strike, boycott, and picket, along with the more familiar right to advocate political change—as manifestations of expressive freedom, worthy of government toleration and perhaps affirmative support. Few, however, defended such activity as an exercise of constitutional rights beyond the scope of permissible regulation. On the contrary, many regarded the Constitution as tainted at its core. Notably, the future founders of the organization that would become the ACLU were among this larger group. If judges blocked efforts to raise wages or improve workplace safety, they argued, the Constitution should be amended or the courts reconfigured; the judiciary was an impediment to personal freedom, not its guardian.

As Americans debated their nation's legal and economic future, calamitous class conflict loomed on the horizon. That efforts by workers to organize for higher wages and greater control often led to death and property destruction was a chilling reality in an age of rapid industrialization. Even so, in 1910, a single sensationalist episode triggered a far-reaching inquiry into the roots of class warfare in the United States, with dramatic consequences for the future of civil liberties advocacy.

✦ ✦ ✦

In the earliest hours of October 1910, an explosion rocked Los Angeles with the force of an earthquake. A blast in an alley adjacent to the *Los Angeles Times* building ignited barrels of flammable ink, fueling a fire that reached the building's gas mains and reduced the structure to rubble. Dozens of people were trapped inside. Twenty-one died and many more suffered agonizing injuries as thousands of spectators looked on helplessly.[5]

The *Times* decried a labor union conspiracy. Although the evidence was inconclusive, the accusation had intuitive purchase. The morning after the explosion, an undetonated bomb was discovered at the home of the company's president, Harrison Gray Otis, an antiunion stalwart. As for the *Los Angeles Times,* the American Federation of Labor (AFL) considered it the "most unfair, unscrupulous, and malignant enemy" of the American labor movement. On street corners, at work sites, and in the pages of the *Times,* Otis and his allies had quashed every effort to organize Los Angeles workers. It was easy to assume, as one journalist put it, that Otis had "us[ed] his newspaper weapon with such venom in beating down his enemies that he created the elements which could find no voice except nitroglycerin to answer the dynamite of [his] language."[6]

In practice, local labor groups had little to gain and much to lose from an attack on the *Times* building. Despite formidable resistance by the city machinery, a union campaign had begun to coalesce in Los Angeles in 1910. Its impetus, as with similar efforts throughout the country, was the power imbalance arising from the consolidation of capital in a modern industrial economy. Unions pressed individual workers, weak in isolation, to enhance their strength by standing together. By combining into associations within particular trades or industries, they urged, working people could voice their demands, improve their wages, and assert control in the workplace. In May, 1,500 Los Angeles metalworkers walked off the job. The *Times* prescribed a brigade, armed with pick handles, to "drive the lawless union laborites, closed-shop, murderous vermin into the sea." The Los Angeles Superior Court, employing more conventional methods, issued a series of injunctions to break the strike. When the union persevered, the city council unanimously adopted an ordinance that banned picketing and boycotts outright, along with "speaking in public streets in a loud or unusual tone."[7]

The *Times* celebrated the hundreds of arrests that followed, but the measure miscarried: the antipicketing ordinance galvanized Los Angeles workers and bolstered their resolve to strike. Meanwhile, free speech demonstrators worked to overwhelm the legal system and flood the city's jails with arrested speakers. Instrumental in this strategy were the city's Socialists, who regarded street speaking as an essential tool in converting the masses to class-conscious political change—that is, to public ownership of the means of production, accomplished through elected representatives as opposed to economic action—and who were seasoned veterans in the legal battle against speech-suppressive laws. In a staggering upset, a Socialist attorney who represented the unions during the strikes won a plurality of votes in the first round of the mayoral election.

The destruction of the *Times* building jeopardized these precarious achievements, and labor sympathizers greeted accusations of union involvement suspiciously. Tensions flared further when private detective William J. Burns (future director of the Bureau of Investigation, the precursor to the FBI) orchestrated the arrests of brothers James B. and John J. McNamara. Burns had been investigating a spate of seventy dynamite attacks on iron manufacturing plants throughout the country when the City of Los Angeles hired him to catch the perpetrators of the *Times* bombing. He quickly linked the two cases, but his high-handed tactics unleashed a national uproar. John McNamara, who was secretary-treasurer of the International Association of Bridge and Structural Iron Workers—an affiliate of the AFL—was arrested in the midst of a meeting of the union's executive board in Indiana and promptly whisked across state lines. Skeptics analogized to the famous 1907 acquittal of William D. "Big Bill" Haywood, whose extradition for the murder of a former governor of Idaho was of dubious legality. (Haywood, whom the *New York Times* would dub "the most hated and feared figure in America," was then secretary-treasurer of the Western Federation of Miners, but the organization would soon expel him for his militancy.)[8]

When the McNamaras proclaimed their innocence, the American labor movement rallied to their defense. Even Samuel Gompers, the AFL's ever-cautious president, decried the prosecution as a frame-up. The AFL billed itself to business as a reliable bargaining partner, opposed to revolutionism as much as exploitation, and Gompers was determined to preserve his organization's reputation. To that end, he persuaded the legendary midwestern lawyer Clarence Darrow to take the McNamaras' case. Darrow, the *Nation* would later observe, "was the country's outstanding defender of labor, at a time when labor was more militant and idealistic and employers more hardened and desperate than ever before or since." It was Darrow who had successfully represented Haywood in 1907, and workers as well as the national press expected another impressive acquittal.[9]

The blow to Los Angeles labor was consequently all the more crushing when, in December 1911, James McNamara admitted to "put[ting] that bomb in Ink Alley, just as the papers have said." In a stunning reversal, both brothers pleaded guilty: James to the charge of murder in the *Los Angeles Times* incident, and his brother John to a separate bombing. James claimed he was dismayed at the human cost of the explosion, and he had never intended to kill. Still, he had deposited the dynamite that was responsible for the deaths. It was an act of principle. "The paper had been fighting us for years," James explained, "and so we decided that something must be done."[10]

The public condemned the McNamaras and anyone who had stood by them. Just four days after the guilty plea, the Socialist mayoral candidate who had assisted Darrow in the legal defense lost his runoff by a sizeable margin. In the months that followed, Los Angeles unions suffered crippling declines in funds and membership. Otis declared victory in his twenty-five-year fight for "industrial freedom"—a principle, he added, that was every bit as vital as religious, political, or personal freedom in a country governed by a "free Constitution." Newspapers throughout the country denounced the McNamaras as ruthless villains and admonished the labor movement to atone for their crimes.[11]

Many labor leaders were responsive to their calls, and Gompers accused the McNamaras of betraying labor. But to Darrow, who was roundly castigated for his role in the McNamara affair and considered it "the greatest strain in [his] life," the brothers' personal guilt was secondary. They were motivated by an unselfish desire to aid their class; their actions were incidental to a "great industrial struggle." Not only did Darrow refuse to condemn them, but he believed them undeserving of the label "criminal." Throughout his life, Darrow would emphasize that James McNamara did not intend the taking of life, a distinction that Darrow considered morally essential, if legally irrelevant. But Darrow was unprepared to denounce unequivocally even intentional violence. "There are other things to consider besides property and other things to consider besides bloodshed," he insisted.[12]

For Darrow, the deaths in Los Angeles were casualties of the class war. Asked whether citizens of a republic in which people enjoyed "political and civil rights and liberty" were entitled to commit acts of war, Darrow resisted the question. He acknowledged that the conflict between capital and labor was tantamount to warfare, but he dismissed the very notion of a right as a manipulable abstraction. Besides, he added, "I don't think we live in a free country or enjoy civil liberties."[13]

✦ ✦ ✦

Clarence Darrow was unusually bold, but he was not alone in linking the *Los Angeles Times* bombing to underlying injustices. Just weeks after the McNamaras pleaded guilty, a delegation of social workers laid much the same case at the feet of Republican president William Howard Taft. On December 30, 1911, Rabbi Stephen S. Wise, a founding member of the NAACP, and Jane Addams, head of Chicago's pioneering Hull House, presented the president with a petition. The document characterized the McNamara case as the consequence of government failure to mitigate class antagonism. The *Times* bombing was merely one manifestation of a brewing class crisis, expressed in unprecedented strikes by garment workers, steel-workers, and coal miners across the United States. With the legal proceedings in Los Angeles now closed, the petition pressed the government to study the social conditions that had prompted the resort to dynamite.[14]

The petition was framed by a deep conviction that desperate acts like the McNamaras' were inevitable in the face of profound economic inequality reinforced by law—that (in the words of progressive reformer Florence Kelley) "the only preventive of violence is justice." Many of its signers had encountered workers' desperation firsthand. Addams, of course, worked tirelessly to relieve class injustice through legislation, social work, and occasionally union activity. Lillian Wald (along with Addams) helped to establish the Women's Trade Union League, which sought to increase women's participation in organized labor. Kelley founded the antisweatshop National Consumers' League. All believed that inattention to injustice was dangerous as well as inhumane.[15]

That was the subject of a December 1911 symposium on the McNamara case in the New York–based *Survey* magazine, a leading progressive journal. Article after article echoed the sentiment expressed by the Socialist labor lawyer and future congressman Meyer London "that a bitter, merciless class war divides society." Most, however, rejected the Socialists' conviction that class war was inevitable. Many contributors allocated responsibility evenly between labor radicals, on the one hand, and conservative industrialists, with their excessive individualism, on the other.[16]

Like other progressives, the reformers who wrote for the *Survey* promoted a unified public welfare, not a struggle between rival classes. They believed, with editor Paul U. Kellogg, that unconstrained conflict would lead to "false balances"—that the "responsibility for sovereign and regulative action rests upon the whole people." They imagined a state that was worthy of deference as well as loyalty, aloof from the competing interests that destructively jockeyed for power. They gathered in the *Survey*'s office to discuss their vision, and they resolved to present it to the public. Signed by some of the nation's most prominent scholars, lawyers, and public figures, in addition to its preeminent settlement workers, their petition to Taft was a set piece for progressive confidence in bureaucratic expertise. What the authors envisioned was a well-staffed commission with the resources to investigate the organization and methods of trade unions and employers' associations, including strikes, as well as the laws and judicial decisions pertaining to labor relations.[17]

The field of study was massive. It extended to the employment effects of technological advances and an expanding workforce, the implications of alternative corporate structures on attitudes toward bargaining, responses to the erosion of traditional social and religious institutions, and the significance of emerging differences in labor's organizing strategies and ambitions. It also encompassed legal change: the need for common law and constitutional principles to accommodate the dramatically shifting circumstances on the ground. Among other tasks, the commission would "gauge the breakdown of our machinery of industrial government" by evaluating the political and judicial treatment of the boycott, the picket, the labor injunction, and the strike.[18]

To proponents of the commission, assessing labor's legal status was among the most crucial functions the new body could undertake. Progressives accused nineteenth-century lawyers and judges of willful blindness to law's political underpinnings. In the service of industry, progressives contended, they had defended private property by reference to abstract rights. That dogmatic insistence on the inviolate autonomy of legal actors—a way of thinking described as legal formalism, legal orthodoxy, and classical legal thought, among other labels—had led modern society astray. In reality, the progressives argued, the public-private distinction was artificial, and the allocation of wealth was a product of shared social norms. The notion that property owners were entitled to disregard the public good was repugnant to progressive values.[19]

It is a perilous enterprise to generalize about the principles of progressivism. Generations of scholars have dissected the tensions among the many programs and ideas assembled under the progressive umbrella. During the early years of the twentieth century, self-described progressives championed such far-ranging projects as tenement housing laws, food and water safety, municipal ownership of public utilities, the income tax, women's suffrage, eugenics, and prohibition. Their disagreements on these and many other issues were sufficiently fundamental to render their common label confusing, if not meaningless. Still, the progressives shared certain antipathies, including toward the federal courts and constitutional rights-based claims. Following Roscoe Pound, the esteemed legal scholar and champion of sociological jurisprudence, they criticized courts for "exaggerat[ing] private right at the expense of public interest." Indeed, the rejection of the autonomous individual was one of the few threads unifying progressive thought.[20]

As to the implications of this insight, there the consensus broke down. Most progressives agreed that a living wage was desirable, if not a necessary precondition of participation in democratic society. Most also endorsed direct government regulation of work hours and labor conditions. On the issue of labor unions, progressives were divided. Unions held out the interests of their constituents as primary and distinctive; their demands for antitrust immunity or the closed shop were at odds with the progressive commitment to social harmony. Still, many progressives accepted unions as a practical counterweight to employers' disproportionate power, and some unequivocally applauded the promise of industrial democracy. The iconic progressive intellectual Herbert Croly argued that the social web of industrial organization would transform individual workers into "enlightened, competent, and loyal citizens of an industrial commonwealth." The freedom of a single worker to bargain for the conditions of his (or, increasingly, her) labor was an obvious fiction in the context of modern labor conditions. Croly and likeminded progressives believed that collective bargaining restored a measure of reality, as well as social consciousness, to the field of labor relations.[21]

Progressive social theorists criticized the legal system for "depriving the weak of the chief weapon by which they may achieve common economic action." Where employers bargained willingly with unions, industrial peace followed. By contrast, powerful industrial groups, including the structural iron trade that the McNamaras targeted, were committed to breaking the unions. Rather than intervening to protect the rights of workers to organize, legal institutions enforced the prerogatives of recalcitrant employers. "The workingman sees the club of the officer, the bayonet of the militia directed against him in the defense of property, and he believes that the hand of the law, strong in the protection of property, often drops listless whenever measures are proposed to lighten labor's heavy burden," the petition to Taft observed. Those who dismissed labor's cries of injustice as "sporadic assaults" on the judiciary were blind to the scale of the struggle. The courts had clung stubbornly to common-law rules crafted for a preindustrial era. By contrast, the new commission might formulate recommendations for reform. The notion of democratic *progress*, according to the petition, "implies the people's freedom to criticize and develop the very civilization which the courts *conserve*."[22]

Although the petition lamented the state's neglect of labor relations, past administrations had made intermittent efforts to diagnose and dampen industrial unrest. In 1898, President McKinley, motivated by concerns about class antagonism as well as the lure of the labor vote, approved the appointment of the Industrial Commission. Its final report, published in 1902 under McKinley's successor, Theodore Roosevelt, foregrounded state legislation to improve labor conditions, as well as the federal regulation of railroad labor. It also evinced moderate support for labor unions, which had emerged as a powerful force in such high-profile actions as the 1892 Homestead Strike and the Pullman Strike two years later. Energized by the unionization drives of the 1890s, workers asserted a right to organize equivalent or superior to employers' rights to bargain freely with nonunion employees. The legal establishment generally rejected such claims. In 1895, the United States Supreme Court upheld a contempt conviction against Eugene V. Debs, the future five-time Socialist presidential candidate, for refusing to comply with a federal injunction against the Pullman boycott—despite the best efforts of Darrow, who abandoned his practice as a railroad attorney to take the case. Still, a growing contingent of anxious officials and sympathetic reformers accepted the reasoning of Oliver Wendell Holmes Jr. in dissent from his colleagues on the Supreme Judicial Court of Massachusetts: "Combination on the one side is patent and powerful. Combination on the other is the necessary and desirable counterpart, if the battle is to be carried on in a fair and equal way."[23]

The Industrial Commission's report helped to shape the agenda for labor reform in the Progressive Era. The years before the First World War were witness to a remarkable explosion of protective labor legislation at the state and, in some cases, federal levels. Fueled by workplace tragedies like the Monongah Mining disaster and (just months after the *Times* bombing) the Triangle Shirtwaist fire, progressive coalitions pushed through workplace safety laws, minimum-wage and maximum-hours laws, employers' liability and workers' compensation reforms, regulation of convict labor, public ownership of utilities, restrictions on child labor, and laws regulating company stores and private employment agencies. Hence the petition to President Taft could plausibly report that political action, while plodding, was open to the working class.

Progress was more equivocal, however, when it came to collective bargaining. The Anthracite Coal Strike Commission, convened by President Roosevelt to mediate a strike orchestrated by the United Mine Workers (UMW), made modest concessions to labor in the form of increased wages and shorter hours, as well as a mechanism for settling worker grievances. But it did not require employers to recognize unions, and it conditioned cooperation on the unions' good behavior. Roosevelt acknowledged that the prevailing labor conditions were unsustainable even as he inveighed against class consciousness. When he mobilized the state to mitigate the worst abuses, his goal was to preserve the sanctity of private property and, in large measure, the existing allocation of wealth.[24]

If the drafters of the 1911 petition were hoping for a radical reformulation of government labor policy, President Taft was an unlikely candidate to initiate reform. Hardly a champion of the progressive labor agenda, Taft nonetheless promised to act on the social workers' proposal—hoping, perhaps, to head off more radical measures. In a special message to Congress, he made good on his word, urging a comprehensive nonpartisan inquiry. Congress responded with a bill that Samuel Gompers helped to frame and that the AFL endorsed, and that called for labor representation on a federal commission for the first time. In March 1912, lawyers, religious leaders, and social workers testified on behalf of the provision before the House Committee on Labor. Committee chairman and UMW veteran William B. Wilson, a year before his appointment by Woodrow Wilson as the nation's first secretary of labor, vowed to secure passage of the bill. With relatively minor concessions on funding, he managed to deliver.[25]

On August 23, 1912, a new Commission on Industrial Relations was charged by statute with "seek[ing] to discover the underlying causes of dissatisfaction in the industrial situation." The nine commissioners, designated by President Wilson rather than his predecessor, represented business, labor, and the public in equal proportions. They were geographically and religiously diverse and included the first woman to serve on a federal commission. The most prominent member was John R. Commons, a labor economist and historian at the University of Wisconsin, who had drafted and administered industrial reforms in addition to investigating them. Wilson selected as chairman Frank P. Walsh, a self-taught Missouri attorney who "fought poverty as a boy—really fought it." Since 1900, when he had ceased all work on behalf of his corporate clients, Walsh had campaigned for "the rights of man rather than the wrongs of property." According to *Harper's Weekly*, it was Walsh's ambition to "put the *law* itself to work for the public service." His dedication to labor would guide the proceedings of the commission as well as its findings.[26]

Between 1913 and 1915, the Commission on Industrial Relations conducted hearings in more than a dozen cities across the United States, and it dispatched researchers to even more. The commissioners heard testimony from more than 700 employers, workers, and public officials. Notable witnesses included industrial giants Andrew Carnegie and Henry Ford, labor leaders Gompers and Bill Haywood, and future Supreme Court justice Louis D. Brandeis. To progressive reformers who regarded the class struggle as an obstacle to social harmony, the complaints aired in the hearings were largely familiar ones. So was the effort to catalog and condemn them. Still, in eleven volumes of testimony, some new and important patterns emerged.[27]

✦ ✦ ✦

What the Commission on Industrial Relations found in Los Angeles and elsewhere was a strong sense among workers that public officials, in the service of employer interests, were trampling their exercise of free speech. Conceptually, this was no new development. Public policing of labor agitation emerged during the nineteenth century as a basic feature of American industrial society. Labor, in turn, claimed a moral and constitutional right to speak and assemble. The anarchists condemned to death in Chicago's notorious 1886 Haymarket affair described their ill-fated rally as an exercise in free speech—a claim that the sentencing judge rejected on the familiar grounds that "liberty is not a license to destroy." Socialists, too, routinely defended their street-corner meetings in free speech terms. When asked to produce their speaking permits, they would hand over reproductions of state constitutions or the text of the First Amendment instead. Initially, local authorities often tolerated Socialist gatherings, as they were, in Eugene V. Debs's words, "too numerously attended by serious, intelligent, and self-reliant men and women to invite interference." But during the twentieth century, governments cracked down. In Harrison Gray Otis's Los Angeles, the city council passed a series of ordinances, beginning in 1901, requiring police permits to speak on public property. When Socialists advertised meetings in private halls instead, the police responded by enforcing a prohibition on the distribution of handbills. One police chief went so far as to advocate the licensing of newspaper sellers, which, according to critics, would have threatened the labor press and conferred an official monopoly on the *Los Angeles Times*.[28]

At first, constitutional claims by street speakers met with modest success in state courts. At the end of the nineteenth century, however, a series of speech-restrictive Massachusetts cases occupied the field. Key among them was an 1895 decision by future free speech luminary Oliver Wendell Holmes Jr. Writing for a majority of the Supreme Judicial Court of Massachusetts in *Commonwealth v. Davis,* Holmes rejected a preacher's asserted right to deliver a public sermon on the Boston Common in violation of the city's permit requirement. "For the legislature absolutely or conditionally to forbid public speaking in a highway or public park," he famously declared, "is no more an infringement of the rights of a member of the public than for the owner of a private house to forbid it in his house." However novel Holmes's formulation when *Davis* was decided, the United States Supreme Court affirmed the preacher's conviction and insulated municipal control over public speaking from meaningful constitutional challenge for nearly half a century. Henceforth, the exercise of free speech meant hiring a private hall or printing in a private mouthpiece. Freedom of speech after *Davis* was contingent on the rights of property.[29]

That bans on public meetings were considered compatible with constitutional principles did not, however, render them desirable as a policy matter. On the contrary, restrictive permitting requirements attracted the ire of many Progressive Era reformers. What made free speech a major source of consternation was a practice of discriminatory enforcement directed against radical groups. And in the early 1910s, the discrepancies became glaringly evident, launching free speech into the center of political and scholarly debate. The cause célèbre was a concerted campaign by a radical labor group, the IWW, to provoke and publicize state suppression. The organization's "free speech fights" were so visible and its corresponding presence so considerable that Louis Brandeis unavailingly advised Wilson to appoint an IWW member to the Commission on Industrial Relations.[30]

Founded in 1905 to organize workers on a class basis, the IWW openly professed its commitment to "abolition of the wage system." Its leaders unequivocally repudiated AFL-style business unionism, with its bureaucratic governance structure and its narrow emphasis on wages and hours. Instead of the skilled workers who established labor unions organized along craft lines, the IWW recruited the unskilled masses, regardless of race, ethnicity, and religion. Although it shared much of its vision with the Socialist movement from which it splintered, the two groups diverged on several important issues, including strategy. Espousing an awkward blend of Marxism, Darwinism, anarchism, and syndicalism, the IWW members, known as "Wobblies," abandoned politics in favor of direct action. That is, they shunned the ballot box in favor of picketing, boycotts, sabotage, and ultimately the general strike, which Bill Haywood described as a total cessation of productive labor that would transfer control of industry from the capitalists to the masses.[31]

The IWW's free speech fights grew out of efforts to attract members to the "One Big Union" through public speaking and literature distribution. When Wobblies were arrested for their recruitment efforts, they invoked the protections of the First Amendment. Like the Socialists, they believed that free speech yielded when "corporation interests are involved." For many Socialists, however, the solution was to reform a judiciary they regarded as broken. The Socialist precursors to the IWW's free speech fights were typically more restrained and more deliberate than their better-known Wobbly counterparts. Organizers orchestrated their protests to maximize their prospects of enlarging access, on the understanding that dissemination of Socialist literature was essential to legislative success. They exalted "the elemental rights guaranteed under the Constitution," and they decried the denial of free speech as "a medieval infringement on the rights of man." By contrast, the Wobblies opted for a flamboyantly confrontational approach. Despite their patriotic rhetoric, most regarded the courts as unalloyed tools of capital and scoffed at the notion of constitutional protection for disempowered minorities.[32]

Still, the free speech fights served tangible goals. Recruitment in urban centers was crucial to channeling migratory labor through IWW hiring halls. The architects of the free speech fights hoped that their rare courtroom successes would open up opportunities for soliciting members on street corners, outside the watchful gaze of employers. Failing that, the partiality of local government and judges would expose American constitutional liberties as fraudulent, attracting adherents indirectly to the IWW.[33]

In practice, the free speech fights met with mixed success. The first fight erupted in Spokane, Washington, where IWW organizers challenged a street-speaking ordinance that targeted "revolutionists." The wave of arrests that followed flooded the city's jails, draining the resources of the courts and correctional system. Reinforcements—including a dynamic young organizer named Elizabeth Gurley Flynn—flocked in from around the country. When the struggle had exhausted everyone involved, the IWW secured access to indoor meeting places and the freedom to sell its news-papers on the city streets. It also managed to reform the employment agency system in Spokane and much of the Northwest. Perhaps most important, the idealism, perseverance, and resolute nonviolence of the Wobbly speakers generated sympathy for their cause.

The outcomes of subsequent fights were more ambivalent. In Fresno, California, after months of passively withstanding torture from mobs and from prison guards, the IWW obtained release of its jailed members and the right to speak on the city streets. Courts occasionally reversed convictions as discriminatory, unsupported by the evidence, or inconsistent with statutory intent. Increasingly, however, these few formal victories seemed inadequate to the task of organizing the workers. The notorious San Diego fight of 1912 led to horrific police and vigilante violence against IWW participants, with little concrete gain. Public opinion, on the whole, was stacked against the IWW. Many commentators celebrated the fundamental principles enshrined in the Bill of Rights but carved radical agitation out of the intended scope of constitutional protection.[34]

Nonetheless, the IWW's efforts, like the Socialist endeavors on which they were modeled, resonated with many progressives. Some supported the legal efforts of Theodore Schroeder's Free Speech League, founded in 1902, which defended the IWW by reference to time-honored American values. Even as courts rejected their constitutional claims, many progressive officials acquiesced to the IWW's demands on policy grounds. New York City's police commissioner believed the best way of "maintain[ing] public order" was to "allow[] public assemblage under conditions which shall conserve the American constitutional rights to free speech." Accordingly, he instructed police officers to protect speakers from unruly crowds, though he considered it essential not to permit the liberty of assemblage "to degenerate into license." Similarly, Attorney General George W. Wickersham resisted encouragement from local law enforcement and President Taft to prosecute the IWW under federal law. Even the Los Angeles City Council, in the wake of the McNamaras' plea, approved (and subsequently expanded) a street-speaking district and erected basic facilities for public addresses.[35]

The free speech fights figured prominently in the proceedings of the Commission on Industrial Relations and in the work of its research division under John R. Commons's guidance. So did the fracas over free speech in

Paterson, New Jersey, which the commission investigated with "unusual thoroughness." While not strictly a free speech fight, suppression of IWW organizing efforts in Paterson launched free speech into the national arena. The trouble began in February 1913, when 13,000 silk workers went on strike. The IWW did not instigate the action, but it quickly took charge and declared an industry-wide general strike. The city responded by ordering closure of all assembly halls, prohibiting outdoor meetings, and preemptively arresting the organization's charismatic representatives, including Haywood and Flynn. As strike funds dissipated, guests at Mabel Dodge's Greenwich Village salon hatched the idea of a Paterson Pageant to publicize the events for New York workers. In a spectacle the *New York Times* denounced as a "mad passion against law and order," striking workers reenacted the most egregious events of the previous months: police raids on peaceful rallies, the silencing of the press, and the tearful sendoff to foster families of 400 Paterson children, many of whom appeared on stage. Madison Square Garden, draped in red, was packed to capacity; the "seditious blaze" of the ten-foot-tall letters "IWW" beamed out overhead as the audience sang the "Marseillaise" and the "Internationale." But the pageant, inspirational to New York's artists and intellectuals, was a financial failure, and Paterson's disheartened workers returned to the mills.[36]

In testimony before the commission, witnesses linked episode after episode of censorship and suppression to the class war. The cataloged complaints included a restraining order against street agitators for language tending to "arouse the anger and incite the antagonism or wrath of the citizens"; the conviction of author and activist Upton Sinclair for engaging in a protest accusing the Rockefeller family of moral culpability in the notorious Ludlow Massacre (itself a major subject of the commission's investigation); and a spate of federal prosecutions for "scurrilous or defamatory" anticapitalist statements on postal wrappers. Prosecutors at every level proceeded against labor agitators under whatever theories they could muster, regularly invoking criminal libel, seditious libel, and obscenity laws, among other statutory and common-law provisions. In short, it was routine, in Schroeder's words, for the "courts [to] lawlessly invade freedom of speech and press when prompted by desire to suppress an agitator."[37]

Such infringements only exacerbated violent episodes like the *Times* bombing, commission witnesses insisted. Some explained that efforts to protect free speech for radicals would reduce the risk of conflict. Many others testified that the silencing of workers bred deep animosity toward law. To be sure, these advocates of free speech had profoundly different long-term goals. Progressives, in the main, believed that expressive freedom was an outlet for class resentment and would serve to defuse more radical tendencies. Others hoped that the freedom to propagandize would shepherd in social change. Schroeder described a radical ideal of compensation based on the social value of labor and believed the first step toward attaining it was "freedom of speech, for [Bill] Haywood and the rest, to defend their dreams."[38]

And yet, the IWW leadership itself was less sanguine than Schroeder about its modest achievements in the realm of free speech. The IWW organ *Solidarity* described the "passive resistance" of the free speech fights as labor's "weakest weapon"; successes in Spokane and elsewhere offered a pale glimpse of what might be achieved "when an industrially organized working class stands forth prepared to seize, operate, and control the machinery of production and distribution." The free speech fights were an exercise in direct action, a prelude to more meaningful struggles. Increasingly, the Wobblies rejected the fights as even an interim strategy.[39]

The IWW was not alone in doubting the utility of the free speech fights. In the opening paragraphs of his iconic progressive tract *Drift and Mastery*, social commentator Walter Lippmann expressed his exasperation with characteristic acerbity. In early 1914, he recounted, government abuses in New York City had created an unparalleled opportunity for agitation. "The newspapers and the police became hysterical, men were clubbed and arrested on the slightest provocation, meetings were dispersed." The public, inured to the injustices of economic inequality, was aroused to defend the rights of free speech and assembly. But the moment of possibility quickly passed. Once their rights were restored, the anarchists who were conducting the agitation lost their followers for lack of a positive program. "They had no message to vie: they knew what they were against but not what they were for." Eschewing radical idealism, Lippmann—who had taken part in the Paterson Pageant the previous spring—lauded the conservative railroad brotherhoods for winning "wages and respect far beyond anything that the IWW can hope for." Industrial democracy was impossible without unions, he mused, but employers and their allies had thwarted organizing by all possible means: "Race is played against race, religion against religion, there are spies, black-lists, lockouts, thugs, evictions." On the long list of obstacles, "the denial of free speech" was almost an afterthought.[40]

Critics within and outside the labor movement believed the true task was to concentrate the power of wage earners, a project largely orthogonal to the free speech fights. Many doubted whether a mere paper right to speech could counteract the forces of capital. What was necessary was not advocacy, but action; not expression, but economic power. Such activity might be accomplished through words, but it was not speech in its conventional legal sense. Still, in the effort to organize American workers, broader claims to expressive freedom promised to play a crucial role.

✦ ✦ ✦

When the Commission on Industrial Relations finally arrived in Los Angeles in the summer of 1914, the McNamara brothers had long since left for San Quentin prison, but the grip of Otis and his antiunion allies was as firm as ever. The commissioners interviewed leaders of local labor and employer organizations, as well as ordinary workers. Again and again, employers affirmed their commitment to the open shop—that is, to an employer's unfettered choice as to whether to hire union or nonunion labor. Nominally, open-shop employees were free to join a union, but in practice, Los Angeles employers used labor spies to weed out those workers who betrayed an impulse to organize for collective bargaining, let alone to picket and strike.

Many of the labor witnesses who appeared before the commission recounted the conditions they had found most frustrating in the months before the bombing. Echoing the articles in the *Survey*, they stressed their sense that public officials were complicit in employers' antiunion practices. It was one thing for employers to counter unions' economic efforts: to fire organizers and hire strikebreakers, as at-will employment clearly allowed. It was another, however, for the city persistently to come to employers' aid.

Efforts to shield employers from agitation took two distinct but related forms. First were outright prohibitions on left-wing political advocacy of the kind that provoked the free speech fights. Measures like these were meant to stanch the dissemination of information or the expression of political views. They targeted soapbox orators and antiestablishment agitators. In the early twentieth century, they were routinely enforced and seldom challenged, though they would fall squarely within the scope of the modern First Amendment.

The second strain is less recognizable as an infringement on free speech. This class of restrictions targeted strikes, pickets, and boycotts—including much activity that consistently was construed as economic rather than political and coercive rather than persuasive. Curtailment of labor activity occasionally originated in city councils and state legislatures, as in the case of the Los Angeles antipicketing ordinance. More often, it came directly from the courts, in the form of labor injunctions. For a brief moment during the New Deal, the First Amendment would expand to encompass speech of this sort. In the 1910s, as after, labor's principal weapons were subject to government regulation.

Progressive Era workers regarded both forms of regulation as incursions on their personal liberty, but when representatives of organized labor endorsed freedom of speech—which they did with unqualified fervor in testimony to the Commission on Industrial Relations—most were motivated by the second category more than the first. They believed that meaningful negotiation required the aggregation of workers' economic strength. The public as well as employers would discount the demands of the weak. Labor organizing was a prerequisite as much as a product of free speech.[41]

Organized labor was therefore deeply committed to a vision of free speech more expansive than a right to political advocacy. In a heated exchange before the commission, Samuel Gompers and Socialist labor lawyer Morris Hillquit jockeyed to establish their respective organizations as more purely or passionately committed to the "absolute freedom of press, speech, and assemblage"—rights they considered to be "inherent" as well as constitutional. Gompers noted that the AFL had taken on tremendous risk to assert and maintain them. He might have added that he had shouldered considerable personal risk, as well.[42]

The fundamental task of the American labor movement was to organize wage earners into unions. Individual workers were powerless to negotiate with employers over the terms and conditions of their employment. Only by banding together could they counterbalance the economic strength of their employers. Whether the goal was a union contract or the wholesale cessation of production, labor organizers relied on a few essential tools. The first, and most basic, was the strike, which the lawyer for the National Association of Manufacturers (NAM) succinctly defined as "a systematic quitting of employment for the purpose of inducing the employer to grant some demand of the striker, accompanied by an effort to prevent others from taking the places of those that quit." In American history, strikes were often stubborn and spontaneous, voicing solidarity and articulating workers' frustrations and ambitions even at the expense of their immediate economic interests. Nonetheless, lawyers, social scientists, and many labor leaders described them primarily in terms of the application of economic pressure. An employer that failed to meet a union's demands risked lost profits, spoilage of goods, contractual damages on missed deliveries, and reputational harms.[43]

By the late nineteenth century, most legal authorities recognized the right of workers to engage in a "simple strike": to quit their jobs collectively for the purpose of raising wages or improving conditions at their own place of employment. Some also tolerated a few peaceful pickets to advise customers and potential strikebreakers of the existence of a labor dispute. Matters were seldom simple, however. Often, employers responded to union demands by replacing recalcitrant strikers with more malleable employees. Many employers hired spies and private security guards to keep picketing safely at bay. Some required their employees to sign "yellow-dog contracts," which prohibited them from joining unions and made potential organizers liable for tortious interference with contract. Meanwhile, in some industries and in some geographic regions, employees proved unwilling to incur short-term loss of livelihood in the interest of long-term systemic gains. Sometimes, local businesses were unsustainable at the wage rates required by union pay scales.

Faced with obstacles like these, unions adopted more aggressive tactics. They stationed mass pickets to dissuade strikebreakers and to inhibit access to employer property, often for the purpose of closing the shop—which necessarily entailed the discharge of nonunion employees. They also wielded conventional tools against unconventional targets. The much-maligned secondary strike placed pressure on "innocent" third parties to cease business relations with the primary target. A company that refused, perhaps because it had entered into a contractual agreement to buy or sell the "unfair" products, would find itself subject to the same sanctions as the primary. Cordial relations between the secondary employer and its workers were no defense against such strikes; unions called their members out regardless. Union members who failed to honor the picket line risked expulsion—which, in a well-organized trade, might mean forgoing future employment. Even family members of strikebreakers were vulnerable to union discipline. Testifying before the commission, one labor witness acknowledged that such tactics occasionally worked real hardships on unwilling participants but explained there were "a great many instances [in which] we are unable to bring any effective pressure to bear on an employer except through this form of discrimination."[44]

And then there was the boycott. Whereas strikes imposed high costs on workers in the form of lost wages, refusal to purchase or handle an unfair good was sustainable for extended periods. Eugene Debs's American Railway Union used the boycott to such stunning effect in support of the 1894 Pullman Strike that the federal government intervened. By the turn of the century, the AFL published a "We Don't Patronize" list in its monthly journal. In response, hat manufacturers in Danbury, Connecticut, formed the American Anti-Boycott Association (AABA), which led a legal campaign to promote "good citizenship, individual liberty, [and] the open shop." The AABA's founders were the plaintiffs in the organization's most notable case, *Loewe v. Lawlor* (the "Danbury hatters' case"), in which the Supreme Court held that a boycott by the United Hatters' Union was an unlawful impediment to interstate commerce under the Sherman Act. On remand, the district court levied treble damages against individual union members for the union's activities and deemed their property in Danbury subject to seizure, with devastating consequences for the defendant hatters, though the AFL ultimately voted an assessment on members of affiliate unions to satisfy the judgment. The Supreme Court affirmed, eliciting Gompers's condemnation and spurring an AFL campaign to exempt labor unions from the antitrust laws. Those efforts, in turn, yielded a declaration in the 1914 Clayton Antitrust Act that "the labor of a human being is not a commodity or article of commerce." Gompers famously celebrated the Clayton Act as labor's "Magna Carta," but in practice, its qualified language offered little protection in the courts.[45]

As an alternative to a legislative solution, some early labor advocates sought to insulate their activity from judicial interpretation of the antitrust laws by grounding it in constitutional rights. Boycotts inevitably included expressive components, and a handful of state courts had proven willing to shield them from regulation on that basis. In 1906, employees at the Buck's Stove and Range Company in Saint Louis, Missouri—a company run by the president of the antiunion NAM—struck to retain the nine-hour day. The following spring, the AFL executive council voted to add the company to its "We Don't Patronize" and "Unfair" lists. Buck's Stove (assisted by the AABA) obtained a sweeping injunction against the boycott, and high AFL officials including Gompers were sentenced to prison for criminal contempt for refusal to comply with its terms. In *Gompers v. Buck's Stove and Range Company,* the Supreme Court reversed the convictions on technical grounds, but it rejected the AFL's argument that its "We Don't Patronize" list was protected by the Constitution, reasoning that speech in furtherance of an illegal purpose was outside the First Amendment's purview. Enjoining a boycott "which, by words and signals, printed or spoken, caused or threatened irreparable damage" failed even to implicate freedom of speech.[46]

As a doctrinal matter, the Supreme Court's casual rejection of Gompers's First Amendment claim in *Buck's Stove* was unremarkable. Protection for free speech was riddled with exceptions, as every lawyer understood. Libel, blasphemy, and obscenity all were denied constitutional protection. So was speech that tended to provoke violence and speech incidental to the commission of a crime. In the case of soapbox oratory by Wobblies and Socialists, the challenge for defense attorneys was to demonstrate that illegal action was not a foreseeable result of their clients' speech. With respect to picketing and boycotts, by contrast, the underlying act was itself unlawful. As James A. Emery reflected on behalf of the NAM, it was no more improper "to enjoin the use of [a man's] hands or his feet or his head to do some unlawful thing . . . [than] to use the injunction in connection with the use of the tongue." Unions' desperate devotion to their economic weapons belied the notion that they were straightforward applications of protected expression as the category was conventionally understood. Indeed, the element of intimidation was what rendered them powerful and prompted labor to maintain them so fiercely.[47]

The Supreme Court's decisions in the Danbury hatters' case and *Gompers v. Buck's Stove and Range Company,* profoundly affected union practices. Gompers considered the decisions to be the most "serious invasion of the rights and liberties of our people" in American history, but he nonetheless felt compelled to submit to them, lest his intransigence bankrupt the labor movement and endanger its members. Compliance may have minimized entanglement with the courts as a stopgap measure, but it did not quiet the clamor for structural change. The fact that employers were free to blacklist union workers but workers could not retaliate in kind fueled the sense, expressed in the 1911 petition to President Taft, that the "channels . . . for economic action to secure industrial justice" were legally foreclosed. More to the point, they confirmed workers' conviction that justice was unattainable in "capitalist court[s]."[48]

Progressive social thinkers worried that labor's complaints were justified. Edward A. Ross, a signer of the 1911 petition to Taft and president of the American Sociological Society (who would eventually serve as national chairman of the ACLU), considered the issue so pressing that he organized the society's 1914 annual meeting on the subject of "Freedom of Communication." Ross lamented what he regarded as widespread government interference with free assemblage, free press, and free speech "at the instigation of an economically and socially powerful class, itself enjoying to the full the advantages of free communication." He traced those rights to the nation's founding struggles and considered them indispensable to the pursuit of "social progress." In Paterson, Spokane, Seattle, and San Diego, American authorities had denied expressive freedom. Censorship sometimes served to prevent the disclosure of local corruption or to shield employers or local officials against allegations of crime. More often, the purpose was "to spare certain employers the risks of a successful strike or the snaffle collective bargaining imposes upon their arbitrary will."[49]

✦ ✦ ✦

In their testimony before the Commission on Industrial Relations, labor leaders and their progressive supporters professed a deeply held belief in freedom of speech, press, and assembly. Many imagined that an abiding American free speech tradition encompassed workers' economic tools as well as their street-corner advocacy. Some thought these values found expression, even if they did not originate, in the state and federal constitutions. And yet, as the free speech fights subsided and *Buck's Stove* ripened into settled law, hardly anyone argued that the solution to labor's woes was to expand judicial protection of expressive freedom. Certainly labor lawyers still invoked the First Amendment, along with other "personal rights" (for example, the right against search and seizure and the right to a jury trial), in appealing criminal convictions. These claims, however, were largely reactive, and they were far less frequent and impassioned than demands to rein in judicial power. Mobilization around judicial enforcement of a labor-friendly First Amendment played a minimal part in the world that the commission brought to light.

It is not enough to explain, as contemporary commentators sometimes did, that the First Amendment cabined only congressional action. It is true that the First Amendment was not yet "incorporated" into the Fourteenth Amendment and was therefore binding only on the federal government, a fact that one of the commission's reports deemed "startling and alarming." The antitrust laws, however, fell squarely within the bounds of federal legislation. Moreover, many prosecutions proceeded under state law in states with constitutional free speech provisions modeled on the First Amendment, with outcomes just as antagonistic to labor—and unions were no more moved to litigate free speech claims in the states than in the federal domain.[50]

Most important, there was promising precedent for fitting free speech within the scope of the Fourteenth Amendment. Adopted during Reconstruction to protect the newly freed slaves, the Fourteenth Amendment did little in practice to shield them from legal or social disability. But it contained a clause prohibiting the states from "depriv[ing] any person of life, liberty, or property, without due process of law," and an equivalent provision in the Fifth Amendment bound the federal government. Federal courts read the two provisions to require not only procedural protections, but also substantive constraints on state and federal power—an approach that subsequent commentators would describe as "substantive due process."[51]

The most notorious application of this doctrine, and a powerful progressive rallying cry, was the Supreme Court's decision in *Lochner v. New York,* which struck down a New York maximum-hours law because it interfered with an implicit constitutional "right to free contract." Revisionist historians have demonstrated that decisions invalidating social and economic legislation were relatively rare at the Supreme Court level during the first two decades of the twentieth century. In many states, however, they were the norm. As Florence Kelley complained in 1905, state courts relied on the Fourteenth Amendment of the United States Constitution to strike down progressive legislation in order to foreclose state constitutional amendment as an antidote to judicial overreaching. Such progressive projects as the minimum wage, the eight-hour day, and workers' compensation all perished at judicial hands.[52]

Judicial invalidation of state labor legislation was premised on the notion that the Fourteenth Amendment insulated certain core rights from government interference by the states as well as the federal government. In its 1897 decision in *Allgeyer v. Louisiana*—the decision that introduced freedom of contract as a constitutional constraint on the states—the Supreme Court reasoned that "liberty" in the Due Process Clause encompassed the "right of the citizen to be free in the enjoyment of all his faculties." This principle plausibly extended to speech rights, as well. A staff member of the Commission on Industrial Relations considered it possible that the Fourteenth Amendment "guarantee[d] free speech and press in the states," in much the same way that it preserved the rights of property.[53]

That analogy, however, rendered the prospect of a judicial strategy deeply troubling to organized labor. Indeed, the small handful of decisions invalidating legislation on the basis of expressive freedom included a Georgia case striking down a prolabor statute that required corporations to inform discharged employees of their grounds for termination, which the court found "violative of the general private right of silence enjoyed in this state by all persons, natural or artificial," as a corollary to "liberty of speech." Whether by class allegiance or pedantic doctrinalism, judges appeared predisposed to vindicate business interests and to suppress innovations designed to improve labor conditions. Just as labor leaders scorned the pursuit of antiemployer injunctions, they were reluctant to promote an expansive vision of a countermajoritarian First Amendment for fear that doing so would legitimate the Supreme Court's constitutional jurisprudence. The lurking specter of "Lochnerism" cast a long shadow over American law.[54]

Judicial solicitude for individual rights threatened unions in other, more pervasive ways as well. Faced with a strike, police typically arrested organizers for misdemeanor offenses such as disruption of the peace, obstruction of traffic, or resisting arrest. When police intervention was inadequate (or, less commonly, was not forthcoming), the courts supplied more drastic measures. By the early 1890s, judges had decisively established their willingness and authority to curtail coercive labor practices—particularly efforts by workers to conduct boycotts or to dissuade strikebreakers—through use of the "labor injunction," the judicially crafted device at the heart of the *Buck's Stove* case. During the first decades of the twentieth century, the pursuit of labor injunctions became a routine affair for beleaguered employers, who invoked the courts' equity power on theories ranging from interference with employment contracts to expected picket line violence. Although some judges exercised restraint, even expressed union sympathies, most were quick to comply with employers' requests, often issuing ex parte restraining orders unsupported by evidence of illegal behavior.[55]

Labor injunctions reflected the same valorization of property rights and liberty of contract that fueled judicial suspicion of progressive legislation. In the decades before the First World War, employers argued that closed shops abridged workers' freedom by conditioning employment on their obligation to join the union and by undercutting the ability of nonmembers to work for an employer of their choosing. Moreover, they maintained that yellow-dog contracts prohibiting workers from joining unions buttressed individual autonomy. With few exceptions, courts agreed on both fronts. As a lower court explained in *Buck's Stove*, "The labor unions and [their] officers meddle into a member's daily affairs deeper than does the law; restrict him in matters that the law leaves free."[56]

To labor, this breed of reasoning appeared unrealistic and insincere. The Supreme Court's decision in the *Buck's Stove* case came just three years after it struck down a statutory prohibition on antiunion discrimination in the railroad industry as a constitutional infringement on workers' freedom of contract under the Fifth Amendment, a holding that it applied to state anti-yellow-dog laws in 1915. The result was that neither state nor federal government could prohibit employers from "unjustly discriminat[ing]" against union members: employers enjoyed a constitutional right to discharge unionized employees at will. As Clarence Darrow told the Commission on Industrial Relations: "They talk about the inalienable right of a man to work," but "the man who stands for the open shop does not care for anybody's rights to work, except the nonunion man." Darrow's sometime cocounsel Stephen S. Gregory, sufficiently well respected to serve as president of the conservative ABA in 1911, made much the same point. "I have no right to go out and file a bill to be permitted to work for whom I choose," he explained, "and if I did, any one of these judges, who sometimes use that language incautiously, would laugh me out of court." The judicial attitude that Darrow and Gregory lamented showed no signs of abating. On the contrary, President Taft's judicial appointments, including five to the Supreme Court, would only exacerbate workers' sense of labor law as "Heads, I win; Tails, you lose."[57]

Against this backdrop, labor's response to cases like *Buck's Stove* was less that the judiciary had misconstrued the First Amendment than that the entire constitutional framework was stacked against them (a reading reinforced by the 1913 release of Charles A. Beard's immensely influential history, *An Economic Interpretation of the Constitution of the United States,* which traced that constitutional framework to the personal financial interests of the Founders). Although their legal reasoning evolved over the early twentieth century, most judges continued to invoke a theory of individual rights based on the sanctity of private property. Courts insisted that such norms were embedded in the Constitution—and labor consequently rejected court-centered constitutionalism, if not the entire judicial enterprise. Put simply, labor leaders were disinclined to pursue a judicial strategy for enforcing union activity as a species of free speech because the judiciary invariably undercut labor's most significant gains. Far better, they thought, to strip the courts of the authority to curtail their activity in the first place.[58]

Organized labor was not the only contingent that was ill disposed toward the judiciary. Progressives, too, denounced *Lochner*-era legalism as excessively doctrinaire or frankly hypocritical. On a pragmatic level, an interventionist judiciary threatened to eviscerate the progressive reform agenda. Theoretically, the problem was its inattention to social facts and the public interest. Both sets of concerns pushed progressives to impugn judicial legitimacy. Their critique of the courts was a necessary corollary of their assault on legal formalism and a central tenet of progressive legal thought.[59]

There were exceptions. Gilbert Roe, a lawyer for the Free Speech League and the former law partner of Wisconsin Republican Robert M. La Follette, was skeptical that courts should be deciding the validity of statutes at all. If they were going to strike them down on the basis of property rights, however, he thought "they ought to apply the same principle to statutes which invade personal rights." His testimony to the commission was consistent with his comments at the American Sociological Society's conference on free speech, where he criticized the other speakers for considering the issue in terms of policy rather than rights. His, however, was a minority view.[60]

✦ ✦ ✦

Critics of the judiciary offered competing explanations for its failings. For some, the problem was the judges, whose minds worked in an "entirely different manner" in the domain of property regulations as opposed to personal liberty or free speech. The cynics, pointing to rampant bribery and corruption in the political branches, blamed graft. Others, more subtly, invoked an "unconscious economic determinism, controlling the judicial intelligence." Samuel Gompers regarded the justices as fallible human beings. Having spent most of their personal and professional lives in the company of "business and financial men," they had inevitably if unwittingly absorbed employers' point of view. Observations of this sort emanated from respected lawyers as well as irate workers. The chief justice of the North Carolina Supreme Court speculated that judges were "unconsciously biased" in favor of the large corporations they used to represent. Even Frank Goodnow, a renowned scholar of administrative law and the newly appointed president of Johns Hopkins University, worried that judges were overly accustomed to the defense of private rights.[61]

Some hoped the system might be redeemable if judges were made more responsive to the political will. That was the impulse behind the judicial recall, a sweeping progressive tool that enabled the replacement of judges regarded as insensitive to industrial realities or especially hostile to workers. As Charles Beard explained, there was no surer way to undermine judicial supremacy than to make judges subject to recall by the same voters who enacted the laws. Incredibly, such assessments attracted widespread popular support. By the time the Commission on Industrial Relations convened, legislators throughout the country were introducing bills to curtail judicial independence. The constitutions of Oregon, California, Nevada, and Colorado all contained provisions for the recall of judges; the last eliminated judicial review (or as contemporaries called it, "the power to enforce constitutional limitations"), as well. President Taft refused to sign the resolution admitting Arizona to the Union until its recall provision was amended to exclude judges, but the state's first legislature promptly reintroduced and overwhelmingly adopted the measure.[62]

The labor movement endorsed such efforts. Gompers believed that the recall, as well as judicial elections, could push judges toward more "democratic views of justice." Some progressives agreed, though they worried about offending the "conservative instincts of the common people." Alternatives included the recall of judicial decisions—a solution espoused by Theodore Roosevelt and incorporated into the Progressive Party's 1912 platform—which would have allowed popular majorities to "veto" judges in cases involving the invalidation of statutes. Roosevelt and his supporters regarded the recall of judicial decisions as a more moderate approach, because it promised to preserve the routine operations of common-law property rights, including the labor injunction, as well as harsh evidentiary rulings against defendants like the McNamaras. Roosevelt was reluctant to interfere with judicial decisions in the ordinary run of cases, but he believed that "when a judge decides a constitutional question . . . the people should have the right to recall that decision if they think it wrong." In that spirit, a joint Senate resolution introduced in the fall of 1912 would have submitted Supreme Court decisions invalidating congressional legislation to democratic override.[63]

Defenders of judicial independence, whether progressive or conservative, occasionally mentioned the threat to personal freedom and minority interests that might follow from efforts at judicial reform. The esteemed attorney and statesman Elihu Root thought judges should be more responsive to changing social circumstances, but he nonetheless believed that judicial enforcement of personal rights protected individuals against government power. President Taft argued that "constitutions are checks upon the hasty action of the majority," essential to respect for minority rights. The progressive Idaho senator William E. Borah cautioned that a servile judiciary "leaves human rights uncertain and worthless." And the Republican Party's 1912 platform rejected judicial recall as unnecessary and ill advised, stressing that independent courts protected "the civil liberty of the individual."[64]

Such statements, however, were both muted and misleading. Opponents of the judicial recall only sporadically invoked personal rights. Free speech, in particular, rarely received more than a cursory nod. Progressives hesitated to legitimate the court's enforcement of individual rights; those who rejected judicial recall instead tended to emphasize, with Woodrow Wilson, that it would undermine the "stability of the State." And conservative advocates baldly relied on the judicial defense of property against radical redistribution. One typical defender of judicial independence worried, in terms that will resonate with modern constitutional scholars, that "in time of great popular excitement and prejudice" a majority might vote to sacrifice the rights of a "small group of men." But the small groups at stake were not the racial minorities or disfavored speakers subsequent generations of judicial enthusiasts would invoke. Instead, the horror the author conjured was a "proposal to take the property of one unpopular corporation and devote it to an unquestioned public good." The courts guarded "civil liberty," to be sure—but the perceived antagonist was socialist confiscation, not state censorship.[65]

It is a largely forgotten feature of judicial politics in the Progressive Era that the ABA played a central role in preserving the independence of the courts. In the ABA's statements and reports, the centrality of property rights was on unabashed display. The organization considered the recall to be "subversive of . . . constitutional democracy," and it assembled the Committee to Oppose Judicial Recall "to spread a general propaganda of education" (including hundreds of thousands of pamphlets) to buttress judicial independence. Attorneys offered their unmitigated support for such efforts, and many appeared before civic groups and city councils to celebrate the integrity of the courts. Although conservative lawyers invoked both personal liberty and property rights, they overwhelmingly emphasized the latter. The bar dismissed the notion of "an oligarchical and despotic judiciary 'whose sympathies are with the propertied class'" as a fantasy of radical agitators. The courts had long served "the mass of the people," one ABA report insisted, and it could be trusted to enforce the interests of the poor as reliably as the rich. "Any man, however poor or humble," could apply to the courts for protection, and it was no reproach upon the courts that they had "extended the same protection to the rich and powerful." On the contrary, "the same law which would deny protection to the rich or confiscate the property of corporations, might take the cottage or the liberty of the humblest citizen."[66]

What the ABA regarded as a commitment to neutrality, radical thinkers rejected as a naked defense of industrial interests. Clarence Darrow believed that the legal remedies the bar touted were meaningless to the weak, who lacked the resources and education to pursue them. A law that applied equally to all, he explained, did not affect everyone alike. After all, the rich had much less cause to trespass, loiter, or steal, and much more property to protect. As for injunctions, it was theoretically possible for workers to obtain one, but Darrow reported that no court would cooperate. Justified or not, Darrow's pessimism found validation rather than qualification in the tone-deaf insistence by employer organizations that "the industrial worker in this country at the present time is privileged under the law." Convinced that the contrary was true, the most militant labor groups foreswore the courts altogether. As one syndicalist publication put it at mid-decade, the "law strike"—defined as "the defense of labor in a capitalist court"—was nearing the end of its usefulness. "When Labor shall have strongly organized on an industrial basis, free from parliamentary law, legal claptrap, judicial fakery, and capitalistic confidence methods there will be no need of hiring lawyers."[67]

In the run-up to the First World War, labor advocates rejected a court-centered strategy for the denial of free speech because they regarded judicial battles as essentially unwinnable. The objection was not, as it would soon become, that the judiciary refused to invalidate state legislation suppressing workers' expressive advocacy. Rather, the problem was the intrusive reach of the court as an arm of the state—the arm most active in stifling workers' self-help and in undermining their political achievements. There was ample reason for labor to forgo an approach that would have strengthened and legitimated the very powers it most resented.

✦ ✦ ✦

In the summer of 1915, the Commission on Industrial Relations issued its findings. By that time, the progressive reformers who spurred its creation had largely lost confidence in the enterprise. Nowhere was the disappointment more keenly felt than in the offices of the *Survey,* where plans for the commission were first conceived. In the early months of the commission's operations, Paul Kellogg had met regularly with Chairman Frank Walsh to offer suggestions and confer on possible paths. The journal reported on the important hearings and dispatched a representative, John A. Fitch, to document and interpret the proceedings. Increasingly, however, Kellogg grew disillusioned with Walsh and vowed to expose the lapses in his leadership, notwithstanding the *Survey's* formative role in convening the commission and continued allegiance to its goals.[68]

The break with the commission reflected emerging divisions among its early sponsors—differences that took on new dimensions when longtime critics and outsiders were suddenly vested with government power. From the outset, Walsh prioritized the commission's hearings over the work of its research department. Conflict over the allocation of resources to the two components of the commission's work temporarily abated when Charles McCarthy, John Commons's Wisconsin associate, took the research reins in the summer of 1914. In time, however, financial pressures rendered the cordial relationship between Walsh and the research division unsustainable. Confronted with a dwindling budget, depleted in large part by his own cavalier spending, Walsh chose to sacrifice the research program in February 1915. Convinced that raising public awareness was the commission's essential task, he slashed McCarthy's staff and ordered him to close his offices.

The dispute between Walsh and McCarthy was ideological as well as methodological. McCarthy, who had headed Wisconsin's pioneering Legislative Reference Bureau for more than a decade, championed the careful crafting of legislation on the basis of scientific investigation, with special attention to such issues as the minimum wage, immigration, and social insurance. His preferred outcome for the commission was the creation of a national mediation board—a solution also favored by the reformers associated with the *Survey*. Although he condemned industrial injustice, McCarthy favored reconciliation through administration. Walsh, by contrast, disparaged McCarthy's unflinching commitment to expert advisory committees. He believed the commission would best serve workers by affording them "an ever-increasing measure of control over the industry in which they are engaged."[69]

The difference in opinion reflected a vexing Progressive Era dilemma. Sophisticated advocates were aware that "paid lobbies are constantly seeking to influence congress and the state legislatures." Nonetheless, many progressives believed that government involvement could serve useful ends. Some rejected the AFL's assertion of "voluntarism": the notion that labor activity should take place outside the realm of state power. Indeed, to some, the AFL's preference for negotiating and enforcing collective-bargaining agreements through economic self-help, divorced from the broader public interest, reproduced the abstractions of laissez-faire liberalism. Even organized labor vacillated over state intervention, though for tactical more than theoretical reasons. The IWW renounced state-centered solutions entirely, but Samuel Gompers and his cohort used government adeptly when it suited their goals.[70]

The desirability of government action was a common theme in testimony before the commission. Theodore Schroeder, for example, favored legislation to promote free speech; he noted that tens of thousands of statutes and ordinances protected private property, but there was no equivalent mechanism "to protect by law [the] constitutional guaranty as to freedom of speech and press." Labor advocates beseeched the "Government [to] take some steps to protect the workers in their right to organize." Notably, the measures they proposed were premised on the assumption that the common-law and constitutional property rights enforced by the courts were creatures of the state, rather than natural conditions independent of its coercive power. One labor witness recommended legislation withdrawing government protection for the property of any employer that denied its employees the right to organize.[71]

Disagreement about the appropriate path forward made its way into the commission's recommendations. Given the commission's tripartite structure, a unanimous report was always unlikely—but after the acrimonious personal clashes and professional disagreements of the commission's final months, it proved impossible even to attain a majority. Instead, the commissioners produced three separate principal reports. The most memorable, written by Basil M. Manly, garnered Walsh's approval as well as the labor commissioners'. Each of the other contingents authored its own statement, though Commons mustered some support from the employers. A complex web of qualifications, critiques, and supplemental statements accompanied the main reports.

Although portions of the Commons report attracted a bare majority of signatures, the document was limited in scope and a weak candidate for constructive reform: "wise but unexciting," according to the *New Republic*. Commons emphasized further inquiry into failure of existing laws, and evaluation of the best methods "of investigating conditions, of enacting legislation, of judicial interpretation, and administrative enforcement necessary to make them worth while as a real remedy." Much of the report summarized the findings by the experts within the research department. It then proposed a permanent array of state and federal industrial commissions, "cooperative between employers and unions," that would administer employment laws and offer nonbinding mediation of labor disputes in cases elected by the parties. Where Walsh rejected the notion of identity across class lines, Commons emphasized the shared interests between employers and employees, even while he acknowledged the persistent reality of class conflict.[72]

The employer report conceded that some employers had "been guilty of much wrongdoing," though it underscored that labor shared the blame for industrial unrest. Despite a forthright endorsement of collective bargaining as the most tenable solution to labor conflict under modern industrial conditions, the employers' representatives denounced labor's most powerful weapons, including output restriction and sympathetic strikes. On the subject of free speech, the employers were noncommittal. Their report included employers' reliance on government officials to suppress freedom of speech and assembly among labor's justifiable grievances, but it offered no suggestions for reform.[73]

Conversely, the Manly report was strongly prolabor and called for "drastic" changes in the allocation of wealth and federal protection of unions' right to collective bargaining as well as federal provisions for social insurance. Walsh considered it the most definitive of the statements, and he boasted that it was "more radical than any report upon industrial subjects ever made by any government agency." It bore the label "staff report," though some of the most respected members of the staff resigned rather than take part in it. Because it appeared first in the printed records of the commission, it was generally treated as the dominant view.[74]

The Manly report reviewed such topics as workplace injuries, unemployment, and agricultural land allocation. It recommended the regulation of private detective agencies, the creation of a bureau of industrial safety, a graduated income tax, and legislation to mandate the eight-hour day. But its overarching theme was judicial hypocrisy. The *Wall Street Journal* summarized its aspirations aptly in its August 23 headline: "Walsh Would Forbid Courts to Interpret Constitution." Judges, the report complained, "allow[ed] their economic bias to influence them in holding laws unconstitutional." Meanwhile, the personal rights of workers—their rights to advocate, organize, and strike, and their rights to legal process when their actions were claimed to cross the line—were little more than paper promises.[75]

From the perspective of Progressive Era reformers, there were two ways to remedy the judiciary's double standard. The first was to elevate freedom of speech and association above property in the constitutional hierarchy, such that courts would have to reject antipicketing ordinances and labor injunctions as unlawful infringements of workers' constitutional rights. The second was to undermine judicial power, leaving the enforcement of constitutional rights and the policing of labor disputes to legislators, regulators, and above all the contending parties. The recommendations of the Manly report favored the latter.

In a section devoted to free speech, the Manly report described the police suppression of unpopular ideas, in public and in private halls, as "one of the greatest sources of social unrest." Rampant interference with "personal rights," it cautioned, "strikes at the very foundation of Government." Manly's language succinctly laid out the progressive case for free speech. "It is axiomatic that a government which can be maintained only by the suppression of criticism should not be maintained," the report asserted; history had demonstrated "that attempts to suppress ideas result only in their more rapid propagation." The answer was to remove all barriers to expressive freedom (explicitly excepting constraints on obscenity and libel). Toward that end, the report outlined a range of recommendations. Some were designed to encourage good governance and promote police impartiality. It was not enough merely to check government abuses. Consistent with witnesses' calls for affirmative government action on behalf of public advocacy as well as labor organizing, the report urged states and municipalities to protect unpopular speakers from molestation by hostile audiences and to open up the schools and other public buildings for lectures and public meetings.[76]

But the report went further. The commissioners who endorsed the Manly report were impressed above all by witness testimony that workers had been "denied justice in the enactment, adjudication, and administration of law"— that constitutional guaranties enacted to safeguard the rights of workers had served as cover for corporate abuses, and that the "whole machinery of Government" had been placed at employers' disposal. Not only had the courts proven far more sympathetic to industry than to labor in the resolution of particular disputes, but they had distorted the sections of the Constitution designed to protect "human rights" and "perverted [them] to protect property rights only," often in contravention of state statutes specifically drafted to protect workers. Meanwhile, they had interpreted the Fourteenth Amendment to incorporate only property rights, not personal rights, and had thereby rendered workers helpless against inroads by the states.[77]

To eradicate these evils and to introduce "justice and liberty" in their place—and, in the process, to avert the strong likelihood that disillusioned workers might assert their collective power to seize the reins of government—the report recommended decisive action. "Personal rights must be recognized as supreme and of unalterable ascendency over property rights," it concluded; any other ordering would doom American democracy to destruction. The proposed solution? "That Congress forthwith initiate an amendment to the Constitution providing in specific terms for the protection of the personal rights of every person in the United States from encroachment by the Federal and State Governments and by private individuals, associations, and corporations." In other words, the amendment the Manly report advocated would have insulated freedom of speech and assemblage against state as well as federal incursions, and against private action as well as government interference. Consistent with their belief that a robust commitment to free speech would require the state to constrain private actors, the commissioners also recommended a long list of restrictions on employer efforts to combat organized labor. Indeed, it called for the inclusion among constitutional rights "of the unlimited right of individuals to form associations, not for the sake of profit but for the advancement of their individual and collective interests." It was only through combination and collective action that workers could secure "economic and political justice."[78]

In the event that legislators overstepped the Manly report's new constitutional rights, claimants would have had to seek vindication elsewhere than the courts. "With full recognition of the gravity of [their] suggestions," the commissioners recommended elimination of the judicial power to invalidate state and federal legislation on constitutional grounds.[79]

✦ ✦ ✦

Reflecting on the *Los Angeles Times* bombing and the class war that produced it, Clarence Darrow told the Commission on Industrial Relations that industrial conflict was ultimately irremediable. Nonetheless, he thought the commission capable of achieving meaningful change. Darrow considered public opinion to be the "greatest force there is in the country," and he deemed it essential to draw people's attention to the injustices of modern labor relations. It was not necessary that the commissioners' recommendations be implemented. From Darrow's standpoint, the crucial thing was to pull back the curtain. "The more fundamental and radical your recommendations are the more good they will do," he advised, "and the more you recognize the division of classes and the injustice of it, the more good it will do."[80]

Measured by Darrow's standard, the Manly report was a success. To be sure, the Commission on Industrial Relations accomplished little in the way of concrete legislation or policy change, at least in the immediate term. The Commons report was noncommittal, and the employer report too friendly to the status quo. As for the Manly report, its bold recommendations failed to attract congressional sponsors or fizzled on the floor. The *New York Times* considered it "superfluous to characterize this frank project of confiscation." The *Philadelphia Inquirer* mused that if Walsh had undertaken the chairmanship "with the determination to set himself down as an ass, he could not have succeeded better." Still, the NAM was too glib when it reported that nothing constructive had come of the commission's work. More than anything, the Manly report served as an organizing tool and rallying cry for disillusioned workers. Labor leaders who agreed on little else converged in their effusive praise of its analysis and recommendations. The AFL officially endorsed it, and the railroad brotherhoods and the IWW expressed approval as well.[81]

The *Survey* was poised to react skeptically when Frank Walsh signed on to the Manly report in the summer of 1915. Even so, its assessment captured general sentiments among progressive reformers. In a series of pieces reviewing the three reports, John Fitch blamed factionalism, jealousies, and mismanagement for the dissension within the commission, which prevented production of a decisive report. He lamented the lack of careful documentation and the sparseness of figures and footnotes—a failing he criticized, in terms that resonated with progressive defenses of free speech, because it inhibited full and informed discussion. He regretted the impression conveyed by the Manly report's recommendations "that the only remedy that amounts to anything is economic action—that is, organization and strikes"; as a dyed-in-the wool progressive, Fitch preferred legislative and administrative solutions. Above all, Fitch chastised the report for its inattention to existing constitutional guaranties for free speech and for its fanciful proposal to abolish judicial review not only of federal legislation—a possibility Fitch deemed feasible and potentially desirable—but of state legislation as well. Fitch was no labor partisan; he worried about unions' monopolistic tendencies and their potentially undemocratic rules of admission. And yet, in language that echoed Darrow's, he considered the Manly report a valuable statement of the "spirit and the bitter resentment of organized labor," unlike any produced previously by any agency of the federal government.[82]

After the commission disbanded, a new Industrial Relations Committee organized to advocate for the proposals contained in the Manly report. Among the tasks it set out to achieve was the passage by Congress of a statute or constitutional amendment prohibiting courts from "declar[ing] laws unconstitutional"—an arrogated power that was "the great barrier to progress and . . . the greatest bulwark of privilege." But the new committee never achieved its ambitions. As the United States inched closer to involvement in the world war, unions sought to sustain public interest in industrial conflict, and they appealed for contributions to the committee's operating expenses. Nonetheless, after limping along for a couple of years, the committee closed its doors in the fall of 1917.[83]

Others organizations soon took up the committee's call. For a generation, the Manly report's scathing attack on the American legal system would stir the imagination of labor leaders and reformers alike. The compiled testimony and factual findings of the Commission on Industrial Relations served as confirmation that the ordinary political channels were inadequate to the task of material economic gains for workers, and that the courts served as inhibitors rather than enforcers of personal rights. Many would come to believe, like Walsh, that well-intentioned bureaucrats could not solve the class war—that only organized labor could advance workers' cause.

Understandably, the significance of the Commission on Industrial Relations for the history of civil liberties has proven difficult to discern. What the commissioners meant when they celebrated free speech bears little resemblance to the understanding that is widely shared today. There was, as yet, no close connection between free speech and "civil liberty"; on the contrary, the latter was more commonly invoked to protect property, and to resist organizing, than the other way around. Nor was there a necessary connection between free speech and the Constitution, though the language of rights regularly appeared. Above all, there was no consensus that enforcement of free speech was primarily a judicial function. On the contrary, from the Progressive Era to the New Deal, millions of ordinary Americans believed that the courts were a menace to freedom and a barrier to justice.

And yet, in the unmitigated rancor of the Manly report, the impetus for the modern civil liberties movement was glaringly apparent. For a time, the social workers and progressive reformers who had urged the creation of the Commission on Industrial Relations continued to insist that a classless society was both possible and desirable—or, at least, that class allegiance was an inappropriate basis for political membership and governance. But a core contingent would come to doubt whether conventional progressive methods were adequate to the task of alleviating inequality, or whether amelioration of the worst injustices would suffice. The fundamental change they ultimately advocated required a robust account of free speech capacious enough to insulate mass picketing and secondary boycotts as well as political advocacy.

In his testimony before the Commission on Industrial Relations, the Socialist Los Angeles lawyer who had helped to represent the McNamara brothers and subsequently lost his mayoral bid reflected that "the act of the McNamaras, unwise as it was, was forced by an enemy, very much as the European war." It was the latter that monopolized debates over free speech as America turned its gaze overseas. The commission's report reflected a sincere commitment to free speech within the left of the progressive establishment.

Perhaps, if the First World War had not intruded, protection for expressive freedom might more quickly have picked up steam. As it happened, the perceived need for patriotic uniformity quelled the prewar awakening of pluralistic tolerance. Still, the commission provided a template. At the outbreak of war, when dissenters were faced with aggressive state and private repression, they had a vocabulary to draw on.[84]

In the years after they petitioned President Taft to investigate the injustices of the American legal system, the very same reformers who launched the Commission on Industrial Relations would pioneer a new approach. The *Survey*'s social workers would go on to found the American Union against Militarism (AUAM), which would give rise to the National Civil Liberties Bureau (NCLB), though not before Paul Kellogg and Lillian Wald resigned in protest. The NCLB would reorganize as the ACLU. Darrow would join the ACLU's inaugural board. So would Jane Addams, Fitch, and Walsh. Crystal Eastman, who was appointed to the commission's research division in 1913 to "take up the constitutional and legal aspects of industrial relations, the courts and the workers," would cofound the new civil liberties organization.[85]

All of these figures cultivated their commitment to free speech in the context of the class war. The great mystery of the modern civil liberties movement is not how or why its leaders came to champion free speech. Rather, it is how the most prominent critics of a hypocritical judiciary came to promote the courts as the last best hope for the class struggle as well as individual rights.

2

The Citadel of Civil Liberty

BURIED in the back of the *Survey*'s November 1917 issue was an inconspicuous announcement. The NCLB, formerly a division of the AUAM, had reorganized as an independent entity for the defense of "constitutional rights." With a network of 150 cooperating attorneys throughout the United States, the civil liberties organization was providing legal aid wherever "the rights of minorities" were under attack. In typical progressive fashion, its leadership was cooperating closely with government officials. The NCLB's underlying concern was to buttress "democratic institutions"—the same objective that justified American involvement in the war, and one that many progressives wholeheartedly endorsed. The notice neglected to mention that the *Survey*'s editor, Paul Kellogg, was a cofounder of the AUAM and regarded the splinter group as a betrayal of his organization's goals.[1]

When the NCLB opened shop as a bureau for the defense of antiwar dissenters, it was venturing onto a lonely field. In the fall of 1917, as the organization declared its commitment to "free speech, free press and public assembly during war-time," patriotic fervor consumed the country. Most Americans dismissed dissent as counterproductive and self-indulgent. Even self-described pacifists insisted that citizens were duty bound to accede to the outcome of majoritarian consensus. To many progressives, the defense of free speech was a backhanded assault on the state.[2]

As the war effort suffused American cultural and political life, the leadership of the NCLB tested the full panoply of prewar precedents for the defense of dissenting speech. In the progressive calculus, dissidence was valuable only insofar as it served broader social interests—and during wartime, the public welfare seemed better served by compliance. Most government officials were unreceptive to outmoded notions of natural rights and unwilling to jeopardize wartime economic production by accommodating unruly agitators. The federal courts, though ostensibly committed to individual autonomy, were too protective of private property and too deferential to military necessity to countenance radical ideas. And the nascent civil liberties advocates were themselves uneasy about their path. As veteran progressive reformers, they had long resented judicial intervention with the products of democratic consensus.

The emergence of the NCLB is widely considered a pivotal moment in the history of civil liberties in the United States, and rightly so. The fledgling group helped lay the foundation for a meaningful civil liberties coalition after the Armistice. The significance of the NCLB's wartime program has, however, been profoundly misunderstood. The suffocating conformity of the First World War has left the impression that what was unusual about the organizational precursor to the ACLU was its adherence to civil libertarian ideals—its unflinching defense of the nation's most reviled speakers in the most repressive of times. At a moment when "the voice of reason [was] not heard," the lonely stalwarts of the NCLB clung to neutral principle.[3]

On the contrary, what made the NCLB so central to the future course of civil liberties was its willingness to compromise consistency in service of its overarching objective, namely, ensuring the continued vitality of American radicalism. Perhaps no feature more fully captured the organization than its ability to adapt, to experiment, and to appropriate the tools and arguments of its perceived antagonists, including the language of court-centered constitutional rights. A group more faithful to progressive precepts would have confined itself to advising heedfulness of free speech in the formulation and enforcement of government policy. But the new organization went further. It asked the judiciary to check the excesses of elected officials. It declared (in language borrowed from a British lord) that "the supreme test of civil liberty is the determination to protect an unpopular minority in a time of national excitement." In so doing, it sought to wrest the notion of civil liberty from its historical entwinement with the prerogatives of property owners—to retool it to accommodate radical propaganda and to counter the suppression of organized labor. As the repressive apparatus of national security caught unruly radicals within its grip, the NCLB reclaimed for labor the conservative commitment to that "citadel of civil liberty, the courts of law."[4]

In the immediate term, the NCLB's efforts were unsuccessful. Pacifists and labor activists landed in prison at an alarming rate. Legal protections for free speech were weaker than before the war. Still, the NCLB's early operations—the organization's defeats, even more than its sporadic successes—would prove critical for the future course of civil liberties advocacy. If the NCLB's failures in the courts were not unexpected, its fruitless negotiations with the Wilson administration on behalf of wartime dissenters and conscientious objectors shook the confidence of the NCLB's leadership in state-centered solutions. Looking forward, those disappointments would push the interwar ACLU to explore alternative avenues of advancing civil liberties goals. The ACLU of the early 1920s was just as wary of the courts as it was of legislators and administrators, but its willingness to challenge progressive orthodoxies about administrative expertise opened space for an eventual alliance with state-skeptical conservatives.

The NCLB's wartime experience is also important for another, more familiar reason. It was during and after the First World War that the *progressive* defense of a court-centered First Amendment was forged. That vision—which was distinct from and only partly compatible with the evolving vision of the NCLB—cast deliberative openness as a prerequisite for informed social change and justified, rather than restricted, the exercise of state power to promote public welfare. Of course, as the labor struggles of the early 1910s revealed, progressives had long urged state actors to tolerate disfavored expression, whether as a "matter of generosity," or—as legal scholar Ernst Freund preferred—"of political prudence." In the course of the war, however, policy interests proved insufficient to safeguard expressive freedom. As the wartime hysteria escalated, so too did discomfort with public and private repression. The agonized debates in progressive journals over the limits of free speech, however inchoate and contradictory, gradually spurred progressives to admit a narrow opening for the operation of judicial review. The possibility that the NCLB's wartime flirtation with constitutional litigation helped to spur the emerging conception is alluring, if ultimately beside the point. What is crucial is that the organization engaged with its proponents as they hashed out its contours. A few years later, the pioneers of the progressive vision would form a critical bloc within the interwar civil liberties coalition. And the leaders of the interwar ACLU would skillfully deploy their understanding, even as they challenged its legitimation of state power.[5]

✦ ✦ ✦

In the fall of 1914, as he was losing confidence in the Commission on Industrial Relations, Paul Kellogg turned his attention to more promising pursuits. Together with social workers Jane Addams and Lillian Wald, he began to formulate strategies for keeping America out of war. Wald was the founder of New York's Henry Street Settlement, and she opened its facilities for a gathering of progressives interested in antiwar activities. The product of that meeting was a new organization. Known initially as the Henry Street Group, it went by a variety of names over the coming years, but its best known, the American Union against Militarism, succinctly captured its underlying objective: to "guard against militarism" and "build toward world federation." Of the seven signers of the petition to President Taft urging creation of the Commission on Industrial Relations, six attended the Henry Street meeting, and the seventh subsequently joined the organization.[6]

Opposition to militarism took on new urgency in 1915, when President Woodrow Wilson—despite early assurances that he would avoid military engagement—embraced a mounting demand for preparedness. Within a year, the AUAM was a sprawling organization with branch offices throughout the United States and 1,500 active members, many of whom had worked together on behalf of the Commission on Industrial Relations. The organization scored some early successes, but its confidence evaporated with Germany's decision in February 1917 to reinstate its policy of unrestricted submarine warfare on vessels carrying supplies to its enemy, Britain.

Within a matter of days, the nation was marching swiftly toward war, and the AUAM was powerless to stop it. The United States Congress declared war on Germany on April 6, 1917, and instituted conscription six weeks later. In June, the AUAM announced its wartime program. One of its components, "a just and lasting peace" premised on robust international cooperation, was the organization's standard fare. But the AUAM introduced a second, surprising set of objectives as well. Under the heading "work against militarism," it pledged opposition to the permanent establishment of conscription, legal advice to conscientious objectors, and, most important, the maintenance of "civil liberty in war time." The new agenda asserted antiwar protests and refusal of military service as legally enforceable rights. That focus on law was evident from the very label "civil liberty," which conjured conservative defenses of property.[7]

The decision to promote "civil liberty" was a controversial one within the AUAM. As an initial matter, the revised strategy threatened to undermine the AUAM's respectable reputation; government hawks and self-styled patriotic groups regarded the strategy as a cover for subversive activity. But many members likely harbored a deeper anxiety about the implications of the new approach. Wald had traveled to Lawrence, Massachusetts, during the IWW's textile strike and came away concerned about legal abuses. Florence Kelley played a seminal role in defending maximum-hours legislation for women against constitutional challenge, and she condemned liberty of contract in unequivocal terms. And few reformers were more cynical about court-centered constitutionalism than the AUAM's executive secretary, Crystal Eastman. The daughter of two Congregational ministers who succeeded Thomas Beecher as pastors of the Park Church in upstate New York, Eastman was practically groomed for progressive activism. Trained as an attorney, she devoted her early career to the sociological study of industrial accidents—first in Pittsburgh, at Kellogg's instigation, and subsequently in New York, when Governor (and future chief justice of the United States Supreme Court) Charles Evans Hughes named her secretary of the commission that drafted one of the country's first workers' compensation statutes. New York's high court soon invalidated that law as an incursion on employers' property rights; a state constitutional amendment would later counter the decision, but the legal defeat was a powerful lesson, made all the more poignant the very next day, when the Triangle Shirtwaist fire took the lives of 146 garment workers and a "constant stirring sense of tragedy and horror . . . sank into [Eastman's] soul."[8]

For the AUAM leadership, then, the decision to resist militarism by invoking individual liberty was a strange turn of events. Most of the organization's veterans regarded the state as an ally in the struggle to achieve industrial harmony. All were suspicious of, if not altogether hostile to, the courts. Probably, all were skeptical of individual rights. And yet, within a matter of months, the Civil Liberties Bureau was the most visible face of the organization's campaign against militarism.[9]

The AUAM's new direction flowed partly from a personnel addition. One month before the impending declaration of war, the board recruited a new member. When Roger Nash Baldwin arrived in New York City in March 1917, Eastman was taking a hiatus to recuperate from a difficult pregnancy that had led to chronic kidney disease. Baldwin seemed an ideal substitute. Like Eastman, he had begun his career as a progressive reformer, committed to social science methods. Baldwin, however, was more pragmatist than ideologue, and his willingness to experiment with alternative approaches would prove momentous for the future course of the organization.

Baldwin was born in 1884 to an affluent family of New England reformers. After an indulgent childhood in Wellesley, Massachusetts, he matriculated at Harvard, where he excelled socially if not academically. After graduation, he met with his father's attorney, Louis Brandeis, to solicit some career advice. The future Supreme Court justice and prominent progressive encouraged the young Baldwin to pursue public service. He also urged him to start his career where Brandeis had started his own: in Saint Louis, Missouri. Over the next ten years, Baldwin held leadership roles in myriad progressive organizations. He built the Department of Sociology at Washington University, headed a settlement house, and helped to establish the Saint Louis Committee for Social Service among Colored People, the city's first interracial organization. He was a founder of the National Probation Officers Association and an authority on juvenile justice. In the course of these endeavors, he grew friendly with the prominent national social workers who eventually attracted him to the AUAM, including Addams, Kellogg, and Wald. He was, in short, the consummate progressive: committed to the existing political and economic systems but determined to help them run as fairly and smoothly as possible.[10]

During his time in Saint Louis, however, two developments drove an entering wedge between Baldwin and his progressive peers. In 1909, Baldwin began a lifetime correspondence with the charismatic anarchist Emma Goldman, whom he assisted in finding a speaking venue after Washington University excluded her from its campus. Anarchists piqued Baldwin's interest. Years later, he explained that he was sympathetic to "their goal of a society with a minimum of compulsion, a maximum of individual freedom and of voluntary association, and the abolition of exploitation and poverty."[11]

Equally important, Baldwin's involvement in a campaign to revise Saint Louis's city charter taught him the pitfalls of progressive reform. The 1914 charter, which Baldwin championed on behalf of the Civic League, instituted the initiative, referendum, and recall. Soon after it was enacted, voters introduced an initiative to mandate segregated housing. Despite Baldwin's best efforts, working in conjunction with the NAACP, the measure passed by overwhelming margins. For the first time, Baldwin faced the basic tension between majoritarian democracy and minority rights that would dominate the rest of his professional life.

With the Civic League, Baldwin participated in a test case challenging the constitutionality of the ordinance in the federal courts. The district court granted a temporary injunction and made it permanent after the Supreme Court's decision in *Buchanan v. Warley*, which invalidated a similar Louisville law on constitutional grounds. To Baldwin's consternation, the basis for that decision was the very provision that progressive reformers so despised: the ordinance, held the unanimous Supreme Court (including the newly appointed Justice Brandeis), was a violation of the seller's Fourteenth Amendment right to dispose of his private property in a manner of his choosing. Troubled but resolute, Baldwin assured local citizens that "in the long run the control of legislation by the whole people is best for all of us, white and colored." He insisted that "a vote of the people" would produce the right result "on almost any other question but one involving race prejudice"—a prediction that would soon prove overly optimistic.[12]

By mid-decade, Baldwin began flirting with a more radical approach to social ills. He was reading the *Masses,* a socialist magazine edited by Eastman's brother Max, and he was sufficiently impressed by interactions with visiting Wobblies to spearhead a new project to open municipal lodging and a soup kitchen in Saint Louis. When the report of the Commission on Industrial Relations came out in 1915, Baldwin wrote to Frank P. Walsh, whom he had befriended through his work on juvenile justice. He told Walsh that the report would "do more to educate public opinion to the truth of existing conditions than any other one document in existence." He was particularly inspired by the testimony of Theodore Schroeder concerning the suppression of workers' speech.[13]

His new attentiveness to industrial inequality predisposed Baldwin to the antimilitarism of the AUAM. Like many of its members, he blamed capitalism for the war. Without the profit motive, he believed, American industry would be less invested in militarism. When the AUAM leadership offered Baldwin a position as national secretary in 1915, he opted to head the Saint Louis branch instead. As war approached, however, Baldwin rightly sensed that local reform work would surrender the stage to national activity. In March 1917, upon receiving a telegram inviting him to take over Eastman's duties, he packed his bags and left for New York.[14]

Baldwin's first undertaking when he arrived at the AUAM was to incorporate broad protections for conscientious objectors into legislation on conscription. There was ample congressional support for the exemption of clergy members and adherents of the well-established peace churches, whom the pending Selective Service Act explicitly recognized. Baldwin's aspirations, however, were more ambitious. Working with Norman Thomas, the Presbyterian minister who would go on to lead the Socialist Party, he urged Congress and the War Department to extend exemptions to Socialists and other potential inductees who approved violence under some circumstances but opposed participation in the world war. Newton D. Baker, Cleveland's former progressive mayor and Wilson's secretary of war, declined to champion a statutory exemption for these "political objectors," and Congress overwhelmingly rejected amendments to enlarge the class of exemptions. In fact, as wartime passions rose, the AUAM's popularity "hit bedrock." Still, the Selective Service Act authorized local draft boards to assess an objector's eligibility for noncombatant service, a significant concession. Moreover, Baker promised the AUAM administrative moderation. Heartened by these opportunities for intervention on behalf of antiwar inductees, Baldwin created a Bureau for Conscientious Objectors within the AUAM.[15]

The new enterprise divided the AUAM's leadership and polarized its membership. Although a majority of the directing committee authorized the proposal, some of the AUAM's most seasoned figures, including founders Wald and Kellogg, were debating whether to resign. In a spirited bid to retain them, Eastman addressed their apprehensions, which centered on the organization's ability to shape future policy if it abandoned its cooperative stance toward the administration. In Eastman's view, such concerns were unfounded. The goals of the new bureau were "liberal" (a term that was quickly if incompletely supplanting "progressive" as the banner of reform-minded advocates and intellectuals), not "extreme radical." In fact, she insisted, the organization's priorities were directly in line with President Wilson's. After all, his appointments to the War Department included Baker and the celebrated progressive commentator Walter Lippmann, along with Columbia University dean Frederick Keppel, who had once served as secretary of the American Association for International Conciliation and announced that "war and civilization can no longer go hand and hand." According to Eastman, the AAUM was perfectly positioned to assist the administration in implementing its commitment to pluralism and tolerance.[16]

Acknowledging that service to conscientious objectors was controversial, Eastman proposed a structural reorganization. In place of the conscientious objectors' bureau, she urged the creation of a "Bureau for the Maintenance of Civil Liberties," which would encompass all of the "fundamental rights in war time—free press, free speech, freedom of assembly, and liberty of conscience." Over the coming months, all of those rights would yield to patriotic zeal. Still, some would prove more palatable than others, and teasing out the differences would help to shape the future civil liberties landscape.[17]

✦ ✦ ✦

Proponents of the AUAM's civil liberties program explained their emerging agenda as a natural outcrop of the organization's prewar effort to promote pacifism through lobbying and publicity. "A Union Against Militarism becomes, during wartime, inevitably a Union for the Defense of Civil Liberty," a September press release explained. In fact, there was nothing inevitable about the organization's new direction. The AUAM's wartime project was a radical reimagining of the relationship between citizen and state.[18]

In defending conscientious objectors, the AUAM embraced a concept of "liberty of conscience" as an "Anglo-Saxon tradition for which our ancestors fought and died." Reliance on Anglo-Saxon tradition was a peculiar tactic for an appeal to progressive officials, many of whom, following Oliver Wendell Holmes Jr., considered it "revolting to have no better reason for a rule of law than that so it was laid down in the time of Henry IV." Equally unusual was the organization's framing of freedom of conscience as an individual right: "Conscience is nothing if it is not individual," an early AUAM pamphlet tendentiously insisted. In the *Survey*, by contrast, references to "conscience" in the 1910s routinely followed the modifier "public." Indeed, for most progressives (as theologian Samuel Zane Batten explained matters), "true liberty mean[t] the voluntary sacrifice of self for the common life."[19]

To be sure, the progressives were well versed in opposition to unjust laws. Their assault on *Lochner*-era due process, though directed at judicial rather than legislative outputs, openly impugned the American legal system.

In addition, they had decried local ordinances prohibiting public meetings and urged police restraint at the level of enforcement. But the solutions they advocated—administrative moderation, legislative reform, constitutional amendment—were state centered and publicly oriented. And while some accepted labor actions outside state channels, most saw the strike as a second-best solution, a collective response to social ills the government had failed to cure. The dangers of second-guessing government policies were all the more acute where, as in the case of conscription, a majority of Americans agreed on a path after vigorous national debate. The Wilson administration's deference to democratic processes made conscientious objection to military service a difficult proposition to defend. In fact, invoking individual autonomy to demand exemption from a duly enacted law threatened to legitimate the very constitutional regime that the AUAM's founders had long condemned.

Cognizant of such objections, the AUAM also insisted that "liberty of conscience" was a means toward "social progress." Here the organization was on firmer ground. One NCLB publication asserted that "progress begins with unpopular minorities, and we endanger society when we imprison heretics and agitators." Another reprinted a tract by a British economist who argued that uncompromising government policies would buttress "despotism" and "arbitrary rule," as well as a popular tendency toward uncritical submission. Perhaps the most explicit account was Norman Angell's *Why Freedom Matters,* which the NCLB circulated in pamphlet form. Angell, a British writer and future Nobel Peace Prize recipient who had spent several years at manual labor in the United States, linked conscientious objection to a pluralist mindset that would enable interrogation of other institutions, including private property. His defense of individual conscience, which the AUAM adopted, was founded on "utility" rather than "abstract 'right.'" Only through the exercise of "private judgment" could citizens cultivate their "public judgment" and participate in political and social betterment. In the absence of heresy, society would suffer.[20]

The AUAM was not alone in advancing such claims. Other progressives, including some within the War Department, suggested similar notions. In the early days of the draft, even the *New Republic* (which Eastman deemed practically the Wilson "administration's own organ") insisted that conscription was imposed for "democratic purposes"—to raise an efficient army—and should not be construed to "coerc[e] unwilling minorities into the firing line." Nonetheless, most progressives were skeptical of exemption. By June, a typical assessment in the *New Republic* criticized conscientious objectors for their "anti-social attitude and mode of conduct." In July, John Dewey elected the same forum for his essay "Conscience and Compulsion," in which he blamed the American legal tradition for elevating "fixed rules and injunctions" over "social conditions and consequences of action." In Dewey's view, conscientious objectors unduly weighted the "inhibitions of inner consciousness." Responding to Dewey directly in an August article for the *Survey,* Norman Thomas cast compulsory service, along with war itself, as more profoundly "anti-social" than the conscientious refusal to serve. But such arguments were quickly falling from favor. A few progressives (including Dewey) remained open to accommodation as a "matter of expedience or of sound public policy," but it was hubris to advocate "recognition of conscientious objection as a matter of democratic right."[21]

At first, the AUAM hoped that policy considerations would be enough. As Eastman put it, the organization's overriding goal was "lenient administration of the Conscription Act," an objective it pursued by asking the state to accommodate dissenters. In a period of patchy government record-keeping, as many as three million "slackers" evaded the draft by simply refusing to register. Despite internal disagreement, the AUAM instead counseled "obedience to law, to the utmost limit of conscience." The organization relied heavily on the methods its leadership had cultivated before the war, including communication with government officials. Roger Baldwin corresponded regularly with Frederick Keppel, the third assistant secretary of war, who assured him that the department appreciated his "spirit of co-operation." Felix Frankfurter, who was serving as a special assistant to the secretary of war, wrote an important memorandum espousing many of Baldwin's suggestions and urging lenience even toward secular objectors. For his part, Newton Baker was cordial to Baldwin and genuinely concerned by reports of discrepancies and injustices in the execution of War Department policies by individual commanders. The NCLB quickly picked up on these cues, and the repressive potential of discretionary power became a central theme of the civil liberties campaign.[22]

Over time, however, informal negotiations proved insufficient to serve the organization's constituency. As the war progressed, reports of "brutality and injustice" against objectors emerged, and Baldwin faced growing resistance from anxious allies who advocated more confrontational methods. In

March 1918, President Wilson issued an executive order that appeared to vindicate Baldwin's trust in the "Administration's liberality." In practice, however, the measure made only a modest improvement. The objectors who mattered most to the subsequent founders of the ACLU were the small contingent motivated by class sentiments to resist a *capitalist* war, whom Thomas described as "pioneers of a new conception of the state." But the Board of Inquiry appointed to interview objectors consistently declared these political objectors insincere.[23]

On balance, the Wilson administration was surprisingly willing to offer alternative service to conscientious objectors who were unequivocally opposed to war, even if their aversion to military service stemmed from secular rather than religious convictions. But to accommodate objectors who were willing to kill for "social revolutions" exceeded the limits of progressive tolerance. As future Supreme Court justice Harlan Fiske Stone reflected, reviewing his service for the Board of Inquiry, the War Department's forbearance applied only to individuals opposed to "all war on principle," not to those who were willing to participate "in a war to exterminate the capitalist and the bourgeois."[24]

In the spring of 1918, Baldwin's cooperative methods finally faltered. The military launched an investigation of Baldwin and his organization (by then known as the National Civil Liberties Bureau), embarrassing Baldwin's administration contacts. War Department officials severed their ties with the group, notwithstanding its willingness to terminate any objectionable practices. By fall, with November's Armistice on the horizon, the emboldened organization cast the administration's attitude toward political objectors as an incursion on individual autonomy. Although it continued to emphasize the "value of minorities in social process," it professed an individual's complete discretion to decide whether any given act was "morally *right* or *wrong*." Recognition of "the value of the individual," it argued, was what differentiated American democracy from the "Prussian doctrine of the total subordination of the individual to the state."[25]

Keppel, answering for the War Department, was dismissive. The administration's tolerance of conscientious objectors was meant to respect "the scruples of those who cannot conscientiously *take human life*." To broaden the category to include selective objectors "would be to admit the right of every man to set himself up as judge of the wisdom of our Government." Such a theory was equivalent to tax resistance and incompatible with progressive values. "What your proposal comes to," Keppel concluded, "is the negation of law, of authority, of government." Any concession to such arguments, Keppel insisted, would jeopardize American democracy as well as public safety. That view followed directly from long-standing progressive principles.[26]

As the war drew to a close, the leadership of the NCLB articulated a theoretical defense of individual conscience rooted in the IWW's hostility to state power. But to read those later pronouncements into the AUAM's earlier endeavors would be anachronistic. There was simply too much faith in Wilson's War Department, and too much formative disillusionment, in the intervening months. Some members, including Thomas, had religiously rooted reasons to defend freedom of conscience. Many, no doubt, invoked the language of conscience primarily for pragmatic reasons. That is, a time-honored tradition of individual rights was the most promising vocabulary for a demand so difficult to square with progressive values. The temerity with which the wartime civil liberties leadership sought administrative recognition of individual rights would later fuel the ACLU's pursuit of collective rights in the courts.[27]

✦ ✦ ✦

The AUAM's Civil Liberties Bureau, formally announced on July 2, 1917, was more than a continuation of the Bureau for Conscientious Objectors. It was a change in tack. Although the organization lumped its defense of "liberty of conscience" together with its "attempt to save free speech, free press and assembly," the latter was more easily reconcilable to the progressive tropes of public welfare and social responsibility. It was one thing to advocate open discussion of democratic laws, and another to countenance defiance of those laws once they were enacted. The *New York Times* captured this sentiment in July 1917 when it described as "indubitable" the "right to disapprove" but counseled that conscientious objectors should accept imprisonment unless they "prevail[ed] upon Congress to change the law."[28]

Under peacetime conditions, most progressives favored robust public discussion and the freedom to organize for political as well as economic change. After all, the Progressive Era had witnessed a staggering ascent of scientific and cultural understandings that were previously taboo. Moreover, suppression typically targeted society's least privileged members and advanced the interests of its most empowered. The AUAM leadership hoped such sentiments would foster support for its wartime program.[29]

In practice, as the "war psychology . . . invaded the home, the street and the market place," many progressives condemned dissent outright or accepted the state's authority to quash it. As Roscoe Pound had earlier admonished, "The individual interest in free belief and opinion must always be balanced with the social interest in the security of social institutions and the interest of the state in its personality." During wartime, estimations of the latter appeared to swamp the former. "It would be a good thing for all of us," one correspondent told Baldwin, "if we emphasized a little more our duties as citizens and were less concerned about insisting upon our 'rights.' "[30]

Still, some progressives—including some very influential ones—were uneasy with the scale of wartime repression. Although they quibbled over specifics, many shared the general sentiment expressed in the *Nation* that "the right to free speech must be upheld, throughout the country"—that "freedom of legitimate criticism" must not be denied. Among the most eloquent exponents of this ideal was John Dewey, whose pained and belated embrace of expressive freedom unfolded in a series of essays for the *New Republic*. In September 1917, Dewey relished the irony of "ultra-socialists rallying to the old banner of Elihu Root with its inscription to the sanctity of individual rights and constitutional guaranties," and he dismissed as implausible the prospect of widespread suppression of "liberty of thought and speech." Two months later, chastened by escalating hysteria (along with a penetrating reproach from his former student Randolph Bourne), Dewey recanted. Like Zechariah Chafee Jr.'s famous defense of free speech in the aftermath of the war, Dewey's wartime writings emphasized pluralism and social welfare as opposed to individual autonomy.[31]

Thus, although there was no national clamoring for free speech in the summer of 1917, moderates within the AUAM were right to regard the Civil Liberties Bureau as more palatable than the Bureau for Conscientious Objectors that preceded it. As the free speech fights and the Commission on Industrial Relations had proven, there was space for progressive discussion about the desirable parameters of free speech. The Civil Liberties Bureau sought to recruit prowar attorneys and supporters who would buttress its credibility—and while many prospective members considered themselves "bound by the national decision," others offered support. After all, the organization explained, the best way to uphold American democracy was to preserve open channels for the ideas that democratic majorities rejected.[32]

The immediate impetus for the AUAM's foray into free speech was the congressional and public debate over the Espionage Act, passed on June 15, 1917. Adopted at Wilson's prompting, the statute made it unlawful to interfere with the recruitment of troops or to disclose information damaging to the military effort. A confluence of zealous prosecution, broad judicial interpretation, and obliging juries eventually resulted in more than a thousand convictions and the exclusion of one hundred publications from the mails. Before passage of the statute, however, few anticipated that defendants would face twenty-year prison terms and $10,000 fines for stray remarks about the inadequacies of the war effort. Rather, discussion centered on a section conferring unilateral authority on postal officials to ban the mailing of any communication unlawful under the statute—a power the postmaster enthusiastically employed.[33]

The First World War precipitated an unprecedented expansion of national power, and the dark side of state building became a leitmotif of the NCLB's wartime civil liberties program. Free speech advocates increasingly argued that concentrating control in the hands of unaccountable bureaucrats "establishe[d] a censorship of the worst kind." The postal censorship provision—together with the Trading with the Enemy Act, passed in October—squarely raised the specter of administrative discretion as a threat to democratic values. In so doing, it seemingly created space for an organization committed to expressive freedom.[34]

In filling that role, the AUAM had a strong model to draw on. During the late nineteenth and early twentieth centuries, groups occasionally organized to defend free speech against governmental incursions—sometimes to protect business interests (especially publishers) and occasionally on ideological grounds. One in particular was well known to the AUAM's leadership. The Free Speech League, founded in 1902 and nurtured by Theodore Schroeder for twenty years, never won a significant judicial victory. But it generated support for free speech at the level of local policy, and it pressed some progressives to question whether a trump on legislative enactments—in the form of the First Amendment—might, under certain circumstances, be made to serve desirable ends. Although much of its work took place in the courts, the league used every strategy at its disposal, including publicity for legal and other disputes, academic and professional advocacy, mass meetings and demonstrations, and correspondence with government officials.[35]

Inspired by the individualist rhetoric of philosophical anarchism, free thought, radical abolitionism, and the women's movement, the Free Speech League defended all expression, regardless of viewpoint or subject matter. Its commitment to personal freedom was a perfect complement to the bohemian culture of early twentieth-century Manhattan, where free speech was not just a platform for legal reform and social change, but a way of life. By the beginning of the war, the Free Speech League was on the decline. Schroeder had been the glue that held it together, and he was increasingly drawn to other interests. Nonetheless, many of the league's most prominent members and allies, including Schroeder and Gilbert Roe, supplied the AUAM's fledgling Civil Liberties Bureau with materials and assistance.[36]

The Civil Liberties Bureau also absorbed the organizational aspirations of Harry Weinberger, an attorney who had worked closely with the Free Speech League and would soon represent the defendant in *Abrams v. United States*. A pacifist and radical individualist, Weinberger had fought against compulsory vaccination in the early 1910s and defended Emma Goldman when she was indicted for distributing birth control literature in 1916. In April 1917, he shared with Baldwin his idea for an American Legal Defense League that would "fight all cases in the United States where free speech, free press or the right peaceably to assemble or to petition the government is invaded." At first, Baldwin was supportive. He had already expressed an interest in expressive freedom, but he was not a lawyer, and he had no concrete program in mind. In May, the Civil Liberties Bureau issued a pamphlet referring victims of constitutional rights violations to the American Legal Defense League, just as Weinberger had requested. Weinberger's group, in turn, attracted an impressive roster of members, along with an enthusiastic announcement in the *New Republic* and an encouraging letter from Newton Baker.[37]

In a move he would repeat often during his ACLU career, however, Baldwin subsequently maneuvered to protect and expand his own organization's turf. At a May 11 meeting, Weinberger agreed that all cases involving conscientious objectors would be left to the Bureau for Conscientious Objectors; although he personally opposed conscription and belonged to Goldman and Alexander Berkman's No-Conscription League, Weinberger's advisory committee was primarily interested in the rights of speech, press, and assembly. In June, Baldwin went further. Withdrawing an earlier promise of financial assistance, he told Weinberger that the AUAM was forming a bureau "to take hold of the work of organizing legal defense throughout the country." The new Civil Liberties Bureau swallowed the American Legal Defense League's entire program. Its goal, according to the press release announcing its formation, was to unite the various groups and individuals committed to maintaining "constitutional liberties" in wartime against government interference. In a revised edition of the pamphlet on constitutional rights, published in July, all references to the American Legal Defense League were gone.[38]

The Civil Liberties Bureau did not entirely abandon the AUAM's standard tactics. When the bureau was first announced, Baldwin emphasized that the board expected to cooperate closely with the federal government in preserving constitutional freedom. Throughout the war, it cultivated relationships with public officials and leaned heavily on well-connected members, including the brother of President Wilson's son-in-law. In mid-July, the bureau organized an emergency conference to address postal censorship of radical publications, including the *Masses*. Participants voted unanimously to send a delegation of lawyers, including Clarence Darrow and Frank Walsh, to discuss the matter with the president and administration officials. But Postmaster General Albert S. Burleson, an antilabor southern segregationist, rebuffed their overtures. If the publishers disagreed with his decisions, he said, they could take up the matter in court.[39]

Despite their inveterate opposition to court-centered constitutionalism, the leaders of the Civil Liberties Bureau accepted Burleson's invitation. Baldwin knew through his experience with the Saint Louis housing ordinance that courts would occasionally act to invalidate oppressive legislation. Moreover, the Free Speech League had unabashedly pursued constitutional litigation as a check on state action, and Weinberger's plans for an independent wartime civil liberties body were themselves modeled on the older organization. Drawing on these examples, Baldwin and his allies devised a plan of action. The organization would operate nationally as a clearinghouse for information and legal aid, providing assistance and legal representation to those individuals whose constitutional rights were violated. If the AUAM's leaders were wary of legitimating the judiciary, they ceded their scruples in favor of results.

A few successful court challenges in the summer of 1917 encouraged pursuit of the legal program, and by September, Baldwin was urging local correspondents to challenge offensive ordinances through litigation. In November, cooperating attorneys throughout the country were assisting in an average of 125 cases per week. The organization was pursuing constitutional cases under the Espionage and Trading with the Enemy Acts and assisting in litigation under local ordinances and state laws in addition to federal legislation. It was also supplying legal and financial aid to needy defendants and supporting local defense committees. Even judicial losses could be made to serve the civil liberties cause. Baldwin observed that most of the bureau's clients did not "want to go to jail or to suffer an expensive trial"—rather, they wanted guidance "as to how far they can go without getting into trouble with the Federal authorities." Still, in the event of an unwelcome conviction, the bureau could "show up miscarriage of justice" in order to generate outrage and stimulate change. In short, the bureau would do everything in its power to prevent "mob-minded judges" (along with overzealous bureaucrats) from "trampl[ing] upon the rights of free speech, free press and public assembly during war-time."[40]

During the summer and fall of 1917, the Civil Liberties Bureau tried its hand at lobbying, propaganda, and grassroots organizing. Increasingly, however, litigation emerged as a defining feature of the organization's campaign. Indeed, the court-centered component of the new project left its stamp on the entity's name. The very notion of a "bureau" invoked a tradition of legal aid bureaus, including the Bureau of Legal First Aid with which it worked closely during the war. The Civil Liberties Bureau would help dissenters to "get their legal rights before the courts."[41]

✦　✦　✦

And what of the "civil liberties" emblazoned on the new bureau's letterhead? Perhaps it would be fairest to accept a policy proposed in an internal memorandum discussing the designation of the American Union against Militarism, namely, to "leave the name out," on the understanding that "it was a makeshift name." In practice, however, the new title mattered to critics as well as supporters of the bureau's platform. When the founders of the Civil Liberties Bureau pledged to uphold the rights of free speech, free press, and public assembly, they were doing more than defining the substantive scope of their wartime work. They were staking out a normative claim.[42]

Of the various American groups that had defended expressive freedom in the past, none had adopted the label "civil liberties." Used almost exclusively in its singular form, "civil liberty" was closely linked with judicial power. As a Maryland judge explained in a 1913 address to the ABA, "Civil liberty cannot be defined without a reference to the law." It was in *Marbury v. Madison,* after all—a case that many progressives denounced as a judicial usurpation—that Justice John Marshall famously characterized the "very essence of civil liberty" as the "right of every individual to claim the protection of the laws whenever he receives an injury." That such injuries most commonly involved property rights was not lost on radical and labor advocates of free speech.[43]

When Crystal Eastman suggested the phrase in her June 1917 letter to the AUAM's executive committee, she was borrowing from Britain's National Council for Civil Liberties (NCCL), founded the previous year. Eastman's second husband, Walter Fuller, was intimately involved in the British group, which furnished an additional, though more attenuated, organizational model for free speech advocacy. The objects of the NCCL were opposition to conscription and to other laws and policies "likely to endanger civil liberty"; the (plural) civil liberties the organization sought to safeguard included freedom of speech and the right of civil trial. Roger Baldwin was very interested in the NCCL's work. Like its American counterpart, the NCCL had strong labor ties, and its leadership included prominent British labor activists and socialist theorists. Despite the affinities and personal connections between the two organizations, however, efforts to coordinate activities faltered during the war. The NCLB shipped its pamphlets and publications to England, but periodic efforts by the NCCL's secretary to return the favor evidently failed to reach their target.[44]

Whatever civil liberties meant to the NCCL and its constituency, it was an incongruous choice for the wavering progressives of the AUAM. As the *New York Times* put it, "Our conception of civil liberty does not make sufficient allowance for changes in economic and social conditions, and is an obstacle to progress." At the outset of the war, the term was typically invoked by conservative lawyers eager to defend the judiciary from political assault and by industry-friendly politicians concerned to forestall state regulation of business practices. Neither group concerned itself with expressive freedom or other personal rights. According to Norman Thomas, the same "rampant individualists" who rejected proposals for the "conscription of wealth" denounced conscientious objectors for their antisocial attitudes. On one point, however, the Civil Liberties Bureau could agree with a former United States attorney general: "Germany is the power which threatens the continuance of civil liberty as our forefathers have established it."[45]

By the beginning of the war, the clamoring for judicial recall and other aggressive court-constraining measures—so salient to the Commission on Industrial Relations—had substantially abated. Already at mid-decade, the ABA's Committee to Oppose Judicial Recall declared that the movement had been "beaten 'to a frazzle.'" A year later, the committee reflected with satisfaction that Theodore Roosevelt had repudiated the judicial recall plank in the Progressive Party platform. The turnabout owed in part, perhaps, to the new sense among progressives that constitutional amendment was possible on both the state and the national levels—along with a new realization that provisions to override judicial enforcement of constitutional provisions would enable local majorities to scuttle progressive achievements. Contemporaries attributed the decline in popular support for such proposals to the ABA's impressive efforts to defeat them, and the Committee to Oppose Judicial Recall eagerly accepted the credit. As one observer concluded with satisfaction, the committee had convinced the American people that attacks on judicial independence stemmed from socialists and subversives.[46]

Once war was declared, however, a new threat emerged. The ABA explained that efforts to "weaken or destroy constitutional safeguards" had become more circumspect in their approach—and were all the more dangerous because they proceeded "under many forms of camouflage." In terms that anticipated the ABA's critique of President Franklin D. Roosevelt's "court-packing plan" two decades later, the Committee to Oppose Judicial Recall denounced a bill authorizing the president to appoint replacements for aging judges as "a menace to the independence of the judiciary." It was even more scathing in reviewing proposals by Socialists, Wobblies, and the Nonpartisan League. And in the campaign against socialism, civil liberty proved an important foil. As long as the power to enforce constitutional limitations inhered in an independent judiciary, a system of government premised on common ownership was impossible—which, on the ABA's account, was precisely why radicals promoted judicial recall. "The judicial function of declaring invalid any statute which contravenes constitutional safeguards to individual rights of property and liberty is, so long as it continues, a barrier to the establishment of a government of Socialism," the committee explained.[47]

The sense that a strong judiciary was crucial to preserving American constitutional governance from a socialist onslaught only intensified after the

1917 Bolshevik Revolution, which promptly dismantled the Russian legal system and abolished nearly all existing courts. Suddenly, antiradicalism took on new urgency, and mainstream politicians and industrial leaders vilified President Wilson's war measures for expanding the reach of the state. The following summer, the Committee to Oppose Judicial Recall warned that the "menace of Socialism" had reached its historical high. The threat was even more acute than the working-class agitation of the early 1910s, because it was accompanied by an unprecedented expansion in government power. The war effort had necessitated the "temporary suspension" of the constitutional protections ordinarily enforced by legislatures as well as the courts; radicals were maneuvering to make those measures permanent, in a ploy to "establish[] a government by human whim in the place of a government by law."[48]

In the summer of 1918, the president of the ABA addressed the association's annual meeting on the subject of "Civil Liberty in America." Employing a rhetorical strategy often adopted by the AUAM, he enjoined his audience to defend their constitutional freedoms, lest the United States become like Germany, where citizens surrendered their individuality to the "great political machine." He conceded that the war effort justified extraordinary executive authority (after all, any other position might have subjected him to liability under the Espionage Act). But he entreated Americans to preserve civil liberty, and he hailed the judiciary as America's most potent weapon in that fight.[49]

On the face of it, then, the Civil Liberties Bureau and ABA shared much common ground. And yet, in their concerns and ambitions, the two groups were diametrically opposed. In the hands of the ABA's president, civil liberty slid into laissez-faire economics (a concept in tension, it should be noted, with the historical understanding of the term as entailing extensive government involvement). Like the Civil Liberties Bureau, he believed that state regulation had made unprecedented incursions on "individual freedom." What he decried as "astonish[ing]," however, was Congress's audacity in "fixing hours of labor and rates of wages upon the transportation system"—not its decision to coerce the unwilling to kill for their country. Even as conservative lawyers condemned the defense of conscientious objectors as "contrary to the ethics of the [legal] profession," they denounced government meddling in economic matters for threatening to "reverse the natural order." In short, civil liberty shielded property rights and "free competition," not personal freedom. The best antidote to "extreme collectivism" was the "calm atmosphere of a court of justice."[50]

In promoting civil liberty as a bulwark of private property, the organized bar was in distinguished company. In September 1918, an Illinois senator portrayed the federal government as a "political autocracy" that was secretly undermining "civil liberty." The infringements he invoked foregrounded purported plots by administration officials, along with Samuel Gompers, to seize physical property and rob enterprising industrialists of their autonomy. The following spring, Columbia University president Nicholas Murray Butler celebrated civil liberty as the source of "all American life and all American success." Lamenting that the wartime expansion of power had opened the door to redistributive regulatory policies, he inveighed against the displacement of "civil liberty and individual opportunity" by the "organized power of the State."[51]

If the AUAM hoped that linking its defense of conscientious objectors and radical dissenters to civil liberty would endear its cause to the public, it was sorely disappointed. To be sure, some conservatives, as Theodore Schroeder once observed, were sympathetic to "unabridged freedom of utterance as a matter of acknowledged natural right." In practice, however, most were quick to condemn radical agitation as a distortion of liberty and an affront to social order. It was no surprise, then, when an Independence Day editorial in the *New York Times* declared (in well-worn terms) that a line must be drawn between "liberty" and "license." The *Times* lambasted the "little group of malcontents" within the Civil Liberties Bureau whose task was to gain "for themselves immunity from the application of laws to which good citizens willingly submit as essential to the national existence and welfare."[52]

During the New Deal, the bald defense of the courts by reference to property would finally give way in the face of economic disaster. To preserve judicial independence against legislative hostility and court-curbing proposals, conservatives would instead acclaim the Bill of Rights. But in the waning years of the Progressive Era, defenders of the status quo squarely pitched civil liberty against the perils of economic redistribution.

✦ ✦ ✦

Notwithstanding this hostile terrain, the erstwhile progressives of the AUAM stubbornly claimed the mantle of civil liberty for their own wartime agenda. To be sure, opting for the plural form allowed them to exclude property rights from the catalog of rights that they defended. Still, for an organizational leadership steeped in labor injunctions and *Lochner*-era constitutionalism, the Civil Liberties Bureau's court-centered defense of constitutional rights, under the banner of a concept valorized by Justice John Marshall and the ABA, was unquestionably a bold departure. It was not a maneuver that the organization officially acknowledged or explained. What mattered most in launching the new bureau, according to one member of the AUAM, was to agree on a "practical program." When it came to "principles," by contrast, the group's founders were "not so seriously concerned."[53]

And yet, with respect to program as well as principles, many within the AUAM were unwilling to go along. The progressive holdouts within the AUAM resisted the creation of the Civil Liberties Bureau because they understood it as an assault on more measured methods of democratic reform. They maintained their faith in "governmental cooperation" and preferred to work through tested progressive channels. Moreover, they believed that the radicals within the Civil Liberties Bureau were more interested in economic reorganization than international collaboration, and that in defending the former, they were endangering the latter. After all, the AUAM's founders were intimately familiar with the attempts by Socialists and the IWW to insulate their propaganda and organizing activities on First Amendment grounds, and their wartime clients often hailed from the same circles as the earlier activists. Many of the organization's cooperating attorneys opposed the Espionage Act because they believed it was a pretext for union busting. Some supported the war but resented its manipulation "for class purposes," to "put down labor organizations and to endeavor to destroy the right of peaceable economic agitation."[54]

Over the summer of 1917, the leadership of the AUAM clashed over the organization's open support for radical causes. Many longtime members, repelled by the board's "impulsive radicalism," threatened to resign. By September, Lillian Wald considered the division to be insurmountable. In a desperate bid to retain her, Crystal Eastman recommended severing the Civil Liberties Bureau from the larger AUAM and "leav[ing] the more conservative minority to continue the work of the organization." Formal separation was recorded in the AUAM's minutes on September 28, following a long and painful debate. Wald left anyway, and after the split, the AUAM was essentially a shell organization. In October, it changed its name to the American Union for a Democratic Peace. Shortly thereafter, it suspended operations.[55]

For the newly independent Civil Liberties Bureau, on the other hand, the path forward was clear. Although it assured AUAM members that its work would remain "exactly the same," the organization was finally free to focus on the issue to which its board was most strongly committed: the "cause of labor."[56]

On October 17, the National Civil Liberties Bureau was announced. The new organization pledged to defend the freedoms of speech, press, and assembly, as well as liberty of conscience and freedom from unlawful search and seizure. Like the Civil Liberties Bureau before it, the NCLB would exert "quiet pressure" on the administration, which was "evidently doing its best under the present law." Roger Baldwin was a savvy organizer, and he was careful to differentiate the new organization from more frankly radical groups. Analogizing to lawyers' defense of unpopular litigants, he consistently distinguished between the advocacy of expressive freedom and approval of the censored speech. He sought to attract respectable members to make the group's claim to neutrality more credible. In December, he refused a request to assist the Socialist Party in federal lobbying, explaining that the NCLB, although "in entire sympathy" with the party's program, was a legal defense organization that did not engage in active propaganda. Other groups were responsible for mobilizing the masses; the NCLB would "keep people's mouths open, and their printing presses free." Its sole function, Baldwin insisted, was to "maintain[] established constitutional rights."[57]

Behind the scenes, however, the NCLB's leaders regarded labor agitation as a substantive good, not merely an instantiation of a generalized right. As Norman Thomas explained to the AUAM's civil liberties skeptics in the run-up to the NCLB's separation, "capitalistic exploitation, militarism, [and] contempt of civil liberties" were entangled "aspects of the wrong basis of our social life." Baldwin expressed the same point more concretely to a potential donor. The "underlying purpose" of the NCLB's attempt to maintain constitutional rights was to preserve a voice for minorities in the "processes of progress," in which "labor of course must in the future play the biggest part."[58]

✦ ✦ ✦

For all its early enthusiasm about constitutional litigation, the NCLB had little success in the courts. In the fall of 1917, much of its energy was devoted to challenging the Selective Service Act. The NCLB did not serve as primary counsel in any of the six consolidated cases that reached the

Supreme Court. In fact, it was Harry Weinberger that agreed to defend Emma Goldman and Alexander Berkman when they were indicted under the statute in June, notwithstanding his earlier concessions to the AUAM. The NCLB nonetheless played an active role under the direction of Walter Nelles, one of Roger Baldwin's Harvard classmates, who had signed on as counsel after reading about the organization in the *New York Times*. Nelles filed an amicus brief arguing that the First Amendment's protection of religious freedom encompassed all conscientious objectors, regardless of whether they were members of religious sects or organizations opposed to the war. That position proved to be a liability for recruitment as well as a nonstarter in the Supreme Court—which, despite its frequent invocation of individual rights in past cases, stressed the broad scope of federal government power.[59]

The draft challenge, like the NCLB's broader defense of conscientious objectors, rested on a claim to individual conscience that many potential supporters considered spurious and antisocial. By contrast, postal censorship continued to trouble mainstream liberals, lawyers, and politicians. In October, Senator Robert M. La Follette famously declared it necessary, in wartime even more than peacetime, "that the channels for free public discussion of governmental policies shall be open and unclogged." Although many denounced La Follette's position as unpatriotic, others were sympathetic. Even President Wilson expressed a preference for moderation—and while the administration was unwilling to abdicate its censorship authority, there was a reasonable chance that the courts would constrain the worst abuses.[60]

Nonetheless, the NCLB's participation in the Espionage Act cases ultimately proved almost as ineffectual as its opposition to the draft. Emblematic of that outcome was its defense of the *Masses,* the suppression of which had helped guide the AUAM's leaders toward civil liberties work when the Espionage Act was first passed. The AUAM had organized a defense fund, and Gilbert Roe had agreed to represent the publication and its staff. Civil liberties advocates were elated in late July when Judge Learned Hand decided, as a matter of statutory interpretation, that the suppression of the *Masses* based on its antiwar editorials and political cartoons exceeded the authority of postal officials under the Espionage Act. But in early November the Second Circuit reversed Hand's decision, and the *Masses,* deprived of its second-class mailing privileges, had no choice but to close its doors. Throughout the country, other courts followed suit.[61]

As war consumed the nation, the broad-based prosecution and conviction of left-wing leaders and organizers threatened the future of the radical and antiwar movements—which, to many within the NCLB, were one and the same. Yet with the radical press largely out of business and many radical leaders in jail, the futility of constitutional litigation was unmistakable. NCLB attorneys and affiliates would continue to intervene in appropriate cases throughout and after the war, but defendants would rarely prevail in court.[62]

The problem was not a generalized decline in the status of individual rights. In December 1917, the Supreme Court issued its divisive decision in *Hitchman Coal and Coke Company v. Mitchell,* upholding a broad injunction against the UMW for attempting to recruit nonunion workers who had signed yellow-dog contracts consistently with their "constitutional rights of personal liberty and private property." The injunction extended to peaceful persuasion, but as usual, the expressive component of picketing raised no constitutional flags. According to the *New Republic,* the decision would "confirm the popular feeling . . . that a majority of the Supreme Court are endeavoring to enforce their own reactionary views of public policy, in direct opposition to the more enlightened views prevailing in legislatures and among the public." It is little wonder that the NCLB's attempt to challenge wartime suppression through constitutional litigation garnered limited progressive support.[63]

For the time being, the most plausible remaining strategy was to mobilize public opinion against repressive laws. Vivid accounts of lawless brutality and vigilante justice—often committed with official encouragement—were alarming to many progressives. Invoking such episodes, along with lingering anxiety over postal censorship, the NCLB convened a mass meeting in defense of "American Liberties in War Time." Its central purpose was to demonstrate why public protest had become necessary. The NCLB hoped to manifest a broad public consensus, but most moderates declined the organization's invitations, either for lack of a liberal critical mass, or because they believed "the world will not be safe for free speech until it is safe for democracy."[64]

In the end, the meeting was attended and its agenda dominated by pacifists and radicals. Denied the use of Carnegie Hall, the NCLB instead opted, appropriately enough, to hold the conference at the Liberty Theatre. Much of the discussion focused on the capitalist underpinnings of the war. The central theme was the unjustified attack on radicalism and the labor movement under the pretext of wartime necessity. "Business interests [were] disloyally using patriotism to intimidate labor and radical movements," and government officials were playing into their hands. In marked contrast to subsequent commentators, conference participants regarded wartime suppression as a predictable continuation of prewar hostility toward radical speech. They considered the recent prosecutions to be more frequent and more flagrant than their prewar analogs. Postal censorship, always concerning, had become more centralized and consequently more threatening. But the basic objectives of the repressors remained the same: to shield the status quo from labor agitation.[65]

When the conference concluded, a committee sent Congress a resolution charging that violations of constitutional liberty were undermining the aspirations of the war. Mob violence had received the sanction of many public leaders. The Espionage Act was being manipulated to quash industrial unrest. Postal censorship was destroying the free press. And businesses were deliberately robbing consumers and strangling labor. "The war has only brought to a sharp focus tendencies hostile to our democratic institutions which have long been evident in the case of such minority groups as the Negro and other races in our national life, as well as many radical and labor movements," the resolution concluded. To unmask business efforts to "use the war as a means to crush labor," the committee members demanded a congressional inquiry. What they wanted, in effect, was a wartime reprise of the Commission on Industrial Relations.[66]

There was, of course, no realistic prospect of congressional action on this resolution, and the press dismissed it as a radical attempt to undermine the war effort. But the conference served a more important function for the NCLB: it marked the organization's reentry into the realm of popular agitation and propaganda. By March, Baldwin was "thoroughly disgusted with the folks at Washington who have given us such hearty assurances," which had failed to translate into tolerant policy.[67] Baldwin thought it time to take a more public stand.

In the weeks after the conference, Baldwin exchanged letters with the national secretary of the Socialist Labor Party of America, who advocated industrial and political organizing instead of congressional resolutions. His view—that the only way to protect working-class rights was to effectuate working-class power—anticipated an ACLU axiom of the 1920s and 1930s.

Baldwin responded that his objective, too, was "working class and radical organization." But there would be "a lot of fighting along the way," and in the course of the struggle, he would use "any existing agency or means" to accomplish the larger mission. Baldwin hoped that other groups—to which, in some cases, he contributed and belonged—would continue to fight the crucial battles. The NCLB would endeavor to protect their right to continue to operate, unmolested by the state and without incurring public condemnation. "The United States Congress isn't a bad tool for purposes of agitation and publicity which is necessary to keep the iron hot," Baldwin mused. The organization was willing to pursue whatever instrument was most effective to accomplish its goals.[68]

✦ ✦ ✦

During the First World War, the extraordinary scale of official intolerance challenged Americans to reevaluate the touted tradeoff between security and freedom. Free speech, they increasingly argued, was no mere personal indulgence, amenable to regulation for the greater good. Instead, reflecting backward on the wartime experience, the pioneering free speech scholar Zechariah Chafee Jr. emphasized the "social interest in the attainment of truth, so that the country may not only adopt the wisest course of action but carry it out the wisest way."[69]

In the spring of 1918, a new breed of free speech constitutionalism began to emerge. Rooted in the uncertain ruminations of a few progressive theorists as well as the passionate exhortations of activists and lawyers, it cast expressive freedom as a precondition of democratic legitimacy, beyond the boundaries of permissible state control. Over the ensuing months, a small cadre of civil liberties luminaries would famously hash out the contours of the First Amendment. Contrary to the prevailing narrative, the progressive theory they fashioned was far from decisive. As the war in Europe wound down, the Supreme Court would uphold a slew of convictions under the Espionage Act, while two stalwart but lonely justices issued stirring dissents. Building a broader consensus on behalf of a countermajoritarian Bill of Rights—the ACLU's achievement in the interwar years—was a much more protracted project, with materially different terms. Indeed, what most accounts have construed as the arrival of the modern First Amendment was merely its prelude.

Still, the war years were foundational to the future course of civil liberties advocacy. The NCLB's defense of radical publications and subversive speakers yielded few concrete victories, but it taught the organization which arguments would prove most persuasive to its progressive partners. It also illuminated unresolved tensions, including lingering progressive anxieties about the courts and individual rights. The wartime agenda of the NCLB was the end of an old era in civil liberties advocacy, not the beginning of a new one. The radical organization that arose from the ashes of wartime civil liberties advocacy was as far removed from the NCLB as from the modern ACLU. And yet, the rhetoric the NCLB tested during the war—a language that was out of step, for the time being, with the values of its intended audience if not its own—provided a model to which the organization could later, more convincingly, return.

The distinguishing characteristic of the NCLB, like its interwar successor, was its willingness to adopt whatever methods were most likely to accomplish its overarching program. Between the First World War and the New Deal, that program was the preservation of labor's right to organize, en route to a general redistribution of economic resources and political power. Perhaps more than anything it was this flexibility that made the NCLB, and later the ACLU, so much more effective than the organizations whose rights it defended. The NCLB's leaders were keenly aware of the prevailing political climate and willing and able to adapt to changing times. They learned from their failures and capitalized on their successes.

By early 1918, it was clear what constituency the NCLB would serve. The urgent and unresolved question for the organization's board was a strategic one: how best to protect that constituency from persecution and prosecution in a time of national crisis.

3

The Right of Agitation

$\mathbb{A}$ T TWO O'CLOCK central time on the afternoon of September 5, 1917, less than half a year after its declaration of war on Germany, the United States government launched a less celebrated internal attack. Its target was the IWW, a labor organization that officials deemed just as threatening to American democracy as any international power. As American troops prepared for combat overseas, hundreds of United States marshals and their deputies, together with agents of the Department of Justice, descended simultaneously on IWW offices throughout the country. They seized five tons of documents, as well as artwork, furniture, and wastebaskets. The raid made headlines throughout the country. In the *New York Times*, it shared front-page billing with an address to the ABA by Charles Evans Hughes, in which the future chief justice of the United States Supreme Court declared that President Woodrow Wilson's contentious wartime policies—including conscription, the regulation of war production, and the suppression of disloyalty—were consistent with the "fighting Constitution" of the United States.[1]

The literature and other materials confiscated in the September raid served as the basis for the federal conspiracy prosecution of the IWW leadership. The Department of Justice secured indictments in areas of significant Wobbly activity, including Sacramento, Kansas City, and the organization's headquarters in Chicago. The Chicago conspiracy trial, whose defendants included IWW head Big Bill Haywood, was the first and most significant. It lasted nearly nine months from indictment to verdict. More than one hundred defendants were marched each day from the Cook County jail to the federal courthouse, enduring verbal abuse and physical violence along the way. The record, purported at the time to be the largest ever filed, contained 33,000 typewritten pages and ten million words. According to prosecution and defendants alike, the Chicago IWW trial was the most important labor case in United States history.[2]

The government's argument in the Chicago trial was that the IWW, by counseling its members not to serve in the military and by organizing strikes in crucial war industries, had conspired to undermine America's war effort. For the defendants, however, these supposed endeavors to obstruct recruitment and war production were mere distractions. In their testimony and in their defense bulletins, the beleaguered Wobblies described the suffering of transient and migratory workers. They recounted the living conditions in the mines and the lumber camps: the inadequate food and water, the lack of access to bathing facilities, the hard straw-covered bunks on which they slept. They explained the methods used to suppress labor organizing, from blacklisting to lynching. The stated goal of the IWW's defense was to put the industrial system on trial.

The IWW trial might seem an unusual episode through which to tell the history of civil liberties during wartime. It was not, after all, a case about free speech as that term is understood today. The liberties at issue—the rights of workers to petition, protest, and strike—were cast in terms of equality rather than autonomy. The IWW did raise a First Amendment argument, but no court entertained it seriously. The case produced no noteworthy doctrinal precedent on which to base future free speech claims; indeed, the Supreme Court denied the defendants' petition for certiorari, and the court of appeals considered itself bound by more memorable wartime decisions. In the conventional civil liberties canon, the IWW trial is nowhere to be found.

And yet, the events in and around that Chicago courthouse had profound implications for the modern civil liberties movement. Among the Wobblies' staunchest defenders was the same small and struggling assemblage of disillusioned progressives that had organized the defense of war critics and conscientious objectors under the banner of the NCLB. Through their involvement with the IWW, the NCLB's leaders came to believe that fundamental change could never occur within the confines of government institutions: on the one hand, because "all of the work that courts do is political," and on the other, because the political branches were just as oppressive as the courts. In their radical conception of civil liberties, workers could organize freely only when judges, mayors, and the National Guard all ceased to enforce employers' constitutional and common-law property rights along with repressive legislation. That is what the Wobblies demanded at their trial and unsurprisingly failed to attain.[3]

Between the First World War and the next, the future founders of the ACLU would gradually reimagine the judiciary as a friendly forum for upholding labor's rights. First, however, they would need to shed their progressive preference for the machinery of the state. What made that trajectory possible was not the legal theory of the IWW defense—theory of any type was never a Wobbly strong suit—but rather the IWW's social and economic vision.

Disillusioned by its own inability to curb repression through diplomatic channels, the NCLB embraced the IWW's millenarian promise of peaceful revolution achieved through unfettered expression. It championed the *right of agitation:* the right of workers to picket and boycott not only for higher wages or a union contract, but also for a fundamental transformation in the relationship between labor and capital. Reflecting backward, the ACLU would call the Chicago IWW trial "the greatest free speech trial of the war."[4]

✦ ✦ ✦

Of the many government abridgments of labor's right to organize over the course of the First World War, the NCLB considered the Chicago IWW trial to be the most troubling. Scores of radical activists and labor leaders were imprisoned under the Espionage Act. Among their ranks was Socialist Party presidential candidate Eugene V. Debs, as well as lesser-known dissenters like Charles Schenck and Jacob Abrams, whose names are familiar only from the Supreme Court cases upholding their convictions. In all such cases, the NCLB leadership believed the government was targeting economic heresies rather than antiwar agitation. The IWW indictments, however, were particularly egregious. After all, the government was threatening to send the entire organizational leadership to jail.[5]

The IWW was no stranger to government persecution. Its free speech fights of the previous decade had emphasized the malleability of constitutional principles and the hypocrisy of the courts. In the face of the Chicago prosecution, its defense committee reached out broadly to socialists and liberals sympathetic to its cause, as it had in earlier cases. The stakes of the Chicago trial were clearly higher, however; its objective was to destroy the IWW, root and branch. In due course, the convictions of Bill Haywood and many of the organization's other leaders precipitated the decline of the IWW as a major force in the American labor movement.

The government had its reasons for targeting the IWW when it did. The wartime economy produced a temporary shift in the balance of power between workers and employers. The combination of increased domestic production, the entry of American workers into military service, and a sharp decline in immigration from Europe meant that unemployment plummeted. Yet though workers were in short supply, their wages did not rise in step with their employers' profit margins. Samuel Gompers and other labor leaders pledged that their unions would not strike while the United States was at war, but they were unable to enforce their promises on the ground. On the contrary, the early months of the war witnessed a steep rise in union organizing and a wave of strikes across all industries. Employers responded by ramping up their antiunion activities.

It was during this moment that the IWW formulated its own wartime labor policy. Unlike its more conservative counterparts, the IWW leadership explicitly called for an escalation of the class war while the Great War raged abroad. IWW recruitment skyrocketed during the spring and summer of 1917. Strikes in such industries as logging and copper mining were responsible for precipitous drops in production, which seemingly threatened the war effort.[6]

Industrial leaders called for a federal crackdown, and local United States attorneys were sympathetic. Attorney General Thomas W. Gregory, a trust-busting southern attorney who had once "brought one of the most powerful combinations of capital in the world to its knees," initially resisted their demands. By late summer, however, the situation had worsened in western states, and federal intervention appeared unavoidable. State law enforcement officials proved incapable of breaking the strikes, and state militias were federalized in the summer of 1917. Meanwhile, vigilante violence was rampant, and IWW pleas for federal protection were curtly dismissed. Loyalty leagues and similar groups comprising off-duty soldiers and angry citizens stormed IWW headquarters, and mobs beat, tarred and feathered, and deported unwanted Wobblies. In July 1917, the sheriff of Bisbee, Arizona, deputized 2,000 townspeople, who rounded up 1,200 alleged Wobblies (supposedly Mexicans, German agents, and subversives), packed them into cattle cars, and shipped them out of state. The Justice Department filed charges against the ringleaders on the theory that the deportation of men legally registered for the draft violated the Selective Service Act. The district court dismissed the indictments, however, and the Supreme Court eventually affirmed.[7]

Employers' associations and state governments were more successful than the IWW in soliciting federal assistance. In July, western governors appealed to the Council of National Defense, which was responsible for coordinating wartime industrial mobilization. Federal troops were dispatched to IWW strongholds like Washington, Oregon, and Arizona to ward off disturbances in production, and despite orders to remain neutral in local conflicts, they generally served employers' interests. Increasingly, federal prosecution appeared a more moderate solution to the IWW problem than active military suppression.[8]

In July 1917, the Department of Justice urged its attorneys to gather evidence against the IWW. Justice agents monitored every IWW move, scouring all of its published circulars and trailing Haywood and other office holders in their daily business. The September raid on IWW offices across the country was the "biggest round-up ever made by the Secret Service forces," according to the *New York Times*. Confident that a jury trial would vindicate them, many of the defendants turned themselves in.[9]

The indictment charged the 166 Wobbly defendants with violations of the Selective Service and Espionage Acts and with conspiring to use the mails to defraud employers, essentially by encouraging employees to engage in a work slowdown. It also alleged conspiracies to hinder the production and transportation of war supplies by means of violent strikes, and to impede constitutional and statutory rights to execute various contracts. During the arraignment proceedings in December 1917, the defense argued that the government's seizure of evidence violated the First and Fourth Amendments to the United States Constitution. That claim predictably failed.[10]

At first, government officials accused the IWW of accepting German funds; IWW stood for "Imperial Wilhelm's Warriors," according to one Arizona senator. Insinuations of espionage and treason quickly collapsed, however. Certainly, the organizational leadership had been staunchly opposed to military intervention in the prewar years. As late as March 1917, it explicitly contrasted its own opposition to war with the AFL's pledge of patriotic service. Even after April, IWW publications implicitly criticized conscription, and some of the organization's most militant organizers went further, advising members to claim exemption on their registration cards based on opposition to war (the same procedure that the NCLB recommended to political objectors). But the organization itself walked a careful line, leaving the decision to individual members. The vast majority of Wobblies who were eligible for the draft chose to register. According to the NCLB, the question of loyalty was always incidental. "The government is attacking primarily not the war-time activities of the organization, but the organization per se," it insisted. The Department of Justice seemingly agreed. Within days of the raid, one United States attorney conveyed his understanding that the purpose of the department's operation was "very largely to put the IWW out of business."[11]

✦ ✦ ✦

As the NCLB understood them, the IWW indictments shared a core feature with other prosecutions under the Espionage Act during the war. The IWW imperiled industrial interests at a time when the federal government was reliant on American industry. On the grounds of military necessity, the Department of Justice was threatening to litigate the organization out of existence. In its November call for contributions, the NCLB articulated the concern at the center of the IWW case and of its own broader agenda during the war years and afterward. "In this prosecution," it declared, "is involved the whole question of the right of agitation by a radical labor body."[12]

The NCLB never defined the right of agitation precisely, but the ACLU espoused it regularly until the Second World War. It was clearly distinct from the dominant progressive conception of expressive freedom, which regarded robust public conversation as a mechanism for advancing knowledge and a prerequisite for democratic legitimacy. Later proponents of free speech, like the Communist Party, claimed a right to advocate revolutionary violence. For the IWW, however, the proscribed activity was not *promotion* of its program; it *was* its program. In broad strokes, the NCLB understood the right of agitation as a right to improve the situation of labor by any means short of physical violence—including, but not limited to, speech. Organizing workers and dissuading strikebreakers were fundamental weapons in the labor struggle. In the words of Elizabeth Gurley Flynn, the prosecution of the IWW "involved the right to strike, organize, and publish the labor press."[13]

After the war, the ACLU frankly declared the right of agitation to be a natural right that preexisted written constitutions. It concluded that the IWW trial was "essentially [a] free speech case[]," insofar as it involved "the right of men to organize, speak, meet, and circulate their propaganda of industrial unionism." But it came to believe, like its labor allies, that "causes get that natural right in proportion to their power to take and hold it." In other words, the interwar ACLU understood power as a prerequisite for freedom, rather than the other way around. For the duration of the war, however, the NCLB was more cautious in its rhetoric, if not in its underlying beliefs. Even while it invoked the right of agitation, the NCLB emphasized to its contributors that the IWW deserved a fair trial. It requested assistance in bringing the IWW's case to the public as a matter of "law and public policy, and of course as protagonists only of American constitutional rights." In short, the NCLB was speaking in two voices. To labor radicals, it promised protection for workers' concerted activity. To the progressives in power, it spoke in conventional reformist terms. Free speech was just the sort of incremental adjustment in the system that would quell widespread social conflict.[14]

As in its defense of conscientious objectors, the NCLB's first recourse was to connections within the administration. While the organization was cautiously optimistic about the prospects for judicial vindication of press freedom in the postal censorship context, it sought to avoid trial in the IWW case. Like the IWW's own defense attorney, who preferred administrative to judicial resolution of the matter, the NCLB regarded the situation as an "administrative problem" for the Department of Labor. The organization cautioned that conviction would only aggravate labor unrest, and it asked insiders to discourage prosecution.[15]

This approach met with limited success. Many of President Wilson's advisers—including Secretary of Labor William B. Wilson, a former secretary-treasurer of the UMW—were receptive to organized labor. But their pro-unionism did not necessarily translate into sympathy for labor radicals, and other members of the administration, such as Postmaster General Albert Burleson, were openly hostile. In August 1917, largely in response to the Bisbee deportations, the president had appointed a mediation commission to evaluate the wartime labor situation and to formulate recommendations in particular disputes. Chaired by Secretary Wilson, the commission included two labor representatives, both AFL, and two moderate employers. Felix Frankfurter, who served as secretary, was initially skeptical of the AFL's dominance. In the course of his investigations, however, he came to agree with Samuel Gompers that the best path to industrial peace was to mandate employer negotiation with AFL unions while officially repudiating radical alternatives like the IWW. The commission's report, issued in January 1918, urged government support for collective bargaining. The same month, John A. Fitch wrote for the *Survey* that government had achieved labor's wartime cooperation "not by suppression of free speech, nor by the jailing of agitators," but rather "by the acceptance . . . of labor's program."[16]

Although the commission's report on the Arizona copper strike traced labor unrest to poor working conditions and low wages, its broader condemnation of radical tactics undercut the NCLB's efforts to negotiate over the IWW indictment. Roger Baldwin believed the Department of Justice preferred to avoid trial in the case, but no one within the administration was willing to take a firm stand. In late February, Baldwin appealed directly to President Wilson, but Wilson had concluded that the IWW deserved to be suppressed.[17]

Indeed, the administration was turning ever more surely away from the NCLB's proposed course. In May, President Wilson endorsed the Sedition Act amendments to the Espionage Act, which explicitly authorized the government suppression of disloyal speech. Western senators were particularly enthusiastic about the new measure, which was based on a Montana statute targeting the IWW. The NCLB cautioned against the increased censorship authority that the bill conferred on the postmaster, explaining that "such arbitrary power in the hands of a single appointed officer" was unprecedented in a constitutional democracy. Others shared the NCLB's concerns. Some senators focused on the dangers of bureaucratic censorship and unsuccessfully sought to introduce protections for truthful criticism. Republicans worried about expanding the authority of Democratic officials, and Theodore Roosevelt openly attacked the Wilson administration for silencing opposition views. Despite these reservations, the original bill passed handily in both houses of Congress, and on May 16, President Wilson signed it into law.[18]

The implications of the Sedition Act for the Chicago trial and for the future of IWW organizing were clear. The new statute forbade all "disloyal, profane, scurrilous, or abusive language about the form of government of the United States," the Constitution, the armed forces, and the American flag. More pointedly, it expressly prohibited advocacy of "any curtailment of production in this country" of anything "necessary . . . to the prosecution of the war." That is, it seemed to outlaw strikes and slowdowns in war-related industries. It also approved the post office's practice of refusing to deliver mail to and from the IWW, a policy that made it virtually impossible for the defense team to raise funds. In fact, one western senator specifically justified the provision as a measure to prevent Haywood and the IWW from receiving contributions by mail.[19]

In June, Senator Thomas J. Walsh, a Montana Democrat and strong supporter of President Wilson, introduced a bill frankly drafted to outlaw the IWW, as many states had already done. The NCLB fought desperately against the measure, which would have criminalized any movement or organization that advocated injury to property as a means of achieving economic change. Opposition to the bill was muted, even in otherwise friendly corners. Senator William E. Borah, an Idaho progressive who often defended free speech, approved the measure on the theory that it would undercut support for the press censorship provision of the Sedition Act; the latter would be unnecessary, he explained, once there was no "IWW organization left to send mail." The Walsh bill passed the Senate without a roll call, but Representative Meyer London of New York, a Socialist, managed to stall it in the House, where eventually it died. Still, the defeat was hardly cause for celebration. By the spring of 1918, it was evident to everyone involved that existing laws were more than adequate to procure convictions of labor radicals in the courts.[20]

✦ ✦ ✦

The twelve jurors who were responsible for deciding the fate of the defendants and with it "the future of American Labor organizations" were sworn in on May 1, 1918. That the trial began on International Workers' Day was not lost on the defendants, who considered it an auspicious sign. Indeed, when the proceedings finally began, the defendants were optimistic. After sitting in their jail cells for months of quiet anticipation, they were excited at the opportunity to state their case publicly at last. The trial, in their view, was the "most monumental" in the history of the international labor movement; it involved not only the rights of the IWW, but also the right to organize and strike more broadly. They hoped that their performance in the courtroom would transform the public's understanding of organized labor, and they were confident that the nation's workers would embrace "the One Big Union and the things it stands for."[21]

The presiding judge, Kenesaw Mountain Landis, was a recognized conservative who would soon leave the federal bench to become the first commissioner of baseball. Despite his distaste for wartime dissenters, he had established a reputation for fairness after a grueling and contentious month of jury selection. He had allowed the defense to question prospective jurors about their economic views, and he had dismissed for cause those panel members who admitted that press coverage predisposed them toward conviction. During the course of the trial, Landis blocked attempts to call witnesses without adequate notice to the defense, chastised reporters for their misrepresentations of witnesses' testimony, and rebuked the prosecution for attempting to filter evidence. Most important, he openly conceded his belief that industry was guilty of "hoggish and unconscionable profiteering."[22]

The case for the prosecution unfolded through the testimony of 150 witnesses over the course of seven weeks. Much of the trial was handled by special prosecutor Frank Nebeker, a corporate lawyer and former district attorney who was a member of the Democratic National Committee. A "cool and resourceful fighter," Nebeker was an "honest lawyer," if (said Roger Baldwin) "utterly without social vision." George F. Vanderveer took charge of the defense. Trained at Columbia Law School, the Seattle prosecutor turned private defense attorney was well known for representing the IWW, though his unsuccessful constitutional challenge to federal wiretapping in *Olmstead v. United States* would ultimately garner him more fame.[23]

Although the government had spent months combing through the mass of evidence seized in the raids, it had been unable to substantiate the popular allegations that Germany had been financing the IWW. Moreover, only one defendant eligible for the draft had failed to register. Furloughed soldiers testified that they had maintained their IWW memberships after they were drafted and had never encountered resistance within the organization. If the IWW leadership had wanted to halt production in crucial industries, Bill Haywood and other witnesses claimed, it could easily have done so. That the war effort was proceeding smoothly was evidence that interference had never been the organization's aim.[24]

On the other hand, the government's review of the evidence had uncovered letters, bulletins, and official publications expressing dissatisfaction with government policies and counseling disruptive conduct. The government introduced evidence that the IWW had urged men to "fight for their jobs and class," that they had organized strikes in war industries, and that they had advocated general strikes and revolution. Although the organization had been careful in its official communications, many of its leaders and members had expressed strong opposition to the war, and some had even proposed sabotage within the armed forces. Haywood himself admitted that he "would have the war stopped today, if it were in [his] power to do it." When pressed, he affirmed his belief that "industrial unionism is anti-military propaganda." Finally, as an NCLB representative put it, "the IWW [had] taken an advantage of the war situation" to improve its bargaining situation—though the organization was quick to invoke findings by the Federal Trade Commission that "the packers, the copper kings, and the lumber barons" had not hesitated to "reap their profits while the world wallows in blood."[25]

The prosecution also devoted considerable attention to the IWW's use of sabotage, ostensibly to hamper preparation for the war. According to the government, it was standard IWW practice to drive spikes into logs, blow up threshing machines, remove machine parts, and destroy food in mills and warehouses. Certainly there was ample reason to attribute such practices to the organization. Indeed, the IWW's general organizer had admitted frankly to the Commission on Industrial Relations that violence in a strike was appropriate if it was effective as a tool. But there was no evidence to substantiate charges of property destruction or personal violence in the criminal records of individual members. In the end, the government relied primarily on the seditious nature of the IWW's principles, expressed in its poetry and songs.[26]

Defense witnesses responded by accusing the prosecution of misunderstanding the concept of sabotage. Sabotage meant adjusting output to suitable levels, they explained: "good pay or bum work." Workers might "bring the strike to the job" by laying down their tools after eight hours of labor, or by refusing to carry a heavy load. Vanderveer cast such tactics as part of the IWW's larger project of shifting the balance of power in labor relations.

The IWW's strikes and organizing campaigns in the summer of 1917 had nothing to do with the war effort, he argued. They were legitimate responses to workers' grievances against oppressive employers, and they were crucial weapons in a class struggle that was both inevitable and desirable.[27]

According to the defense, Wobblies were the victims of violence, not the perpetrators. Witnesses recounted the horrific story of the Speculator Mine fire that cost 168 lives and precipitated the IWW's strike in Butte, Montana, which the government alleged was an effort to cripple the wartime production of copper. One defendant had visited the morgue in the wake of the fire; he recounted "that the fingers of some of the corpses were worn to the second joint, with the bone protruding, as the result of the men clawing at the bulkheads." Witnesses and perpetrators described the Bisbee deportations, the mounted machine guns trained on the men—many of whom owned Liberty Bonds, and hundreds of whom were registered for the draft—who were forced into automobiles and loaded into cattle cars covered in inches of manure. Testimony of this kind moved several of the jurors and spectators to tears. It was introduced over the government's objections, to prove that mistreatment, rather than hostility toward America's war aims, had jumpstarted IWW recruitment in the early months of the war.[28]

In late July, the government finally halted the flood of heart-wrenching testimony in the only way it could. It admitted that "evil social and economic conditions" had obtained in the northwestern lumber camps, Butte, and Arizona. As for the persecution of the IWW, Nebeker argued it was a consequence rather than a cause of the organization's militancy. He did not condone vigilantism, but he asked the jury to ponder what kind of conduct could be so vexing that "in practically every state in this union, these fellows get into trouble." Notably, Nebeker cited the IWW's free speech fights as an example of this phenomenon. By overwhelming the municipal court systems and forcing their release, Nebeker reasoned, the IWW were practically asking for extralegal justice.[29]

✦ ✦ ✦

The IWW's defense team directed its "economic defense" of the IWW to the broader public as much as the jurors. Indeed, the "propaganda value" of the courtroom testimony was always central to the organization's trial strategy, occasionally at great personal cost to the defendants. A few defendants, including Elizabeth Gurley Flynn, secured dismissals of their indictments by renouncing support for the IWW's methods. Flynn urged others to do the same. She also advised the defense team to resist the blanket indictment, which made conviction much more likely. They opted instead for the spectacular publicity of a mass trial.[30]

In the fall of 1917, the IWW's Chicago headquarters organized a general defense committee and launched the *Defense News Bulletin,* which reported on developments in the case. But their attempts to mobilize external assistance faced formidable obstacles. The post office routinely held IWW mailings and donations, and IWW offices were subject to periodic raids. Outside groups, including the NCLB, were less susceptible to government meddling. To aid in the efforts, the NCLB housed a member of the IWW's General Defense Committee in its New York office, and it appointed a fund-raising committee—chaired by *Survey* editor John Fitch—to enlist support from respected liberals.[31]

That spring, the NCLB printed a call for funds in the *New Republic.* An early draft would have accused the government of foul play in its prosecution of the case, but potential supporters were reluctant to express hostility toward the government's war policy. In any case, the *New Republic* would not accept the advertisement if "interference by officials" was included. The NCLB complied, and the revised version—signed by John Dewey, among others—instead emphasized the "right of a fair trial." Even then, the Department of Justice threatened to revoke the *New Republic's* second-class mailing privileges if it reprinted the advertisement in future issues.[32]

Roger Baldwin anticipated that the commercial press would issue distorted reports of the trial, and he was determined "to put the burden of guilt where it belongs, on the shoulders of private capital exploiting the workers." He arranged to send a reporter to Chicago to produce "truthful and accurate" accounts of the trial. The socialist reporter who took the job confirmed Baldwin's view that newspaper coverage was frivolous, malicious, and inattentive to social and economic issues. Finding the "front door to fair publicity" to be "shut and locked," his solution (which he borrowed from the Christian Scientists) was to circulate a compendium of press misrepresentations to supporters and ask them to write letters to local newspapers correcting the record. With Haywood's approval, the NCLB implemented the plan, but its actual effect was minimal.[33]

In its fund-raising and publicity efforts, the NCLB was honing techniques it had developed during its AUAM days and used to good effect in earlier Espionage Act cases. What was distinctive about the NCLB's involvement in the IWW case was a project at the heart of its service to the IWW: its preparation of a pamphlet, *The Truth about the IWW,* intended to dispel misconceptions about the organization's goals. The NCLB's objective in the pamphlet was to document the "campaign by war-profiteers and employing interests to use the war to crush this labor organization." Citing sociological evidence, the NCLB attributed the IWW's radical ideology to the brutalities of industrial capitalism. Much of the pamphlet consisted of corrective quotations by academics and government officials, including a War Department labor representative who believed migratory workers were deprived of legal and social rights. As Norman Thomas subsequently explained, the NCLB considered it crucial to a fair hearing for the IWW "that the public shall be informed of the facts which newspapers do not give."[34]

In *The Truth about the IWW,* the NCLB hardly touched on a speaker's First Amendment right to espouse noxious ideas—the position that would become the hallmark of the ACLU's free speech program. If there was a constitutional guarantee at stake in the government's treatment of the IWW, it was not the liberty to speak, but rather "equality before the law." In fact, the NCLB barely understood the case as implicating disfavored speech at all. What troubled the organization instead was the suppression "of the normal economic protest-*activities* of the IWW." The government's position was objectionable because it was misguided; it sought to attack the symptom of industrial oppression rather than the disease.[35]

In the spring of 1918, the NCLB staked its reputation on a robust, substantive defense of an organization that was almost universally reviled. It agreed to raise bail for Bill Haywood. It convened half a dozen conferences to generate support and publicity for the IWW's cause. It provided legal assistance in preparing the defense. And it distributed *The Truth about the IWW* to every individual, group, and public official conceivably interested in the trial. The NCLB committed its support in any case "where the issues of the right of agitation are involved." As Baldwin told a potential donor, "I doubt whether anything more can be done to aid the IWW from the outside [than] has been done by this committee."[36]

Indeed, the NCLB's justification of the organization's revolutionary beliefs came sufficiently close to an endorsement to prompt a judge to condemn it for "teach[ing] the doctrine of sabotage and industrial terrorism." When the NCLB issued its pamphlet in May, the government moved almost immediately to suppress it. Postal officials declared it non-mailable, and the Department of Justice advised express companies not to deliver it.[37]

In defending the IWW, the NCLB sometimes spoke the language of constitutional liberties. Its true goal, however, was more ambitious. As Baldwin freely admitted, "A fair trial for these men [was] of the greatest public necessity to the industrial future of America."[38]

✦ ✦ ✦

By the defendants' own account, a fair trial was exactly what they got. Judge Landis "proved himself to be impartial in all respects," and he allowed the defense to present a robust picture of the injuries that the IWW had suffered at the hands of employers. One evidentiary dispute stood out as especially important. George Vanderveer's broad ambition, as he and Roger Baldwin had been proclaiming for months, was to put the industrial system on trial. In furtherance of that goal, he marshaled the findings of the Commission on Industrial Relations. When it first convened, Bill Haywood had dismissed that commission as a "tragic joke." But its hearings and recommendations had defied the organization's early expectations, and its indictment of industrial and governmental abuses rendered it an ideal recruitment tool, the "Bible of the IWW." Judge Landis refused to admit the full report into evidence, but the IWW had printed a condensed version for distribution to its supporters. In that abbreviated form, Landis agreed to let it in.[39]

Vanderveer recited the report's most salient findings to the jury. Seventy-nine percent of working families were unable to support themselves, he said. The working people, 65 percent of America's population, owned less than 5 percent of the nation's wealth. The wealthiest 2 percent owned two-thirds of the country's real and personal property. Large corporations were earning monopoly profits. Industry was trampling on workers' health as well as public safety. These conditions were unjust, but they were not irremediable, Vanderveer explained. The goal of the IWW was to counter the concentration of industrial strength by organizing the workers. The capitalists understood the danger that a powerful workers' movement posed, and they were doing everything possible to shut it down.[40]

Frank Nebeker denounced the report as blatantly partisan, a "forum for cranks and fanatics," and he was desperate to minimize its significance. According to Nebeker, the case had nothing to do with industrial conditions in the United States. Workers had no business taking matters into their own hands, particularly in a time of national emergency. In Nebeker's view (albeit one he moderated in closing argument), the right to strike was suspended during wartime. The activities of the IWW constituted an attack on the United States government precisely when it most required support.[41]

To Vanderveer, Nebeker's reasoning was symptomatic of a deeper misapprehension of syndicalist ideology and of the IWW's goals. The organization was not attempting to overthrow the government. It was not "aimed at the government" at all, he explained, but rather at exploitation—it was "social" rather than "political." Although Vanderveer understood that the legal system structured and regulated economic exchange, he emphasized that there was no law setting wages at any particular level. On the contrary, any such law would be struck down as unconstitutional. After all, the courts' view was the one that Nebeker himself had endorsed in his opening statement: that the "wage system" was a matter of negotiation between contending parties, a product of that "fundamental right," both natural and constitutional, "of all men to contract with each other." Employers appropriated the profits that belonged to the workers because they had the economic power to do so.[42]

Just as there was "no law which gives the right to exploit," Vanderveer continued, there was "no law which stays a man in his effort to prevent it." The IWW sought to counter exploitation through industrial organizing. Workers and their employers were locked in a simple power struggle, and there was no middle ground. If the workers cut employers' profits low enough, the profit system would fall. On the other hand, if employers "cut our wages low enough, then our morals and our civilization will topple and fall." In this conflict, labor's most effective tool was *direct action*, the IWW's signature method. The IWW was not opposed to democratic processes, Vanderveer clarified. In fact, it "believe[d] so completely and absolutely in our form of government, that it want[ed] to extend it to industry." But there was no reason to resort to political action to accomplish something nonpolitical. In the perennial contest between labor and capital, the IWW wanted the government to stay out.[43]

In his closing argument, Nebeker flatly declared that "the industrial system of this country is not on trial." He condemned war profiteering, and he acknowledged that there were people in the United States who were living in need. These circumstances, however, were "no legal justification" for the IWW's militancy. Nebeker insisted that the government had no desire to criticize any "honest" and "patriotic" labor organization (implicitly, the AFL). He conceded that many members of the IWW were sincere and hardworking, including the soldiers who had testified on the organization's behalf. But these rank-and-file members did not understand the true purposes of the organization. The defendants, with their "soft hands and hard faces," were of a different breed. In concluding, Nebeker described a recent flowering of "progressive legislation" intended to ease economic injustice. Denying the capacity of American political institutions to solve the problem of wealth inequality was in Nebeker's estimation a declaration that American institutions had failed—a conclusion he trusted the jury would not reach.[44]

Inexplicably, Vanderveer declined to make a closing argument. Reporters, observers, and historians have debated whether he was overconfident, defeatist, or simply convinced that the evidence would speak for itself. Certainly, many of the defendants expected to be acquitted. Throughout the summer, the radical press had reported that the IWW had the stronger case, and courtroom spectators agreed. But if Vanderveer found the principles of IWW ideology so convincing that he believed a wartime jury could be persuaded to embrace them, the swift and unanimous verdict taught him otherwise.[45]

On August 17, 1918, the jury in the Chicago trial returned a verdict of guilty on all counts and as to all defendants, after half an hour of deliberation—which, as Vanderveer observed, amounted to five seconds of consideration per verdict. To the defendants, the jury's decision was "a shock, a thunderbolt from a clear sky." Haywood considered it "one of the greatest blunders ever committed in a court of justice," and he pledged to uphold the principles and purposes of the IWW after his release. Baldwin echoed the IWW's outrage, though he conceded that such results were predictable in wartime. Juries in earlier Espionage Act cases had convicted defendants far less reviled on evidence far less damning.[46]

✦ ✦ ✦

For all of his reputed fairness during trial, Judge Landis thought the jury got it right, and the sentences he handed down were harsh. He gave Bill

Haywood, along with fourteen others in the organization's highest leadership, the legal maximum of twenty years in prison. Thirty-three more were sentenced to ten-year terms. All told, ninety-three of the defendants were bound for Leavenworth, in what constituted the largest single arrival of prisoners in its history.[47]

Frank Nebeker, of course, celebrated the government's successful resolution of "America's greatest criminal case." In the wake of the trial, he advised the Department of Labor to treat migratory and foreign workers sympathetically, "to the end that they will feel no need for such an organization as the IWW." At the same time, he urged state and national governments to enact legislation explicitly prohibiting "revolutionary movements of all kinds." Although he had managed to secure a conviction under wartime legislation, he thought existing laws were inadequate to combat such organizations as the IWW during times of peace. Press coverage of the convictions suggests that many Americans agreed. Not one AFL affiliate publicly denounced the verdict.[48]

In October 1920, two years after the Armistice, the Seventh Circuit rejected the defendants' appeal. George Vanderveer claimed, as he had throughout the proceedings and in his unsuccessful motion for a new trial, that the evidence was inadequate to connect the defendants to a conspiracy to obstruct the war effort or to interfere with the draft. He also argued that the convictions were constitutionally flawed. Among other theories, he suggested that the warrants supporting the raids on IWW offices were issued without probable cause and failed to describe the articles to be seized. The court agreed, but it nonetheless declined to exclude the evidence on Fourth Amendment grounds because the seized property belonged to the organization while the defendants were indicted as individuals (in 1923, the American Law Reports cited the case for the rule that evidence unlawfully seized from a voluntary association was not inadmissible against its individual members). Vanderveer denounced the legal system's disregard for the defendants' "most fundamental constitutional liberties." The government, in turn, chastised the defendants for attempting to evade responsibility for their criminal conduct by contesting the validity of the warrants.[49]

Vanderveer raised a final argument at trial and on appeal. He argued that the defendants' convictions were unconstitutional because the evidence on which they were based—the speeches, literature, and private correspondence articulating the IWW's position on militarism and conscription—was expressive. Vanderveer had requested an instruction to the jury on "the right of free speech as defined in the First Amendment." Judge Landis refused, however. He acknowledged a right to oppose American militarism in times of peace, but he believed that "once war is declared, this right ceases." The Seventh Circuit presumably agreed, as its opinion did not address the defense's First Amendment argument. The notion that the IWW's opposition to war or compulsory military service might merit constitutional protection evidently fell in the category of claims "of trivial consequence," not sufficiently plausible to require express consideration.[50]

The Seventh Circuit did reverse the defendants' convictions under the peacetime federal criminal code. It rejected the theory that the IWW, by organizing strikes against producers with whom the government expected to contract, violated sections of the penal code prohibiting conspiracies to hinder the execution of United States laws or to interfere with the exercise of rights or privileges guaranteed to citizens. Such an interpretation might have rendered virtually any strike illegal under federal law, even during peacetime, a position that the Seventh Circuit was unwilling to endorse. On the other hand, the court considered the evidence under the wartime statutes so abundant that the "verdict was inevitable." Those who still desired freedom for the IWW's leadership would have to pursue nonjudicial channels to secure their release.[51]

✦ ✦ ✦

The NCLB was at the forefront of the interwar efforts to aid the IWW defendants. Like the IWW itself, the organization stressed procedural irregularities surrounding the case, with particular emphasis on administrative abuses. Prior to the convictions, the NCLB had been careful not to antagonize potential allies in the administration. Afterward, with little left to lose, it accused the Department of Justice of deliberate and lawless interference with the IWW's defense.[52]

In September 1918, the NCLB issued an open letter to President Wilson charging federal agents with using expired warrants, interfering with the delivery of defense news literature by express companies as well as United States mail, and intimidating defense witnesses. These methods, it claimed, were "unparalleled in modern criminal prosecutions." But the administration was unmoved by the NCLB's appeal for executive clemency. On the contrary, even while it suspended other prosecutions under the Espionage Act, it relentlessly pursued the IWW. In January 1919, dozens of members were convicted in Sacramento. All but three of the defendants chose to underscore the injustice of the American legal system by making no defense in court. Twenty-seven more Wobblies were convicted in Wichita, Kansas, after languishing in jail for more than two years; NCLB documentation of the horrible conditions there eventually moved the Department of Justice to order the prisoners transferred while awaiting trial. Like the Chicago case, the Sacramento and Wichita verdicts were unsuccessfully appealed. Certiorari to the Supreme Court was denied in all cases. The estimated cost of litigating the three federal conspiracy cases to conclusion was $225,000, "a larger sum than ha[d] ever been spent by a labor organization in defending itself in a criminal trial." To the end, the NCLB assisted in raising funds.[53]

While these trials were pending, the NCLB pursued its final strategy for helping the beleaguered IWW: it mounted a national amnesty campaign on behalf not only of the IWW prisoners, but of all prisoners convicted under the Espionage and Sedition Acts. At first, the organization was optimistic about the prospects for amnesty at the end of the war. Several respected liberals were urging better treatment for "political prisoners," and a proposed amnesty for court-martialed prisoners attracted broad-based support. The NCLB hoped to translate this sentiment into a movement for the Espionage Act prisoners' release. But the NCLB's efforts to create amnesty committees in local communities were denounced as unpatriotic, and its attempted mass meetings were sparsely attended. President Wilson was favorably disposed toward a partial amnesty but consistently deferred to his advisers, who were staunchly opposed.[54]

The advent of the Red Scare only exacerbated matters. In the summer of 1919, Wilson communicated his intention to pardon "all American citizens in prison or under arrest on account of anything they have said in speech or in print concerning their personal opinions." A. Mitchell Palmer, who replaced Thomas Gregory as attorney general in March 1919, was adamant that no such cases existed. Although there was considerable support within the Department of Justice for amnesty for convicted Socialists (though not the IWW), he persuaded Wilson to resist mounting pressure for the release of Eugene Debs and other sympathetic prisoners. In fact, he initiated new Espionage Act prosecutions for, among other things, the distribution of amnesty literature, and he publicly advocated a peacetime sedition law.[55]

All told, the amnesty campaign dragged on for fifteen years. In 1921, President Warren G. Harding met with representatives from the (by then reorganized) ACLU and commuted the sentences of Debs and over twenty others, including several members of the IWW. But in the face of threats of vigilantism by the American Legion and professed patriotic societies, exacerbated by mounting industrial unrest, Harding refused to do more. Internal disagreement among the IWW prisoners, many of whom refused to file individual petitions, made action on their behalf even more difficult. So did the decisions of nine defendants, including Bill Haywood, to jump bail when the Supreme Court declined their request for certiorari—an action that Baldwin condemned, to the disappointment of his more radical allies. For the rest of the decade, the ACLU, along with the Joint Amnesty Committee that the organization helped create, exerted quiet pressure on Washington, securing the release of a few prisoners at a time. Only in 1933, when President Franklin D. Roosevelt issued a blanket Christmas amnesty, were the remaining wartime prisoners finally released and their citizenship and voting rights restored.[56]

✦ ✦ ✦

In February 1918, an IWW publicity agent wrote to Roger Baldwin that the federal government, local officials, and "unofficial thugs" had worked together to undermine "every right that is supposedly guaranteed by the American Constitution." By the end of the Chicago IWW trial, that assessment appeared to Baldwin to be well founded. The great lessons of the IWW trial were, first, that "civil rights hardly exist for the IWW," and second, that the perceived deprivation of justice in the courtroom was a powerful mobilizing force.[57]

Baldwin abhorred the verdict, but he was adamant that the end of the trial did not portend the demise of the radical labor movement. On the contrary, he believed that outrage against legal injustice would unify an otherwise divided and disorganized constituency in favor of "economic freedom." As one influential progressive observed in the wake of *Debs v. United States*, the Supreme Court's contortion of the First Amendment was evidence of its determination to "protect the old order," "in war times and class-war times" alike. The NCLB made a similar point, in a revealing reference to Justice Oliver Wendell Holmes Jr.'s dissent in *Lochner v. New York*. Its pamphlet on the *Debs* case acknowledged that criticism of the law occasionally provoked law breaking, particularly when the criticism was justified. But in the NCLB's vision, the risk was well worth taking. When Justice Holmes declared that "the Fourteenth Amendment does not enact Mr. Herbert Spencer's Social Statics," he had signaled the importance of legislative openness and peaceful democratic change. A constitutional right to agitate might have served the same interest Holmes had honored and progressives had endorsed. "We have been used to suppose that the desirability of an open door for long-range progress outweighs at all times the danger to present policy from free criticism," the NCLB explained. "We have believed that social statics could not be enacted—that the First Amendment embedded an insurance against social statics in the walls of American democracy."[58]

To civil liberties advocates, the judiciary's refusal to vindicate the constitutional commitment to democratic progress came at great social cost. Workers' perception that "the law and the courts are not for them on equal terms with the wealthy" had driven them to self-help and violence. The Espionage Act decisions were of a piece with a long line of labor decisions that the Commission on Industrial Relations had condemned. As a result, the solution to the persecution of the radical labor movement was "not to be found in written constitutions," but rather in the will of the people and in just economic relations free from the machinery of the state.[59]

Unlike their prewar precursors, however, the radical wing of an emerging civil liberties movement considered Congress and the president to be just as blameworthy as the courts. Of course, labor unions were already familiar with the coercive potential of state power. The conservative unions affiliated with the AFL benefited from federal policy during the war, but their radical counterparts felt its grip even more keenly than before. As witness after witness recounted in the IWW trial, workers had regularly experienced the crushing force of the state in the form of compulsory arbitration, military intervention, and labor injunctions. For the progressives, *the state* and *the courts* were vastly different creatures. For the radical labor movement, they were faces of the same beast.[60]

Over the course of the IWW trial, the NCLB's core leadership came to absorb this view. George Vanderveer's exchange with Frank Nebeker over direct versus political action—and the corresponding relevance of the

Commission on Industrial Relations—made such a strong impression on the organization that it published it in pamphlet form. For Baldwin, the most appealing of the IWW's methods was the free speech fight. As he reflected years after the war, "Far more effective is this direct action of open conflict than all the legal maneuvers in the courts to get rights that no government willingly grants. Power wins rights—the power of determination, backed by willingness to suffer jail or violence to get them."[61]

Tellingly, the IWW trial coincided with the termination of the War Department's cooperative posture toward the NCLB on the issue of conscientious objectors. Colonel R. H. Van Deman, chief of the Intelligence Section of the War College in Washington, DC, had initiated an investigation of Baldwin in December 1917, and by the spring, the NCLB was being closely monitored. Many within the military believed that the NCLB's activities verged on "direct conflict with the Government." In a desperate bid to preserve cordial relations, Baldwin voluntarily submitted the NCLB's printed materials and mailing list for inspection, with the hope that an official inquiry would clear the organization's name. Van Deman nonetheless recommended that Baldwin be prosecuted under the Sedition Act, and Frederick Keppel was sufficiently concerned to sever ties with the NCLB, despite his personal connections to members of the executive board.[62]

Other government departments were also gathering information on the NCLB and its leadership. Over the summer, postal officials declared fourteen NCLB pamphlets nonmailable, despite conceding to the Department of Justice that they did not explicitly violate the Espionage Act. On August 13, Walter Nelles sued in federal district court for an injunction directing the New York postmaster to mail them. A few weeks later, after government counsel declined to oppose the NCLB's application, Judge Augustus Hand—Learned Hand's older cousin, and himself an emerging champion of free speech—ordered the post office to deliver the pamphlets.[63]

Meanwhile, in late August, the government began a series of interviews with Baldwin concerning his opinion of the IWW and the funding of the NCLB's publicity work in the case. A few days later, six agents arrived at the NCLB offices to collect evidence for an Espionage Act prosecution. In the ensuing days, Walter Nelles wrote to the organization's close associates. He attributed the operation to complaints from local patriotic societies (whose representatives accompanied the federal agents during the raid) and from intelligence officers concerned with the organization's work on behalf of conscientious objectors, along with its involvement in the IWW trial. Although there was ample demand for an indictment, the NCLB's connections, including John Nevin Sayre (brother of President Wilson's son-in-law), helped dissuade the Department of Justice from prosecuting.[64]

On November 11, 1918, hostilities in Europe ceased. With the Armistice, the Selective Service and Sedition Acts lapsed, although a few pending prosecutions under the Espionage Act continued. President Wilson turned his attention to negotiations for a lasting peace, but his diminishing political clout impeded his efforts, and the Treaty of Versailles would never pass the American Senate. According to Gilbert Roe, Wilson's ill-fated Fourteen Points were a casualty of his own approval of the Espionage Act. The administration's suppression of liberal criticism had served only to empower the critics of internationalism and to undermine support for the president's peace plans.[65]

✦ ✦ ✦

For Roger Baldwin, the fallout from the war extended well beyond the Armistice. By August 1918, he was disillusioned. He had been confident in the ability of his new organization to moderate government policies toward pacifists and radicals. When a year of cooperation with various government agencies definitively failed to yield results, he was ready for more radical methods. He had, moreover, discovered the potential of courtroom spectacle as a platform for radical propaganda—even, or especially, when conviction seemed certain.

In the summer of 1918, the draft age was raised to forty-five, and Baldwin, at thirty-four, became eligible for conscription. Baldwin announced his intention to resign as director of the NCLB so that he would be free to take a "personal stand" against the draft. In mid-September, he declined to appear for his physical examination and declared in a written statement that he would refuse all compulsory service, regardless of its nature. In October, at his own request, a government agent was sent to his apartment to arrest him, and he was indicted for violation of the Selective Service Act.[66]

Less than two weeks before the cessation of hostilities in Europe, Baldwin appeared in the Southern District of New York before Judge Julius Mayer, who had presided over the convictions of Emma Goldman and Alexander Berkman the previous year. In his statement to the court, Baldwin articulated a strong commitment to "individual freedom," distinct from arguments about pluralism, democratic decision making, and the public interest. He emphasized that his resistance rested on the precepts of individual conscience. He asserted a right to abide by his internal beliefs, unconstrained by state power. He was particularly opposed to military conscription because it served the purpose of war, to which he was unequivocally opposed.[67]

Baldwin's autobiographical narrative, which he prepared in advance and read aloud in the courtroom, neatly captured the transformation in his thinking. He began by describing his upbringing, his education, and his early career as a social worker and progressive reformer in Saint Louis. Over the years, he explained, he had become "more and more impatient with reform." He claimed to have come to New York to work for the AUAM because he had grown discouraged by the ineffectiveness of incremental change at the local level and had awakened to the cause of labor radicalism. He linked himself to a "great revolt surging up from the people—the struggle of the masses against the rule of the world." In short, he was engaged in a fight against the "political state itself."[68]

To Judge Mayer, Baldwin's insistence on individual autonomy was incompatible with democratic government. Mayer was no stranger to Progressive Era arguments about the limits of state power. In 1905, in his capacity as New York's attorney general, he had unsuccessfully defended his state's maximum-hours law before the United States Supreme Court in *Lochner v. New York*. In Mayer's view, Baldwin's attitude endangered a government that remained, despite its imperfections, "a real people's Government." He admonished Baldwin that the republican liberties he celebrated rested on obedience to law. Channeling the prevailing progressive understanding, he told Baldwin that "the freest discussion" should be permitted and encouraged prior to enactment of a statute and, once it passed, "as to the methods of [its] administration." The democratic process, however, could not countenance disregard for duly enacted laws. Accordingly, he pronounced his sentence: one year in prison, the maximum provided by law.[69]

Baldwin listened to Judge Mayer with a "friendly smile," and, when the proceedings were over, his supporters streamed past him, one by one, shaking his hand and congratulating him. Many of the most notable figures of the American Left celebrated Baldwin's stand. Over the coming months, they initiated efforts to secure Baldwin an executive pardon, but Baldwin insisted that he would leave jail only under a general amnesty, not as a "favor obtained by politically influential friends."[70]

Notwithstanding his somewhat grandiose declaration of his willingness to suffer for his beliefs, Baldwin fared relatively well over the coming months. After a brief stay at the Tombs in lower Manhattan, he arrived at Essex County Jail in Newark, where he devoted his days to reading and writing, conversing with his fellow inmates and frequent visitors, and organizing a Prisoners' Welfare League. In May, Baldwin was transferred to the county prison in Caldwell, New Jersey, a work farm designed for short-term prisoners. While he was in residence, the warden attended the annual meeting of the National Conference of Social Work, where Florence Kelley nominated Baldwin to a committee. He lost by a margin of 262 to 216, but he won the warden's vote.[71]

Baldwin was released from Caldwell on July 19, 1919. He reported that his time in jail had been valuable and that he was "leaving more of a radical than [he] went in." The state was "not a sacred institution," whatever his progressive allies believed. The notion that government policy reflected "determined majority opinion" was misguided and naive; in reality, he explained, it reflected "controlling economic interests." Baldwin planned to cease all civic participation, including jury duty and the vote. He announced his intention to join the "revolutionary labor movement," since the world had "passed so-called political democracy" by.[72]

Over the course of the Chicago proceedings Baldwin had developed close relationships with Bill Haywood and other IWW leaders. He admired their philosophy and determination, and he resolved in jail to experience the life of an itinerant worker. Although Haywood thought Baldwin's time and energies could be spent more profitably on fund raising and publicity, he obligingly sponsored him for IWW membership. Baldwin traveled the country by hopping railroad trains, and he tried his hand at manual labor. After a few months, satisfied with his new credentials but convinced that he would never rise to prominence in an organization for unskilled workers, he returned to New York to undertake a new project: transforming the NCLB into the most influential force in the interwar civil liberties movement, the ACLU.[73]

✦ ✦ ✦

Out of the NCLB's central engagements in 1917 and 1918 emerged several crucial features of the interwar reconfiguration of rights, constitutionalism, and legal advocacy. Most obviously, the early leaders were fundamentally devoted to economic redistribution of a kind more radical than they confessed to liberal members and correspondents. The primary right they advocated was a capacious and malleable right of agitation. Although they invoked the rhetoric of constitutional rights from the outset, there is reason to believe such rhetoric was more tactical than heartfelt. Baldwin stated his attitude in a leaked letter often quoted by conservative critics: "We want to also look like patriots in everything we do. We want to get a lot of good flags, talk a good deal about the Constitution, etc."[74]

Equally important, the First World War produced in the NCLB's core leadership a lasting aversion to state power. Just a few years before the war, the founders of the AUAM, and the broader network of progressive reformers connected to the *Survey,* had criticized the Manly report of the Commission on Industrial Relations for privileging public opinion and economic self-help over administrative intervention. As wartime suppression escalated, NCLB supporters had tried repeatedly to elicit moderation from government officials. They corresponded with low-level bureaucrats, friends and acquaintances in the president's cabinet, even Wilson himself. But all too often, in these early years and after, the organization's highly placed contacts delivered disappointing results.

By April 1918, Roger Baldwin had come to question whether anything meaningful could be accomplished by "working on legislation or administrative orders affecting civil and religious liberties." Government channels were closed to radicals and their advocates. "The situation at Washington is not one which lends itself at all to any influences from the outside," he observed. President Wilson was in "complete control," and Congress was "willing to pass any legislation demanded by the Executive." With a handful of exceptions, administrative actors had been more inclined to engage in censorship than to temper it. The Department of Justice and the Post Office Department had proven eager to exercise their discretion in the service of repression. Effective dissent, like effective defense work, was practically impossible. In combating the Espionage Act, the NCLB was "dealing with the shifting policies of autocratic and arbitrary officials," not "with law."[75]

As administrative moderation receded as a tenable civil liberties program, the most important influence on the NCLB was the very set of labor radicals they mobilized to protect. Between the First World War and the late New Deal, anxieties about a strong state would mark off the NCLB's leadership from progressive advocates of civil liberties within and outside the organization. Even as they acknowledged the hazards of administrative discretion, most progressives would continue to endorse legislative and regulatory solutions to America's social problems. They would promote free speech not as an alternative to state power, but as a prerequisite to its intelligent exercise. By contrast, the NCLB was beginning to develop a radical theory of civil liberties that resisted the very state machinery that the AUAM's founders had helped to create. The veteran leaders of the NCLB rejected legislative, administrative, and judicial approaches in equal measure, on the understanding that "the processes of law and the constitutional guarantees of personal liberty are absolutely dead letters in the United States where private business interests control city government, city police and courts." The answer they proposed instead was the assertion of working-class economic power. Whereas the early NCLB borrowed methods and arguments from the Free Speech League, its later iteration looked to the tactics of the IWW, which "blazed the trail . . . for free speech which the entire American working class must in some fashion follow." The vision of civil liberties it espoused was modeled on direct action, not the "voting of wise decisions."[76]

The NCLB was acutely aware that mere absence of state suppression would not ensure equality of opportunity for dissenters. Many of the greatest obstacles to workers' organizing efforts stemmed from private sources, including denial of access to private meeting halls, vigilante violence, and employer-friendly reporting in the corporate press. The progressives, recognizing the same structural disparities, endorsed government programs to improve public discussion and increase access to unpopular ideas. As Zechariah Chafee Jr. later mused, "It may be necessary for the community not to rest content with a negative attitude of hands off but to adopt in addition positive measures to ensure that argument and counter argument on vital issues will have full play." But the NCLB no longer trusted the government to level the playing field. In this, it found itself aligned with industry and the ABA against progressive reformers.[77]

Despite its suspicion of social and economic regulation, the NCLB's concept of civil liberties diverged in fundamental ways from its conservative counterpart. It evinced no concern for private property, and it was exercised collectively rather than individually, through the assertion of group power. Still, the kinship was evident even to contemporaries. As Leon Whipple, the ACLU's official theoretician, reflected in 1927, "Libertarians on principle have been few and far between, and have generally belonged to three queerly mated groups: the Quakers, the Anarchists, and the lawyers."[78]

The first two groups were among the NCLB's primary constituencies during the First World War. Finding common ground with the third would be the organization's central project during the 1920s. In significant ways, the resonances between its antistate radicalism and the conservative tradition of state-skeptical constitutionalism would enable the ACLU's eventual success where progressives continued to fail, namely, in the courts.

4

Dissent

F IVE YEARS after his release from the Caldwell penitentiary, Roger Baldwin readied himself for a return to prison. This time, the charge was unlawful assembly. Baldwin had organized a procession to support striking silk workers in Paterson, New Jersey, in defiance of local police.

To seasoned civil liberties advocates, the 1924 episode was an uncanny echo of a familiar and foundational event in the history of expressive freedom. In 1913, the police suppression of the Paterson silk strike had catapulted free speech into the national spotlight. At that time, interference with IWW organizing efforts attracted the assistance of lawyers and activists, as well as the indignation of the Commission on Industrial Relations. For attempting to speak to the strikers, a local magistrate sentenced Bill Haywood to six months in county jail. The charges included disorderly conduct, as well as parading in violation of a 1796 New Jersey unlawful assembly statute that had languished for over a century. The conviction was set aside, however, on a writ of habeas corpus to a free-speech-friendly justice of the New Jersey Supreme Court, "the one bright spot on the side of the state authorities during the strike." The justice decided the case as a matter of common-law interpretation and statutory construction, not constitutional law. He nonetheless counted free speech among the inalienable rights secured by the state and federal constitutions.[1]

A decade later, thousands of Paterson silk workers were again on strike, seeking nearly the same concessions they had demanded in 1913. Mill owners again turned to local officials, including judges, to put an end to the picketing. The ACLU, organizational heir to the wartime NCLB, came to the strikers' defense. On October 16, 1924, Baldwin marched with the protesters from the headquarters of the Associated Silk Workers (ASW) to the city hall steps, where a union leader read from the Bill of Rights. With "brutality" that Baldwin considered blatant and unprovoked, police arrested instigators and dispersed the crowd. Baldwin volunteered himself for prosecution, and the chief of police obliged, charging Baldwin and nine of the strikers under the very same statute deemed inapplicable to Haywood in 1913. In December, without a jury and without opinion, a trial judge found Baldwin and his codefendants guilty of unlawful assembly within the meaning of the New Jersey act. Like Haywood before him, Baldwin was sentenced to six months in prison.[2]

In 1927, an appellate court upheld Baldwin's conviction for unlawful assembly. The "inflamed state of a public mind in the midst of a strike," it explained, was bound to prompt a breach of the peace. One year later, New Jersey's high court, the Court of Errors and Appeals, unanimously reversed. Among the justices who decided the case was the very justice who had reversed Haywood's conviction in 1913. Once again, the opinion rested on common-law and statutory interpretation: the protesters were unarmed and quietly submitted to arrest, it was the police who instigated violence, none of the participants threatened public peace. Once again, constitutional principles played a muted role.[3]

Notwithstanding the auspicious parallels to 1913, the ACLU's eventual victory in Paterson was no foregone conclusion. Arthur T. Vanderbilt, a future president of the ABA and chief justice of New Jersey's highest court, took charge of the appeal. But Vanderbilt was not yet the distinguished leader of the profession he would one day become, and in the months before the decision, Baldwin fully expected to serve out his sentence. When the opinion was handed down, the ACLU celebrated the New Jersey decision as its first vindication of civil liberties and "the most notable free speech decision from a state supreme court since the war."[4]

In broader context, the Paterson case was important less in terms of legal interpretation—Socialists and Wobblies had managed similar fact-based reversals in scores of cases before the First World War—than as a turning point in interwar civil liberties strategy. The years between the Armistice and Baldwin's Paterson protest were formative ones for the American civil liberties movement, but their importance cannot be measured in judicial outcomes. The overwhelming majority of civil liberties cases decided during this period privileged state security over expressive freedom. At the Supreme Court, Justices Oliver Wendell Holmes Jr. and Louis D. Brandeis awoke to the democratic value of free speech. Their dissents, however, were only that. Their persistent and impassioned insistence that the First Amendment encompassed subversive speech failed to persuade their fellow justices and afforded no protection to disfavored speakers.

Historians have long cast the great Holmes and Brandeis dissents as harbingers of an emerging constitutional commitment to expressive freedom. And yet, throughout the 1920s, the dissenters on the bench were just as overpowered as the dissenters in the public square, and there was little cause for optimism about future trajectories. After all, Holmes and Brandeis were persistent holdouts with respect to the Supreme Court's due process doctrine, with little to show for their perseverance. Indeed, in *Lochner v. New York,* Holmes had issued a dissent every bit as biting as his subsequent paeans to free speech. In the years since, his insistence that "a constitution is not intended to embody a particular economic theory" had become a rallying cry for progressive reformers as well as revolutionists. But the court had only amplified the valorization of property rights and freedom of contract that Holmes had castigated. Judicial dissents made useful mobilizing tools, perhaps, but they did not betoken imminent legal change.[5]

Even so, the Holmes and Brandeis dissents, along with a handful of speech-protective decisions in the lower courts, reflected a renewed endorsement of expressive openness within the liberal legal establishment. And that broader shift, though not immediately manifested in Supreme Court decisions, had significant implications for the future of civil liberties. Many former progressives and administrative enthusiasts had come to regret their wartime approval of ideological conformity. They recognized the value of expressive freedom in guiding democratic policy, as they had in the early 1910s. Despite decrying *Lochner*-era judicial overreaching, some went so far as to advocate an increased role for the judiciary in preserving personal rights. Meanwhile, few conservatives yet promoted free speech for perceived subversives, and most wholeheartedly supported the postwar wave of state sedition laws. They were increasingly troubled, however, by the wartime growth of federal authority—an expansion that receded with the Armistice but would never revert to its prewar levels. And they were as enthusiastic as ever about the courts.

As for the ACLU, the core leaders remained adamant that broad-based economic reordering was desirable in the United States and that the right of agitation could facilitate peaceful change. For a time, they flirted with the patent radicalism they had absorbed from the IWW. As massive strikes roiled the American economy and working-class activism surged throughout the world, they hoped and believed that peaceful revolution was possible if only the workers would cease to work and the state would stay its repressive hand. Still, from the beginning, they sought to enhance the organization's credibility by partnering with respected officials and academics and by appealing to American constitutional traditions.

Between the world wars, the cases the ACLU litigated produced some of the most stirring of the Holmes and Brandeis dissents. Yet in its early years, the very organization that pioneered the modern civil liberties strategy doubted that a speech-protective majority would ever coalesce on the Supreme Court. After all, even a decade earlier, at the height of the progressive assault on the judiciary, judges had overwhelmingly refused to recognize labor's legal claims. For the first half of the 1920s, the ACLU pursued constitutional litigation primarily to discredit the courts and, by extension, the labor injunctions they issued; the notion that the judiciary might soon preserve civil liberties against oppressive majoritarian laws seemed no more plausible than persuading those majorities to embrace revolution.

By the time it argued Baldwin's appeal in Paterson, the ACLU was struggling to answer the "fundamental question of what briefs in civil liberties cases are written for." In a period marked by economic prosperity, the immediate outlook for radical social and economic change was dim. When Baldwin marched in Paterson, the ACLU harbored no illusion that a mere right to assemble would yield dramatic results on the ground: the right to strike is of little value in the absence of economic power. As a matter of long-term policy, however, the organization came to consider the incremental expansion of expressive freedom to be a worthwhile investment—one that promised to pay dividends when meaningful agitation again became possible. It was that hope that motivated the organization's leadership as it sought to convince court-friendly conservatives that civil liberties would serve their interests, too. Within the ranks of the ACLU leadership, deep ambivalence toward the judicial strategy persisted for another decade. For the time being, few within the organization believed that the best way to advance civil liberties was to litigate constitutional cases. Nonetheless, a sizeable contingent was beginning to prefer judicial victories to the alternative, namely, the dubious proposition of "promoting propaganda by defeats in court."[6]

✦ ✦ ✦

In January 1919, civil liberties advocates anticipated a stormy future for free speech. As Gilbert Roe observed, President Woodrow Wilson promised deregulation of American businesses after the Armistice, but he offered no similar assurances in the domain of expressive freedom. During the war, when restrictive measures like the Espionage and Sedition Acts were debated in Congress, apologists insisted that patriotic consensus was essential to the country's military efforts; peace, they promised, would bring with it a complete restoration of civil liberties. But as the NCLB and other critics had predicted, the cessation of hostilities abroad failed to stem the hysteria at home.[7]

The end of the war ushered in a climate of heightened social tensions, including rampant anti-immigrant sentiment, race riots, and widespread labor unrest. The interwar civil liberties movement understood these trends to be related, and they denounced them all in unequivocal terms. Still, for most, the suppression of labor organizing and the persecution of radical activists were especially troubling.[8]

The Wilson administration's wartime support for AFL unions, driven largely by labor shortages, had empowered organized labor to make unprecedented demands on employers as well as the state. Even as it condemned the labor radicals within the IWW, the administration had courted mainstream unions for both political and policy ends. The National War Labor Board, chaired by Frank P. Walsh and William Howard Taft, advanced labor's interests considerably. With official sanction, union membership swelled to unprecedented levels. By 1919, Samuel Gompers was "demand[ing] a voice," at President Wilson's First Industrial Conference, "in the determination of the conditions under which we will give service . . . not only as supplicants but by right."[9]

Labor's new optimism was, however, short lived. The labor supply expanded rapidly as soldiers returned to the civilian workforce and immigration resumed. Foreign-born workers, popularly denounced as the source of radical agitation, were summarily deported. At the same time, a shortage of civilian goods during the reconversion process led to high inflation and increased cost of living, fueling both support for and fear of labor radicalism. The taste of power had emboldened labor, precipitating industrial conflict on a scale previously unimaginable in the United States. The recentness of the Russian Revolution amplified the perceived dangers, and in the face of thousands of strikes involving four million workers, it seemed that the labor struggle was on the brink of tearing the country apart. In the spring of 1919, revolutionary anarchists mailed bombs to prominent politicians and government officials. One of the bombs was meant for Attorney General A. Mitchell Palmer; another, for Frank Nebeker, who had prosecuted the IWW in Chicago.[10]

The result was the "wholesale denial of civil rights." The NCLB leadership celebrated the coal and steel strikes in the fall of 1919 for their unparalleled demonstration of working-class power. Wilson, however, deployed federal troops to break the steel strike in September 1919. Then, the administration obtained a federal injunction against striking coal miners in November—a move that the NCLB denounced as a "grave blow at the liberties of the American workingman, probably without precedent in our history." In fact, ever since Republicans had gained control of Congress in 1918, the president had made mounting concessions to industry. He continued to endorse responsible unionism and demanded a comprehensive federal reform agenda, but he openly criticized labor radicalism as well as strikes by public employees, most notably the Boston police strike of 1919—a failed attempt to secure union recognition and better wages and working conditions—which he branded a "crime against civilization."[11]

In addition to suppressing strikes, the Wilson administration did its part to silence those advocating radical ideas. Historically, much social policing in the United States was accomplished through private and informal means. During the war, vocal opposition to lynchings and other lawless tactics of the sort publicized by the NCLB had the effect of legitimating administrative and prosecutorial alternatives at the local and federal levels. In the late 1910s, even while it condemned mob violence, the government consolidated its coercive powers and called for official suppression and an expanded investigatory bureaucracy. Increasingly, such vigilante groups as the Ku Klux Klan, the American Legion, and the National Security League pursued their objectives through public channels. And public officials were eager to oblige. In June, Attorney General Palmer assigned the young J. Edgar

Hoover to investigate alleged subversives as head of the newly organized General Intelligence Division of the Bureau of Investigation. Between November 1919 and January 1920, the federal government arrested several thousand suspected radicals and deported hundreds of foreign nationals, including Emma Goldman and Alexander Berkman, in the notorious Palmer Raids. In the mainstream press, reactions to the raids were generally favorable. According to the *Washington Post,* there was "no time to waste on hairsplitting over infringement of liberty when the enemy [was] using liberty's weapons for the assassination of liberty."[12]

Congress, too, succumbed to antisubversive pressures. Among its noteworthy flourishes was the November 1919 refusal by the House of Representatives to seat Wisconsin Socialist Victor Berger, who was appealing a twenty-year prison term under the Espionage Act for his opposition to the war. The Supreme Court ultimately vindicated Berger's claim that Judge Kenesaw Mountain Landis—who, having recently wrapped up the proceedings in the Chicago IWW case, presided over the trial—improperly disregarded an affidavit of prejudice after expressing his vitriolic distaste for people of German descent. Despite the specious circumstances of his conviction, a House committee adjudged Berger "traitorous" and "disloyal" and professed a constitutional duty to exclude him. The House, with only one vote in opposition, enthusiastically accepted the committee's recommendation.[13]

In 1919 and early 1920, at the urging of Attorney General Palmer, Congress debated and came close to passing peacetime sedition legislation. In the spring of 1919, the Senate's Overman Committee helped to manufacture popular and congressional enthusiasm for federal action. Its operations were heavily influenced by the testimony of Archibald Stevenson, who sought to parlay wartime anti-German sentiment into postwar antagonism toward labor radicals and the Bolshevik threat. To Stevenson, who had spearheaded the wartime raid on the NCLB's New York offices, the need for sedition legislation stemmed not from "small groups which seek to use the torch and bomb," but rather from "those quasi-political and economic organizations which teach that the workers should organize into revolutionary industrial unions." That is, the danger was not terroristic violence (though the anarchist bombings of fall 1919 would make useful fodder for the anti-Red agenda), but the "coercive power of the general strike" to trump common-law prerogatives and political will.[14]

In February 1919, a strike in Seattle's shipyards provoked a wave of union sympathy strikes that shut the city down. Sensationalist press coverage of the Seattle General Strike lent credibility to claims like Stevenson's, and in the wake of the Overman Committee's June report, Congress consolidated seventy sedition bills into a single measure. According to the NCLB, it would have passed were it not for the intervening expulsion of Socialists from the New York legislature, which prompted a critical letter from Charles Evans Hughes on behalf of the New York Bar Association and (reported *Literary Digest*) provoked an outcry from "Republican, Democratic, and Socialist newspapers alike." In the NCLB's estimation, "the statesmen . . . suddenly realized that they did not *know* where all this led to," and the "opposition to sedition legislation crystalized almost overnight."[15]

If the United States Congress evinced a modicum of caution in its legislative program, the states were more audacious. Between the beginning of the war and the height of the Red Scare, dozens of state legislatures passed criminal syndicalism, criminal anarchy, Red flag, and sedition statutes. Some tried to push through antistrike and antipicketing laws as well, but failed; criminal syndicalism measures were a more politically palatable way to "shut up the agitators and keep them off the job."[16]

Invoking their old mantra, "Liberty is not license," a broad coalition of politicians and public figures approved the new laws. They affirmed their dedication to an American tradition of free speech while endorsing strict government regulation of radical expression—which, they claimed, threatened to undermine the very system that made civil liberties possible. To be sure, there were some notable exceptions. The distinguished Columbia political scientist and constitutional theorist John Burgess denounced the Espionage Act and state sedition laws (along with labor's "still more contemptible methods of social ostracism and business boycott") for impeding individual freedom. He linked his belief that the First Amendment embodied "the fundamental principle of American political philosophy" with his confidence in judicial supremacy. Such assessments, however, remained marginal on the Right. The official journal of the ABA urged local bars to "purge the rolls of unworthy members," that is, to disbar lawyers who engaged in "extreme utterances and activities" in aid of strikes. There was no place in the profession, the journal emphasized, for attorneys who impugned the institutions they had sworn to maintain and who thereby exceeded the limits of free speech.[17]

For the time being, two competing tendencies in conservative thought in the early 1920s—the old insistence that a broad police power was incompatible with the robust property rights on which civil liberty rested, and a simultaneous desire for government intervention to suppress class-conscious agitation—maintained a delicate equilibrium. As the philosopher John Dewey later explained, the Holmes and Brandeis dissents were based on the relationship between unfettered expression and the public welfare, as opposed to "anything inherent in the individual as such." By contrast, laissez-faire liberals rejected government intrusions on business practices but remained "almost uniformly silent in the case of even flagrant violations of civil liberties—in spite of lip service to liberal ideas and professed adulation of the Constitution." According to Dewey, the apparent contradiction was easy to explain: "Business interests have been and still are socially and politically dominant. . . . Only those individuals who are *opposing* the established order ever get into trouble by using the right to free inquiry and public discussion."[18]

Sometimes, conservatives' dueling commitments were voiced in a single breath. In 1922, the president of the ABA echoed familiar concerns about the concentration of government power in Washington and emphasized the need for a strong judiciary to prevent bureaucratic overreaching. Even in the states, he considered the encroachment of the "so-called police power" on constitutional limitations to be profoundly troubling. There was, however, a notable exception to his plea for limited government. Where speakers exceeded the bounds of acceptable debate, it was the duty of every patriot to support government officials and invite the maximum punishment under law, including deportation of foreign-born agitators. There was "no place for so-called class consciousness in America," he warned. "Upon the rostrum, in the press, and above all, in our schools of every grade, our people should be taught that our constitution and laws and the courts that interpret them do not destroy but preserve their liberties."[19]

James H. Tufts, a philosophical pragmatist at the University of Chicago who collaborated and coauthored with Dewey, provided a prescient, if premature, analysis of the incipient realignment in attitudes toward civil liberties and American institutions. Tufts observed that the compatibility of democracy with judicial review was "not so violently under discussion" as in the prior decade, when Justice Holmes's dissent in *Lochner*, among other factors, had pushed the issue to the fore. In fact, the circumstances of the war had precipitated an "interesting shift in the attitudes of conservative and liberal groups toward majority rule expressed through legislation on the one hand and constitutional guarantees as supported by the courts on the other." As a historical matter, constituencies that failed to prevail in the legislatures had turned to the courts to implement their policy preferences as constitutional mandates. Prior to the war, liberals had endorsed majority rule, while conservatives invoked constitutional protections for private property. Beginning with the war, however, legislative majorities had frequently targeted the rights of free speech and free press, which were purportedly protected by constitutional guarantees. In this new domain, it was conservatives who espoused majority rule.[20]

✦ ✦ ✦

If conservatives had begun to appreciate the advantages of government power, liberals were rediscovering its perils. The peacetime incursions on labor organizing and radical advocacy were sufficiently troublesome to prompt a sizeable contingent of progressives and liberal intellectuals to reevaluate their deference to the state regulation of speech. Respectable outlets such as the *Nation* warned that the continued repression was transforming ordinary workers into "dangerous radicals and extreme direct actionists"—echoing arguments often invoked during the free speech fights but largely forgotten during the war. Indeed, while reminding readers of the *Nation*'s steadfast opposition to socialism, an editorial espoused the right of every person "to present for public consideration his ideas, no matter how erroneous they may appear." That right, it claimed, was the basis of democracy; and the forces denying it, rather than the Socialists or the IWW, were the "most dangerous enemies of the social order today."[21]

Other former supporters of President Wilson's war policy agreed. Even Wilson claimed always to have believed that "the greatest freedom of speech was the greatest safety." In March 1919, the socialist *New York Call* ran an article titled "The Liberals Wake Up," in which it welcomed the news that American liberals were finally promoting political democracy.[22]

Established labor groups, whose activity was significantly threatened for the first time in a decade, also reawakened to the dangers of suppression. In January 1918, Roger Baldwin had complained that the NCLB's efforts to attract union support were stymied by Samuel Gompers's insensitivity to personal and minority rights. By the following summer, AFL leaders were attacking state sedition laws and pronouncing free speech the "answer to the Steel Trust"; at their annual convention, they urged complete revocation of all restrictions on freedom of speech, press, assembly, association, and travel. In the summer of 1919, labor activists and sympathizers from around the country assembled in Chicago for an American Freedom Convention to discuss the maintenance of civil and political rights. Baldwin spoke and was asked to put together a national amnesty group. Also among the speakers was Albert DeSilver, a close friend of Baldwin's who had assumed control of the NCLB in fall 1918 when Baldwin resigned as director, and who played a formative role in the organization until his early death in 1924. Independently wealthy, DeSilver graduated from Yale and served as editor of the *Columbia Law Review* before the allure of wartime civil liberties work seduced him away from his promising law firm career. Although socialists and radical unionists dominated the conference, moderates attended as well. The group condemned the convictions of Eugene Debs, Victor Berger, and the IWW. It demanded the repeal of antisedition legislation and broad recognition of free speech and free press. In August, the NCLB published a leaflet featuring the many free speech resolutions by labor bodies. As the organization had predicted during the war, outrage at the legal system had served to "solidify otherwise discordant groups of wage workers" into a solid phalanx for free speech.[23]

To many mainstream liberals who were ambivalent about the administration's suppression of radical agitation, the massive roundups of the Palmer Raids crossed the line. The Justice Department's violent methods and indiscriminate arrests endangered such well-established constitutional protections as the rights against search and seizure along with more amorphous claims to expressive freedom. A group of twelve prominent lawyers and academics, including Felix Frankfurter, Zechariah Chafee Jr., Ernst Freund, and Roscoe Pound, were sufficiently outraged to write a *Report upon the Illegal Practices of the United States Department of Justice*, which condemned the recent wave of warrantless searches and arrests and other unlawful methods. Although the authors explicitly declined to discuss free speech, they echoed concerns often invoked in debates over expressive freedom. "There is no danger of revolution so great," they argued, "as that created by suppression, by ruthlessness, and by deliberate violation of the simple rules of American law and American decency."[24]

For Frankfurter and Chafee, the report grew out of a broader campaign against arbitrary official action. Much of its content was based on materials they had gathered in preparing an amicus brief in *Colyer v. Skeffington,* a case involving deportations for membership in the Communist Party. In an opinion issued a few weeks after the report, a federal judge chastised public officials for their "lawlessness" and observed that "a mob is a mob, whether made up of government officials acting under instructions from the Department of Justice, or of criminals, loafers, and the vicious classes." The decision in favor of the deportees was eventually overturned by the court of appeals. In the meantime, however, it exercised a moderating influence on the Department of Labor and prompted a concession by the *Christian Science Monitor* "that what appeared to be an excess of radicalism on the one hand was certainly met with something like an excess of suppression."[25]

Frankfurter and Chafee hoped that advances in the domain of procedural rights would carry over to judicial support for free speech. During 1919 and 1920, the two Harvard Law professors—with the help of distinguished intellectuals and jurists, including Harold Laski and Judge Learned Hand— managed to secure many converts to the free speech cause, most notably Justice Holmes. Chafee's 1919 article "Freedom of Speech in War Time," expanded to book form in his 1920 *Freedom of Speech,* is widely regarded as the template for the interwar theory of expressive freedom and a prominent influence on Holmes's evolving position. In the summer of 1919, Laski arranged a private meeting between Holmes and Chafee. A few months later, Holmes, joined by Justice Brandeis, issued the first of his iconic dissents. "When men have realized that time has upset many fighting faiths, they may come to believe even more than they believe the very foundations of their own conduct that the ultimate good desired is better reached by free trade in ideas," he hopefully declared in *Abrams v. United States.* The longtime skeptic of laissez-faire constitutionalism concluded that truth was the strongest basis for sound public policy and that truth was best tested in the marketplace of thought.[26]

The Holmes and Brandeis dissents in the remaining wartime speech cases galvanized liberal support for free speech. There were details to be worked out. During the 1920s, the unsettled progressives within the civil liberties coalition appreciated the dangers of excessive emphasis on the public interest, majority will, and administrative consensus. Moreover, they knew that sound social science required openness to new theories and new methods. They acknowledged, with the *New Republic,* that "the successful operation of democratic governments depends upon the ability of public opinion to get at and prefer the truth." Most, however, accepted the administrative state as an abiding feature of modernity. Some fretted about "bigness" in government as an analog to the industrial consolidation of wealth, but they never made a concerted effort to turn the tide of central state growth. Instead, they sought to introduce protections for inadequately represented groups into the exercise of federal power. Chafee explained in his seminal work on civil liberties that constitutional rights protected both individual and social interests, and the trick was to balance the two. The prewar progressives had celebrated bureaucrats for their insulation from political will, but neutrality had proved illusory (industrial interests, among others, had consistently managed to assert their influence). Interwar civil libertarians instead sought to ensure that the state, despite and because of its unprecedented reach, would be responsive to new ideas and interests—accessible, mutable, and open to structural change.[27]

The liberal solution to the wartime expansion of state authority was not to undo it, as conservatives and anarchists both claimed. Rather, it was the necessity of a strong state in a modern industrial society that made a broader commitment to civil liberties crucial. As British civil libertarian Norman Angell explained, "The very fact that we do need more and more unity of *action*—regimentation, regulation—in order to make a large population with many needs possible at all, is the reason mainly which makes it so important to preserve variety and freedom of individual thought." The surrender to government of authority over the minutiae of daily life made the open and ongoing discussion of social priorities imperative.[28]

Many of the strongest advocates for expressive freedom continued to harbor deep reservations about advancing their agenda in the courts. After all, it was a "commonplace among progressive jurists" that the Supreme Court had transformed the Fourteenth Amendment into an "instrument whereby the preferences of certain judges about public policy may be substituted for the preferences of legislatures." Frankfurter worried about expanding judicial oversight of the political branches and advocated administrative tolerance instead. Freund, though more skeptical of administrators than his friend Frankfurter, distrusted the courts in equal measure. He criticized the Supreme Court's Espionage Act decisions for swapping an "arbitrary executive" with "arbitrary judicial power." Chafee emphasized that the First Amendment constrained Congress as well as, indeed more than, the courts. He considered the constitutional provision to be "much more than an order to Congress not to cross the boundary which marks the extreme limits of lawful suppression." In language that presaged later calls for constitutionalism outside the courts, he cast the First Amendment as "an exhortation and a guide for the action of Congress," a "declaration of national policy in favor of the public discussion of all public questions."[29]

For the time being, such squabbles remained in the background. Dissenters, after all, need not agree on a positive program. And however compelling their rhetoric, the great dissenters resolutely failed to sway their fellow justices, or conservative sentiment more broadly. As a correspondent complained to Chafee in 1921, "It seems the hardest thing in the world to straighten out the honest conservative American mind on this question of free speech."[30]

✦ ✦ ✦

In the fall of 1919—as Attorney General Palmer launched his raids, Justice Holmes drafted his *Abrams* dissent, and hundreds of thousands of workers went on strike—the NCLB's leaders contemplated the future direction of their organization. From their perspective, government and industry had jointly engineered the suppression of labor agitation through a combination of antilabor and antiradical legislation, administrative action, vigilante lawlessness, injunctions against labor practices and boycotts, and judge-made law. Facing a broad array of opposition forces, none of their conventional tactics seemed adequate to the task ahead. "The situation calls for a dramatic campaign of service to labor in the areas of conflict, by those who see the vital need of freedom of expression for orderly progress," a memorandum making the case for reorganization explained.[31]

Like the labor groups it represented, the NCLB had come to claim that rights could be secured only by "ceaseless agitation and sacrifice," and that they could be maintained only through "organized power." Every measure to suppress free speech was at its heart an attempt to suppress the class struggle. The targets of such initiatives were not just radicals, but established trade unions as well.[32]

To meet the emerging challenges, the national committee needed new personnel, split evenly among union leaders, labor activists, and liberals interested in both civil liberties and the industrial struggle. Walter Nelles put the group's overarching objective succinctly. "We are frankly partisans of labor in the present struggle," he said, and "our place is in the fight." In January 1920, the NCLB leadership endorsed the plan to reorganize. The name of the NCLB's successor, the American Civil Liberties Union, was meant to capture its transition from "a bureau of legal service to a propaganda organization."[33]

What were the rights to which the ACLU would be committed? On the surface, they involved familiar constitutional principles like freedom of speech, press, and assembly. But if there were variations in the ways that mainstream liberals understood and advocated those principles, the radical project contemplated by the ACLU was fundamentally distinct. Among the rights promoted in the ACLU's earliest literature were a "right of workers to organize in organizations of their own choosing," which should "never be infringed by law"; a right to picket, free from court order or police edict; and a right of workers to strike "at all times and in all places"—a right the ACLU considered "inviolate," even among public employees. It was with these goals in mind that the ACLU concluded, in language far more palatable than the underlying agenda it reflected, that in the struggle for industrial democracy, "the issues of free speech, free press, lawful assemblage, and peaceful picketing are everywhere involved."[34]

Shaped by their wartime experience, the erstwhile progressives of the interwar ACLU no longer assumed that quiet negotiations and political pressure could accomplish fundamental change. Perhaps because the old progressive convictions were so strongly ingrained, the early ACLU did reach out to government agencies and public officials in opposition to restrictive legislation and in pursuit of amnesty for political and industrial prisoners. When mobs and vigilantes beat dissenters, it called on officials to intervene, notwithstanding its concerns about government abuses. More tellingly, when local officials aligned with courts to quash local labor struggles, even Roger Baldwin was tempted to enlist state and federal assistance in leveling the playing field. On the whole, however, the leaders of the ACLU were intensely distrustful of administrative governance. Mindful that legal rights were most salient when buttressed by public opinion, they preferred publicity campaigns and grassroots organizing to administrative oversight.[35]

Notably, constitutional adjudication also played a minimal role in the ACLU's proposed program. That the NCLB had even attempted a legal strategy was a departure from its leaders' long-standing principles. Most had heartily endorsed the judicial recall and other efforts, reflected in the reports of the Commission on Industrial Relations, to cabin judicial power. As a general rule, labor advocates were no friendlier to the courts in 1919 than they were at the beginning of the decade. On the contrary, they believed that "our courts [are] today, and have been for years, inclined toward big business, or corporate influence." The NCLB had been willing to appropriate the conservative language of individual rights and to pursue civil liberties in the courts if that was the best means of serving its clients. But the wartime failures only confirmed initial doubts about the legal strategy. First in the ACLU's long list of factors contributing to the suppression of civil liberties in the wake of the war were "the reactionary decisions of federal and state supreme courts." The *Abrams* case, Justice Holmes's dissent notwithstanding, had left "the status of civil liberty hopeless so far as it is the concern of the courts of law."[36]

Mounting worries about the wartime excesses within the judiciary as well as the administration emphasized a point that labor leaders had long understood, namely, that the outcomes and effect of judicial decisions were closely related to public opinion. As an initial matter, it was evident that popular support affected the odds of acquittal or successful appeal in particular legal disputes. As a result, the organization sought to generate sympathy for defendants through newspaper advertisements (as it had in the IWW case) and even letter-writing campaigns. Some correspondents, including Learned Hand, Felix Frankfurter, and Roscoe Pound, worried about the propriety of efforts to influence the judiciary. "After a good deal of thought," however, the leadership concluded that "because of the character of political cases, which in their very nature involve much publicity unfavorable to the defendant, it is, or should be, permissible and ethical even for a member of the bar, to endeavor to secure publicity for the other side of the facts."[37]

Even more important, the ACLU believed that judicial defeats, as much if not more than victories, could generate sympathy for the civil liberties cause. At the height of the Progressive Era, it was the Supreme Court's perceived hypocrisy that undergirded bids for judicial recall and constitutional amendment. Given the improbability of a marked change in judicial personnel or ideology in the foreseeable future, the best hope for the civil liberties movement was to emphasize just how unreasonable the federal judiciary could be. To that end, "the job of reporting trials," as compared with litigating them, had "much more probability of result." The new organization would orchestrate nationwide publicity of noteworthy struggles and events. It would also dispatch speakers and organizers to centers of industrial conflict, where they would provoke arrest under local regulations that conflicted with constitutional principles. There was to be no detachment between the advocates of civil liberties and the "struggle in the field."[38]

As planned, the ACLU national committee attracted a mix of labor leaders, advocates, and respectable liberals. Harry Ward chaired the organization and would continue to do so for almost twenty years. Born in England, Ward was a Methodist minister who had served as head resident of the Northwestern University Settlement House before embracing more radical methods of social activism. Duncan McDonald, president of the Illinois State Federation of Labor, agreed to serve as a vice-chair, along with the antiwar activist and former member of Congress Jeannette Rankin. Baldwin and DeSilver were codirectors. William Z. Foster—a former Wobbly and veteran of the Spokane free speech fight who had recently (after a brief flirtation with the AFL and a formative trip to Moscow) become a leader of the American Communist Party—considered the struggle for civil liberties so important that he made an exception to his general policy of belonging only to trade union organizations. Much of the original leadership of the AUAM (and by extension, many signers of the petition to President Taft on behalf of the Commission on Industrial Relations) became members within the first year of operations. The executive and national committees included Jane Addams, Florence Kelley, Herbert S. Bigelow, Crystal Eastman, John A. Fitch, and Norman Thomas. Even Lillian Wald approved of the reorganization, though she did not join. Clarence Darrow was an inaugural member. Ernst Freund and Harold Laski joined, as did Felix Frankfurter, with some coaxing. Other notable members included John Dewey, Helen Keller, and Upton Sinclair.[39]

Although Baldwin expressed a willingness to include conservatives, he did not think it likely that they would join. He did, however, acknowledge the need to temper the ACLU's partisan rhetoric, at least in its official communications. In the first year of the ACLU's existence, the more cautious members urged the leadership to restore the neutral posture cultivated by the NCLB, which was crucial to broader support. To that end, the ACLU modified its publications to emphasize the democratic value of political expression as a means toward "orderly social progress." It seized on Justice Holmes's endorsement of a marketplace of ideas, in which the most compelling theories and thinkers would inexorably prevail. Although much of the ACLU leadership remained convinced that radicalism would ultimately triumph, the organization consistently assured audiences that airing revolutionary ideas was the best way to assure their defeat. In June 1920, the statement of principles was amended to convey "the social value of the principle of civil liberty at all times, not only when a class is struggling for expression."[40]

The organization also argued over the limits of expressive freedom. While much of the core leadership believed that speech advocating violence should be protected—Baldwin, after all, considered "political action under representative government" to be "the very heart of violence"—others disagreed. Invoking Mahatma Gandhi, playwright Zona Gale (who eventually resigned over the issue) deemed the renunciation of revolutionary violence a morally warranted sacrifice of "personal liberty," no different in kind from the abridgment of personal freedom effected by Prohibition.[41]

What emerged from these internal debates in the ACLU's first year was the closest the organization would come to a theoretical defense of the right of agitation, loosely modeled on a proposal made by Nelles the previous year. According to Nelles, it was crucial to channel the alienation experienced by modern workers into productive change. "When agitation is outlawed," he reasoned, "the unrest which it might have made a force for constructive betterment is diverted in bitterness toward retaliation." Nelles was not arguing, like his progressive counterparts, that censorship made martyrs of radical speakers or made their dangerous ideas more alluring. Rather, he believed that legal suppression of labor organizing—the sort of direct action with the potential to produce peaceful but revolutionary economic reordering—would leave workers with no choice but to resort to the bloodier Bolshevik methods that few Americans desired. The ACLU's first official report on its objectives and activities laid out the organization's "social philosophy" in similar terms. An appeal to civil liberties in the farmer-labor campaigns of the 1920 election cycle was "buried under the Republican landslide." As a result, many workers had embraced "the ultimate necessity of armed resistance," and industrial conflict of epic proportions loomed on the horizon.[42]

Against this backdrop, the two major goals of the ACLU were, first, "the reorganization of our economic and political life," and second, "the demand for the 'rights' of those minorities and individuals attacked by the forces of reaction." Although many activists on the Left believed that the existing power structure would yield only to superior force, civil liberties could soften the conflict. "We realize that these standards of civil liberty cannot be attained as abstract principles or as constitutional guarantees," the ACLU explained. Legal rights securing the right of agitation would never be conceded while class conflict threatened, as "economic or political power is necessary to assert and maintain all 'rights.'" Nonetheless, the "mere public assertion of the principle of freedom of opinion in the words or deeds of individuals, or weak minorities, helps win it recognition, and in the long run makes for tolerance and against resort to violence."[43]

The early ACLU believed the class struggle was inevitable. Civil liberties, however, could minimize the bloodshed. The right of agitation might advance the economic status of the working class by peaceful means. The only alternative was violent revolution. The civil liberties championed by the early ACLU were not legal rights conferred by the state to secure the expression of individual conscience, nor did they reflect a policy commitment to rational discussion of optimal social conditions in the marketplace of ideas. Rather, civil liberties were a byproduct of group struggle, rooted in power and only incidentally inscribed in law.[44]

✦ ✦ ✦

When Roger Baldwin went to Paterson in the fall of 1924, he was doing exactly what the ACLU's early literature had promised: inserting the organization "directly into the struggles of labor and radical groups . . . by send[ing] free speech organizers and speakers to conduct demonstrations." A radical journalist who served as the ACLU's publicity director in 1924 captured the organization's method in colorful terms. First, "the police of Ameba, New Jersey, let us say, broke up a strike meeting held outdoors and beat up the speakers." Second, at the ACLU's urging (and after a "stinging communication" to the Ameba chief of police), the strikers held a test meeting; they read, perhaps, from the Declaration of Independence, with similarly suppressive results. Third, the ACLU arranged its own challenge of the ban. "This time the speakers were not strikers and labor organizers, but a prominent lawyer, a famous bishop, a celebrated senator, two well-known editors of respectable journals and a wealthy lady of liberal views." The distinguished guests stressed constitutional rights rather than the strikers' demands. Sometimes, officials stood their ground. More often, "the Ameba police listened with profound respect to these good people who were well dressed and spoke in modulated tones," and the ACLU "sent out releases to the newspapers announcing that free speech had scored a victory in New Jersey."[45]

The organization achieved some notable successes pursuing this path, which was reminiscent of the IWW's free speech fights. In its first year of operations, it secured the right of the Amalgamated Textile Workers of America to meet in Passaic, New Jersey, by sending Norman Thomas, Albert DeSilver, and Harry Ward to stage a gathering. When the police turned off the meeting hall lights, the ACLU representatives read from the New Jersey Constitution by candlelight, insisting on workers' right to assemble without a permit. The Passaic police, wary of negative publicity, acceded to their claims.[46]

In May 1922, ACLU attorney Arthur Garfield Hays traveled to Vintondale, Pennsylvania, alongside representatives of the UMW. A successful New York lawyer who attributed his "so-called radicalism" to the close friendship between his grandfather and the freethinker Robert Ingersoll, Hays was known for an "intense sense of justice which [made] it impossible for him to indict a class or a group, or to see all the good only on one side." Hays campaigned against capital punishment and believed imprisonment was often unwarranted—an issue that took on a personal meaning when company officers and local officials in Vintondale attacked and jailed him. He managed to secure indictments against them for assault and battery and, in the process, to vindicate the rights to meet and to speak.[47]

For two years, the ACLU was on the front lines of the labor struggle, marching, picketing, and organizing, outside the factory gates and in the Alabama and West Virginia coalfields. In these early campaigns, the organization forthrightly acknowledged its enthusiasm for the underlying objectives of the unions it defended. As events unfolded, however, the ACLU's radical rhetoric proved just as ephemeral as the revolutionary moment that produced it.

The Republicans who came to office in the 1920 election vocally opposed the labor policy of their Democratic predecessors, and they were eager to reverse any remaining wartime advances. Meanwhile, the postwar depression undermined labor's demands for higher wages and put unions on the defensive. By 1921, union membership had declined by 1.5 million and the open shop was the rule. The next year, the Warren G. Harding administration was faced with two major strikes, and in both cases it threw its support to employers. Beginning in April 1922, a nationwide coal strike involving more than half a million miners threatened to interrupt the country's coal supply. Though Harding initially professed neutrality, he encouraged producers to resume operations with strikebreakers, and he denounced John L. Lewis and the UMW (which rebuffed his invitation to submit to compulsory arbitration) for attempting to organize nonunion mines. After four exhausting months, the miners returned to work; although they secured modest short-term concessions, their bleak long-term outlook was painfully evident.[48]

The Great Railroad Strike of 1922 was even more devastating to labor. It was prompted by pay cuts announced by the Railroad Labor Board, an institution created when the Transportation Act of 1920 returned the railroad industry to private hands after it was nationalized by executive order during the First World War. The cuts targeted nonoperating railroad workers, who were less skilled and more replaceable than their counterparts in the established railroad brotherhoods, and whose unions eventually voted to strike. The Harding administration condemned the strikers as a lawless minority, and it pledged to keep the trains running and "sustain the right of men to work." Judge James H. Wilkerson dealt a further blow to the already doomed strike with his notorious shop-craft injunction, secured on the president's orders. Among its many far-reaching provisions, the injunction prohibited any member or agent of the union from "encourag[ing]" any person to "abandon" or "refrain from entering" the employment of a railroad, by picketing, in the press, or in private communications—indeed "in any manner whatsoever"—through "suggestion" or "persuasion." Harding boasted that it was the most sweeping injunction ever secured.[49]

Although most Americans supported the injunction, some thought it went too far. In Congress, an Arkansas senator decried the judiciary for betraying the "fundamental safeguards of liberty." Charles Fremont Amidon and George M. Borquin—the same federal judges who had proven most sympathetic to Espionage Act defendants—issued parallel decisions that relied on the Clayton Act to refuse injunctions against the striking railroad workers. Still, such critics were rare. The *ABA Journal* suspended its ordinary silence on ongoing judicial matters to defend Wilkerson's order, and it dismissed the argument that the injunction infringed on expressive freedom as "loose talk and loose thinking."[50]

The Supreme Court's labor decisions in the early 1920s, under its newly appointed chief justice William Howard Taft, were only marginally more restrained than Wilkerson's. In a report on the civil liberties situation between 1921 and 1923, the ACLU included only two cases under the heading "United States Supreme Court": *Duplex Printing Press Company v. Deering* and *Truax v. Corrigan*. Both dismantled legislative protections for organized labor, and neither expressly invoked the Bill of Rights. In the first, the Supreme Court declared secondary boycotts unlawful under federal antitrust laws, notwithstanding the protective language of the Clayton Act, and authorized the use of injunctions to block them. In the second, it struck down a state anti-injunction law as an unconstitutional violation of equal protection and due process. Other decisions effectively outlawed any activity "bear[ing] the sinister name of 'picketing'" and made unions subject to high damages for restraint of interstate commerce. And in 1926, three years after invalidating Kansas's compulsory arbitration law because it unduly burdened businesses, the Supreme Court upheld a conviction under the same Industrial Court Act prohibiting a strike. In language that was unusually blunt but substantively unremarkable, the unanimous opinion clarified that "neither the common law nor the Fourteenth Amendment confers the absolute right to strike." As the ACLU understood, such decisions gave license to judges like Wilkerson to undermine labor organizing at will. It is a telling measure of their perceived importance that an ACLU pamphlet, *The Supreme Court vs. Civil Liberty,* featured Justice Brandeis's dissents in *Hitchman Coal* and *Duplex Printing Press* alongside the better known First Amendment decisions.[51]

Unions, of course, were not wholly powerless during the 1920s. Well-established unions like the railroad brotherhoods retained considerable strength. The Republican Party offered up various concessions, including immigration restrictions, high tariffs, and the Railway Labor Act of 1926, which officially recognized railroad workers' right to bargain collectively. Still, by the mid-1920s, strong government support for labor (for example, of the kind envisioned by the Nonpartisan League) was off the table, and mass mobilization through direct action had come to appear hopeless.[52]

Counterintuitively, the ACLU believed that liberal backlash against the Palmer Raids only weakened the prospects of protecting labor activity in the legislatures and the courts. By the spring of 1921, Albert DeSilver and Zechariah Chafee Jr. agreed that the expulsion of the New York Social-

ists marked "high tide in the assault on civil liberty." Thirty-five states retained suppressive legislation, and there were continued rumblings for a
federal sedition law. The Supreme Court's speech cases stamped out any
hope of securing new protections for constitutional rights in the short term,
and juries continued to return convictions. Still, the hysteria appeared to
be slowly receding.[53]

But from the ACLU's perspective, the bigger problem was the "open shop
campaign," which was still in full swing. That antiunion activism had out-
lived the frank repression of the Red Scare was no accident. When the political liability of the Palmer Raids discouraged further prosecutions for
dissenting expression, industry and its government allies resorted to the
direct suppression of labor through injunctions. The upshot was a "transfer
of the real conflict outside the arena of litigation." Liberal opinion might be
marshaled on behalf of silenced socialists, but press coverage of picket-line
violence and the threat of economic disruption had effectively undermined
public support for strikes. Meanwhile, those who were most sympathetic to
unions remained wary of constitutionalism as a trump on state economic
policy and were therefore hesitant to defend labor activity in constitutional
terms. The result, according to the ACLU, was that "the power of injunctions, backed by a propagandized public opinion increasingly hostile to all
new ideas, assail[ed] civil rights at every point."[54]

✦ ✦ ✦

In Paterson, New Jersey, the new labor landscape was on prominent display. In 1924, thousands of the city's weavers went on strike. Paterson was
well acquainted with such strikes, which had occurred there almost annu-
ally since the city became a dominant silk producer in the 1870s; the 1913
strike and another in 1919 were only the most prominent examples. The
1924 action nonetheless stood out as a last gasp for desperate workers in a
dying industry.[55]

In the summer of 1924, manufacturers increased the number of looms
that Paterson weavers were expected to operate, a change that threatened
to decrease total employment in Paterson and to increase hours (without a
corresponding increase in pay) for those workers who retained their jobs.
The ASW, an independent local union, supported the spontaneous walkout
that resulted. It was no surprise to union leaders when officials sought an
injunction against picketing in Paterson. Two years earlier, the state's

highest court had authorized the restriction of peaceful picketing if its tendency was to intimidate, over a stinging dissent by Justice James F. Minturn (the judge who had dismissed Bill Haywood's conviction in 1913), who chastised his colleagues for suppressing "peaceable and constitutional economic agitation." In the 1924 strike, judges issued a series of ex parte temporary injunctions prohibiting the strikers from picketing or congregating in crowds. Meanwhile, the police made mass arrests under New Jersey's Nuisance Act, and by midmonth, the indicted workers were convicted and fined.[56]

The ASW enlisted the assistance of the ACLU, but it advised the organization to keep a low profile and to refrain from engaging outside counsel, lest it antagonize local judges. When strikers were arrested for violating the injunctions, the ACLU expected to defend their right of peaceful picketing in court. Hearings on the injunctions were delayed, however, and further picketing in the interim was risky. Then, on September 24, Paterson's chief of police—just like officials in the 1913 strike—suspended the strikers' access to Turn Hall, the private hall that the union had rented for its daily meetings. And on October 6, the injunction was made permanent.[57]

The same day, Roger Baldwin arrived at the ASW's headquarters in Paterson for a scheduled free speech meeting at Turn Hall. Hearing that police had blocked entry to the building, he attempted to secure another private venue. Unsuccessful, he settled on City Hall Plaza, where disruption to traffic would be minimal. About thirty protesters set out from Turn Hall, marching by twos behind a pair of socially prominent sisters who carried American flags. By the time they arrived at their destination, only a block and a half away, hundreds of strikers had joined the procession. According to the police estimate, the crowd that gathered at City Hall Plaza eventually numbered between 2,000 and 3,000. When one of the strikers began to read from the Bill of Rights, the police descended in force and made several arrests. Baldwin was not among them, but he turned himself in, and on October 31 a grand jury indicted him for unlawful assembly along with several of the strikers. Baldwin elected a bench trial to force a decision on the legal claims.[58]

The judge sentenced Baldwin to six months in prison and fined the other defendants. In a prepared statement that the court declined to consider, Baldwin boldly articulated his understanding of the Paterson events. The case was an outcrop of the class struggle, he explained; the strikers were indicted because they were trying "to get their rights." They were all the more vulnerable because many were immigrants (in fact, local officials threatened that continued participation in the strike would lead to deportation), and because their independent union lacked the "powerful political and industrial backing" of the AFL. In the sort of provocative language that official ACLU communications would soon eschew, Baldwin linked his indictment to the "long struggle of the working-class for the rights to organize and strike"—a struggle in which "police almost everywhere side with the propertied employing interests as against the workers."[59]

In 1918, when he stood trial for refusing to submit to the draft, Baldwin had used his courtroom performance as a platform for propagating his beliefs. Having lost faith in state and court alike, he all but invited conviction. His statement in the Paterson case suggests that 1924 found him no more eager to compromise; even if the judge had agreed to hear it, it is hard to imagine that its naked class politics would have swayed him in the defendants' favor. For the time being, Baldwin's intended audience was well outside the courthouse.

A few anxious liberals heard his call. A week after he received his sentence, the thousand-member New York Civic Club nominated Baldwin as its president. The *Baltimore Sun* regarded the conviction as a betrayal of American ideals. And yet, the Paterson affair hardly provoked a public outcry. The *New York Times,* after describing the rally as a "riot" in initial coverage, adopted a neutral tone. In Paterson, locals resented the invasion of New York rabble-rousers. Samuel Untermyer, the respected civic leader and corporate attorney who volunteered to argue Baldwin's appeal, blamed Americans' indifference on gambling, boxing, baseball, and crossword puzzles, along with the "struggle for existence." Baldwin himself believed that employment and reasonable wages had seduced the workers into complacency. "Enough of our workers can buy second hand cars to ward off class-consciousness," he lamented at mid-decade. "All they need for contentment is the price of gasoline."[60]

Despite the many similarities, the resemblance between Baldwin's 1924 prosecution and its better-known 1913 antecedent was only surface deep. This time, the strike was defensive—a last-ditch effort to reverse mounting losses rather than an ambitious attempt to gain new ground. Additionally, conflict between Socialists and Communists, as well as ethnic tensions among German, English, and Polish Jewish weavers, undermined solidarity. In the weeks after the October protest, Paterson officials permitted the strikers to hold meetings. At first they excluded outside speakers, but the ACLU (adhering to its usual script) scheduled a meeting featuring addresses by an Episcopal bishop and other "distinguished people." That meeting and a second one proceeded undisturbed. The ACLU reported that the "right of free speech was completely vindicated," and it attributed the about-face to its own involvement. More cynically, the city capitulated because the threat to industry, as compared with 1913, was substantially less acute. Even as the ACLU organized its free speech meeting, Paterson's striking weavers were returning to work.[61]

Only a few years after it set up shop, the ACLU was forced to reassess its methods. Expert bureaucrats, legislative majorities, and organized working-class power all had failed to preserve the right of agitation. Constitutional litigation yielded only prison terms and poetic dissents. Tellingly, in the same year that Baldwin marched in Paterson, the ACLU endorsed a proposal by progressive presidential candidate Robert M. La Follette to curtail judicial review. In stark contrast to the analagous measure advocated by Theodore Roosevelt in the early 1910s, the new demand garnered little popular or elite support. Both the Republican and Democratic candidates staunchly defended a role for the judiciary in checking majoritarian excess, echoing the earlier arguments of the ABA. Calvin Coolidge, who had succeeded to the presidency upon Warren Harding's death in 1923, called the Supreme Court "the very citadel of justice" and warned that an unconstrained Congress would trample people's rights. Like Charles Evans Hughes, who stumped on his behalf, he counted free speech among the constitutional values dependent on an independent court. Indeed, as president of the ABA in 1925, Hughes expressly rejected both legislatures and administrators as feasible enforcers of the Bill of Rights; the only mechanism adequate to the task, he declared, was "the judgment of impartial and independent men learned in the law and experienced in its application, placed in judicial tribunals and charged with the duty of enforcing the Constitution as the supreme law."[62]

In practice, such appeals to the judicial enforcement of personal rights did not contemplate the protection of radical agitation. Still, the ACLU might have seized on the emerging rhetoric to press for judicial protection of free speech, as it would during the New Deal. Instead, it chose to castigate the courts. The organization advised voters that the courts had violated civil liberties as flagrantly as the political branches. The civil liberties guaranteed in the state and federal constitutions were only paper rights. If anything, courts were more apt to curtail the rights to strike and picket than they had been a decade prior. Rather than protecting freedom of speech and assembly, they were themselves the worst offenders.[63]

The ACLU's 1925 annual report laid out the organization's new understanding. Despite a perception of improvement in the civil liberties situation, intolerance persisted. The decline in violence of the 1920 variety only reflected the dwindling opposition: "No serious conflict or minority activity has aroused the latent forces of repression." In the antilabor climate of the mid-1920s, the best the ACLU could hope for was incremental improvement for beleaguered unions at the local level. It was in that spirit that its attorneys debated strategies for briefing Baldwin's appeal in the New Jersey courts.[64]

✦ ✦ ✦

To the ACLU, appealing Baldwin's conviction mattered less as a matter of legal principle than as a means of "arous[ing] to action the slumbering conscience of our people." As Samuel Untermyer explained in a protest meeting on Baldwin's behalf, the key to rolling back the wartime repression was to unify public support for civil liberties across class and political lines. As a tactical matter, that meant extracting the fight for free speech from the labor struggles in which it was embedded.[65]

Argument in the New Jersey Supreme Court was delayed until May 1927 due to Untermyer's poor health. In the meantime, the ACLU leadership had ample opportunity to refine its approach. The legal brief, which was drafted by New York attorney Samuel D. Smoleff with the assistance of Walter Nelles, Felix Frankfurter, and others, was technical, academic, and abundant in ancient British authority. In the ambivalent assessment of Arthur Garfield Hays, who thought the ACLU's briefs "ought to be at least as effective as [its] pamphlets," it was excessively legalistic and insufficiently inspirational. To Frankfurter, for whom the goal of a brief was a favorable outcome rather than a landmark decision, that "pedestrian" quality was precisely the point. Frankfurter disregarded the possibility that it would serve civil liberties better "to have Baldwin go to jail than to have his conviction reversed." In his view, the legitimate objective of any litigation was to win.[66]

The challenge, in the authors' opinion, was to nudge the courts in a more liberal direction without raising alarm bells or conjuring slippery slopes. To that end, the brief accepted the power of the New Jersey legislature to proscribe those restraints on assembly recognized at common law. Baldwin was hesitant to concede too much. To a conservative court, he told Nelles, the brief's endorsement of the common-law test was an invitation to abridge the right of assembly on less favorable facts. It offered little cover for the kinds of meetings he wanted most to protect. "Certainly *any* meeting during a strike may lead to disorder," he complained. Nelles responded that a right to assemble under circumstances "alarming to men of firmness and courage" might be defensible as a matter of libertarian principle, but not of constitutional right. The radical vision of civil liberties advanced by the ACLU was simply untenable in court.[67]

Instead, the brief cast the October 1924 meeting as the paragon of peaceful and orderly assembly. As an initial matter, no permit was required to meet publicly in Paterson, and so the ACLU's failure to secure one did not render the meeting unlawful. More important, Judge Minturn's decision in the *Haywood* case had required a showing of alarming conduct, and there was nothing in the record to support such a finding. Baldwin had advised participants to acquiesce to police orders, and by every indication they had done so. If there was physical resistance on the part of the strikers, it was only after the order to disperse, and only in response to unprompted violence by the police. The whole point of the episode had been to generate a legal test of the organization's rights, and the brief sought to capitalize on this "naive faith in the courts."[68]

The authors of the brief understood the constitutional protections for speech and assembly as important undergirding principles, but they made no sweeping demands for revising prevailing tests. After all, constitutional limitations were relevant only if the meeting ran afoul of state law. Certainly there was room for aggressive argument in the domain of statutory construction. Perhaps the court might be persuaded to hold that speakers were accountable only for the alarming acts they instigated, as opposed to the hostile reaction of police or thugs or passers-by. But there was broad-based agreement among the lawyers that the best approach on appeal was to argue the case on its sympathetic facts. "Constitutional questions are more effective in the background than as protagonists," Nelles explained.[69]

This reserved and forward-looking approach initiated a new phase in the ACLU's civil liberties campaign. True, the ACLU had never altogether abandoned litigation of constitutional claims, despite its distrust of the judiciary. In fact, the organization's attorneys argued the most important First Amendment decisions of the 1920s, including *Gitlow v. New York* and *Whitney v. California*. From the perspective of the ACLU leadership, however, those cases played a bit part in a broader propaganda campaign. *Gitlow* involved a Communist former member of the New York State Assembly convicted under New York's Criminal Anarchy Act of 1902 (enacted in the wake of the William McKinley assassination) for publishing his "Left Wing Manifesto." In 1925, the Supreme Court upheld the conviction over a Holmes and Brandeis dissent. Because the majority signaled that it would "incorporate" the First Amendment into the Fourteenth, thereby imposing federal constitutional constraints on the ability of states to regulate speech, subsequent generations would hail the decision as a victory for civil liberties. At the time, though, incorporation appeared to be a modest concession. Most state constitutions formally protected speech in language at least as vigorous as the First Amendment, yet the state courts were no more likely than the federal judiciary to protect radical speech on constitutional grounds.[70]

In the second case, which reached the Supreme Court on the merits in 1927, the justices unanimously upheld Anita Whitney's conviction under California's Criminal Syndicalism Act for helping to organize California's Communist Labor Party in 1919. Justice Brandeis (who also wrote for Justice Holmes) concurred in the judgment because the relevant constitutional claims were not preserved at trial. Still, his separate opinion has long been celebrated for its stirring and eloquent defense of free speech. As an attorney and advocate, Brandeis had lambasted judicial reliance on the Fourteenth Amendment's Due Process Clause, and his opinion in *Whitney* expressed his enduring discomfort with the doctrine. Given the reality of judicial review, however, he insisted that "the power of the courts to strike down an offending law is no less when the interests involved are not property rights, but the fundamental personal rights of free speech and assembly"—a point he had made as early as his 1920 dissent in *Gilbert v. Minnesota*. In language that absorbed an array of justifications proffered by free speech advocates in the Progressive Era and after, he attributed to the framers of the First Amendment the understanding "that order cannot be secured merely through fear of punishment for its infraction; that it is hazardous to discourage thought, hope and imagination; that fear breeds repression; that repression breeds hate; that hate menaces stable government; that the path of safety lies in the opportunity to discuss freely supposed grievances and proposed remedies, and that the fitting remedy for evil counsels is good ones."[71]

Reflecting backward, the ACLU cast *Gitlow* and *Whitney* as steps along a carefully plotted journey for judicial recognition of free speech. In the moment, even though it briefed the pivotal First Amendment tests of the 1920s, the organization never put much stock in the results. Few within the ACLU imagined that the Supreme Court might reverse Gitlow's or Whitney's conviction on constitutional grounds; Nelles was forthright about his intentions in the cases, namely, to raise public awareness about injustice in the courts.

In the Paterson case, by contrast, the ACLU's attorneys had other opinions about the best path forward for the civil liberties cause. As Nelles understood the problem, there were two potential approaches to the brief. One might pepper it with history and "libertarian philosophy" in an effort to produce propaganda on behalf of the organization's underlying ambitions, as the NCLB had done during the war. Or one might downplay ideological commitments to enhance the likelihood of a successful outcome. With some reluctance, Nelles advised the second path, and he cautioned Baldwin not to "wav[e] a red rag in the face of any bull judge." The notion that judges would recognize a robust right to assemble under the First Amendment or its state equivalent was unthinkable to the attorney who—together with fellow ACLU attorney Walter Pollak—had argued and lost the most notable First Amendment challenges since the war. Judges had steadfastly resisted claims to liberty by "subversive movements." Best, then, to mask the implication that the defendants' demonstration "was in the aid of a strike."[72]

Frankfurter echoed Nelles's concerns. It was foolish and futile to transform the case into a *cause célèbre* in the fight for civil liberty," he advised. To Frankfurter, the ACLU's habit of pursuing losing cases for propaganda purposes was misguided. In fact, Frankfurter had disapproved of Nelles's decision to take Benjamin Gitlow's case to the Supreme Court, and he hoped the Supreme Court would refuse jurisdiction in the *Whitney* case, lest it affirm her conviction as well. "Of course I believe in asserting the principles of freedom and keeping libertarian convictions alive through publicity," he told Nelles. "But I count very low the publicity of cumulative adverse decisions by the Supreme Court." In this he differed not only from the ACLU's radicals, but from many nonlawyer liberals. In 1925, the *New Republic* expressed its continuing disdain for constitutional test cases but acknowledged the usefulness of convictions in "obtaining publicity" to promote repeal of undesirable laws.[73]

By contrast, both Frankfurter and Nelles had come to believe that judicial losses had heavy attendant costs. Their cautious calculations were a direct repudiation of the wartime strategy of the NCLB. In his 1917 challenge to the constitutionality of the Selective Service Act, Nelles recounted, he had expressed his unvarnished view of the issues involved, with "complete indifference" toward the outcome. Over time, however, he had muted the radical thrust of his work in the interest of occasional victories for his clients, who preferred to avoid spending time in jail. The prospect of systemic change through the courts was dim, and Nelles was increasingly unwilling to treat the client as an instrument for raising popular awareness. And yet, unable to abandon completely his commitment to civil liberties advocacy, he had resorted to compromise briefs that disserved defendents along with the cause. What he valued most in the Paterson brief was "its thorough-going concentration upon the single matter of winning the case." If the challenge proved successful, he explained, "that is itself the best possible propaganda." And if it failed, "the whole out of court world" could hold protests and write pamphlets.[74]

✦ ✦ ✦

For all its practicality, the ACLU's brief to the New Jersey Supreme Court did not persuade the justices to overturn the convictions of Roger Baldwin and his fellow defendants. Without addressing the constitutionality of the New Jersey statute, the court concluded that a meeting to emphasize disapproval of police conduct was bound to trigger police hostility, and consequently a breach of the peace. That was enough to render the meeting an unlawful assembly within the meaning of New Jersey's prohibition. "The situation created by the defendants presented an analogy to a fire with obvious danger of a conflagration if not checked," the court explained, taking up an analogy often invoked by the United States Supreme Court.[75]

The unanimous affirmance was disappointing, but it was not surprising. The panel that heard the appeal was, according to Samuel Smoleff, among the most conservative on the bench. In the New Jersey Court of Errors and Appeals, fifteen fresh judges would hear the case, and the unsympathetic judges who had sat on the Supreme Court would be excluded from the panel.[76]

The first pressing question for the next appeal was who would argue it. It was a decision debated in the absence of Baldwin, who (while out on bail) was traveling across Europe and Soviet Russia to investigate political persecution and its antidotes abroad. The remaining leadership worried that involvement by a prominent New York attorney implied either that local lawyers were incapable or that the merits were so hopeless that the only option was to "overawe" the court. Samuel Untermyer reluctantly relinquished the case, but it proved difficult to find a replacement. When all of the ACLU's top choices for the job had demurred, Felix Frankfurter proposed an up-and-coming Newark lawyer named Arthur Vanderbilt, and he urged Baldwin to investigate whether the justices were likely to regard him favorably. Baldwin arranged a meeting with Vanderbilt and walked away impressed. He was a "perfect trump," Baldwin reported—the first candidate "with real convictions in our favor" who satisfied the ACLU's specifications. A "young chap" with a large practice and a "very liberal viewpoint," he was well versed in New Jersey politics as well as an able attorney. Vanderbilt agreed to take the case for the cost of his office overhead. Upon his advice, the names of all New York lawyers were removed from the brief.[77]

Vanderbilt argued before New Jersey's high court on February 7, 1928, more than three years after Baldwin's arrest. In the interim, much had changed. The Red Scare had receded from view. The radical labor politics that spawned the ACLU had foundered on widespread economic prosperity and the appealing promises of welfare capitalism. No longer consumed by anti-Communist hysteria, judges ceased to rubber-stamp the convictions they reviewed. As before the war, they demanded meaningful evidence that the radical defendants before them had engaged in criminal conduct. Vanderbilt was optimistic. While he was not so rash as to predict a favorable result, he felt the defendants had allies on the bench who were "inclined to their view of the case as a matter of constitutional law."[78]

What the ACLU sought in New Jersey was not a bold pronouncement on constitutional limitations. Vanderbilt thought the case was the first in the state to raise squarely the boundary between unlawful assemblage and the constitutional right to expressive freedom. But he did not argue that statutory or common-law restraints on assembly conflicted with the New Jersey constitution, let alone the First Amendment. Nor did the organization plan to pursue a constitutional pronouncement from the United States Supreme Court. With *Gitlow* as a guide, Baldwin assumed there was a federal question in the case. He nonetheless considered his chances of reversal in the federal courts to be negligible, and he had no intention of taking further appeals.[79]

Indeed, in 1928, the ACLU declared that the "clear and present danger test," to which Holmes and Brandeis stubbornly clung though the rest of the Supreme Court ignored it, had proved a failure. More to the point, the organization saw "no possibility of a successful appeal from further convictions on the ground of constitutionality"—though the court's decision in *Fiske v. Kansas,* overturning a conviction under a Kansas criminal syndicalism statute premised solely on the IWW preamble, indicated that judgments might occasionally be set aside for insufficient evidence. The lesson from *Fiske* was that the best prospect for preserving the right of agitation was to argue the case on the facts, a more palatable route for sympathetic judges. That was precisely the course the ACLU adopted in Paterson.[80]

Still, the ACLU's ambitions in New Jersey were not insignificant. The organization conceded that neither unlawful assemblage nor constitutional liberties were capable of precise definition. It hoped, however, that the court might signal its refusal to interpret the facts in a way that would altogether undermine the constitutional guarantees at stake. After all, constitutional protections could be nullified just as effectively by basing an indictment on "trivial or isolated circumstances . . . as by denying them outright."[81]

The brief to the Court of Errors and Appeals was modest in its approach. In staging its test meeting, it argued, the ACLU had turned to the courts as the proper arbiter of the perennial conflict between the power of the police and the rights of the citizen. There was no evidence of threats, weapons, or previous disturbances in Paterson that would justify unusually repressive measures. If there was violence, it was only because the police themselves had resorted to force. As for the strike that precipitated the test, it had been exceptionally orderly and lawful, but that was immaterial. The court was not deciding whether "the prohibition of *strikers'* meetings . . . [was] justifiable or not." Rather, Baldwin's conviction raised the unrelated question whether the free speech advocates acted unlawfully when they engaged in public discussion of police repression.[82]

Crucially, the brief sharply distinguished between the ACLU's interest in free assembly and the substantive goals of the strikers whose rights it defended. It cast Baldwin as the impartial head of a well-respected national organization, whose 6,000 members included "some of the most distinguished and public-spirited citizens of the land." The ACLU's only objective in Paterson was to preserve the priceless liberties of the citizen against the encroachments of public officials. "Neither the defendant, Baldwin, nor the American Civil Liberties Union or any of its members," stressed the brief, "were in any way connected with the Paterson strike."[83]

In May, the New Jersey court issued an opinion for a unanimous bench overturning the convictions of Baldwin and the other defendants. According to the ACLU, it stood out as the first "liberal" civil liberties decision in a state high court in recent memory. Judge Samuel Kalisch accepted the ACLU's argument practically in total. He took it as given that the constitutional rights to free speech and assembly extended only to "peaceful and law-abiding conduct." But the common-law prohibitions incorporated by the New Jersey statute were the limits of legitimate police interference. A finding of unlawful assembly required conduct that would "reasonably create in the minds of firm and courageous persons a well-founded fear of threatening danger to the public peace." The court found no evidence that the meeting had any such character.[84]

To the ACLU's surprise, the press celebrated Baldwin's vindication. The *Newark Evening News,* warning that suppression encouraged insurrection, called the decision a "sweeping verdict against the misuse of police authority and the denial of rights." The *New Republic* pronounced it the most "wholesome victory for civil liberties" since the war. The *St. Louis Post-Dispatch* hoped it augured "a revival of liberty all over the country." And the *New York World* thought one such success per year was enough to justify the existence of the ACLU. "We seem to have touched off a lot of latent disapproval of police methods in New Jersey existing in unexpected quarters," Smoleff reported to Baldwin. Even the "ultra-conservative" *Newark Sunday Call* issued a favorable editorial on the case.[85]

Gilbert Roe thought the court's decision would "help[] the cause of free speech more than anything which has occurred since we entered upon the World War." But Baldwin was more measured, even disappointed. He agreed that the case was significant, but he stressed it was an outlier. Aberrations aside, the courts remained overwhelmingly antagonistic to civil liberties claims by workers and radicals. As an ACLU pamphlet explained, the Paterson decision was "only an exception to the general rule that such verdicts in labor cases are not righted." In Justice Kalisch's opinion, the *New York Times* rightfully reported, "everything hinged on matters of fact." The ACLU's victory in Paterson offered little cover to striking workers, for whom neither lawful purpose nor peaceful conduct could reliably be established. Baldwin had avoided prison, but judicial vindication of the right of agitation remained a distant dream.[86]

5

The New Battleground

I F THERE is a single case that defines the interwar ACLU in the popular imagination, it is *State of Tennessee v. John Thomas Scopes*. In the summer of 1925, iconoclastic attorney Clarence Darrow sparred with populist hero and three-time Democratic presidential nominee William Jennings Bryan over the legal status of the Tennessee antievolution law that Bryan himself had inspired. Their dramatic showdown in the otherwise unremarkable town of Dayton, Tennessee, pitted (said observers) science against sectarianism and freedom against forced conformity. Journalists, historians, even playwrights and screenwriters have masterfully told the story of the Scopes "monkey trial," to borrow H. L. Mencken's colorful coinage. None of them, however, fashioned the narrative of the trial more deliberately than the ACLU itself.[1]

The *Scopes* trial was many things to many people. To John T. Scopes, the affable young teacher turned national celebrity who accepted the ACLU's invitation to challenge the law, it was an entrée to exclusive social circles and grist for a budding flirtation with radical causes. To Bryan, who considered religion the foundation of morality, it was a capstone in a decades-long crusade against the pernicious effects of social Darwinism, "the merciless law by which the strong crowd out and kill off the weak." To Mencken, the journalist and scathing social critic who sensationalized the trial, it was a chance to lampoon southerners and humiliate Bryan. And to Darrow, who took the case pro bono, it was a grand stage for exposing the "absurdities" of the Bible. Many years after the McNamara bombing trial, Darrow still believed that Americans clung to Christianity because it was "cheaper to pay workingmen in religious dope" than in decent wages. "Christianity functions as a sop to keep people satisfied, and almost nothing else," he explained.[2]

To the ACLU, which sponsored and managed the case, the *Scopes* trial was an opportunity to raise its profile, enhance its credibility, and expand its donor base. Although much of its membership shared Darrow's substantive views, the organization disclaimed any attack on religion. According to a public statement, it was participating in the case as an advocate of academic freedom, not evolution. In a fund-raising letter, Roger Baldwin was more candid about his ambitions. "Persons who have not contributed before to the defense of civil liberty, will do it now on such an issue as this," he predicted. Always savvy about appearances, he established a separate fund to bank and handle contributions under the auspices of the "distinguished committee" that the ACLU had assembled for publicity purposes. "Supporters of educational and scientific work will be interested, of course and some liberal spirits in the churches," Baldwin mused. Best of all, "they need not fear contamination with the defense of reds!"[3]

A Tennessee jury found Scopes guilty of violating the state's antievolution law in July 1925, just six months after Baldwin was convicted of unlawful assembly in New Jersey. From the perspective of the ACLU's litigation program, it was an important half year. In the conservative climate of the mid-1920s, there were few strikes left to suppress. Flagrantly oppressive tactics were no longer necessary to quash worker militancy; "widespread prosperity and the consequent absence of industrial strife" had already accomplished that task. The labor movement had lost its ambitious campaign of the immediate postwar period, and as the ACLU's approach in Paterson attested, the organization's options for that now-quiet front were limited. Still, according to the ACLU, the longer war still raged. "The efforts to impose majority dogma by law and intimidation have shifted from the industrial arena to the field of education," the 1925 report concluded.[4]

When it was founded in 1920, the ACLU had promoted the right of agitation through "propaganda." It had sought to generate public outrage toward structural inequality, and it hired publicity agents to propagate its ideas. An information service distributed its news releases, statements, and pamphlets to a national network of cooperating speakers and writers. Although it managed to arouse opposition to the most patently abusive practices of federal administrators and local officials, however, the ACLU's charges of judicial hypocrisy neither mobilized the masses nor convinced the courts. Framed against this forgotten phase in the ACLU's history, the oft-told saga of the *Scopes* trial takes on new meaning and importance. Baldwin's march through Paterson was something of a last gasp for the ACLU's first and most radical period. The new labor landscape called for a revised set of civil liberties commitments, and Tennessee's antievolution law provided an ideal introduction. Indeed, in its brief appealing Baldwin's conviction in New Jersey, the ACLU explicitly referenced its involvement in the *Scopes* case as evidence of the organization's respectable goals.[5]

In practice, the *Scopes* trial confounded the ACLU's careful choreography. Darrow was not the organization's choice of counsel, and his strong personality and provocative tactics upstaged the ACLU's intended message. Bryan's death just days after Darrow humiliated him on the witness stand left the unfortunate impression that he was "spiritually and literally crucified . . . on the cross examination." The very features that made the trial so memorable to future generations exasperated the ACLU. And yet, even after the Dayton debacle, the ACLU's constitutional challenge to Tennessee's antievolution law attracted sympathetic commentary from both the AAUP and the ABA. Newspapers that had recently denounced the ACLU as a revolutionary front celebrated its defense of modern science. Liberal educators, researchers, and religious leaders wholeheartedly endorsed its message of open-minded exploration for the sake of social progress. Even conservatives—long accustomed, after all, to opposing Bryan—condemned the Tennessee law as an infringement of individual liberty.[6]

During the mid-1920s, disputes over education played an increasingly central role in the ACLU's agenda. The organization continued to defend the handful of anarchists and Communists prosecuted under state criminal syndicalism laws. It challenged immigration laws that targeted radicals, and it opposed alien registration and deportation bills. It also combatted racial discrimination, and it undertook an investigation of lynchings. But it made primary and secondary education its most visible focus. Faced with workers' waning energy and diminished strength, the ACLU tied the long-term success of organized labor not only to the tools of collective activity, but also to advocacy and instruction in their use. Education was "the new battle ground," according to the ACLU's 1925 report. And if the *Scopes* case was a representative example, it featured more level terrain.[7]

✦ ✦ ✦

As with free speech more broadly, organized advocacy for academic freedom was rooted in the labor problem. To be sure, the notion that scholars should be free to question received wisdoms stretches back into antiquity. Separately, states and localities had long debated the propriety of compulsory education and religious education in the public schools. But the professional educators who launched the struggle for academic freedom during the early twentieth century were concerned, above all, to shield university professors against retaliation for articulating economic ideas incompatible with the interests of the wealthy trustees who filled and funded their positions.[8]

It is a neat historical accident that one of the first notable conflicts over academic freedom in an American university involved the investigation of evolution in Tennessee; in 1878, Vanderbilt University dismissed a geologist whose views on evolution posed a threat to religious values. Such cases, however, were relatively rare. Most of the prominent controversies instead involved instructors with radical or prolabor sympathies. Progressive economist Richard T. Ely nearly lost his chair at the University of Wisconsin in 1894 for his allegedly socialist views, though the state's board of regents eventually retained him. His student, progressive economist and labor historian John R. Commons, did not fare as well; Syracuse University dismissed him for his critique of capitalism in 1899, and he joined Ely at Wisconsin a few years later. A University of Chicago economist who espoused a preference for state regulation of industry likewise lost his position.[9]

In 1900, yet another economist suffered dismissal for voicing heretical views, with sweeping consequences. A decade before he signed the *Survey's* petition to President William Howard Taft on behalf of the Commission on Industrial Relations, Edward A. Ross incurred the antagonism of Stanford University's founding family for promoting municipal ownership of public utilities and for criticizing the railroad industry that generated its fortune. Ross's transgressions, according to the *San Francisco Chronicle*, also included his endorsement of the free coinage of silver and, appropriately enough, his personal friendship with William Jennings Bryan. Although Stanford's president fought to retain him, Ross was ultimately forced out, and several of his colleagues resigned in protest. Like Commons before him, Ross eventually found his way to the University of Wisconsin, where he organized the American Sociological Society's 1914 annual meeting on the subject of free speech.[10]

Among the professors moved by Ross's predicament to resign from Stanford University was philosopher and historian Arthur O. Lovejoy, whose appeal to fellow academics to create a society devoted to the institutional needs of the profession resulted in the founding of the AAUP in 1915. Together with Columbia economist Edwin R. A. Seligman, he drafted the 1915 Declaration of Principles on Academic Freedom and Academic Tenure, the inaugural policy report of the new AAUP and the foundational text of the modern program for academic freedom in the United States.

According to the declaration, research universities (as opposed to "proprietary institutions") were meant to "advance knowledge by the unrestricted research and unfettered discussion of impartial investigators." To police that responsibility, the AAUP created the Committee on Academic Freedom and Tenure, or Committee A, to investigate potential transgressions of its policies. In its first years of operation, many of its cases involved allegations of radicalism in the classroom or in public discourse. One professor claimed that the impetus for his dismissal was his labor-friendly testimony before the Commission on Industrial Relations, though the AAUP did not validate his claim. Another, economist Scott Nearing, lost his position at the University of Pennsylvania's Wharton School when alumni complained that he "aroused class prejudice" by endorsing redistribution. Though it did not save Nearing's job, the AAUP's involvement prompted the university to reform its procedures.[11]

The 1915 declaration was saturated in progressive ideology. It was premised on the assumption that academic knowledge was capable of objective assessment and was properly evaluated by peers within a scholar's discipline rather than by lay trustees, who were motivated by politics and ideology. "The claim to freedom of teaching is made in the interest of the integrity and of the progress of scientific inquiry," the document explained (without adding that empirical scholarship was itself presumptively progressive), and it was therefore available only to those who adopted scientific methods. The AAUP was primarily concerned with ideas expressed in scholarship and in the classroom, not with political activities outside of academic institutions. In fact, the declaration expressly rejected the suggestion that "individual teachers should be exempt from all restraints as to the matter or manner of their utterances." On the contrary, it assumed that reasonable restrictions were appropriate both within the university and without.[12]

✦ ✦ ✦

The ACLU's conception of academic freedom was of a different ilk. Early on, the organization identified schools as unusually sensitive to accusations of radicalism, and freedom for radical teachers was a core component of its agenda beginning in its NCLB days. At the outset of the war, Leon Whipple, whose historical and theoretical writings on free speech during the 1920s were funded by the ACLU, was discharged from the University of Virginia after espousing pacifism and celebrating Russia in a speech at a neighboring women's college. Scott Nearing, who joined the AUAM after his 1915 dismissal from the University of Pennsylvania, lost his subsequent position at Toledo University as well. In the spring of 1917 he moved to New York, where he assisted in creation of the NCLB.[13]

Nearing played a crucial role in the NCLB's early activities on behalf of academic freedom. He was intimately involved with the Rand School of Social Science, a Socialist institution for the education of workers. For six years, Nearing lectured at the Rand School in economics and sociology, alongside a set of influential academics that included Charles A. Beard, who had resigned his own position at Columbia University to protest the expulsion of two professors for their purported disloyalty. The government began targeting the Rand School early in the war, and the postwar Red Scare only intensified efforts to suppress the institution's message.[14]

After the war, the Rand School attracted the attention of the New York's legislature's Joint Legislative Committee to Investigate Sedition Activities, or Lusk Committee—the same entity that promoted the infamous expulsion of Socialist representatives from the state assembly. The instigator of the campaign against the Rand School was the Lusk Committee's counsel, Archibald Stevenson, the Red hunter who had urged the Department of Justice to prosecute the NCLB the previous year. In June 1919, fifty men ransacked the school's facilities in pursuit of papers and materials and then returned to search the safe for its financial records. Although the raids produced little actionable evidence (the most sinister finding reported in the *New York Times* was "that persons identified with the Rand School had interested themselves in the defense of William Haywood and other I.W.W. leaders convicted in Chicago"), the attorney general of New York initiated charges to cancel the school's charter, cheered on by the press. Samuel Untermyer—before defending Roger Baldwin in New Jersey—represented the Rand School in the legal proceedings. He denounced the Lusk Committee for distorting evidence and holding sham hearings, and he pledged to put both Clayton R. Lusk and Stevenson on the stand to account for their criminal lawlessness.[15]

According to the NCLB, the attack on the Rand School was a wakeup call for "liberal Americans." In August, three months before Justice Oliver Wendell Holmes Jr.'s dissent in *Abrams v. United States,* the organization prepared a statement by prominent non-Socialists urging the state to stand down. If the Rand School's teachings were unsound, exposing them to public scrutiny was the best remedy. Such reasoning fit neatly into the progressive model of free speech that had receded during the war but was reemerging among liberal lawyers and academics. In communications with government officials and potential contributors, the NCLB emphasized the value of political expression as a means both of buttressing democratic legitimacy and of facilitating "social progress." It attracted mainstream support by celebrating (along with Justice Holmes) a marketplace of ideas, or (before Justice Louis D. Brandeis) the centrality of open discussion to democratic decision making. In the NCLB's assessment, the true danger was "the immeasurable harm which . . . coercion of minority opinion does to the processes of orderly discussion of public affairs."[16]

Although the NCLB issued its statement while the legal proceedings in the Rand School case were pending, it was a general pronouncement on the government's policy, not the merits of the legal case. By the same token, when the case eventually collapsed, the Lusk Committee continued to lambast the Rand School just as vigorously. In 1920, it proposed legislation prohibiting the state from licensing any private school teaching the doctrine "that organized government shall be overthrown by force, violence or unlawful means." Had the bill stopped there, it might have avoided controversy. But the Lusk laws went much further. They also required public school teachers to demonstrate that they were "loyal and obedient" to the state and federal governments; any teacher who had ever advocated change in the form of either was to be denied a certificate of fitness. The bill passed, but Governor Alfred E. "Al" Smith vetoed it, explaining that it targeted teachers for their thinking instead of their teaching, and that it would invest the commissioner of education with dictatorial power.[17]

Despite Smith's denunciation, the legislature passed the bill again in 1921—and Smith's successor, Governor Nathan L. Miller, signed it into law. The Rand School responded by refusing to apply for a license and, when the state filed suit, challenging the validity of the statute. Socialist leader and labor lawyer Morris Hillquit, a member of the new ACLU's national committee, argued the case. Among his central contentions was a claim about the constitutional limits of state regulatory power: New York's licensing requirement, he argued, trampled the Rand School's rights to liberty and property under the Due Process Clause of the Fourteenth Amendment. The irony was apparent to observers. Zechariah Chafee Jr. mused that "class rooms of the Rand School must have frequently echoed to denunciations" of *Ives, Jacobs, Lochner,* and other notorious examples of judicial review. Now the Rand School was citing those very cases to extend constitutional protection to its own unpopular activities. After its "foot was pinched by state regulation," he speculated, the Rand School "understood better the irritation which other kinds of business feel under government regulation."[18]

Notwithstanding the venerable constitutional authorities Hillquit cited, a New York court rejected his constitutional challenge in a 2–1 decision, invoking the Reconstruction-era Slaughterhouse Cases as evidence of a state's power to adopt appropriate licensing requirements in the public interest. Only one year later, the United States Supreme Court adopted an argument markedly similar to Hillquit's to strike down Nebraska's prohibition on foreign-language instruction. But in the meantime, the Lusk laws had the imprimatur of constitutional validity, and the state enforced them with gusto. In September 1921, New York administered oaths to 57,000 public school teachers, even though the law did not require it. In November, the commissioner of education required principals to report on the "morality and loyalty" of their teachers. In the spring of 1922, he appointed a five-member advisory council, led by Stevenson, to decide contested cases in secret meetings. The anonymous evaluations and closed proceedings proved too much for many New Yorkers to bear. Newspapers denounced the law and, even more fervently, its administration. Most tellingly, the *Nation* acknowledged the public's "callous indifference to the civil liberties of workers" but hoped that an attack on education might attract popular outrage. In an atmosphere of fear, hypocrisy, and servility, it explained, it was impossible to "make good citizens." In May 1923, at the urging of newly reelected governor Smith, both the public school law and the private school licensing provisions were repealed.[19]

The fight over the Lusk laws taught the ACLU that academic freedom, unlike the rights of anarchist immigrants or radical workers, commanded mainstream support. It also foregrounded the possibility of appropriating constitutional argument for radical ends. Both lessons resurfaced in a controversy over another restrictive education law, which was then working its way up through the federal courts. That law effectively abolished private education in the state of Oregon, and the surrounding litigation culminated in the Supreme Court's heavily cited decision in *Pierce v. Society of Sisters,* which recognized parents' authority over their children's education and disclaimed the "power of the State to standardize its children by forcing them to accept instruction from public teachers only." For the ACLU, the Oregon public school law was a curious foray into the field of academic freedom. Backed by the Ku Klux Klan, the law was meant to abolish Catholic schools, which were widely regarded as an impediment to the assimilation of immigrant children. As a rule, neither the Klan nor anti-immigrant sentiment was popular within the ACLU. Still, most of the ACLU leadership personally opposed parochial education, and the Oregon law served arguably progressive purposes in addition to reactionary ones.[20]

William S. U'Ren, an ACLU national committee member, was among Oregon's most notable progressive reformers. He counseled the ACLU's executive committee to ignore the public school law, because it raised no issue of "civil or religious liberty." U'Ren advised the committee that the state's governor was a "liberal" who respected citizens' constitutional rights; if he had accepted the endorsement of the Ku Klux Klan, it was only for political purposes. More to the point, U'Ren thought the measure would raise the quality of the public school system and mitigate class differences in education. "If every normal child must go to the district public school through the first eight grades, then every parent, whether rich or poor, Jew or Gentile, Catholic or Protestant, saint or sinner, will have the highest possible selfish parental interest in making the best possible school," he explained.[21]

To U'Ren's surprise, the ACLU's executive committee uniformly rejected his reasoning and pledged its support to the opposition. The leaders of the ACLU considered the Oregon school law to be incompatible with "the right to worship according to the dictates of one's conscience." But as Baldwin subsequently clarified, they did not understand the law's menace primarily in terms of religious freedom, or even (as later Supreme Court decisions would cast it) of individual liberty or family autonomy. "We've got a number of experimental private schools in and near New York which are infinitely more valuable to the future of education than anything the public schools are doing," Baldwin told U'Ren. "Under such a law as you have in Oregon, they would be wiped out."[22]

When it discussed *Pierce v. Society of Sisters* publicly, the ACLU invoked religious freedom and parental rights. It emphasized that compulsory public schooling would eliminate the private schools "to which persons of means send their children," along with the "experimental" alternatives that the organization did not identify by name. Through its circumspect approach, the ACLU made new allies among conservatives and, perhaps, helped to secure a unanimous decision in the Supreme Court. At bottom, however, the members of the ACLU's executive committee opposed the Oregon school law because it threatened the future of the Rand School and projects like it. They believed that control of the curriculum was a more insidious version of the violently repressive machinery of the First World War. Industrial interests were purging radical teachers, dictating lesson plans, and prohibiting private education—all to ensure that the public school system would inculcate children with the values of the dominant capitalist culture. By contrast, radical education, if it were only sheltered from state suppression, had the potential to awaken the masses.[23]

✦ ✦ ✦

In the fall of 1924, just months before the *Scopes* trial commenced, the ACLU launched its first formal committee: the Committee on Academic Freedom. When the ACLU addressed the issue of academic freedom as a potential area of activity in June 1924, it openly acknowledged its concern—namely, "propagandists' efforts to distort education in the interest of a particular conception of political and economic thinking," of which the Lusk Committee's effort to shut down the Rand School was the most prominent example. Such laws, the ACLU insisted, were "special interest" measures to promote industrialist propaganda and thereby undermine the broader public interest.[24]

Over the summer, the ACLU explored potential avenues of involvement in academic freedom work, for the purpose (as Roger Baldwin told Ernst Freund) of "preventing further inroads upon the agitation of radical and labor issues in the colleges." It regarded a possible alliance with the AAUP as particularly appealing. That association remained concerned primarily with ideas expressed in scholarship and in the classroom. The ACLU, by contrast, was most interested in communication outside the classroom, where the "public interest is peculiarly involved." An organization like the ACLU could not properly defend a teacher who used the classroom, the proper domain of education professionals, to disseminate propaganda. Conversely, it was patently the ACLU's concern to ensure that educational institutions did not attempt to impede teachers in their exercise of "the common rights of citizens, including the right of expressing their views on political and economic issues, in speech or in print."[25]

The ACLU also resolved to protect the right of students to hear radical speakers and organize radical activities and groups on campus. Such issues were largely outside the AAUP's domain. Moreover, the AAUP advanced academic freedom only in colleges and universities. The ACLU extended its efforts to secondary education, as well. In that endeavor, ACLU executive committee member Henry R. Linville, who also served as president of the Teachers Union of New York City, played a formative role. A trained zoologist, Linville was largely responsible for developing the modern high school biology curriculum. At New York's DeWitt Clinton High School, he worked closely with George W. Hunter, who authored the textbook that Tennessee mandated for use in its high school science classrooms (until the state textbook commission replaced them in June) and from which John Scopes dutifully taught. Within the ACLU, Linville took a lead role in the academic freedom campaign and coauthored the organization's official statement on the issue with Harry Ward.[26]

An October 1924 announcement clarified the ACLU's interests in academic freedom. Its new committee would resist rules restricting "liberal and radical activities," in addition to preserving teachers' and students' "freedom of opinion" outside the classroom. It would also oppose laws limiting teachers' autonomy in the classroom, such as those prohibiting teaching of pacifism, critiques of capitalism, and—in a concession to Linville's particular concerns—evolution. In the Oregon public school controversy, the ACLU's nod to inviolate traditions and family values had garnered conservative sympathy. In the evolution context, the notion that experimentation and diversity in intellectual inquiry were the source of democratic progress resonated with progressive audiences.[27]

Although the last issue was a relative latecomer to the ACLU's platform on academic freedom, it soon took center stage. In the spring of 1925, Tennessee passed the Butler Act, which prohibited the teaching of evolution in any state-funded college or school. The statute was part of a wave of antievolution measures proposed during the early 1920s, and Kentucky had already passed similar legislation. The ACLU had been monitoring the antievolution movement, and when the Tennessee bill passed, it issued a press release pledging its assistance to any teacher willing to challenge the law in the courts. Officials and interested citizens in Dayton—hoping to attract attention and tourism to their town—answered the ACLU's call.

✦ ✦ ✦

By all indications, the *Scopes* trial should have been exactly the kind of "friendly test case" the ACLU anticipated. George Washington Rappleyea, a New York metallurgical engineer who managed the Cumberland Coal and Iron Company in Dayton, convinced the chairman of the town's school board and the superintendent of schools to cooperate with the ACLU in testing the law. The county attorneys (brothers Sue and Herbert Hicks), who were sympathetic to the Butler Act but doubted its constitutionality, offered to participate as well. No one in the town harbored animosity toward John Scopes. On the contrary, the young science teacher and part-time football coach was a friend of Sue Hicks's. Although his father was an outspoken socialist and agnostic, Scopes was guarded about his own views. In fact, he was not sure he had ever even taught evolution. That minor complication aside, he was, by all accounts, an ideal defendant—well liked, unmarried, and unattached to Dayton—and he cheerfully agreed to volunteer himself for indictment.

The ACLU envisioned a constitutional test of the Butler Act in the appellate courts, and it expected the trial to proceed rapidly to conviction. Just a few months earlier, the organization had rejected litigation as a strategy for advancing academic freedom, and it had planned to operate through protests and publicity instead. The struggle over antievolution laws, however, seemed to lend itself to legal challenge. In its pamphlet on the *Scopes* case, the ACLU presented the Butler Act as one among many recent legislative restrictions on public teaching, which included compulsory Bible reading, loyalty oaths, and laws against employment of radical and pacifist teachers (of which the Lusk laws "were the first of the new crop"), in addition to antievolution laws. The *Scopes* case was important because it presented a "clear legal test of the right of a majority acting through the legislature to determine what shall or shall not be taught in public school." A constitutional victory would help to abet the "tyranny over minority and unpopular views" that had only accelerated after the war. As a legal and policy precedent, it would carry over from the field of education to "freedom of opinion in general."[28]

To buttress the credibility of its constitutional claims, the ACLU hoped to enlist the legal services of the 1924 Democratic presidential nominee John W. Davis, who was a skilled Supreme Court litigator, or (as Felix Frankfurter preferred) the eminent lawyer and statesman Charles Evans Hughes. Very quickly, however, events escaped the organization's control. In May, William Jennings Bryan offered to assist the prosecution, though he had not practiced law for over thirty years. Clarence Darrow, in turn, approached Scopes about appearing on behalf of the defense, together with the liberal activist and divorce attorney Dudley Field Malone, who had briefly served under Bryan in the Department of State. From the ACLU's perspective, Darrow and Malone were disastrous choices, but Scopes accepted their overtures.[29]

After the McNamara case, Darrow had fallen out of favor among labor groups, but his fame had only increased. Tennessee's attorney general considered him the "greatest criminal lawyer in America" and chastised him for using his talents for evil ends. A staunch opponent of capital punishment, Darrow had just made national headlines for his defense of confessed child-killers Nathan Leopold and Richard Loeb. In the 1924 sentencing hearing, he convinced the judge to impose life in prison in lieu of execution by, in part, attributing their depravity to their intense engagement with the writings of Friedrich Nietzsche. To Bryan, the sinister effects of an amoral education were precisely the problem that the antievolution laws attempted to redress.[30]

Despite his deeply felt allegiance to the antievolution cause, and his own hand in the law's passage, Bryan's theory of the case sidestepped the debate over the law's prudence or desirability. In Bryan's view, the authority to set the public school curriculum inhered in the voters and taxpayers, not individual teachers or elite intellectuals. Bryan was convinced that "Biblical truth [could] hold its own in a fair field," but he refused to afford evolutionists an unfair advantage on taxpayers' dime. In this, he echoed Senator Lusk, who defended New York's teacher loyalty laws on the understanding (according to the *New Republic*) "that while men and women as citizens may advocate peaceful changes in government, 'they have not the right to do it while they subsist on public funds.'" By the same token, Bryan reasoned at trial that a teacher "has the right to say anything he wants except in the school room where he is an employee of the State." Scopes, he complained, had the audacity to demand that the state furnish him an audience of impressionable children to hear him promote a message inconsistent with the preferences of the people who paid him.[31]

Bryan's framing of the case as a battle between the masses and the privileged few might have appealed to a younger Darrow—who, after all, had campaigned tirelessly for the "Great Commoner" in the 1896 presidential election. To Bryan, the notion that academic consensus rather than popular will should control the curriculum undermined American democratic values. It was as if a "scientific soviet is attempting to dictate what shall be taught in our schools," he complained a year before the *Scopes* trial began. On this limited interpretation of the case, Bryan attracted some notable supporters. Samuel Untermyer was among them, even as he joined the ACLU's national committee, and he advised Bryan to avoid entangling the case in the debate over evolution.[32]

Darrow's participation made Untermyer's advice untenable. Darrow was an outspoken opponent of the antievolution laws and of religious fundamentalism more broadly. Despite his respect for Bryan's political accomplishments, he had attacked him publicly for his antievolutionist activism. According to Darrow, the problem with Bryan's approach was not his religious faith; Darrow insisted that he "never tried to impose [his] views on religion on any human being." But laws like Tennessee's, as Darrow understood them, suffered from exactly that vice. Just as Bryan did not dispute the right of a teacher to be agnostic or atheist, Darrow believed strongly in the right of individuals to propound their own religious principles. But he resented what he regarded as a legislative campaign by a religious majority to force its dogma on others.[33]

As Darrow conceived the defense, the weight of scientific authorities was overwhelmingly in his favor. Well before passage of the Butler Act, the American Association for the Advancement of Science had condemned antievolution laws for inhibiting "humanity's search for truth" and for "denying the freedom of teaching and inquiry which is essential to all progress." It had also pronounced the evidence for evolution practically irrefutable. It is no wonder, then, that Darrow produced respected biologists, zoologists, and other experts from throughout the country to testify on Scopes's behalf. Bryan, by contrast, could not find a single scientist to testify for the prosecution. As for the religious authorities, many mainstream Christian denominations accepted the evolutionary origins of the species, and respected theologians assured Americans that evolution was compatible with the Bible.[34]

But Darrow's distinguished witnesses never had an opportunity to testify. The court denied a motion by the defense to quash the indictment on constitutional grounds. The unsuccessful arguments raised by the defense (and, later, made central on appeal) invoked free speech, religious establishment, procedural guarantees, and even a Tennessee constitutional clause enjoining the state legislature to cherish science and education. Adopting Morris Hillquit's technique in the Rand School case, Arthur Garfield Hays—the only representative from the ACLU's inner circle to participate on the defense team—emphasized the unreasonableness of the statute under the due process clauses of the state and federal constitutions. Although Hays preserved space for state discretion in controlling the curriculum, he argued that the Butler Act crossed the line by demanding that a subject be taught "falsely." Such claims might have justified expert testimony on behalf of evolutionary science, but the judge rejected Hays's argument along with the others.[35]

The balance of the trial therefore turned on the textual argument that the Butler Act forbade the teaching of evolution only when accompanied by an explicit rejection of the Bible. The statute declared it unlawful for any teacher in a school or university receiving state funds "to teach any theory that denies the story of the Divine Creation of man as taught in the Bible, and to teach instead that man has descended from a lower order of animals." Teaching evolution was only half of a criminal act, according to the defense; unless evolutionary science inherently denied the divine origins of the species, merely teaching evolution was not unlawful. It was in this spirit that Darrow persuaded Bryan to take the witness stand as an expert on the Bible. For his part, Bryan submitted to questioning because he "want[ed] the Christian world to know that any atheist, agnostic, unbeliever, can question me anytime as to my belief in God, and I will answer him."[36]

Examining Bryan before thousands of spectators (Judge John T. Raulston moved the trial to the courthouse lawn to accommodate the larger crowds), Darrow mercilessly derided Bryan's "fool religion," his "fool ideas that no intelligent Christian on earth believes." Despite his belligerent manner, however, Darrow's interrogation of Bryan served a legal purpose. As Malone explained—adding that he considered himself "as good a Christian" as Bryan—the point was to demonstrate that biblical passages were capable of both general and literal constructions. If the Bible could accommodate competing interpretations, then a law against contradicting it was inherently indefinite and unreasonable. More centrally, a blow against biblical literalism from such a storied adherent of revealed religion as Bryan would validate the modernist understanding that divine creation was compatible with evolution. On that score, Darrow managed to elicit some dramatic concessions from Bryan, including Bryan's abiding belief that the six days of creation referred to "periods," not twenty-four-hour days.[37]

Such concessions failed to impress Judge Raulston, who suspended questioning. In his view, further testimony would benefit neither the jurors nor the appellate court. The only issue before the jury was whether Scopes had taught that "man descended from a lower order of animals." With nothing to offer on that point, Darrow rested his case. His last-minute maneuver robbed the disappointed Bryan of the chance to deliver a closing argument he had been preparing for three months, and Bryan beseeched the press to print it instead. The statement sounded the same notes he had emphasized throughout the trial. "This law does not violate any rights guaranteed by any constitution to any individual," he insisted in his published speech. "It deals with the defendant, not as an individual, but as an employee, an official or public servant, paid by the state, and therefore under instructions from the state."[38]

On July 21, after nine minutes of deliberation, the jury dutifully entered a guilty verdict. The abrupt conclusion was fitting for a trial, according to the *New York Times*, "in which nothing has happened according to schedule except the opening of court each morning with prayer."[39]

✦ ✦ ✦

When the *Scopes* trial was over, no one was certain which side had won. A similar ambiguity surrounded popular perceptions of the ACLU. Without question, the event was a publicity bonanza for the organization and its agenda. Reporters from major newspapers descended on Dayton and telegraphed thousands of words daily to readers across the world. H. L. Mencken's acerbic accounts polarized American households. In an unprecedented technological feat, WGN Radio broadcast the proceedings live. Initial press coverage of the *Scopes* trial inclined toward the defense, and antievolutionists lamented the disparity. For the first time in the ACLU's history, press bias favored the organization instead of the other way around.[40]

Over the course of the trial preparations and proceedings, however, Clarence Darrow's perceived attack on religion dampened public enthusiasm for the ACLU. The public relations problem became particularly acute when William Jennings Bryan died in his sleep five days after the trial concluded. His death, as Arthur Garfield Hays observed, made it difficult for the ACLU to talk about the case. Darrow's interrogation of Bryan, which had elicited laughs and applause along with some indignation, was recast as a vicious assault on an ailing hero. Fundamentalists hailed Bryan as a martyr to his righteous cause. Commentators charged that Darrow had alienated potential sympathizers, and they predicted that more antievolution bills would soon follow.[41]

The majority of the ACLU leadership was distressed by Darrow's attack on Christianity and desperate to replace him on appeal. The organization had never meant to bill itself as an advocate of evolution. Its concern was the fact of legislative censorship, not the content of the ideas suppressed. "If similar legislation were aimed at the teachings of a religious group in the U.S.," it emphasized, "it would be equally obnoxious to those who advocate civil liberties." The ACLU's interest in the case diverged irreconcilably from Darrow's. For Darrow, the main thing was to bring the battle over evolution to the country's attention, and in that, he believed the trial was an unequivocal success.[42]

By August, the "Darrow personality" was a clear liability for the ACLU, and Forrest Bailey reported that the prospect of Darrow arguing the case in the Tennessee Supreme Court gave the organization's officers "chills and fever." Much like in Baldwin's New Jersey case, Felix Frankfurter emphasized the preference for Tennessee lawyers in the Tennessee courts. Walter Nelles was cautious, too. At the trial stage, he had valued the opportunity for propaganda over the limited prospect of legal victory. In the appellate courts, by contrast, he thought the best path to "popular education" was also the best chance for winning the case: turning over the defense to a committee of distinguished lawyers. As Bailey paraphrased his proposal, "It was Nelles' idea that we might enhance our respectability, so to speak, by annexing to ourselves a group of conservatives headed by [Charles Evans] Hughes and that this arrangement would facilitate the raising of money."[43]

Darrow was willing to cooperate with Tennessee counsel, but he refused to withdraw altogether, and the ACLU leadership reluctantly conceded it could not force him out. Only Hays stood staunchly behind him on substantive grounds as opposed to appearances or obligation. "I am not willing to have conservative lawyers and conservative organizations reap the benefit of work done by liberals or radicals," he complained. In Hays's experience, only the latter were willing to undertake controversial cases at the outset, when public opinion was uncertain. Once it appeared that involvement might generate "publicity or honor," offers of assistance poured in. If Hughes was willing to take the case, Hays concluded, it was only because the ACLU was likely to win.[44]

Hays was uncharacteristically confident about the ACLU's chances. He believed the brief to the Tennessee Supreme Court, which he drafted, would persuade the justices to strike the Butler Act down. When the court postponed oral argument, observers reasoned that the justices, who were up for reelection in the fall, expected to declare the law unconstitutional and did not want to jeopardize their chances. After all, George Rappleyea explained, they owed their jobs to the "very same yokels" who enthusiastically endorsed the antievolution law. Critics of the judiciary had long pushed for judicial accountability to democratic will—but in cases like *Scopes*, popular pressures cut the wrong way.[45]

In the domain of elite opinion, on the other hand, there was ample reason for optimism. In a June 1925 commencement address, Columbia president Nicholas Murray Butler equated antievolution laws with Prohibition and condemned both for fostering disrespect of law. Sounding like the ACLU, he castigated majoritarianism and lamented that "courage" had "give[n] way to conformity to type, to a sort of spineless corporate opinion which . . . aims to reduce all individuality, whether of mind or character, to a gelatinous and wobbling mass." Distinguished academics and administrators shared in Butler's assessment, including several university presidents. Of the twenty prominent educators the ACLU invited to serve on its Tennessee Evolution Case Fund advisory committee, all accepted. The AAUP pledged to coordinate groups opposed to legislative incursions on freedom of teaching and the separation of church and state. Respectable conservatives voiced legal objections to the Butler Act as well as policy concerns. A July 1925 article in the ABA's journal considered antievolution laws to be unconstitutional for precisely the reasons the defense team raised at trial and articulated in its brief to the Tennessee Supreme Court.[46]

It was Hughes's very public endorsement that most heartened the ACLU leadership. As president of the ABA, he delivered his annual address in 1925 on the subject of "liberty and the law." In his remarks, Hughes lamented the "growth of an intolerant sprit," inconsistent with "the American spirit of civil and religious liberty." True liberty, he emphasized, often required incursions on individual will: the complexities of modern society made much regulation inevitable and desirable. He nonetheless worried that the growth of state power had inured Americans to the potential tyranny of democracy. Hughes reminded them that enforced uniformity came at a price.[47]

Like the ACLU, Hughes regarded academic freedom as a core concern. Without it, he argued, it would be impossible to cultivate an informed public opinion. And so, turning to the *Scopes* case (though he did not identify it by name), he assailed the recent campaign to "lay hands on our public schools and State universities to set obstacles in the path of knowledge." Hughes saw law and liberty as intertwined, and he doubted the constitutionality of the antievolution laws. Regardless of their legal status, however, he staunchly opposed the statutes on policy grounds. The organized bar evidently agreed. When a session chair invited adherents of Hughes's ideals to stand, the entire audience rose. According to the organization's journal, Hughes's address was among "the most timely, useful, fearless, patriotic and able utterances" that an ABA president had ever delivered.[48]

Such sentiments found affirmation in recent judicial decisions. In its 1923 decision in *Meyer v. Nebraska,* the Supreme Court struck down a Nebraska law prohibiting foreign-language instruction as a violation of the Due Process Clause of the Fourteenth Amendment. To Justice Holmes, who thought "a teacher might be forbidden to teach many things," the Nebraska statute was not so unreasonable as to exceed constitutional bounds. As in so many other due process decisions, however, Holmes's opinion was a dissent. Writing for the majority, Justice James Clark McReynolds acknowledged that "the state may do much, go very far, indeed, in order to improve the quality of its citizens, physically, mentally and morally," but he insisted that the "individual has certain fundamental rights which must be respected." Just one month before the *Scopes* trial, McReynolds relied on his reasoning in *Meyer* to invalidate the Oregon public school law. In *Pierce v. Society of*

Sisters, the Supreme Court held that the Oregon statute abridged the constitutional liberty of parents and guardians to control their children's education. This time, the decision was unanimous.[49]

Both *Meyer* and *Pierce* involved prohibitions on private schooling rather than control of the public schools. Still, the defense team in *Scopes* made much of the court's misgivings about the "power of the state to standardize its children." In fact, constitutional claims were the whole of the ACLU's case. As a result of a missed filing deadline, only the initial constitutional challenges were preserved on appeal. All of Darrow's wrangling with Bryan was suddenly irrelevant: the Tennessee Supreme Court would not consider his claim that the Butler Act was compatible with teaching evolution. The ACLU had no choice but to ask the justices to invalidate the law.[50]

The first class of arguments pertained to religious establishment. In promoting the Butler Act, Bryan had argued that it embodied religious neutrality. Since state constitutional limitations prohibited teachers from propagating fundamentalist explanations of creationism, the Butler Act simply imposed equal treatment. The state invoked Bryan's justification at trial and on appeal. By contrast, John Scopes's lawyers argued that the Butler Act established Christianity at the expense of other religions, and a particular Christian sect, Evangelism, instead of others. At the time, the prohibition on religious establishment in the United States Constitution applied only to the federal government, and the analogs in state constitutions were narrowly construed to forbid only sectarian preferences. Like many other states, Tennessee mandated daily readings of Bible verses in public schools; because the provision proscribed commentary on the verses, neutrality among denominations was thought to be satisfied. In fact, the attorney general of Tennessee baldly asserted at trial that "the King James version of the Bible is a recognized one in this section of the country," and that "the laws of the land recognize the law of God and Christianity as a part of the common law." In subsequent decades, antievolution laws would fit squarely within the Supreme Court's Establishment Clause doctrine, but that day had not yet come.[51]

The defense team raised a litany of claims under the state and federal constitutions, attacking everything from the specificity of the indictment to the clarity of the statute's title to the vagueness of the purported offense. The brief argued that the Butler Act deprived evolutionist teachers of the equal protection of the law, and that it introduced a preference for private schools over public schools and for nonscience subjects, which were governed by teachers' discretion, over scientific ones. Just as Bryan had charged, Scopes's lawyers sought to import elite assessments of scientific knowledge into the Constitution. They urged the court to look to books, encyclopedias, and other compendiums of scientific consensus. They relied heavily on esteemed authorities, including a 1922 letter from Woodrow Wilson stating that he, "like every other man of intelligence and education . . . believe[d] in organic evolution." Above all, they embraced the progressive vision of academic freedom. They emphasized that the pursuit of knowledge was fundamental to social progress, and that education was the basis on which scientific research was built.[52]

And yet, the heart of Scopes's appeal—counterintuitive though it may seem to modern eyes—turned on the very *Lochner*-style arguments that progressives had long decried. Relying on *Meyer* and *Pierce,* the defense team maintained that legislatures were confined to "limited purposes," and that dictating scientific and religious conclusions was not among them. It also impugned the Butler Act for depriving Scopes of his "right properly to practice his profession," a standby in antiregulatory challenges stretching back to Reconstruction.[53]

When the *Scopes* case finally came up for oral argument in May 1926, various members of the defense team made statements to the court. But it was Hays who emphasized the liberty and property interests on which the defense case rested. In fact, despite his opposition to enlisting conservative assistance in arguing the *Scopes* case, he quoted several pages from Hughes's address to the ABA. To be sure, Hays asserted the ACLU's tested defenses of free speech: "The majority of today may be a minority of tomorrow," he recited, and "the theory of our Constitution is that in the competition of ideas, truth will prevail." Still, the arguments he emphasized stood in stark tension with the ACLU's earlier attacks on the courts. As the *New Republic* critically reflected, the ACLU's reliance on constitutional arguments might "vindicate certain ambiguous individual rights," but only "at the expense of the wholesome functioning of certain clear and desirable popular political responsibilities." Mainstream liberals continued to believe that the "right of Tennessee to pass a foolish law [was] quite as much in need of defense as the right of a soap-box orator to utter a foolish or dangerous speech."[54]

Before the Supreme Court of Tennessee, the defenders of the Butler Act, channeling Bryan, touted the *"police power* of the State's constitutionally chosen and elected *legislative* representatives as to what is required for the public welfare." For the ACLU, on the other hand, Hays made a forthright plea for countermajoritarian intervention. "The court is the barrier which protects the minority from vicious, or even well-intended legislation, the effect of which is inimical to the State," he proclaimed, echoing the time-tested justification for constitutional limitations on the pernicious effects of redistributive democracy. According to Hays, legislators were unduly vulnerable to electoral pressures and popular whims. It was not to the people, but to the "men of the Supreme Court Bench, conscientiously avoiding emotion or passion, removed by training and thought from the influence of popular demands," that the ACLU presented its plea for the preservation of American institutions.[55]

✦ ✦ ✦

On January 15, 1927, the Supreme Court of Tennessee issued its long-awaited decision. According to the plurality opinion, John Scopes, as an employee of the state, was subject to whatever terms the state prescribed. The Butler Act, unlike the laws considered by the United States Supreme Court in *Meyer* and *Pierce,* regulated neither the conduct nor contracts of individuals or private entities in their mutual dealings. The state was acting as a proprietor or employer—and the United States Supreme Court had approved a broad range of state practices setting wages, limiting hours, and otherwise regulating public employees. As for religious establishment, the very fact that Protestants, Catholics, and Jews all evinced a range of beliefs about evolution belied the claim that antievolutionism favored any particular religious sect. In short, the legislature of Tennessee had "not crossed . . . constitutional limitations." Substantiating the enduring progressive belief that elected judges would prove more deferential to the people's will, the court gave the Butler Act "the benefit of any doubt."[56]

Although it upheld the Butler Act, the court overturned Scopes's conviction on a technicality. Both parties had consented to Judge Raulston's decision to assess the minimum fine of one hundred dollars authorized by the statute, but the Tennessee constitution formally required fines of that size to be determined by the jury. On the basis of that seldom-enforced provision, the defense lost the opportunity to challenge the Butler Act in the United States Supreme Court. Scopes might have been retried, but the Tennessee court advised against it. "We see nothing to be gained by prolonging the life of this bizarre case," the court concluded, and it urged the attorney general to suspend prosecution.[57]

Decades later, Roger Baldwin would recall that the ACLU "lost the best-publicized case it ever handled—the test of the anti-evolution law in Tennessee in 1924—but it ended the drive in the South to write Genesis into law." In reality, the *Scopes* case did not stem the tide of antievolution legislation. Many contemporaries complained that it energized the movement, though it may have confined it to southern states. By the end of the decade, Mississippi, Arkansas, Louisiana, and Texas all adopted antievolution legislation of various kinds. School boards throughout the South followed suit, and the ACLU's annual reports continued to catalog antievolution activity.[58]

Yet in another sense, the *Scopes* trial was a tremendous breakthrough for the ACLU. Whatever its effect on antievolution legislation, the ACLU's engagement in *Scopes* had the unmistakable effect of bolstering the organization's legitimacy. Certainly the leadership would have preferred that Clarence Darrow adopt a more respectful tone. It had no desire to alienate religious believers, and it regretted that donors were holding back contributions as a result of Darrow's antics. The ACLU repeatedly assured correspondents that its purpose in the *Scopes* case was neither to denigrate religion nor to eliminate moral instruction in the schools. Rather, it was to preserve American liberty by preventing the "complete standardization" of the "intellectual life of [the] nation." The enemy was "force[d] conformity"—which was why the ACLU could advocate the right of Catholics to private education in Oregon and the right of Tennessee school teachers to explain evolution in the same breath.[59]

Still, it was one thing to be faulted for religious insensitivity, and another to be accused of complicity in radical agitation. If the press denounced the ACLU for antireligious elitism rather than revolutionism, that was itself a public relations victory. For the time being, the transition remained incomplete. Long after the Lusk Committee was discredited, critics continued to cite its conclusion that the ACLU, "in the last analysis, is a supporter of all subversive movements, and its propaganda is detrimental to the interests of the state"—more to the point, that the ACLU attempted not only to protect the rights of dissenters, but also "to encourage attacks upon our institutions." During the *Scopes* proceedings, these old accusations resurfaced, and the ACLU worked hard to dispel them. Indeed such concerns, perhaps even more than the attack on William Jennings Bryan's "fool ideas," motivated the organization's effort to replace Darrow on appeal. In the estimation of the ACLU leadership, *Scopes* was "not a radical case and [did] not require a man whose economic philosophy is radical to handle it." The ideal lawyer—a lawyer, that is, like Charles Evans Hughes—would impress the Supreme Court, not predispose the justices against the case. Even Darrow acknowledged "possible prejudice" against himself and Arthur Garfield Hays, though he considered the ACLU as an organization to be significantly more disreputable. As he told Forrest Bailey, the state's lawyers argued at length about the ACLU's intentions, and "in this discussion, the Lusk report was read very freely."[60]

Over the course of the *Scopes* proceedings, however, the revolutionist reputation of the ACLU gradually receded. When the *Iron Trade Review* accused the ACLU of radicalism in 1925, George Rappleyea conveyed his confidence that the organization would be a better partner in labor disputes than the "agitators" of the AFL. After their principled defense of Scopes, he reported, "I know that I could go to their leaders who are as well educated as I am, and who draw no salaries, and who are God fearing, peace loving people." Two years later, when the ACLU disclaimed substantive support for the striking silk workers it defended in New Jersey, its brief to the New Jersey Court of Errors and Appeals invoked the *Scopes* case as the standout example of the organization's commitment to expressive freedom as a neutral value. By 1928, the ACLU observed in its annual report that "the attitude of the newspapers to our activities, judging by editorials, grows more favorable."[61]

As Baldwin told the prominent Communist James P. Cannon, the ACLU had a particular crowd to reach in the overarching struggle for economic equality. It was up to the "liberals"—or, as Baldwin preferred to call them, "Libertarians"—to "fight for civil liberty as a principle of progress." To that end, the ACLU's pamphlet on the *Scopes* trial lumped antievolution laws together with compulsory Bible reading and restrictions on radical teachers. "All of them," it claimed, "involve precisely the same issues as the laws punishing opinion passed during the war, and the criminal syndicalism and sedition laws passed in 35 states during and just after the war." All were part of an immense and unprecedented effort "to regulate public opinion and to penalize minority and heretical views," and they were bound to narrow human understanding. Such rhetoric was effective. In the fall of 1926, Baldwin recounted that "the Scopes evolution case in Tennessee [had] opened the eyes of hundreds to the growth of intolerance and brought them into camp."[62]

✦ ✦ ✦

By the time the Tennessee Supreme Court issued its opinion in *Scopes*, the ACLU was firmly committed to the fight for academic freedom. The stakes of excluding unconventional ideas from the schools were painfully evident to the organization, which considered a prohibition on its own meetings in the New York Public School to be the "most important free-speech fight" of 1927. But the demand for academic freedom was also spilling over into other areas of social regulation. According to Zechariah Chafee Jr., who daily encountered the municipal censorship that made "Banned in Boston" a household phrase, the very same intolerance that fueled antievolution laws and restrictions on parochial education also underlay the suppression of birth control meetings in Boston. As Leon Whipple put it, there was a threat to social progress from the "steady extension of the police power over health, morals, and personal habits"—the "slow encroachment" of the state onto all aspects of personal liberty.[63]

Still, there were some restrictions, within and outside the educational context, that the ACLU had quietly accepted since its founding. In the NCLB's first year of operations, Theodore Schroeder had urged Roger Baldwin not to neglect intrusions on "personal liberties," but Baldwin dismissed such issues as irrelevant to the "wider political question" the new organization was pursuing. After the war, the Lusk Committee noted the ACLU's acceptance of libel and slander laws, as well as restrictions on "licentious or immoral speech or writing." Despite the long-standing association of radicalism with "free love," the ACLU had studiously avoided the field of obscenity, except to oppose prior restraint or the use of obscenity prosecutions to "punish persons for their political views."[64]

In the wake of the *Scopes* case, however, a growing contingent within the ACLU believed the organization's absence from the field of obscenity was misguided. Chief among them were the organization's new general counsels, Arthur Garfield Hays and Morris Ernst. Hays, of course, had an established relationship with the ACLU, and—despite a lucrative corporate law practice and a propensity to defend the integrity as well as the legal interests of his business clients—eagerly participated in the organization's free speech fights. Ernst, too, often assisted in ACLU cases. A feature in *Life* magazine would later describe Ernst as an "unlawyerlike lawyer" who relished unorthodoxy—a "smallish" man with an "inability to match socks, tie and handkerchief," whose ability to "first-nam[e] the famous" was unparalleled in the United States. Ernst used those connections to good effect in his three decades of service to the ACLU. Born in Uniontown, Alabama, he spent the bulk of his childhood in New York City before matriculating at Williams College. A "jumping-jack-of-all-trades," he attended New York Law School's night program while working in a furniture store; *Life* attributed his frenetic activity and insatiable ambition to the "knowledge that he did not attend, as did his partners, a first-class law school, that he never made Phi Beta Kappa in college, that he was never much of a muchness until he was over 30." Ernst declined the ACLU's 1926 invitation to become the organization's chief counsel, preferring to serve in an informal capacity, but he signed on as associate general counsel in 1930.[65]

Both Hays and Ernst were skeptical of state morals regulation, and both had experience in obscenity cases. In their private law practices, both defended periodicals and publishing houses against obscenity charges, and like their clients, they had financial as well as ideological reasons to distrust the state. In October 1928, Hays championed liberalism over radicalism in a debate at the Ford Hall Forum. Both Hays and Ernst were the children of Jewish immigrants and resisted the "'squeamishness' in the field of censorship" that purportedly followed from their colleagues' New England upbringings and "puritanical instinct[s]."[66]

The ACLU's reluctance to enter the obscenity fray did not dissuade Hays or Ernst from tackling the subject. In 1927, Ernst unsuccessfully attempted to convince a New York jury that a censored book was not obscene. Determined to do better, he published a systematic study of obscenity censorship in America, *To the Pure: A Study of Obscenity and the Censor,* which attacked the obscenity laws as arbitrary and inconsistent with the pursuit of knowledge. Hays, meanwhile, had more luck. While the *Scopes* appeal was pending, he helped H. L. Mencken stage a celebrated confrontation with Boston's Watch and Ward Society. On Hays's advice, Mencken provoked arrest by selling an issue of his literary journal, the *American Mercury,* containing a story about a small-town prostitute. Hays defended Mencken against criminal charges, and when postal officials nonetheless refused to mail the magazine's April issue, he secured an injunction compelling its circulation.[67]

Indirectly, it was Hays's representation of Mencken in the postal matter that finally pushed the ACLU to tackle the new terrain. Inspired by his victory, the influential birth control advocate Mary Ware Dennett sought Hays's assistance in restoring the postal circulation of her sex education pamphlet, *The Sex Side of Life*. Dennett had served as secretary of the NCLB and had close personal relationships with many members of the ACLU's executive and national committees. Though Hays was sympathetic, he declined the case, explaining that courts were deferential to administrative decisions and unlikely to issue an injunction, especially given the explicit descriptions in the pamphlet. Dennett nonetheless remained optimistic. In 1928, she turned to Ernst instead, and found him more responsive. While he pondered potential strategies, postal authorities grew tired of Dennett's defiance of the ban. In December 1928, she was indicted under the 1873 Comstock Act, which empowered the post office to censor "lewd" materials, along with publications deemed immoral for, among other transgressions, criticizing the institution of marriage or endorsing the use of contraception. Ernst volunteered to represent her pro bono, and he quickly persuaded the ACLU to sponsor the case.[68]

For the ACLU, the Dennett defense was an ideal introduction to obscenity regulation. As Ernst and Dennett both emphasized, it raised many of the same considerations at issue in *Scopes*. Far from being obscene, the ACLU argued, the pamphlet reflected the objectives of the social hygiene movement, which employed scientific methods to regulate sexual behavior and control the spread of venereal disease. The piece had been printed in the *Medical Review of Reviews* and circulated by the YMCA and the Bronxville, New York, public schools, and it was "in complete accord with modern scientific thought." In the ACLU's statement, increasing its availability would promote knowledge, dispel misconceptions, and encourage responsible behavior. Moreover, as with foreign-language instruction and private schooling, suppression of the pamphlet interfered with the rights of parents to control the education of their children. Finally, there was reason to believe that the postmaster targeted the pamphlet for exclusion not because of its content, but because of Dennett's outspoken criticism of postal censorship under the Comstock Act. According to Ernst, the censorship of *The Sex Side of Life* was a "test-case of vital importance."[69]

As in *Scopes,* the ACLU solicited statements and letters from prominent scientists, educators, and public leaders endorsing the pamphlet (also as in *Scopes,* the judge excluded expert testimony). Like John Scopes, Dennett was convicted; she was fined $3,000 and pledged to serve time in prison instead. In the end, her resolve was not tested. Her conviction, too, was overturned on appeal—this time, on the merits. True, Judge Augustus Hand, writing for a three-judge panel, rejected Ernst's constitutional claims. The Comstock Act neither exceeded federal power under Article I, Section 8 nor contravened the Bill of Rights. The Supreme Court had ruled in *Ex parte Jackson* that the First Amendment did not apply to the mails, and even a sympathetic Second Circuit panel was unwilling to extend the reasoning of the Holmes and Brandeis dissents to the obscenity context, as Ernst had urged. Still, Judge Hand implicitly modified the prevailing *Hicklin* test, which conditioned a work's obscenity on its potential to deprave the youngest and most corruptible of readers. Reasoning that the dissemination of knowledge outweighed the "incidental tendency to arouse sex impulses," he held that a work must be judged in its entirety—that a few explicit passages would not render a "manifestly serious" contribution to sex education obscene. Although *Dennett* was no sweeping constitutional victory, it paved the way to the Supreme Court's midcentury extension of First Amendment protection to sexually explicit speech.[70]

What distinguished *Dennett* most starkly from the *Scopes* case it followed was an overwhelming outpouring of public approval of Dennett and her cause. Ernst and the ACLU effectively choreographed the public presentation of the proceedings, and neither the defendant nor the defense strategy attracted significant criticism. Three months after offering Dennett its support, the ACLU created the Mary Ware Dennett Defense Committee. Like its precursor in the *Scopes* case, the committee drew from educational, religious, and scientific leaders. Chaired by John Dewey (after several months under the leadership of Scripps-Howard newspaper publisher Roy Howard), it promptly launched a national campaign. The effort yielded spectacular results. Prominent public figures, respected associations, and universities all issued statements on Dennett's behalf, and hundreds of strangers sent letters and donations, along with orders for *The Sex Side of Life.* Newspapers throughout the country—cognizant, presumably, that a more lenient obscenity standard served their financial interests—celebrated Dennett's victory. The positive press coverage, in turn, generated even more enthusiasm for Dennett and the ACLU. Lewis Gannett of the *New York Herald Tribune* called *Dennett* a "historic case, a landmark in the history of America's attitude toward sex," and he sounded a call for broad-based reform of obscenity laws and postal censorship.[71]

The ACLU was well positioned to heed that call. In 1929, its national committee approved increased attention to anticensorship work. Guided by Ernst, the organization used the *Dennett* case as an opportunity to challenge "the whole method of determining obscenity, the rules of evidence in trials, and the constitutionality of the law under which the Post Office Department operates its censorship." In the wake of the Second Circuit's decision, it capitalized on its victory, literally and figuratively. In May 1929, it convened a meeting at New York's famed Town Hall to discuss the *Dennett* case and its broader implications. The 1,500 people who attended demanded freedom of instruction on "sex subjects" and recommended the creation of a permanent agency to study censorship and its policy implications. The ACLU obliged by creating the National Committee for Freedom from Censorship (NCFC), which it financed from a budgetary surplus in the Dennett defense fund. Especially after the stock market crash, the fund-raising potential of the new censorship work was evident to the ACLU. Under the direction of Pulitzer Prize–winning playwright Hatcher Hughes, the NCFC launched a "drive against censorship in all its forms," based on a combination of legislative lobbying and test case litigation. Its first targets included post office censorship, state movie censorship laws, the New York state theater padlock law, and the pernicious influences of private vice societies.[72]

Along with a new organizational apparatus, the ACLU developed a more ambitious program for its anticensorship work. In his conclusion to the *Dennett* brief, Ernst argued that *The Sex Side of Life* deserved protection "even if [it] were not educational, even if it were utterly worthless." When the ACLU first sponsored Dennett's case, few within the organization's leadership shared that view. By the early 1930s, however, Ernst's approach had adherents in the courts as well as the ACLU. Ernst litigated dozens of obscenity cases during the 1920s and 1930s, winning most of them. The early prosecutions involved materials like Dennett's that most contemporaries considered wholesome. By building gradually on favorable precedent (often citing dissents in past cases, many of which he litigated, to exaggerate the indecency of materials previously protected), he defended written and visual works that verged increasingly on pornographic. Eventually, many members and supporters of the ACLU understood this assault on obscenity regulation as essential to the civil liberties campaign.[73]

✦ ✦ ✦

The expansion in the civil liberties agenda entailed a corresponding shift in civil liberties theory. Early advocates of artistic freedom and sex education argued that censorship was out of step with the cultural experimentalism of the Roaring Twenties. As the class of protected materials became more vulgar and more explicit, appeals to its underlying value dwindled in number. In political cases, ACLU lawyers defended "freedom for the thought that we hate"—for example, the Ku Klux Klan's right to rally in Boston—by arguing that bad ideas would be less powerful if they were subjected to scrutiny; good ideas, even if they elicited initial skepticism, would prove their worth in the marketplace of thought. But in the realm of sexually explicit speech, legal authorization seemed certain to increase the availability and consumption of undesirable materials. Some advocates, including Mary Ware Dennett herself, insisted that smut was less alluring when it was freely available (in 1929, she complained that "sexual knowledge [was] being conducted on a bootleg basis"). Few contemporaries agreed, however, and Dennett and her allies often invoked alternative justifications for easing legal restraints. At a basic level, their new argument was definitional. The very concept of obscenity was culturally dependent and, in language that anticipated the Supreme Court's later doctrine, "varie[d] ridiculously from time to time and from place to place." In addition to line drawing obstacles and chilling effects, the slipperiness of social norms posed problems for centralized, top-down enforcement of community standards.[74]

In building the new understanding, Morris Ernst and the ACLU drew on an emerging antipathy toward administrative intrusion on personal privacy and daily life. In 1929, as vice crusaders in Boston and New York ramped up their attacks on purportedly immoral expression, the ACLU included the censorship of books, plays, and talking movies among the important new civil liberties problems. The onset of the Great Depression only exacerbated matters. To attract audiences, publishers and producers pushed the limits of legal and cultural propriety. In New York State, the ACLU helped to defeat a 1931 censorship bill, modeled on one already in place for motion pictures, that would have made all plays subject to approval by a bureau within the Board of Education. Civil liberties advocates seized on public criticism of the proposal to generate support for a campaign to repeal censorship laws outside the theater context, including postal censorship and the restrictive regulation of the airwaves by the Federal Communications Commission.[75]

In contrast to criminal prosecutions for political speech under state sedition acts, administrative censorship raised familiar concerns about prior restraints and unbridled authority. As isolated bureaucrats, unelected censors were unresponsive to changing social norms. Moreover, their relative insulation from political accountability rendered the threat of arbitrary power particularly troublesome. An earlier generation of reformers had valued administrators for their expertise and their service to elite priorities, and they had trusted them to make appropriate allowances for unconventional speech. Civil liberties supporters of the 1930s—who had witnessed rampant wartime censorship, wholesale deportations of immigrants, and, most recently, the gross abuses of Prohibition enforcement—were less sanguine about administrative power. Whereas *Scopes* pitted scientific consensus against the will of the people, *Dennett* and its progeny pitted aloof administrators against an emerging popular consensus.[76]

It is no surprise, then, that the ACLU's initial efforts to rein in obscenity regulation focused on administrative censorship. Among its early victories was the NCFC's reform of customs censorship. During the 1920s, the Customs Office barred the importation of thousands of medical, scientific, and artistic works. In response, the NCFC helped to draft amendments to the tariff bill that transferred the authority to assess the obscenity of imported materials from the Customs Office to the federal courts and, by extension, to federal juries. In a stark departure from their Progressive Era roots, ACLU operatives preferred judicial to administrative resolution of a contentious civil liberties problem.[77]

As events unfolded, the new tariff law became the vehicle for the next major advances in the censorship fray. Drawing on Judge Hand's opinion in *Dennett,* Judge John M. Woolsey of the Southern District of New York decided two formative obscenity cases in the Southern District of New York under the Tariff Act of 1930, which prohibited the importation of any material "which is obscene or immoral." The first involved sexually explicit advice for married couples. The second, in which Woolsey admitted a book describing the history and practice of contraception, made it lawful to import birth control information for the first time in forty years. Ernst argued both cases with the assistance of his colleague Alexander Lindey and on behalf of the NCFC. In both cases, Ernst emphasized public desire for open discussion of sex, especially in light of the risks of suppression. As in past cases, his office solicited letters of support from sympathetic public figures. As Ernst explained, obscenity was ultimately a measure of public opinion, and "public opinion could best be crystallized in getting the opinions of representative persons in the community."[78]

Judge Woolsey's decisions signaled a new judicial openness to eroding administrative censorship power, but they were not without limits. The court patently rejected Ernst and Lindey's First Amendment arguments, reasoning that freedom of the press meant merely freedom from prior restraints. Moreover, the customs law was narrower than its postal equivalent, which explicitly prohibited the circulation of birth control materials in the mail. Perhaps most important, the decisions applied to medical and scientific works of the kind at issue in *Dennett*, as opposed to literary or artistic productions. The NCFC was ready to tackle that issue, but it was cautious about potential test cases. Ernst's office preferred to "take only those cases where the cards [were] stacked in [their] favor, and where a favorable decision would establish precedent for an entire class of literature heretofore prohibited." In fact, the ACLU was reluctant to defend any book written in the twentieth century and preferred to begin with the "old classics."[79]

In his private practice, however, Ernst was less discriminating. On behalf of booksellers and publishing houses, he defended works that were sexually explicit, profane, and decidedly modern. As it happened, the first major victory for artistic freedom involved a book that was all three. Random House, which Ernst represented, contracted with James Joyce to publish an American trade edition of his modernist masterpiece, *Ulysses*. Despite its celebrated critical status, *Ulysses* was a favorite target for vice crusaders, and the book was banned in the United States for its first ten years in print. A test case proved necessary to clear the book for circulation, and Ernst arranged for Judge Woolsey to preside over the proceedings. Ernst emphasized the book's artistic merit and, without even raising a First Amendment claim, insisted that there was nothing obscene about its stark depictions of human language and behavior. Judge Woolsey agreed, and in *United States v. One Book Entitled Ulysses,* he explicitly repudiated the *Hicklin* test. Extending *Dennett*'s reasoning to literary works, he held that a book must be judged by its aggregate effect (not isolated passages) on a person with "average sex instincts." Highlighting the follies of government "intolerance," Ernst predicted that the month of the decision would "go down in history for two repeals, that of Prohibition and that of squeamishness in literature."[80]

A few months later, the Second Circuit affirmed, heralding a new era in obscenity regulation. The prosecution of *Ulysses* was an embarrassment for the Herbert Hoover administration: at the height of the Great Depression, censorship of sexually explicit materials seemed trivial, misguided, and a waste of government resources. As Ernst put it in 1934, "In this period while men's stomachs have been empty, there appears to have been less fear of writings dealing with sex." Persuaded by newspaper coverage and political pressure, the Customs Service retained a special adviser on obscenity matters and curtailed its censorship activities. Laxer regulation and mounting popular tolerance were mutually reinforcing: in the wake of the Second Circuit's decision, American consumers accessed a flood of foreign books that were previously unavailable, and in turn recalibrated their attitudes toward the limits of acceptable sexual content. Reflecting on the sea change that followed the case, a 1938 *Harvard Law Review* article called *Ulysses* a "new deal for literature."[81]

There were other beneficiaries of relaxing standards on sexual censorship besides modernist literature. In the years after *Ulysses*, Ernst—who played a formative role in Planned Parenthood as well as the ACLU—scored some dramatic successes in easing government regulation of contraceptives. During the Depression, strained household finances brought home the benefits of family limitation, and public support for birth control climbed sharply. As with obscenity regulation, however, the legislatures lagged behind public opinion. In a notable departure from *Lochner*-era wisdoms (and in stark contrast to subsequent preoccupation with the "counter-majoritarian difficulty"), Ernst believed that institutional features made the courts better metrics of popular will than the political branches. That was the lesson of *Scopes*, *Dennett*, and other cases involving suppression of avant-garde ideas.[82]

In his ACLU work and on behalf of private clients, Ernst solicited public letters because he believed they influenced judges. Legislators were beholden to special interests and powerful lobbies, but judicial tenure freed the courts to conform to elite opinion, if not majoritarian preference. Ernst's solution was the "nullification" of birth control regulation, a process that turned on executive nonenforcement and the judicial invalidation of restric-tive laws. And in 1936, in *United States v. One Package*—another Second Circuit decision written by Judge Augustus Hand—he secured a pivotal ju-dicial victory for the importation of contraceptives. Although many states continued to restrict access to contraceptives, Margaret Sanger celebrated the decision as "the end of birth control laws," "an emancipation proclama-tion to the motherhood of America." In its earliest years, the ACLU had brought its cases to the courts with the expectation of losing and the hope of arousing popular outrage. By the early 1930s, the organization's lawyers were appealing to public support for civil liberties, with the hope that re-spectability would convert the courts to their point of view.[83]

It was due in large part to their successes that the ACLU was gradually coming to regard the civil liberties it supported as judicially enforceable rights. When the ACLU was founded, only three of its twenty executive committee members were lawyers. Over the course of the decade, that number steadily grew. Certainly the ACLU's lawyers, like their contempo-raries who came of age in the Progressive Era, remained cynical about the courts. Felix Frankfurter staunchly opposed the pursuit of civil liberties through constitutional litigation and considered the Supreme Court's "occa-sional services to liberalism" to be a dangerous step toward judicial legisla-tion. As late as 1927, Walter Nelles rehearsed perennial progressive critiques of the judiciary. "Judges are chosen from lawyers of standing at the bar, and standing is attained by devoted service to important property inter-ests," he intoned. "It is extraordinary when a judge can slough off the pre-possessions which his practice has engendered." In 1928, the ACLU counted *Meyer* and *Pierce* as the only two cases in which the Supreme Court had upheld civil liberties.[84]

Still, the organization's lawyers continued to make constitutional claims. And over time, the combination of periodic state-court successes, Holmes's and Brandeis's powerful Supreme Court dissents, and victories in nonlabor cases were making the courts a more inviting venue. In its new approach, the ACLU parted ways with some of its closest collaborators, who enthusi-astically endorsed expressive freedom on policy grounds. Many labor unions declined to back the *Scopes* defense, and influential progressives expressly criticized the constitutional approach. "Why should the Civil Liberties Union have consented to charge the State of Tennessee with disobeying the Constitution in order legally to exonerate Mr. Scopes?" the *New Republic* poignantly asked. "They should have participated in the case, if at all, for the purpose of fastening the responsibility for vindicating Mr. Scopes, not on the Supreme Court of the United States, but on the legislature and people of Tennessee." The latter path would have hewed more closely to the ACLU's founding values. The organization remained deeply opposed to both *Lochnerism* and labor injunctions, and given the chance to cabin judicial authority, most of its members would have eagerly signed on. Taking the world as they found it, however, the leaders of the ACLU had come to believe that the judiciary could become an important, if unwitting, abettor of the civil liberties cause.[85]

✦ ✦ ✦

When the ACLU first embraced academic freedom, its leaders predicted that radical propaganda would pave the way to peaceful revolution. By the end of the decade, the organization's communications more commonly emphasized autonomy and individual rights. Such seminal cases as *Scopes* and *Dennett* shifted internal influence to the lawyers and pushed the organization's activity toward the courts. Many of the ACLU's new members supported civil liberties because they felt that people's beliefs and behavior were best left to private control. They celebrated what a 1934 NCFC statement labeled "personal choice."[86]

Although the ACLU's radicals often adopted the same language, their true objectives remained more ambitious, and occasionally they came out. In Roger Baldwin's understanding, "the Klan's attempt to compel all children to go to public schools" and the "Fundamentalist attack on scientific teaching" were instances of a more general phenomenon, namely, "the effort of all groups in power to hold on to their privileges, and to write those privileges into law." Baldwin invoked familiar progressive tropes even while he speculated that "political liberalism [was] dead." In the "hopeful days" of the Progressive Era, he had believed that popular majorities could control the "privileged classes." But he had since come to recognize that there "is no 'Public'; the 'People' as a political party are unorganizable." In place of the public interest there were only economic classes. Industrial autocracy had taught Baldwin that "the only power that works is class-power."[87]

Correspondents regularly reminded Baldwin of the many advocates of expressive freedom who were not sympathetically inclined toward organized labor. It undermined the civil liberties struggle, they told him, when he championed the goals of labor unions as opposed to their right to speak. The same critique applied to much of the organization's inner circle. Forrest Bailey revealed his personal predilections in a letter admonishing the field secretary of the ACLU's Southern California branch to be more discreet in his public statements: "Let me be perfectly clear on this point," he wrote. "I too am a radical and am as much concerned as you can possibly be to see the end of the capitalist system." But the national leadership objected to "giv[ing] out the overthrow of the capitalist system as one of the aims about which this organization is concerned."[88]

Baldwin acknowledged that patent partisanship was unseemly in the ACLU leadership—in fact, he conceded that greater detachment "would make the philosophy of free speech stand on firmer ground." He also insisted that the official ACLU position was exactly what his critics demanded. "As an organization," he said, "we stand for everybody's civil rights, and I think we have never failed to defend all comers impartially." Channeling the lessons he had learned in Paterson, he began to treat radicalism as a viewpoint rather than a calling. To that end, he often invoked Justice Holmes's dissenting proclamation in *Gitlow v. New York:* "If in the long run the beliefs expressed in proletarian dictatorship are destined to be accepted by the dominant forces of the community, the only meaning of free speech is that they should be given their chance and have their way."[89]

By the end of the 1920s, the ACLU no longer figured in public conversation as a front for seditious activity. In 1927, Frankfurter described a "slowly-growing tide in our favor." Although the organization had not yet convinced a court to overturn the conviction of a radical defendant on First Amendment grounds, it had scored some modest successes by emphasizing faulty pleadings and insufficient evidence, including its New Jersey victory. Soon, it hoped, the defense of labor radicals would seem no more subversive than the defense of sex education: merely one facet of a larger project to protect disfavored ideas. At the end of the decade, the ACLU reported that "public opinion [was] more responsive, chiefly because the issues to arouse opposition [were] varied enough to make wider appeals."[90]

Critics alleged that the ACLU expanded its activities into the realm of personal freedom for the express purpose of enhancing its credibility, and that "genuine Liberal[s]" joined the ACLU under illusions about its underlying objectives. If so, it was a risky strategy for the organization's leadership. As Baldwin freely admitted, he was "not troubled . . . about any issues of theory or principles." Throughout his career, he was more concerned with achieving results than with ideological consistency. Yet that adaptability exacted a toll. By the dawn of the New Deal, civil liberties were something more than an implement of economic redistribution, and the ACLU's radicals were losing control over the movement they had founded.[91]

6

Old Left, New Rights

I N THE SPRING of 1937, the ACLU issued a statement assessing "how far the Court has been a defender of civil liberties." The results were not encouraging. Although the justices had occasionally protected personal rights in line with their "widening conception" of the Due Process Clause, they had "more often failed to protect the Bill of Rights than preserve it," and the comparatively rare exceptions involved less vital issues. Nor was there comfort in deference to bureaucratic expertise. Like lower courts, "administrative officials . . . follow[ed] the Supreme Court more consistently in protecting property than personal rights."[1]

At the height of the New Deal, as the future of judicial review hung in the balance, civil liberties enjoyed unprecedented support. As the nation reeled from the Great Depression, lawyers, labor advocates, and members of Congress claimed the mantle of civil liberties as their own. While they clashed over the legality and desirability of the New Deal state, these disparate celebrants of civil liberties all endorsed the rights of workers to engage in peaceful picketing. And yet, the most decorated veterans of the interwar civil liberties movement still harbored serious reservations about judicial enforcement of the Constitution. Indeed, some eagerly anticipated the demise of liberal legalism in the United States.

On the future of the federal judiciary, the ACLU took no definitive stand. The organization's indecision was understandable, given its close ties to organized labor and its long antagonism toward the federal courts. Within a decade, there would be few stronger advocates for an independent and active judiciary—but when the Supreme Court was most vulnerable, the ACLU remained steadfastly noncommittal.

And yet, though it issued from other sources, a powerful cry for court-centered civil libertarianism proved instrumental in rehabilitating judicial review in the public imagination. In the weeks after President Franklin D. Roosevelt announced his ill-fated Judicial Procedures Reform Bill, it was the ABA, not the ACLU, that denounced court packing as a threat to free speech and minority interests. To save the federal judiciary, conservative lawyers embraced a vision of civil liberties that the ACLU had equivocally advanced, as a check on state suppression and a safeguard of personal rights. In promoting that vision, they publicized the very speech-protective decisions that the ACLU had litigated and defended and that much of the bar had opposed. Their about-face—which, like the ACLU's ambivalence, is largely absent from existing histories of civil liberties—played a crucial role in linking the judicial enforcement of civil liberties to American constitutional liberalism. Eventually, the Supreme Court countenanced the new regime.

When the decade began, there were few hints of the pending realignment. According to the ACLU, the onset of the Depression prompted a short-lived spike in free speech prosecutions and vigilante violence against "Negroes, strikers, and Communists." The antispeech ardor diminished, however, when it became evident to officials that "there was not much to repress." As strikes and protests both dropped off, so did efforts to stifle them. The Supreme Court's 1931 decision in *Stromberg v. California,* subsequently heralded as a First Amendment icon, was characteristic of this guarded benevolence. The opinion extolled the virtues of democratic debate while preserving ample space for the state policing of radical agitation. As the California court had put it, "Change . . . may be permitted as a means of political evolution, but not of revolution." The ACLU, which helped to litigate the case, regarded the decision as a limited victory that offered "no hope for voiding the laws in principle."[2]

In short, the Great Depression notwithstanding, there was little to distinguish either the civil liberties situation or the ACLU's strategy in the last years of Herbert Hoover's presidency from that of the preceding decade. That continuity, however, was on the verge of rupture. Roosevelt's election ushered in a period of instability and uncertainty in the civil liberties campaign. Across the political spectrum, the architects of the emerging order were about to rethink their relationships toward state power and judicial review.

✦ ✦ ✦

The decade opened with a more modest assault on the federal judiciary, about which the ACLU expressed no hesitation at all: the curtailment of courts' power to issue injunctions against labor activity. As in years past, the labor injunction was the "principal weapon" used by employers to combat serious strikes. When the opportunity arose, the organization poured its resources into legislative action to contain it.[3]

In 1930, the ACLU founded the National Committee on Labor Injunctions with an appropriation from the American Fund for Public Service, or Garland Fund, which Roger Baldwin had helped to organize a decade prior. Under the leadership of former federal judge Charles Fremont Amidon, the committee "focused interested forces for the first time on legislative relief." It consulted closely with ACLU members Felix Frankfurter and Nathan Greene, whose pathbreaking book, *The Labor Injunction,* generated support for legislative reform. It upbraided the courts for upholding the "liberty of contract" between a massive employer and a single worker, "a liberty that in reality does not exist." And it helped to produce a draft anti-injunction measure agreeable to the AFL, labor lawyers, and law professors ensuring that no acts "which involve only workers' rights to meet, speak, [or] circulate literature" would be enjoined.[4]

Sponsored by Nebraska senator George W. Norris and New York representative Fiorello H. La Guardia, the final bill acknowledged that individual workers lacked meaningful liberty of contract, and it sharply limited the circumstances under which federal courts could issue injunctions against labor activity. It also provided for jury trials in many contempt actions and declared yellow-dog contracts unenforceable as against public policy. Within a year, the ACLU celebrated the 1932 Norris–LaGuardia Act as the only significant change in federal or state law involving civil liberties. The National Committee on Labor Injunctions had played an "active part" in its passage, and AFL president William Green arranged for the ACLU to assist in the preparation of state anti-injunction bills, as well.[5]

On its surface, the ACLU's role in promoting the Norris–LaGuardia Act appears at odds with its pursuit of judicial redress in constitutional cases. The ACLU's leadership had spent fifteen years whittling away at adverse precedent in the domain of free speech. Invigorating the First Amendment as the organization urged would require increased judicial oversight of legislative and bureaucratic abuses. By contrast, the object of anti-injunction laws was to stop judicial "law-making." That is, the purpose of the Norris–LaGuardia Act was to restrain judicial power.[6]

Such tensions were evident to the ACLU's conservative critics. According to the *ABA Journal,* organized labor might have claimed its rights in the courts, but it had spurned the judiciary in favor of "trial by legislature"—an approach incompatible with due process of law. By endorsing the anti-injunction bill, the members of the "so-called Civil Liberties Union" were discarding the Constitution in service of their prolabor agenda. By urging judicial enforcement of First Amendment freedoms while simultaneously advocating anti-injunction laws, they revealed themselves to be fair-weather constitutionalists who were "for their own liberties and against those of others."[7]

The ACLU, on the other hand, regarded the two tactics as branches of a common campaign. Its attorneys explicitly equated labor injunctions, imposed by courts, with the historically disfavored practice of prior restraint, where aggrieved parties sought judicial enforcement of the First Amendment. That an order issued from judicial rather than administrative hands did not ameliorate its gravity, in light of judges' evident economic biases. In fact, of all of the ACLU's targets, labor injunctions imposed the "most extensive restrictions on free speech and assemblage" and had proven to be the hardest to combat.[8]

In the 1930s, the ACLU's reasoning found unexpected vindication in the country's highest tribunal, albeit not in a labor case. The ACLU understood *Near v. Minnesota*—the celebrated challenge to Minnesota's 1925 "gag law," which authorized judges to enjoin the publication of malicious or scandalous newspapers—as directly analogous to injunctions in the industrial arena. When a Minnesota judge relied on the law to issue an ex parte injunction against Jay M. Near's antisemitic invective, the ACLU made preparations to defend him, though it eventually ceded the matter to the better funded *Chicago Tribune* and the American Newspaper Publishers Association. In 1931, the Supreme Court invalidated the statute in a decision that underscored the role of press freedom in policing government power. Drawing on property and contract cases, Chief Justice Charles Evans Hughes's majority opinion located free speech and free press squarely within the liberty safeguarded against state action by the Due Process Clause of the

Fourteenth Amendment. In curtailing the injunctive power of the lower courts, the decision dramatically expanded the scope of judicial review.[9]

Despite the real significance of "incorporation," *Near* had limited implications for labor speech. The decision applied only to prior restraints and allowed for exceptions even within that limited category. The majority reaffirmed the decisions in the Espionage Act cases and approved government censorship of obscenity. Quoting *Gompers v. Buck's Stove and Range Company,* it also reiterated that "the constitutional guaranty of free speech does not 'protect a man from an injunction against uttering words that may have all the effect of force.'" In short, the Supreme Court's condemnation of antispeech injunctions did not extend to strikes and boycotts.[10]

Still, the labor injunction could not have been far from the justices' minds. What was particularly pernicious about the statute's operation, in the majority's view, was the same feature that labor advocates habitually condemned: it rendered noncompliance with the court's order "punishable as a contempt of court." That is, it promised to silence the speaker completely, without the benefit of a jury trial. The "mere procedural detail[]" that censorship authority rested with a judge rather than an administrative official did not alleviate the majority's concerns.[11]

Perhaps it was the majority's indifference to the unique evils of bureaucratic power that animated the vigorous dissent by Justice Pierce Butler, for whom judicial injunctions and administrative censorship were conceptually and constitutionally distinct. In Butler's view, the Minnesota statute did not operate as a prior restraint on publication. Far from the administrative tyranny exercised by licensors and censors, the statute simply "prescribe[d] a remedy to be enforced by a suit in equity." The notion that judicial action might violate the Constitution rather than preserve it was scarcely conceivable to the conservative justices, who had held in *Truax v. Corrigan* that employer access to the injunctive relief in labor disputes was constitutionally required.[12]

✦ ✦ ✦

Ironically, at precisely the moment that a Supreme Court majority awoke to the dangers of judicial repression, the ACLU was inching closer to Justice Butler's view. Despite its deep antipathy toward labor injunctions, the organization had scored real successes in the courts in the years between passage of the Minnesota gag law and the Supreme Court's decision in *Near.* In its sex education and artistic freedom cases, it had persuaded judges to exercise restraint where postal and customs censors charged ahead, and it had sponsored legislation to transfer censorship authority from administrators to the federal courts. Prominent members of the ACLU's national committee believed the organization's principal purpose was "the preservation of the constitutional rights of the individual against arbitrary exercise of officials."[13]

In fact, one of the most distinctive features of the ACLU's interwar program was its affirmative use of the courts. Labor lawyers had always been called to defend their clients against civil charges and criminal prosecutions, but the ACLU used law as a sword as well as a shield. The organization filed test cases to challenge state and federal legislation and threatened libel suits against its critics. Roger Baldwin would have preferred to rely on grassroots agitation and direct action, but he had resigned himself to the fact that "the middle-class mind works legalistically"—that "whenever rights are violated, the first thing they want to do is get a lawyer and go to court."[14]

It was with this impulse in mind that the ACLU had employed and advocated a technique about which organized labor harbored serious doubts: it had sought to turn employers' most potent weapon against them, by securing prolabor injunctions in state and federal court. Arthur Garfield Hays pioneered the new tactic during the ACLU's direct action days. In 1922, he gathered a group of reporters and UMW officials in a Pennsylvania mining town, and, when local officials obligingly arrested him, secured an injunction against them for interference with the exercise of civil rights. By 1925, successes like these prompted him to propose a study of "affirmative legal action" on labor's behalf. The ACLU's executive committee urged the Garland Fund to sponsor the iconoclastic account, which became a coauthored volume, *Don't Tread on Me.*[15]

A 1930 ACLU pamphlet on *Legal Tactics for Labor's Rights* condensed the book's analysis and laid out a new policy for advancing labor's rights through the courts. Aimed at labor groups, the pamphlet argued that lawsuits generated positive publicity and produced "a good moral effect." The ACLU was no judicial booster, and it did not overestimate the prospects of legal success. Courts routinely withheld injunctive relief, especially against public officials. But the ACLU believed that even defeats could be turned to labor's advantage, at least in the long run. It hoped that the pursuit and denial of injunctions would convince the public that law had wrongfully oppressed labor. Employers were adept at generating public sympathy by complaining of disorder. Workers, in response, could "stir up the cry of repression of civil liberty." To that end, the ACLU encouraged attorneys to appeal all strong cases, even after a strike had ceased. An occasional victory would build favorable precedent, and the more typical failures would buttress labor's allegations of judicial bias. The principal benefit of litigation, according to the pamphlet, was "*not the winning of legal actions, but the bringing of them.*"[16]

The ACLU shared labor's conviction that the injunction should be abolished, and it acknowledged labor lawyers' reluctance to validate it by using it. In the end, however, it dismissed such concerns as overly scrupulous. "It is almost like saying to the employers 'we won't use this because you do,'" one ACLU publication protested. Of course, unions were hesitant to compromise their independence by relying on judicial generosity rather than self-help. As a tactical matter, however, the ACLU considered legal remedies to be perfectly compatible with strong organization.[17]

The ACLU understood its investment in injunctive relief as a second-best alternative, and in the same year that it issued *Legal Tactics for Labor's Rights,* it enthusiastically embraced the legislative charge to cabin the courts' power to enjoin union activity. Passage of the Norris–LaGuardia Act, in turn, made the judicial strategy even more appealing. Whatever dangers labor's pursuit of injunctions had posed during the 1920s, it offered clear advantages under the new regime, in which the courts' authority to enjoin picketing and boycotts had drastically diminished. On the brink of the New Deal, undesirable injunctions were "pretty well hedged in."[18]

As the ACLU warmed to the judiciary, it intensified its critique of administrative power. In a world populated by the conservative administrative appointees of the 1920s, on the one hand, and federal judges with the benefit of life tenure—many of whom had been on the bench since the Progressive Era—on the other, the ACLU leadership had long since shed its reflexive enthusiasm for bureaucratic expertise. Developments since the world war were "fast abolishing the mores of democracy," and the organization's lawyers (channeling William Graham Sumner) had come to consider it a virtue that judges were "behindhand." Administrators, by contrast, were on the vanguard of repression.[19]

During its first decade, the ACLU had challenged exclusions and deportations of radical aliens on due process grounds. It had advocated the unfettered use of radio airwaves for public debate, lest the "censorship of broadcasting" pave the way to the "censorship of newspapers." At every level of government, it had called on its allies to constrain unbounded bureaucrats. "From the State Department to local police and Mayors arbitrary authority is exercised without restraint," the organization lamented in the mid-1920s. "More significant than the issues of law," the ACLU concluded, "are the arbitrary and lawless invasion of civil rights by administration officials."[20]

In their skepticism toward centralized state power, the leaders of the ACLU parted ways with their progressive allies. The antistatism of the IWW had always infused their attitudes toward legislative and administrative meddling in social and economic conflict. Certainly, they had shared progressives' aversion to the courts. But they were far more antagonistic to labor injunctions, which cabined direct action, than to the *Lochner*-era due process decisions, which targeted political action. Many liberals worried that a constitutional approach to insulating union activity would validate constitutional attacks on minimum-wage and maximum-hours laws. For the ACLU's state skeptics, however, that was an acceptable risk.

During the 1920s, when radicals and progressives were shut out of power, disagreements like these posed little threat to a unified civil liberties campaign. In the 1930s, by contrast, such differences came to a head. Over the course of the decade, ACLU supporters would split over the desirability of radio censorship, the extension of free speech to Nazi marches, and the propriety of racial discrimination in public accommodations. But the most important fracture in the civil liberties alliance involved the right of agitation and the New Deal state.

✦ ✦ ✦

For over a decade, the ACLU had promoted a robust right of agitation—the right of organized labor to challenge the existing industrial and political order through direct action, without government interference. For the organization's state-skeptical view, the Norris–LaGuardia Act was the crowning achievement as well as a last gasp. During the New Deal, government institutions legitimated workers' efforts to organize, and labor leaders, in turn, embraced government institutions. A new breed of interventionists dismissed voluntarism as an "archaic philosophy." In a modern industrial economy, they argued, strong unions went hand in hand with a strong state.[21]

Certainly there were holdouts, even within the mainstream labor movement. While most industrial unionists welcomed state support in organizing unskilled workers, some craft unions fared well under the old regime and bristled at administrative meddling. But from the perspective of the ACLU leadership, the salient risks were of a different sort. At a fundamental level, their anxieties about New Deal labor policy stemmed from a deeply rooted distrust of state power. More concretely, they worried that established unions would tilt the law in their own favor, as they had during the First World War with disastrous consequences for the IWW. Since the 1920s, for example, the ACLU had supported left-wing miners in their struggle to unsettle John L. Lewis's control of the UMW. In mining as in other industries, the ACLU understood that exclusive bargaining rights would freeze out the radical minority. That is, if entrenched unions were empowered to negotiate union security agreements with employers excluding nonmembers from employment, radical unions would collapse—a point that AFL unions and their bargaining partners both understood. Such concerns became a basis for cooperation with the Far Left, which was vocally opposed to the New Deal's state-centered labor policy until mid-decade.[22]

Although the ACLU was neither a front nor an apologist for the Communist Party, the two groups were closely connected. To some extent, their link was situational. Over the course of the 1920s, the Communists supplanted the IWW as the "objects of official persecution," and as the ACLU often emphasized, they bore the brunt of interwar repression. In addition, many ACLU board members were attracted to the Soviet experiment. Only Elizabeth Gurley Flynn officially joined the Communist Party, but several made regular financial contributions and expressed sympathy for Communist ideology, if not party practices. Baldwin assured the head of the International Labor Defense, a Communist-affiliated legal defense organization that provided assistance to workers, "I want the same results as you do, and I have one crowd to reach and you another—both of whom should be pulling together, each in their respective best ways."[23]

Despite Baldwin's aspirations, the ACLU and its Communist clients often worked at cross-purposes. At a basic level, Soviet policy was inconsistent with the ACLU's formal position on civil liberties. In the mid-1920s, free speech emerged as a foil to Soviet-style regimentation. Even while conservatives continued to urge prosecution of subversives at home, the United States Chamber of Commerce reprinted statements by Samuel Gompers and by disabused Communist sympathizers denouncing Soviet Russia for its suppression of dissenting speech. From the ACLU's perspective, such proclamations were self-serving and hypocritical. Conservative unionists were no more tolerant of dissent and had instigated prosecutions against Communists and other radicals. In fact, the ACLU had requested the resignation of seamen's leader Andrew Furuseth from its national committee for invoking California's criminal syndicalism law against the IWW. Still, the ACLU acknowledged concerns about Communists' intolerance.[24]

The first major rift arose when the ACLU openly chastised the Workers Party for breaking up meetings of Socialists and Soviet dissenters. In response, the Communist leadership advised the ACLU to confine its activities to state censorship. The controversy created a troubling dilemma for the ACLU, which desired both to preserve the right of pickets to heckle strikebreakers and to insulate labor meetings against interference by employers and patrioteers, without falling back on the prerogatives of private property. As it later emphasized, the realities of private oppression made it impossible to adopt "any legalistic view of civil liberties." In the end, the organization hedged. It accepted booing and hissing but not large-scale disruptions. It also urged self-restraint, lest Communists alienate liberal support for their own free speech. To American Communists, however, the "liberalism" the ACLU touted was merely "the face of imperialistic oppression."[25]

Tensions heightened at the end of the 1920s as a result of ACLU activities in North Carolina, where the organization assisted the ILD in appealing the conviction of seven strikers who were accused of killing the Gastonia chief of police. The North Carolina controversy cost the ACLU $10,000, more than any other recent engagement, but what irked the organization was an unintended expense. Since the late 1920s, the ACLU had administered a bail fund on behalf of the Garland Fund. In that capacity, it authorized nearly $40,000 in bail for five of the Gastonia defendants. Before the North Carolina Supreme Court issued its decision, the defendants (including, most famously, Fred E. Beal) set sail for the Soviet Union, as Bill Haywood had done a decade earlier. In an official statement, the ACLU voiced pragmatic concerns: the difficulty of raising future funds, the prospect of excessive bail in subsequent cases, and the betrayal of friends and sympathizers whose contributions were forfeited. Many members, however, also condemned bail jumping as a legal and ethical breach, and the organization refused to authorize further bail in Communist cases unless the Communist leadership rejected the practice. William Z. Foster, the general secretary of the Communist Party, resigned his membership in the ACLU in protest.[26]

One month after Foster's resignation, the ACLU announced a new policy for handling Communist cases. Henceforth, it would cooperate with the ILD only if the ACLU retained full authority over legal decisions. Despite the conspicuous timing, the change in course purportedly reflected tactical differences rather than the bail issue. The ACLU believed that the ILD was pouring money into "hopeless legal work," where an adverse outcome appeared certain. More fundamentally, the two organizations had different goals. The ILD's courtroom emphasis on "class and economic issues" was often "detrimental to the civil liberties questions" involved.[27]

Despite the growing gulf between them, the ACLU and ILD continued to collaborate. In fact, over the next half decade, they cooperated on such foundational First Amendment cases as *Stromberg v. California, DeJonge v. Oregon,* and *Herndon v. Lowry.* The ACLU also played a central role in the ILD's legal campaign on behalf of racial justice, notwithstanding the failure of a 1929 proposal by the ACLU's executive committee to expand the organization's "aid to Negroes" and to defend "the rights of defendants in criminal cases," among other issues. The plan's opponents included Felix Frankfurter, who had argued that the only appropriate role for the ACLU in connection with "the protection of negroes" was to preserve the freedom to espouse it; although he personally supported such causes, he believed that ACLU involvement would dilute the organization's message and deplete its resources. Others agreed, and the ACLU had consequently detached itself from the campaign for "negro civil rights." In fact, the organization had arranged for former Georgia governor Thomas W. Hardwick to argue the Gastonia case in the North Carolina Supreme Court, and Hardwick subsequently joined the national committee upon assurances that his racial views—namely, that neither "political [n]or social equality is possible between the races"—would not disqualify him from membership. As Baldwin explained, the ACLU took "no stand on social equality as such," only the "right to advocate it."[28]

To be sure, the ACLU's leaders were actively involved in the NAACP and other organizations committed to racial equality. ACLU board members were instrumental in organizing and disbursing the Garland Fund, which made major appropriations for NAACP activity. In 1931, both Morris Ernst (who chaired the Garland Fund's Committee on Negro Work) and Arthur

Garfield Hays accepted invitations to serve on the NAACP's legal committee, and Frankfurter was a member as well. Representatives of the NAACP leadership routinely sat on the ACLU board, and as of 1930, there were "two Negroes on the national committee." Occasionally the ACLU issued statements on racial violence, including the 1931 pamphlet *Black Justice,* which prompted Hardwick's resignation from the national committee just one year after he joined. Still, as a matter of formal policy, the ACLU "regarded the struggle for the civil rights of Negroes and against lynchings as more or less the exclusive province of the NAACP and . . . did not wish to encroach upon it."[29]

Sometimes, though, the ACLU made exceptions. One such occasion arose in March 1931, when nine black teenagers, the so-called Scottsboro boys, were pulled from a train traveling through Alabama and accused of raping two white women while on board. Barely two weeks later, an all-white jury sentenced eight of the defendants to death—a verdict that Alabama officials stubbornly defended despite abundant evidence that the charges were fabricated. The ACLU helped the ILD to generate publicity in the case. It also served as an intermediary between the ILD and the other organization that vied (belatedly) to represent the defendants, the NAACP. Whereas the NAACP worked to mitigate racial bias in the legal system, the ILD condemned the courts altogether, as "instruments of ruling class injustice." The ACLU straddled the middle and, working with the NAACP's Charles Hamilton Houston, managed to unite the contending parties in the Scottsboro Defense Committee by the fall of 1935. Perhaps most important, the ILD invited ACLU litigator Walter Pollak to argue two cases involving the defendants in the Supreme Court. He won both, securing a decision that incorporated part of the Sixth Amendment's right to counsel into the Due Process Clause of the Fourteenth Amendment for the first time. The Scottsboro victories, like the ACLU's free speech cases, would soon play a pivotal part in the effort by the organized bar to rehabilitate the Supreme Court and save judicial review.[30]

In the first half of the 1930s, the three groups made common cause on another issue, as well—one that distanced them from their New Deal allies, rather than binding them, as Scottsboro did, to an emerging left-liberal consensus. Notwithstanding their competing views of the courts, the NAACP, the Communist Party, and the ACLU all harbored grave reservations about New Deal labor policy.

✦ ✦ ✦

In the early months of Franklin D. Roosevelt's presidency, the ACLU was optimistic. The new administration was practically teeming with "friends of Civil Liberty." Before Roosevelt even took office, the ACLU sent him a series of proposals for federal action. It urged the administration to restore the rights of those convicted under the Espionage Act, issue passports without regard to political views, and allocate radio airtime for minority viewpoints. It also outlined legislative programs to eliminate postal censorship, prohibit wire tapping, and admit pacifist aliens to citizenship, among other issues. When ACLU member Harold L. Ickes was appointed secretary of the interior, Baldwin suggested "half a dozen problems affecting Indians and the Colonies where issues of civil liberty have been unhappily neglected."[31]

But the ACLU had always considered the conflict between labor and capital to be the "central struggle involving civil liberties," and in that domain, the early New Deal was a distinct disappointment. In 1933, Roosevelt signed the National Industrial Recovery Act (NIRA), which authorized employers to enter into cooperative codes of fair competition standardizing prices and working conditions and created a National Recovery Administration (NRA) to implement its provisions. To attract labor support, the statute included a provision, Section 7(a), affirming the right of employees to organize in code industries. In July, the ACLU pledged its support in policing antilabor practices under the act. Although employers were flouting the statute, the organization believed that federal officials would address the violations if "the facts [were] plainly put to them." The ACLU's confidence proved unfounded. In practice, employer recalcitrance was quietly accepted, and the effect of Section 7(a) was to buttress strong unions while abandoning the most vulnerable. Far from protecting the right to strike, the NRA administrators charged with enforcing the statute had hastened "to get workers back to work by accepting some form of government mediation or arbitration, usually to their disadvantage."[32]

The shortcomings of the NIRA were particularly troubling to the leftists on the ACLU board, including Roger Baldwin, Harry Ward, and Corliss Lamont, a celebrated philosopher and lifelong civil liberties activist who was born into wealth but "cast his lot into the arena of radical causes." In consultation with radical unionists, they advocated absolute freedom to strike, regardless of the terms of applicable NRA codes. They also condemned racial discrimination by unions, an issue that was especially troubling where employers agreed to hire only union members in good standing. A closed-shop agreement with a racially exclusive union rendered minority workers ineligible for employment. "Exploited by the employers in the hardest and lowest-paid jobs, they are also excluded from most unions," Baldwin explained. Without the ability to "organize and fight in independent unions," no code could improve their situation. "Negro Workers' rights—N.R.A. or no N.R.A.—[were] pretty near zero."[33]

When Baldwin wrote to President Roosevelt and the head of the NRA demanding proportional representation for minority unions—whether racial or otherwise—much of the ACLU's labor contingent balked. To longtime progressive labor experts like John A. Fitch and John R. Commons, Baldwin's position appeared profoundly misguided. To the ACLU's seasoned unionists, it verged on treason. Exclusive representation ensured that an employer would recognize and bargain with the union that the majority of workers in a bargaining unit supported, not with individual employees or contending unions. Labor advocates worried that minority group recognition would prop up company unions—which one assistant secretary of labor helpfully defined as a union "confined to a single company, more or less supported by management, and, above all, offering as representatives for labor only employees of that company," who were beholden to the employer for their livelihoods. Morris Hillquit threatened to resign over the issue, and had he not died shortly after issuing a second ultimatum, he may well have followed through. Baldwin eventually conceded the point, albeit only as long as company unions posed a threat.[34]

The difference in opinion penetrated to the core of the ACLU leadership. For the board's committed New Dealers, the key to preserving civil liberties was to staff "responsible positions" with "fair-minded men"; in Morris Ernst's view, as long as the newspapers, radio, and movies remained free, the problem of labor relations would take care of itself. Debating Ernst over NBC's Blue Network, Baldwin offered a more measured assessment. In the absence of focused opposition, he acknowledged, Roosevelt had demonstrated tolerance toward aliens, American Indians, the unemployed, and political dissenters. With respect to labor, however, the New Deal had been detrimental and far reaching.[35]

Opposition to New Deal economic policy stemmed from two principal sources. On the Right, it came from "employers still wedded to laissez-faire economics." Baldwin's resistance derived from the Left, those "radicals who oppose state capitalism as a form of economic fascism, denying to the working class a chance to develop its power." Among the ACLU's broader network of supporters, neither view found much support; even the workers and farmers had curbed their criticism in exchange for doles and subsidies. Still, according to Baldwin, government could not be trusted to safeguard labor's interests. On the contrary, "the state [was] always an instrument of violence and compulsion in the hands of the dominant economic class." Despite protests from the ACLU and others, the Roosevelt administration had declined to outlaw company unions. It had curtailed the right to strike and discriminated against left-wing unions. It had withheld union representation on the code authorities—a right in any case far less valuable than the rights to organize, convene mass meetings, and hold a picket line. "The governmental industrial machine" was contriving to "take labor into camp . . . and thereby to lull opposition to sleep." But workers could not rely on government largesse. During the New Deal, as before, the workers who had accomplished most were the ones who had struck hardest. "The real fight is on the job," Baldwin concluded, "not in Washington."[36]

In articles, interviews, and public lectures, Baldwin sounded a consistent message. "Against the extension of repressive powers inherent in the New Deal, against the dangers of wholesale suppression and regulation by the newly-created federal machinery," he declared, "a relentless struggle must be carried on for freedom to agitate and to organize." Baldwin reiterated his abiding belief that preserving the "channels of agitation" for competing political forces was the only means of avoiding bloodshed when struggle inevitably unfolded. And for a time, his view was the institutional position of the ACLU. The organization's 1934 annual report cautioned that the "enormous increase of the power of the federal government under New Deal policies carries with it inevitable fears of inroads on the rights of agitation." Raising the specter of "dictatorship by the President," it railed against the dramatic expansion of federal economic power and a dangerous encroachment on states' rights.[37]

✦ ✦ ✦

In the same state machinery that Roger Baldwin decried, others saw the potential for buttressing labor's strength. In March 1934, Senator Robert F. Wagner introduced his Labor Disputes Act, which would have authorized the National Labor Board (NLB), initially established in August 1933, to enforce the labor-protective measures of Section 7(a) of the NIRA. Wagner's bill imposed majority rule and exclusive representation, and it prohibited company unions. While it made mediation and arbitration voluntary and guaranteed the right to strike, it was premised on the belief that protecting labor's rights meant giving the state more power, not less. The bill faced vehement business opposition, but it received enthusiastic support from the AFL as well as the Socialist Party. The Communist Party, meanwhile, condemned it as a tool to break strikes and cripple working-class agitation.[38]

Mary van Kleeck, who chaired the ACLU's new Committee on Workers' and Farmers' Rights, adopted the Communist line. Like Baldwin, she believed that economic planning that aimed to ameliorate the dangers of capitalism would undercut the class struggle and lead America down a path to fascism. Together with a representative of the International Juridical Association (IJA), a left-wing labor lawyer group, she explained her opposition to the ACLU board. The board, in turn, conveyed those reservations to Massachusetts senator David I. Walsh, chairman of the Senate labor committee. Administration of the NIRA had demonstrated that any state machinery for the conciliation of conflict, no matter how well intentioned, was bound to undercut the rights of labor to organize and strike in the long run.[39]

If Wagner's Labor Disputes Act favored industry, industry evidently did not know it. The bill provoked bitter business opposition that rendered passage in its original form impossible. Senator Walsh's committee offered an amended version that expressly disavowed class antagonism and jettisoned the prolabor provisions of the original. The revised bill made collective bargaining voluntary and permitted company unions, and an ACLU communication urged members of Congress to oppose it as a "sham and a fraud" that would eviscerate organized labor. Although it garnered political approval, the amended bill never reached a vote. Roosevelt, convinced by a wave of strikes in the late spring that some kind of immediate action was necessary, pushed his National Industrial Adjustment Act, or Public Resolution No. 44, through Congress. The resolution authorized a National Labor Relations Board to conduct investigations, hold elections, and issue orders in furtherance of Section 7(a). Wagner thought it best to accept the stopgap measure while building support for a more aggressive proposal. A permanent resolution would have to wait for the new Congress.[40]

Meanwhile, the summer and fall of 1934 witnessed a wave of violent strikes by radicals as well as established AFL unions. The ACLU joined a coalition of leftist organizations including the IWW and the ILD in denouncing "a trampling upon workers' constitutional and civil rights" worse than any since the Red Scare. The first NLRB proved inadequate to the task of administering national labor policy. Employers summarily ignored its decisions, and when the Department of Justice finally overcame its reluctance to sue for enforcement, it lost in the federal courts. In January 1935, Roosevelt announced that the NLRB would not operate in industries already governed by code authorities. In February, a federal district court issued a decision in a case involving an NLB order, holding that manufacturing did not fall within Congress's power to regulate interstate commerce. Frank Nebeker, two decades after prosecuting the IWW in Chicago, argued and lost the government's case. By March 1935, NLRB chairman Francis Biddle pronounced that Section 7(a) was a mere "paper right, a sort of innocuous moral shibboleth."[41]

It was under these disheartening circumstances that self-described civil libertarians met in Washington in December 1934 to discuss "Civil Liberties under the New Deal." The purpose of the ACLU-sponsored conference was to recommend federal legislation, changes in federal regulations, and test cases in the courts "to protect rights of labor and minorities and to assure freedom of expression." The final program included representatives from a broad range of liberal and radical organizations, including the American Federation of Teachers, the ILD, the National Urban League, and the NAACP. Government officials were invited to respond to participants' arguments and data.[42]

The organizers sought to present a comprehensive picture of civil liberties in all its permutations. Panels touched on such far-ranging issues as antilynching legislation (carefully framed to preclude its use against striking workers), tribal autonomy for American Indians, transfer of colonial possessions from naval to civilian rule, and the rights of the unemployed. Participants debated proposals to expand asylum for political refugees, provide jury trials in postal censorship cases, and mandate airtime for radio rebuttals on controversial questions. There were occasional differences of opinion. Members of the panel on radio censorship clashed over the dangers of administrative discretion and the tradeoffs between private and public control of the airways. NAACP representatives refused to endorse a resolution protesting the Scottsboro convictions until language applauding the ILD's efforts was modified. On the whole, however, the delegates "showed surprising unanimity of opinion on fundamentals."[43]

Notwithstanding the persistence of Baldwin's small radical wing, the consensus largely carried over to the labor question. Even on contentious issues—for example, the collective bargaining rights of agricultural workers and discrimination against black workers under the NRA—disagreements were often more strategic than substantive. Labor representatives were critical of the manner in which Section 7(a) had been administered but held out hope for reform rather than revolution. So did the conference's predominantly Socialist Committee on Labor's Rights, which submitted a report condemning the NRA and regional labor boards for declining to enforce Section 7(a) but withholding criticism of Roosevelt and the NLRB. The statement was "vigorously debated" on the floor and passed, in amended form, with several opposing votes.[44]

The conference participants had "no illusions as to the place of law in achieving civil liberties," but they nonetheless proposed legislation that would undercut the influence of industrial interests. The recommendations they sent to Congress were familiar ones: to prohibit company unions and to require employers, in agriculture as well as industry, to bargain collectively with representatives of the majority of their workers. In fact, the resolutions were so compatible with mainstream liberal sentiment that many members of Congress promised their support.[45]

✦ ✦ ✦

By the spring of 1935, persistent labor tensions, coupled with a newly elected Congress, made meaningful labor legislation a realistic possibility for the first time. In February, Senator Wagner introduced his National Labor Relations Act (NLRA) in Congress. Wagner told Roger Baldwin that he had drawn on ACLU suggestions in drafting it. The new bill, which came to be known as the Wagner Act, was a revised version of the earlier iteration, with a preamble to ensure against constitutional challenge. As a measure of state involvement, it reflected a compromise approach. It shielded workers from employer retaliation for concerted activity, and it forced employers to the bargaining table when a majority of workers voted in a union. It also created a three-member quasi-judicial board to police unfair labor practices and made its orders enforceable by the federal courts. At the same time, however, the statute left the parties to negotiate their own substantive terms as a function of their relative bargaining strength. It legitimated the resort to economic weapons and explicitly preserved the right to strike.[46]

As with Wagner's earlier bill, labor endorsed it wholeheartedly: as one senator noted during debate over the bill, it codified the very provisions that the Commission on Industrial Relations had endorsed two decades before. The president once again waffled. Employers were just as adamant that it be defeated, and they were eagerly assisted in their propaganda efforts by the recently founded American Liberty League, an organization of conservative Democrats and other New Deal opponents who deemed the bill an affront to the American constitutional tradition.[47]

For the ACLU, debate over the Wagner Act was a defining event. The organization's labor committee remained skeptical of the New Deal state. Its dominant members included left-wing lawyer Carol Weiss King and Nathan Greene, coauthor with Felix Frankfurter of *The Labor Injunction,* whom Baldwin would later describe as a "fellow traveler with the Communist opposition." Both were also members of the IJA, which prepared a memorandum on the statute's faults. After considering the IJA's analysis, the ACLU board voted to oppose the proposed legislation.[48]

In a letter to Senators Wagner and Walsh, Baldwin expressed several concrete objections that would eventually become major civil liberties concerns. He criticized the exclusion of agricultural workers, who were disproportionately drawn from racial minorities and were arguably most in need of statutory protection. He also condemned the bill's failure to prohibit "discrimination on account of sex, race, color or political convictions." In so doing, he echoed concerns voiced by black unionists and civil rights groups as well as the Communist Party. The NAACP and the National Urban League each proposed amendments to address race discrimination in the Wagner Act, but labor advocates consistently rebuffed them. Some harbored patently racist views. Others were sympathetic but believed that "racial discrimination, etc. will only be eliminated after economic injustices are corrected." Even John P. Davis, executive secretary of the Joint Committee on National Recovery and cofounder of the National Negro Congress, advised Baldwin not to press the point, since prohibitions on discrimination "would be unenforceable in any real sense" and would "be used by the industry as another weapon to defeat the solidarity of the trade-union movement." In Davis's view, the ACLU would help more by urging the union rank and file to abandon segregation.[49]

In the coming years, such matters would demand resolution, with profound consequences for the relationship between the civil rights and labor movements in the United States. For the time being, however, the Wagner Act eschewed regulation of union membership criteria, and Wagner declined to discuss the issue with Baldwin. After all, Baldwin's fundamental opposition to federal regulation of labor relations rendered further discussion fruitless. Wagner explained, "Whether we will it or not, government in every country is going to be forced to play a more important role in every phase of economic life, and for that reason it seems to me more useful to attempt to direct the nature of that role rather than merely to state the truism, that government is likely to be influenced by the forces in society that happen to be strongest." More to the point, Wagner saw the state as the only feasible counterweight to powerful private interests. Over "a decently long period of time," appropriate state policies would buttress labor, not quash it. In fact, in Wagner's view, even Section 7(a) had proven to be "a galvanizing force."[50]

After fifteen years, the ACLU faced a fundamental quandary. The Wagner Act was premised on the progressive understanding that state institutions could advance labor's interests. The ACLU's right of agitation presupposed a hostility to state power that labor itself had abandoned and had never, in any case, held inviolate. For the ACLU, by contrast, state-skepticism permeated the civil liberties program. In *Scopes, Dennett,* and countless other cases, its lawyers had accentuated the dangers of government oversight of ideas. Its initial preference for direct action in labor disputes had generated a broader campaign against government interference with minority viewpoints, personal morality, and private life.

At the same time, in constructing a civil liberties coalition, the ACLU had channeled its antistate impulses into a circumscribed assault on government infringement of "personal rights," as opposed to labor activity in general. Within and outside the ACLU, competing visions of civil liberties vied for dominance. Baldwin's radical view, which cast the state as a tool of industrial interests, was quickly losing ground. In fact, the ACLU's radical core had paved the way to its own marginalization. The right of agitation began as a revolutionary right to restructure society through the exercise of collective power. The ACLU's work, on this model, entailed two basic assumptions: first, "that civil liberties constitute an inalienable right," and second, "that they are a necessary instrument of social change." By hitching its ambitions to the First Amendment, the ACLU had galvanized support for labor's right to strike. But the liberals it persuaded, and who increasingly influenced the organization's governing structure, foregrounded other constructions. Like the radicals, they regarded government interference with pickets and boycotts as illegitimate and unconstitutional. But they emphasized workers' freedom to communicate their ideas, not to reconstitute the state. On this understanding, Judge Amidon, head of the ACLU-sponsored National Committee on Labor Injunctions, worried that the organization would compromise its usefulness if it engaged in "campaigns against economic wrongs." Others agreed. Free speech theorist Alexander Meiklejohn, a member of the ACLU's national committee, criticized "the tendency of the Board to engage in industrial disputes instead of fighting for the maintaining of civil liberties in connection with them." Civil liberties might be employed to reshape society, but socioeconomic reordering was not an independent civil liberties goal.[51]

New Deal liberals recognized the risk of state overreaching. The Espionage Act prosecutions, arbitrary deportations, postal censorship, and other interwar practices had taught them the dangers of unchecked discretion. Still, most regarded administrative power as essential to modern governance. No less a First Amendment enthusiast than Zechariah Chafee Jr. thought that "social legislation," except in egregious cases, should be left to the "elected representatives of the people." Indeed, civil liberties were a means of legitimating state power, not undermining it. As Leon Whipple explained in a study sponsored by the ACLU, "The modern idea grants liberty to men not for the sake of their natural rights, but for the sake of the state."[52]

Just as civil liberties served the state, so the state served civil liberties. Many New Dealers believed that government regulation was a necessary prerequisite for a robust marketplace of ideas. "Social control, especially of economic forces," wrote philosopher and ACLU member John Dewey, "is necessary in order to render secure the liberties of the individual, including civil liberties." To adherents of that view, the notion that labor relations should be isolated from state intervention smacked of *Lochner*-era economic liberty, which (said Dewey) subjugated the underprivileged in the name of freedom. Advocates of the Wagner Act—a statute, after all, that promised administrative protection of the right to strike—were quick to translate such lessons into concrete terms. "You sound a little, I confess to say, like the Liberty League," Francis Biddle told Baldwin. "If that doesn't stop you I don't know what will."[53]

Biddle's criticism struck close to home. Baldwin had worked hard to distinguish the board's objections to federal labor legislation from employers'.

In fact, he hesitated to use the word "liberty," which the American Liberty League had recast as the "right to exploit the American people without governmental interference." Baldwin regarded that organization's agenda as antagonistic to the ACLU's, which linked liberty to the "freedom to agitate for social change without restraint." The ACLU's concerns were "human rights," not property rights, and they were expressed collectively, not atomistically. True, "reactionary employers" also opposed the Wagner Act, but as Baldwin assured Wagner, the ACLU's objections stemmed from "diametrically opposite grounds."[54]

Baldwin's vigorous protestations betrayed an underlying insecurity. The Wagner Act's defenders rejected Baldwin's objections as "too damned theoretical"—and Baldwin was hardly an exemplar of theoretical rigidity. As his labor allies poignantly reminded him, the courts had denied the rights of free speech, assemblage, and press, and yet it was no longer ACLU policy to "fight against the courts and to seek to strike down the rights guaranteed in the constitution." On the contrary, the organization had sought to invigorate the Bill of Rights, using the courts to their fullest advantage. If government agencies had often abridged labor's rights, the answer was to "release such agencies from the grip of the employing class," not to abandon state action altogether. Framed appropriately, legislative recognition of labor's rights could facilitate social change. As long as the ACLU operated on the "theory that social advances *can* be made within the present system," it would have to rely on the "instrumentalities of law" to pursue economic justice.[55]

✦ ✦ ✦

Pressed hard enough, Roger Baldwin and the board backed down. In May 1935, the ACLU held a referendum on the Wagner Act among the members of the national committee and local branches. The majority of the returns supported the proposed statute in some form, and the board voted to retract its opposition and take no official position on the bill. Wagner cordially acknowledged the development, though it had little practical effect. The Committee on Education and Labor reported favorably on the bill, and it passed both houses of Congress with decisive majorities. When the Supreme Court unanimously declared the code-making authority conferred by the NIRA to be unconstitutional in *Schechter Poultry Corporation v. United States*, it was clear that a new measure was necessary. And on July 5, 1935, President Roosevelt signed the Wagner Act into law.[56]

Even before the Wagner Act made its way into the statute books, left-liberal opposition to it evaporated. Communists abandoned their antagonism toward the New Deal in favor of an antifascist united front. The NAACP continued to advocate amendments to mitigate the Wagner Act's racially discriminatory effects, but it denounced conservative attempts to scrap the statute. And labor leaders wasted little time in using the new mandate to their fullest advantage. In the months after its passage, John L. Lewis and other AFL labor veterans turned aggressively to organizing unskilled workers in the mass production industries. When the AFL rebuffed their strategy in its 1935 convention, Lewis assembled his allies in the new Committee for Industrial Organization (CIO). He also worked closely with New Deal Democrats, who enacted additional protections to foster CIO efforts.[57]

In a curious repudiation of the ACLU's arguments during the early 1930s, the upsurge in support for New Deal labor policy was itself regularly framed in civil liberties terms. Emblematic of that development was the Senate Civil Liberties Committee, empowered by the Senate to conduct hearings and issue reports on employers' violations of labor's rights. In the spring of 1936, Wisconsin senator Robert M. La Follette Jr. called for an investigation of "violations of the rights of free speech and assembly and undue interference with the right of labor to organize and bargain collectively." To his surprise, the Senate acted on his resolution. La Follette (whose famous father had once been a law partner of the Free Speech League's Gilbert Roe) went on to chair the subcommittee, which was organized within the Senate's Committee on Education and Labor. Its task was to investigate interference by detective agencies, employer associations, and employers with "the formation of outside unions, collective bargaining, rights of assemblage and other liberties guaranteed by the Constitution." Lawyers might have quarreled with the notion that private employers could impede constitutional rights, but the slippage reflected a new permeability in understandings of state action. Just as the state channeled private interests (though perhaps not in the vulgar Marxist way the Communists implied), unpoliced private action bore the imprimatur of the state. There was no reason that employers, too, should not be constrained by the Constitution.[58]

Known as the La Follette Committee, the new body cast civil liberties as synonymous with the rights of labor, whether statutory or constitutional. Several members of the ACLU, including Morris Ernst, Norman Thomas, and Washington-based Gardner Jackson, helped to fashion the committee and formulate its program. The ACLU suggested situations that warranted investigation, and it recommended appropriate witnesses and offered to pay their travel expenses. Like La Follette, Baldwin thought employer interference with labor organizing should be the committee's focus. Newly reconciled to state intervention, he envisioned a full slate of federal legislation protecting the rights of labor against public and private curtailment. The La Follette Committee borrowed much of its staff from the NLRB, whose chairman, J. Warren Madden, was the first witness at the preliminary hearings. Underscoring the need for congressional assistance, Madden observed that "the right of workmen to organize themselves into unions has become an important civil liberty."[59]

Employing a proven civil liberties tactic, the La Follette Committee pitched its agenda as a foil to totalitarianism. "We are unquestionably the most powerful agency against Fascism in this country," one staff member wrote, casting the committee as a bastion of American democracy. Testifying at the congressional hearings, NLRB member Edwin S. Smith invoked the familiar ACLU argument that the suppression of civil liberties would provoke popular unrest. Efforts to forestall revolution through repression were self-defeating. "You cannot suppress freedom of expression," he admonished, "without rapidly undermining democracy itself."[60]

But if La Follette and his staff emphasized the time-honored value of expressive freedom, their true ambitions were more radical. As Smith explained in an address to the ACLU, "Civil liberties are not abstractions which hover above the passions of contending groups and can be successfully brought to earth to promote the general welfare." By the same token, La Follette believed that "the right of workers to speak freely and assemble peacefully is immediate and practical, a right which translates itself into the concrete terms of job security, fair wages and decent living conditions." Even as the ACLU shifted toward a value-neutral conception of free speech, the La Follette Committee envisioned civil liberties as a vehicle for economic justice.[61]

In the coming years, the ACLU would do its utmost to sustain the work of the La Follette Committee through publicity, lobbying, and letter-writing campaigns. Indeed, the organization considered it the single most important agency in exposing employer violations of workers' rights. And the ACLU would defend the Wagner Act, too, as an essential safeguard of labor's rights to strike, picket, and organize. Still, the perceived threat of state suppression would linger in the background. New Dealers like La Follette and Madden acknowledged the long shadow of court-ordered injunctions and police oppression, but they were concerned above all to constrain "private interests." By contrast, the ACLU harbored an enduring suspicion of state power. Eventually, that wariness would justify its defense of *employers'* "personal rights," in the form of constitutional protection for employer speech.[62]

✦ ✦ ✦

If policy debate over New Deal labor law fundamentally shaped the articulation of civil liberties theory during the 1930s, it was the legal fate of New Deal labor law that forged the modern relationship between civil liberties and the courts. Today, the New Deal settlement is thought to contain two entangled components: first, the relaxation of constitutional constraints on Congress's power to regulate the economy, and a corresponding curtailment of judicial review in those domains; and second, a dramatic expansion in judicial enforcement of the Bill of Rights. The latter is presumed to legitimate the former by ensuring that democratic policy reflects robust public debate, with adequate protections for minority interests.

Looking forward from the mid-1930s, however, the new arrangement was scarcely conceivable. In the absence of constitutional amendment, contemporaries assumed that judicial enforcement of expressive freedom went hand in hand with judicial policing of property rights, liberty of contract, and Congress's commerce power. Accordingly, civil liberties advocates faced a troubling dilemma: whether to risk invalidation of the Wagner Act and invest in judicial enforcement of the First Amendment, or, rather, jettison the courts and trust that legislators and administrators would adequately protect labor's rights.

For their part, employers were certain that their best hope lay in the courts. After passage of the Wagner Act, employers baldly refused to comply with the new legislation. They flagrantly opposed organizing efforts and routinely used such patently prohibited antilabor practices as industrial espionage and private policing. As in years past, they turned to the judiciary for vindication. The most visible face of the legal campaign was the American Liberty League's National Lawyers Committee, a group of corporate lawyers who argued that the Wagner Act was unconstitutional and would soon be invalidated. The organization offered free legal services to any client that agreed to "buck" New Deal legislation on constitutional grounds. Defending the practice as a matter of legal ethics, the ABA explicitly analogized the Liberty League's approach to the ACLU's. "Lawyers, farmers and mechanics alike enjoy the right of free speech and a free press and the right peaceably to assemble and petition the government for a redress of grievances," concluded the ABA.[63]

As soon as the Wagner Act took effect, dozens of challenges to the statute began making their way up through the federal courts. The NLRB, acknowledging the likelihood that the Supreme Court would vindicate the Liberty League's views, channeled much of its energy during 1935 and 1936 into crafting a legal defense. In May 1936, the Supreme Court declared in *Carter v. Carter Coal Company* that labor provisions in the Bituminous Coal Conservation Act were an unconstitutional extension of Congress's commerce power. Relying on *Carter Coal,* corporate attorneys easily convinced judges that the Wagner Act was inconsistent with a century of settled judicial precedent. Unlike Progressive Era legislation, which was often ambiguous, the Wagner Act was unmistakably protective of unions in its statutory language. It was also carefully drafted to weather judicial review. Courts nonetheless proved ready and willing to invalidate it on constitutional grounds. Lower court decisions severely undercut the NLRB's authority to issue orders in all but the most clearly interstate industries, such as transportation and communications. Industry and labor alike considered it a matter of time until the Supreme Court took up the Wagner Act and expressly declared a broader application unconstitutional.[64]

President Roosevelt was determined to forestall that outcome. With the help of Labor's Non-Partisan League, formed by John L. Lewis to mobilize labor voters, the 1936 presidential election resulted in a landslide victory for Roosevelt. The president considered the results a mandate for the New Deal, and he pledged to do whatever was necessary to preserve his labor policies. With the NLRB mired in constitutional litigation, its legitimacy squarely rejected by industry and its lawyers, preserving those labor policies meant doing something about the courts.

In February 1937, Roosevelt recommended a bill that would have authorized the appointment of an additional justice to the Supreme Court for every sitting justice who had not retired within six months after reaching the age of seventy, up to a maximum of six. Had the bill passed, Roosevelt would have been able to appoint six new justices. Although it was clearly designed to ensure a pro–New Deal majority, Roosevelt publicly justified the measure on the basis that the current justices were unable to meet the demands on their resources.[65]

The proposal polarized supporters of the New Deal. Organized labor endorsed it, as did many within the NLRB. Robert La Follette Jr. favored a constitutional amendment but thought Roosevelt's statutory measure was warranted as a stopgap measure. He acknowledged the importance of preserving civil liberties but argued that "no kind of legal guaranty has ever been able to protect minorities from the hatreds and intolerances let loose when an economic system breaks down." Similarly, the IJA endorsed the president's plan in the immediate term, though it hoped eventually for a constitutional amendment prohibiting any state or federal court from invalidating any legislation on constitutional grounds. "Judicial protection for civil liberties by means of the power to invalidate laws cannot be separated from judicial protection for the selfish interests of large property," it argued, nor from "dangerous restraints upon legislative authority to provide for the general welfare." With unmitigated confidence in majoritarian democracy, the pamphlet concluded that "there can be no true enforcement of the Bill of Rights in the interests of persons instead of wealth, except by the elected representatives of the people."[66]

The IJA pamphlet made a greater impact because it bore the stamp of the newly founded National Lawyers Guild, an organization of liberal and radical lawyers who supported the New Deal and distrusted the courts. The Guild's early executive committee included many prominent officials, academics, and politicians, as well as attorneys for both the AFL and CIO. Its first president—who lived to see the Roosevelt administration implement many of the measures he had championed for the Commission on Industrial Relations before his death from a heart attack in 1939—was Frank P. Walsh.

Also on the executive committee was the ACLU's Morris Ernst, who was instrumental in organizing and promoting the new organization. Ernst was an outspoken critic of the ABA, which he considered a force of reaction. He had refused to join as a young lawyer when he learned that the organization excluded black applicants. Ernst imagined the Guild as an opportunity for a segment of the legal profession to advance the causes that he himself promoted in his private legal work and public service for the NAACP and CIO, as well as the ACLU. As the Guild's "Call to American Lawyers" explained, the organized bar had shirked its responsibility to improve social conditions and protect civil rights. Worse, it had acted to block the will of the people as expressed in popular legislation. It had pandered to the interests of a minority of the profession, for whom "concern for liberty" was "secondary to its concern for property."[67]

The Guild's concern for liberty led it to support rather than oppose the judiciary reorganization bill. Although some of its members considered the plan "dangerous to Civil Liberties," they capitulated after discussion. Citing the collapse of civil liberties abroad and the corresponding need for vigilance in protecting them at home, the Guild adopted a series of resolutions on behalf of free speech and labor's rights. But the measures it advocated were justified by reference to policy goals, not constitutional limitations. At its first annual convention, Guild representatives appointed a committee to study proposed amendments to check the "unwarranted exercise of judicial power." In the interim, they urged Congress to pass the president's proposal.[68]

For other liberals, the potential dangers of the plan were not so easily overcome. Despite disagreeing with the Supreme Court on discrete constitutional issues, many regarded an independent judiciary as an important institution. Some supported efforts to curb the power of judicial review in economic cases through such means as constitutional amendment or statutory limitations on federal jurisdiction. But the president's proposal raised concerns about an unfettered executive in lieu of judicial power, and the bill's deceptive framing exacerbated reservations even among critics of the courts.

The ACLU, which had never resolved its own relationship to the judiciary, found it difficult to settle on a position. Despite its early doubts, the leadership had come to consider the Wagner Act a crucial civil liberties victory. On the other hand, the organization had increasingly adopted a judicial strategy for the vindication of civil liberties. Especially after Norris–LaGuardia, the federal courts had proven a favorable forum for the ACLU's efforts. While equivocal, such successes as *Stromberg* and Scottsboro hinted at the possibilities of a court-centered approach, particularly in cases involving infringements by state courts and legislatures. And in January 1937, the Supreme Court unanimously incorporated freedom of assembly into the Fourteenth Amendment in *De Jonge v. Oregon,* involving a Communist Party organizer convicted under Oregon's criminal syndicalism law. ACLU attorney Osmond K. Fraenkel argued the case, which was handled jointly with the ILD. Although it was decided on narrow grounds—the indictment had charged Dirk De Jonge with mere assistance of a Communist-run meeting—the ACLU called it "one of the most significant free speech decisions in recent years."[69]

Within the ACLU, discussion of judicial independence centered less on the plan itself than on the general desirability of judicial review. A few members spoke publicly about the president's proposal. John Haynes Holmes rejected it for its failure to face squarely "the problem of the Constitution and the Court," though he supported a constitutional amendment empowering Congress "to regulate commerce, protect public health and safety, and safeguard economic security," as the 1936 Democratic platform had proposed. Norman Thomas shared Holmes's reservations about the plan but would have voted the other way. He deemed it likely that a Supreme Court packed with pro–New Deal justices would be sympathetic to free speech and minority rights. Addressing concerns that court packing would pave the way to totalitarianism, he speculated that "a democracy impotent to act because it is paralyzed by a . . . judicial oligarchy would be more likely to invite a strong man to step in as Dictator." Still, he considered the president's solution deeply inadequate as a policy matter. What he feared most was not executive aggrandizement, but rather the misguided notion that a particular crop of justices, rather than the Constitution, was at fault. "It is amazing," he reflected, "to find organized Labor, with its traditional distrust of government by courts, waxing so enthusiastic for fifteen judges instead of nine."[70]

Thomas was adamant that a constitutional amendment should preserve the "right of the Court to defend civil liberty." True, the Supreme Court had rarely protected civil liberties against congressional encroachment. On the other hand, it had proven willing to intervene in cases involving repressive state legislation. Indeed, Thomas thought that stripping the court of all review power would prompt "a flood of legislation, especially in Southern states, of . . . a Ku Klux Klan sort." Others were even more adamant. "Have they forgotten the Oregon school case?" one member asked, imploring the board to condemn the president's plan. "The Scottsboro case? The De Jonge case? I hope a small group of New Dealers and socialists on the committee will not be permitted to overlook the point . . . that when the courts are subservient to the executive all hope of democracy dies."[71]

During the spring of 1937, debate within the ACLU intensified. Critics of the Supreme Court accused their opponents of whitewashing its record, while defenders of judicial review thought the detractors were exaggerating the justices' missteps. In an attempt to formulate a position, the ACLU circulated a survey to ten prominent lawyers, including Arthur Garfield Hays, Ernst, and

Thomas, requesting their views of the most commonly cited suggestions for curbing the courts. Although the returns were collected after the president's plan was unveiled, the survey predated it, and none of the participants addressed it. They did, however, offer their opinions of other proposals.[72]

The responses ran the gamut. Most of those polled thought the Supreme Court should retain its power to invalidate acts of Congress as well as state legislation on constitutional grounds. Several thought it acceptable to require a supermajority of the justices in decisions invalidating federal laws. The participants split over suggestions to permit a two-thirds congressional veto of constitutional decisions or to make the constitutional amendment process less demanding. Notably, all expressed willingness to endorse a carefully crafted provision restricting due process to procedural matters while making the Bill of Rights binding on the states. That is, even the staunchest supporters of an independent judiciary were willing to limit judicial review in the ordinary run of cases, as long as the courts continued to protect personal rights from legislative encroachment. In effect, that was the compromise that the Supreme Court itself ultimately adopted.[73]

The participants' comments illuminate the various tensions among self-described civil libertarians with respect to state and judicial power. Some thought the importance of the courts in safeguarding civil liberties was exaggerated, despite concerns about administrative abuse. Others thought the principal danger facing the country was the "expansion of the executive power into dictatorship" and defended the Supreme Court as "the greatest safeguard we have against executive arbitrariness." Ernst felt that some check on the Supreme Court was necessary, but he favored a congressional override and wrote a book advocating just that. Lloyd K. Garrison, dean of the University of Wisconsin Law School and the first chair of the original NLRB, thought that all of the measures posed some danger to civil liberties and cautioned against "giving majorities too much say over minorities." Thomas preferred a constitutional amendment authorizing Congress to legislate in "economic and social matters" and restricting judicial review only in those domains. He emphasized that a simple count of Supreme Court decisions would underestimate the effectiveness of the federal judiciary in fostering civil liberties. He accentuated the "psychological effect of the review power of the Court," which he judged more significant than critics of the judiciary appreciated.[74]

In May, the ACLU issued an analysis of the Supreme Court's record in civil liberties cases, in an effort to educate the public regarding the pending proposals. Prepared by Fraenkel, who had represented two of the Scotts-boro defendants as well as De Jonge, the report tallied the court's decisions in such far-ranging areas as military trials, slavery and peonage, searches and seizures, freedom of religion, education, aliens and citizenship, freedom of speech, and labor relations. Pointing to decisions sustaining convictions under the Espionage Act and state criminal syndicalism laws, Fraenkel con-cluded that the justices had succumbed to "popular hysteria." Nonetheless, he held out hope for future gains. In responding to the board's survey on proposals for limiting judicial power, he emphasized that "so long as we be-lieve in safeguarding the rights of minorities, the power of review is essen-tial to protect these rights."[75]

More than ten years after the ACLU championed Robert La Follette Sr.'s proposal to curtail the authority of the courts, and more than two decades after demands for judicial recall failed to sway national majorities, a coali-tion of liberals, radicals, and labor leaders pushed the judiciary to the brink of institutional overhaul. Since its founding, the ACLU had sought to shield the labor movement from the arbitrary exercise of judicial power. And yet, on the cusp of victory, the organization faltered. Citing substantial disagreement among its members, the ACLU remained neutral on the ju-diciary reorganization plan, just as it had withheld official judgment on the Wagner Act. On the New Deal's momentous challenge to judicial review, the nation's staunchest organizational advocate for civil liberties took no position.

✦ ✦ ✦

Although the ACLU was noncommittal, debate over the court-packing plan featured an unexpected champion for the judicial enforcement of civil lib-erties. In the face of the president's proposal, conservative lawyers, most of whom had resisted the Supreme Court's speech-friendly turn, evinced a sudden enthusiasm for judicial enforcement of the Bill of Rights.

Even before the court-packing controversy erupted, there were hints of the new direction. For decades, conservatives had lambasted legislative and administrative incursions on their business prerogatives. Often, they cast regulatory initiatives as threats to American freedom. Sometimes, as in *Meyer* and *Pierce,* they professed a broader concern for individual rights. A few distinguished lawyers courted labor support for the judiciary by com-paring administrative intrusion on property rights with administrative abuses of radical deportees.[76]

Still, conservative endorsements of civil liberties remained a rarity until the mid-1930s. In 1935, Archibald Stevenson (who had railed against the ACLU for decades) acknowledged that any proposed sedition statute would be "decried as destructive of political freedom and its authors ridiculed as 'Red baiters.'" He voiced the dominant conservative sentiment when he dismissed such characterizations as misguided, emanating either from the targets of suppression or from well-meaning interlopers who "fail[ed] to understand what that freedom really is." Assessing the field the same year, the president of the Association of American Law Schools observed, "There is heard on every side much talk of the Constitution, but practically nothing is heard of the Bills of Rights."[77]

But the New Deal presented fresh challenges. To be sure, it was property rights that corporations most staunchly defended, as they had during and after the First World War. And on that score, existing constitutional measures—for example, the Commerce Clause and liberty of contract—provided adequate cover against administrative meddling. Still, a growing conservative contingent was exploring the appeal of other angles.

Some incursions were particularly amenable to the new frame. The corporate press had long defied censorship on policy and constitutional grounds, and when New Deal regulation threatened, media lawyers were quick to raise the banner of the First Amendment. The new appeals existed alongside the old. "You don't have any liberty in any country where you don't have property rights," maintained Elisha Hanson, who served as counsel to the American Newspaper Publishers Association and to the reactionary media magnate William Randolph Hearst. But the old allure of private property as the anchor of American freedom was quickly fading, and so Hanson frequently denounced government regulatory efforts as infringements on First Amendment freedoms, instead. In the domain of advertising, for example, he condemned regulation for "restricting the freedom of the press," rejecting arguments by the ACLU and other entities that media consolidation and corporate influence made meaningful free speech impossible. Indeed, in a move that anticipated the Supreme Court's reasoning nearly half a century later, he defended advertising for its salutary social function, namely, the "dissemination of information about the goods, services and ideas of those who are sufficiently interested in getting this information to the public to pay to have it disseminated." Besides, as business groups understood, advertising promoted not only goods and services, but also the "American way."[78]

On Hanson's account, advertising revenues served another useful purpose, as well: they funded hundreds of millions of dollars in expenditures on news service and employment. Given the demands of modern media operations, advertising was the only alternative to the old British practice of taxing newspapers. In Hanson's view, such taxes ran afoul of the First Amendment. Invoking the old maxim that "the power to tax is the power to destroy," he railed against efforts by Louisiana's Huey Long to tax state newspapers into submission—an anti-censorship position validated by a unanimous Supreme Court in its 1936 decision in *Grosjean v. American Press Company.* By the same token, Hanson opposed all efforts to regulate child labor in the newspaper industry, including the NRA newspaper code and proposed constitutional amendments. Evoking *Meyer* and *Pierce,* he rejected Congress's power to "direct the course of life of any one else's sons or daughters." But he also made (in Roger Baldwin's estimation) a "false appeal" to press freedom.[79]

Above all, the corporate media drew a sharp line between government regulation, which it opposed, and private influence, which it celebrated. The ACLU consistently fought state censorship of conservative speech, including Kansas's attempt to suppress a film opposing the court-packing plan. At the same time, it had long complained about the biases of the corporate press. "You cannot have genuine freedom when you have two radio chains controlling these great means of communication, nor a motion picture monopoly nor a highly organized press, all responsive to the owners of property," Baldwin explained. In fact, Baldwin considered private censorship in service of business interests to be "vastly more important" than the government variety.[80]

Representatives of the media, notwithstanding their affinities for the ACLU's anticensorship campaign, could not have disagreed more sharply. The founding president of the National Broadcasting Company attributed the popularity of American radio to the "freedom of speech and entertainment available on the air," which he equated with lax government regulation. Louis G. Caldwell, the first general counsel of the Federal Radio Commission and chairman of the ABA's Special Committee on Administrative Law, explicitly distinguished between government censorship and private control. Contrary to "certain statements published in the name of the American Civil Liberties Union," he advised, the First Amendment extended only to the former. From Caldwell's perspective, the effects of advertising and corporate power on programming were antidotes to censorship, not a cause. "In my opinion," he advised, "there is no better way of bringing on a Hitler regime over radio in this country than by having the government attempt to interfere with private censorship—which, in most cases, is simply perfectly legitimate editorial selection—and by seeking additional governmental interference with broadcast programs." If content was unduly homogenous, the solution was market competition between the radio and the press.[81]

During the Red Scare, progressives had chastised conservatives for defending business autonomy while abridging freedom of speech. When the tables turned, it was conservatives who rebuked the liberals for their hypocrisy. They emphasized that misleading expression often posed a greater danger than the misbranding or adulteration of consumer goods. Even more worrisome, the regulation of business would pave the way to censorship of the press. "We cannot have regimentation of any sort without also regimenting ideas," Hanson argued.[82]

Outside the media context, conservative targets of New Deal regulation ordinarily clung to tested constitutional claims. Before the 1930s, "conservative members of the legal profession" (as a Philadelphia lawyer observed in the *ABA Journal*) believed the Supreme Court's decisions adequately insulated the speech rights of an "honest man." As the decade wore on, however, perceived abuses often presented as infringements on personal rights. The most prominent example involved the Senate's Special Committee to Investigate Lobbying Activities, established in July 1935. Chaired by Hugo Black, an Alabama senator and future justice of the Supreme Court, the committee's tactics prompted a strong public protest from the ACLU. In 1935, in the course of investigating a lobbying campaign by the utility companies in opposition to the Wheeler-Rayburn Act, the committee ordered Western Union to turn over telegrams transmitted on the companies' behalf. Its revelation that the companies had sent millions of letters and telegrams to Congress in the names of concerned citizens contributed to passage of the statute, which imposed drastic restrictions on utilities. The following year, the Black committee expanded its sweep and subpoenaed telegraphs by prominent opponents of the New Deal. The Chicago law firm Winston, Strawn and Shaw—targeted by the probe because partner Silas Strawn, a past president of the ABA, had ties to the American Liberty League—successfully claimed that the mass subpoenas were invalid on Fourth Amendment grounds. Washington attorney Frank J. Hogan, who would soon become ABA president, served as counsel to the firm and denounced the committee's actions as "one of the numerous attempts by congress to destroy the guarantees under the bill of rights."[83]

Increasingly, lobbying itself was cast as an exercise of free speech. As with any perceived affront to civil liberties, the nature of the transgression was a matter of perspective. When corporate influence over Washington came under attack in the 1920s, business boosters hastened to defend the practice in *Nation's Business,* the official organ of the Chamber of Commerce of the United States. One author defended "propaganda" as "merely the exercise of freedom of speech by a citizen in a manner which some other citizen does not like," and "lobbying" as "merely the exercise of the right of petition to Congress by somebody whose cause is thought by somebody else to be a poor and bad one." The Chamber of Commerce was clear about its function as a lobbying group, devised to sway legislation and administration as well as public opinion.[84]

When the business-friendly policies of the Roaring Twenties yielded to the regulatory impulse of the 1930s, conservatives briefly tempered their enthusiasm for concentrated interest-group power. Some attributed the "socialist tinge" of Depression-era legislation to the undue influence of "organized minorities" clamoring for their share of subsidies and rewards. But changing political winds, along with the Senate's lobby committee and other attacks on conservative propaganda, soon shifted the scales. By the end of the decade, the Committee on Public Relations of the National Association of Manufacturers reported that American demand for the "conservative viewpoint" was exceeding the organization's supply. In 1938, when the La Follette Committee exposed a National Association of Manufacturers "propaganda campaign," the press defended the expenditures as a justifiable response to tax-funded government publicity programs and decried the announcement as an attack on free speech. According to the *Cincinnati Times-Star,* Robert M. La Follette Jr. was "interested in protecting the civil liberties only of those on his side of the political fence."[85]

In a curious turn of events, the Senate's lobby committee followed up its aggressive investigations of conservative lobbyists with a more classic threat to freedom of the press. Indiana senator Sherman Minton, who chaired the committee after Black's 1937 appointment to the United States Supreme Court, focused the committee's efforts on the national newspaper conglomerates. According to Minton (himself a future Supreme Court justice), corporate advertisers and large financial institutions were dictating newspaper content and manipulating political debate: under cover of press freedom, they were "control[ling] thought . . . by their command of money." Minton led charges against the Hearst press, which had roundly condemned the committee's subpoena orders, and subsequently against media mogul Frank E. Gannett, who in turn accused Minton of dictatorial methods. The spat with Gannett eventually prompted Minton to introduce legislation making it unlawful to "publish information known to be false"—a measure that even Minton's fellow New Dealers rejected for infringing on press freedom. It is no accident that Gannett's response to the court-packing plan was to organize a Committee to Uphold Constitutional Government, which attacked the New Deal for "abrogat[ing] the constitutional guarantee of free speech" and hailed the courts as the guardian of Jews, factory workers, and the "colored race."[86]

For many conservatives, it was the New Deal assault on the judiciary itself that motivated a reevaluation of personal rights. As early as 1935, the American Liberty League celebrated the lawyer's duty to "to defend the individual against the tyranny of the majority," and it pledged the pro bono services of its attorneys in constitutional cases (an offer that prompted one Liberty League lawyer to express his "sympathy for the work of [the] Civil Liberties Union in defending constitutional rights"). The following year, the president of the ABA, speaking at the annual meeting of the Chamber of Commerce of the United States, invoked the horror of totalitarian abuses to counter jurisdiction-stripping proposals that would have impeded judicial review. But the true turning point was the announcement of President Roosevelt's court-packing plan. The ABA staunchly opposed any restriction on the power of the federal courts. In the 1910s, the organization had campaigned throughout the country against the evils of judicial recall. Two decades later, it mobilized a massive publicity drive that substantially weakened the prospects for passage of the president's bill. In convincing Congress and the American people to preserve judicial independence, the Supreme Court's recent decisions upholding civil liberties were indispensable tools.[87]

In the spring of 1937, an ABA committee brainstormed methods for arousing popular hostility toward reorganization of the judiciary. Its "best idea" was to develop a series of radio broadcasts featuring "famous case[s] in which personal rights have been upheld by the Supreme Court." The same approach carried over to the ABA's written materials. In the two issues of the *ABA Journal* devoted to the court-packing plan, danger to the Bill of

Rights was a dominant theme. One author advised minority groups, including organized labor, that an independent judiciary was "their best friend." Another charged that labor leaders, by attacking the court, were undermining their own future strength; he assumed that the right to organize required freedom of press and assembly and cautioned that an unfettered Congress could someday outlaw unions. William Joseph Donovan (later a founder of the Office of Strategic Services) devoted an entire article to "the question whether the existence of an independent judiciary in this country has protected the civil liberties of minority groups." Citing *Pierce v. Society of Sisters, Meyer v. Nebraska,* the Scottsboro cases, and *De Jonge v. Oregon,* he concluded that they had.[88]

Even as New Dealers decried the ABA's position as a self-serving assault on majoritarian will, the appeal to the Bill of Rights proved persuasive. Testifying before Congress against the court-packing plan, speaker after speaker raised civil liberties concerns. "The rights of all racial groups and religions, all minorities, in America, are not asserted in the Congress, or our States, or our legislatures," pronounced New York senator Royal S. Copeland, invoking free speech for Communists and "those poor Negro boys" in Scottsboro, Alabama. "They are asserted in the Constitution and enforced by the courts of justice." Also citing Scottsboro, along with *Meyer* and *Pierce,* David I. Walsh (succeeded as chairman of the Senate's labor committee by Black) considered an "independent judiciary" to be the only meaningful check on "tyrannical interferences with the liberties of the individual." Even Charles C. Burlingham, an esteemed lawyer and civic reformer who counted Learned Hand and Felix Frankfurter among his friends, believed "the Court, and especially the present Court, [had] stood strongly and consistently for free speech, free press and free assembly."[89]

✦ ✦ ✦

Defenders of an independent judiciary habitually assumed that judicial protection of personal rights also entailed the judicial protection of property. Preserving one without the other appeared unlikely in practice, if not undesirable as a matter of policy. It was a surprise to nearly everyone, then, when the Supreme Court—just months after reversing Dirk De Jonge's conviction under Oregon's criminal syndicalism statute—upheld a minimum-wage law from neighboring Washington. Two weeks later, when the court decided *NLRB v. Jones and Laughlin Steel Corporation*, it embarked on a new era in American constitutional law.[90]

For three long months during the spring of 1937, as the public debated the president's court-packing plan, the justices deliberated over five cases testing the constitutionality of the Wagner Act. In April, Chief Justice Hughes—who had once declared that "no one has a vested right in the common law"—wrote for a five-member majority in upholding the broadest construction of the statute. All of the companies in question, he insisted, operated within interstate commerce, and the NLRB's procedures were consistent with due process. Employers and unions were not required to agree on a contract, he concluded, but they could lawfully be compelled to try.[91]

In upholding the Wagner Act, the Supreme Court upended employers' common-law prerogatives and came astoundingly close to recognizing a right of agitation. To be sure, it upheld the statute as a legitimate exercise of Congress's commerce power, not as a means of enforcing a constitutional right to organize under the First Amendment. Although labor lawyers and New Deal lawmakers often invoked constitutional language, the NLRB had chosen to frame its legal claims on less controversial grounds. Still, Justice Hughes cast the "right of employees to self-organization" as a "fundamental right." Indeed, it was every bit as important as an employer's right "to organize its business."[92]

The ACLU's Morris Ernst opined during the New Deal that "the decisions of the courts have nothing to do with justice"—that "the point of view of the judge derives from the pressure of public opinion." Ever since 1937, critics and commentators have debated whether the "switch in time that saved nine" reflected popular pressures of that sort. Among the cynics, few were more scathing than Felix Frankfurter, who famously berated the justices for their lawlessness. Frankfurter construed Justice Owen Roberts's about-face as conclusive proof that the "Court is in politics." The Wagner Act decisions, he reported two weeks later, "do not make me feel any better about the institution, whatever I may feel about the results of the cases."[93]

For Frankfurter, as for others within the ACLU, the Supreme Court's 1937 decisions reflected a concession to political realities. For the ACLU leadership, though not for Frankfurter, they reinforced the view that the judiciary might be made to serve progressive ends. The crucial thing, as President Roosevelt had come to understand, was to populate the courts with sympathetic judges. "Before any person is appointed to the bench in the future, there should be a very stringent cross examination by the proper committees of Congress as to the man's economic faith," Ernst had counseled at mid-decade. "It is about time that we got away from the idea that there is such a thing as a good lawyer or a bad lawyer. He is either a man of our prejudices or of other prejudices."[94]

For the future of civil liberties, what mattered most was not why the Supreme Court reversed course, but what the new path portended. And in the immediate term, the answer remained uncertain. For one thing, the controversy over judicial review was far from settled. Even after *Jones and Laughlin Steel*, opponents of the court-packing plan were "amazed" it was defeated. More than half a year later, they thought it "possible, even likely," that a new constitutional crisis would emerge, and with it a renewed assault on the judiciary. The Supreme Court would hear "several crucial cases" over the coming months involving public utilities regulation, national wage and hour legislation, and the Tennessee Valley Authority. It seemed plausible that the justices would prove unwilling to uphold New Deal initiatives in all of them, and "if even in one case, the law was held void . . . it might mean that the President would return to the attack."[95]

More fundamentally, the Supreme Court's decisions prompted yet another reevaluation of the ACLU's court-centered strategy for First Amendment claims. In the challenge to the Wagner Act, it was conservatives rather than liberals who invoked the First Amendment. In *Associated Press v. NLRB*, decided the same day as *Jones and Laughlin Steel*, the Supreme Court held that the Associated Press (AP) operated in interstate commerce and was thus within the reach of the statute. The AP, however, had attempted an alternative defense. Elisha Hanson had argued since passage of the Wagner Act that application of its provisions to the press was an unconstitutional abridgment of the First Amendment. To permit the government to "exercise a direct control over the gathering and dissemination of information" by interfering in newspapers' employment practices was to subject America to totalitarian tendencies better suited to "the dictator-ridden countries of Europe."[96]

Testing Hanson's arguments before the Supreme Court, the AP repudiated its obligation to bargain with unionized workers as incompatible with the First Amendment. "Freedom of expression" was just as vital as the due process of law, the brief proclaimed, and the Constitution prohibited the government from controlling or even influencing it. Ernst disagreed. Squaring off against the AP on behalf of the American Newspaper Guild he helped to found, Ernst dismissed the notion that the First Amendment authorized discrimination against unionized newspaper employees. In fact, he considered abrogation of the duty to bargain a graver First Amendment threat, and he implied that government might owe a constitutional duty to protect labor's rights. Labor strife would only undercut expressive freedom: a free press required a strong union.[97]

Justice Roberts's opinion in *Associated Press v. NLRB* dismissed the notion that a newspaper publisher has special immunity from generally applicable laws. The First Amendment, the court's majority concluded, confers "no special privilege to invade the rights and liberties of others." But Justice George Sutherland was not convinced. In a dissent joined by Justices Willis Van Devanter, James Clark McReynolds, and Pierce Butler, he hailed the First Amendment freedoms as "cardinal rights" and stressed the need to "preserve them against any infringement, however slight." The same justices who regarded the Wagner Act as an unconstitutional incursion on freedom of contract enjoined their colleagues to resist any encroachment on the First Amendment, no matter how trivial—"For the saddest epitaph which can be carved in memory of a vanished liberty is that it was lost because its possessors failed to stretch forth a saving hand while yet there was time."[98]

Then, one month after *Jones and Laughlin Steel,* another landmark case reached the United States Supreme Court. Instead of the right to organize into unions, it involved the right to organize for the Communist Party. In 1932, Angelo Herndon was convicted of "inciting insurrection" in Atlanta, Georgia, for distributing literature urging unemployment relief and racial equality, among other causes. The ILD took charge of the case, with ACLU assistance. It cast the conviction of the "young Negro" and Communist organizer as a "challenge to the Negro people of the country" as well as "to all American labor." Sympathetic liberals and northern conservatives emphasized the racial dimensions of the case, but the ACLU attorney who argued it in the Supreme Court focused on First Amendment objections.[99]

In *Herndon v. Lowry,* the tables turned. As in *Associated Press,* Justice Roberts wrote for the majority. Justice Van Devanter wrote a dissent, in which Justices McReynolds, Sutherland, and Butler joined. This time, it was Justice Roberts who heralded the First Amendment. When the decision came down, the *New York Times* reported "conflict of opinion among lawyers as to whether the Roberts opinion merely held that the Reconstruction Law had been illegally applied to Herndon, or whether the statute had been invalidated by the Supreme Court." Either way, the majority's language signaled increased concern for expressive freedom. "The power of a state to abridge freedom of speech and of assembly is the exception, rather than the rule," Roberts wrote, and "the judgment of the Legislature is not unfettered." Just weeks after inhibiting the application of the Fourteenth Amendment to employers' hiring practices, the liberal majority extended it to subversive speech. And Justice Van Devanter, who had so recently feared the slippery slope to authoritarianism, insisted that "the constitutional guaranty of freedom of speech and assembly does not shield or afford protection for acts of intentional incitement to forcible resistance to the lawful authority of a state."[100]

A few keen observers perceived the contradictions, but Frankfurter was not surprised. "The fact of the matter is that the Justices who resist the social obligations of property, and apply Herbert Spencer's 'Social Statics' instead of the Constitution, are also the Justices who have had no respect for civil liberties, i.e., for the protection of views that they regard as dangerous," he told his friend Charles C. Burlingham. "To think of Butler and Co. as safe-guards against fascism is really funny," he reflected, in an assessment that resonates with today's understandings.[101]

Yet Frankfurter's assessment was too glib. After extolling the Supreme Court's civil liberties decisions to defeat the president's reorganization plan, some conservatives had come to believe their own rhetoric. A March 1937 editorial in *Nation's Business* presented police noninterference with a massive Communist meeting in New York as the essence of American democracy. "Never was free speech freer," it proclaimed. "What passes for 'liberalism' comes to its fullest expression under the protective wing of the tolerant 'conservatism' it so roundly abuses." Even more presciently, the influential industrialist and former Wisconsin governor Walter J. Kohler mused at the annual meeting of the Chamber of Commerce of the United States in April (in an address warning against the "destruction of civil liberties") that "freedom of enterprise and personal freedom are but expressions of one and the same thing." Statements like these would soon became commonplace. Faced with dwindling public enthusiasm for unchecked economic competition, the NAM launched a public relations programs to "re-create a public understanding of the vital inter-relationship between private competitive business and personal and political freedom," that is, "freedom of assembly, freedom of speech and the press, freedom of religion, and freedom to choose their rulers." For the time being, however, the uses to which a conservative First Amendment might be put remained inchoate.[102]

Two months after the Wagner Act decision, the Supreme Court inched even closer to the ACLU's foundational goals. In *Senn v. Tile Layers Protective Union*, it upheld a Wisconsin statute that authorized labor picketing and prohibited employers from obtaining injunctive relief, effectively reversing its decision in *Duplex Printing Press*. In its amicus brief defending the statute it had helped to draft, the ACLU did not even mention the First Amendment. Nonetheless, Justice Louis D. Brandeis, writing for the majority, invoked constitutional principles. He concluded that union members were entitled to publicize the facts of a labor dispute, "for freedom of speech is guaranteed by the Federal Constitution." It is no wonder that the future Supreme Court justice Robert H. Jackson called the "avalanche of victories" in the spring of 1937 "a legal revolution, as real and meaningful as any ever fought on field of battle." In Jackson's assessment, "these were the greatest days in labor's legal history."[103]

The Supreme Court's transformation in the spring of 1937 has rightly been labeled a revolution, even as its most radical dimensions have largely been forgotten. That summer, the eminent political scientist and constitutional scholar Edward S. Corwin reflected on its implications in the *New Republic*. American constitutional law had "undergone a number of revolutions," he observed, "but none so radical, so swift, so altogether dramatic as that witnessed by the term of Court just ended." What made the new approach radical was less its deference to congressional judgment than its bold reimagining of "liberty" to require the assistance of the state. In Corwin's account, a majority of the justices had recognized liberty "as something that may be infringed by other forces as well as by those of government; indeed, something that may require the positive intervention of government against those other forces." Corwin, who had testified on behalf of the court-packing plan before Congress, had long castigated the judiciary for its outmoded adherence to laissez-faire. That the Supreme Court had finally awakened to social and economic reality "mark[ed] a development of profound significance in our constitutional history."[104]

The ACLU was never quite so bold as Corwin about the scope of the Supreme Court's holdings. In December 1937, Roger Baldwin described the Bill of Rights as "a defensive document guaranteeing the citizen protection against the invasion of his rights by the government." By contrast, "the more positive program for civil rights [was] to be found in the Labor Relations Acts and the other guarantees under which democratic organization in industry becomes not only a defensive but a positive force." And yet, for the first time, the two branches were components of a single civil liberties project. The coupling of *Senn* with *Jones and Laughlin Steel* liberated the ACLU at long last to pursue a constitutional strategy, without fearing its tendency to legitimate liberty of contract or judicial review.[105]

Assessing the state of civil liberties as 1937 drew to a close, the ACLU was more optimistic than ever before. Far from creating a "federal dictatorship," Baldwin told a conservative critic, the New Deal state was admirably serving civil liberties goals. The La Follette Committee had proven the "most helpful single agency in exposing violations of labor's rights by employers." As for the Wagner Act, the ACLU "accept[ed] the reasoning of the Supreme Court."[106]

7

The Civil Liberties Consensus

R ESIDENTS of Jersey City during the 1930s had little doubt about the attitude of their municipal government toward labor relations. Their mayor, Frank Hague, had staked the economic vitality of the New Jersey industrial center on its employer-friendly reputation. Signs posted on the major thoroughfares made Hague's commitments unmistakable. "This Is Jersey City," they boldly proclaimed. "Everything for Industry."[1]

By most accounts, Hague's opposition to organized labor was a matter of convenience rather than conviction. Hague was among America's last and most powerful political bosses, and for the first half of his thirty-year reign he had courted endorsements from labor groups. In the early 1930s, however, Jersey City was struggling. Hague had raised taxes on local industry even while the Depression chiseled away at its profits, and by mid-decade, the situation had reached a breaking point. His solution was to lure New York–based employers to Hudson County by clamping down on unions. "We took a hand and reorganized labor without regard for national heads of organized labor themselves," he reassured prospective employers in 1934. "The leaders who planted a feeling of hatred in the minds of the men are gone, and in their place are leaders with whom you can deal."[2]

Labor's dramatic successes over the course of the 1930s emboldened union organizers to challenge Hague's new orientation. Hague, however, was determined to stand his ground. His police force harassed, beat, and arrested agitators and shut down union picketing, meetings, and leafleting— even after Congress as well as the state and federal courts had made it unlawful to do so. Initial efforts to challenge local ordinances and police

226

practices in the courts were thwarted when Hague refused to make arrests. Agitators were simply deported across city lines by southbound buses or by ferry or the Hudson Tubes to Manhattan—a policy, according to Arthur Garfield Hays, that violated the "fundamental right of the American citizen to be arrested."[3]

Hague's hostility toward organized labor would have been unremarkable a decade earlier, but it was unusual for a vice-chairman of the Democratic National Committee during the New Deal. It prompted highly ranked Democratic officials to challenge Hague's fitness for office and, less publicly, Franklin D. Roosevelt's integrity. Still, when the liberal establishment and much of mainstream opinion turned against Hague in the late 1930s, it was not because of his labor policies. Indeed, in the public relations battle over Hague's suppressive activity, critics of Jersey City's policies were quick to point out their own indifference toward the broader labor issues involved.

The ACLU was the surprising pioneer of the new approach. At mid-decade, Roger Baldwin still considered "the struggle of capital and labor [to be] the most conspicuous and vital application of the free speech principle." The ACLU routinely sent its representatives into the field alongside union organizers, as it had throughout the 1920s. Indeed, in 1934, board member Corliss Lamont was arrested in Jersey City for picketing. And yet, just a few years later, ACLU leaders carefully divorced advocacy of free speech from the underlying messages of the radical groups they were defending. At trial and in interviews, they stressed the rights of fascists and conservatives as well as radicals. In their courtroom arguments and briefs, the enemy was censorship, not inequality or capitalist oppression.[4]

By the late 1930s, Hague's insistence that a "real American" would never invoke the Bill of Rights sounded outdated, even unpatriotic. Dozens of prominent national organizations condemned his flagrant disregard for rule of law. Free speech advocates emphasized the similarities between Hague's autocratic practices and similar speech restrictions under Adolf Hitler and Joseph Stalin. Like Father Charles E. Coughlin and Huey Long, Boss Hague was emblematic of dangerous totalitarian tendencies within the United States. His oft-quoted pronouncement, "I am the law," was palpable evidence that fascism could happen at home. Indeed, the eminent theologian Reinhold Niebuhr regarded "Mayor Hague's defiance of our laws [a]s one of the most flagrant pieces of fascism in the modern day."[5]

With the force of public opinion behind it, the ACLU adopted a bold strategy in Jersey City. When Hague prohibited CIO leafleting and rejected meeting requests by the ACLU and the Socialist Party, ACLU attorney Morris Ernst sought and secured an injunction in federal court. The litigation culminated in the Supreme Court's 1939 decision in *Hague v. CIO*, which affirmed the district court's order. The organization's victory, though limited, was celebrated throughout the country.[6]

That reaction reflected a sea change in popular and political understandings of civil liberties. By the time *Hague* was decided, the ACLU had helped to establish that some modes of censorship—in the realms of academic freedom, sex education, and literature, for example—were more damaging than edifying. With the *Hague* case, for the first time, many Americans enthusiastically endorsed the judicial protection of radical speech, as well. Most tellingly, the ABA, known for its conservative politics, created a Committee on the Bill of Rights in 1938. Its first action was to file an amicus curiae brief on behalf of free speech in *Hague v. CIO*. Mainstream newspapers celebrated the ABA's intervention and denounced Mayor Hague as a menace to American democracy.[7]

The ACLU's disavowal of radicalism was effective, but it precipitated a deep rift with the Left. In time, it eclipsed the radical origins of the civil liberties movement, just as its proponents hoped it would.

✦ ✦ ✦

"For a great many years," according to the *New York Herald-Tribune*, the United States Constitution was "a dead letter in Jersey City." Frank Hague repeatedly won reelection by overwhelming margins, and there was little vocal opposition to his administration. Born in 1876 to Irish immigrants, Hague spent his youth (as he perpetually reminded his constituents) in the slums of Jersey City's Horseshoe district, and he was intimately familiar with the gritty realities of Hudson County governance. Graft and election fraud were staples of the Jersey City tradition, and although Hague presented himself as a municipal reformer, he adeptly turned them to his advantage.[8]

Control and expansion of the municipal payroll was a core feature of Hague's influence, and it was expensive. During the Depression, companies could not afford to pay the city's high tax rate, and many relocated. Federal assistance helped some, notwithstanding Hague's complicated relationship with President Roosevelt. Although he had favored Al Smith for the 1932 Democratic nomination, Hague delivered New Jersey for Roosevelt by a margin of 30,000 votes. The president disliked him, but he understood his importance, and Hague claimed to receive 500,000 federal dollars a month for distribution to the needy.[9]

Still, Hague faced a dramatic shortfall in the municipal budget. His solution was to ensure that businesses could offset high taxes by paying low wages to unorganized workers. In his early years, Hague had declared himself "a friend of labor" and had regularly defended strikes. By the early 1930s, however, organized labor was no longer consistent with Hague's design for Jersey City. When the New Jersey Senate considered a state anti-injunction bill like those passed by neighboring states, Hague denounced it as a threat to New Jersey industry and ensured that it would never reach a vote. Meanwhile, Jersey City passed a series of measures restricting public meetings and handbilling, including the 1930 ordinance at the heart of *Hague v. CIO,* which forbade public assembly without a permit and authorized denial of a permit to prevent riots or "disturbances." And the state's Disorderly Persons Act of 1936 permitted the arrest of any person who could not "give a good account of himself"; under the statute, pickets were arrested and jailed, often until the relevant strike was broken. Union halls were closed for building code violations, leaders were deported, and property and pamphlets were seized. In February 1936, the chamber of commerce boasted that Jersey City was more than 80 percent open shop.[10]

Over the coming months, the city's open-shop policy became increasingly difficult to maintain. In late 1936, a massive seamen's strike spread from the West Coast to the Hudson County waterfront. Jersey City prohibited picketing at its piers, and representatives from Robert M. La Follette Jr.'s Senate Civil Liberties Committee concluded that the Bill of Rights, "as far as Labor [was] concerned, . . . [did] not exist in Jersey." The ACLU attempted to intervene, but the strike settled before Arthur Garfield Hays could obtain an injunction in court.[11]

Hays subsequently arranged for a test case involving two AFL picketers who were ejected by subway to Manhattan. At an injunction hearing before federal district judge William Clark, Jersey City officials were remarkably candid about their antilabor policies. Daniel Casey, the acting commissioner of the Department of Public Safety, admitted to blocking recognitional picketing and instructing the police to remove troublemakers from the city. He also accused the ACLU of Communist agitation, prompting Hays to emphasize the organization's strict neutrality. Indeed, the ACLU received funds from the "most ardent reactionaries," and Hays had personally defended the right of the Nazi Party to march in Hudson County. Judge Clark was sympathetic, and he awarded the unions a temporary injunction, but Jersey City secured a stay on appeal. The appellate court delayed for more than a year before dismissing the case as moot because one of the plants had declared bankruptcy and the other had settled with the striking workers.[12]

By that time, national attention was fixed on a Jersey City injunction far greater in scope—one directed not only at labor's right to picket, but at the meaning of civil liberties in a constitutional democracy. In November 1937, half a year after the Supreme Court upheld the Wagner Act in *NLRB v. Jones and Laughlin Steel Corporation*, the CIO announced a Jersey City organizing drive. Local newspapers proclaimed an imminent "invasion." When CIO organizers tried to gather at their headquarters on November 29, police blocked their entry and seized meeting announcements informing residents of their rights under the Wagner Act. Officers were stationed at the Hudson Tube stations to prevent entry to Jersey City of all CIO members arriving from New York City or Newark. A few made it past the blockade, but the police muscled them into squad cars, drove them to the city border, and ordered them not to return. Those who persevered were arrested and, within hours, made to stand trial. The city magistrate who presided over the proceedings promised to "go to the limit" to keep the CIO out. He refused to consider a motion for adjournment to prepare a defense, denied a jury trial, and excluded facts challenging the court's jurisdiction and the constitutionality of the city's ordinance. Then he sentenced seven of the defendants to five days in jail.[13]

At the invitation of CIO counsel Lee Pressman, Morris Ernst agreed to assist with the legal challenge. Ernst seemed the ideal candidate for the job. In 1933, he had helped to found the journalists' union, the American Newspaper Guild, which had recently affiliated with the CIO. For Ernst, however, the legal problem in Jersey City was not one simply, or even primarily, of labor organizing. It presented a natural extension of the principles he had defended in cases involving sex education, artistic freedom, and birth control: the right to be free from the arbitrary control of an intrusive and irresponsible state authority. As he emphasized during the early New Deal and again during the court-packing controversy, the reality of totalitarianism abroad made the threat of government overreaching at home all the more palpable. In Jersey City, that threat emanated not from the Post Office Department or the Customs Bureau, as in past cases, but from a local despot.

In his capacity as special counsel, Ernst (along with the law firm of Isserman and Isserman) appealed the convictions, which the Hudson County Court of Appeals had declined to review on the basis that the controversy was moot. More important, Ernst orchestrated a broader approach to the Jersey City legal campaign. Drawing on established ACLU methods, Ernst arranged for the CIO to file a request for a meeting permit, with the expectation of challenging a denial in court. But the centerpiece of Ernst's program was an omnibus injunction suit in federal court, in which the ACLU itself, not just the CIO, was a plaintiff. In the past, virtually every civil liberties case that reached the Supreme Court, and the vast majority of the ACLU's legal work, involved defense against criminal prosecution. In *Hague v. CIO*, the ACLU sought to marshal the authority of the federal judiciary rather than to cabin it.[14]

✦ ✦ ✦

In mid-December, the civil liberties forces launched a "siege" on Jersey City. Mayor Hague struck back by casting his critics as Communist interlopers. According to Hague, Roger Baldwin was a "leading communist," and Morris Ernst was his second in command. "From behind the scenes," he alleged, the two Communist masterminds were "directing the whole CIO program."[15]

For the most part, the leadership of the Jersey City free speech effort answered Hague's attacks by disclaiming affiliation with the Communist Party. Dean Spaulding Frazer of the Newark Law School, who would serve as counsel for the CIO in the Supreme Court, pleaded, "Let us not be misled by any herrings dragged across the trail, even though they be red ones." William J. Carney, regional director of the CIO for New Jersey, pronounced himself a devout Catholic and dismissed the red-baiting as a distraction. Baldwin disavowed any sympathy for violent revolution, and his appearance at a church in Bayonne, New Jersey, was an orchestrated display of antitotalitarian, God-loving Americanism.[16]

Still, Baldwin was unwilling to vilify Communists outright. Despite misgivings about the Stalinist suppression of civil liberties, he believed the Soviet economic program to be laudable and had even declared in a 1935 Harvard class book that "communism is the goal"—though he always insisted he meant "economic communism" rather than its political counterpart. When Ernst urged him to invoke the names of prominent anti-Communists and to announce himself opposed to "any form of dictatorship—right or left," Baldwin refused. In the winter of 1937–1938, before the Molotov-Ribbentrop Pact shattered his remaining hopes for the Soviet experiment, Baldwin declined to equate the Soviet Union with Nazi Germany. Instead, he criticized Hague for his "high-handed dictatorship," which was incompatible with the commitments of the Roosevelt administration that Hague claimed to support.[17]

This basic strategic difference was a source of tension among the various organizations challenging Hague's repressive policies. Carney's goal in Jersey City was to "tell the world that the fundamental issue is that of the right to organize." The ACLU's lawyers, on the other hand, were eager to dissociate the civil liberties campaign from the substantive demands of their labor clients. Arthur Garfield Hays told the *New York World-Telegram* that the ACLU would oppose violence committed by organized labor against unorganized workers, just as it would protest employer or police abuses. Ernst was even more emphatic. Drawing on his experience with sex education and artistic freedom cases, in which public opinion had proved to be a powerful influence on judicial decision making, he assembled a new Committee on Civil Liberties in Jersey City composed of sixty-four of the country's "front-page figures" in the arts, sciences, law, religion, journalism, and academia. Labor leaders were notably absent from the group. In his letter to potential members, Ernst emphasized that while the current fight involved the CIO, Hague had employed the same tactics against the AFL. "It does not matter where you stand on the question of industrial versus craft unionism, or even as between organized and unorganized labor," he told them. "The real issue in Jersey City is democracy versus dictatorship."[18]

When Ernst labeled Hague "the greatest radical of our day" in a radio address, CIO organizers thought he had gone too far. The goal in Jersey City was to facilitate a successful organizing campaign, complained a CIO organizer, not "to show the world how really respectable you are." The CIO's steering committee believed that Ernst's "red-baiting" and publicity stunts were harming rather than helping the organizing drive. Months later, that sentiment was even stronger. Other than Carney, the CIO leadership had concluded that "the civil liberties angle was of no use to them."[19]

Ernst dismissed such complaints as misguided meddling by "bad tacticians." But the dispute was about something more than mere tactics. Ernst was increasingly focused on the right of the CIO to voice its views, not the likelihood that its message would ultimately triumph. And the right to speak, by the late 1930s, was an effective rallying cry. The battle over President Roosevelt's judiciary reorganization bill, still fresh in public memory, had strengthened the association between free speech and American values. When Ernst enlisted journalist and political commentator Dorothy Thompson to the cause, a CIO correspondent complained that Thompson was uninterested in helping organized labor. But to Ernst, that was what made her an ideal ally. In the *New York Tribune*, Thompson told readers she felt duty-bound to speak out in Jersey City for the same reason that she had fought the court-packing plan: because she believed that "the basic rights guaranteed to individuals under the Constitution should not be left to the interpretation of a 'kept' Court, switched into line—to use the Nazi phrase—with the policy of this or that Administration." By the same logic, Walter Lippmann argued that proponents of an independent judiciary were bound to join him in condemning the denial of civil liberties in Jersey City. To make the case for broad popular resistance to Hague's autocratic policies, Ernst enlisted support from such disparate groups as the National Lawyers Guild and the Republican Party.[20]

Rule of law was a particularly persuasive argument in Jersey City in light of developments in international politics. At a moment when Americans daily confronted accounts of totalitarian purges and propaganda—when, faced with Hitler, Stalin, Franco, and Mussolini, many believed that democracy in Europe was poised to topple altogether—the slippery slope from Mayor Hague to fascist dictatorship seemed plausible. Although Hague carefully avoided antisemitic rhetoric, the mayor's supporters did not fail to notice that many of his most outspoken detractors—including attorneys Hays, Ernst, and Abraham Isserman—were Jewish, and the resulting "Jew-baiting" brought the threat of totalitarian violence that much closer to home.[21]

Ernst decried the "Hudson Hitler" at every opportunity, and a radio speech in December prompted dozens of congratulatory letters. Others in the ACLU also adopted the line. Hays compared Germany's imprisonment of Communists in concentration camps to Jersey City's policy of expelling them to Hoboken. Norman Thomas, in a speech titled "Hagueism Is Fascism," charged that Hague's "process of working the masses up into a patriotic, nationalist frenzy, is characteristically fascist." And the CIO declared that "'I am the Law' Frank Hague, Mayor of Jersey City, is playing the role of [Adolf] Hitler."[22]

Arguments like these made the Jersey City situation resonate broadly, and Ernst believed he had "done a swell job in taking a handful of arrests and developing a national issue out of the situation." As *Life* magazine explained, the CIO and its supporters were answering the charges of "'Red Communists!' by "roaring back 'Fascist' and 'Dictator' at Hague"—and "out of the tumult, the Mayor of Jersey City has suddenly burgeoned big and menacing on the political horizon of America." The CIO may have felt ambivalence toward Ernst's approach, but it accepted assistance from "progressive and liberal elements," including consumers' groups, women's clubs, and fraternal organizations, as "the genuine sentiment of the foremost citizens of the State." That sentiment was substantial. The Liberal Ministers' Club cautioned "that Fascism can happen here" and issued a resolution enthusiastically endorsing the work of the ACLU. The Newark diocese of the Protestant Episcopal Church implored American citizens to stand together for the freedom of speech, press, assembly, and religion.[23]

Certainly Hague had his share of supporters. The working-class electorate of Jersey City consistently handed him landslide victories, and his rallies and demonstrations reliably attracted massive crowds. Skeptics argued that many of the spectators were motivated by fear of job loss or retaliation, and the *New York Post* reported that "scores of letters [were] pouring in from Jersey readers too scared to sign." Privately, however, the ACLU acknowledged that "the people of Jersey City, through fear and ignorance, are to a great extent back of Hague and have been right along." The apparent fervency of local support led the *New York Times* ruefully to conclude, "There is in Jersey City a large population which is satisfied with things as they are and which really believes that radicalism represents a menace to the United States."[24]

As for organized labor, unsurprisingly, it was divided. By late 1937, the AFL and the CIO were embroiled in a bitter organizing battle, and the AFL was reluctant to come to its rival's defense. Hague tried his best to retain AFL support. The New Jersey State Federation of Labor was so hostile to the CIO that it sided with Hague, and William Green, president of the AFL, "held his peace." Still, some AFL unions agreed to overcome sectarian differences in pursuit of a common goal. In January 1938, a gathering of AFL and CIO unions resolved "that this un-American censorship cease at once, by Federal intervention if necessary." The same month, the presidents of three AFL unions sought to revoke an honorary AFL membership that Samuel Gompers had conferred on Hague and condemned the mayor's manipulation of the schism between the AFL and CIO to mask his underlying "anti-labor purposes."[25]

In the wake of a national CIO organizing campaign marked by radical methods—most notably, a wave of sit-down strikes in spring 1937—Hague could credibly query whether his adversaries had "any regard for constitutional rights, or for any law" when they took possession of factories or blocked employees from getting to work. He had ample company in claiming that such techniques were not legitimate labor tools and that the CIO was actually "trying to seize power by creating violence and disorder." Indeed, in a sense, the question is not why so many of Hague's constituents supported him, but rather why so much of America condemned him. After his anti-CIO rally at the Jersey City armory in January 1938, Hague reportedly received hundreds of congratulatory letters and telegrams from throughout the United States. Had he limited his attack to the CIO—had he permitted speeches by liberal groups, members of Congress, and the ACLU even while resisting CIO organizing efforts—he would very likely have garnered considerable sympathy. When the ACLU challenged his despotic practices, many of his advisers encouraged him to do just that. Hague, however, ignored their suggestions. He adopted policies so extreme as to seem a caricature; journalist Heywood Broun (a friend of Ernst's since their school days at Horace Mann) aptly likened Jersey City officials to "vulgarized" versions of the characters in Marc Blitzstein's Broadway labor opera, *The Cradle Will Rock*. Urged on by business groups, Hague denounced free speech itself as a Communist ploy. In 1938, that was no longer a palatable strategy.[26]

✦ ✦ ✦

In the four months before the injunction proceedings commenced, sundry supporters of the ACLU's civil liberties campaign attempted to speak publicly against Hague and his policies in Jersey City. The Hague administration denied meeting permits to these would-be speakers, whatever their topic or political bent. While some were radicals or labor advocates, others were not. For example, a Princeton University student group wanted to host a speech by Senator William E. Borah, and the Independent Speakers' Association of New York City, whose members included New York City mayor Fiorello La Guardia and future New York governor Thomas E. Dewey, sought permission to hold an open-air meeting to discuss free speech. These proposals and many others were summarily rejected.

In February, the civil liberties forces decided to circumvent the permit requirement and, appropriating Hague's own terminology, "invade" Jersey City. At a meeting convened by an ACLU affiliate, 250 Hague opponents crowded into a rented hall (too small, but the only one they could secure) to hear addresses by United States representatives Jerry J. O'Connell, a Montana Democrat, and John T. Bernard of the Minnesota Farmer-Labor Party. The next step was to challenge Hague's bans on gathering in public spaces and on circulation of handbills. In its March decision in *Lovell v. City of Griffin*—at the urging of the ACLU as amicus curiae—the United States Supreme Court invalidated a municipal license requirement for the distribution of printed materials. The ACLU immediately informed Hague that Jersey City's permit requirement was unconstitutional, and the city reluctantly conceded the point, though it insisted that unlawful assemblage would still be prohibited.[27]

In May, the International Labor Defense announced an outdoor test meeting featuring a repeat performance by O'Connell and Bernard. Tens of thousands of public employees, veterans, AFL members, and other Hague supporters assembled in Journal Square. Concerned that vigilante violence was inevitable, the two representatives decided to cancel their appearance. According to the *New York Daily News*, the civil liberties contingent was convinced "that direct action should be abandoned and an appeal made to the Federal courts." Despite the change of tack, O'Connell vowed to return to Jersey City to deliver his speech; when he appeared before an equally hostile crowd of 10,000 to 15,000 people in late May, he was promptly whisked away by the police.[28]

Meanwhile, the deportation of Norman Thomas at a Socialist Party rally made national headlines. When Thomas tried to address a May Day Eve meeting at Journal Square, police seized him, pushed him into a car, drove him to the ferry dock, and forced him onto a boat bound for New

York. The episode triggered a flood of newspaper editorials condemning Mayor Hague. Public figures expressed outrage, including Alf M. Landon, the 1936 Republican presidential nominee, who told Thomas that he was shocked by "such a gross violation of our sacred right of free speech." According to the *New York Post,* criticism poured in from Republicans and Democrats, conservatives and radicals.[29]

The critics clamored all the more loudly because Arthur T. Vanderbilt's Newark law firm agreed to represent Thomas in the matter, without financial compensation. A decade after representing Roger Baldwin in Paterson, Vanderbilt had established a national reputation, and he was serving as president of the ABA. Although the *New York Post* labeled him "an extremely conservative man," his demonstrated commitment to civil liberties had lent credibility to the ABA's defense of judicial review during the court-packing controversy. It had also undercut allegations that the bar was a corporate pawn. "It just so happens that I have spent a good many years in liberal movements and have taken more body blows in these fights than have most of the men who are leading the National Lawyers' Guild," Vanderbilt explained to an ABA colleague. "I have even been so brash as to represent the American Civil Liberties Union in our court of last resort. Think of that!"[30]

Vanderbilt was the ideal spokesperson for a value-neutral model of free speech. The new president firmly believed in "personal and civil liberties" and had "given freely of his services to defend these rights in the Courts." Just as his track record in civil liberties cases had allowed him to champion the Bill of Rights without provoking charges of hypocrisy from New Dealers, his status as head of the eminently conservative ABA belied Hague's claim that free speech was simply a vehicle for Communist agitation. Vanderbilt confidently brushed aside such allegations, explaining that "Mr. Hague does not yet understand that the lawyers of the country are deeply concerned with the preservation of civil liberties guaranteed by our Federal and State Constitutions."[31]

Lawyers at Vanderbilt's firm organized a comprehensive legal challenge on Thomas's behalf. In federal court, they sought damages from city officials. They also filed new permit applications with the city, and when those were denied by Commissioner Casey—who cited a threat of violence by hostile spectators, anticipating decades of municipal reliance on the so-called heckler's veto—they sued in state court for a writ of mandamus. At oral argument, Vanderbilt insisted that Thomas should be permitted to speak "even if a riot were to ensue," but the New Jersey Supreme Court deemed the permit ordinance constitutional and upheld Casey's right to exclude him. Vanderbilt appealed to the state high court, which refused to hear the case before the following spring.[32]

The most unusual component of Vanderbilt's legal strategy was his pursuit of a federal prosecution under a Reconstruction-era civil rights law. Title 18, Section 51 of the United States Code, along with its companion provision, Section 52, were passed during Reconstruction to protect black southerners, though as a prominent black newspaper pointed out, no attorney general had sought to use the laws "when colored people were concerned." In 1938, the two provisions were among just a handful of federal statutes criminalizing the deprivation of civil liberties. Their use, according to the *New York Times,* raised "the problem of the affirmative powers of the Federal Government to protect constitutional guarantees against alleged infringement."[33]

Section 51 provided for a $5,000 fine and up to ten years in prison for conspiracy "to injure, oppress, threaten or intimidate any citizen in the free exercise or enjoyment" of any right "secured by" the United States Constitution or a federal statute. Although the law seemingly implicated a broad range of private interference with such rights, the courts had interpreted it narrowly. The Department of Justice rescued Section 51 from disuse in the fall of 1937, when it obtained an indictment against dozens of coal companies, executives, and public officials in Harlan County, Kentucky, for conspiracy to violate the Wagner Act. Harlan County had been the site of publicly sanctioned antiunion terrorism for a decade, and in 1937, the La Follette Committee had uncovered murders, assaults, and interference with UMW organizing efforts on the part of the county's "coal barons and deputized thugs." All efforts to curb the violence and secure miners' rights in state courts—by the ACLU, among other actors—had failed. As the Department of Justice considered possible courses of action in the Thomas case, its attorneys in Harlan County were about to go to trial.[34]

And yet, although Attorney General Homer Cummings announced that he was considering a similar action in Jersey City, the investigation proceeded halfheartedly. According to Thomas, the Roosevelt administration was reluctant to antagonize Mayor Hague, who had become one of the staunchest and most reliable supporters of the president and his agenda. In the end, two special assistants to the attorney general, Welly K. Hopkins and Henry A. Schweinhaut (both of whom had assisted in the Harlan County prosecution), assembled indictments. The grand jury, which was drawn from Hudson County, declined to indict, but Hopkins and Schweinhaut promised a new and more sweeping investigation before jurors from the entire state. Responding to a Department of Justice request, the ACLU and New Jersey Civil Liberties Union submitted descriptions of eighty-nine court cases, directly involving nearly 2,000 people and organizations, related to civil liberties violations in Hudson County between 1930 and 1938. The ACLU was frustrated with the pace of the federal investigation but confident that the attorney general would give its report appropriate consideration.[35]

Civil liberties advocates applied equivalent pressure to other political bodies and officials, with similarly unimpressive results. Members of Congress called for Hague's appearance before the House Special Committee to Investigate Un-American Activities, presumably without expecting his compliance. Meanwhile, labor groups and politicians asked President Roosevelt to censure Hague, but Attorney General Cummings advised him not to get involved. At first, the ACLU was hesitant to pressure Roosevelt. Many board members were staunch New Dealers, and Morris Ernst was a frequent correspondent of the president, as well as an occasional houseguest in Hyde Park. But in early May, when Roosevelt dismissed the issue as a "local police matter," a vocal minority within the organization demanded an ACLU response. On May 26, the board urged Roosevelt to oust Hague as vice-chairman of the Democratic National Committee. Eventually the president addressed the situation, but only obliquely. In a move with which the *New York Times* conjectured that "all thoughtful Americans, 'conservatives' and 'liberals,' supporters and opponents of the Administration, [could] wholeheartedly agree," he announced in a fireside chat that "the American people [would] not be deceived by any one who attempts to suppress individual liberty under the pretense of patriotism." Although there was "no possibility of misunderstanding" the passage, Roosevelt declined to rebuke Mayor Hague by name.[36]

The La Follette Committee, too, disappointed the free speech forces. After repeated pleas from Thomas and the ACLU, the committee indicated that it would launch an investigation over the summer if funds permitted. When the Senate approved the committee's requested appropriation (with significant help from an ACLU publicity campaign), Baldwin assumed that its future work would cover Jersey City. By September, however, the committee's continued inaction was apparent. A letter from sixty prominent liberals urging an investigation of the "extraordinary and open defiance of constitutional guarantees" in Jersey City was also fruitless, despite the inclusion of eight members of Congress. In November, Baldwin concluded that no Senate inquiry was forthcoming; La Follette claimed that funds were limited and professed a desire not to intrude where other federal actors were already involved. At the height of the New Deal, the ACLU had reconsidered its long-standing distrust of the state. Despite the leadership's early opposition to the Wagner Act, the organization had begun to imagine the government as a potential protector of civil liberties. The Roosevelt administration's tepid response to Mayor Hague pushed the ACLU, once more, toward the federal courts.[37]

✦ ✦ ✦

Hague v. CIO went to trial on June 1, 1938, after early attempts to reach a settlement fell apart. Judge Clark, who had decided Arthur Garfield Hays's injunction suit in the ACLU's favor the previous year, was assigned to hear the case. The complaint described in detail the thwarted CIO organizing drive of November 1937—with its deportations, illegal searches, and confiscation of CIO literature—along with other efforts by the ACLU and CIO to hold meetings and distribute materials in Jersey City. It was later amended to include Representative O'Connell's and Norman Thomas's speeches, as well. The plaintiffs argued that Jersey City's leaflet and meeting ordinances were unconstitutional, and they sought to enjoin municipal officials from interfering with public and private meetings, picketing, the distribution of literature, and lawful CIO labor activity.[38]

As expected, Judge Clark was sympathetic to the anti-Hague forces. He repeatedly admonished Hague and the defense team to adopt a more respectful tone, and he made a number of interjections on behalf of the plaintiffs. On one occasion, reflecting on "the difference between actual government and paper constitutions," he quoted the free speech provisions of the Soviet constitution. "I don't know whether I will be accused of being a Communist," he added wryly.[39]

The courtroom testimony unfolded along predictable lines. Witnesses recounted numerous episodes of interference with CIO meetings, leaflet distributions, and other organizing activities, and the deportations, violence, and other abusive practices employed by the Jersey City police. To the ACLU, the city's prophylactic denial of permits to forestall rioting was a patently unconstitutional example of prior restraint. It was also a bridge to totalitarianism. "The operation of preventive devices in anticipation of overt acts is the threshold of a dictatorship, no question about it," Morris Ernst declared. "It is the Hitler, the Stalin, the Mussolini, the Japan of today."[40]

The climax of the trial was the four-day examination of Mayor Hague, who appeared as the plaintiffs' principal witness. Ernst and Spaulding Frazer hoped that Hague's sense of infallibility would prove self-defeating, and they were not disappointed. The mayor frequently referred to himself in the third person, and he routinely answered questions over the objections of his own counsel. Though he professed to "have no desire to stop anybody from talking," he openly conceded his restrictive policies and practices, with the sole exception of coercing hall owners not to rent to CIO speakers. In his view, the seizure of subversive literature and the prevention of radical meetings were wholly justified in the interest of public safety. The proper method of dealing with potential insurgents was to "suppress them," he explained. On the issue of deportation, he insisted that eviction was a favor compared with arrest.[41]

Hague was cooperative on the witness stand as long as Frazer handled the questioning. Once Ernst took over, however, Hague abandoned the "congenial manner" he had assumed during the first two days. "At times the scene took on the aspect of a Donnybrook fair," reported the *New York Times*, "with the Mayor and Mr. Ernst both shouting at each other, and the Mayor's lawyers also yelling at the top of their voices in a bedlam through which nothing could be clearly heard." When Ernst attempted to contain Hague's long-winded answers, Hague scornfully accused the lawyer of attempting to curtail his freedom of speech.[42]

To Hague (as the *New York Times* put it), "Americanism and law and order, not free speech and constitutional rights," were the values at stake in Jersey City. According to Hague, who had spent a few days in Russia in 1936 and considered himself an expert on Communism, all of the CIO's leaders except John L. Lewis were Communists. So were Thomas, Representatives Bernard and O'Connell (who was "ten Communists"), Roger Baldwin, and the worst offender, Ernst. Indeed, Hague was sufficiently concerned by the imminent threat of Communist invasion to advocate the deportation of alien radicals from the United States and the creation of a concentration camp in Alaska for citizen "Reds."[43]

After such a strong showing, the plaintiffs hoped for a quick decision. Much to their disappointment, Judge Clark announced that none would be issued before fall. In the interim Mayor Hague's spin fell just as flat outside the courtroom as it had within it. In early June, the Hague administration mounted a massive "Americanism" demonstration to display its continued popularity in Jersey City. The *New York Times* estimated that half of Jersey City's 300,000 residents turned out for the two-hour event. Nationally, however, Hague faced increasing criticism across the political spectrum. Newspaper rhetoric comparing Hague to Hitler and Mussolini was ubiquitous during the trial, and the Americanism rally only exacerbated matters. A *Washington Post* editorial predicted that students of modern dictatorship would observe that the gathering "contained, in embryonic form, many of the attributes of those Fascist or Nazi demonstrations which accompanied the overthrow of democracy in Italy and Germany." Hague's credibility further plummeted when a Nazi radio broadcast praised Hague as a "man fighting for the cause in the United States." Even veterans groups began to denounce Hague for his un-American suppression of constitutional rights.[44]

For the ACLU, which received a flood of congratulatory letters and contributions during the proceedings, the challenge was to maintain its momentum over the summer. Despite widespread optimism about the outcome, holding the various civil liberties groups together was proving to be increasingly difficult. Ernst left for vacation in July and beseeched Baldwin to manage the various factions in his absence, and to begin preparations for disseminating 100,000 copies of the decision once it was handed down.[45]

Judge Clark finally issued his opinion on October 27, 1938. The front page of the *New York Times* announced that Hague had lost the fight, but the reality was somewhat murkier. Judge Clark had held that the meeting ordinance was unconstitutionally administered, but to Ernst, who saw the *Hague* case as a "chance to upset all of the damn ordinances," that was not enough. Ernst conceded that municipalities could legitimately consider traffic in regulating public gatherings, but in his view, that was the limit of their discretion. He argued at trial that the recent First Amendment cases—*Near v. Minnesota, De Jonge v. Oregon,* and *Lovell v. City of Griffin*—had rendered any law providing for "precensorship of what a man may say" unconstitutional. Judge Clark, however, appeared unwilling to go that far.[46]

Issued over a week before the formal injunctive decree, Clark's written opinion embraced Zechariah Chafee Jr.'s celebration of "the discovery and spread of truth on subjects of general concern." Following Chafee, Clark acknowledged that unfettered expression might interfere with other legitimate purposes of government (including "order, the training of the young, [and] protection against external aggression"). As with other matters of "political science," he explained, there was a need for balancing, and the trouble was to achieve the right "adjustment of the scales." That Clark framed the issue in these terms was significant. In the years since the First World War, political scientists had traded in their idealistic vision of the public welfare for a hard-boiled model of interest-group pluralism. In fact, to many, the erasure of difference in the service of the public interest was the distinguishing feature of totalitarianism. Fragmentation and friction were fundamental to American democracy, and they were best facilitated by freedom of speech.[47]

Clark was no relativist. He believed that some ideas, some forms of government, were better than others. In particular, he considered Communism "economically unworkable" and the methods employed in its propagation "abhorrent to all true believers in democracy," though he was loathe to make martyrs of its advocates. He also believed that productive political conversation required civilized public discourse, and to that end, he thought the state might be justified in curtailing speech where riot was truly likely to ensue. Judge Clark was clear that Jersey City's existing practice of denying permits to all CIO and ACLU speakers—a policy of deliberate discrimination to which Mayor Hague and Commissioner Casey freely admitted—violated the constitutional right to free assembly. He was equally explicit, however, that a municipality was entitled to require permits for meetings in order to ensure public enjoyment and safety. As Clark later conceded, he was worried that "events in Europe [would] cause the pendulum to swing too far in the direction of license." Perhaps it was with that concern in mind that he concluded, relying on English case law, that if a speaker's past conduct was sufficiently provocative, the city could bind the speaker over to keep the peace, or even censor the speech.[48]

To the Jersey City authorities, Judge Clark's decision was an invitation to continue denying meeting permits to the ACLU and CIO. But Ernst was confident that the "*obiter dicta* in regard to reading of speeches in advance was merely *dicta*"—a prediction that proved to be right. The final judgement and decree enjoined city officials from excluding or deporting the plaintiffs; from restraining them except in connection with a lawful search or seizure; and from interfering with their rights to distribute leaflets, converse with passersby in public places, or carry placards. On the crucial issue of public meetings, it forbade the city from preventing assemblies in the "open air and parks" as long as a permit application was submitted three days in advance. The city could refuse a permit only if the designated time or place for the meeting would undermine the public recreational purpose of the parks, reasonably construed. Ernst got everything he requested.[49]

In fact, he got more. Judge Clark did not merely require the city to stay out. He set the further condition, unprecedented in the federal courts and rarely followed in subsequent decisions until the civil rights era, that the city actively prevent "interruption by such persons as may be present." In other words, he required the police to *protect* the plaintiffs against interference by hostile spectators, to the extent consistent with public safety. Judge Clark's affirmative guarantee of access had its limits. He implied that the city could lawfully adopt a policy prohibiting meetings on the public streets and thoroughfares—a narrowing that could be used to proscribe union organizing efforts adjacent to employer property. Still, in those public parks that were "dedicated for the purposes of the general recreation of the public," the plaintiffs were entitled to speak their minds.[50]

Civil liberties groups were justifiably elated. The ACLU called the injunction a "clear-cut victory." The *New York Post,* which had harshly criticized Judge Clark for his initial opinion, was "happy to pay tribute to him . . . for his splendid and unequivocal final decree." Although the fight against Hague's "dictatorial lawlessness" was not yet over, the ACLU was confident that "the power of a federal court order [would] go far toward winning it."[51]

✦ ✦ ✦

The months between Judge Clark's decree in November and the appellate court's decision affirming it in January were momentous ones. Procedurally, a few unusual developments attracted newspaper attention (for example, when the plaintiffs challenged an effort to "pack" a Third Circuit panel with Hague supporters). But the truly noteworthy development came in the form of an amicus brief. According to the *New York Times,* it was a brief that "ought to stand as a landmark to American legal history." Its author was the ABA's newly minted Committee on the Bill of Rights.[52]

That committee, little studied by historians but integral to the emergence of the modern understanding of civil liberties, had its origins in a public relations initiative under ABA president Arthur Vanderbilt. Vanderbilt began contemplating proposals to improve the ABA's image in early 1937. In February of that year, Reginald Heber Smith of the association's Committee on Legal Aid Work wrote to request additional funds. He advised Vanderbilt that the ABA, out of a gross income of almost $250,000, "devotes to the whole subject of legal aid for poor persons the sum of $500." Smith thought people would be appalled by the figure if it were made public. Vanderbilt was sympathetic, but he felt constrained to turn Smith down. He explained that in light of a budget deficit made worse by the court-packing controversy, no additional funds would be available in the foreseeable future. Still, Smith persisted. In July, he tried to convince Vanderbilt that increasing legal aid would detract attention from the new National Lawyers Guild. The Guild, he emphasized, had already formed a Committee on Legal Aid and approached the National Association of Legal Aid Organizations to offer its assistance. Smith hoped the ABA would not "fumble the ball and let the Guild pick it up."[53]

Although Vanderbilt did not act on Smith's request, he found his argument compelling. The National Lawyers Guild distinguished itself from the ABA by endorsing programs and reform proposals "designed to promote human welfare," such as the Child Labor Amendment, social security legislation, minimum-wage laws, and protections for collective bargaining—all of which the ABA had opposed. Vanderbilt was determined to level the playing field, and in the winter of 1937–1938, he launched a new "Public Relations" program and convened a conference on the issue. To Vanderbilt, the ABA's public relations problem was twofold. The first difficulty was the relationship between the organization and the membership of the bar. The ABA leadership formulated strategies for undercutting the Guild's recruitment in law schools and among dissatisfied attorneys. But the second, more pressing issue was the negative perception of lawyers, and the ABA in particular, among the general public. Increasing legal aid was one potential solution to this problem, but it was expensive. The ABA eventually opted for a thriftier way to redirect the National Lawyers Guild's positive press: creation of a new and high-profile Committee on the Bill of Rights.[54]

Vanderbilt proposed a committee on constitutional rights to the ABA's board of governors in January 1938—the same month as his conference on public relations—but the "more conservative members . . . 'saw red' and voted the suggestion down." Half a year later, a second opportunity presented itself, courtesy of Wall Street lawyer Grenville Clark. Clark was a frequent correspondent of Felix Frankfurter's who was actively involved in public service throughout his life. He was often called a conservative, and he acknowledged that he would qualify under a "broad definition [of] the term." Still, an associate at his law firm described him as an "independent liberal." He was raised a Republican but considered Roosevelt a close friend and voted for him in the 1932 and 1936 elections. Moreover, he disliked the Supreme Court's "economic royalist" attitude and was open to the prospect of judicial reform. In fact, even before the court-packing plan was announced, he corresponded with Lloyd K. Garrison—a newly appointed ACLU national committee member, as well as the dean of the University of Wisconsin Law School and the former chair of the first NLRB—about drafting a constitutional amendment to increase the power of the federal government. Speculating that "there may come a time when the liberals will be the ones who will most wish the protection of the Supreme Court and the Constitution," he considered it crucial to preserve "the protection of the courts with regard to civil rights."[55]

Despite Clark's sympathies with the New Deal project, he thought the president's judiciary reorganization bill was an "essentially illiberal proposal in the long view." Together with his friends Charles C. Burlingham and Monte Lemann, he organized a National Committee for Independent Courts to assist the ABA and other groups in defeating the plan. The founders were careful to distinguish their position from that of groups like the American Liberty League, and membership was conditioned on having voted for Roosevelt in the 1936 election. The organization eventually comprised 250 members, including the ACLU's Walter Pollak, as well as Roscoe Pound. A core element of its campaign was the belief that "protection of civil liberty rests with the judiciary." After the defeat of the reorganization bill, Clark thought that view had been vindicated. "An important by-product of this court discussion," he told the American Academy of Political and Social Science in December 1937, "has been a strengthening of the cause of civil liberty."[56]

In June 1938, Clark made the same point more boldly when he delivered an address on "Conservatism and Civil Liberty" to the annual meeting of the Nassau County Bar Association. Clark told his audience that the problem of civil liberties in America was evolving in crucial ways. It had become fashionable to contrast civil liberties in the United States with totalitarianism in Europe, but Clark considered such appraisals to be somewhat beside the point. The importance of "reconciling authority with individual freedom" stemmed not primarily from the rise of dictatorships overseas, but from the inevitable growth of "governmental interference with the social and economic life of the citizen" at home. As he explained in a subsequent address, the federal government had rapidly regulated such fields as agriculture, securities, housing, unemployment relief, and labor relations, to name just a few. The solution, however, was not to roll back the state, but rather to "reconcile its powers with the essentials of our civil rights." True civil liberty, Clark told the Nassau bar, required both democratic self-government and rule of law, that is, nonarbitrariness in government action.[57]

According to Clark, it was up to conservatives, not liberals or radicals, to strike the appropriate balance. Conservatives wanted reform to come "gradually and with a minimum of friction," in a fashion that preserved past insights. In practice, however, "the active defense of civil liberty [had] been allowed to drift very largely into the hands of the elements of 'the Left.'" Many Americans had come to believe that conservatives were more interested in the protection of property than the vital protections of the First Amendment (Clark himself believed that "purely personal liberties" had "superior sanctity" to property rights, though he considered that a controversial position). Clark emphasized that the ACLU deserved credit for defending unpopular causes—a charitable characterization that captured a dramatic transformation in the organization's reputation since the beginning of the decade. Still, he had reservations. He believed that by cornering the field of civil liberties so completely, the ACLU's radical leadership had created the "public impression that the active defense of civil liberties is not a matter of primary concern with those of more moderate views."[58]

The time had come, in Clark's assessment, for conservatives to reclaim the mantle of civil liberties. That conservatives themselves, under the New Deal, were facing the purported deprivation of civil rights for the first time was evidence of the need for a neutral defense of constitutional rights. There had been ample protests against the methods of Sherman Minton's lobby committee, which in essence were no different from Mayor Hague's. But American conservatives could not "have it both ways," Clark cautioned. If they countenanced the oppression of minorities while conservatives were "in the ascendant," they should expect their own rights to be suppressed when the situation reversed. The only feasible position was to defend all constitutional rights, in all cases, "irrespective of whether we approve or disapprove the sentiments and policies of the persons affected."[59]

In promoting that ideal, the legal profession had a particularly crucial role to play. After all, lawyers were conservative by nature and training. They had led the defense of civil liberties for generations, and despite their quiescence in recent decades, they had rediscovered the central importance of constitutional rights. What, Clark asked, was the secret of lawyers' powerful drive against the court-packing plan? "It was their conviction, arrived at both by reason and instinct, that the proposal . . . was fundamentally a threat to our civil liberties." He concluded with an exhortation: "This zeal and power that manifested itself in the crisis of a year ago ought not to be permitted to lapse but should be better organized for opposition to other attacks on civil liberty that are constantly occurring."[60]

Clark's pronouncements resonated within and outside the bar, and they were widely publicized in professional journals and the popular press, including the *ABA Journal*, which reprinted his remarks in full. Clark received numerous letters applauding his suggestion. Future chief justice Earl Warren asked for a copy of his "splendid address," and Walter Lippmann read the speech with the "greatest admiration and agreement." Vanderbilt was also impressed, and he hoped to channel the positive public reaction into action on his proposed committee on constitutional rights. Vanderbilt thought Clark's support might sway the ABA board, and he asked Clark whether he "would feel free, without referring to the correspondence we have had, to write me a letter urging the desirability of the appointment of such a committee by the American Bar Association." Three days later, Clark obligingly wrote Vanderbilt to advocate the creation within the ABA of a committee "exclusively concerned with the question of the protection of civil liberties," stressing the bar's long tradition of service in the field. He added that the National Lawyers Guild already had one; creating it was among that organization's first priorities, and it was approved at the inaugural national convention.[61]

Armed with Clark's letter, Vanderbilt put the matter on the agenda when the ABA's board of governors met in Cleveland in July—though at the request of his successor, Frank J. Hogan, he left the matter for the subsequent board, which acted promptly to implement the recommendation. In his annual address as ABA president, Hogan admonished the organization's membership to be vigilant in defending individual rights. Hogan himself claimed a lifelong commitment to civil liberties work. Twenty years earlier, he had delivered a lecture denouncing wiretapping, unlawful searches, and privacy incursions by legislative committees. In the intervening decades he had ruefully observed that individuals opposed only the suppression of their own views. Hogan echoed Clark's statement that civil liberties were worth protecting even when the idea conveyed was offensive or its expounder unlikable. He insisted that "violations of the Bill of Rights are intolerable, no matter whom they affect," and whether emanating from a Senate committee, an administrative tribunal, or the "mayor of an American city." Rhetorically, he adopted precisely the same line as the proponents of neutrality on the ACLU board, who were constantly called to justify their defense of conservatives and reactionaries.[62]

For Hogan, however, property rights clearly still remained within the ambit of constitutional protection. Hogan considered the Supreme Court's spring 1937 decisions to be "the most devastating destruction of constitutional limitations upon Federal power" in American history, and he doubted that a "government which may arbitrarily control the individual's economic freedom [could] be relied on permanently to keep safe his civil and political liberties." Moreover, like other outspoken defenders of free enterprise, he was explicitly motivated by New Deal encroachments on conservative interests. Among the violations that most troubled him were the Senate's seizure of legal correspondence from the office of ABA secretary and former aviation regulator William P. MacCracken Jr., suspected of collusion in an airline contract; the cancelation of government contracts by presidential proclamation; and the confiscation of corporate property upon order of the attorney general (only an injunction, which Hogan helped to procure, prevented that particular "trampling on the Bill of Rights"). Indeed, Hogan reported that his own telephone wires were tapped by the Department of Justice, and he had led the legal battle against the Minton committee's telegram subpoenas on behalf of his close friend Silas Strawn. In his address to the ABA, Hogan portrayed the businessmen threatened by reform initiatives at the turn of the century as the unheralded victims of gross authoritarian abuses. "Perhaps, because the trampling recently sometimes has been upon well-worn shoes," he mused, "the hurt done thereby has been considered more important than when the crushed toes were encased in patent leather footwear of the wealthy, or the rights denied or the privacy invaded were those of the business corporation." It is little wonder that initial reactions to the ABA's announcement evinced skepticism toward the organization's underlying objectives.[63]

Still, Hogan's examples achieved their effect. Later that day, the ABA House of Delegates adopted a resolution creating a Special Committee on the Bill of Rights (Hogan thought the term "civil liberties" was too contentious). The new committee would ensure the availability of competent legal representation whenever provisions of the Bill of Rights were violated. Where necessary, it would intervene to protect civil liberties by filing amicus briefs, educating the public, and cooperating with state and local bar associations. Clark was appointed chair of the committee. Vanderbilt chose not to participate in light of his involvement in the Norman Thomas case, but Zechariah Chafee Jr., concerned that "the bar associations [had] been bad offenders against civil rights," agreed to serve. Perhaps the most notable member, aside from Chafee and Clark, was Joseph A. Padway, general counsel for the AFL. The CIO's Lee Pressman was also invited to join, but gruffly declined.[64]

The ACLU leadership was gratified by the ABA's emerging interest in civil liberties. There was reason for caution, of course; in Chafee's words, many observers expected the committee "to oppose all the policies of the New Deal on the ground that they deprive American citizens of all their rights, the most important of which appears to be the right to be taxed low." And yet, as right-wing critics quickly realized, the ABA's involvement promised to make civil liberties work truly respectable, with evident implications for civil liberties fund raising and advocacy. The ACLU was especially heartened by Clark's involvement; Clark had already attempted to organize conservative support for the ACLU, and he joined the organization in 1939. In a press statement, the ACLU offered its complete cooperation with the ABA's new committee—though it pointedly suggested that the ABA "lift its membership ban on Negroes as the initial act on behalf of minority rights," much to the distress of ABA members already nervous about the new venture.[65]

The Committee on the Bill of Rights reciprocated the ACLU's interest. Immediately after the committee's announcement, its members were flooded with requests from criminal defendants complaining about denial of process. The committee considered these cases to be of primarily local concern, however, and it recommended the appointment of local committees to assume responsibilities for such matters. The national committee, by contrast, wanted to reserve its services for issues of national significance. To that end, Clark asked Arthur Garfield Hays to suggest areas in which it could most usefully intervene. The ACLU board, after discussion, recommended a few issues of particular importance, including compulsory flag salute laws, radio censorship, and third-degree legislation. But the first and most pressing concern was clear: the ACLU invited the ABA to join the battle against Jersey City's Mayor Hague.[66]

✦ ✦ ✦

At the ACLU's urging, the Committee on the Bill of Rights agreed at its first meeting, in November 1938, to file an amicus brief in *Hague v. CIO*. Clark thought the civil liberties issues in the case "had become confused in the public mind with the labor issue and the 'red' issue," and he felt that ABA involvement would help clarify the constitutional questions. The committee was particularly concerned with the city's arbitrary refusal to issue meeting permits, which implicated "the right of public assembly"—a constitutional liberty that the Supreme Court had not yet considered.[67]

Grenville Clark assumed primary responsibility for drafting the brief. Zechariah Chafee Jr. was an active collaborator, and the other committee members contributed occasional suggestions. Within his law offices, Clark also had the able assistance of an unusually insightful associate, Louis Lusky, whose scholarly reputation would someday rival Chafee's in the field of constitutional law. Fresh from a clerkship with Justice Harlan Fiske Stone—whom Clark had once described as a "conservative in the true sense"—Lusky had thought carefully about the future of the First Amendment. Indeed, in aiding Justice Stone with an otherwise unexceptional case called *United States v. Carolene Products Company*, the recent graduate of Columbia Law School had helped to craft the most famous legal footnote of all time.[68]

When Clark's firm hired him, both the footnote and Lusky—in stark contrast to Mayor Hague's antics—were relative unknowns. On April 26, 1938, the day after *Carolene Products* was handed down, the *New York Times* contained three references to events in Jersey City. On page six, the paper devoted half a column to the legal travails of "Hague Foe" Jeff Burkitt. Page twenty-two informed readers, "Jersey Methodists Join Critics of Hague." And in a telling measure of the regnant perception of judicial review, the front-page coverage of New York's constitutional convention reported on "labor's proposed new 'Bill of Rights,'" which included (as the headline pronounced) a "Severe Curb on Court Power to Void Legislative

Acts," along with a right to distribute handbills, "which in recent months was challenged in New Jersey by Mayor Frank Hague." Buried on page forty, by contrast, was the paper's only reference to Stone's opinion: "The United States, applt., v. Carolene Products Co. Appeal from the United States District Court of the Southern District of Illinois. Judgment Reversed and cause remanded." The *Times* made no mention whatsoever of the opinion's fourth footnote, which so succinctly encapsulated the future trajectory of judicial review in the United States.[69]

The omission is not surprising. As Lusky later explained, the footnote was clearly dicta, and it "did not purport to *decide* anything." Lusky subsequently regretted that Justice Stone had not taken more care to elaborate the thesis, captured in its second paragraph, that courts should apply "more exacting" constitutional scrutiny to legislation "which restricts those political processes which can ordinarily be expected to bring about repeal of undesirable legislation." Nor did Justice Stone, who was deeply influenced by the specter of Nazism, explain why legislation targeting "discrete and insular minorities" might similarly call for "more searching judicial inquiry." Worse yet, Justice Stone opened the footnote, in a concession to a suggestion by Justice Charles Evans Hughes, with a separate justification for favoring free speech and other civil liberties over property rights, namely the applicability of "*a specific prohibition of the Constitution*, such as those of the first ten amendments, which are deemed equally specific when held to be embraced within the Fourteenth."[70]

If Lusky lamented his missed opportunity to refine the Supreme Court's rationale for "bifurcated review," the ABA's brief in *Hague v. CIO* presented him with a second chance. From the beginning, Lusky was intimately involved in the intellectual and administrative operations of the Committee on the Bill of Rights. In November, he wrote Clark with an attempt to define *civil rights*. In "popular terminology," he began, the term ordinarily encompassed the freedoms of speech, press, and assembly, and other guarantees contained within the first eight amendments to the Constitution. And yet, not all of the rights within those amendments were civil rights—nor, as he would often emphasize in future writing, were all equally implicated in the rationales for searching judicial inquiry that he had proposed to Justice Stone. By the same token, there were some rights, including the right to vote, that might be counted as civil rights but were not enumerated in the first eight amendments.[71]

The distinction was not the relative importance of the rights in question; from an individual's perspective, Lusky observed, the right not to be killed or robbed was just as crucial as freedom of speech. There were some rights, however, that were "essential to the health of a democratic state" but particularly prone to abuse. Among those rights, the most important was the "free communication of political ideas, in order that governmental policies may be subjected to effective peaceful revision at the polls." Repressive majorities were often inattentive to the broader value of free expression, focusing instead on the "quite different question of the *rightness* of the ideas," as well as the short-term benefits of containing disorder and preserving state institutions. Similar problems plagued freedom of religion and assembly and the right of petition, all of which were instrumental to "peaceful social change." In such cases, it would not do to defer to popular majorities. That was why the Constitution protected civil rights, and it was the legal profession's "noblest responsibilit[y]" to enforce them. Lusky hoped to fulfill that responsibility through his work for the ABA committee, including his contributions to its amicus brief in *Hague v. CIO*.[72]

Despite its conservative branding, the ABA's brief in *Hague* espoused a fundamentally progressive theory of free speech—an unsurprising result, in light of its principal authors. Doctrinally, the brief deemed the Supreme Court's recent First Amendment decisions to have altered the constitutional balance between state authority and liberty of expression. It distinguished Justice Oliver Wendell Holmes Jr.'s foundational decision in *Commonwealth v. Davis,* which made government discretion to curb speech on public property commensurate with that of private property owners. In one of the brief's few concessions to the ABA's conservative constituency, it described Holmes's theory in *Davis* to be particularly dangerous at a time when the government was acquiring large quantities of property and "carrying on enormous activities" (tellingly, shortened from *business* activities in the draft). If such enterprises as the Tennessee Valley Authority were permitted the power of exclusion that Holmes had extended to public parks, opponents of government policy "would find many aspects of their lives at the mercy of a property owner (nation, state or city), possessed of vast and arbitrary power." Political outsiders could be foreclosed "from selling their products to the government or from doing work for it in fields where there might no longer be any customer worth mentioning." That is, in a world marked by the consolidation of federal power and the displacement of private enterprise, Holmes's proprietary theory of public property would put the authors' corporate clients at the mercy of the New Deal state.[73]

As for the Supreme Court's recent deference under the Fourteenth Amendment's Due Process Clause, the brief did not mention it. In fact, every case it cited that was decided since March 1937 involved free speech or minority rights—with the sole exception of a reference to *Wright v. Vinton Branch*, a decision impelling courts to adopt a constitutional construction of a statute where possible, which caused Morris Ernst great "heartache" because it soft-pedaled the issue of whether Hague's permit ordinance was facially unconstitutional.[74]

On the whole, the ABA committee deferred to the ACLU's lengthy brief for coverage of case law, and focused instead on the more capacious theoretical and policy questions at stake. The authors argued that freedom of assembly was worthy of constitutional protection because it was essential to the "American democratic system." That system, in turn, was premised on popular consent, which was only meaningful when secured through open debate. Legislation passed in the absence of robust public discussion could not command popular support and would lack legal legitimacy. Moreover, oversight by an engaged constituency provided a check on administrative abuses. While there were many available forums for public debate— including print media, radio, and movies—the face-to-face encounter of a meeting on the street corner or at the town square performed a unique and crucial role in the production of public opinion. This was particularly true in the context of unpopular minorities, who often had limited financial resources and whose ideas were otherwise unlikely to be heard. Indeed, the brief pronounced the outdoor meeting the "most *democratic* forum of public expression," in a line it borrowed directly from a memorandum submitted by Lusky.[75]

The brief's authors were adamant that the unpopularity of an idea could not justify suppressing it. Indeed, they considered "the right to express unpopular opinions and to hold unpopular meetings" to be the "essence of American liberty," which was fundamentally premised on tolerance. This principle, the brief emphasized, applied not only to determinations by officials that a particular idea was dangerous or undesirable, but also to the perceived hostility of a crowd. Whether spontaneous or orchestrated, a threat of disorder by opponents of a speaker (as opposed, potentially, to a threat by the speakers themselves) was no reason to prohibit a public appearance. Rather, the right response on the part of the authorities was to furnish adequate police protection in the event that violence indeed occurred. Government actors were bound not only to tolerate dissenting speech, but to take reasonable measures to protect the speaker from private disruptions. "Let the threateners be arrested for assault, or at least put under bonds to keep the peace," the brief proposed. After all, "it is they who should suffer for their lawlessness, not he."[76]

For the authors, free speech ensured both the legitimacy and optimal outcome of the democratic process. That was why it was not enough for the courts to prohibit state discrimination against disagreeable speakers—why the government needed to prevent interference by hecklers, too. By the same token, a city could not elect to close all of its property to public meetings. In the Supreme Court, the ABA would argue that to "safeguard the guaranteed right of public assembly," the government was obligated "to provide adequate places for public discussion." The committee wanted the state to do more than stay out. It was advocating an affirmative role for government in providing unpopular speakers with an opportunity to air their views, if not the means to make them heard.[77]

As Clark had hoped, the committee's involvement in the *Hague* case was well received. In fact, editorial comments were "unanimous" in commending the ABA for its contribution. Judge William Clark thought the committee "did a much better job than the Civil Liberties Union," which he considered "a somewhat irritating body" despite esteeming their cause. Four days before his appointment to the Supreme Court, Felix Frankfurter told Grenville Clark that the "symbolic significance" of the brief made it "a document of first importance." William Ransom, president of the ABA from 1935 to 1936, despised Ernst, Roger Baldwin, Norman Thomas, and the CIO for their "obnoxious collectivism." Nonetheless, he thought the committee's brief was one of the ABA's most impressive achievements, and he told Clark that it would stand "for years to come [as] an historic document, often referred to and quoted by those who are trying to fulfill the responsibility of so-called conservatives for the maintenance of civil liberties and free institutions."[78]

On the legal front, too, the ABA's intervention was a success. On January 26, 1939, the Third Circuit sustained Judge Clark's injunction. On the issues of deportation, searches and seizures, unlawful arrests, the posting of placards, and the distribution of leaflets, the court of appeals unanimously approved Judge Clark's reasoning and considered his findings to be amply supported by the record. The central question, about which the judges on the panel disagreed, was the constitutionality of the meeting ordinance. The dissenting judge thought the issue was not "primarily free speech at all." But the decision of the two-judge majority was even more protective of expressive freedom than the district court's. Not only was the ordinance unconstitutional as administered; the majority deemed it unconstitutional on its face.[79]

Citing *Near v. Minnesota,* Judge John Biggs Jr., a recent Roosevelt appointee, condemned the prior restraint of speech as patently unconstitutional. The threat of violence was not a legitimate basis for curtailing speech. Rather, it was the obligation of the police to protect the speaker. As for Judge Clark's suggestion that Jersey City could close all streets to public meetings, the Third Circuit majority disagreed. In Judge Biggs's view, a municipality owned and administered its streets and parks as trustees for the people, and the people had an affirmative right to access them for the purpose of public debate. "Fundamental civil liberties must not be tampered with," the court concluded, "if our system of democratic government is to survive."[80]

The press hailed the Third Circuit's discussion as it had the ABA's brief. It was clear, however, that the true test would take place in the Supreme Court, which promptly granted certiorari in the case. In the interim, the ABA was building on its newfound popularity. In the January 1939 issue of the *ABA Journal,* the Committee on the Bill of Rights urged all state and local bar associations to form their own committees to operate in local matters, with ample representation from younger lawyers. The national committee, meanwhile, arranged to file an amicus brief in the Supreme Court. Both Arthur Vanderbilt and Frank Hogan supported the endeavor, and with minimal internal opposition and the approval of both parties to the litigation, the committee submitted a brief that was substantially identical to its earlier version. Again, acclaim for the committee's work rolled in. At the Supreme Court, "very nice things were said about [the] Committee," and the gossip was the "brief would have attention." Reflecting on the case in 1940, Grenville Clark surmised that the briefs had "influenced both Courts in declaring Hague's ordinance and actions unconstitutional."[81]

The ABA Committee on the Bill of Rights had accomplished precisely what it was supposed to. In February, Hogan noted to Vanderbilt that the

National Lawyers Guild, for all its publicity, was shrinking rather than growing. Vanderbilt attributed the Guild's failure in large part to the ABA's stand on civil liberties. Hogan agreed, and he unreservedly endorsed the committee's work in a letter to the ABA board. The brief had prompted praise from every region of the United States, he observed. In fact, he added, there had been no press criticism whatsoever.[82]

To Hogan and Vanderbilt, the *Hague* brief was only the beginning. In the spring, the Carnegie Foundation (headed by Frederick Keppel, the NCLB's correspondent in the War Department during the First World War) awarded the ABA a grant to support the "editorial and publication program" of the Special Committee on the Bill of Rights. That grant funded the ABA's *Bill of Rights Review,* which was intended to connect the hundreds of lawyers and dozens of bar committees devoted to civil liberties work. Meanwhile, the committee's legal work continued. In the coming months, it would intervene in a variety of important cases, including *Minersville School District v. Gobitis.* Its efforts drew adulation from Frankfurter, who "kn[e]w of nothing in the Association's history that [was] more commendable than the establishment of this Committee on Civil Liberties," as well as the next Supreme Court appointee, William O. Douglas, who lauded the ABA's "contribution to civilized government." "It is not too much to say," Hogan wrote in reference to the committee's involvement in *Hague,* "that the good 'public relations' reaction which has come to the Association from (a) the creation of the Bill of Rights Committee, (b) the personnel of that Committee, and (c) its brief, has been of more value, along the much discussed line of public relations, than anything since our stand in opposition to the proposal to pack the Supreme Court." By the summer, he went even further. He told the board that nothing the ABA had done in recent years, not even its "remarkably fine work" in opposition to the court-packing proposal, had produced "such excellent public relations."[83]

✦ ✦ ✦

As Americans awaited the Supreme Court's decision in *Hague v. CIO,* civil liberties advocacy was already a confused and crowded field. In the spring of 1939, yet another actor entered the arena, and Frank Hogan somewhat grandiosely took the credit. When the ABA "went on record militantly for recognition of the sacred guaranties of the Bill of Rights," he declared, "the Department of Justice woke up and created a Civil

Liberties Unit." In reality, the new development reflected longer steeping commitments.[84]

On January 2, 1939, an old ACLU ally succeeded Homer Cummings as attorney general of the United States. As mayor of Detroit from 1930 to 1933, Frank Murphy had advocated for the unemployed. He quickly became one of the New Deal's "most enthusiastic supporters," for which the president rewarded him with an appointment as governor-general of the Philippines (and subsequently, United States high commissioner). In 1936, Murphy was elected governor of Michigan. Shortly after he took office, his refusal to break a UAW sit-down strike with state troops fostered the rise of the CIO. Murphy subsequently explained that Michigan workers resented employers' noncompliance with the Wagner Act, including the use of industrial espionage to discourage unionization. Their seizure of employer property was "honest" if misguided; they were "defending their own rights against what they believed to be the lawless refusal of their employers to recognize their unions." Murphy advised union representatives that sit-downs were illegal and unwise, but he considered it crucial to address the cause of workers' defiance, not merely to "enforce the law."[85]

Murphy carried those convictions to the Department of Justice. He had witnessed the contributions of the Senate Civil Liberties Committee in Michigan and elsewhere, and he shared Robert La Follette Jr.'s view that employer suppression of workers' rights exacerbated class antagonism, particularly when government officials intervened on employers' behalf. At the same time, Murphy maintained that other rights also warranted protection. He identified civil liberties in all aspects of life, "social, political, and economic." He drew from such disparate ideas as self-governance, individual self-expression, and freedom of conscience. Like Grenville Clark, Murphy accepted that governmental regulation was "necessary for an orderly society" and thought the modern state could accommodate expressive and religious freedom. Moreover, he deemed such rights equally applicable to "the business man and the laborer," to "the Jew and the Gentile," to "people of all racial extractions." Murphy's vision of civil liberties was neither the laissez-faire conception of Frank Hogan nor the ACLU's right of agitation. "Civil liberty," for Murphy, was "the idea of human dignity—translated into actuality," and he believed it to be America's "finest contribution . . . to civilization."[86]

Murphy made civil liberties enforcement a priority the moment he took office. Within weeks, he arranged a radio program on the federal government's protection of civil liberties and a speaking engagement with the National Lawyers Guild. He told Roger Baldwin that the opportunity to advance civil liberties was one of the "great satisfactions" of his new position, and he was "anxious that the weight and influence of the Department of Justice should be a force for the preservation of the people's liberties."[87]

One month after Murphy was sworn in, his office made an announcement: a Civil Liberties Unit had been created within the Criminal Division of the Department of Justice. Headed by Henry Schweinhaut—who had distinguished himself during investigations in both Harlan County and Jersey City—the new entity would prosecute violations of the constitutional and statutory guarantees extending "civil rights to individuals." Among its priorities were violence, denial of workers' rights, and interference with freedom of speech and assembly. Acting on recommendations by the La Follette Committee, the Civil Liberties Unit would ensure that those rights were respected. It would throw the "full weight of the Department" behind the "blessings of liberty, the spirit of tolerance, and the fundamental principles of democracy." In time, Murphy mused, the Civil Liberties Unit would prove "one of the most significant happenings in American legal history."[88]

The ACLU board wrote immediately to offer its support. It expressed confidence that the department of Justice could do much to help redress deprivations of the rights of citizens under federal law. The organization had often sought to involve the department in cases that seemingly fell under federal jurisdiction, but the absence of designated channels had hampered effective action. Recent efforts in Harlan County and Jersey City hinted at what the Civil Liberties Unit might accomplish with the appropriate internal machinery.[89]

By the spring of 1939, there were many bodies devoted to advancing civil liberties, including the La Follette Committee and the ABA Committee on the Bill of Rights, in addition to the ACLU. Still, the Civil Liberties Unit was particularly important. It was equipped not only to identify violations of civil liberties, but also to mobilize state power to rectify them. And its mechanism for enforcement was formidable. The NLRB, too, could command compliance with the law, at least in cooperation with the courts, but the Civil Liberties Unit had the authority to prosecute a broad range of offenses. At a nationwide gathering of United States attorneys in Washington, DC (the first such conference ever held), Murphy advised the federal prosecutors to exercise that authority responsibly. In a period marked by scapegoating and economic desperation, only deliberate state action could forestall the repression of minorities. Civil liberties had never before been so important.[90]

Murphy imagined an ambitious program for the Civil Liberties Unit. By targeting abuses, it would send a message to local officials who might be tempted to engage in arbitrary or unsavory practices. And yet, the new body could not "do the whole job," due to jurisdictional and practical constraints. In lynchings, beatings, and vigilante violence, the worst abusers were often private individuals whom federal prosecutors could not reach. More to the point, the surest way to preserve civil liberties was through tolerant public opinion. The Golden Rule, Murphy quipped, could not be implemented by United States marshals. The only true solution was "an overwhelming public determination that it must not happen here."[91]

Murphy hoped that over time the Civil Liberties Unit might expand its mandate. Department staff was studying the constitutional and statutory provisions that were potentially applicable to civil rights enforcement, including prohibitions on kidnapping, peonage, and mail fraud. The most promising possibilities were the ones the ACLU had promoted in Jersey City (and about which Grenville Clark harbored "a good deal of doubt"): Title 18, Sections 51 and 52 of the United States Code. The department hoped to invoke the statutes often, but it acknowledged their limitations. Section 52 applied only to deprivations of civil liberties under color of state laws. Section 51 was passed to curb the Ku Klux Klan, which rendered it "a somewhat difficult statute, for psychological reasons, to prosecute under." Moreover, while it authorized prosecutions for violations of constitutional rights, few constitutional guarantees implicated private action. Both sections also faced a final hurdle, namely, they criminalized interference with rights "secured by" the Constitution or federal statutes. Defendants were quick to argue—as they had, unsuccessfully, in Harlan County—that the language contemplated coverage of new rights "created" by the Constitution, not existing rights that the Constitution merely "guaranteed," including the rights of free speech and assembly. Given these limitations, the Civil Liberties Unit planned to recommend updated legislation.[92]

Until such legislation was passed, however, the Civil Liberties Unit would make do with existing options. The Civil Liberties Unit fielded hundreds of complaints within its first month. It reviewed such violations as lynchings, interference with meetings, police abuses, and denial of voting rights. It also considered filing prosecutions under Section 51 for unlawful employer practices under the Wagner Act. Even where it could not proceed, the mere suggestion of "violations of the Federal Civil Rights Statute" sometimes prompted local officials to release detained strikers or to settle labor disputes. Among the many requests that the Civil Liberties Unit received, one was particularly tempting. A week after the new body was announced, delegates from the Workers Defense League of New Jersey met with Schweinhaut to discuss the situation in Jersey City. They asked the department to continue its investigation of the Hague administration and to pursue an indictment for, among other things, the deportation of Norman Thomas.[93]

Jersey City, of course, was very much on Murphy's mind. He considered filing an amicus brief in the *Hague* case, with an eye to action in future civil liberties cases. In the end, he decided not to, reportedly because a favorable outcome was expected without the department's intervention. Still, the interest of the Civil Liberties Unit was evident to all involved, including the Supreme Court.[94]

✦ ✦ ✦

In its brief to the Supreme Court, Jersey City disputed only two significant points: federal jurisdiction and the constitutionality of the meeting ordinance (both facially and as applied). On the latter issue, it repeated the same arguments it had made in the two courts below. Municipal officials, it claimed, have the authority and duty to maintain public spaces for the enjoyment and tranquility of the public. Relying heavily on the *Davis* decision, it insisted that there was no "catch-all" concept of "free expression" in the Constitution, as the ACLU and CIO implied. Rather, rights were specific and idiosyncratic, tied to the "particular time, place and circumstance of the particular attempted type of 'expression.'" In public places, the boundaries of acceptable communication were constrained by the rights of the greater community.[95]

Morris Ernst and Spaulding Frazer likewise reiterated their earlier arguments. They rehearsed the many abuses to which the ACLU and CIO were subjected and argued that broad injunctive relief was justified notwithstanding the city's concessions. They reviewed the Supreme Court's recent First Amendment decisions to make a case for a robust freedom of assembly. And they argued that the right to speak in public places was a basic feature of democratic governance. In fact, it had become "so integral a part of American democracy" that a number of state courts had already moved to protect it by striking down permit requirements much like the one in Jersey City.[96]

The Supreme Court, which issued a decision in *Hague* on June 5, 1939, barely touched on these arguments. The monthly bulletin of the International Juridical Association lamented that the justices' reasoning was largely technical and lacked the lucidity and urgency of the great free speech cases; in contrast to the eloquent dissents of Justices Oliver Wendell Holmes Jr. and Louis D. Brandeis and the recent decisions in *De Jonge* and *Lovell*, fewer than half a dozen paragraphs over five separate opinions discussed the nature of the rights at issue and their significance to democratic governance. The bulletin declined to add that the opinions were as muddled as they were dry—a feature that likely explains the relative obscurity of the case in the subsequent development of First Amendment law.[97]

Of the seven justices who participated in the case (Justices Frankfurter and Douglas, newly appointed, did not take part), five voted to modify but affirm the district court's order, and two, Justices Pierce Butler and James Clark McReynolds, dissented. Two competing theories were advanced on behalf of the majority's conclusion that the meeting ordinance was facially unconstitutional. Justice Owen Roberts, in an opinion joined by Justice Hugo Black, considered the city's policy to be an abridgment of the privileges or immunities of citizens of the United States. Justice Stone, in a decision joined by Justice Stanley Reed, analyzed the case through the lens of due process instead. Justice Hughes split the difference.[98]

Both opinions concluded that the plaintiffs—with the exception of the ACLU, which was a corporation rather than a natural person—had stated a cause of action under a measure that originated in the Civil Rights Act of 1871. That provision, then codified at Title 8, Section 43 of the United States Code, and now familiar to civil rights lawyers as Section 1983 of Title 42, created a private cause of action for the denial under color of law of "rights, privileges, or immunities secured by the Constitution." Both opinions also located the district court's jurisdiction over the claim in Section 24(14) of the Judicial Code, a provision that conferred federal jurisdiction over suits to redress the deprivation, under color of law, "of any privilege or immunity secured by the Constitution of the United States, or of any right secured by any law of the United States providing for equal rights."

From there, however, the two opinions diverged widely. Justice Roberts limited his analysis to a "narrow question." The relevant inquiry, he reasoned, was whether freedom to discuss the Wagner Act was within the scope of the Privileges or Immunities Clause of the Fourteenth Amendment and thus covered by the civil rights provisions. Concluding that it was, he deemed it unnecessary to address the city's contention that the rights at stake preexisted the United States Constitution and thus were not "secured by" it within the meaning of the statute. Freedom to discuss federal legislation was an attribute of national citizenship, and thus safely within the protective ambit of the federal courts. The Jersey City meeting ordinance was unconstitutional because it infringed the privilege of citizens to use the streets and parks to communicate their views on national issues.[99]

Relying on the Privileges or Immunities Clause had a number of pitfalls, as Justice Stone was quick to point out. First, the provision applied only to citizens of the United States and thus limited freedom of speech in an unprecedented fashion. Second, there was no basis in the record for assuming that the CIO had ever intended to discuss the Wagner Act itself, as opposed to the merits of unionizing. Justice Roberts's decision seemingly opened the door to an expansion of the Privileges or Immunities Clause beyond the rule laid down in the 1873 Slaughterhouse Cases, which had confined its application to rights arising out of the relationship of United States citizens to the national government—and which, for a time, had sharply limited businesses' ability to challenge state social and economic legislation on constitutional grounds. Justice Roberts, by loosely construing the rights of "national citizenship," was inadvertently "enlarg[ing] Congressional and judicial control of state action" and endangering the "rightful independence of local government."[100]

Justice Stone's opinion turned on the Fourteenth Amendment's Due Process Clause instead. Freedom of speech and assembly were rights of personal liberty, he reasoned, and they applied to all persons, regardless of their citizenship. They were also squarely among the rights for which Section 43 of Title 8 provided a federal cause of action; as Ernst and Frazer had argued in their brief, earlier cases to the contrary all predated the Supreme Court's incorporation of the First Amendment. The only open question, according to Justice Stone, was whether due process claims could be maintained in the federal courts under Section 24(14) of the Judicial Code. After reviewing the legislative history of that provision, he concluded that they could.[101]

That the ACLU and other organizations could sue in federal court for injunctive relief had obvious implications for future litigation strategy.

Previously, the vast majority of ACLU cases had originated in the state courts, generally as criminal defenses. The new rule gave the ACLU an option to initiate test case litigation in federal court. Except in criminal cases, the organization and its allies could henceforth avoid those state courts whose independence was compromised—not just under circumstances like *Hague*, but in cases involving the civil rights of racial minorities, particularly in the South. When the ACLU was founded, one of its central objectives was to curb the injunctive power of the federal courts. Twenty years later, it was responsible for a momentous extension of that precise power, which it would invoke often in subsequent years when seeking vindication of civil liberties claims.

The Supreme Court's decision had ramifications for another body, as well. Henry Schweinhaut, reflecting on Hague's implications for his Civil Liberties Unit of the Department of Justice, was "elated" by the decision and considered it an invitation for prosecution under the criminal provisions of the Reconstruction statutes. Justice Stone's opinion implicitly rejected the narrow interpretation of Section 51 in *United States v. Cruikshank,* an 1876 case growing out of the mob murder of more than a hundred black Republicans in Reconstruction Louisiana. *Cruikshank* was just the sort of case that Section 51 was designed to cover. The defendants were convicted of conspiracy to deprive citizens of the United States of their rights to assemble and bear arms, among other charges. The Supreme Court reversed the convictions on the theory that such rights were not protected by the Fourteenth Amendment. Justice Stone's opinion suggested that *Cruikshank*, at least in part, was no longer good law.[102]

Of course, the court's decision left one fundamental limitation of the civil rights legislation intact. In October 1939, Assistant Attorney General O. John Rogge spoke about *Hague* at the ACLU's National Conference on Civil Liberties, which—in a telling homage to the new civil liberties landscape—honored the public servants of the Civil Liberties Unit, the La Follette Committee, and the NLRB. As Rogge explained, rights under the Due Process Clause of the Fourteenth Amendment did not extend to private action. The state action requirement expressed in *Cruikshank* and other cases meant that the statute was inapplicable to "the great mass of civil liberties cases" the department would otherwise have pursued. Rogge assured the audience that the Civil Liberties Unit was evaluating those cases, and if it deemed them unsound, it would have "no hesitation" in asking the Supreme Court to overrule them.[103]

There was one category of private action that Section 51 could be made to reach without a radical revision of existing case law. The Department of Justice interpreted the decision in *Hague* to authorize prosecution under Section 51 for the deprivation of a private right conferred by federal statute, including private violence affecting statutory rights "under the recently extended commerce clause." The Wagner Act was the most obvious candidate, and its curtailment by employers was the theory of the Harlan County case. In the department's view, *Hague* was a call for additional indictments under the statute, and the CIO announced that it would solicit federal prosecution of anyone who interfered with its organizing activities "by violating the civil rights of workers." Over the coming years, the department actively pursued the new strategy, albeit with uneven results.[104]

In the meantime, Frank Murphy was confident that the Supreme Court's decision would bolster efforts by the Department of Justice to prosecute infringements of constitutional rights. Indeed, he predicted that the Civil Liberties Unit would soon "grow into something very important." Americans had come to recognize the value of the fundamental rights the unit was designed to protect. "It has been obvious for some time in our country," he observed, "that our people are becoming increasingly civil liberties conscious, as they should."[105]

Murphy was right. By the spring of 1939, civil liberties had a popular salience that would have astounded dissenters during the First World War. Public approval of the outcome in *Hague* was a foregone conclusion. The dominant sentiment in press coverage of the decision was that the Supreme Court had not gone far enough.[106]

✦ ✦ ✦

In the wake of their Supreme Court victory, the civil liberties forces were jubilant. On June 12, the ACLU convened a mass meeting to celebrate free speech in Jersey City. The announcement for the celebration called the decision "a clear mandate to American citizens to exercise their rights of freedom of speech and assembly," as well as "a mandate to local officials not to interfere with those rights." The purpose of the gathering was not to espouse "radicalism or foreign doctrines," the ACLU emphasized. Rather, the audience would include Republicans and Democrats; Catholics, Protestants, and Jews. "This," the statement declared, "is fundamental Americanism."[107]

Between 7,000 and 8,000 people attended the meeting, by the ACLU's estimate. The Hague administration, at last, had determined that it was time to cut its losses. City officials aided in preparations and assisted at the event. "It was a wondrous sight to behold," an ACLU representative mused, "all those heads close together and not a nightstick coming down on any one of them; all the police on hand to help—not to pull down a speaker."[108]

Future meetings proceeded just as smoothly. In July, Jersey City adopted a new meeting ordinance, and the ABA called it "a model municipal enactment." The *Washington Post* thought that Hague's capitulation to the Supreme Court's decision was an "occasion for rejoicing": the distinguishing feature of a democracy was "the readiness of the people voluntarily to submit to the law's dictates." By September, an update in the ACLU's *Civil Liberties Quarterly* was titled "Jersey City Open to Free Assembly" and began with a heartening assessment: "All's quiet on the Jersey City front."[109]

In addition to its implications for free speech generally, the *Hague* decision was an unmistakable "go signal," as California's state bar journal put it, for labor organizing in Jersey City and elsewhere. In the days after the decision, the CIO relocated its offices to Jersey City and launched a massive organizing campaign. William Carney, in a public statement on June 5, announced that the 30,000 CIO members in Hudson County had "enlisted for the duration of the war" and would not give up until Hague was "either in jail or in political oblivion."[110]

As it turned out, the parties came to terms much more easily than Carney expected. Less than two months after the Supreme Court's decision, CIO representatives visited Mayor Hague's office and emerged with assurances that city hall was "always open" to them. The next day, the Hague administration sided with a local CIO affiliate in a labor dispute. Hague, who proclaimed a few days later that he was "one hundred percent" for a Roosevelt third term, had determined that cooperation with local labor leaders was a more profitable strategy than defiance. The Roosevelt administration reciprocated. Shortly after Hague's endorsement, reports emerged that the Civil Liberties Unit was dropping its investigation in Jersey City. Frank Murphy, who had spearheaded anticorruption efforts within the Department of Justice and was widely regarded as self-righteously moral (he did not smoke, drink, swear, or eat meat, according to the *Baltimore Sun*), was accused of selling out.[111]

A few hours before he was sworn in as associate justice of the Supreme Court, on January 18, 1940, Murphy issued a statement on his "unfinished business" as attorney general. In it, he denied that he had avoided proceeding against Hague for political purposes and attributed his inaction to insufficient evidence instead. Morris Ernst, who by 1940 was a close personal adviser to President Roosevelt, went further. He reported that he had worked with the criminal division and knew it had made a comprehensive inquiry. "Not only was there no suppression of the investigation," he added, "but the only way they could have prosecuted Hague would have been by violating the Mayor's civil liberties."[112]

The battle with Mayor Hague was a last gasp for the ACLU's founding commitment to fighting in the trenches alongside its labor allies. For two decades, the ACLU leadership had stood at the head of the rallies and picket lines that precipitated the organization's major court challenges. Roger Baldwin was convicted of marching with striking silk workers in Paterson, just a few miles away from Hudson County. As late as May 1938, Arthur Garfield Hays invited arrest by making an impromptu address from the roof of a Jersey City car. But as the litigation in *Hague v. CIO* unfolded, Ernst and the ACLU decided that it was more effective to stand aloof from the fray.[113]

By the time Judge Clark began hearing testimony in *Hague*, ACLU attorneys had convinced the courts and the public that free speech was an important American value. Hague himself, while insisting that free speech was not implicated in Jersey City, agreed during trial that nobody "should be denied the right to talk." Over the course of the legal proceedings, however, the broader civil liberties project was still very much in flux. Increasingly, the ACLU took steps to ensure its "neutrality." It publicly and ardently disavowed labor issues as appropriate organizational concerns. As in its academic and artistic freedom cases, it insisted that the rights at stake were the right to air disfavored ideas and the right to be free from the censor's arbitrary and autocratic reach. At the public celebration following the Supreme Court's decision in *Hague*, William Callahan, an editor for the *Catholic Worker*, reminded his audience that the judicial victory was "only a small part of the larger, grander work of securing the fruits of democracy for the millions to whom they are yet denied." But Callahan's determination to use the case as a "springboard towards a larger, more generous freedom" was becoming a marginal view within the ACLU, which explicitly dissociated its free speech meeting from the organizing efforts of the CIO.[114]

As the La Follette Committee yielded the spotlight to Martin Dies Jr.'s House Special Committee to Investigate Un-American Activities, the ACLU stripped civil liberties of their radical valence. Even Baldwin began to abandon the radical rhetoric he had so resolutely voiced since the First World War. At the outset of the litigation, Baldwin linked the ACLU's objectives in Jersey City to the ascendance of organized labor under the new wave of labor-friendly legislation and court decisions. Around that time, a correspondent offered Baldwin some revealing advice: "I know you're a Marxist and all that, and I know the argument that civil liberties and economic liberties are all of one piece and are as inseparable as the Trinity. Well, from my point of view that's good theology, but damn poor tactics." One year later, Baldwin still believed that "the real issue" at stake in Jersey City "was the right of independent trade unions to organize in what has been proudly heralded as an open shop town." He nonetheless assured his audience that the ACLU defended everyone's rights without distinction and had "no 'ism' to promote except the Bill of Rights." The ACLU, he insisted, was no more concerned with the rights of labor than the rights of employers. The organization would "open doors" that were closed to unions, but it was up to the workers "to walk through the doors after they are opened."[115]

All told, Ernst estimated that the *Hague* case absorbed more of his firm's time than the rest of his ACLU cases put together. The legal bill, which included only expenses, came to thousands of dollars and led to a spat between the plaintiffs as to which group should pay. The dispute over reimbursement, however, was the least important of the many disagreements that the *Hague* case spawned between the ACLU and the CIO.[116]

From the perspective of the ACLU's dwindling labor constituency, the Jersey City campaign had been most costly in nonfinancial terms. *Hague v. CIO* was the first time that an ACLU legal action on behalf of organized labor attracted widespread public support. But its popular resonance stemmed precisely from the erasure of labor issues from its central terms. As the *Yale Law Journal* observed, "When practically every shade of public opinion became outraged at what appeared to be a blatant denial of fundamental rights, emphasis shifted from specific attempts by one group at raising abnormally low Jersey City working conditions to the more basic issue of whether constitutional guaranties of free speech, free press, and free assembly apply to union sympathizers as well as to other citizens."[117]

Right-wing critics had feared that support for the civil liberties cause by self-described conservatives, and particularly such eminent bodies as the ABA, would make the ACLU more respectable—and indeed it did. Their fear, however, was largely misplaced. Respectability attracted new members and new allies to the ACLU. In turn, it created new expectations. After *Hague v. CIO*, the ACLU would rarely defend its labor clients on anything other than generally applicable First Amendment grounds. The next step was to extend those same rights to the very individuals and entities whose dominance the ACLU was founded to resist. In 1940, the ABA's Committee on the Bill of Rights announced its intention to file its next amicus brief in a case involving the right of employers to free speech, asserted against the coercive apparatus of New Deal labor law. Its position on the matter was squarely in line with the ACLU's.[118]

8

Free Speech or Fair Labor

O N MAY 26, 1937, representatives of the United Automobile Workers of America (UAW) assembled peacefully near the Ford Motor Company's River Rouge plant in Dearborn, Michigan, to distribute union leaflets. They were greeted by Ford agents and, in the presence of peaceful observers and press representatives, brutally beaten. The message was clear: the Ford Motor Company would not be organized.

The "Battle of the Overpass," as the events of May 26 came to be known, was a pivotal episode in negotiations between the Ford Motor Company and the UAW, and it features prominently in accounts of industrial unionism in America. The River Rouge assault tarnished Henry Ford's reputation for industrial benevolence and revived support for workers' efforts to secure union recognition. But an equally important legacy of the Battle of the Overpass has been largely lost to history. Ford's attack on UAW organizers occurred just six weeks after the Supreme Court upheld the constitutionality of the Wagner Act. Newly empowered, the NLRB swiftly condemned Ford's labor policies, precipitating a second and more protracted clash in the courtroom instead of on the shop floor.

Under NLRB scrutiny, Ford's attorneys were hard pressed to defend the company's response to organizing efforts in Dearborn. Instead, they launched a legal and public relations campaign against the NLRB itself. Their indictment of its procedures undermined public confidence in the adjudicative capabilities of the NLRB and helped to lay the groundwork for the Taft-Hartley Act ten years later.

270

The most original contribution of Ford's lawyers, however, was not in the field of procedure, where a battle between industry and the NLRB was already raging, but rather in the ongoing struggle over the meaning of civil liberties. In the spring of 1937, the Supreme Court had signaled a new deference to government regulation of the economy. In the altered constitutional landscape, employers no longer could count on the federal courts to strike down prolabor machinery for encroaching on the property rights of employers. They would need instead to whittle away at state power by invoking those checks capable of mustering broad popular and political support. The ABA's belated but successful endorsement of civil liberties during the court-packing controversy had established free speech as the most promising possibility. And so, seizing on civil libertarian rhetoric of the past two decades, Ford introduced a new twist on old rights. By dictating the terms of employers' communications with their employees, it argued, the NLRB was trenching on freedoms that were guaranteed by the Constitution to protect democratic processes. The NLRB was curtailing employers' freedom of speech.

Conservatives quickly assimilated the new argument into their antilabor arsenal. Soon, the ABA and the National Association of Manufacturers counted the Wagner Act's encroachment on "an employer's freedom of oral and written expression" among the most pressing defects of the New Deal's labor law regime. Organized labor and the Left staunchly disagreed. Although they acknowledged free speech as an important value, they insisted that antiunion statements by employers were coercive and thus outside the protection of the First Amendment. To hold otherwise, they protested, would be subversive of social progress in precisely the same fashion as the judicial enforcement of liberty of contract, which the Supreme Court had so recently abandoned.[1]

For the ACLU, the issue was more complicated. Longtime ACLU secretary Lucille Milner told an NLRB regional director that the question of employer free speech was the most contentious one that the ACLU board had ever considered. In fact, the ACLU's leadership had never been "so completely at loggerheads on any issue since the organization ha[d] been in existence." This time, the contest was not primarily over institutions, though the old arguments about which branch of government would most reliably serve labor's interests were involved. Rather, the dispute over the

NLRB's order in the *Ford* case challenged the ACLU to reassess the meaning and limits of free speech—indeed, to question whether free speech was always in fact a desirable goal. Its resolution hardened the mature commitments of the ACLU, as well as the modern understanding of civil liberties in the United States.[2]

✦ ✦ ✦

During the winter of 1936–1937, America's attention was sixty-some miles from Dearborn, Michigan, in Flint. After a sensational forty-four-day sit-down strike, the General Motors Company (GM), the world's largest industrial corporation, begrudgingly recognized the UAW-CIO as the exclusive bargaining representative of its workers. Even the union was surprised by that outcome. GM had secured an injunction against the strikers, but Michigan's new governor, Frank Murphy, refused to deploy state power on the company's behalf. Two years before he created the Civil Liberties Unit of the Department of Justice as attorney general of the United States, Murphy was already grappling with the appropriate role of government in policing contests over rights. Like President Franklin D. Roosevelt, he conceded that the seizure of GM property was illegal—but so too, he insisted, was GM's violation of the Wagner Act. Murphy mobilized the National Guard troops but ordered them to maintain the peace and protect the strikers from local law enforcement and vigilantes rather than break the strike.[3]

Nationally, the victory generated a mix of outrage and admiration. Labor justified the sit-down strike as a remedy for employers' ongoing disregard of New Deal labor law, as well as the logical culmination of a wholesale reallocation of rights. According to UAW attorney Maurice Sugar, federal legislation had utterly unsettled employers' common-law prerogatives. All that distinguished the sit-down strike from other activity authorized by the Wagner Act was its location.[4]

Like other radical labor leaders, Sugar regarded the sit-down strike as an essential weapon in labor's arsenal. It promoted solidarity and impeded the use of replacement workers. It also discouraged police and security personnel from employing violence against the strikers, lest they inadvertently damage employer property. By the spring of 1937, sit-downs had directly affected 400,000 workers, and UAW membership had reached a quarter million. As the pioneer of the new strategy, the CIO had become a formidable opponent. In March, United States Steel entered into a collective bargaining agreement with the Steel Workers Organizing Committee–CIO, no strike necessary. Even as they vilified the strikers, business leaders and their attorneys reluctantly conceded the lack of "direct precedent as to the legality of the sit-down strike." After all, the Wagner Act had conferred on strikers an unprecedented right to engage in concerted activity on employer property, and the Supreme Court had deemed it constitutional. There was a realistic possibility— notwithstanding the "plainest principles of common law"—that courts might deem sit-downs, too, to be protected by the Wagner Act and consistent with the Constitution.[5]

By late spring, however, the tide had begun to turn against labor. Almost one-quarter of America's nonagricultural workers were unionized, and the majority, for the time being, belonged to CIO-affiliated unions. But the CIO was already struggling to maintain its power and legitimacy. The economy had contracted sharply as a result of Roosevelt's fiscal policy, fueling frustration and desperation by industry and workers alike. Public and political figures expressed concern at unions' aggressive attitude. By summer, fear of sit-downs was pervasive, and the Senate had roundly condemned the practice.[6]

Sit-down strikes were only the first congressional casualty. The failure of Roosevelt's judiciary reorganization bill had suggested that New Deal labor law, newly safe from constitutional challenge, was vulnerable to legislative attack. Republican opponents of the administration partnered with southern Democrats who feared that federal involvement in labor disputes might spread to Jim Crow. At the same time, the AFL charged the NLRB with favoring the CIO. New Deal Democrats countered with evidence from Robert M. La Follette Jr.'s Senate Civil Liberties Committee of rampant employer abuses. By the summer of 1937, however, the committee's staff was regularly fielding demands that it investigate labor unions in addition to employers. Its correspondents blamed striking workers for picket-line violence and the NLRB for forsaking employers. One outraged citizen pointedly suggested that the La Follette Committee investigate President Roosevelt for his court-packing plan.[7]

In this antiunion tempest, the ACLU was adrift. Ever since its debate over the Wagner Act, the ACLU had been struggling to define its underlying objectives. Over the past decades, the organization had restored a measure of credibility to the courts. It had convinced many Americans, including many judges, that state suppression of speech stifled democratic change and unduly burdened individual autonomy. It had done all this to preserve the rights of labor to picket, boycott, and strike, "in any circumstances, by any method, in any numbers" (that is, mass picketing and secondary activity in addition to simple strikes). But as organized labor attained unprecedented economic power, the ACLU leadership questioned how the right of agitation squared with civil liberties concerns. The CIO's new tactics were not obviously about speech or expression. Nor was the ACLU board's endorsement of the Wagner Act or the NLRB. And increasingly, the mainstream press and the ACLU's own members, many of whom had recently joined, were critical of the organization's identification with the labor cause.[8]

In March 1937, the ACLU board of directors took a first cut at clarifying its position. It pronounced in a statement that the organization's only purpose was "the maintenance of democratic rights." In the past, ACLU annual reports had always proclaimed the organization's special concern for the civil liberties of labor. This time, the ACLU professed to have no "economic direction" or connection with any "economic movement." To be sure, the organization continued to defend nonviolent "agitation" as well as propaganda. But the emphasis was different. As it had for years, the board explained the disproportionate representation of radicals in the ACLU leadership as a function of conservative indifference. This time, however, it resolved to correct the imbalance. It promised not only to welcome individuals with divergent economic views, but also to give them leadership positions. It stressed the organization's willingness to defend the constitutional rights of conservatives, reactionaries, and even ("if occasion required, as it does not") of nonunion workers.[9]

These general pronouncements masked bitter disagreements within the ACLU leadership, but the controversy over sit-down strikes laid them bare. A statement on the issue prepared by a board subcommittee simply summarized the case for both sides. The attempt to preserve the ACLU's neutrality pleased no one. By failing to follow Congress and the press in condemning the tactic outright, the compromise approach alienated the board's conservative bloc. It was attacked just as vigorously from the Left, which believed that the courts might soon recognize the sit-down strike as a lawful labor weapon. Both of the ACLU's attorneys balked, though for different reasons. Morris Ernst argued, as he had in debates over the Wagner Act, that economic equality was outside the sweep of civil liberties advocacy. Like Ernst, Arthur Garfield Hays thought his sympathy for labor had no place in the ACLU. His concerns, however, ran deeper. Although he was personally inclined to celebrate the UAW's impressive achievements in Michigan, he worried that the sit-down strike might undermine the "civil liberties" of employers, or the "right of non-union men to work"—extraordinary anxieties for someone willing to provoke his own arrest to defend the right to strike.[10]

The national committee proved even more polarized than the core leadership. To its conservative faction, the issue was simple: workers who engaged in sit-downs and slowdowns were trespassing on employer property. Labor's claim to a countervailing property right in one's job was untenable in the absence of an employment contract that so provided; sit-downs were a stepping-stone to revolution and dictatorship. At the other end of the spectrum, Elizabeth Gurley Flynn was bewildered that the statement credited the crippling of essential services as a legitimate concern when the ACLU had so often rejected that objection in the past. One correspondent equated the board's position with the American Liberty League's. Perhaps the most telling response came from a longtime member who personally thought the sit-down justifiable but considered the issue largely moot. "With the Labor Relations Act in force," he said, "there should be little provocation for sit-down strikes."[11]

Disagreement about sit-down strikes was only the beginning; soon, the ACLU's acrimonious debate extended to the Wagner Act and its administration. The Supreme Court's decision upholding the statute emboldened the NLRB, and within a few months, it had more than tripled its caseload. Very often, it ruled against employers. When congressional opponents first introduced statutory amendments to soften the Wagner Act, the ACLU opposed them on the anemic basis that they had not been sufficiently studied. But calls for amendment only intensified over the coming months. In the summer of 1937, Republican senator Arthur H. Vandenburg suggested provisions that would have restrained unions and introduced new employer rights. Many similar proposals followed, fueled by the increasingly bitter struggle between the AFL and the CIO (which prompted AFL president William Green to complain that the CIO was "brutally prevent[ing]" workers "from exercising their civil rights of free speech, free assemblage and freedom to organize"). The AFL felt that NLRB policy favored the CIO, and at its October convention, it recommended a slate of amendments to the Wagner

Act. In 1938, the AFL leadership allied with business to oppose the NLRB—going so far as to collaborate with former American Liberty League attorneys who were representing the NAM. Although congressional efforts to curb the NLRB were unsuccessful, public and political opposition to the Wagner Act and its administration was mounting.[12]

Within the ACLU, controversy erupted over every pressing issue in the rapidly changing world of labor relations. Although the organization consistently professed neutrality, conservatives bemoaned "the Union's partiality toward union labor." The ACLU's statement on violence in strikes claimed that "the Civil Liberties Union does not take sides in the industrial struggle" and would act against violence by organized labor just as vigorously as attacks by employers. It insisted, however, that allegations of union violence were usually fabricated.[13]

Many of the efforts to counteract the increased power of organized labor focused on bringing unions under greater government control. In January 1938, the ACLU came out squarely in opposition to proposed legislation providing for compulsory incorporation of trade unions and publication of financial statements. This was exactly the sort of strangulation through regulation that Roger Baldwin had worried about when the Wagner Act was first introduced: compulsory incorporation would transform the right to organize into a licensed privilege contingent on good behavior. According to the statement, the true purpose of the proposed amendments was to restrict legitimate trade union growth. By the same token, the ACLU opposed empowering the NLRB to police coercive union practices. Regulating unions, the organization argued, was an unwarranted extension of state power more intrusive than the vanquished labor injunction.[14]

As in the earlier debate over passage of the Wagner Act, many within the ACLU pushed back against the organization's stated position, complaining that a civil liberties group had no business interfering with government regulation of labor relations. Then, the incipient separation of civil liberties and social policy had moved the organization to accept state control over ostensibly economic matters, as long as the rights to strike, picket, and boycott were preserved. This time, some took a further step. A growing contingent thought the organization should be supporting amendments to temper the administrative power of the NLRB, on the one hand, and to protect the constitutional rights of employers and nonunion employees, on the other. There was a strong kinship, if not a causal link, between the

ACLU's early attacks on administrative discretion and the late–New Deal demands for administrative law reform. Like many within the latter movement, the members of the ACLU worried about unchecked administrative discretion, even while they believed that administrative expansion was an inevitable outcrop of modernity. The call to administer the new machinery in a manner consistent with the framework of American constitutional democracy hardly seemed objectionable from a civil liberties standpoint. Indeed, at that very moment the ACLU was opposing legislation to curb fascist activity in the United States because it raised the specter of improper administrative enforcement against radicals and religious minorities. Once labor policy became an unexceptional application of administrative authority, there was little principled basis for distinguishing the NLRB from the Post Office Department or the Federal Communications Commission, whose censorship the ACLU had routinely opposed. The ACLU's labor sympathizers sidestepped this problem by claiming that the NLRB, unlike those other entities, had operated responsibly and within the bounds of constitutional law. A vocal minority of the organization's membership found that response unconvincing.[15]

Even more divisively, some within the ACLU believed the Wagner Act curtailed the civil liberties of nonunion members. Their first target was the closed shop. Concerned ACLU members demanded action on behalf of workers "who through no fault of their own—except in the refusal to contribute to an organization of which they disapprove—are denied the right to work in the jobs they have held for so many years." The ACLU had always considered the discharge of an employee for union membership to be a violation of civil liberties, explained William G. Fennell, the lone labor skeptic on the organization's Committee on Labor's Rights (which, at Fennell's request, was eventually renamed the Committee on Civil Rights in Labor Relations). Fennell felt that the ACLU was bound to defend with equal vigor the right of employees not to join a union. At a time when the ACLU's defense of value-neutral rights had become axiomatic, Fennell's argument reflected the unintended consequence of the organization's legal strategy. From its founding through *Near v. Minnesota,* the ACLU had linked the right to organize to the First Amendment. And it had often argued that interference with that right—even by injunction—abridged the Bill of Rights. The ACLU's theory that judicial enforcement of a private contract providing for the abrogation of one party's constitutional rights was unconstitutional state action would have required an expansive construction of state action rarely endorsed and almost never effectuated. As events unfolded, passage of the Norris–LaGuardia Act rendered such a reading unnecessary. But as compared with judicial contract enforcement, administrative authorization of a collective bargaining agreement prohibiting the employment of non-members made the state more palpably complicit in their exclusion.[16]

Rather than address this argument, the ACLU avoided it. As it had in the case of the sit-down strike, it issued a statement relating competing points of view on the closed shop. It was the ACLU's conclusion that the civil liberties of nonunion workers were threatened only in cases of arbitrary restrictions on union membership, such as racial discrimination. In those situations, it promised—without explaining why—that the organization would defend the right of nonmembers to continued employment "by recourse to the courts."[17]

✦ ✦ ✦

The ACLU's increasing ambivalence toward administrative enforcement of the Wagner Act precipitated a momentous but underappreciated episode in the history of civil liberties: the controversy over employer free speech. The issue first attracted the ACLU's notice in the fall of 1937, when the NLRB's purported interference with press freedom in two cases caused a media uproar. In the first incident, the NLRB accused an employer of influencing speculation in a local newspaper that unionization would lead to loss of jobs. In the second, it subpoenaed the editor of a trade magazine to testify about its negative coverage of the board's investigation of an employer, in an effort to determine whether the employee had encouraged or written the critical article.[18]

Newspapers and politicians were quick to condemn the NLRB for its "open attack[] on the freedom of the press," and ACLU members began asking for a statement of the organization's position. Nathan Greene, co-author with Felix Frankfurter of *The Labor Injunction*, was chairman of the Committee on Labor's Rights, and he drafted a response to the charges. A staunch labor advocate, he sprang unflinchingly to the defense of the NLRB. Most states denied journalists a privilege to withhold confidential communications about unlawful conduct, and for Greene, that settled the matter. An important antecedent of Greene's position was the assumption that employers themselves could be prevented from expressing antiunion views. Of this fact, Greene had no doubt. Like the NLRB, he believed that antiunion speech by an employer curtailed employees' right to organize under the Wagner Act. Employers' antiunion propaganda amounted to an order rather than reasoned argument, he explained, and the ACLU would "not defend speech when it is but the velvet glove that conceals the iron fist." That was an unusual qualification for an organization founded to protect radicals, as critics soon pointed out. But Roger Baldwin was convinced by Greene's disposition of the matter and secured the board's approval to redraft it as a letter, send it to the chairman of the NLRB, and issue it as a news release. Citing *Associated Press v. NLRB*, it emphasized that past experience had taught the ACLU to be suspicious when employers invoked the freedom of the press.[19]

Once again, conflict erupted within the ACLU's national committee. The labor bloc believed it was impossible for the NLRB to guarantee the rights of labor in the face of employer "coercion." In the past, the ACLU had supported legislation prohibiting employers from circulating political advice in pay envelopes, and employers' intervention in union elections seemingly raised the same concerns. But many ACLU members disagreed, and they conjured practical as well as theoretical considerations. After all, the ACLU had steadfastly opposed the issuance of injunctions against union pickets on the grounds that they were coercive. If union activity was unfair, they had argued, the appropriate remedy was to denounce it, not to enjoin it. Someday, the state might once again target speech by unions rather than employers. When it did, the ACLU would be best served by a consistent record of the rigorous protection of all expression, no matter how persuasive.[20]

Faced with a barrage of comments like these, the board agreed to address the issue of employer free speech head on. In January, it requested an advisory vote on two memoranda: a "proposed statement on employers' rights in industrial conflict," together with a minority report. The former reiterated Greene's earlier arguments about the coercive nature of the employer-employee relationship, and to assuage fears of administrative censorship, it stressed that NLRB orders were unenforceable in the absence of judicial approval. Roger W. Riis (the son of muckraker Jacob Riis) submitted the minority report because he felt that the board had abandoned its motivating principles. In his assessment, which anticipated one of the central questions in scholarly debate over free speech, defenders of the

NLRB distrusted "the free competition of the market." They professed neutrality, but they wanted to amplify weaker voices, that is, "to bring about a more equitable propaganda-balance between employer and employee." And for Riis, laudable as the board's desire was, it was not a legitimate objective for an organization devoted to civil liberties.[21]

The committed leftists rejected Riis's reasoning, but many members of the national committee, including reliable labor advocates, shared his concerns. Some worried about administrative overreaching. Others emphasized appearances. Morris Ernst, about to go to trial in *Hague v. CIO*, cautioned that the rationale of the majority report would jeopardize the ACLU's effort in Jersey City. Lloyd K. Garrison preferred to leave the thorny problem for the courts, and he counseled against any statement at all.[22]

In practice, however, ignoring the issue was no longer a feasible option. The circulation of the majority and minority reports touched off a firestorm in the ACLU that would not be quieted until 1940, with the expulsion of Communists from the ACLU board. In the meantime, a heated exchange of letters between two major players in that controversy—Harry Ward, longtime chairman of the ACLU board, and John Haynes Holmes, who replaced him in that capacity once the anti-Communist resolution was passed—captured the brewing tension within the leadership. Holmes thought the majority report was "the most specious document" the ACLU had ever produced. The ACLU, he said, was "face to face with fundamentals." Like many members of the organization, Holmes supported the labor movement and belonged to organizations committed to protecting its rights. The ACLU, however, was about civil liberties, not the class struggle. According to Holmes, accepting the board's position would mean promoting fascism; it would destroy the ACLU and leave him no choice except to resign. For the time being, Holmes was "not asking for any excommunications." But he could not sanction an approach that had made free speech a means to an end.[23]

Ward flatly denied the premise of Holmes's argument. He believed the true conflict was between free speech, on the hand, and a constitutionally protected right to organize, on the other. Within the board, he argued, there was an honest disagreement as to where to strike the balance. By questioning the motives of those who would strike it differently, Holmes would only exacerbate the conflict within the organization.[24]

Holmes was right to regard the cleavage within the board as a turning point. Nothing in the ACLU's past had raised so basic a challenge to its theory of civil liberties. To be sure, the organization had defended speech that its leaders reviled. But the rights of the Ku Klux Klan to rally in Catholic Boston or of the Nazi Party to march in New Jersey were the rights of disfavored minorities to organize for social change, however repugnant.[25]

Before the New Deal, it was practically inconceivable that the state, with judicial approval, would silence capital vis-à-vis labor. In the early 1930s, radicals within the ACLU had opposed the Wagner Act because they believed the state would inevitably suppress the right to strike in the service of industrial interests. Even in 1937, state and local governments routinely targeted labor activity, and a full 40 percent of the cases handled by the ACLU involved unions. But the NLRB had defied the expectations of the ACLU's state-skeptics, and as a result, the conflict over employer free speech turned the organization's ordinary arguments on their head. The NLRB was curtailing employer expression in order to facilitate union organizing. For the first time, defending free speech threatened labor's substantive gains. Upholding the right to speak meant undercutting the right of agitation.[26]

Some within the ACLU thought that the controversy over employer speech was exaggerated. They assumed that an employer's distaste for unionization would be known to employees regardless of whether it was explicitly articulated, and that it was far better to "err on the side of free speech," both in the immediate term (to forestall attacks on the Wagner Act) and as a general policy. The crucial thing, they insisted, was to eradicate coercive employer conduct like espionage and discriminatory discharge. This view, of course, hinged on a belief that radical speech—whether in the form of picketing and boycotts or advocacy of political change—was capable of making a concrete difference in political and economic conditions. It also assumed that workers would not be persuaded by their employers' pronouncements on the perils of organization.[27]

The other side, which began as the progressive view, was voiced by an increasing contingent of political activists and academics over the coming years. It emphasized that free speech, in a society dominated by commercial media, was never really free, and that radical proposals were bound to be drowned out in a marketplace of prepackaged ideas. It danced around the edges of a theory of false consciousness, harking back to the master-servant relationship and insinuating that the oppressed were no longer capable of perceiving their chains. Ever since the IWW trial, the ACLU leadership had been aware that private checks on expressive freedom were at least as repressive as the state's. The Wagner Act was an effort to protect workers' speech from private curtailment. Like the La Follette Committee and the Civil Liberties Unit of the Department of Justice, the NLRB was promoting, for this brief moment, a vision of free speech as a substantive right to be heard.

In the end, citing an even split within the leadership as well as the national committee, the board tabled both the majority and minority reports. Instead of issuing a statement, it finally heeded the lawyerly advice that Felix Frankfurter had given the board a year earlier, when the controversy over the Wagner Act first erupted—namely, to establish its policy in particular applications rather than issuing abstract statements of principle.[28]

The case that it chose to examine had been brewing since the fall, and it had been invoked in support of both positions on employer free speech. That case pitted the Ford Motor Company against the NLRB.[29]

✦ ✦ ✦

An outspoken proponent of welfare capitalism, Henry Ford often touted his company's excellent wages and employee benefits. In 1914, the Ford Motor Company announced a profit-sharing plan. It introduced the forty-hour workweek in 1926. But Ford was also a true believer in the individualist creed of the *Lochner* era, and on the issue of unions, he would not budge.

Indeed, Ford was determined to forestall unionization of the Ford Motor Company at any cost. The task of combating the UAW fell to the Ford Service Department, whose head, Harry Bennett, was known for his unsavory connections with organized crime. Bennett's "Servicemen" used espionage, intimidation, and violence to dissuade workers from organizing. As strikes rocked the auto industry, Ford invested thousands of dollars in guns and tear gas and increased the size of the Service Department for good measure.[30]

Nonetheless, in the spring of 1937, the UAW resolved to take on its most formidable adversary. In Michigan, as in the rest of the country, public opinion had turned against labor. Aggressive UAW actions in Detroit prompted powerful police responses, and neither the state nor the federal government was willing to intervene on labor's behalf. To the UAW leadership, the new reality made organizing the Ford Motor Company all the more important. Not only had Ford kept unions out of its own plants, but it had stood in the way of efforts to organize its purchasers and suppliers. UAW organizer Richard Frankensteen, took charge of the Ford campaign and announced that 200,000 workers would assist in the effort.[31]

Ford's River Rouge plant in Dearborn was a crucial organizing target, and the UAW planned to distribute literature to the largely insulated employees from an overpass connecting the factory gates to a nearby streetcar stop. When they arrived at River Rouge on May 26, 1937, the organizers were not expecting a fight. If anything, Walter Reuther, the UAW's future president and Frankensteen's rival for control of the organization, had been unusually cautious. He secured a permit for the event and ensured attendance by respected observers, including clergy members, the local press, and La Follette Committee staff. To further discourage violence, he designated a women's auxiliary to pass out the union pamphlets, which were precleared by the Dearborn city clerk. Of course, union organizing was always a risky endeavor, particularly in Dearborn. But leafleting was constitutionally protected activity, and there was no reason to suspect any more than the usual trouble.

When Reuther and Frankensteen posed for a photo outside the plant gates, however, a menacing group of Ford Servicemen told them that they were trespassing on company property and ordered them to leave. Although the overpass was actually public property (the company had constructed it but leased it to the Detroit Street Railway Commission), the two organizers peacefully turned to comply. They only made it a few steps before they were attacked from behind. Reuther was beaten severely in the face, chest, and groin and then picked up and dropped onto the concrete seven or eight times. Frankensteen was pummeled repeatedly and thrown down three flights of stairs. The women distributing the leaflets were punched, albeit less forcefully, and were "called all manner of vile names usually attributed to women of the streets." Some participants lost consciousness, and one suffered a broken back. Many spent days in the hospital recovering.[32]

Wary of bad press, Ford Servicemen tried to seize and destroy all records of the event, but a few photographers manage to retain their plates and films. Among them was a *Detroit News* photographer whose iconic images of the attack inspired the Pulitzer committee to introduce a prize for photography. In the span of a few hours, the Ford Motor Company extinguished its worker-friendly reputation and opened itself up to a powerful organizing drive.[33]

In the days after the Battle of the Overpass, as UAW organizers sought to capitalize on a rare wave of favorable publicity, Maurice Sugar prepared a lengthy complaint for a hearing before the NLRB. The complaint accused the Ford Motor Company of a host of unfair labor practices besides the River Rouge assault, including intimidation and threats, soliciting members for a company union, and discriminating against three dozen employees on the basis of union status. Finally, it charged the company with distributing statements and propaganda that criticized unions and discouraged membership.[34]

The hearings before an NLRB trial examiner began on July 6, and the bulk of the testimony focused on the Battle of the Overpass. Witness after witness described the callous brutalities in vivid detail. Frankensteen recalled being "bounced, thrown, dragged and knocked down three flights of stairs." An observer filled in the gaps, describing how Frankensteen was "kicked in the groin and kidneys and knocked down, . . . lifted to his feet and then knocked down and beaten again." A member of the women's auxiliary saw a group of men leaning over one victim shouting, "Kill him! Kill him!" while blood poured out of his nose and mouth. A reporter who had been covering the events summed things up neatly in his testimony: "Everywhere you looked there was someone getting kicked around."[35]

As a public relations tool, the hearings were a resounding success for the UAW. Newspapers reprinted large portions of the testimony documenting Ford's history of spying, intimidation, blacklisting, and other unlawful practices, as well as the harrowing events of May 26. The UAW, by contrast, was cast as peaceful and law abiding. For the first time in months, the NLRB figured as a forum where the trampled underclass could secure justice against industrial tyranny. The generosity of Ford's wages no longer excused its autocratic methods. As the NLRB's chairman pointedly observed, depriving the "employees of benevolent employers" of the right to organize was no less objectionable than "leaving [the slaves] of benevolent masters in slavery."[36]

Legally, too, the UAW scored an important victory. The trial examiner's voluminous report, which served as the basis for the NLRB's order in the case, was highly favorable to the UAW. The local lawyer representing Ford did a barely passable job, according to the attorneys at Cravath, de Gersdorff, Swaine, and Wood, the white-shoe New York law firm that represented the company on appeal. Many of the charges, and many descriptions of damaging conversations and events, were never answered or refuted. Ford's Cravath lawyers thought there was ample evidence to sustain any findings the NLRB was likely to make. The statement of what happened on May 26 accorded fully with the testimony, and the record rendered it utterly impossible to deny that the UAW organizers "were beaten without provocation."[37]

Ford's new lawyers faced a difficult task, but they did not lack for legal talent. The partners on the case included a one-time railroad attorney who was "one of the ablest trial lawyers and advocates of the country," and a former assistant United States attorney whom a prominent journalist had denounced as an "exponent of rapacious capitalism" for his challenges to New Deal regulation. After meeting with their clients in late December, the lawyers began to formulate their strategy. They spoke extensively with Bennett's second in command at the River Rouge plant, who oversaw the Servicemen's preparations for the scheduled UAW literature distribution. Alarmed by the spring sit-down strikes, he had been preparing for the possibility of "actual invasion of the plant." If Ford's lawyers could convince the courts to take judicial notice of the prevailing hysteria in May 1937, they could perhaps provide a measure of justification for the brutality with which the company shut down a peaceful UAW organizing event.[38]

Still, given that the case appeared unfavorable on the facts, the heart of Ford's legal plan was to attack the NLRB itself. Ford's lawyers accused the board of acting as a prosecutor rather than an unbiased tribunal. They insisted that the administrative machinery developed for trade and commerce was ill suited to labor relations, where emotions ran high, and they questioned whether the quasi-judicial function could be fulfilled "by handing down quasi-decisions based upon a quasi-record which has been fabricated out of quasi-evidence unearthed at a quasi-hearing."[39]

Ford's legal team was realistic about its chances. By 1938, the federal judiciary was a comparatively friendly forum for labor. According to the NAM, the Supreme Court had traded in "our historic liberties" for the "theories of sociological jurisprudence," leaving Congress as the "only bulwark . . . between the American people and the ultimate loss of their freedom." Given the courts' reluctance to overturn NLRB orders and procedures, Ford's lawyers advised a cautious approach. They discussed the situation at length with Edsel Ford, president of the company and Henry Ford's son, whose opposition to organized labor was less obstinate than his father's. They explained that a frank constitutional challenge to the Wagner

Act was off the table, but the courts might be open to arguments about administrative bias or procedural irregularities.[40]

First, however, the company would have to exhaust its remedies before the NLRB. In its December 22 order, the board accepted virtually all of the trial examiner's findings. The Ford Motor Company had demonstrated patent "ruthlessness" in resisting UAW organizing efforts, and the NLRB ordered it to cease and desist from interfering with the right to organize, whether by issuing threats, establishing a company union, or engaging in antiunion violence. To that end, it forbade the company from "circulating, distributing or otherwise disseminating among its employees statements or propaganda disparaging or criticizing labor organizations or advising its employees not to join such organizations." Among the materials it targeted was a pamphlet presenting Henry Ford's critique of organized labor and cards featuring his famous "Fordisms," which condensed his views into memorable quotations.[41]

Ford promptly filed a petition to vacate the decision. It sought an opportunity to present additional testimony on rehearing, including evidence of industrial unrest in spring 1937. For the most part, however, it focused on questions of law. The company claimed that it was denied due process because the trial examiner had never issued an intermediate report to which it could file exceptions. It also argued that the NLRB's order, by barring the dissemination of antiunion views, was an unconstitutional infringement on Ford's free speech.[42]

It was the last argument that attracted the most attention, though Ford's attorneys did not invent it from whole cloth. In fact, business groups had suggested a free speech justification for employer propaganda almost as soon as *NLRB v. Jones and Laughlin Steel Corporation* was decided. In the summer of 1937, the monthly magazine of the United States Chamber of Commerce conceded the right to organize as "fundamental" but assured employers that a little education would persuade employees to reject unions' overtures. In the New Deal's antibusiness climate, it was crucial to cast industry "as the friend of individualists and minorities, a bulwark of freedom." True, the NLRB was attempting to curtail antiunion propaganda, but any attempt to prohibit employers from conversing with their employees was inconsistent with the "right of free speech." And it was "obvious," according to the NAM, that "between the right to strike and the right of free speech," the latter merited greater protection. Calculations of this type proliferated in the ensuing months. With growing conviction, conservative commentators decried NLRB regulation of union organizing campaigns as abridgments of employers' free speech.[43]

And yet, as the NLRB observed, constitutional arguments of this sort were largely confined to the "public press." After all, the courts had long since upheld the power of the Federal Trade Commission to prohibit oral or written methods of unfair competition. Many states prohibited employers from influencing their employees' votes in political elections, and a federal statute prohibited "advice" by members of the armed forces that would interfere with the free exercise of suffrage. Most relevant, the Supreme Court had already considered and rejected a First Amendment challenge to the Wagner Act, in *Associated Press v. NLRB*. In light of this legal landscape, the Supreme Court appeared unlikely to invalidate a regulatory measure on First Amendment grounds. One Ford attorney wrote in a 1937 internal memorandum that the NLRB could probably limit speech when it infringed on other fundamental rights—including the "fundamental right to self-organization." A few months later, another lawyer read and summarized every Supreme Court decision involving freedom of speech and press (which, in 1938, was still a manageable task). He concluded that while Henry Ford might be entitled to make public statements about his views, communications with employees was likely outside the scope of constitutional protection.[44]

It was no surprise, then, when the NLRB denied Ford's petition and filed in the Sixth Circuit for enforcement of its order. Before the court could act, however, the Supreme Court issued a decision in an unrelated case, invalidating a rate-fixing order of the secretary of agriculture due to lack of a "full hearing," and the NLRB filed a motion for leave to withdraw its enforcement petition in the Ford case and remedy any potential defects in the record. The Sixth Circuit granted the NLRB's motion a few days later, but Ford challenged it on procedural grounds. For the next half year the case would be stalled, until the Supreme Court finally held in January 1939 that the Sixth Circuit's judgment was proper.[45]

In the meantime, the legal team continued to prepare the company's case. It investigated the legislative history of the Wagner Act and discovered that a House amendment explicitly preserving First Amendment protections for freedom of speech and the press was dropped in conference as unnecessary. In Senate debate, David I. Walsh, who chaired the Committee on

Education and Labor, asserted that employers and employees would retain the right to discuss the merits of any organization. "Indeed," he clarified, "Congress could not constitutionally pass a law abridging the freedom of speech."[46]

The more Ford's lawyers researched, the more confident they became that the NLRB's order violated the First Amendment. The Supreme Court's March 1938 decision in *Lovell v. City of Griffin*—which the ACLU was using to such great effect in its campaign against Mayor Frank Hague in Jersey City—provided additional ammunition. In a May 1938 draft brief, Ford's lawyers quoted from Zechariah Chafee Jr.'s scholarship and from Justice Oliver Wendell Holmes Jr.'s dissent in *Abrams v. United States*, as well as the Supreme Court's newer entries in the First Amendment debate, including *Stromberg v. California* and *Grosjean v. American Press Company*. To connect these cases to employer speech, they invoked the metaphor of industrial democracy so often promoted by labor. It was the premise of the Wagner Act that "workers should have the same freedom of action in determining the manner of their organization as citizens have in the sphere of politics," they argued. If free speech was crucial to the appropriate and informed exercise of rights in the political sphere, it was just as essential to the intelligent exercise of the right to organize. The CIO and UAW had been actively engaged in recruitment and had made their views known in the national press as well as in the plant. What could be objectionable, they asked, about advising workers to consider the potential disadvantages of joining a union before they made up their minds? By the summer of 1938, the Ford Motor Company and its lawyers considered the free speech argument to be the strongest element of their case.[47]

✦ ✦ ✦

When the NLRB's order in the *Ford* case erupted onto the public stage, demands for ACLU comment immediately poured in. The case was bound to cause controversy within the already divided organization. It coincided with the ACLU's effort to reach out more vigorously to "outwardly conservative characters," as well as an increasing willingness to chastise New Dealers for civil liberties abuses. And it brought together all of the elements about which the ACLU's board and its national committee had been fighting. It was closely tied to the sit-down strikes of spring 1937 and implicated employer efforts to safeguard their property. It involved the procedural limitations of the Wagner Act in the immediate aftermath of the constitutional revolution. Above all, it squarely raised the question whether the Constitution protected antiunion speech by employers.[48]

For the ACLU, the Ford Motor Company was a familiar adversary. Roger Baldwin had corresponded at length with Maurice Sugar after the "Ford Massacre" of 1932, in which the Dearborn police, assisted by Harry Bennett and his Servicemen, opened fire on hunger marchers outside the River Rouge plant and killed four members of the Young Communist League. Baldwin had made multiple visits to Detroit and worked diligently with Sugar and the International Labor Defense to assemble a damages suit, but they were unable to collect sufficient evidence and eventually abandoned the effort. In the mid-1930s, the ACLU worked closely with local civil rights groups, including the Conference for the Protection of Civil Rights and the Professional League for Civil Rights. The former organization, which became the Civil Rights Federation in the summer of 1937, handled publicity after the Battle of the Overpass, and the ACLU helped it translate public sympathy for the UAW into a broader organizing drive. When the organization issued a pamphlet on the *Ford* case in August 1937, Baldwin only regretted that it did not include the names of the ACLU's national committee.[49]

In short, throughout the 1930s, the ACLU had attacked the Ford Motor Company for its flagrant interference with civil liberties. By contrast, the NLRB's decision pushed the organization to consider whether employers had corresponding rights of their own. Arthur Garfield Hays seized the opportunity to apply the arguments he had been working toward in his general statement on employer speech. In a draft statement on the case, he reasoned that the NLRB could lawfully prohibit direct threats or acts of coercion, and he emphasized Ford's many unfair labor practices. But he carved out the "expression of opinion" as a different matter, protected by the Constitution. Nathan Greene bitterly disagreed, and his interpretation— that the literature distributed at River Rouge was speech "implemented by force," a "promise of beatings to come"—found expression in a substitute statement endorsed by the Committee on Labor's Rights. Both options were on the table at a special meeting of the ACLU board in March 1938. After lengthy discussion, the majority concluded that no limitation on the "expression of views" was justifiable. Significantly, the tally of the national committee's votes on the majority and minority statements on employer free speech were reported at the same meeting. The majority report had received sixteen votes, and the minority report fifteen. Two members had counseled against any statement at all. The ACLU, it seemed, was evenly divided.[50]

As the ACLU board had instructed, Roger Baldwin sent a copy of Hays's statement to the NLRB. Baldwin was sympathetic to the labor committee's position, and he sought to frame the ACLU's intervention as a mere request for clarification that Ford's language had been "coercive in effect." A concession of that sort might have quieted critics like the labor consultant for McKinsey, Wellington and Company, who believed (observing that "Henry Ford and the Civil Liberties Union make strange bedfellows") that there were "plenty of rugged individualists among employees" and that workers often disregarded their employers' advice on the subject of unions.[51]

To the NLRB, however, such distinctions misconceived the employer-employee relationship. Chairman J. Warren Madden believed employers' economic power rendered their antiunion pronouncements to employees "coercive per se." That is, to distinguish between coercive communications and expressions of opinion would "draw a line where none in fact exists." It would also undermine the NLRB as an institution, which was doing more than any other entity to preserve civil liberties. Madden believed what the Commission on Industrial Relations had concluded twenty-five years prior: that incursions on civil liberties almost invariably occurred when employers and local officials colluded to quash organizing or break strikes. Rather than suppressing free speech, it was the NLRB that made expressive freedom possible. In fact, to Madden, the First Amendment argument in *Ford* was simply *Lochner*-era legalism in modern dress. In Justice Holmes's formulation, the goal of Progressive Era labor law had been "to establish the equality of position between the parties in which liberty of contract begins." The Wagner Act, in turn, sought "to establish the equality of position between the parties in which *liberty of speech* begins."[52]

Impressed by Madden's vehemence, the ACLU board invited NLRB counsel Charles Fahy to attend one of its meetings. Although Fahy did not manage to persuade the majority, he found an ally in Harry Ward, who threatened to voice his opposition publicly in a dissenting opinion if the board persisted in its views. To Ward, as to the NLRB, joining a union was a civil liberty in its own right, and it deserved more deference than free speech as a matter of law as well as "social necessity." Ward explicitly resisted the organization's embrace of individual rights–based justifications of free speech. In Ward's view, civil liberties were "an instrument of social progress," but Ward's was not the progressive defense of free speech as a prerequisite for informed democratic debate. Preserving civil liberties was not a matter of maintaining open channels in a dispute between competing economic interests. Instead, it was the ACLU's duty to make space for "orderly social advance" as against the status quo. Organizing the workers was the way forward, and anything that impeded it could be curtailed. In a desperate ploy to preserve organizational unity, the ACLU board adopted Ward's proposed statement as an addendum to the original. For many members of the ACLU, the combined statements went too far in protecting employers' antiunion utterances; for many others, they did not go far enough. For the time being, the board chose to gloss over these fundamental differences.[53]

The truce held for the summer months. In September, the renamed Committee on Civil Rights in Labor Relations took up two new cases. The first involved industrial espionage and clear-cut discharge for union activity, and the board accepted the committee's conclusion that the employer's distribution of antiunion pamphlets was coercive in broader context. The same reasoning applied in the second case, in which the company distributed materials critical of the CIO. In each case, the NLRB considered the employer's antiunion statements as part of an unlawful course of conduct but declined to prohibit the future dissemination of literature. The ACLU announced that neither case violated employers' free speech.[54]

Subsequent NLRB decisions, however, impinged more boldly on employer expression, and the shaky equilibrium in the board soon began to break down. In October, Baldwin sent Nathan Greene a copy of the Labor Relations Report, with a notice of a federal appellate decision refusing to enforce an NLRB order. Superintendents of the employer, Union Pacific Stages, had told employees that union membership was not advantageous. The Ninth Circuit found that there was no substantial evidence of discharge for union membership, and thus there was no adequate ground for prohibiting employer speech. Although the court considered the right to organize to be "a natural right of equal rank with the great right of free speech, protected by the Constitution," it rejected the union's argument that an employer's expression of opinion infringed it. *NLRB v. Union Pacific Stages* was the first federal court decision on employer speech under the Wagner Act, and Baldwin thought it warranted favorable ACLU comment.

After all, the opinion was a monumental judicial concession to the right of agitation. And yet, the court had failed to appreciate that the right to organize was a product as well as a prerequisite of worker power. As a result, it understood coercion in terms of post hoc interference with workers' informed and independent choices, rather than the source of those choices in the first place. In other words, the court did not have to decide whether the First Amendment trumped the right to organize, because speech simply enriched employees' decision-making calculus. Here was the logical conclusion of Justices Holmes's and Louis D. Brandeis's canonical dissents, which the ACLU had long endorsed. More speech, in the court's view, was better for everyone.[55]

Labor leftists considered this formalistic understanding of rights to be fundamentally incompatible with their own, which was rooted in power. Their critique of disembodied rights echoed labor's earlier rejection of liberty of contract, updated for the realm of free speech. In early cases, including *Ford*, employers' clearly abusive conduct had obscured the distance between the two theories of civil liberties. Even if one believed that rational and autonomous decision making was possible—that is, that underlying power disparities in the employment relationship did not render such choices illusory—frank violence crossed the line. As employer interference with organizing became less flagrant, however, underlying tensions between the two accounts of coercion loomed large. And for the NLRB, that made a clash between the Wagner Act and the First Amendment inevitable. In formal communications, the NLRB invoked the Constitution to defend labor activity. It insisted not only that the Wagner Act "impose[d] no limitations on the right to strike," but that any attempt to do so "would no doubt be unconstitutional." Still, as member Edwin Smith explained, constitutional rights were not absolute. The Wagner Act was meant to ensure "that the working population may attain a fuller life within the framework of the democratic state." That substantive goal was the very heart of civil liberty and justified the occasional suppression of free speech. For the NLRB, the abrogation of an employer's right to communicate with employees was no different from the right to hire and fire at will. Both had been protected by the Constitution as interpreted by the federal courts, and both were expendable in the interest of social progress.[56]

By the fall of 1939, conservatives had learned how best to respond to claims like these. Speaking at an ACLU conference in October 1939, one of the Cravath partners involved in the Ford litigation answered the NLRB's appeal to industrial democracy with the assertion that "every invasion of free speech ha[d] been defended on the ground that those inviting it believed that the larger public good would be advanced." However important the right to organize, he insisted, it was something other than the exercise of free speech. And "the right of free speech may be subordinated to no right, if we expect the freedom and liberties of the people to continue and democratic processes to go on."[57]

Within the ACLU, many members agreed. No longer was free speech merely one among many attributes of democracy, subject to balancing in the interest of social progress. Certainly, there was a time in the 1920s when such an interpretation might have been possible—when "free speech" was a component of "civil liberties," not its core value. That moment, however, had long since passed. The ACLU could no longer accept, like the NLRB, that free speech ranked lower in the hierarchy of rights than did a substantive interest in the improvement of workers' lives.

If the ACLU acknowledged that speech might be oppressive on its own terms, the face-off between speech and agitation would become unavoidable. It was left with an unstable compromise, a distinction between coercion and opinion that seemed bound to collapse. The organization was trying to maintain its underlying commitment to the rights of labor to agitate—to challenge the existing allocation of resources, and with it the basic social structure—while preserving a neutral right of expression as a political tool. Eventually, the ACLU would have to choose.

✦ ✦ ✦

When the Supreme Court handed down its decision on the procedural issue in the *Ford* case in January 1939, the NLRB was under attack. In the 1938 Democratic primaries, anti–New Deal candidates overwhelmingly defeated Roosevelt's supporters, and the general elections swept almost one hundred Republican candidates into Congress and many more into state and local office. Among the casualties was Frank Murphy, who ran for reelection as Michigan's governor and suffered a stinging defeat.[58]

In early 1939, a congressional coalition of Republicans and southern Democrats introduced a host of amendments designed to curb the authority of the NLRB. Concurrently, David I. Walsh proposed a more moderate bill, which was backed by the AFL and commanded considerable support. On the whole, the ACLU opposed the amendments as it had earlier ones. And yet, there were two provisions that prompted ACLU debate. First, the Walsh bill provided for more robust judicial review of NLRB decisions. Arthur Garfield Hays was sympathetic to the proposal, and he convened a committee to study quasi-judicial boards. Although he considered it inadvisable to single out the NLRB for special requirements, he lamented the growing trend toward "trial by commissions" and believed that citizens should have the same protections before commissions as before the courts. Hays thought the commissions were censoring business, "which [was] just as bad as a censorship over literature."[59]

Another of Senator Walsh's suggestions was even more pressing: a provision guaranteeing an employer's right to free speech. The free speech amendment capitalized on liberal disquiet over the free press cases, *Union Pacific Stages,* and, of course, *Ford.* J. Warren Madden's testimony before the Senate Committee on Education and Labor only amplified support for the bill. Madden told the committee that an employer's antiunion statements in the context of a stable, long-term bargaining relationship might be acceptable, but the same assertions would be coercive where a new union faced a recalcitrant employer. Robert A. Taft, the newly elected Ohio senator who would someday sponsor the Taft-Hartley Act, pointed out that Madden's distinction effectively meant that "you could call an A.F. of L. union anything, but you cannot call a C.I.O. union anything"—an implication that Madden acknowledged but dismissed as irrelevant. Even bolder, Madden suggested that an employer's accurate statement that the leaders of a union were Communists might discourage an employee from joining and accordingly constitute interference with organizing. "The fact that it is true," he insisted, "does not keep it from being coercive." Referencing the law of labor injunctions, he reminded his interlocutors that truthful statements enjoyed no special privilege when they destroyed other rights.[60]

From the ACLU's perspective, "Brother Madden['s]" position jeopardized the decade's most valuable civil liberties gains. Despite staunch opposition from longtime labor allies (and enthusiastic support for a free speech amendment among business groups), even veteran board members were open to legislative action. In the end, the ACLU opposed all of the proposed amendments as "either unnecessary or dangerous to the fundamental purpose of the act." It did not, however, endorse Madden's understanding of employer speech. Instead, it cast the *Ford* case as an opportunity to test its theory that existing limitations were sufficient. The ACLU would ask the NLRB to modify its order to comport with constitutional concerns. If it proved unwilling to do so, the federal courts would serve as an adequate check.[61]

Thus in January 1939, when the NLRB issued an order setting aside its original findings, Baldwin wrote to Madden to reintroduce the ACLU's familiar free speech concern. A few weeks later, the NLRB issued its new proposed order, which was practically identical to the original. A Ford press release noted that the only changes pertained to the employer speech provisions, which had been subject to "severe criticism from many sources, including a stinging rebuke from the Civil Liberties Union." In the earlier version, the NLRB had required Ford to cease and desist from the dissemination of antiunion views. In the revised order, this clause was slightly qualified; the company was prohibited from "interfering with, restraining, or coercing its employees in the exercise of the rights guaranteed in Section 7 of the Act" *by* engaging in the communications it had previously proscribed.[62]

As the ACLU's staff attorney observed, the meaning of the change in wording was ambiguous. It was unclear whether the NLRB would construe mere expressions of opinion as permissible, or rather would consider all antiunion communications to fall within the qualifying clause, as its public statements had suggested. That is, the NLRB had limited its prohibition to communications that interfered with employees' rights under the Wagner Act, without clarifying whether employers' antiunion speech to employees could ever avoid impeding the right to organize.[63]

That uncertainty allowed the ACLU to extend its impasse awhile longer, though in fact its leaders had never been further apart. Hays, for example, had come to believe "that an expression of opinion is lawful under any and all circumstances," even when accompanied by unlawful acts. To prevent him from imputing that position to the ACLU, the board assigned Osmond Fraenkel to draft the ACLU's brief to the NLRB. The final version hewed to the middle course. It affirmed the ACLU's commitment to free expression for all speakers, "powerful or weak," and it contended (citing *De Jonge v. Oregon*) that a statement must be "in fact intimidatory" to justify curtailment. In taking this position, the ACLU was flatly rejecting the possibility that the employment relationship itself was a constitutionally relevant species of economic coercion—that unadorned speech, to an average worker, was coercive per se. At the same time, it stopped short of Hays's strict line between words and deeds. Distribution of antiunion literature would constitute an unfair labor practice if and only if Ford continued to engage in prohibited nonspeech antiunion activity. The ACLU announced its conclusion in the same press release in which it reaffirmed its opposition to amending the Wagner Act. Its timid chastisement of the NLRB was enough for the *New York Times* to proclaim, "Liberties Union Again Aids Ford"—an assessment that the NAM echoed in testimony to Congress.[64]

Meanwhile, the Ford Motor Company's defense of employer speech was growing ever bolder. The lawyers knew the case had weaknesses. They worried about the limits of corporate personhood, citing none other than the Supreme Court's newly issued decision in *Hague v. CIO*. But their primary obstacle was the body of proindustry labor injunction cases that had plagued labor for so many years. These decisions had shut down efforts to organize, picket, and boycott—especially, but not exclusively, in the context of mass picketing and secondary activity—whenever unions amassed too much power. Judges regarded picket signs and "We Don't Patronize" lists as coercive rather than expressive, emphasizing the broader context in which such communications occurred and the practical inability of strikebreakers and employers to resist union demands. One Ford memorandum concluded from pre-1937 cases that advice was constitutionally protected only if it preserved the listener's "free right to choose" whether to comply. That "freedom" encompassed a pragmatic judgment about individuals' ability to withstand social and economic pressure, of a piece and yet at odds with its formalist incarnation in constitutional cases like *Lochner v. New York*. This was a test with obvious limiting implications for employer speech.[65]

Still, Ford's lawyers were optimistic about their chances. In internal documents and communications to the NLRB, they quoted frequently and fervently from the free speech decisions that the ACLU had fought so hard to promote and defend. One memorandum declared that "the nearest approximation to truth is arrived at by the clashing against each other of rival theories." Employers made the "most effective cross-examiners of the proponents of labor unions," and to prevent the expression of their opinions would be to impoverish the marketplace of ideas.[66]

After several months of deliberation, the NLRB issued its final order in the *Ford* case in August 1939. The last iteration omitted an earlier finding that Ford Motor Company had "deliberately planned and carried out" the

Battle of the Overpass to crush unionization in the plant. On the free speech issue, however, the order was virtually unchanged. In a press release, the NLRB acknowledged public concerns about employer free speech but explained that the company's circulation of literature had to be considered in context. Ford's statements had denounced labor organizations and characterized their leaders as liars and racketeers. Under the circumstances, they were not "directed to the reason of the employee." Rather, their "unmistakable purpose and effect" was to warn employees that joining a union likely would undermine their opportunities for advancement.[67]

Responses to the decision within the ACLU fell along predictable lines, though an air of resignation had settled on both camps. Nathan Greene rightly assumed that "those who quarreled with the proposed order [would] quarrel with this one," and he predicted a strong attack in the courts. Still the NLRB had clarified that it was concerned only with communications that were coercive in intent and effect. With John Haynes Holmes dissenting, the ACLU board deemed that good enough to render the order consistent with the Constitution. At the end of October, the ACLU released a public statement explaining its position and its decision not to a file a brief in the federal courts.[68]

When the NLRB filed for enforcement of its new order in the Sixth Circuit, Ford's brief raised the familiar free speech claims. According to Ford, either the order exceeded the NLRB's statutory authority, or the Wagner Act itself violated the First Amendment. The brief made much of international events, which underlined the importance of the vigorous protection of First Amendment principles. "There are *no* qualifications whatever to the provisions of the First Amendment," it emphasized, in language that would have bewildered labor lawyers two decades earlier. Citing *Lovell v. City of Griffin* and *Schneider v. New Jersey*, it celebrated the important place of pamphleteering in American history and culture, a practice that the Supreme Court had declared "vital to the maintenance of democratic institutions." The NLRB's order, Ford's lawyers cautioned, amounted to a prior restraint on utterance and threatened the heart of the constitutional guarantee of free speech.[69]

The NLRB found itself in the unlikely situation of defending the curtailment of free speech by relying on cases that had haunted labor for generations. It invoked the "verbal act" cases, including *Gompers v. Buck's Stove and Range Company*, as well as the *Schenck v. United States* line. In arguing that freedom of speech for employers should be no greater than that afforded employees, it risked undercutting the tremendous gains secured for labor speech in the past decade. Ford's attorneys, conversely, denounced the same antilabor decisions as encroachments on First Amendment liberties. "It is generally admitted that those cases went too far in restraining legitimate union activities," they reasoned, "and it is surprising to find the Board arguing, in effect, that past injustices to unions should now be matched by corresponding injustices to employers." They pointed to the Supreme Court's recent decision in *Senn v. Tile Layers Protective Union,* the first in an unfolding series of cases reversing the earlier judicial understanding. Prior courts had resisted legislative efforts to protect labor speech, enjoining pickets and boycotts and trampling on the First Amendment in the process. Now, Ford was asking the court to undercut legislative protection for labor once again, only this time by invoking free speech.[70]

The irony must have been as distressing and confusing to labor advocates as it was to the ACLU. The reversal of opinions in these cases is, of course, standard fare for legal argument. It is a neat bookend to the ACLU's appropriation of constitutional language at the outset of the First World War, at a time when individual rights and personal liberty were watchwords of labor's oppression. In the *Ford* case, however, the shift in positions indicated something more than the malleability of legal doctrine. It reflected a fundamental realignment in the relationship of various American constituencies to the courts, the Constitution, and the state.

✦ ✦ ✦

In its statement on the NLRB's revised order in the *Ford* case, the ACLU had only forestalled the inevitable. Within a matter of months, the temporary calm within the organization erupted into full-fledged crisis, culminating in the expulsion of Communists from the ACLU's board of directors and the resignations of Harry Ward and many other seasoned leaders and members of the ACLU.

The controversy over employer free speech was crucial to the conflict, though it was not the only source. The Molotov-Ribbentrop Pact, and the corresponding deterioration in relations between American Communists and their liberal allies, was a crushing blow to many Soviet sympathizers, including Roger Baldwin. In the wake of the agreement, the board's centrists became increasingly suspicious of Communist influence. In addition, the board divided over the House Special Committee to Investigate Un-American Activities, chaired by Representative Martin Dies Jr., a Texas Democrat. The Dies Committee was directed toward foreign subversive activity in the United States, including Nazi propaganda. In practice it focused on alleged Communist collaboration (including by the CIO and the NLRB), prompting a wave of anti-Communist hysteria and the passage of the 1940 Smith Act, a federal peacetime sedition law.[71]

As the ACLU debated the *Ford* case, the Dies Committee was scrutinizing many members of the ACLU board, along with the Popular Front organizations to which they belonged. The most notable victim was Ward, who was serving as chairman of the American League for Peace and Democracy. After he testified before the Dies Committee on behalf of the American League, many members of the ACLU's leadership demanded his resignation; Norman Thomas counted him among "six or seven Communists or fellow travelers" within the ACLU leadership and cautioned that Stalin's apologists should not be entrusted with the defense of civil liberties in America. Those fellow travelers, in turn, accused Morris Ernst and Arthur Garfield Hays of striking a deal with Dies to forestall an investigation of the ACLU (and, in Ernst's case, the National Lawyers Guild, from which he resigned because of its Communist ties, as well). In October, Dies publicly absolved the ACLU of Communist collaboration. Whether he received anything in return was the subject of intense speculation for decades. Certainly, the ACLU's official criticism of the Dies Committee was halfhearted and equivocal—an approach that the board's moderates justified as "pragmatic liberalism" or "political realism" and their adversaries denounced as hypocritical.[72]

After months of mounting tension at ACLU board meetings—depending on who was present, slim majorities would alternately pass and rescind anti-Communist statements—the board passed (and the national committee approved) its notorious "1940 Resolution" in February. The resolution affirmed that the ACLU would "defend[] the right to hold and utter any opinions" and would not disqualify general members on the basis of political or economic views. For the governing committees and staff, however, it established a "test of consistency in the defense of civil liberties in all aspects and all places," and it presumed that the requisite consistency was lacking in anyone willing to "justify or tolerate the denial of civil liberties by dictatorship abroad." It therefore excluded from leadership positions any individual who publicly supported totalitarian dictatorship in any country or who belonged to an organization that did.[73]

The resolution was ostensibly meant to "create greater harmony" by clarifying existing ACLU policy, but the members and supporters of the ACLU immediately erupted into bitter debate. Ward—lamenting that "the Civil Liberties Union which did this is not the Civil Liberties Union with which I have been glad to work for twenty years"—resigned as chairman. In an open letter, seventeen prominent liberals counseled the ACLU to "restore civil liberties" by rescinding the resolution. More than thirty members resigned. Local committees condemned the resolution or considered it unnecessary; only one approved.[74]

The ACLU insisted that the decision was not a concession to outside pressure, and it disclaimed the desire "to become 'respectable' to conservatives." Still, there was "no question but that the Union ha[d] been greatly strengthened in public opinion by this action," as the overwhelming approval of newspaper editorials (the radical press excepted) had clearly revealed. Opponents of the resolution could not help but notice an April memorandum from the chair of the ACLU's Membership Advisory Committee: "This seems the ideal time to promote our old plan to increase the membership of the Union. The organization has never been more highly regarded by the press and public than now, and a determined effort will bring us declared adherents in larger numbers and contributions in larger volume than at any period in our twenty years."[75]

If the February resolution was contentious, the board's enforcement of its terms—its expulsion of its one openly Communist member—was a declaration of war. Elizabeth Gurley Flynn was a founding member of the ACLU and had been a consistent advocate for civil liberties ever since her IWW days. For almost three decades, she had argued unflinchingly for the rights of dissenters, at great personal cost; during that period, she reminded the board, the organization's conservatives had never once "been in jail for free speech." Although she harbored serious reservations about Stalinist methods, Flynn joined the Communist Party in 1936, and in the summer of 1938, she became a member of its national committee. She was nonetheless reelected to the ACLU board in 1939, after disclosing her Communist affiliation.[76]

When the ACLU passed its 1940 resolution, Flynn refused to resign. She shared Ward's view that the ACLU had abandoned its founding values, and she described a "steady infiltration of new elements"—including lawyers, businessmen, and ministers, "but not a single representative of organized labor"—whose "anti-labor, anti-union attitude" had led the organization astray. These interlopers were responsible for the ACLU's attacks on the NLRB, its opposition to the sit-down strike, and its defense of Ford's free speech. Flynn dismissed as metaphysical her critics' contention that she believed in civil liberties not "in a vacuum of pristine purity, but as a means to an end." In Flynn's view, those members who were most rigid about abstractions were most willing to capitulate on the "practical issues, especially where labor is concerned."[77]

On May 7, 1940, after a brief postponement in light of the death of Flynn's son, the ACLU's board of directors convened proceedings to expel her from its governing body. As the anti-Communists openly conceded, no one questioned Flynn's personal loyalty to the civil liberties cause. Rather, she was a "symbol" of a struggle to define the ACLU's attitude toward collaboration with Communists. At 2:20 a.m., after hours of debate over procedural matters, organizational politics, and the principles of free speech, the board voted. Nine members (including Ernst and Roger Riis) favored expulsion; nine members (including Osmond Fraenkel and Hays) opposed. John Haynes Holmes, as chair, broke the tie in favor of removal.[78]

Much has been made of the intemperance of the ACLU's purge: its inexplicable curtailment of dissent and presumed capitulation to popular pressures in a period when Communists were most in need of the organization's support. In fact, Flynn's expulsion was regarded as such a black mark in ACLU history that in 1976 the organization posthumously restored her membership. Baldwin, however, consistently defended the board's decision. Throughout his life, he argued that decisive action had been necessary to prevent the Communists and fellow travelers within the board from standing in the way of the ACLU's commitment to free speech. He claimed in public statements and private letters that the new policy was merely an affirmation of the organization's commitment to civil liberties as an independent principle rather than a tool.

Historians and ACLU insiders have long assumed that Baldwin's defense was insincere—that he was motivated by the Dies Committee, fund-raising efforts, the investigations and aspersions of red-baiters, and other seemingly petty concerns. As Abraham Isserman complained upon leaving the ACLU in solidarity with Flynn, the ACLU was increasingly consumed with "what the public thinks" and "what the Gallup polls say."[79]

However valid such criticisms may be, the crisis within the board needs to be understood against the backdrop of conflict over employer free speech and the NLRB. In correspondence with Alexander Meiklejohn, who staunchly opposed the resolution and considered resigning over it, Baldwin explained that the board was at an impasse; expressly excluding Communists was "an unhappy way out of a bad mess." Holmes was even more adamant. The board had been paralyzed for months by a "militant minority," he explained. The resolution was painful, but circumstances had left the board with no choice. For the first time, there were individuals within the ACLU who did not believe in the ACLU's civil liberties work—who were "moved consciously or unconsciously to oppose it, to block it, and to defeat it from within." Their expulsion from the board, Holmes reported in April, settled the ACLU's priorities and freed the organization to move forward.[80]

The conventional understanding of the 1940 events is based on a modern view of free speech as a right to hold and disseminate unpopular ideas. Historians have interpreted the board's action as a prelude to McCarthyism, an abandonment of the ideal of protection for distasteful expression. They have rejected Baldwin's explanation that the move was primarily organizational and that the ACLU remained fully committed to the defense of Communist speech. They have presumed, in short, that those who favored expulsion rejected freedom of speech for all.[81]

The *Ford* case is an important corrective to this well-worn story. Above all, the expulsion of Communists needs to be understood as a fundamental shift in the underlying objectives of the ACLU—not from the defense of all to the defense of some, as critics have long charged, but from the complicated calculus of the "right of agitation" to a streamlined civil libertarianism that was impervious to inequalities in the marketplace of ideas. The ACLU retained its hostility toward state overreaching, even as the New Deal demonstrated that industrial interests were separable from state power.

Against this backdrop, even such vocal critics as Meiklejohn were not as far away from the authors of the resolution as they now seem. Most emphasized only its tendency to curtail debate: to exclude minority opinions that might have enriched the ACLU's policy agenda. For them, labor equality had become a viewpoint rather than a goal. But the targets of the purge understood its import as a repudiation of the ACLU's founding principles. During the proceedings, Flynn expressed her belief that some of the board's members were "in blissful ignorance of what the ACLU really stands for," and she blamed the veterans for failing to educate them properly. Flynn charged that those members who were "abandoning . . . the fight for labor's rights" did not belong on the board. But by 1940, it was Flynn who no longer belonged.[82]

In due course, the reconfiguration of the ACLU board prompted a re-evaluation of the organization's position on employer free speech. In January, the board rejected a recommendation of the Committee on Civil Rights in Labor Relations and voted to protest the NLRB's treatment of antiunion communications in a recent decision. That same month, in a Massachusetts case against the Ford Motor Company, the NLRB called free speech a "qualified" rather than absolute right. It based its finding of unfair labor practices in the case exclusively on antiunion expression by chief inspectors and supervisory officials and surveillance by supervisory foremen. There were no violent assaults, no proven attempts to organize a company union, no discharges or demotions because of union membership. Notwithstanding resistance by the board's "fellow-travelers," Holmes thought the ACLU's "mission as a civil liberties organization" required an aggressive repudiation of the NLRB's order, which was precisely the same as in the Michigan case. Hays wrote to the NLRB to convey the organization's position: "You have held in effect that the distribution of literature to employees as such, violates their rights under the Act." That is, the NLRB had "construed mere language in print as coercive." That was a position that the ACLU could not condone. In February, the same month that it passed the 1940 resolution, the ACLU announced its "strong objections" to the NLRB's order.[83]

✦ ✦ ✦

Despite the organization's new vigilance in employer speech cases, there were never more than a few conservatives in the ACLU's ranks. John Haynes Holmes was a Socialist. Arthur Garfield Hays had proven his mettle in many labor battles, and he personally favored the CIO. When the House considered more than twenty amendments to the Wagner Act in March 1940, the ACLU opposed all of them. It rejected the measure protecting employer free speech because it might have been construed to require more than the constitutional baseline. The ACLU was adamantly against "giving employers' speech more protection than the speech of others."[84]

Even in the wake of the 1940 resolution, the leaders of the ACLU who defended employers' antiunion speech trusted that doing so, in the long run, would better serve the rights of labor. Twenty years of civil liberties work on behalf of labor gave them plenty of cause for that belief. Time and again, courts had enforced injunctions against picketing and boycotts. In so doing, they had rejected ACLU claims that labor's methods were expressive and thus deserving of constitutional protection. But in 1940, for the first time, robust First Amendment protection for labor activity seemed plausible. That spring, the Supreme Court handed down two monumental decisions on labor and free speech. In *Thornhill v. Alabama*—the first Supreme Court case to link protection for freedom of speech to the theory articulated in *United States v. Carolene Products Company*—the justices were nearly unanimous in upholding the right to picket as an expression of ideas within the ambit of constitutional protection. "Free discussion concerning the conditions in industry and the causes of labor disputes," the majority concluded, citing *Hague v. CIO,* was "indispensable to the effective and intelligent use of the processes of popular government to shape the destiny of modern industrial society." *Thornhill's* companion case, *Carlson v. California*, added that peacefully "publicizing the facts of a labor dispute . . . by pamphlet, by word of mouth or by banner" was also within the "liberty of communication" insulated against abridgment by the state.[85]

Thornhill and *Carlson* were argued in the Supreme Court by, respectively, Joseph A. Padway, AFL general counsel, and Lee Pressman, CIO general counsel. Padway had argued *Senn v. Tile Layers Protective Union,* and his service on the ABA's Committee on the Bill of Rights reflected his openness toward the courts. Pressman, who had worked closely with the ACLU in Jersey City, shared J. Warren Madden's view that expression of an employer's distaste for unionism was equivalent to a threat of discharge, and he vigorously supported NLRB regulation of employer speech. At the same time, cases like *Hague* had persuaded Pressman to temper his earlier hostility to constitutional litigation. By 1940, he believed that a strong First Amendment might counterbalance the judicial protection of property rights, and like the ACLU, he celebrated *Thornhill* and *Carlson* as dramatic victories for labor. Both opinions, appropriately enough, were authored by Justice Frank Murphy, just months after his appointment as an associate justice of the Supreme Court. In the span of a decade, Murphy had served as (among other roles) mayor of Detroit, governor of Michigan, and attorney general of the United States. He had corresponded regularly with the ACLU in each of those capacities, and he was sympathetic to the organization's views. It was gratifying, if not surprising, that his opinions in *Thornhill* and *Carlson* vindicated the ACLU's long-standing position.[86]

And yet, constitutional protection for labor's most effective methods—including mass picketing and the secondary boycott—remained far fetched. The University of Chicago law professor and influential labor scholar Charles O. Gregory offered a telling assessment of the emerging doctrine in the *ABA Journal*. Gregory acknowledged that a massive transformation in the judiciary's attitude toward labor had rendered common-law restraints on nonviolent union activity obsolete. In earlier decades, the Supreme Court had been wrong to attempt to check that shift; its effort to do so in such cases as *Truax v. Corrigan* "still baffle[d] good lawyers." But while it was one thing for courts to tolerate state protection for union activity, it was another to insulate that activity from legislative interference. Picketing was about coercion rather than argument, and to shield it from regulation on First Amendment grounds was a "perversion of an American ideal."[87]

Those ACLU veterans like Hays who tried to hold the speech versus conduct line understood that the recent First Amendment victories were precarious: the notion that labor's economic weapons were immune from state policing was arguably incongruous with the New Deal settlement, as well as deeply threatening to the political order. Just as they feared, a rapid retrenchment in First Amendment protection for labor activity followed on *Thornhill* and *Carlson*'s heels. In 1941, the Supreme Court's decision in *Milk Wagon Drivers Union v. Meadowmoor Dairies* upheld a state court injunction against picketing by a union with a record of violence and property destruction. "Utterance in a context of violence can lose its significance as an appeal to reason and become part of an instrument of force," Justice Frankfurter explained, two years after his appointment to the court; future picketing, even if peaceful, could constitutionally be curtailed. Reflecting on *Meadowmoor* in an internal memorandum, one Ford lawyer thought it plausible "that Justice Frankfurter was encouraged to go so far in limiting peaceful picketing because the ruling would establish a precedent which would sustain the Labor Board's position on free speech." To most observers (that is, to those who had abandoned the notion that organizing was a protected good independent of expressive or associational freedom), the parallel between the two scenarios was inescapable. Gregory thought it "disquieting to hear proponents of organized labor applaud [*Thornhill* and *Carlson*] and then condemn a manufacturer who, contrary to the terms of the Wagner Act, insists upon telling his employees exactly what he thinks of a certain labor union and why." One way of squaring the two was to preserve a sphere for legislative action: to deny constitutional protection to workers as well as employers in the face of democratic efforts to regulate their behavior. The ACLU espoused the opposite solution. Like the DC Circuit—which, in a case argued by some of Ford's Cravath lawyers, upheld the right of the Bethlehem Steel Company to circularize its employees—it reasoned that the Supreme Court's expansive view of the First Amendment in *Thornhill* and *Carlson* "extends to employers as well as to employees."[88]

In October 1940, the Sixth Circuit agreed. In its opinion in *NLRB v. Ford Motor Company,* the court took judicial notice of the sit-down strikes that had swept through Michigan between December 1936 and March 1937. It condemned the seizure of property as illegal and noted that it had been recognized as such by the Supreme Court. It accepted then-governor Murphy's description of the events as "the greatest industrial conflict of all times," and it acknowledged that legal remedies had been unavailable to the owners of property. Under those circumstances, it considered Ford's increased security to be a reasonable precaution. Still, the court accepted the NLRB's findings that the Service Department's reaction to the UAW's organizing efforts was excessive, and that the Ford Motor Company had interfered with employees' rights to organize under Section 7 of the Wagner Act.[89]

With these preliminary matters out of the way, the court turned to "the major issue, at least from the point of view of the public interest." Ford expected its lawyers to "win on this point, if no other," and it was not disappointed. The court considered the right of employees to organize and engage in concerted activity to be "so clearly recognized as a fundamental right that citation [was] superfluous." But according to the court, the right to express views on controversial questions had "even more venerable sanction." The circulation of pamphlets was an important American tradition and one that had proven effective in the dissemination of ideas. Ford Motor Company's communications expressed disapproval of unions, to be sure. But neither their words nor the company's conduct was sufficiently egregious to justify abridgment of constitutionally protected speech.[90]

Ironically, by securing statutory rights to employees, the Wagner Act had made the NLRB's claim about the coercive effect of employer speech untenable. In the past, the court acknowledged, the power relations between employer and employee, namely that of master over servant, might have given an employer's statement disproportionate influence. But the Wagner Act—upheld as constitutionally valid, strictly enforced by the NLRB, and liberally construed by the courts—undercut any argument about inherent coercion in labor relations. "The servant," declared the court, "no longer has occasion to fear the master's frown of authority or threats of discrimination for union activities, express or implied."[91]

The court concluded with a panegyric to freedom of speech. The right to speak, it insisted, was the basis for the rights secured by the Wagner Act. Quoting the Supreme Court's decision in *Thornhill v. Alabama,* it emphasized that "the dissemination of information concerning the facts of a labor dispute must be regarded as within that area of free discussion that is guaranteed by the Constitution." The court entered a decree enforcing the NLRB's order in every other important respect, but it pronounced the Ford Motor Company free to circularize its employees.[92]

✦ ✦ ✦

On June 20, 1941—four years after the Battle of the Overpass—the Ford Motor Company signed a contract with the UAW-CIO covering 123,000 employees. Recognizing the union was a condition of settling its pending cases, and Ford's attorneys thought the victory on employer free speech was the most the company could hope for from the courts.[93]

If the Battle of the Overpass was a seminal turning point in organizing the Ford Motor Company, the *Ford* case was a flashpoint in the larger war over administrative authority, New Deal labor policy, and constitutional interpretation. By 1940, the NLRB's infringements on employer speech resonated with Americans as a symbol of administrative overreaching. That February, the *New York Herald-Tribune* printed a piece entitled "Muzzling the Employer," and the *Chicago Daily Tribune* lamented the NLRB's bureaucratic disposition to disregard constitutional rights, including the "right of free speech" as well as the "right of fair trial." When the Sixth Circuit issued its October decision, the *New York Times* reprinted it practically in full. Dozens of bar journal and law review articles gave detailed consideration to *Ford* and the issue of employer free speech. Dean James M. Landis of Harvard Law School considered the issues so novel and significant that he made them the basis of the law school's moot court case.[94]

The organized bar, too, understood the stakes of the Ford dispute. Even before the ABA's Committee on the Bill of Rights was created, Grenville Clark (though a "strong advocate of unionism") felt that the NLRB was "overstepp[ing]" in abridging employer speech. He had attended an ACLU meeting at which the issue was discussed, and he was impressed with the organization's apparent evenhandedness, as well as the dangers of administrative censorship. In a peculiar twist, Clark imagined the *Ford* case as a chance to prove that his committee was similarly nonpartisan—that is, that it was willing to defend "persons publicly identified with the 'Right.'"[95]

In framing its agenda at the dawn of the new decade, the Committee on the Bill of Rights walked a fine line. The outside world continued to insinuate that ABA lawyers cared only about their clients' bottom line. That cynicism prompted an "urgent request[]" by the chairman of the ABA's Public Relations Committee to avoid mention of the Ford matter as an example of Clark's committee's work. And yet, the ABA's broader membership voiced the opposite concern. At the organization's January meeting, a stream of delegates stood to decry the committee's inattention to "individual workmen," "acts of violence directed not against radicals or Communists but directed against our own people," who asserted the "inalienable right" to labor under conditions of their choosing. To stanch criticism of this type, ABA president Charles A. Beardsley went so far as to advise the committee to protest "interference with the right to work."[96]

Compared with the alternative, *Ford* seemed an ideal compromise. The ACLU's stance in the case made intervention palatable to liberals. At the same time, attacking the NLRB assuaged conservative critics within the ABA. As Frank Hogan told Clark, supporting the Ford Motor Company could serve as an "antidote to the statement that we act only in left-wing cases." With these benefits in mind, the committee explored the possibility of filing a brief in the matter. A twenty-four page memorandum prepared by several members carefully weighed the issues involved and, endeavoring to remain "absolutely impartial," determined that the NLRB had unjustifiably curtailed Ford's speech. In January 1940, as the ABA's conservatives maneuvered to abolish the Committee on the Bill of Rights, Clark conferred with Zechariah Chafee Jr. about the merits of the case. He concluded that the NLRB's abridgment of employer speech implicated a "vital issue of civil rights"; the committee's intervention was desirable "on the merits" and also "as a matter of policy, to counteract any impressions that we have been one-sided."[97]

As President Roosevelt's judiciary reorganization bill receded from view, the benefits to the bar of a court-centered civil liberties program subtly shifted. In the debate over the court-packing plan, celebrating the Supreme Court's civil liberties decisions had helped to improve the judiciary's public image. The ABA had cast the courts as a protector of minority rights as opposed to industrial interests. But by the end of the decade, President Roosevelt had lost his hold on political and popular power, and the courts no longer needed rehabilitation. The ABA's inaugural issue of its *Bill of Rights Review,* published in the summer of 1940, devoted an article to the "The Labor Board and Free Speech." It reported that the committee had voted to file an amicus brief in an appropriate Supreme Court test case, which was poised to "establish a landmark in the history of the Bill of Rights." Past ABA president William Ransom was candid about the allure of the new approach. "Come what may in the form of judicial decisions where issues of legislative policy are offered for adjudication," Ransom was confident that the Supreme Court would "enforce resolutely against all agencies of government the substance and the verities of the historic freedoms." That is, despite the demise of liberty of contract, businesses retained the Bill of Rights.[98]

In the end, the NLRB did not seek review of the Sixth Circuit's free speech holding, and the Supreme Court declined the Ford Motor Company's petition for writ of certiorari on the other elements in the case. The *Bill of Rights Review*'s second issue described the Sixth Circuit's decision in detail and interpreted it as imposing upon the NLRB the burden of proving that employer speech would in fact constitute coercion. According to the ABA, that rule appeared to be a justifiable one.[99]

Over the ensuing years, the NLRB developed a policy that was almost indistinguishable from the ACLU's stated position. When J. Warren Madden's term as chairman expired in August 1940, President Roosevelt appointed a more conciliatory replacement. The NLRB revised its policies and procedures to accommodate complaints by the AFL, employers, and the general public, and the Supreme Court upheld the new, more speech-protective approach.[100]

Fittingly, it was Justice Murphy who authored the Supreme Court's first decision on the issue. In 1941, less than a year after his opinions in

Thornhill and *Carlson* extended First Amendment protection to picketing, he took up employer free speech in *NLRB v. Virginia Electric and Power Company.* Murphy's opinion clarified that the NLRB, in considering whether an employer had "interfered with, restrained, and coerced" its employees under the Wagner Act, was permitted to inquire into its communications as well as its conduct. He concluded, however, that language must be actually coercive or part of a coercive course of conduct to justify curtailment by the NLRB. In the case under consideration, the employer had stated its opinion that unions were undesirable but had indicated that it would not retaliate against employees who chose to join. The NLRB had considered this expression of views to be unlawful without situating it in a broader complex of unlawful activities. Murphy left ample room on remand for the board to buttress its order with concrete findings ("Perhaps," he wrote, "the purport of these utterances may be altered by imponderable subtleties at work which it is not our function to appraise"). On their own terms, however, the employer's views did not rise to the level of constitutionally regulable coercion.[101]

Murphy's opinion in *Virginia Electric,* its formal protection of free speech coupled with broad interpretive deference to the NLRB, set the stage for that agency's decisions over the next five years, until Congress finally delineated the parameters of employer expression in the Taft-Hartley Act. The NLRB's understanding of "coercion" was predictably broad, and employers continued to complain about interference with their First Amendment rights. Still, by 1944, the secretary of the Labor Relations Committee of the Chamber of Commerce of the United States described a principle "emerging from the Courts . . . by which the First Amendment (of the Constitution) protects an employer's mere expression of opinion about unions."[102]

For its part, the ACLU never again wavered in its defense of employer free speech. The organization's leadership proclaimed an unflinching commitment to preserving government neutrality in the contest between workers and industry over public opinion and public policy. That contest, both labor and capital believed that they could win.[103]

Epilogue

A S THE 1930S drew to a close, free speech was indisputably an American value. Across the United States, newspapers, business leaders, and government officials celebrated the nation's commitment to expressive freedom. As German troops marched through Poland, Attorney General Frank Murphy assured Americans that the Department of Justice would respect their civil liberties, come what may. In countering espionage, the government would not align with "private industrial organizations which are concerned primarily with industrial disputes and labor problems," as it had during the First World War. Instead, domestic law enforcement would remain in the hands of trained government agents instructed to respect the people's rights. The United States would do its utmost to protect minorities and preserve free speech.[1]

Speaking at the sesquicentennial of the first Congress in March 1939, President Franklin D. Roosevelt and Chief Justice Charles Evans Hughes each exalted the First Amendment as fundamental to American democracy. The National Association of Manufacturers endeavored to "link free enterprise in the public consciousness with free speech, free press and free religion"; if any one component were weakened, it warned, "the whole structure of our Freedom [would] collapse." According to the ACLU, practically everyone, from high federal officers to local officials and private individuals, was united "in a common crusade." "Never in American history," the organization declared two weeks after the Japanese attack on Pearl Harbor, "has our Bill of Rights rested upon such a firm foundation of law."[2]

In practice, of course, there were transgressions. In 1940, the ACLU criticized Attorney General Murphy for his prosecutions of minority political groups. By 1941, Murphy's successor, Robert H. Jackson, urged the deportation of dangerous Communists and bemoaned the circulation of subversive materials in the mails. In the administration's assessment, aggressive enforcement of the Smith Act of 1940, the first federal peacetime sedition law since 1798, was necessary to forestall state and local oppression by vigilantes and overeager officials. Congress repeatedly acted to deport radical labor leader Harry Bridges, in a targeted fashion that offended even the ABA. Francis Biddle—who inherited the attorney general's office when Jackson, like Murphy before him, was appointed to the Supreme Court—advised United States attorneys to curtail civil rights only when "absolutely necessary" to the "military and economic war effort." He nonetheless authorized the prosecution of Minnesota Trotskyists for their alleged plot to overthrow the government of the United States. Even O. John Rogge, who had promised civil liberties advocates that the Department of Justice would "not become an instrument of oppression," pursued the prosecution of nearly three dozen accused fascists, though the charges eventually were dropped.[3]

It was the United States Supreme Court, among the nation's governing institutions, that best withstood the wartime hysteria. In a series of speech-protective decisions, it blocked the deportation of Bridges, overturned convictions for subversive speech, and sharply limited the definition of treason. Not even the court, however, was immune to patriotic pressures. Its decision in *Ex parte Quirin* conferred expansive powers on the president to try unlawful combatants in military tribunals in lieu of civilian courts. Most notoriously, it acquiesced to the internment of Japanese Americans, even while it embraced the notion that racial classifications were "suspect" and subject to "the most rigid scrutiny."[4]

The wartime experience—notwithstanding its ambivalent character—reflects a triumph for the ACLU's mature vision of civil liberties. To be sure, the Supreme Court weighed security against freedom in interpreting the First Amendment, as it always would. Still, the threshold for suppression was considerable. "The First Amendment does not speak equivocally," the Supreme Court proclaimed in 1941. "The substantive evil must be extremely serious and the degree of imminence extremely high before utterances can be punished." Even when judges and government officials sanctioned suppression, they acknowledged the limitations imposed by the Bill of Rights.[5]

✦ ✦ ✦

During the 1920s and 1930s, industry, labor, government officials, and the ACLU all had experimented with alternative understandings of civil liberties. As the new structure of state power coalesced, they scrambled to redefine freedom for a modern industrial economy. President Roosevelt famously counted both "freedom of speech" and "freedom from want" among America's most fundamental values. Even as the New Deal faded into history, the dictates of democracy encompassed economic security along with the liberty to demand it. And yet, there was a yawning conceptual gap between the "essential human freedoms" that Roosevelt so enthusiastically endorsed. Economic rights were a matter of government policy, conditioned on democratic deliberation. By contrast, free speech was a "civil liberty," and thus grounded in the Bill of Rights. An adequate standard of living was "positive," but aspirational; expressive freedom was a "negative" guarantee, asserted against the state.[6]

To the partisans of organized labor, the new arrangement manifested misplaced priorities. When business ranked a "free mind and an unfettered soul" above a "full stomach," it was simply repackaging the lapses of the *Lochner* era. Liberty was a dangerous abstraction, and economic power was a prerequisite for free speech. Nathan Greene—writing not for the ACLU but for the International Juridical Association—stressed the malleability of terms like *liberty,* which for so long had been invoked on employers' behalf. "We believe speech and the other civil liberties are meaningful only to men who dare to use them," Greene explained. "And that before 'daring' come bread and water, come roots in the community, comes respite from fear." Labor leaders made the same point more bluntly. Speaking at a mass meeting of Ford workers, one organizer recounted that twenty-five years earlier "the employers refused to speak to us because we were just that many nobodies, men and women without rights."[7]

The administrators of New Deal labor law, like its beneficiaries, believed the primary impediment to economic justice was consolidated industrial strength. In their view, even organized labor was vulnerable to employer abuse. The NLRB's Edwin Smith thought that strong unions were the key to democracy, and that to survive they must "receive from the government firm protection." In 1939, Robert La Follette Jr. at last introduced his bill to prohibit "oppressive labor practices." Had it passed, it would have made espionage, industrial munitions, private police, and strikebreaking punishable by fine or imprisonment. William Green and John L. Lewis both supported the bill. So, "heartily," did Attorney General Murphy, who believed "that the Federal Government has a definite role to play in the preservation of civil liberties."[8]

To J. Warren Madden, what workers deserved was a new and fundamental right—"a liberty to emerge from a condition of economic helplessness, and dependence upon the will of another, to a status of having one's chosen representative received as an equal at the bargaining conference table." According to Madden, that was what the Wagner Act had provided. In contemplating the appropriate label for the "new right," he emphasized its origins in a statutory framework that "restrains the private interests which formerly could and did prevent unionization, rather than by an act of self-denial on the part of the government itself, pledged in the text of the Constitution." He continued,

> Is it, for that reason, inaccurate to call it a civil liberty? I should suppose that the year 1935 was as propitious a year for the birth of a civil liberty as the year 1789. . . . In each of these years 1789 and 1935 the Federal Government placed in the body of its law the guarantee of the aspirations of multitudes of its citizens, for which they had struggled for decades. But let us not quibble about names. However it may be classified it is a new right which millions of Americans are exercising who never did so before. They have joined A.F. of L. unions, C.I.O. unions and unaffiliated unions. No one longer denies that they have a moral right to do so. And no one can successfully deny that they needed the protection of the government in order to be free to exercise this moral right.

Madden lamented the frequent fate of legislation meant to advance labor's legal rights: its vitiation by the lawyers and other officials whose "backgrounds and training made them incapable of a sympathetic administration of the law." It was Madden's singular objective to insulate the Wagner Act against that outcome. The statute demanded more than the passive toleration occasionally afforded labor by sympathetic progressives. In Madden's view, labor's decades-long struggle to organize had culminated in attainment of a right enforceable by the state at the expense of private interests. When the demise of court-centered constitutionalism was a realistic possibility, labor's legislative mandate was every bit as powerful as—indeed, more so than—induction into the Bill of Rights.[9]

Yet by the end of the decade, debates over employer speech had made the cost of exclusion from the Constitution apparent. In discussing the accomplishments of the statute he had drafted, Robert F. Wagner desired to remedy that deficiency. The Wagner Act did more than recognize a "legitimate economic interest," he explained. It also conferred freedom to workers in their daily lives and at the ballot box. "As we celebrate the 150th Anniversary of our democracy," he counseled, "we do well to include the right to organize among those fundamental expressions of the human spirit guaranteed, against impairment, by the Bill of Rights."[10]

✦ ✦ ✦

If the labor movement and its allies privileged the right to organize over free speech, the legal establishment squarely embraced the ACLU's elevation of expressive freedom to the top of the constitutional hierarchy. In the *Bill of Rights Review*, the ABA heralded the emergence of "civil liberties" as a "distinct field of law." Although the label remained informal, it captured (said the head of the Civil Liberties Unit of the Department of Justice) "such varied matters as freedom of speech, press, assembly and the ballot, unreasonable searches and seizures, religious freedom, censorship of the arts, and minority rights in general." That is, civil liberties meant virtually what it means today. The ABA encouraged law schools to offer classes in the subject. It also urged the adoption of an annual Bill of Rights Week throughout the United States, and it recommended daily study of the Bill of Rights in all American schools.[11]

On economic issues, the conservative bar retained its perennial aversion to regulation. In part, it shifted its efforts to procedural reform in lieu of freedom of contract or congressional power. The Administrative Procedure Act, enacted in 1946 after years of pressure for reform from the ABA, did little more than codify agencies' existing best practices. But as the ABA understood, the Bill of Rights offered an independent check on administrative excess. In enforcing those great amendments, the courts could ensure equal treatment for all Americans, including beleaguered employers.[12]

Freedom, of course, had its limits. In 1939, Grenville Clark mused that the Bill of Rights was becoming "fashionable," "almost too much so." As America readied for war, it necessarily imposed more onerous duties on its citizens, and the balance between liberty and responsibility shifted toward the latter. This "principle of relativity" subjected such privileges as the "so-called 'right to strike'" to moderation. Indeed, Clark went so far as to invoke the old axiom that "unbridled liberty degenerates into intolerable license"—and the rest of the ABA's Committee on the Bill of Rights, with the partial exception of Zechariah Chafee Jr., agreed. There was only one issue on which Clark was entirely unwilling to give ground to wartime exigencies. The "independence of the courts from domination by either the executive or the legislature," he cautioned, "must be jealously preserved."[13]

The onset of war initiated a massive expansion of federal power as well as a dramatic upsurge in popular acceptance of state authority. Still, Clark and his committee rejected the naked assertion of national necessity as a basis for curtailing personal freedom. Most famously, they denied the government's authority to compel its citizens to salute the American flag, before and during the war. In 1939, when *Minersville School District. v. Gobitis* first made headlines, there was reason to believe the Supreme Court would affirm the lower courts in holding that the expulsion of two Jehovah's Witnesses from the Pennsylvania public schools for refusing to salute the flag was unconstitutional. Judge William Clark, who had authored the district court opinion in *Hague v. CIO*, told Grenville Clark he considered such laws to be "utterly vicious," and he "hope[d] the Supreme Court [would] have the guts to put an end to them." With one dissenter, the Committee on the Bill of Rights voted to file an amicus brief—though in a testament to the decade's priorities, Chafee considered *Hague* to be "obviously" a more important case.[14]

Drafted largely by Louis Lusky, the committee's brief argued that legislation infringing on religious and expressive freedom should undergo "more exacting judicial scrutiny" than legislation regulating business or property—as Justice Harlan Fiske Stone, with Lusky's help, had suggested in footnote 4 of *United States v. Carolene Products Company*. Writing for the court over Stone's lone dissent, Justice Felix Frankfurter disappointed his old civil liberties allies. Frankfurter's long leadership in the ACLU (which filed its own amicus brief in *Gobitis*) reflected the organization's earlier aversion to judicial meddling in labor relations as opposed to its later enthusiasm for the Bill of Rights, and he remained deeply wary of judicial overreaching. His views, however, were increasingly out of step with professional opinion as well as recent precedent. Just three years later, in *West Virginia State Board of Education v. Barnette,* a Supreme Court majority reversed course and deemed the compulsory flag salute an abridgment of First Amendment freedoms. In an amicus brief, the Committee on the Bill of Rights distinguished a legislative contest between two "powerful economic groups," where a court could comfortably defer to democratic processes, from the flag salute controversy, which involved a weak minority subject to majoritarian whims. It was up to the judiciary to ensure that the rights of that minority were respected.[15]

At the peak of wartime fervor, when the impulse to trade liberty for security was most acute, the ABA maintained a formal commitment to expressive freedom. When members of the organization's House of Delegates were asked in 1943 to choose war-related activities to promote in their communities, more than one-third selected the Committee on the Bill of Rights. And yet, most were moving steadily further from the right of agitation. Even as it pushed the court to strengthen its scrutiny of legislation that infringed the Bill of Rights, the legal profession excluded labor picketing from the domain of expression. In 1943, even Chafee "doubt[ed] whether the picketing involved in the Thornhill case should be constitutionally protected," and he contended that "invitations to boycott persons whose connection with the controversy is exceedingly remote should not be deemed privileged free speech."[16]

In the bar's evolving understanding, labor picketing (despite the soaring language of *Thornhill v. Alabama*) was not necessary to the fair operations of democratic processes, nor was organized labor a small and beleaguered minority deserving of special judicial protection. On the contrary, if there were two quintessential "powerful economic groups," they were industry and labor. In a world divided between ordinary economic legislation and the curtailment of personal freedom, restrictions on labor organizing fell squarely on the economic side of the line.

By the mid-1940s, the ABA's enthusiasm for its Committee on the Bill of Rights was waning. In 1943, the committee suspended publication of the *Bill of Rights Review.* Despite its best efforts, the editorial staff was unable to solicit funding to replace the Carnegie grant, which the foundation had declined to renew. In any case, the editor and business manager had both entered government service, and Clark was immersed in wartime work. The committee continued for a time. It took up such subjects as the distribution of Communist literature, the denial of second-class mailing privileges to *Esquire* magazine, and the rights of the incarcerated to habeas corpus. But as the world war gave way to the Cold War, the allure of suppression reemerged. At the height of McCarthyism, the ABA succumbed to anti-Communist hysteria.[17]

By then, however, the New Deal coalition had accomplished its goal: the Bill of Rights was doctrinally ensconced as a check on government repression, though it was sometimes a slender reed in practice. The justices of the Supreme Court, whose tenure partly shielded them from changing political winds, never fully capitulated to the Second Red Scare. In 1949, the Committee on the Bill of Rights described "the marked solicitude of the courts for the protection of any individual who complains that he has suffered an encroachment of his civil rights." In fact, the committee worried that disproportionate concern for individual freedom endangered the "civil rights of the citizens as a whole," and it recommended legislation to authorize the government to combat subversive groups. As Clark reflected, the "Committee had become 'perverted,' in that it seemed actually to encourage or condone rather than to fight against obviously unjust and oppressive practices." The critique extended to the bar as a whole. In 1951, the publisher of the *Washington Post* chastised the legal profession for neglecting to defend constitutional rights. Even business groups, he said, were more attuned to the importance of individual freedom. The same year, President Harry S. Truman pleaded that "lawyers in the past have risked the obloquy of the uninformed to protect the rights of the most degraded," and unless they continued to do so, "an important part of our rights will be gone." In 1952, the ABA appointed a Special Committee on Individual Rights as Affected by National Security. As a member of the ACLU's national committee, Clark hoped, "but hardly expect[ed]," that it would "amount to something."[18]

Over the course of the 1950s, a new threat to legal legitimacy emerged. In the Golden Age of Capitalism, there was little cause to fear the trampling of industrial interests. But increasingly, the legal sanction of southern apartheid belied America's commitments to its democratic ideals, and the nation's diplomatic and propaganda interests fueled a new concern for racial equality. In the wake of *Brown v. Board of Education,* it was Justice Frankfurter who defended the integrity of the Supreme Court.[19]

Twenty years after it was founded, the Committee on the Bill of Rights requested its own dissolution, professing that there was nothing for it to do. Clark decried the absurdity of that assessment "in view of the steady stream of vital civil rights cases . . . before the courts, various legislative bodies and the public at large." In the face of massive resistance and the Southern Manifesto, Clark lamented "the lack of any desire on the part of the present Committee to grapple with any of these tough problems, especially the racial one which [was] the hardest but also the most important of all." Partly at his urging, the ABA intensified its commitment to civil rights. In 1964, the ABA announced a new committee to protect individual rights. At eighty-one, Clark agreed to serve.[20]

At the height of Warren Court liberalism, the Bill of Rights became a potent tool for advancing the interests of the disenfranchised. Increasingly, its provisions bound the states. The due process revolution countered race-based injustices for criminal defendants. At the same time, the Supreme Court read the Equal Protection Clause expansively and, relying on footnote four of *Carolene Products*, extended its reach to women as well as racial minorities. Scholars and social critics have long debated the trade-offs of a strategy rooted in legal rights: the ease with which color-blind constitutionalism eviscerated affirmative action, the costs to solidarity of court-centered change, and the emptiness of formal equality in the absence of meaningful redistribution.[21]

It took somewhat longer, however, for similar skepticism to emerge around the First Amendment. For the civil rights movement, a strong First Amendment shielded protests, pickets, boycotts, even the litigation program of the NAACP. Free speech was a banner of anti-Vietnam activism and a license for 1960s counterculture. But in the 1970s, when economic stagnation tempered the social and cultural turmoil of the preceding decade, the First Amendment served other ends. Citing their rights of free speech, advertisers, political donors, and eventually employers chipped away at the reach of the regulatory state.[22]

✦ ✦ ✦

And what of the right of agitation? When court-based constitutionalism was most vulnerable, an unlikely alliance between conservative lawyers and state-skeptical radicals had helped to save judicial review. The constituents of that united campaign had little in common, but all agreed on one basic principle: in the workplace struggle between labor and industry, the First Amendment required the government to stay out. But as the ACLU's labor contingent had foreseen, the compromise they struck proved unsustainable.

When the Supreme Court decided *Thornhill v. Alabama* and *Carlson v. California* in 1940, the world took note. At a symposium on civil liberties in 1941, the renowned legal scholar Herbert Wechsler described the Supreme Court decision incorporating the religion clause of the First Amendment as unimportant in comparison with the labor picketing cases, which were of "major significance." To University of Chicago law professor Charles O. Gregory, writing in the *ABA Journal*, the cases marked a dangerous development. Picketing achieved its effect through annoyance and social ostracism, not the dissemination of ideas. "True liberals in this country no longer look askance at economic compulsion," Gregory explained, but that was no reason to "call such coercion constitutionally guaranteed freedom of speech." In an assessment that astutely captured the import of the judiciary's interwar trajectory, Gregory concluded, "For years the 'Old Court' was under fire because of its doctrine of 'substantive due process' developed to make possible the invalidation of local legislative experiments. It now seems from the picketing cases of last Spring that the 'New Court' is perpetuating this error by using the Fourteenth Amendment to establish its conception of the guaranties of liberty set forth in the First Amendment." That, of course, was precisely the outcome the ACLU and its allies had advanced.[23]

Liberal critics worried that the Supreme Court's invigoration of the First Amendment would reopen the door to judicial usurpation of the police power. Their misgivings were well founded. In his opinion in *Thornhill*, Justice Murphy compared labor picketing with commercial advertising, and by implication "invest[ed] both types of publicity pressures with the dignity of freedom of speech." Just months after the decision came down, *Nation's Business* highlighted the potential benefits of constitutional protection for commercial speech. Soon, the Newspaper Publishers Committee sent Grenville Clark examples of its weekly advertisements, printed in newspapers throughout the country, advising their readers about "the importance of a free press in maintaining our kind of Democracy." And in June 1941, Samuel B. Pettengill admonished his audience at the annual meeting of the Chamber of Commerce of the United States to uphold the "rights of the individual and of the minority." Pettengill denounced the closed shop and defended the right of strikebreakers to cross the picket line. The chamber, he explained, supported the simple strike. But the "equal right to work" was "the first right of all." A few months later, the organization's president proclaimed the right to work to be a *"fifth freedom,* quite as important as . . . worship, speech, the press and assembly." In time, industry would learn to frame that fifth right, too, by reference to the First Amendment.[24]

Increasingly, business fought to extend expressive freedom to corporations as well as individuals. In *Hague v. CIO,* Justice Stone had considered free speech to be a right of "natural, not artificial persons." But Stone's was not a majority opinion, and the press cases pointed toward an alternative path. In *Grosjean v. American Press Company,* the Supreme Court had recognized the right of newspaper corporations to challenge Louisiana's tax law under the First and Fourteenth Amendments (a result that Sherman Minton denounced for transferring the stewardship of expressive freedom to "soulless creations of the law"). The ACLU considered it "unthinkable" that corporations were "not entitled to the benefit of the liberty clause of the Fourteenth Amendment," given that three-quarters of the nation's daily and Sunday newspapers were corporate entities. If corporate entities flooded the marketplace of ideas, so much the better. According to Attorney General Jackson, all of that advertising inured Americans to the dangers of totalitarian propaganda.[25]

Against this backdrop, it is all the more striking how quickly and completely labor activity fell out of the First Amendment. In 1947, with the voice of industry behind them, congressional conservatives at last succeeded in amending the NLRA. That June, the Taft-Hartley Act was enacted over the veto of President Truman. On many issues, it implemented the very proposals that the ACLU had come together to oppose in the spring of 1940, at a time when it was otherwise so thoroughly divided. The new statute introduced a slate of union unfair labor practices parallel to the restrictions on employers. It prohibited secondary activity, and it abolished the closed shop. It required union leaders to file affidavits denying membership in the Communist Party. It authorized states to outlaw agency fees (that is, to pass "right-to-work" laws). It extended the supervisory authority of the courts. It empowered the NLRB to seek injunctions against statutory violations, and it required the NLRB to pursue injunctions to block secondary activity by unions.

The ACLU denounced Taft-Hartley as a "direct violation of labor's rights." It warned that the act's provisions were "fraught with peril to the maintenance of civil liberties in labor disputes." Its next annual report jettisoned the optimistic outlook of the late 1930s and 1940s. Citing Taft-Hartley, among other setbacks, it expressed "justified skepticism concerning the immediate future of our democratic liberties as instruments of progress." It described the popular desire, expressed in the 1946 elections, to supplant state power with "the presumably sound leadership of private business." The Taft-Hartley Act accomplished that goal not only by altering the basic framework of the Wagner Act, but by increasing the review power of the judiciary. Mounting skepticism toward state economic regulation had "produced an atmosphere increasingly hostile to the liberties of organized labor, the political left and many minorities." But the ACLU's protest came too late. However much the organization willed it to be otherwise, legislators had injected the prerogatives of employers and nonunion workers into the centerpiece of New Deal labor policy.[26]

Labor law was a staple of postwar legal culture. Before Congress, judges, and the NLRB, the parameters of industrial pluralism were gradually hashed out. But the great cases in the law of industrial relations turned on statutory construction and administrative interpretation, not the Constitution. On the infrequent occasions when courts considered First Amendment limitations, they departed nonchalantly from principles established in other domains, where picketing and boycotts enjoyed increasing constitutional protection. On the issue of employer free speech, the Taft-Hartley Act amended the Wagner Act to provide that the expression of opinion, in the absence of threat of reprisal or force or the promise of benefit, would neither constitute nor provide evidence of an unfair labor practice under the statute. Although the Supreme Court famously described the clause as "merely implement[ing] the First Amendment," it emphasized workers' dependency on their employers and their corresponding ability to discern subtle meanings in apparently innocent statements. After Taft-Hartley passed, an amendment was proposed to ease restrictions on union contributions to political campaigns, in a concession to "freedom of speech and of the press." But such accommodations merely nudged the margin. In upholding a state injunction against peaceful picketing in *Teamsters Union v. Vogt,* Justice Frankfurter explained on behalf of the Supreme Court majority that labor activity was not immune from state regulation. The dissent described the opinion as a "formal surrender." The law was back where it started, "when *Senn v. Tile Layers Union* was decided."[27]

Over the course of the twentieth century, strikes, boycotts, and picketing were carefully hemmed in: recognitional picketing, secondary activity, and union discipline were recast as unlawful infringements on employer interests and the rights of nonunion employees. It was not until the new millennium, when union density had plummeted and organized labor had lost much of its political power—when unions, that is, had lost the capacity to coerce—that the courts evinced a renewed openness to constitutional challenges in the labor law domain. In 2016, the Supreme Court divided evenly over a claim by California school teachers that a public sector "right-to-work" regime is required by the First Amendment.[28]

✦ ✦ ✦

More than any other entity, it was the ACLU that crafted the constitutional compromise of the post–New Deal era. By investing in the Bill of Rights, the ACLU produced its most influential victories: the Supreme Court decisions of the 1930s, which protected the rights of radicals to articulate their views without interference by the state. Well after 1937, the judges, academics, and activists who came of age in the Progressive Era remained wary of judicial review. The new vision of court-based constitutionalism would take years to find a firm hold among postwar liberals. Still, by 1940, former progressives who were sympathetic to free speech routinely decried administrative censorship but "[took] comfort in evidences of an enlightened judiciary."[29]

Seizing on the conservative rhetoric of time-honored individual rights, the ACLU had attracted supporters within and outside the courts. The majority within the ACLU had convinced themselves, employers, and the ABA that freedom of speech meant freedom from government censorship. It was a right held by all equally, worker and employer alike. An estimated 2,000 people attended the ACLU's National Conference on Civil Liberties in October 1939, representing a sweeping range of political and economic views.[30]

By the 1940s, the ACLU's "battleground [was] chiefly in the courts." Its volunteer attorneys had carried "scores of civil liberties issues" to the United States Supreme Court, "where decisions in case after case [had] firmly established the interpretations of the Bill of Rights which the Union supports."

Over the following decades, the ACLU would continue to pursue such non-judicial methods as lobbying, grassroots organizing, and cooperation with administrative agencies. At times, when the courts seemed unusually un-friendly to civil liberties claims, it would emphasize legislation or education. But the organization's mature view was unmistakable: "The whole court system, top to bottom, federal and state, is the proper and natural ally of citizens' rights, and for the ACLU, with its appeal to law, it is the essential forum."[31]

The constitutional strategy came at a cost. In 1940, the labor press accused the ACLU of "turning against labor," citing a long list of changes in ACLU policy, including its position in the *Ford* case. The ACLU's labor allies chastised the organization for abandoning "a large part of the field of battle for civil liberties." As it entered the new decade, the ACLU professed a commitment to the legal protection of strikebreakers in "their right of access to places of employment," and it applied for funds to study "auto-cratic" union practices. Several of its prominent members denounced the closed shop as a threat to civil liberties. Some commended the Dies Committee for its investigation of "destructive" trade union activity. Over time, the ACLU expressed support for the "democratic rights" of workers to be free of union discrimination based not only on race (as in earlier years) but also on "political views or opposition to union administration." It asked the police to protect the civil rights "not only of organized workers but of non-union workers and managers in their right of access to places of employment." It created a Committee on Trade Union Democracy to monitor union compliance with these principles, and in 1947, it sponsored legislation to promote union democratic practices, though its bill never left committee. "Unions should be democratic," the ACLU reasoned, "because the power which they hold over the individual worker is largely derived from government."[32]

In the 1940s, preserving civil liberties meant promoting and protecting speech, not correcting it. The ACLU proved consistent in enforcement of that principle. It continued to criticize violent interference with the right to organize and strike. But it held labor to the same standard. It admonished pickets to "keep traffic open for pedestrians and vehicles, to insure access to places picketed, to prevent the use of fraudulent signs, and to maintain order." In place of the right of agitation, the ACLU touted the marketplace of ideas. Workers were free to express their discontent. They could reason with strikebreakers. But frank union "coercion," like its employer counter-part, had no claim to civil liberties status.[33]

The same principle applied in other domains. The ACLU envisioned the Bill of Rights not only as a shield, but also as a "sword cutting through private restraints on the market-place of thought." Toward that end, it en-couraged government to promote conversation. It urged public officials to prosecute hecklers and to create public forums for expression. It also invited action by the Civil Liberties Unit of the Department of Justice, though that body, like the ACLU, was transitioning to new priorities. In 1941, the Civil Liberties Unit became the Civil Rights Section. The name change (notwithstanding the enduring fluidity of both terms) reflected a new focus on racial inequality, and in particular, on the plight of ex-ploited black farmworkers—a program of patent importance in unsettling America's racial hierarchy, yet which the department deemed less radical than abetting strikes and pickets by industrial workers. The ACLU con-tinued to urge federal protection of union speech from lawless officials and recalcitrant employers. On the section's new understanding, however, such situations "fail[ed] to indicate the violation of any Federal Criminal statute warranting action by the Department."[34]

Over time, the ACLU experimented with alternative methods for in-creasing access to unpopular speech. Morris Ernst persuaded President Roosevelt to introduce a discounted postage rate for printed matter, which facilitated "a flow into the market place of great additional diversity of points of view." He also advocated ACLU legal action against newspaper owners for restraint of trade, and although the ACLU did not follow him quite that far, it met him partway. In 1945, the board formally adopted a new policy extending its "traditional principles" to contexts in which "private agencies rather than public authorities" restricted freedom of speech. It opposed restraints on expression by motion picture distributors, for example. Even-tually, it would add company towns and shopping malls.[35]

More contentiously, the ACLU also adopted Ernst's long-standing posi-tion on broadcast radio. In 1946, it endorsed the Federal Communications Commission's new standards for granting and renewing radio licenses, which required stations to allocate time for the discussion of "important public questions" and to cover all sides of controversial issues. The revised rules, it reasoned, provided for "more speech, not less." In practice, of course, expanding access for marginal figures came at the expense of existing speakers. The radio industry denounced the measures as censorship, but the ACLU disagreed. After all, if the government sought to withhold radio licenses based on the quality of programming, the station owners had recourse to the courts.[36]

Some within the ACLU wanted the government to enhance the value of speech in addition to its volume. Alexander Meiklejohn, voicing the old progressive line, thought that government ownership of the airwaves would serve the "public interest" and enrich the quality of radio programming. On that point, however, the board of directors staunchly disagreed. John Haynes Holmes decried public ownership as "the first step in the direction of totalitarianism" and an "invasion of what we have called 'the free market in thought.'" It was one thing for government to regulate public utilities, and another to regulate the "distribution of opinion." Ernst warned that government-run newspapers and radio stations would completely undermine free speech. An ACLU pamphlet expressed the organization's position: "The evils of big business ultimately invite government correction, a cure as bad as the disease. Once the government enters to correct, it will remain to control. And government domination of the public mind cannot be reconciled with democracy."[37]

The ACLU approved efforts to multiply speech, but never to curtail it. It countenanced no consideration for the relative worth of speech, however provocative, hateful or abusive. It even condemned distinctions between commercial and noncommercial speech. That the organization adhered to its position with tremendous consistency over the span of decades accounts in part for its continued vitality. When the Supreme Court decided *Citizens United v. Federal Election Committee* in 2010, the ACLU issued a statement. "The ACLU does not support campaign finance regulation premised on the notion that the answer to money in politics is *to ban political speech*," the organization announced. It was not the role of government to decide what speech the people were entitled to hear.[38]

So too in the context of labor. As Roger Baldwin told Meiklejohn, the ACLU advocated complete freedom of expression for both unions and employers. Restricting both sides was no solution to disparities in bargaining power, he advised. "You know we are of course opposed to restraints on either."[39]

By the early 1940s, civil liberties were no longer radical. Invoking recent prolabor decisions and prior prolabor dissents, employers and their lawyers transformed them into a potent weapon against state control over industry.

Such is the standard course in a legal system built on precedent; corporations hired the most skilled and best trained of lawyers, who availed themselves of every argument in their arsenal. Even so, their embrace of civil liberties was not simply a fallback to the least bad alternative. The ACLU had naively hoped, in an era when revolution seemed possible, that a mere right to agitate would pave the way to substantive change. Implicit in their position was the confidence that radicalism would prevail in the marketplace of ideas. By the 1940s, employers understood that no free exchange in ideas existed. They understood that a right to free speech would ordinarily favor those with superior resources. As Nathan Greene put it, employer speech was "a *protected* commodity in a *monopoly* market."[40]

The New Deal's constitutional compromise guaranteed Congress far-reaching control over economic regulation, subject only to the constraints of the most fundamental American liberties, including free speech. *Lochner*-style substantive due process no longer impeded progressive legislation. Like the ACLU leadership, the courts had come to accept state regulation of the economy as a positive force that served the public interest. No longer would they regard freedom of contract or the rights of property as trumps on social progress. But they would demand, lest America slide into dictatorship, that the state remain neutral in the realm of thought. In short, industry was free to dominate the marketplace of ideas. It could marshal all of its economic might to lobby government and to disseminate its views in the workplace and the public forum. And the First Amendment would ensure that no one would stand in its way.

Looking backward from 1940, Constance L. Todd, a radical journalist who was married for two decades to the ACLU's early representative and press correspondent in Washington, DC, reflected nostalgically on the organization's origins: "Twenty years ago," she wrote to Baldwin, "you . . . showed such diabolical ingenuity in devising an organization which would compel (and I use the word advisedly) the comfortable intelligent to work for socialism in the name of Consistency and the Bill of Rights." According to Todd, the genius of the ACLU was its eclecticism, its ability to entertain competing theories while committing to none—to "balanc[e] on two ropes and draw[] together strange bedfellows." That strategy, she recalled, "worked for us, and against them; though before 1914, the Bill of Rights had worked for them and against us." Yet in Todd's view, the ACLU's success was also its downfall. To attain respectability, it had disavowed its underlying ideals.[41]

Baldwin consistently denied the charges that the ACLU had gone conservative. When pressed by former friends and colleagues, he fell back on his pre–Wagner Act belief that the best protection for workers was a strong union, not the state. He reasserted his distrust of state power, which had always operated before to trample the rights of the least empowered. The true goal, for Baldwin, had always been to "keep[] the public authorities neutral in . . . strikes."[42]

Such arguments, however, were quickly fading into the background; the ACLU's emerging program emphasized other ideas. In the 1940s, "race relations . . . occup[ied] first place in the struggle for civil liberties." Also central were religious liberty, immigration, and women's rights. In addressing these issues, the ACLU stressed its utter impartiality. The organization, it claimed, had no "'isms' or other objects to serve." It defended the freedoms to speak, worship, and assemble as essential to American democracy. The right to picket was an application of a general commitment to free speech. "We are neither anti-labor nor pro-labor," Baldwin insisted in 1940. "With us it is just a question of going wherever the Bill of Rights leads us."[43]

Abbreviations

AABA   American Anti-Boycott Association

AAUP   American Association of University Professors

ABA   American Bar Association

ACLU   American Civil Liberties Union

ACLUM   American Civil Liberties Union Records and Publications, 1917–1975, Microfilming Corporation of America (Glen Rock, NJ, 1977)

ACLUR   American Civil Liberties Union Records, Roger Baldwin Years, 1917–1950, Seeley G. Mudd Manuscript Library, Princeton University, Princeton, NJ

ACLUS   Records of the American Civil Liberties Union, Swarthmore College Peace Collection, Swarthmore, PA

AFL   American Federation of Labor

AGHP   Arthur Garfield Hays Papers, Seeley G. Mudd Manuscript Library, Princeton University, Princeton, NJ

AMP   Alexander Meiklejohn Papers, 1880–1969, Wisconsin Historical Society, Library-Archives Division, Madison, WI

ASW   Associated Silk Workers

ATVP   Arthur T. Vanderbilt Political, Professional, and Judicial Papers, Collection 1000-186, Special Collections and Archives, Wesleyan University, Middletown, CT

AUAM   American Union against Militarism

AUAMR   American Union against Militarism Records, 1915–1922, DG 004, Swarthmore College Peace Collection, Swarthmore, PA

CCUSR   Chamber of Commerce of the United States Records, Accession 1960, Hagley Museum and Library, Manuscript and Archives Department, Wilmington, DE

CEP   Crystal Eastman Papers, 1889–1931, Schlesinger Library, Radcliffe Institute, Harvard University, Cambridge, MA

CIRRT   United States Commission on Industrial Relations, *Final Report and Testimony Submitted to Congress by the Commission on Industrial Relations*, 11 volumes, 64th Congress, 1st session (Washington, DC, 1916)

CIRP   U.S. Commission on Industrial Relations, 1912–1915: Records of the Division of Research and Investigation: Reports, Staff Studies, and Background Research Materials (microfilm)

CIO   Congress of Industrial Organizations

CJR   American Bar Association Committee to Oppose the Judicial Recall

DOJR   Records of the Special Executive Assistant to the Attorney General, 1933–40, Subject Files, 1933–1940, General Records of the Department of Justice, Record Group 60, National Archives and Records Administration, College Park, MD

FDRP   Franklin D. Roosevelt Papers, Franklin D. Roosevelt Presidential Library, Hyde Park, NY

FMCLP   Ford Motor Company Legal Papers, Ford Motor Company and UAW before the NLRB, Benson Ford Research Center, Dearborn, MI

GCP   Papers of Grenville Clark in the Dartmouth College Library, ML-7, Rauner Special Collections Library, Hanover, NH

GJP   Gardner Jackson Papers, 1912–1965, Franklin D. Roosevelt Presidential Library, Hyde Park, NY

IJA   International Juridical Association

ILD   International Labor Defense

ILDP   Papers of the International Labor Defense on Microfilm, Collection 5815 mf, Kheel Center for Labor-Management Documentation and Archives, Cornell University, Ithaca, NY

IWW   Industrial Workers of the World

IWWC   Industrial Workers of the World Collection, Series V: Legal Problems, Trials and Defense, US v. Haywood et al., Accession 130, Walter P. Reuther Library, Archives of Labor and Urban Affairs, Wayne State University, Detroit, MI

LMP   Lowell Mellett Papers, 1938–1944, Franklin D. Roosevelt Presidential Library, Hyde Park, NY

MLEP   Morris Leopold Ernst Papers, Harry Ransom Center, The University of Texas at Austin, Austin, TX

MSC   Maurice Sugar Collection, Accession 232, Walter P. Reuther Library, Archives of Labor and Urban Affairs, Wayne State University, Detroit, MI

MWDP   Mary Ware Dennett Papers, 1874–1947, MC 392, Schlesinger Library, Radcliffe Institute, Harvard University, Cambridge, MA

NAACP   National Association for the Advancement of Colored People

NAM   National Association of Manufacturers

NAMP   National Association of Manufacturers Papers, Accession 1411, Hagley Museum and Library, Manuscript and Archives Department, Wilmington, DE

NARA DC   National Archives and Records Administration, National Archives Building, Washington, DC

NARA M-A   National Archives and Records Administration, Mid-Atlantic Region, Philadelphia, PA

NARA NE   National Archives and Records Administration, Northeast Region, New York, NY

NCCL   National Council for Civil Liberties

NCFC   National Committee for Freedom from Censorship
NCLB   National Civil Liberties Bureau
NIRA   National Industrial Recovery Act
NLRA   National Labor Relations Act
NLRB   National Labor Relations Board
NRA   National Recovery Administration
NYT   *New York Times*
PWP   Philip Wittenberg Papers, 1932–1934, Collection 5237, Kheel Center for
    Labor-Management Documentation and Archives, Cornell University Library,
    Ithaca, NY
RTFC   Richard T. Frankensteen Collection, Accession 14, Walter P. Reuther
    Library, Archives of Labor and Urban Affairs, Wayne State University, Detroit, MI
UAW   United Automobile Workers of America
UMW   United Mine Workers of America
WGRP   William Gorham Rice Papers, Wisconsin Historical Society, Library-
    Archives Division, Madison, WI
ZCP   Zechariah Chafee Jr. Papers, 1898–1957, Harvard Law School Library,
    Harvard University, Cambridge, MA

Notes

Introduction

1. ACLU, *The Fight for Free Speech* (New York, 1921), 5.
2. Ibid., 3.
3. "Civil Liberties—A Field of Law," *Bill of Rights Review* 1 (Summer 1940): 7–9. Critics of the positive-negative distinction emphasize government's role in enforcing so-called negative rights and in structuring putatively private relationships. Nonetheless, participants in the interwar civil liberties movement regularly invoked the concepts. On historical usage of the terms by advocates of constitutional rights, see Emily Zackin, *Looking for Rights in All the Wrong Places: Why State Constitutions Contain America's Positive Rights* (Princeton, NJ, 2013), 42–47.
4. Francis Lieber, *On Civil Liberty and Self-Government* (London, 1853), 9, 40, see also 298 ("A weak government is a negation of liberty"); Henry Campbell Black, *A Dictionary of Law* (Saint Paul, 1891), 208 (citing Blackstone's *Commentaries*); William Blackstone, *Commentaries*, vol. 1 (Oxford, 1765), 121–122; "Address on Legal Procedure and Social Unrest," *Ohio Law Bulletin* 48 (1913): 381 (Judge N. Charles Burge to the ABA; "excessive individualism"); Ernst Freund, *The Police Power, Public Policy and Constitutional Rights* (Chicago, 1904), 23; Christopher G. Tiedeman, *A Treatise on State and Federal Control of Persons and Property in the United States,* vol. 1 (Saint Louis, 1886), 67 (approvingly quoting Daniel Webster's observation that "it is an error to suppose that liberty consists in a paucity of laws").
5. Charles de Secondat, baron de Montesquieu, *The Spirit of the Laws* (New York, 1900), 232; Thomas M. Cooley, *A Treatise on the Constitutional Limitations which Rest upon the Legislative Power of the States of the*

American Union (Boston, 1868), 429; Herbert Spencer, *Social Statics, or, The Conditions Essential to Human Happiness Specified, and the First of Them Developed* (London, 1851), 148–153.

6. William Blackstone, *Commentaries*, vol. 4 (Oxford, 1769), 151; Leonard Levy, *Emergence of a Free Press* (New York, 1985). The Supreme Court famously endorsed this view in *Patterson v. Colorado*, 205 U.S. 454 (1907). On Lincoln, see Michael Kent Curtis, *Free Speech, "The People's Darling Privilege": Struggles for Freedom of Expression in American History* (Durham, 2000); Mark E. Neely, *The Fate of Liberty: Abraham Lincoln and Civil Liberties* (New York, 1991), 160–184. On civil liberties during wartime, see Christopher Capozzola, *Uncle Sam Wants You: World War I and the Making of the Modern American Citizen* (New York, 2008); Paul Murphy, *World War I and the Origin of Civil Liberties in the United States* (New York, 1979); Richard Steele, *Free Speech in the Good War* (New York, 1999); Geoffrey R. Stone, *Perilous Times: Free Speech in Wartime from the Sedition Act of 1798 to the War on Terrorism* (New York, 2004). On civil liberties advocacy before World War I, see David M. Rabban, *Free Speech in Its Forgotten Years, 1870–1920* (New York, 1997).

7. Freund, *Police Power*, 11; "Peace-Time Sedition Law," *Cincinnati Tribune*, August 18, 1919. On liberty and license, see, for example, "Criticism of the Judiciary," *Law Notes* 8 (July 1904): 307 (describing "liberty is not license" as a "hackneyed phrase"); Zechariah Chafee Jr., "Freedom of Speech in War Time," *Harvard Law Review* 32 (1919): 932–973, 943 ("'license' is too often 'liberty' to the speaker, and what happens to be anathema to the judge"). The incorporation cases include *Gitlow v. New York*, 268 U.S. 652 (1925) (speech, in dicta); *Near v. Minnesota*, 283 U.S. 697 (1931) (press); *Cantwell v. Connecticut*, 310 U.S. 296 (1940) (free exercise of religion). On the pervasiveness of state morals regulation during the nineteenth century, see William Novak, *The People's Welfare: Law and Regulation in Nineteenth-Century America* (Chapel Hill, NC, 1996), 149–189.

8. Abrams v. United States, 250 U.S. 616, 630 (1919) (Holmes, J., dissenting). See, for example, Paul L. Murphy, *The Meaning of Freedom of Speech: First Amendment Freedoms from Wilson to FDR* (Westport, CT, 1972), 8–9; Rabban, *Forgotten Years*, 1 (describing the dominant view that "the creation of the modern First Amendment" began with the passage of the Espionage Act of 1917).

9. Scholarship highlighting the relationship between labor radicalism and civil liberties in the early to mid-twentieth century includes Jerold Auerbach, *Labor and Liberty: The La Follette Committee and the New Deal* (Indianapolis, 1966); Robert Cottrell, *Roger Nash Baldwin and the American Civil Liberties Union* (New York, 2000); Cletus Daniel, *The*

ACLU and the Wagner Act: An Inquiry into the Depression-Era Crisis of American Liberalism (Ithaca, NY, 1980); Donna T. Haverty-Stacke, *Trotskyists on Trial: Free Speech and Political Persecution since the Age of FDR* (New York, 2016); Murphy, *Freedom of Speech;* James Gray Pope, "The Thirteenth Amendment versus the Commerce Clause: Labor and the Shaping of American Constitutional Law, 1921–1958," *Columbia Law Review* 102 (2002): 1–123, 99–123; Jennifer Luff, *Commonsense Anticommunism: Labor and Civil Liberties between the World Wars* (Chapel Hill, NC, 2012); John Wertheimer, "Free Speech Fights: The Roots of Modern Free-Expression Litigation in the United States" (PhD diss., Princeton University, 1992). In addition, the labor literature has investigated the uses of civil liberties rhetoric and First Amendment advocacy to defend and buttress labor organizing. On the IWW's free speech fights, see, for example, Melvyn Dubofsky, *We Shall Be All: A History of the Industrial Workers of the World* (Chicago, 1969); Philip S. Foner, *History of the Labor Movement*, vol. 9, *The T.U.E.L. to the End of the Gompers Era* (New York, 1991); Philip S. Foner, ed., *Fellow Workers and Friends: I.W.W. Free Speech Fights as Told by Participants* (Westport, CT, 1981). On the boycott and picketing cases of the 1910s and 1920s, see Daniel R. Ernst, *Lawyers against Labor: From Individual Rights to Corporate Liberalism* (Urbana, IL, 1995); William E. Forbath, *Law and the Shaping of the American Labor Movement* (Cambridge, MA, 1991); Philip Taft, *The A. F. of L. in the Time of Gompers* (New York, 1957); Christopher Tomlins, *The State and the Unions: Labor Relations, Law, and the Organized Labor Movement in America, 1880–1960* (New York, 1985).

10. Gompers v. Buck's Stove and Range Co., 221 U.S. 418 (1911) (see Chapter 1). For summary and analysis of the common justifications for the differential treatment of labor speech, as well as counterarguments, see Cynthia Estlund, "Labor Picketing and Commercial Speech: Free Enterprise Values in the Doctrine of Free Speech," *Yale Law Journal* 91 (1982): 938–960; Catherine Fisk and Jessica Rutter, "Labor Protest under the New First Amendment," *Berkeley Journal of Labor and Employment Law* 36 (2015): 277–329; James Gray Pope, "The First Amendment, the Thirteenth Amendment, and the Right To Organize in the Twenty-First Century," *Rutgers Law Review* 51 (1999): 941–970; Pope, "Thirteenth Amendment," 99–123; Mark D. Schneider, "Peaceful Labor Picketing and the First Amendment," *Columbia Law Review* 82 (1982): 1469–1497.

11. In exploring these sources, *The Taming of Free Speech* joins a growing body of scholarship, building on Rabban, *Forgotten Years*, linking legal and cultural understandings of civil liberties through the organizations and social movements that advocated for them within and outside the

courts. Recent examples include Risa Goluboff, *Vagrant Nation: Police Power, Constitutional Change, and the Making of the 1960s* (Cambridge, MA, 2016); Sam Lebovic, *Free Speech and Unfree News: The Paradox of Press Freedom in America* (Cambridge, MA, 2016); Leigh Ann Wheeler, *How Sex Became a Civil Liberty* (New York, 2013); John Fabian Witt, *Patriots and Cosmopolitans: Hidden Histories of American Law* (Cambridge, MA, 2007).

12. John Dewey, "Liberalism and Civil Liberties," *Social Frontier* 2 (February 1936): 137. On the progressive understanding, see generally Mark Graber, *Transforming Free Speech: The Ambiguous Legacy of Civil Libertarianism* (Berkeley, 1991).

13. Frank J. Hogan, "Justice, Sure and Speedy, for All," address to ABA annual meeting, July 29, 1938, GVP, box 83, folder 45 ("rights denied"). On the conservative civil libertarian tradition, see David Bernstein, *Rehabilitating Lochner: Defending Individual Rights against Progressive Reform* (Chicago, 2011); Kenneth I. Kersch, *Constructing Civil Liberties: Discontinuities in the Development of American Constitutional Law* (New York, 2004); Jeremy K. Kessler, "The Early Years of First Amendment Lochnerism," *Columbia Law Review* 116 (forthcoming); Lebovic, *Unfree News;* Laura Weinrib, "The Liberal Compromise: Civil Liberties, Labor, and the Limits of State Power, 1917–1940" (PhD dissertation, Princeton University, 2011).

14. Samuel Walker's encyclopedic volume, *In Defense of American Liberties: A History of the ACLU* (New York, 1990), remains an invaluable resource on the ACLU. See also Cottrell, *Baldwin;* Daniel, *ACLU;* William Donohue, *Politics of the American Civil Liberties Union* (New Brunswick, 1985); Donald Johnson, *Challenge to American Freedoms: World War I and the Rise of the American Civil Liberties Union* (Lexington, KY, 1963); Judy Kutulas, *The American Civil Liberties Union and the Making of Modern Liberalism, 1930–1960* (Chapel Hill, NC, 2006); Peggy Lamson, *Roger Baldwin, Founder of the American Civil Liberties Union: A Portrait* (Boston, 1976). Freund and Laski were founding members of the national committee, and Dewey and Meiklejohn both subsequently joined. Chafee declined to sit on the national committee because he believed it would compromise his perceived scholarly objectivity, but he made donations, worked closely with the ACLU leadership, and guided the activities of the Civil Liberties Union of Massachusetts.

15. Grenville Clark, "Conservatism and Civil Liberty," *ABA Journal* 24 (1938): 640–644, 641 (ACLU), 644 ("enlightened").

16. ACLU, "Guardians of Freedom," accessed March 22, 2016, https://www.aclu.org/guardians-freedom; William Pickens, *Lynching and Debt Slavery* (New York, 1921), 1 (published by the ACLU); Roger Baldwin,

"Memorandum on the South as Observed in a Trip in May and June 1920," ACLUR, reel 23, vol. 166.

17. Gitlow v. New York, 268 U.S. 652 (1925); Whitney v. California, 274 U.S. 357 (1927); Pierce v. Society of Sisters, 268 U.S. 510, 535 (1925); Scopes v. Tennessee, 152 Tenn. 424 (1925).

18. See, for example, Ernst, *Lawyers against Labor*; Forbath, *American Labor Movement*; Victoria C. Hattam, *Labor Visions and State Power: The Origins of Business Unionism in the United States* (Princeton, NJ, 1993); Christopher L. Tomlins, *Law, Labor, and Ideology in the Early American Republic* (New York, 1993).

19. Jones v. Opelika, 316 U.S. 584, 608 (1942) (Stone, C. J., dissenting) ("preferred"); United States v. Carolene Products Company, 304 U.S. 144, 152n4 (1938). The expansive literature on the New Deal settlement and the origins and implications of the "preferred freedoms" formulation includes Bruce Ackerman, *We the People* (Cambridge, MA, 1991), 105–130; Jack M. Balkin, "The Footnote," *Northwestern University Law Review* 83 (1989): 275–320; Richard A. Epstein, *How Progressives Rewrote the Constitution* (Washington, DC, 2006), 7–9, 52–83; Barry Friedman, "The History of the Counter-majoritarian Difficulty, Part Four: Law's Politics," *University of Pennsylvania Law Review* 148 (2000): 971–1064, 974; Howard Gillman, "Preferred Freedoms: The Progressive Expansion of State Power and the Rise of Modern Civil Liberties Juris-prudence," *Political Research Quarterly* 47 (1994): 623–653; Larry D. Kramer, *The People Themselves: Popular Constitutionalism and Judicial Review* (New York, 2004), 122; G. Edward White, *The Constitution and the New Deal* (Cambridge, MA, 2000), 128–164, 227–232. Although social movement activism predated the rise of totalitarianism, international developments certainly influenced the salience of civil liberties claims, as described in Chapter 7. On the role of totalitarianism, see, for example, William Edward Nelson, *The Legalist Reformation: Law, Politics, and Ideology in New York, 1920–1980* (Chapel Hill, NC, 2001); Richard Primus, *The American Language of Rights* (New York, 1999); Edward Purcell, *The Crisis of Democratic Theory: Scientific Naturalism and the Problem of Value* (Lexington, KY, 1973).

1. Freedom of Speech in Class War Time

1. See, for example, "Report of the Committee to Oppose the Judicial Recall," *ABA Annual Report* 37 (1912) (hereafter CJR 1912).

2. Zechariah Chafee Jr., "Freedom of Speech in War Time," *Harvard Law Review* 32 (1919): 932–973.

3. My discussion of the prewar period is deeply indebted to David Rabban's influential account of the Free Speech League and the IWW's free speech fights. David M. Rabban, *Free Speech in Its Forgotten Years, 1870–1920* (New York, 1997). Rabban, however, regards the ACLU's early program (and the interwar understanding of civil liberties more broadly) as a sharp departure from the Free Speech League's and, accepting Roger Baldwin's own much later reconstruction of his organization's wartime activities, minimizes the relationship between the ACLU's conception of civil liberties and its prewar antecedents (307–315). My account, which explores the legacy of *labor's* prewar understandings as opposed to the individualist alternative of the Free Speech League, underscores the direct influence of the IWW's antistatism on the corresponding state-skepticism of the ACLU, and in particular, the latter organization's emphasis on securing labor activity against state regulation. Recovering the labor orientation of the interwar civil liberties movement (and, by extension, revising the conventional attribution of the modern First Amendment to the repression of the First World War) integrates the Progressive Era debates that Rabban revealed into the longer history of civil liberties advocacy and enforcement.

4. For examples of early class consciousness, see Alan Dawley, *Class and Community: The Industrial Revolution in Lynn* (Cambridge, MA, 1976); Leon Fink, *Workingmen's Democracy: The Knights of Labor and American Politics* (Urbana, IL, 1983); Lawrence Goodwyn, *Democratic Promise: The Populist Moment in America* (New York, 1976); Alexander Gourevitch, *From Slavery to the Cooperative Commonwealth: Labor and Republican Liberty in the Nineteenth Century* (New York, 2015); Herbert G. Gutman, *Work, Culture, and Society in Industrializing America: Essays in American Working-Class and Social History* (New York, 1976); David Montgomery, *The Fall of the House of Labor: The Workplace, the State, and American Labor Activism, 1865–1925* (New York, 1987); Sean Wilentz, "Against Exceptionalism: Class Consciousness and the American Labor Movement, 1790–1940," *International Labor and Working Class History* 26 (1984): 1–24; Sean Wilentz, *Chants Democratic: New York City and the Rise of the American Working Class, 1788–1850* (New York, 1984). Older literature, beginning with Selig Perlman, *A Theory of the Labor Movement* (New York, 1928), emphasized the underlying conservatism and narrow objectives of the American labor movement. See also John Patrick Diggins, "Comrades and Citizens: New Mythologies in American Historiography," *American Historical Review* 90 (1985): 614–638.

5. The literature on the *Times* bombing and surrounding labor struggles in Los Angeles includes Sidney Fine, *"Without Blare of Trumpets": Walter*

*Drew, the National Erectors' Association, and the Open Shop Movement,
1903–1957* (Ann Arbor, 1995); Philip S. Foner, *History of the Labor
Movement in the United States,* vol. 5, *The AFL in the Progressive Era,
1910–1915* (New York, 1980); John H. M. Laslett, *Sunshine Was Never
Enough: Los Angeles Workers, 1880–2010* (Berkeley, 2012); Grace
Heilman Stimson, *Rise of the Labor Movement in Los Angeles* (Berkeley,
1955); Mark H. Wild, *Street Meeting: Multiethnic Neighborhoods in
Early Twentieth-Century Los Angeles* (Berkeley, 2005).

6. *Report of the Proceedings of the Twenty-Seventh Annual Convention of
the American Federation of Labor* (Washington, DC, 1907), 322; Frederick Palmer, "Otistown of the Open Shop," *Hampton's Magazine* 26
(1911): 31.

7. Editorial, *Los Angeles Times,* June 11, 1911; Los Angeles Ordinance No.
20586 (New Series), adopted July 16, 1910, reprinted in *Blacksmiths
Journal* 11 (1910): 31.

8. "Big Bill Haywood Dies in Moscow," *NYT,* May 19, 1928. On the national
response, see Luke Grant, *The National Erectors' Association and the
International Association of Bridge and Structural Ironworkers: Report
for the Commission on Industrial Relations* (Washington, DC, 1915). For
a comparison to Haywood's trial for the murder of Frank Steunenberg,
see Frank E. Wolfe, *Capitalism's Conspiracy in California: Parallel of the
Kidnapping of Labor Leaders Colorado-California* (Los Angeles, 1911).
On Haywood's trial, see Melvyn Dubofsky, *"Big Bill" Haywood* (New
York, 1987), 42.

9. "Burns and Gompers Dispute," *Guthrie Daily Leader,* May 12, 1911
(reporting Gompers's statement); David E. Lilienthal, "Clarence Darrow,"
Nation, April 20, 1927, 417.

10. "James B. McNamara's Confession," *NYT,* December 2, 1911.

11. "Otis Warns Labor to Purge Its Ranks," *NYT,* December 2, 1911; "Murder
for 'Principle,'" *NYT,* December 3, 1911.

12. "Gompers Is Amazed by the Confessions," *NYT,* December 2, 1911
(Gompers); "Both M'Namaras Plead Guilty to Los Angeles Dynamiting,"
NYT, December 2, 1931 ("greatest strain"); Clarence Darrow, May 18,
1915, CIRRT, vol. 11, 10811. For criticisms of Darrow, see John Wigmore,
"The Limits of Counsel's Legitimate Defense," *Virginia Law Register* 17
(1912): 743; "Does the American Bar Stand for It?," *Bar* 19 (1912): 8–12.

13. Clarence Darrow, May 18, 1915, CIRRT, vol. 11, 10786.

14. "For a Federal Commission on Industrial Relations," petition to the
president of the United States, reproduced in *American Federationist* 19
(1912): 158–159 (hereafter Petition); Graham Adams Jr., *Age of Industrial
Violence 1910–1915: The Activities and Findings of the United States*

Commission on Industrial Relations (New York, 1966), provides a comprehensive account of the founding of the Commission on Industrial Relations and its subsequent work.

15. Florence Kelley, "Justice the Only Preventive," *Survey,* December 30, 1911, 1419. See, for example, Louise W. Knight, *Citizen: Jane Addams and the Struggle for Democracy* (Chicago, 2005), 213 (Addams); Nancy Schrom Dye, *As Equals and as Sisters: Feminism, the Labor Movement, and the Women's Trade Union League of New York* (Columbia, MO, 1980) (Wald); Kathryn Kish Sklar, *Florence Kelley and the Nation's Work: The Rise of Women's Political Culture, 1830–1900* (New Haven, CT, 1995), 147–148, 255–264 (Kelley).

16. Meyer London, "Confession," *Survey,* December 30, 1911, 1421. The arguments for shared accountability included Edwin R. A. Seligman, "The Reactionary and the Radical Fanatic," *Survey,* December 30, 1911, 1419.

17. Paul U. Kellogg, "Conservation and Industrial War," *Survey,* December 30, 1911, 1412.

18. Petition, 159; for a contemporary analysis, see Paul U. Kellogg, "The Field before the Commission on Industrial Relations," *Political Science Quarterly* 28 (December 1913): 593–609.

19. Morton J. Horwitz, *The Transformation of American Law, 1870–1960: The Crisis of Legal Orthodoxy* (New York, 1992); Duncan Kennedy, *The Rise and Fall of Classical Legal Thought* (Washington, DC, 2006); Morton White, *Social Thought in America: The Revolt against Formalism* (New York, 1949); William M. Wiecek, *The Lost World of Classical Legal Thought: Law and Ideology in America, 1886–1937* (New York, 1998). For a critique of the progressive characterization of nineteenth-century legal thought, see David M. Rabban, *Law's History: American Legal Thought and the Transatlantic Turn to History* (New York, 2013).

20. Roscoe Pound, "Liberty of Contract," *Yale Law Journal* 18 (1909): 454–487, 461. See Peter Filene, "An Obituary for the Progressive Movement," *American Quarterly* 22 (1970): 20–34; Daniel T. Rodgers, "In Search of Progressivism," *Reviews in American History* 10 (December 1982): 113–132.

21. Herbert David Croly, *Progressive Democracy* (New York, 1914), 379. In *Muller v. Oregon,* 208 U.S. 412 (1908), the Supreme Court upheld a maximum-hours law applicable to women. In *Adkins v. Children's Hospital,* 261 U.S. 525 (1923), however, it struck down federal minimum-wage legislation for women as an unconstitutional infringement on liberty of contract. On the tensions within progressivism between class-conscious labor advocates and advocates of class reconciliation, see Eldon J. Eisenach, *The Lost Promise of Progressivism* (Lawrence, KS, 1994); Leon

Fink, *Progressive Intellectuals and the Dilemmas of Democratic Commitment* (Cambridge, MA, 1997); Ruth O'Brien, *Workers' Paradox: The Republican Origins of New Deal Labor Policy, 1886–1935* (Chapel Hill, NC, 1998); Shelton Stromquist, *Re-inventing "The People": The Progressive Movement, the Class Problem, and the Origins of Modern Liberalism* (Urbana, IL, 2006); Clarence E. Wunderlin, *Visions of a New Industrial Order: Social Science and Labor Theory in America's Progressive Era* (New York, 1992).

22. Edward A. Ross, "Freedom of Communication and the Struggle for Right: Presidential Address," in *Publications of the American Sociological Society: Papers and Proceedings, Ninth Annual Meeting*, vol. 9 (Chicago, 1915) (hereafter *American Sociological Society Proceedings*), 5 ("depriving the weak"); Petition, 158 (emphasis added).

23. Vegelahn v. Guntner, 167 Mass. 92 (1896).

24. His concessions satisfied moderate labor leaders like John Mitchell, president of the UMW, who came to regard the state as a crucial tool for labor reform. Marc Karson, *American Labor Unions and Politics* (Carbondale, IL, 1958), 90.

25. Message of the President of the United States, Transmitting Data of the Work of the Interior Department, February 2, 1912, United States Congressional Serial Set, Issue 6320, 133; "To Urge Labor Board," *Washington Post*, March 22, 1912; see generally Adams, *Industrial Violence*.

26. U.S. Statutes, 62nd Congress, 2nd Session, Public, 351; "Editorial Grist: Industrial Relations Commission," *Survey*, July 5, 1913, 453 (on Commons); Dante Barton, "Frank P. Walsh," *Harper's Weekly*, September 27, 1913, 24. For a description of the commissioners, including Florence J. Harriman, see Adams, *Industrial Violence*, 67.

27. "Introduction," *Research Collections on Labor Studies: U.S. Commission on Industrial Relations, 1912–1915*, ed. Melvyn Dubofsky (Frederick, MD, 1985), xii. The witnesses were evenly split among employers, labor, and unaffiliated. "Three Reports by Walsh Board," *Boston Globe*, August 23, 1915, 9.

28. Freemont O. Bennett, *The Chicago Anarchists and the Haymarket Massacre* (Chicago, 1887), 141 ("liberty is not"), 134 (quoting Sam Fielden's statement that the First Amendment "gives every man the right to speak"); Eugene V. Debs, "Outlook for Socialism in the United States," *International Socialist Review* 1 (September 1900): 129–135, 131. On socialists' free speech fights, see John Wertheimer, "Free Speech Fights: The Roots of Modern Free-Expression Litigation in the United States" (PhD diss., Princeton University, 1992).

29. Commonwealth v. Davis, 162 Mass. 510, 511 (1895); Davis v. Massachusetts, 167 U.S. 43 (1897). Because the First Amendment had not yet been
incorporated into the Fourteenth Amendment and thus made binding on
the states, the case was decided by reference to property rights instead.
See generally Tabatha Abu El-Haj, "The Neglected Right of Assembly,"
UCLA Law Review 56 (2009): 543–589.

30. Adams, *Age of Industrial Violence*, 58. Literature on the IWW free
speech fights includes Melvyn Dubofsky, *We Shall Be All: A History of
the Industrial Workers of the World* (Chicago, 1969); Philip S. Foner,
ed., *Fellow Workers and Friends: I.W.W. Free Speech Fights as Told by
Participants* (Westport, CT, 1981); Philip S. Foner, *History of the Labor
Movement*, vol. 9, *The T.U.E.L. to the End of the Gompers Era* (New
York, 1991); Joyce L. Kornbluh, ed., *Rebel Voices: An I.W.W. Anthology*
(Ann Arbor, 1964); Rabban, *Forgotten Years*.

31. William D. Haywood, May 13, 1915, CIRRT, vol. 11, 10599. See
Dubofksy, *We Shall Be All*, 85–97.

32. *Social-Democratic Herald*, August 2, 1902 ("corporation interests"); J. Stitt
Wilson to Hiram W. Johnson, 7 July 1913, CIRP, reel 1, folder "Civil
Liberties" ("elemental rights"); "Ringing Resolutions," *Party Builder*, July 19,
1913, 1 ("medieval infringement").

33. Dubofsky, *We Shall Be All*, 174–188; Rabban, *Forgotten Years*, 84–86.

34. Rabban, *Forgotten Years*, 90–99, 115–120. For discussion of early judicial
decisions, see Wertheimer, "Free Speech Fights," 195–215.

35. Arthur Woods, "Reasonable Restrictions upon Freedom of Assemblage,"
in *American Sociological Society Proceedings*, 29–41, 35; Dubofsky, *We
Shall Be All*, 195 (Wickersham); "Victory for Free Speech," *Party Builder*,
May 9, 1914, 7.

36. Daniel O'Regan, "Free Speech Fights in San Diego, California," 14
December 1917, CIRP, reel 1, folder "Civil Liberties" (free speech
fights); report of Basil M. Manly, August 9, 1915, CIRRT, vol. 1 (here-
after Manly Report), 11–152, 55 ("unusual thoroughness"); "Two
Pageants—A Contrast," *NYT*, June 9, 1913; Mabel Dodge Luhan,
Movers and Shakers (New York, 1936), 203 ("seditious blaze"). A
plurality of commissioners considered Paterson's persecution of the
IWW to be inconsistent with the "fundamental principles of American
Government." Manly Report, 55n1. Neither Haywood nor Flynn was
ultimately imprisoned.

37. Theodore Schroeder, Additional Statement, May 27, 1915, CIRRT, vol. 11,
10873–10895. In upholding Sinclair's conviction, the court distinguished
the acquittal of Haywood in Paterson. People v. Sinclair, 86 Misc. 426,
439 (N.Y. Misc. 1914). Roe defended Sinclair.

38. Arthur Woods, May 12, 1915, CIRRT, vol. 11, 10550; Theodore Schroeder, May 27, 1915, CIRRT, vol. 11, 10850.

39. Quoted in Dubofsky, *We Shall Be All,* 105.

40. Walter Lippmann, *Drift and Mastery: An Attempt to Diagnose the Current Unrest* (New York, 1914), 1, 98.

41. As Gompers put it, "Liberty can be neither exercised nor enjoyed by those who are in poverty." Rowland Hill Harvey, *Samuel Gompers: Champion of the Toiling Masses* (Stanford, CA, 1935), 131 (quoting Gompers in a 1905 address).

42. Samuel Gompers and Morris Hillquit, May 22, 1914, CIRRT, vol. 2, 1504.

43. James A. Emery, May 18, 1915, CIRRT, vol. 11, 10832. On alternative uses and understandings of the strike, see Josiah Bartlett Lambert, *"If the Workers Took a Notion": The Right to Strike and American Political Development* (Ithaca, NY, 2005).

44. E. B. Ault (Seattle Union Record), August 12, 1914, CIRRT, vol. 5, 4199. For a vivid account of such hardships, see Daniel R. Ernst, "The *Danbury Hatters'* Case," in *Labor Law in America: Historical and Critical Essays,* ed. Christopher L. Tomlins and Andrew J. King (Baltimore, 1992), 180–200.

45. Clarence Elmore Bonnett, *Employers' Associations in the United States: A Study of Typical Associations* (New York, 1922), 451 ("good citizenship"); Loewe v. Lawlor, 208 U.S. 274 (1908); Samuel Gompers, editorial, *American Federationist* 15 (1908): 180–192, 181. See generally Daniel R. Ernst, *Lawyers against Labor: From Individual Rights to Corporate Liberalism* (Urbana, IL, 1995); Ernst, *"Danbury Hatters."*

46. Gompers v. Buck's Stove and Range Co., 221 U.S. 418 (1911). Mitchell (a vice president of the AFL) and AFL secretary Frank Morrison were also convicted. For early cases see Brief for Appellant, AFL v. Buck's Stove and Range Co., No. 1916 (DC Court of Appeals, 1908), 33–38; Genevieve Lakier, "The Invention of Low Value Speech," *Harvard Law Review* 128 (2015): 2166–2233, 2182; Joseph Tanenhaus, "Picketing as Free Speech: Early Stages in the Growth of the New Law of Picketing," *University of Pittsburgh Law Review* 14 (1953): 397–418.

47. James A. Emery, May 18, 1915, CIRRT, vol. 11, 10823.

48. Samuel Gompers, "To Organized Labor and Friends," *American Federationist* 15 (1908): 193 ("serious invasion"); Petition, 158 ("channels"); Theodore Schroeder, Additional Statement, May 27, 1915, CIRRT, vol. 11, 10896 ("capitalist court[s]," quoting article in syndicalist newspaper).

49. Edward Alsworth Ross, "Freedom of Communication and the Struggle for Right," in *American Sociological Society Proceedings,* 4–5.

50. Manly Report, 47.

51. On the emergence of the term *substantive due process,* as well as its limitations, see G. Edward White, *The Constitution and the New Deal* (Cambridge, MA, 2000), 241–268.

52. Lochner v. New York, 198 U.S. 45 (1905); Florence Kelley, *Some Ethical Gains through Legislation* (New York, 1905), 141. Notably, Kelley, citing *Holden v. Hardy,* 169 U.S. 366 (1898) (upholding a Utah law limiting hours for miners and smelters), considered the United States Supreme Court to be more "reasonable" in its approach. The Commission on Industrial Relations assembled a long list of statutes invalidated by courts on constitutional grounds. Manly Report, 44.

53. Allgeyer v. Louisiana, 165 U.S. 578 (1897); Rabban, *Forgotten Years,* 125 (quoting B. F. Moore).

54. "A Corporation's Right of Privacy," *Weekly Law Bulletin and Ohio Law Journal* 34 (1895): 211; Wallace v. Georgia, C. & N. R. Co., 94 Ga. 732 (1894).

55. See Ernst, *Lawyers against Labor;* Daniel Ernst, "The Yellow-Dog Contract and Liberal Reform, 1917–1932," *Labor History* 30 (1989): 251–274, 268–270; William E. Forbath, *Law and the Shaping of the American Labor Movement* (Cambridge, MA, 1991).

56. Transcript of Record, Gompers v. Buck's Stove & Range Co. (D.D.C. Dec. 23, 1908) (No. 372), 627. For an early analysis of the dominant approach and its exceptions, see "Strikes and Boycotts," *Harvard Law Review* 34 (1921): 880–888.

57. Adair v. United States, 208 U.S. 161 (1908) (further holding that the provision exceeded Congress's power under the commerce clause); Coppage v. Kansas, 236 U.S. 1 (1915); Erdman Act, Section 10 ("unjustly discriminat[ing]"); Clarence Darrow, May 18, 1915, CIRRT, vol. 11, 10806; Stephen S. Gregory, May 11, 1915, CIRRT, vol. 11, 10538; Theodore Schroeder, Additional Statement, May 27, 1915, CIRRT, vol. 11, 10895 ("Heads, I win"). Like Darrow, Gregory was a member of the legal team that defended Debs after the Pullman Strike.

58. Charles A. Beard, *An Economic Interpretation of the Constitution of the United States* (New York, 1913). Old justifications were fading by this period, to be replaced by the pluralism of the mature AABA, but courts were relatively slow to follow. Ernst, *Lawyers against Labor.* Gompers was somewhat ambivalent about the desirability of enforcing bargaining agreements against employers through legal remedies in addition to economic weapons; in practice, unions seldom attempted to enforce such agreements in court. O'Brien, *Workers' Paradox,* 20–26; see also Public Documents of Massachusetts, No. 15, Incorporation of Trade Unions (1907), 148–150.

59. See, for example, Pound, "Liberty of Contract," 461–463; Horwitz, *Crisis;* Daniel T. Rodgers, *Atlantic Crossings: Social Politics in a Progressive Age* (Cambridge, MA, 1998), 58; White, *Social Thought in America.*

60. Gilbert Roe, "Our Judicial Oligarchy," *La Follette's Weekly Magazine* 3 (June 24, 1911): 7–9; Gilbert Roe, May 10, 1915, CIRRT, vol. 11, 10474. In a conference manuscript of nearly two hundred pages, the term "First Amendment" appears fewer than a dozen times, and all in a single paper: Henry Schofield, "Freedom of the Press in the United States," *American Sociological Society Proceedings* 9 (1914): 67–116.

61. Theodore Schroeder, May 27, 1915, CIRRT, vol. 11, 10847 ("entirely different"); Theodore Schroeder, Additional Statement, May 27, 1915, CIRRT, vol. 11, 10896 ("unconscious economic"); Samuel Gompers, editorial, *American Federationist* 15 (1908): 180–192; Graham R. Taylor, "Labor and the Law as Viewed by Those Who Represent Each," *Survey,* May 29, 1915, 193 (quoting Walter Clark, "unconsciously biased"). Taylor, ibid., discusses progressive critiques of the judiciary before the commission.

62. Charles A. Beard, *Contemporary American History, 1877–1913* (New York, 1921), 287; "Report of the Committee to Oppose Judicial Recall, to Be Presented at the Meeting of the ABA, September 4–6, 1917," in Rome G. Brown, *Addresses, Discussions, Etc.* (Minneapolis, 1917). On judicial recall, see Kenneth P. Miller, *Direct Democracy and the Courts* (New York, 2009), 191–199; William G. Ross, *A Muted Fury: Populists, Progressives, and Labor Unions Confront the Courts, 1890–1937* (Princeton, NJ, 1994), ch. 5; Jed Handelsman Shugerman, *The People's Courts: Pursuing Judicial Independence in America* (Cambridge, MA, 2012), 161–166; Stephen Stagner, "The Recall of Judicial Decisions and the Due Process Debate," *American Journal of Legal History* 24 (1980): 257–272; Michael Wolraich, *Unreasonable Men: Theodore Roosevelt and the Republican Rebels Who Created Progressive Politics* (New York, 2014), 220–226. Many important statements were compiled in Edith M. Phelps, ed., *Selected Articles on the Recall* (New York, 1913).

63. Samuel Gompers, editorial, *American Federationist* 18 (1911): 458–465, 463 ("democratic views"); Ross, *Muted Fury,* 128 ("conservative instincts," quoting Edward A. Ross); Theodore Roosevelt, "A Charter of Democracy," February 21, 1912, Senate Doc. No. 348 (62nd Congress, 2nd Session) (Washington, 1912), 14 ("when a judge"); "Report of the Committee to Oppose the Judicial Recall, to Be Presented at the Meeting of the American Bar Association, September 1–3, 1913," in Brown, *Addresses* (Senate resolution). See also Samuel Gompers, editorial, *American Federationist* 15 (1908): 180–192; Samuel Gompers, May 22, 1914, CIRRT, vol. 2, 1505.

64. Elihu Root, "Judicial Decisions and Public Feeling," *New York State Bar Association Proceedings* 35 (1912): 148–167, in Phelps, *Recall;* William Howard Taft, "Recall of Judges," *West Publishing Company's Docket* 1 (1912): 550–553, 551 (Taft message of August 15, 1911) (Taft); William E. Borah, "Recall of Judges Unwise," *Maine Law Review* 5 (1912): 123–150, 147; John Kirby Jr., "Political Platforms," *American Industries* 13 (August 1912): 9–14, 9.

65. Woodrow Wilson, address to Kansas City Knife and Fork Club, quoted in "Survey of the World," *New York Independent,* May 11, 1911, 1; Charles H. Hamill, "Constitutional Chaos," *Forum* 48 (July 1912): 45–60. Free speech typically appeared on lists of the many liberties protected by the courts. See, for example, CJR 1912.

66. "Report of the Committee to Oppose the Judicial Recall, to Be Presented at ABA Meeting, October 20–22, 1914," in Brown, *Addresses* (hereafter CJR 1914) ("subversive"); CJR 1914 ("oligarchical"); CJR 1912 ("mass"). On the origins of the committee, see CJR 1912; Edson R. Sunderland, *History of the American Bar Association and Its Work* (1953), 155–157, also contains a brief description of the committee. The ABA acknowledged that judicial decisions were increasingly out of step with popular demands, but its solution was procedural reform, and it hoped that simplifying the rules of procedure in the federal courts would undermine the campaign for the recall of judges. CJR 1912.

67. Clarence Darrow, May 18, 1915, CIRRT, vol. 11, 10786 (compare John Dewey and James H. Tufts, *Ethics* [New York, 1908], 439); James A. Emery, May 18, 1915, CIRRT, vol. 11, 10832 ("industrial worker"); Theodore Schroeder, Additional Statement, May 27, 1915, CIRRT, vol. 11, 10896 ("law strike," quoting recent article in syndicalist newspaper).

68. Editorials, *Survey,* November 14, 1914, 175. On divisions within the commission and the *Survey* controversy, see Adams, *Age of Industrial Violence;* Fink, *Progressive Intellectuals,* ch. 3; Shelton Stromquist, "Class Wars: Frank Walsh, the Reformers, and the Crisis of Progressivism," in *Labor Histories: Class, Politics, and the Working Class Experience,* ed. Eric Arnesen, Julie Greene, and Bruce Laurie (Urbana, IL, 1998), 97–124; Wunderlin, *Industrial Order.*

69. Adams, *Age of Industrial Violence,* 210; Stromquist, *Re-inventing "The People,"* 166 (quoting Walsh).

70. Taylor, "Labor and the Law," 193 (quoting Judge Walter Clark). By contrast, Gompers invoked Roscoe Pound and his principles of sociological jurisprudence in defending voluntarism for its vindication of social interests. Samuel Gompers, "Labor by Law, Not by Discretion," *Federationist* 21 (January 1913): 45; Samuel Gompers, "A Perverted Conception of Rights," *Federa-*

tionist 20 (June 1912): 466. This argument is developed in O'Brien, *Workers' Paradox,* 19–21; Michael Rogin, "Voluntarism: The Political Functions of an Antipolitical Doctrine," *Industrial and Labor Relations Review* 15 (July 1962): 521–535, 524–526. For representative discussion of labor attitudes toward state power, see Melvyn Dubofsky, *The State and Labor in Modern America* (Chapel Hill, NC, 1994); Karen Orren, *Belated Feudalism: Labor, the Law, and Liberal Development in the United States* (New York, 1991); Christopher Tomlins, *The State and the Unions: Labor Relations, Law, and the Organized Labor Movement in America, 1880–1960* (New York, 1985). On the AFL and the state, see Nelson Lichtenstein, *State of the Union: A Century of American Labor* (Princeton, NJ, 2002), 12; Nick Salvatore, introduction to *Seventy Years of Life and Labor: An Autobiography,* by Samuel Gompers (Ithaca, NY, 1984). Despite early misgivings, Wilson developed a strong relationship with organized labor. See, for example, Joseph A. McCartin, *Labor's Great War: The Struggle for Industrial Democracy and the Origins of Modern American Labor Relations, 1912–1921* (Chapel Hill, NC, 1997), 15–16; David Montgomery, *The Fall of the House of Labor: The Workplace, the State, and American Labor Activism, 1865–1925* (New York, 1987), 363–369; Arthur S. Link, *Wilson,* vol. 1, *The Road to the White House* (Princeton, NJ, 1947), 527.

71. Theodore Schroeder, May 27, 1915, CIRRT, vol. 11, 10845; E. B. Ault (Seattle Union Record), August 12, 1914, CIRRT, vol. 5, 4192–4193.

72. "Industrial Conflict: Four Articles on the Reports of the Industrial Relations Commission," *New Republic,* August 28, 1915, 91; Report of Commissioners John R. Commons and Florence J. Harriman, CIRRT, vol. 1, 169–247, 171–172.

73. Report of Commissioners Weinstock, Ballard, and Ainston, CIRRT, vol. 1, 231–248, 233–234. Harris Weinstock, who had been appointed by the California governor to investigate the IWW's free speech fights, concluded that the police should not be permitted to curtail free speech on the grounds of anticipated abuse. Daniel O'Regan to Charles McCarthy, August 19, 1914, 5, CIRP, reel 1, folder "civil liberties."

74. Quoted in Dubofsky, *State and Labor,* 55; see also "A Follow-Up Committee on Industrial Relations," *Survey,* November 13, 1915, 156.

75. "Walsh Would Forbid Courts to Interpret Constitution," *Wall Street Journal,* August 23, 1915; Manly Report, 43.

76. Manly Report, 98–100.

77. Ibid., 38, 47.

78. Ibid., 59–61, 67.

79. Ibid., 61. Labor advocates had long pursued constitutional amendments in the states. See Emily J. Zackin, *Looking for Rights in All the Wrong*

Places: Why State Constitutions Contain America's Positive Rights (Princeton, NJ, 2013).

80. Clarence Darrow, May 18, 1915, CIRRT, vol. 11, 10803.

81. "The Walsh Commission," *NYT,* August 23, 1915; "The Manly Report," *Survey,* December 18, 1915, 320 (quoting *Philadelphia Inquirer*); editorial, *American Industries* 16 (September 1915): 9 (NAM).

82. Manly Report, 322; "The Manly Report," *Survey,* 320 ("spirit"). For *Survey* coverage, see John A. Fitch, "Probing the Causes of Industrial Unrest: A Series of Three Installments Reviewing the Reports Issued by the United States Commission on Industrial Relations," *Survey,* December 18, 1915, 317–333; *Survey,* January 1, 1916, 395–402; *Survey,* January 8, 1916, 432–434.

83. Report of Proceedings of the Thirty-Fifth Annual Convention of the American Federation of Labor (Washington, DC, 1915), 205; Kenneth E. Miller, *From Progressive to New Dealer: Frederic C. Howe and American Liberalism* (University Park, PA, 2010), 231–232. The committee's members included Frederic Howe and Amos Pinchot, along with Walsh, the three labor commissioners, and other labor representatives. For an example of union support, see "Two and a Half Million Trade Unionists Back Walsh Committee," *Commercial Telegraphers' Journal* 14 (January 1916): 40. The UMW was a major sponsor.

84. Job Harriman, September 15, 1914, CIRRT, vol. 6, 5809.

85. "Industrial Relations Statistics or a Program?," *Survey,* November 8, 1913, 152. Eastman's appointment was widely reported, but information on her subsequent relationship to the commission is sparse. Eastman also testified before the commission on behalf of the Congressional Union for Woman's Suffrage; she told the commission that the vote was an essential tool but that women "must raise their wages as men have raised their wages, by organization." Crystal Eastman Benedict, May 17, 1915, CIRRT, vol. 11, 10782.

2. The Citadel of Civil Liberty

1. "Civil Liberties in War Times," *Survey,* November 3, 1917, 130–131.

2. "Civil Liberties Bureau," *New York Evening Post,* October 17, 1917.

3. Ernst Freund, "The Debs Case and Freedom of Speech," *New Republic,* May 3, 1919, 13. On the manufacture of public consensus on behalf of the war effort, see David M. Kennedy, *Over Here: The First World War and American Society* (New York, 1980). The ACLU itself encouraged this view. By 1941, it traced its origins to "hysterical attacks upon opponents of war and of conscription" and declared itself "the first non-partisan

national organization in American history dedicated to the maintenance of the Bill of Rights for everybody without exception." According to the statement, "labor's civil rights" was among the "wide fields" of activity it had entered as a result of subsequent developments. ACLU, *Presenting the American Civil Liberties Union, Inc.* (New York, 1941), 2.

4. "Civil Liberties in War Times," 130–131 (quoting Charles Cripps, 1st Baron Parmoor); Walter George Smith, "Civil Liberty in America," *ABA Journal* 4 (1918): 551–566, 562.

5. Freund, "Debs Case," 13. On the progressive understanding see, for example, Mark Graber, *Transforming Free Speech: The Ambiguous Legacy of Civil Libertarianism* (Berkeley, 1991), 2; David M. Rabban, *Free Speech in Its Forgotten Years, 1870–1920* (New York, 1997), 4. On the distance between the progressive vision and alternative theories of free speech during the 1920s and 1930s, see Laura M. Weinrib, "From Left to Rights: Civil Liberties Lawyering between the World Wars," *Law, Culture, and the Humanities* (prepublished May 18, 2016, DOI: 10.1177/1743872 116641871); Laura M. Weinrib, "Civil Liberties outside the Courts," *Supreme Court Review* 2014 (2015): 297–362. The many accounts identifying these debates and the Espionage Act cases (especially the great Holmes and Brandeis dissents) as the source of the modern First Amendment include Harry Kalven Jr. and Douglas H. Ginsburg, "Ernst Freund and the First Amendment Tradition," *University of Chicago Law Review* 40 (1973): 235–247, 236; Graber, *Transforming,* 2 (emphasizing Chafee).

6. AUAM pamphlet, AUAMR, reel 10-1. On the Henry Street Group's early activities, see C. Roland Marchand, *The American Peace Movement and Social Reform, 1898–1918* (Princeton, NJ, 1972); Kenneth E. Miller, *From Progressive to New Dealer: Frederic C. Howe and American Liberalism* (University Park, PA, 2010). The overlap between the Henry Street Group and the Commission on Industrial Relations is mentioned in Allen F. Davis, "The Campaign for the Industrial Relations Commission, 1911–1913," *Mid-America* 45 (1963): 211–228, 228.

7. "Past Programs of the American Union against Militarism (for Reference)," AUAMR, reel 10-1.

8. Ives v. South Buffalo Railway Company, 94 N.E. 431, 439 (N.Y. 1911); Crystal Eastman to Max Eastman, April 1911, CEP, folder 190. Eastman's work for the Pittsburgh Survey, which was sponsored by the Russell Sage Foundation and headed by Kellogg, culminated in Crystal Eastman, *Work-Accidents and the Law* (New York, 1910). On New York's Wainwright Commission, see John Fabian Witt, *The Accidental Republic: Crippled Workingmen, Destitute Widows, and the Remaking of American Law* (Cambridge, MA, 2004), 127. For discussion of Eastman's

career, see Sylvia A. Law, "Crystal Eastman: Organizer for Women's Rights, Peace, and Civil Liberties in the 1910s," *Valparaiso University Law Review* 28 (1994): 1305–1326; John Fabian Witt, *Patriots and Cosmopolitans: Hidden Histories of American Law* (Cambridge, MA, 2007), ch. 3. See Crystal Eastman to the executive committee, 14 June 1917, AUAMR, reel 10-1 (hereafter Eastman Memorandum), for a discussion of concerns related to the AUAM's credibility and reputation. Wald discussed Lawrence in Lillian D. Wald, *The House on Henry Street* (New York, 1915), 278. Kelley elaborated her views on the judiciary in Florence Kelley, *Some Ethical Gains through Legislation* (New York, 1905), 141. The Brandeis brief in *Muller v. Oregon,* 208 U.S. 412 (1908), upholding Oregon's maximum-hours law for women, was partly modeled on Kelley's unsuccessful brief to the Illinois Supreme Court in *Ritchie v. People,* 155 Ill. 98 (1895).

9. On the progressive reluctance to invoke rights to undermine state policy, see Graber, *Transforming,* 65–66.

10. On Baldwin's early life, see Robert Cottrell, *Roger Nash Baldwin and the American Civil Liberties Union* (New York, 2000), 1–30. Progressives imagined the juvenile courts as an alternative to classical legal thought. See Michael Willrich, *City of Courts: Socializing Justice in Progressive Era Chicago* (New York, 2003).

11. Quoted in Cottrell, *Baldwin,* 31.

12. Quoted in ibid., 42. On the implications of *Buchanan v. Warley,* 245 U.S. 60 (1917), see Richard A. Epstein, "Lest We Forget: *Buchanan v. Warley* and Constitutional Jurisprudence of the 'Progressive Era,'" *Vanderbilt Law Review* 51 (May 1998): 787–796; David E. Bernstein, "Philip Sober Controlling Philip Drunk: *Buchanan v. Warley* in Historical Perspective," *Vanderbilt Law Review* 51 (May 1998): 797–879; Michael J. Klarman, "Race and the Court in the Progressive Era," *Vanderbilt Law Review* 51 (May 1998): 881–952.

13. Quoted in Cottrell, *Baldwin,* 45.

14. Ibid., 48–49. The AUAM's view of war and capitalism is articulated in Announcement of Anti-Militarism Committee, AUAMR, reel 10-1; Norman Thomas, *The Conscientious Objector in America* (New York, 1923). For discussion of such arguments, see Marchand, *Peace Movement,* 244–248; James Weinstein, *The Decline of Socialism in America, 1912–1925* (New York, 1967), ch. 3.

15. C. T. Hale to the members of the executive committee, 6 May 1917, ACLUR, reel 3, vol. 16, 284. Representative AUAM statements and correspondence include "Suggestions for Dealing with Men of Conscription Age Who Are Conscientious Objectors to War," 28 June 1917,

ACLUR, reel 3, vol. 16; Lillian Wald, Jane Addams, and Norman Thomas to Hon. Newton Baker, 12 April 1917, ACLUR, reel 3, vol. 16; Norman Thomas, "War's Heretics: A Plea for the Conscientious Objector," *Survey,* August 4, 1917, 391–394. The practice of excusing Quakers, Mennonites, and other members of the historic peace churches from military service, typically conditioned on payment of a fine or procurement of a substitute, was well established. See, for example, Michael W. McConnell, "The Origins and Historical Understanding of Free Exercise of Religion," *Harvard Law Review* 103 (1990): 1409–1517, 1500–1503. On the unpopularity of exemptions for conscientious objectors, see Christopher Capozzola, *Uncle Sam Wants You: World War I and the Making of the Modern American Citizen* (New York, 2008), 55–56. The ACLU's defense of political objectors is the subject of Laura M. Weinrib, "Freedom of Conscience in War Time: World War I and the Civil Liberties Path Not Taken," *Emory Law Journal* 65 (2016): 1051–1137. On the attitudes of administration officials during the drafting process, see Donald Johnson, *Challenge to American Freedoms: World War I and the Rise of the American Civil Liberties Union* (Lexington, KY, 1963), 17–18; Jeremy Kessler, "The Administrative Origins of Modern Civil Liberties Law," *Columbia Law Review* 114 (2014): 1083–1166.

16. Eastman Memorandum ("liberal"); Frederick P. Keppel, "How to Interest the General Public in International Affairs," in *Proceedings of Second National Conference, American Society for Judicial Settlement of International Disputes* (Cincinnati, OH, 1911), 88 ("war and civilization"). On the transition from progressivism to liberalism, see Alan Brinkley, *End of Reform: New Deal Liberalism in Recession and War* (New York, 1995), 9; James T. Kloppenberg *Uncertain Victory: Social Democracy and Progressivism in European and American Thought, 1870–1920* (New York, 1986), 299.

17. Eastman Memorandum.

18. Proposed Announcement for Press, 24 September 1917, AUAMR, reel 10-1.

19. AUAM, "Conscription and the Conscientious Objector to War," May 1917, AUAMR, reel 10-2 ("liberty of conscience"); Oliver Wendell Holmes Jr., "The Path of the Law," *Harvard Law Review* 10 (1897): 457–478, 469 ("revolting"); AUAM, "Conscription" ("nothing if it is not individual"); "Tariff Revision and Wage Cuts," *Survey,* May 24, 1913, 261 ("The public conscience demands that they work under healthy conditions"); "Potlach vs. Sociology," *Survey,* July 26, 1913, 543 ("The public conscience is waking up"); Eldon J. Eisenach, *The Lost Promise of Progressivism* (Lawrence, KS, 1994), 189 ("true liberty," quoting Batten). Traditional justifications for conscientious objection emphasized corporatist religious

interests or, in some cases, personal religious belief. See, for example, Kent Greenawalt, "The Significance of Conscience," *San Diego Law Review* 47 (2010): 901–918, 901; McConnell, "Free Exercise," 1492–1503; John Witte Jr., *Religion and the American Constitutional Experiment: Essential Rights and Liberties* (Boulder, CO, 2000), 39. Neither theory provided cover for political objectors.

20. Norman Thomas and Roger Baldwin to the Conference Committee on the Army Bill, 1 May 1917, ACLUR, reel 3, vol. 16, 263 ("liberty of conscience"); NCLB, "A Sympathetic Strike in Prison," New York, undated, ACLUS, box 1 ("progress begins"); John A. Hobson, "The World Safe for Democracy," NCLB, New York, undated, ACLUS, box 1 ("despotism"); Norman Angell, *Why Freedom Matters* (London, 1918; issued by NCCL), 15.

21. Eastman Memorandum ("administration's own organ"); "The Success of Selective Service," *New Republic,* June 9, 1917, 149 ("democratic purposes"); Arthur O. Lovejoy, "A Communication," *New Republic,* June 16, 1917, 189 ("anti-social"); John Dewey, "Conscience and Compulsion," *New Republic,* July 14, 1917, 297–298; Thomas, "War's Heretics" (1917), 391–394. Jeremy Kessler has linked the openness to claims by conscientious objectors among some War Department officials to progressives' endorsement of national self-determination. Kessler, "Administrative Origins," 1115.

22. Eastman Memorandum ("lenient administration"); AUAM statement, 23 May 1917, AUAMR, reel 10-1 ("obedience to law"); Frederick Keppel to Roger Baldwin, 24 May 1917, ACLUR, reel 6, vol. 47 ("spirit of cooperation"); Newton Baker to Roger Baldwin, 7 July 1917, ACLUR, reel 2, vol. 15. The negotiations with the War Department are documented in Cottrell, *Baldwin,* 53–82; Johnson, *Challenge,* 30–36. On Frankfurter's memorandum, see Kessler, "Administrative Origins," 1111–1123. On "slackers," see Capozzola, *Uncle Sam,* 30.

23. Roger Baldwin to Newton Baker, 22 November 1917, ACLUR, reel 2, vol. 15 ("brutality"); Lenetta Cooper (American Liberty Defense League) to Roger Baldwin, 12 March 1918, reel 4, vol. 16 (criticizing Baldwin's approach); John Codman to Roger Baldwin, 27 March 1918, ACLUR, reel 3, vol. 25 ("Administration's liberality"); Norman Thomas, "War's Heretics," *Survey,* December 7, 1918, 319–323, 323. The executive order permitted objectors to elect alternative service under civilian command; absolutists, who refused alternative service, particularly experienced abuses. See Johnson, *Challenge,* 33–39; Robert Zieger, *America's Great War: World War I and the American Experience* (Lanham, MD, 2000), 62. The three board members were Major Walter G. Kellogg for the army,

Judge Julian M. Mack (an AUAM supporter before the war), and Columbia dean and future Supreme Court justice Harlan Fiske Stone.

24. L. Hollingsworth Wood, Norman Thomas, John Haynes Holmes, and John Lovejoy Elliott to Newton Baker, 14 September 1918, ACLUR, reel 5, vol. 44 ("social revolutions"); Harlan Fiske Stone, "The Conscientious Objector," *Columbia University Quarterly* 21 (1919): 253–271, 267. See also Roger Baldwin to Newton Baker, 30 June 1917, ACLUR, reel 2, vol. 15 (noting undue limitation of religious exemption).

25. L. Hollingsworth Wood, Norman Thomas, John Haynes Holmes, and John Lovejoy Elliott to Newton Baker, 14 September 1918, ACLUR, reel 5, vol. 44. On the military investigation, see Roy Talbert Jr., *Negative Intelligence: The Army and the American Left, 1917–1941* (Jackson, MS, 1991), 78–81.

26. Frederick Keppel to L. Hollingsworth Wood, Norman Thomas, John Haynes Holmes, and John Lovejoy Elliott, 2 October 1918, ACLUR, reel 6, vol. 47; see also Newton Baker to L. Hollingsworth Wood, 15 July 1918, ACLUR, reel 6, vol. 47. Keppel indicated that he did not actually write the letter but that it captured his attitude. Frederick Keppel to L. Hollingsworth Wood, 9 October 1918, ACLUR, reel 6, vol. 47.

27. On the Protestant roots of Thomas's commitment to individual conscience, see Louisa Thomas, *Conscience: Two Soldiers, Two Pacifists, One Family: A Test of Will and Faith in World War I* (New York, 2011), 163–178. On Christian pacifism during the First World War, see Joseph Kip Kosek, *Acts of Conscience: Christian Nonviolence and Modern American Democracy* (New York, 2009), 16–48.

28. Eastman Memorandum ("liberty"); "Topics of the Times," *NYT,* July 18, 1917.

29. Leon Whipple, *The Story of Civil Liberty in the United States* (New York, 1927), 327 (explaining emergence of progressive interest in civil liberties).

30. Thomas, "War's Heretics" (1918), 323; Roscoe Pound, "Interests of Personality" (pt. 2), *Harvard Law Review* 28 (1915): 445–456, 453–455; Joseph Byers to Roger Baldwin, 25 June 1918, ACLUR, reel 3, vol. 26.

31. "The Case of Columbia Professors," *Nation*, October 11, 1917, 388; John Dewey, "Conscription of Thought," *New Republic*, September 1, 1917, 128–130, 129; John Dewey, "In Explanation of Our Lapse," *New Republic,* November 3, 1917, 17; Zechariah Chafee Jr., "Freedom of Speech in War Time," *Harvard Law Review* 32 (1919): 932–973, 958. On the *New Republic* essays, see Graber, *Transforming*, 98–103; Rabban, *Forgotten Years*, 243–245. For discussion of Dewey's debate with Bourne, see Kennedy, *Over Here,* 50–53, 90–92; Robert B. Westbrook, *John Dewey and American Democracy* (Ithaca, NY, 1991), 202–212.

32. Philip Willett to Roger Baldwin, 21 August 1917, ACLUR, reel 5, vol. 35 ("bound"); Civil Liberties Bureau to the editor of the *New York Tribune*, 28 August 1917, ACLUR, reel 3, vol. 18 (explaining "patriotic duty" to "keep democracy alive at home"); Charles Ellwood to Roger Baldwin, 8 January 1918, ACLUR, reel 1, vol. 3 (offering support if the goal was "to secure free and adequate public discussion of every public policy before a decision is reached on that policy, so that the decision shall represent the untrammeled expression of rational public opinion").

33. Most prosecutions (approximately 2,000) arose under title 1, section 3, and judges typically applied the common-law "bad tendency" test, which held speakers criminally accountable for statements likely to lead to prohibited conduct. The postal provision was title 11, "Use of Mails." See Paul Murphy, *World War I and the Origin of Civil Liberties in the United States* (New York, 1979), 80, 98–103; Rabban, *Forgotten Years*, 250–255; Harry Scheiber, *The Wilson Administration and Civil Liberties* (Ithaca, NY, 1960); Geoffrey R. Stone, "The Origins of the Bad Tendency Test: Free Speech in Wartime," *Supreme Court Review* 2002: 411–453.

34. Gilbert Roe to Roger Baldwin, 30 June 1917, ACLUR, reel 3, vol. 26. Roe favored a judicial determination of excludability. For similar criticism from Walsh, see Johnson, *Challenge*, 59.

35. See Rabban, *Forgotten Years;* Janice Ruth Wood, *The Struggle for Free Speech in the United States, 1872–1915: Edward Bliss Foote, Edward Bond Foote, and Anti-Comstock Operations* (New York, 2008).

36. See Theodore Schroeder, *Constitutional Free Speech Defined and Defended* (New York, 1919), iv; Rabban, *Forgotten Years*, 308–309. On New York bohemian culture, see Christine Stansell, *American Moderns: Bohemian New York and the Creation of a New Century* (New York, 2000), 74.

37. Harry Weinberger to Roger Baldwin, 28 April 1917, ACLUR, reel 5, vol. 35; AUAM, *Constitutional Rights in War Time* (New York, 1917), in ACLUR, reel 5, vol. 43; Newton Baker to Harry Weinberger, quoted in "Secretary of War Denounces Military Rowdyism—Militarism the Same the World Over," *Locomotive Firemen's Magazine* 63 (July 15, 1917): 3. The notable members of the American Legal Defense League included Charles C. Burlingham, Theodore Schroeder, Gilbert Roe, Clarence Darrow, and New York governor Charles S. Whitman, along with several AUAM board members. "Defense of Free Speech," *New Republic,* May 12, 1917, 54; "The American Legal Defense League," *Nation,* May 31, 1917, v. On Weinberger's early career, see Richard Polenberg, *Fighting Faiths: The Abrams Case, the Supreme Court, and Free Speech* (New York, 1987), 79.

38. Memorandum of conference between Roger Baldwin and Harry Weinberger, 11 May 1917, ACLUR, reel 5, vol. 35; Roger Baldwin to Harry Weinberger, 18 June 1917, ACLUR, reel 5, vol. 35; AUAM press release, 2 July 1917, AUAMR, reel 10-2; Civil Liberties Bureau (AUAM), *Constitutional Rights in War Time*, rev. ed. (New York, July 1917), in ACLUR, reel 5, vol. 43. I discuss Baldwin's appropriation of the American Legal Defense League's agenda in greater detail in Weinrib, "Freedom of Conscience," 1086–1091. Baldwin was also concerned about organizational overlap with the Emergency Peace Federation and wanted that group to concede national efforts to the AUAM. Roger Baldwin to Oswald G. Villard, 11 April 1917, AUAMR, reel 10-1.

39. Baldwin hoped that the participation of John Nevin Sayre would undercut efforts by "super-patriots" to accuse the organization of "pro-Germanism." Roger Baldwin to John Codman, 7 May 1918, ACLUR, reel 3, vol. 25. On the emergency conference, see Crystal Eastman to American union members, local committees and affiliated organizations, 13 July 1917, AUAMR, reel 10-2. Targeted publications included the *Masses*, the *International Socialist Review*, the *American Socialist*, and the *Milwaukee Leader*. For Burleson's response, see Johnson, *Challenge*, 58–59.

40. Roger Baldwin to Mrs. Leo Simmons, 21 September 1917, ACLUR, reel 5, vol. 36 (on litigation); NCLB, statement to members of the AUAM, 1 November 1917, AUAMR, reel 10-1 (summarizing operations); Roger Baldwin to Harry Weinberger, 3 May 1918, ACLUR, reel 5, vol. 35, 190 ("jail"); NCLB, "The Need of a National Defense Fund," 15 November 1917, ACLUR, reel 3, vol. 26 ("miscarriage of justice"); "Civil Liberties Bureau," *New York Evening Post*, October 17, 1917 ("mob-minded judges").

41. Roger Baldwin to John Codman, 11 October 1917, ACLUR, reel 3, vol. 25.

42. Memorandum (undated and unsigned), AUAMR, reel 10-1.

43. Roger Baldwin, introduction to ACLU, *American Civil Liberties Union Annual Reports*, vol. 1 (New York, 1970), iii (origins of plural form); N. Charles Burge, "Address on Legal Procedure and Social Unrest," *Ohio Law Bulletin* 58 (1913): 381 ("reference to law"); Marbury v. Madison, 5 U.S. 137, 163 (1803); "Report of the Committee to Oppose Judicial Recall," *ABA Journal* 4 (July 1918): 400 (hereafter CJR 1918) (describing opposition to *Marbury*). John Fabian Witt has argued that the plural form "promised to break down the abstraction of 'civil liberty' into its specific and concrete component parts," that is, it "substitute[d] for the older idea of 'civil liberty' in a new Hohfeldian age of pragmatic skepticism about legal abstractions." John Fabian Witt, *Patriots and Cosmopolitans: Hidden Histories of American Law* (Cambridge, MA, 2007), 195.

44. NCCL, *Objects and Principal Activities* (London, 1918) ("likely to endanger"); Roger Baldwin to B. N. Langdon-Davies, 5 January 1918, ACLUR, reel 3, vol. 26; "The Week," *Nation*, February 15, 1919, 240 (describing connection to labor groups); B. N. Langdon-Davies to Leon Whipple, 20 June 1918, ACLUR, reel 3, vol. 26 (pamphlets not received). Members of the NCCL included William Crawford Anderson, Robert Smillie, Ethel Snowden, Henry William Massingham, and John A. Hobson. Baldwin later identified the NCCL as the source of the name. Baldwin, introduction, viii.

45. "How the World Governs Itself," book review of *Principles of Constitutional Government*, by Frank J. Goodnow, *NYT*, August 13, 1916; Thomas, "War's Heretics" (1917), 393; "Urges Insurance Men to Buy War Stamps," *NYT*, February 15, 1918 (quoting George W. Wickersham).

46. "Report of the Committee to Oppose Judicial Recall, Presented at the Meeting of the ABA, August 17–19, 1915," in Rome G. Brown, *Addresses, Discussions, Etc.* (Minneapolis, 1917) (hereafter CJR 1915) ("frazzle"); "Report of the Committee to Oppose Judicial Recall, to Be Presented at the Meeting of the ABA, August 30–September 1, 1916," in Brown, *Addresses* (hereafter CJR 1916) (on Roosevelt; the platform retained a provision for the recall of judicial decisions); CJR 1916 (accepting credit). Commentators singled out as particularly influential the efforts of Rome G. Brown, the Minneapolis attorney who chaired the ABA Committee to Oppose Judicial Recall beginning in 1912. Hugh H. Brown, "Rome G. Brown," *Lawyers Magazine* 22 (August 1916): 26–257. The ABA also acknowledged the work of a special committee of the New York State Bar Association. "Report of the Committee to Oppose Judicial Recall, to Be Presented at the Meeting of the ABA, September 4–6, 1917," in Rome G. Brown, *Addresses, Discussions, Etc.* (Minneapolis, 1917) (hereafter CJR 1917). On the danger to progressive legislation, see CJR 1915 (explaining progressive concerns that Denver, a wet city, would be able to repeal a Supreme Court decision applying the statewide alcohol ban to it).

47. CJR 1917 ("weaken"; "judicial function"; "menace"); CJR 1918 ("camouflage"). The attorney general evidently supported the bill, which would have allowed the replacement of judges who had reached the age of seventy and served for ten years, and were therefore eligible for retirement at full pay under the Judiciary Act. CJR 1918, 400. The bill, sponsored by Georgia senator Hoke Smith, has received little scholarly attention. For a brief account, see Dewey W. Grantham, *Hoke Smith and the Politics of the New South* (Baton Rouge, 1958), 303–304. Because the Smith bill (unlike its New Deal counterpart) would have enabled the

forced retirement of existing judges, opponents relied on Article III, Section 1, providing that federal judges "shall hold their offices during good behavior," to impugn the constitutionality of the proposal.

48. Richard Pipes, *The Russian Revolution* (New York, 1990), 797; CJR 1918, 400.

49. Smith, "Civil Liberty in America," 551. Notably, Smith conceded a need for procedural reform but insisted such efforts should aim to strengthen the courts, not to belittle them.

50. Ibid. ("individual"); "Addendum: Employment to Secure Exemption from Draft Unethical," *ABA Journal* 3 (1917): 558 (reporting resolution of Illinois State Bar Association ("contrary")).

51. "Assails Wilson as an Autocrat," *NYT*, September 4, 1918 (describing remarks by Lawrence Yates Sherman, who would soon help to scuttle United States participation in the League of Nations); "America Not Safe Yet, Says Butler," *NYT*, April 20, 1919.

52. Theodore Schroeder, "Liberal Opponents and Conservative Friends of Unabridged Free Speech," *Mother Earth*, March 13, 1910, 96; "Topics of the Times: Jails Are Waiting for Them," *NYT*, July 4, 1917. For an analysis of conservative academic writing on free speech, see Graber, *Transforming;* Charles L. Barzun, "Politics or Principle? Zechariah Chafee and the Social Interest in Free Speech," *Brigham Young University Law Review* 259 (2007): 259–325.

53. Memo (undated and unsigned), AUAMR, reel 10-1.

54. Eastman Memorandum ("governmental cooperation," quoting Lillian Wald); Arthur LeSueur to Crystal Eastman, 6 July 1917, ACLUR, reel 4, vol. 32 (union busting); Austin Lewis to Roger Baldwin, 9 July 1917, ACLUR, reel 5, vol. 39 ("class purposes").

55. Lillian Wald to Crystal Eastman, 26 August 1917, AUAMR, reel 10-1 ("impulsive radicalism"); H. R. Mussey to Crystal Eastman, 27 September 1917, AUAMR, reel 10-1 (threatening resignation); Lillian Wald to committee, 13 September 1917, AUAMR, reel 10-1; AUAM minutes, 13 September 1917, AUAMR, reel 10-1 ("conservative minority"). Controversy centered on the decision to send delegates to a conference organized by the radical People's Council. In the end, the meeting location was moved, and the AUAM delegates were unable to attend. AUAM minutes, 13 September 1917, AUAMR, reel 10-1. Notably, the First Amendment Conference for Democracy and Terms of Peace had included a resolution to protect "American liberties," including the freedom of speech, press, and assembly. People's Council of America for Democracy and Peace, *Resolutions of the First American Conference for Democracy and Terms of Peace, May 30 and 31, 1917* (New York, 1917).

56. Norman Thomas to Crystal Eastman, 27 September 1917, AUAMR, reel 10-1; NCLB, statement to members of the AUAM, 1 November 1917, ACLUR, reel 5, vol. 43 ("exactly"). An early draft of a press announcement was more forthright in declaring it "essential for leadership in the fight of civil liberty in war time to come from the heart of the minority itself." Proposed Announcement for Press, AUAMR, reel 10-1.

57. Roger Baldwin to Scott Nearing, chairman, People's Council, 13 October 1917, ACLUR, reel 3, vol. 26 ("quiet pressure"); NCLB to citizens registered with the Civil Liberties Bureau, 1 November 1917, ACLUR, reel 5, vol. 43 ("evidently"); Roger Baldwin to Adolph Germer, 10 December 1917, reel 1, vol. 3 ("entire sympathy"); Roger Baldwin to George Edwards, 10 November 1917, ACLUR, reel 5, vol. 36 ("keep"); Roger Baldwin to John Codman, 11 October 1917, ACLUR, reel 3, vol. 25 ("maintain[]"). Despite his efforts, Baldwin received criticism from prospective supporters for the disproportionate representation on the committee of radicals and people of "foreign extraction." For example, Lawrence Brooks to Roger Baldwin, 21 September 1917, ACLUR, reel 4, vol. 32.

58. Norman Thomas to Crystal Eastman, 27 September 1917, AUAMR, reel 10-1; Roger Baldwin to Fay Lewis, 30 January 1918, ACLUR, reel 5, vol. 39.

59. Opposition to the draft appeal included Lawrence Brooks to Roger Baldwin, 21 September 1917, ACLUR, reel 4, vol. 32 ("Fighting the draft and attempting to repeal it merely discredits an organization which indulges in the pastime without doing the slightest good."); John Codman to Roger Baldwin, 25 October 1917, ACLUR, reel 3, vol. 25 (expressing desire not to "be connected" with a challenge to the draft). Weinberger's argument invoked a Thirteenth Amendment right against involuntary servitude as well as a First Amendment claim on the theory that sectarian exemptions infringed religious liberty. Transcript of record, Arver v. United States, 245 U.S. 366 (1918) (No. 681), 5. For Nelles's argument, see Brief of Walter Nelles and for the NCLB as Amicus Curiae, Ruthenberg v. United States, 245 U.S. 480 (1918); AUAM, *Some Aspects for the Constitutional Questions Involved in the Draft Act* (New York, 1917). I discuss the legal issues, the NCLB's amicus brief, and public perception of the case in Weinrib, "Freedom of Conscience," 1099–1106.

60. Robert La Follette, "Free Speech in Wartime," U.S. Senate, 65th Congress, 2nd Session (October 6, 1917); Laurence Todd to Roger Baldwin, 25 October 1917, ACLUR, reel 3, vol. 25 (reporting " 'inside' information that the President had been induced to order Burleson to soft-pedal the press control scheme"). By contrast, even Chafee accepted conscription

and ascribed the constitutional challenge to "extreme views." Chafee,
"War Time," 937.

61. Masses Publishing Company v. Patten, 244 F. 535, 538 (S.D.N.Y. 1917),
reversed, 246 F. 24 (2d Cir. 1917). On the *Masses* case, see Gerald
Gunther, "Learned Hand and the Origins of the Modern First Amendment Doctrine: Some Fragments of History," *Stanford Law Review* 27
(1975): 719–773; Gerald Gunther, *Learned Hand: The Man and the Judge*
(New York, 1994). Burleson's censorship practices were upheld by the
Supreme Court in *Milwaukee Publishing Company v. Burleson,* 255 U.S.
407 (1921). A few federal judges rejected the dominant approach, including George M. Borquin (District of Montana) and Charles Fremont
Amidon (Eighth Circuit Court of Appeals). Most judges, however,
capitulated to popular pressures. See Murphy, *Origin of Civil Liberties,*
179–247; Geoffrey Stone, "Bad Tendency Test."

62. Crystal Eastman to Oswald G. Villard, 16 November 1917, AUAMR, reel
10-1 ("The only great movement against war must be the radical
movement").

63. Hitchman Coal and Coke Co. v. Mitchell, 245 U.S. 229, 251 (1917);
"Breaking the Labor Truce," *New Republic,* December 22, 1917, 197.

64. Circular, ACLUR, reel 1, vol. 3; William English Walling to L. Hollingsworth Wood, 7 January 1918, ACLUR, reel 3, vol. 24. Correspondence
indicating reservations about the conference includes Mary White
Ovington to Roger Baldwin, 11 December 1917, ACLUR, reel 1, vol. 3
(explaining that the NAACP was divided on the war question); Beatrice
Hale to Mary Ware Dennett, 9 January 1918, ACLUR, reel 1, vol. 3 ("You
know how we used to feel in Suffrage—until you can have an effective
affair, don't have one at all!"). Vigilante episodes included a vicious attack
on the AUAM's own Herbert S. Bigelow, a pacifist minister and outspoken
opponent of "big business." NCLB, *The Outrage on Rev. Herbert S.
Bigelow of Cincinnati, Ohio* (New York, 1918); Herbert Shapiro, "The
Herbert Bigelow Case: A Test of Free Speech in Wartime," *Ohio History*
81 (Spring 1972): 108–121. On reactions to vigilantism, see Capozzola,
Uncle Sam.

65. Mary Ware Dennett to friends, 5 January 1918, ACLUR, reel 1, vol. 3
("Business interests"). The assumption that attacks on labor were proceeding "under the cloak of patriotism" was central to the NCLB's wartime
rhetoric. Roger Baldwin to Fay Lewis, 30 January 1918, ACLUR, reel 5,
vol. 39; see also NCLB to friends, 5 January 1918, ACLUS, box 1; telegram
from NCLB to Woodrow Wilson, 26 September 1917, ACLUR, reel 3, vol.
26 (opposing the Trading with the Enemy Act on the basis that the war
power was being used "to stifle legitimate agitation by labor"). Chafee

famously cast wartime censorship as a departure from earlier tolerance. Contrast circular, ACLUR, reel 1, vol. 3, with Chafee, "War Time," 937.

66. Resolution, ACLUR, reel 1, vol. 3.

67. Roger Baldwin to Edmund Evans, 16 March 1918, ACLUR, reel 3, vol. 25; see also Roger Baldwin to Scott Nearing, 30 January 1918, ACLUR, reel 5, vol. 35.

68. Arnold Peterson to Roger Baldwin, 31 January 1918, ACLUR, reel 5, vol. 35; Roger Baldwin to Arnold Peterson, 2 February 1918, ACLUR, reel 5, vol. 35; ACLU, "Maintain Your Rights," undated, ACLUR, reel 7, vol. 69 (explaining that groups maintained rights "only by insisting upon them"). Meanwhile, pacifists worried that narrow exceptions for conscientious objectors would prolong the war by "ameliorating [its] horrors." James Warbasse to Roger Baldwin, 9 November 1917, ACLUR, reel 3, vol. 25.

69. Chafee, "War Time," 958–959.

3. The Right of Agitation

1. "War Power Ample, Hughes Declared," *NYT,* September 6, 1917; "Big Raid on I.W.W. and Socialists," *NYT,* September 6, 1917. Chapter 1 contains a brief overview of the IWW's prewar activities, including the free speech fights.

2. For example, NCLB circular, 3 January 1918, ACLUR, reel 4, vol. 27. For descriptions, see "Judge Landis Brings Joy to Tobacco-Chewing I.W.W.," *New York Tribune,* April 4, 1918; "Pauper's Petition to Be Filed in Haywood Case," *New York Tribune,* May 27, 1919.

3. William Haywood, 10 August 1918, IWWC, box 117, folder 3, a14h.

4. ACLU, "The Greatest Free Speech Trial of the War," ACLUS, box 1. On the IWW's underdeveloped social and economic theory and its millenarian impulses, see Melvyn Dubofsky, *We Shall Be All: A History of the Industrial Workers of the World* (Chicago, 1969), 85–97.

5. Schenck v. United States, 249 U.S. 47 (1919); Abrams v. United States, 250 U.S. 616 (1919); Debs v. United States, 249 U.S. 211 (1919).

6. Dubofsky, *We Shall Be All,* 376–397.

7. Stanley Meade Reynolds, "Attorney General Thomas W. Gregory, '84," *Alumni Bulletin of the University of Virginia* (Charlottesville, 1915), 34. On the summer 1917 events, see Dubofsky, *We Shall Be All,* 380–388. A significant number of the Bisbee deportees had never belonged to the IWW, and some were AFL members. In *United States v. Wheeler,* 254 F. 611 (D. Ariz. 1918), affirmed, *United States v. Wheeler,* 254 U.S. 281 (1920), the district court held that the Selective Service Act did not require registrants to remain within their state of residence, and the

deportation of the victims across state lines was otherwise insufficient to implicate federally cognizable rights; the unlawful behavior of the vigilantes fell within the jurisdiction of state law (which, as a matter of politics, meant no case would proceed). On the ACLU's efforts to facilitate federal prosecution in such cases, see Chapter 7.

8. Melvyn Dubofsky, *The State and Labor in Modern America* (Chapel Hill, NC, 1994), 67.

9. "103 I.W.W. Leaders Face Judge Landis," *NYT*, December 16, 1917. Many of the indictments were subsequently dismissed for insufficient evidence.

10. For a detailed account of the legal claims raised at various stages of the case, see Laura Weinrib, "The Liberal Compromise: Civil Liberties, Labor, and the Limits of State Power, 1917–1940" (PhD dissertation, Princeton University, 2011), ch. 2.

11. 55 Congressional Record 6104 (1917) (Henry Ashurst); NCLB, "The Need of a National Defense Fund," 15 November 1917, ACLUR, reel 3, vol. 26 ("government"); Dubofsky, *We Shall Be All*, 233 ("very largely," quoting United States attorney). See generally Dubofsky, ibid., 354–358; NCLB, Memorandum regarding the Persecution of the Radical Labor Movement in the United States (undated), ACLUS, box 1.

12. NCLB, "Defense Fund."

13. Elizabeth Gurley Flynn, A. Giovannitti, and Carlo Tresca to Roger Baldwin, undated, ACLUR, reel 4, vol. 27.

14. ACLU, *The Persecution of the I.W.W.* (New York, 1921) ("essentially"); ACLU, *The Fight for Free Speech* (New York, 1921), 5 ("causes"); NCLB, "Defense Fund" ("law and public policy").

15. George Vanderveer to Roger Baldwin, 6 February 1918, ACLUR, reel 4, vol. 27; Roger Baldwin to Laurence Todd, 26 February 1918, ACLUR, reel 3, vol. 25; Roger Baldwin to Carlton Parker, 8 February 1918, ACLUR, reel 4, vol. 27; Roger Baldwin, Memorandum on the IWW Prosecutions, 9 February 1918, ACLUR, reel 4, vol. 27.

16. John A. Fitch, "Labor in World Politics," *Survey*, January 19, 1918, 440; "Finds Many Causes for Labor Unrest," *NYT*, February 10, 1918.

17. Roger Baldwin to John Graham Brooks, 14 March 1918, ACLUR, reel 4, vol. 27; Roger Baldwin to Carlton Parker, 8 February 1918, ACLUR, reel 4, vol. 27; Roger Baldwin to Woodrow Wilson, 27 February 1918, ACLUR, reel 4, vol. 27.

18. "Gives Power to Stop Mail Delivery," *New York Evening Post*, April 30, 1918 ("arbitrary power"); "Senators Flay Gag Bill as Hit at U.S. Liberties," April 5, 1918, clipping, ACLUR, reel 6, vol. 53. The bill was modified very slightly to address criticism. "Senate Makes Slight Change in Gagging Bill," *New York Call*, April 9, 1918. On the debate over the Sedition Act,

see generally Geoffrey R. Stone, *Perilous Times: Free Speech in Wartime from the Sedition Act of 1798 to the War on Terrorism* (New York, 2004), 183–191.

19. Sedition Act of 1918, 40 Stat. 553 (1918); NCLB to President Woodrow Wilson, 27 September 1918, ACLUR, reel 5, vol. 43 (citing Utah senator William King).

20. "Senate Passes Bill Aimed at the I.W.W.," *NYT*, May 7, 1918; Laurence Todd to Roger Baldwin, 3 May 1918, ACLUR, reel 3, vol. 25 (citing Borah); Donald Johnson, *Challenge to American Freedoms: World War I and the Rise of the American Civil Liberties Union* (Lexington, KY, 1963), 97–98.

21. IWW Defense News Service, 2 May 1918, ACLUR, reel 4, vol. 28; IWW daily bulletin 7, 9 April 1918, IWWC, box 123, folder 18; IWW daily bulletin 2, 2 April 1918, IWWC, box 123, folder 13.

22. IWW trial bulletin, 4 July 1918, ACLUR, reel 4, vol. 28 ("hoggish," referring to the lumber industry); "Defense Wins New Point in IWW Case," *New York Call*, April 19, 1918; IWW defense bulletin, 18 April 1918, ACLUR, reel 4, vol. 28; "Anti-IWW Witnesses Are Halted by Landis," *New York Evening Call*, May 29, 1918; IWW trial bulletin 27, 15 May 1918, IWWC, box 123, folder 37; "Malicious IWW Yarn Is Scored by Court," *New York Evening Call*, May 17, 1918. On the other hand, Landis scolded the IWW (outside the presence of the jury) for an article in the *Industrial Worker* that implicitly threatened the judge, jurors, and prosecutors with reprisal should a guilty verdict be returned. "I.W.W. Threat Draws Warning from Judge at Chicago Trial," *New York Tribune*, May 8, 1918.

23. Paul Hanna to Roger Baldwin, 4 April 1918, ACLUR, reel 4, vol. 28 ("cool"); Roger Baldwin to Mildred B. Wertheimer, 10 July 1918, ACLUR, reel 4, vol. 27 ("utterly"); Olmstead v. United States, 277 U.S. 438 (1928). The prosecution team also included Charles Clyne (the United States attorney for the Northern District of Illinois), Claude Porter, and William C. Fitts. The IWW had hoped that Clarence Darrow or Frank P. Walsh could be convinced to handle the defense, but Darrow was preoccupied with other legal matters, and Walsh—who would soon be appointed as cochair of the National War Labor Board—was unwilling to jeopardize his productive relationship with administration officials. Jack Law to Roger Baldwin, 15 January 1918, ACLUR, reel 4, vol. 27. Vanderveer was assisted by W. B. Cleary, an Arizona attorney who had been deported along with Bisbee strikers; Otto Christensen, a Chicago Socialist; and Caroline Lowe, a Socialist organizer and veteran of the IWW's free speech fights who enrolled in law school at the age of forty and had

recently been admitted to the bar. On Vanderveer, see Lowell S. Hawley and Ralph Busnell Potts, *Counsel for the Damned: A Biography of George Francis Vanderveer* (New York, 1953).

24. F. M. Bailey, IWWC, box 11, folder 103, 618 (German finances); NCLB, *The Truth about the IWW* (New York, 1918), 55 (registration); "Chicago Trial Enters Last Month," *Labor Defender*, July 20, 1918, ACLUR, reel 5, vol. 42 (soldiers' testimony); David Karsner, bulletin 6, 19 August 1918, ACLUR, reel 4, vol. 28 (Haywood).

25. "End of IWW Trial Far Off," *New York Evening Post*, June 24, 1918 ("fight for their jobs"); William Haywood, 10 August 1918, IWWC, box 117, folders 2–3, c35c, e26; David Karsner, "The IWW Case—An Idea on Trial" (draft), ACLUR, reel 4, vol. 28 ("taken an advantage").

26. "End of IWW Trial Far Off," *New York Evening Post*, June 24, 1918; Vincent St. John, May 21, 1914, CIRRT, vol. 2, 1451; IWW trial bulletin 35, 10 June 1918, IWWC, box 123, folder 45; "Jurors Hear IWW Songs as Evidence," *New York Evening Call*, May 10, 1918.

27. "Editor of 'Solidarity' on the Witness Stand in IWW Trial," *New York Weekly People*, July 20, 1918 ("good pay," reporting testimony of Ralph Chapin); Karsner, "IWW Case" ("bring the strike," recounting testimony on lumber strike). See also David Karsner, bulletin 6, 19 August 1918, ACLUR, reel 4, vol. 28; clipping, *New York Evening Call*, July 12, 1918 (quoting testimony of James Rowan).

28. "Court Probes Fire in IWW Case," *New York Evening Call*, July 3, 1918 ("fingers"); "Nebeker Fails to Stop IWW Recital," *New York Evening Call*, June 27, 1918. For discussion of the Speculator disaster, including analysis of the more complicated cause of the deaths, see Arnon Gutfeld, "The Speculator Disaster in 1917: Labor Resurgence at Butte, Montana," *Arizona and the West* 11 (Spring 1969): 27–38. On Bisbee, see Dubofsky, *We Shall Be All*, 435.

29. "U.S. Admits 6 Vital Points in IWW Trial," *New York Call*, July 24, 1918; Frank Nebeker, closing argument, 17 August 1918, IWWC, box 130, folder 2, c9h (hereafter Nebeker Closing Argument).

30. George Vanderveer to Roger Baldwin, 1 April 1918, ACLUR, reel 4, vol. 27. Flynn, who was indicted for translating Emile Pouget's classic tract on sabotage, believed the government would be unable to maintain a case against each of the individual defendants on each count. Elizabeth Gurley Flynn, Carlo Tresca, and Joseph Ettor to friends and sympathizers, ACLUR, reel 4, vol. 27. Based on his reading of the Department of Justice records in the IWW case, Melvyn Dubofsky concluded that Flynn's optimism about the prospects for dismissal was misguided, if not disingenuous. Dubofsky, *We Shall Be All*, 427.

31. For example, Roger Baldwin to Amos Pinchot, 6 February 1918, ACLUR, reel 4, vol. 27. At the IWW's request, Baldwin made many efforts to raise funds from contacts in New York, Boston, and elsewhere; see, for example, Roger Baldwin to friends of liberty in wartime, 19 March 1918, ACLUR, reel 4, vol. 27. See also Robert Cottrell, *Roger Nash Baldwin and the American Civil Liberties Union* (New York, 2000), 73.

32. J. G. Phelps Stokes to Roger Baldwin, 19 April 1918, ACLUR, reel 4, vol. 28; Roscoe Pound to George West, 24 May 1918, ACLUR, reel 4, vol. 28; J. E. Dumars to Roger Baldwin, 9 May 1918, ACLUR, reel 4, vol. 28; revised draft of *New Republic* advertisement, ACLUR, reel 4, vol. 28; Roger Baldwin to Robert Hallowell, treasurer, *New Republic,* 16 July 1918, ACLUR, reel 4, vol. 28.

33. Roger Baldwin to Paul Hanna, 1 April 1918, ACLUR, reel 4, vol. 28; Paul Hanna, Report to Roger Baldwin, 13 April 1918, ACLUR, reel 4, vol. 28; sample circular, ACLUR, reel 4, vol. 28. Several correspondents who were assigned the task abdicated the position. Baldwin finally reached an arrangement with a Chicago correspondent for the *New York Call,* David Karsner. David Karsner to Roger Baldwin, 5 June 1918, ACLUR, reel 4, vol. 28. Baldwin separately agreed (not on behalf of the NCLB) to assemble a committee of reporters in New York and Washington who would produce balanced accounts of the proceedings. Roger Baldwin to Bill Haywood, 27 March 1918, ACLUR, reel 4, vol. 27.

34. NCLB, *Truth,* 10–11; *Proceedings of the Judiciary Committee of the Assembly,* vol. 2 (New York, 1920), 1682 (Norman Thomas).

35. NCLB, *Truth,* 46 (quoting Robert Bruere), 12 (emphasis added).

36. Memorandum on IWW Cases, 14 February 1918, ACLUR, reel 4, vol. 27; Roger Baldwin to George Vanderveer, 26 March 1918, ACLUR, reel 4, vol. 27 ("where the issue"); Roger Baldwin to Jessie Ashley, 20 March 1918, ACLUR, reel 4, vol. 27 ("I doubt").

37. C. H. Libby to Walter Nelles, 19 July 1918, ACLUR, reel 5, vol. 36 (reporting that his clients had been convicted for distributing the pamphlet); Johnson, *Challenge,* 95.

38. Roger Baldwin to Jessie Ashley, 20 March 1918, ACLUR, reel 4, vol. 27.

39. "Haywood Says Trial Was Fair," *New York Call,* August 22, 1918; undated bulletin, ACLUR, reel 4, vol. 28 ("proved himself"); W. D. Haywood, "Working Class Commission of the Whole," *Survey,* August 2, 1913, 580; George Vanderveer, 24 June 1918, IWWC, box 108, folder 7, A5h–6h ("Bible"); "Evidence for Defense Begins at IWW Trial," *New York Weekly People,* July 13, 1918.

40. George Vanderveer, 24 June 1918, IWWC, box 108, folder 7, a5h–6h.

41. "I.W.W. Can't Use Industrial Report," *New York Call*, June 25, 1918 ("forum for cranks," quoting Nebeker); George Vanderveer, 24 June 1918, IWWC, box 108, folder 7. Compare Frank Nebeker, 24 June 1918, IWWC, box 108, folder 7, F1c–F2c, with Nebeker Closing Argument, C2c.

42. George Vanderveer, 24 June 1918, IWWC, box 108, folder 7, A9h, D4h, D5h–6h; Frank Nebeker, opening statement, 2 May 1918, IWWC, box 103, folder 6, b13h.

43. George Vanderveer, 24 June 1918, IWWC, box 108, folder 7, B3c–B5c, D5h–D6h. Similarly, Haywood testified that the IWW was nonpolitical rather than antipolitical, and that many of its members took part in political action. He also noted that many of the least privileged workers were denied the vote, including migratory workers, black workers, and children. William Haywood, 9 August 1918, IWWC, box 116, folder 5, F3h–F5h.

44. Nebeker Closing Argument, C2h–C6h.

45. For example, Mildred S. Wertheimer to Roger Baldwin, 26 July 1918, ACLUR, reel 4, vol. 27 (reporting perceptions of case).

46. Argument on Defendants' Motion for a New Trial, 27 August 1918, IWWC, box 118, folder 4, 12348–12349 (five seconds); undated bulletin, ACLUR, reel 4, vol. 28 ("thunderbolt"); sentencing, 29 August 1918, IWWC, box 118, folder 6, B3m ("greatest blunders"); Roger Baldwin to Bill Haywood, 26 August 1918, ACLUR, reel 4, vol. 27. Landis had concluded that there was insufficient evidence to support the government's fifth count, conspiracy to violate the postal laws, and he removed it from the jury's consideration.

47. Clipping, *Chicago Weekly People*, September 21, 1918, ACLUR, reel 5, vol. 42. Landis thought "the jury could not have done anything else on this evidence but find a verdict of guilty," though he did not direct a verdict. Sentencing, 29 August 1918, IWWC, box 118, folder 6, A27h–A28h, A35h–A36h. Haywood expressed that Landis had been "absolutely square throughout the whole trial." Undated bulletin, ACLUR, reel 4, vol. 28.

48. "The Closing Chapter," *New Haven Register*, August 31, 1918. For representative press responses, see "The Guilty IWW Leaders," *Republican* (Springfield), August 18, 1918; "The Guilty IWW," *Herald News* (New Britain, CT), August 19, 1918; clipping, *Norwich Record* (CT), August 21, 1918, ACLUR, reel 5, vol. 42. On the AFL's response, see Dubofsky, *We Shall Be All*, 437.

49. "Admissibility of Evidence Obtained by Illegal Search and Seizure," 24 A.L.R. 1408 (1923); Supplemental Reply Brief of Plaintiffs in Error, Haywood v. United States, 268 F. 795 (7th Cir. 1920), No. 2721, IWWC,

box 122, 21; Supplemental Brief and Argument for Plaintiff in Error, Haywood v. United States, 268 F. 795 (7th Cir. 1920), No. 2721, IWWC, box 122, 67. The posttrial motions are described in Weinrib, "Liberal Compromise," ch. 3.

50. Reply Brief for Plaintiffs in Error, Haywood v. United States, 268 F. 795 (7th Cir. 1920), No. 2721, IWWC, box 122, 60; Petition for Rehearing, Haywood v. United States, 268 F. 795 (7th Cir. 1920), No. 2721, IWWC, box 123, folder 2; sentencing, 29 August 1918, IWWC, box 118, folder 6, A36h–A38h; Haywood v. United States, 268 F. 795, 807 (7th Cir. 1920). The government considered *Abrams v. United States,* 250 U.S. 616, 621 (1919), to be dispositive. Supplemental Reply Brief of Plaintiffs in Error, Haywood v. United States, 268 F. 795 (7th Cir. 1920), No. 2721, IWWC, box 122, 107.

51. Haywood, 268 F. at 799–800, 807. The court rejected the second count, based on Section 19 of the Penal Code, applicable in cases of conspiracy to injure citizens of the United States in the exercise of any "right or privilege secured to [them] by the Constitution and laws of the United States." The government alleged that the IWW had run afoul of this provision by preventing producers from fulfilling their contracts with the government for war munitions and supplies. The court stated decisively that "to produce, to sell, to contract to sell to any buyer, are not rights or privileges conferred by the Constitution and laws of the United States." Ibid., 801.

52. IWW bulletin, 26 July 1918, ACLUR, reel 4, vol. 27.

53. NCLB to President Wilson, 27 September 1918, ACLUR, reel 5, vol. 43; press release (undated), ACLUR, reel 25, vol. 181 ("larger sum"); *Nation* advertisement, ACLUR, reel 25, vol. 181; ACLU press release, 8 March 1921, ACLUR, reel 25, vol. 181. On Sacramento, see Dubofsky, *We Shall Be All,* 438–431; Johnson, *Challenge,* 101–104. On Wichita, see Johnson, *Challenge,* 105–109; Clayton R. Koppes, "The Kansas Trial of the I.W.W., 1917–1919," *Labor History* 16 (1975): 339–358; Earl Bruce White, "The United States v. C. W. Anderson et al.: The Wichita Case, 1917–1919," in *At the Point of Production: The Local History of the IWW,* ed. Joseph R. Conlin (Westport, 1981), 143–164.

54. Upton Sinclair to Newton Baker, undated, ACLUR, reel 6, vol. 50; clipping, *New York Call,* January 28, 1919, ACLUR, reel 5, vol. 41; Johnson, *Challenge,* 109–118. Both Thomas Gregory and A. Mitchell Palmer were willing to consider leniency in particular cases. The NCLB considered a general amnesty to be the "only possible solution." "Liberties Bureau Takes Issue with Gregory," clipping, ACLUR, reel 5, vol. 43.

55. Woodrow Wilson to Joseph P. Tumulty, June 28, 1919, in *The Papers of Woodrow Wilson,* vol. 61, ed. Arthur S. Link et al. (Princeton, NJ,

1966–1994), 351–352; "Political Prisoners in U.S. Total 1,500, Estimates Bureau," *New York Tribune,* March 10, 1919.

56. ACLU, *A Year's Fight for Free Speech: The Work of the American Civil Liberties Union from Sept. 1921 to Jan. 1923* (New York, 1923); "Legion Warns Harding against Freeing Debs," *NYT,* July 29, 1921; Elizabeth Gurley Flynn (for Workers Defense Union), general letter, 30 July 1921, ACLUR, reel 25, vol. 181 (internal disagreement); Carl Haessler to Roger Baldwin, 2 May 1921, ACLUR, reel 23, vol. 166 (bail).

57. Frederick Esmond to Roger Baldwin, 21 February 1918, ACLUR, reel 4, vol. 30; ACLU, *Persecution.*

58. Roger Baldwin to Bill Haywood, 26 August 1918, ACLUR, reel 4, vol. 27 ("economic freedom"); Amos Pinchot, "Protecting the Old Order," *New York Call,* March 12, 1919; Lochner v. New York, 198 U.S. 75 (1905) (Holmes, J., dissenting); NCLB, "The Law of the Debs Case," undated, ACLUS, box 1. On *Debs,* see Ernest Freeberg, *Democracy's Prisoner: Eugene V. Debs, the Great War, and the Right to Dissent* (Cambridge, MA, 2008). The IWW complained that Debs, as a Socialist, garnered significantly more popular support. Otto Christensen, Statement Submitted to the Attorney General of the United States concerning the Present Legal Status of the IWW Cases, IWWC, box 131, folder 2, 23.

59. NCLB, "The Right to His Day in Court," undated, ACLUS, box 1 (quoting Arthur Le Sueur); "Denounce Debs Decision," *New York Call,* March 12, 1919.

60. William Haywood, 10 August 1918, IWWC, box 117, folder 3, A14h.

61. NCLB, *The Meaning of "Industrial Action"* (New York, 1918); Roger Baldwin, "Free Speech Fights of the IWW," in *Twenty-Five Years of Industrial Unionism* (Chicago, 1930), 15 ("far more").

62. Frederick Keppel to Roger Baldwin, 26 February 1918, ACLUR, reel 2, vol. 15 ("direct conflict"); Roger Baldwin to Nicholas Biddle, 8 March 1918, ACLUR, reel 2, vol. 15; Ralph H. Van Deman to Frederick Keppel, 9 March 1918, ACLUR, reel 2, vol. 15. See also Cottrell, *Baldwin,* 66–67.

63. NCLB press release, 17 October 1918, ACLUS, box 1, folder 1918; Johnson, *Challenge,* 74–75.

64. L. Hollingsworth Wood to friends of the bureau, 17 September 1918, AUAMR, reel 10-1; John Nevin Sayre to Albert DeSilver, 18 October 1918, ACLUR, reel 6, vol. 47; Cottrell, *Baldwin,* 82; Johnson, *Challenge,* 76–77.

65. Gilbert E. Roe, "Repeal the Espionage Law: An Address Delivered before the Civic Club of New York, December 3, 1918," *Dial,* January 11, 1919, 21–22.

66. Roger Baldwin to the directing committee, 10 August 1918, ACLUR, reel 3, vol. 25; *The Individual and the State: The Problem as Presented by the*

Sentencing of Roger N. Baldwin (New York, 1918), 6. Baldwin intended to refuse to register, but the raid on the NCLB offices prompted him to delay action until the "critical period" had passed.

67. "Convict Berkman and Miss Goldman," *NYT*, July 10, 1917; *Individual and the State*, 6.

68. *Individual and the State*, 9–10.

69. Ibid., 13. Mayer filed a cursory brief in *Lochner,* prompting speculation that he either underestimated the likelihood that the law would be invalidated or was unenthusiastic about defending the statute. See David Bernstein, *Rehabilitating Lochner: Defending Individual Rights against Progressive Reform* (Chicago, 2011), 32; Paul Kens, *Judicial Power and Reform Politics: The Anatomy of Lochner v. New York* (Lawrence, KS, 1990), 112.

70. "Baldwin Gets Year for Draft Act Defiance," *New York Call*, October 31, 1918; NCLB press release, 7 March 1919, ACLUR, reel 5, vol. 43; Roger Baldwin to Albert DeSilver, undated, ACLUR, reel 5, vol. 423.

71. See Cottrell, *Baldwin*, 94–100.

72. "Roger Baldwin Free from Jail, Urges Amnesty," *New York Call*, July 20, 1919 ("leaving more"); clipping, *New York Telegram*, July 20, 1919, ACLUR, reel 6, vol. 45 ("revolutionary"); Roger Baldwin to Albert DeSilver, 5 March 1919, ACLUR, reel 5, vol. 44 ("not a sacred"); clipping, *New York Telegram*, July 20, 1919, ACLUR, reel 6, vol. 45 ("revolutionary").

73. Cottrell, *Baldwin,* 73, 108–110.

74. *New York Legislative Documents, 144th Sess., 1921,* vol. 18, part 2 (Albany, 1921), 1981.

75. Roger Baldwin to Harold Evans, 13 April 1918, ACLUR, reel 3, vol. 25 ("working on"); Roger Baldwin to I. C. Herendeen, 10 September 1917, ACLUR, reel 5, vol. 36 ("dealing with"). Compare Reuel Schiller, "Free Speech and Expertise: Administrative Censorship and the Birth of the Modern First Amendment," *University of Virginia Law Review* 86 (2000): 1–101, 3–4 (locating transformation after World War II).

76. NCLB, *The "Knights of Liberty" Mob* (New York, 1918); 16; Ralph Chaplin, *Wobbly: The Rough-and-Tumble Story of an American Radical* (Chicago, 1948), 151 (quoting Baldwin); Alexander Meiklejohn, *Free Speech and Its Relation to Self-Government* (New York, 1948), 25. Meiklejohn was active in the ACLU during the interwar period and his famous formulation, though articulated after World War II, captures the spirit of the progressive defense of free speech during the 1920s and 1930s.

77. Paul Hanna, Report to Roger Baldwin, 13 April 1918, ACLUR, reel 4, vol. 28; Zechariah Chafee Jr., introduction to *Civil Liberty,* ed. Edith M.

Phelps (New York, 1927), 49. See also Bertrand Russell, *Free Thought and Official Propaganda* (New York, 1922), 41 ("Equality of opportunity among opinions can only be secured by elaborate laws directed to that end"). The question whether government should redress inequalities in the "marketplace of ideas" has troubled free speech theorists since the First World War. See, for example, Meiklejohn, *Free Speech*; Owen Fiss, *Liberalism Divided: Freedom of Speech and the Many Uses of State Power* (Boulder, CO, 1996); Cass R. Sunstein, *Democracy and the Problem of Free Speech* (New York, 1993); Mark Graber, *Transforming Free Speech: The Ambiguous Legacy of Civil Libertarianism* (Berkeley, 1991). During the interwar period, the ACLU included many committed progressives within its ranks, and the organization would consistently split over progressive measures designed to increase the quantity of speech. As a whole, however, it would cast state power as more oppositional than facilitative. For conservative opposition toward state regulation of the media, see Chapter 6.

78. Leon Whipple, *Our Ancient Liberties: The Story of the Origin and Meaning of Civil and Religious Liberty in the United States* (New York, 1927), 137.

4. Dissent

1. Henry Marelli, June 16, 1914, CIRRT, vol. 3, 2532 ("one bright spot," describing Justice James F. Minturn); "State v. Haywood et al.," *New Jersey Law Journal* 36 (1913): 146–150, 149. Section 215 of the Crimes Act listed "unlawful assemblies" among an array of offenses "of an indictable nature at common law, and not provided for in or by this or some other act of the legislature," which were made misdemeanors under New Jersey law. Henry Marelli represented Haywood in Paterson, and his testimony to the commission detailed the events and the proceedings before James F. Carroll, recorder of the City of Paterson. The city argued that Haywood had not secured a permit for the procession as required by law, and was therefore engaged in unlawful assembly under the statute. Minturn determined that the protesters had proceeded haphazardly (as the city alleged in a separate disorderly conduct charge, also subsequently dismissed), and consequently were not parading. "State v. Haywood et al.," *New Jersey Law Journal,* 149.

2. ACLU, *"Unlawful Assembly" in Paterson: The Trial and Conviction of Roger N. Baldwin and Seven Silk Strikers under a Law Passed in 1796* (New York, 1925), 5 ("brutality"); "ACLU Statement on Civil Liberty Situation in America at Present," 29 August 1925, ACLUR, reel 41, vol. 285.

As in 1913, the broad-silk weavers were seeking two looms and eight-hour days. The Paterson strike and Baldwin's trial are discussed in Nancy Fogelson, "They Paved the Streets with Silk: Paterson, New Jersey, Silk Workers, 1913–1924," *New Jersey History* 97 (1979): 142–146; Martha Glaser, "Paterson 1924: The ACLU and Labor," *New Jersey History* 94 (1976): 155–172; Steve Golin, *The Fragile Bridge: Paterson Silk Strike, 1913* (Philadelphia, 1998), 201–202; Paul L. Murphy, *The Meaning of Freedom of Speech: First Amendment Freedoms from Wilson to FDR* (Westport, CT, 1972), 151–153; Arthur T. Vanderbilt II, *Changing Law: A Biography of Arthur T. Vanderbilt* (New Brunswick, 1976), 48–53.

3. State v. Butterworth, 104 N.J.L. 43 (1927); State v. Butterworth, 104 N.J.L. 579 (1928).

4. Roger Baldwin to John Larkin Hughes, 28 January 1928, ACLUR, reel 58, vol. 346; ACLU, *The Fight for Civil Liberty, 1927–1928* (New York, 1928), 9.

5. Lochner v. New York, 198 U.S. 75 (1905) (Holmes, J., dissenting).

6. Walter Nelles to Roger Baldwin, 23 January 1926, ACLUR, reel 22, vol. 159A; Felix Frankfurter to Walter Nelles, 25 January 1926, ACLUR, reel 22, vol. 159A (expressing distaste for pursuing publicity through judicial defeats).

7. Gilbert E. Roe, "Repeal the Espionage Law: An Address Delivered before the Civic Club of New York, December 3, 1918," *Dial,* January 11, 1919; "Danger Ahead," *Nation,* February 8, 1919, 186.

8. For example, Frederic Howe, a member of the ACLU's inaugural national committee, observed, "The 'immigration problem,' so called, has always been and always will be an economic problem." Frederic C. Howe, "The Alien," in *Civilization in the United States: An Inquiry by Thirty Americans,* ed. Harold E. Stearns (New York, 1922), 337–350, 341. See also William Pickens, *Lynching and Debt Slavery* (New York, 1921), 1 (on lynching, race, and class); Roger Baldwin, "Memorandum on the South as Observed in a Trip in May and June 1920," ACLUR, reel 23, vol. 166 (on race and class).

9. "The Industrial Conference: How Representatives of Capital, Labor, and the Public Sought a Solution of Wage Problems," *Current History* 2 (November 1919): 197 (quoting Gompers). Taft's unexpected cooperation tempered labor's opposition when President Warren G. Harding appointed him to the Supreme Court. Melvyn Dubofsky, *The State and Labor in Modern America* (Chapel Hill, NC, 1994), 72; David Montgomery, *The Fall of the House of Labor: The Workplace, the State, and American Labor Activism, 1865–1925* (New York, 1987), 442–446.

10. "Find More Bombs Sent in the Mails," *NYT,* May 2, 1919.

11. ACLU, *The Fight for Free Speech* (New York, 1921), 6 ("wholesale"); Albert DeSilver to A. Mitchell Palmer, 6 November 1919, ACLUR, reel 7,

vol. 69 ("grave blow"); *The Papers of Woodrow Wilson*, vol. 63, ed.
Arthur S. Link et al. (Princeton, NJ, 1966–1994), 196 ("crime"). See David
Brody, *Labor in Crisis: The Steel Strike of 1919* (Philadelphia, 1965);
Austin K. Kerr, *American Railroad Politics, 1914–1920: Rates, Wages,
and Efficiency* (Pittsburgh, 1968), 204–227; Robert K. Murray, *Red Scare:
A Study in National Hysteria, 1919–1920* (Minneapolis, 1955), 122–134;
Joseph Slater, "Public Workers: Labor and the Boston Police Strike of
1919," *Labor History* 38 (1989): 7–27.

12. "The Red Assassins," *Washington Post,* January 4, 1920, 26. On changing
attitudes toward vigilante violence, see Christopher Capozzola, *Uncle Sam
Wants You: World War I and the Making of the Modern American Citizen*
(New York, 2008).

13. *Hearings before the Special Committee Appointed under the Authority of
House Resolution No. 6 concerning the Right of Victor L. Berger to Be
Sworn in as a Member of the Sixty-Sixth Congress,* vol. 1 (Washington,
DC, 1919), 70; "Berger Conviction Reversed by Court," *NYT,* February 1,
1921; Berger v. United States, 255 U.S. 22 (1921). Berger was subsequently
reelected on a special vote, and again excluded, this time with six votes in
opposition. Murray, *Red Scare,* 227–229.

14. Archibald E. Stevenson, "The World War and Freedom of Speech," review
of *Freedom of Speech* (New York, 1920), by Zechariah Chafee Jr., *NYT,*
February 13, 1921; see also Archibald E. Stevenson, "Circular," in *Civil
Liberty,* ed. Edith M. Phelps (New York, 1927), 150 (arguing, in response
to a June 1925 editorial on *Gitlow,* that advocating amendment of the
United States Constitution to establish a soviet form of government would
be lawful, but advocating a change in government through the general
strike or violence "constituted the highest crime against the principles of
civil liberty and democratic governance"). On the Overman Committee,
see Regin Schmidt, *Red Scare: FBI and the Origins of Anticommunism in
the United States, 1919–1943* (Copenhagen, 2000), 136–146.

15. Graham-Sterling Bill, 66 Cong. Rec. (2d. Sess.) 1338–1343, 2207; NCLB,
"This Little Story Is Entitled 'God Bless the Lusk Committee,'" 28 January
1920, ACLUS, box 1; "Albany's Ousted Socialists," *Literary Digest,*
January 24, 1920, 19. The brief by the Special Committee of the Association of the Bar of the City of New York, of which Hughes was a member,
opposed the expulsion on the theory that tolerance of dissent was "the
most efficient safety-valve against resort by the discontented to physical
force." Chafee, *Freedom of Speech*, 189 (quoting brief).

16. Murphy, *Freedom of Speech,* 42 (quoting Benjamin W. Oppenheim); see
also William Preston, *Aliens and Dissenters: Federal Suppression of
Radicals, 1903–1933* (Cambridge, MA, 1963).

17. James A. Emery (general counsel, NAM), "Building a Political Platform for Industry," *American Industries* 20 (1920): 36–38, 37 ("There is, therefore, a danger in restricting liberty, not in controlling license"); William H. King, " 'Bloc' Menace in Law Making," *Nation's Business,* November 1921, 11 ("They are those who would make of the liberty which the Government guarantees a license to destroy the Government which is the very source of liberty"); John W. Burgess, *Recent Changes in American Constitutional Theory* (New York, 1923), 26; "Current Events," *ABA Journal* 6 (1920): 131–132.

18. John Dewey, "Liberty and Social Control," *Social Frontier* 2 (1935): 41–42; see also Nicholas Murray Butler, "The Changing Foundations of Government," *ABA Journal* 8 (1922): 7–11, 8 ("Property is an attribute of personality, and individual property is essential to liberty").

19. Cordenio A. Severance, "The Constitution and Individualism," *ABA Journal* 8 (1922): 535–542, 542 (address at ABA annual meeting).

20. James H. Tufts, "The Legal and Social Philosophy of Mr. Justice Holmes," *ABA Journal* 7 (1921): 359–363, 361.

21. "Danger Ahead," *Nation,* 186.

22. Woodrow Wilson, *The Triumph of Ideals: Speeches, Messages and Addresses Made by the President between February 24, 1919, and July 8, 1919* (New York, 1919), 78; "The Liberals Wake Up," *New York Call,* March 24, 1919. Wilson's remarks echoed sentiments he expressed in his prewar book, Woodrow Wilson, *The New Freedom: A Call for the Emancipation of the Generous Energies of a People* (Chicago, 1913).

23. Roger Baldwin to Fay Lewis, 30 January 1918, ACLUR, reel 5, vol. 39 (discussing Gompers); "Labor Federation Demands Death of Sedition Bill," *Public Ledger* (Philadelphia), June 21, 1919 ("answer," quoting John Fitzpatrick); "Resolution Adopted by the Annual Convention of the American Federation of Labor," June 1919, ACLUR, reel 7, vol. 69; "Amnesty Meet Forming New Liberty League," *New York Call,* September 28, 1919; "Freedom Meet to Represent All Parts of U.S.," *New York Call,* September 20, 1919; NCLB press release, 1 August 1919, ACLUR, reel 5, vol. 43; NCLB, *The Truth about the IWW* (New York, 1918), 46 ("solidify," quoting Robert Bruere). See also Frank L. Grubbs Jr., *The Struggle for Labor Loyalty: Gompers, the A. F. of L., and the Pacifists, 1917–1920* (Durham, NC, 1968); Ernest Freeberg, *Democracy's Prisoner: Eugene V. Debs, the Great War, and the Right to Dissent* (Cambridge, MA, 2008), 196–199. DeSilver died when he fell from a moving express train in December 1924. See ACLU, *Free Speech in 1924: The Work of the American Civil Liberties Union January to December 1924* (New York, 1925), 3; "Albert DeSilver," *Obituary*

Record of Yale Graduates, 1924–1925 (New Haven, CT, 1925), 1442–1443.

24. National Popular Government League, *Report upon the Illegal Practices of the United States Department of Justice* (Washington, DC, 1920), 8. In 1921, the ACLU reported that "in respect to freedom from unlawful searches and seizures, . . . a liberal interpretation of the constitutional provision is now assured." ACLU, *The Supreme Court vs. Civil Liberty* (New York, 1921), 1.

25. Colyer v. Skeffington, 265 F. 17 (D. Mass., 1920), 43, 22; Skeffington v. Katzeff, 277 F. 129 (1st Cir. 1922); editorial, *Christian Science Monitor,* June 25, 1920, 16. See Murray, *Red Scare,* 250–251; Donald L. Smith, *Zechariah Chafee Jr., Defender of Liberty and Law* (Cambridge, MA, 1986), 47–50; Jeremy Kessler, "The Administrative Origins of Modern Civil Liberties Law," *Columbia Law Review* 114 (2014): 1083–1166, 1152.

26. Zechariah Chafee Jr., *Freedom of Speech* (New York, 1920). For the conversations and correspondence among Hand, Laski, Chafee, and Holmes, among others, see David M. Rabban, *Free Speech in Its Forgotten Years, 1870–1920* (New York, 1997), 299–315; Thomas Healy, *The Great Dissent: How Oliver Wendell Holmes Changed His Mind—And Changed the History of Free Speech in America* (New York, 2013). The concept of the "marketplace of ideas" is generally attributed to Justice Holmes's dissent in *Abrams v. United States,* though he did not explicitly use the phrase. Abrams v. United States, 250 U.S. 616 (1919) (Holmes, J., dissenting). For problems with the market analogy, see Vincent Blasi, "Holmes and the Marketplace of Ideas," *Supreme Court Review* 2004:1–46, 6–13.

27. "The Conduct of the Scopes Trial," *New Republic,* August 19, 1925, 332 ("successful operation"); Chafee, *Freedom of Speech,* 32–35. On "bigness," see Morris Ernst, *Too Big* (Boston, 1940), planned by ACLU attorney Morris Ernst in consultation with Brandeis as an update to Louis D. Brandeis, *The Curse of Bigness: Miscellaneous Papers of Louis D. Brandeis,* ed. Osmond K. Fraenkel (New York, 1934). On Osmond K. Fraenkel, also an influential ACLU attorney, see Chapter 6.

28. Norman Angell, *Why Freedom Matters* (London, 1918), 29.

29. "Scopes," *New Republic,* 331 ("commonplace"); Ernst Freund, "The Debs Case and Freedom of Speech," *New Republic,* May 3, 1919, 13 ("arbitrary"); Chafee, *Freedom of Speech,* 3–6 ("much more"). Freund framed *Debs* in terms of the "freedom of agitation in war time" but focused on political "opinion," not labor advocacy. Freund, "Debs Case," 13. On Freund and Frankfurter, see Daniel R. Ernst, "Ernst Freund, Felix Frankfurter, and the American *Rechtstaat:* A Transatlantic Shipwreck,

1894–1932," *Studies in American Political Development* 23 (2009): 171–188. Literature discussing the ways in which noncourt actors interpret and implement the Constitution includes Sophia Z. Lee, "Race, Sex, and Rulemaking: Administrative Constitutionalism and the Workplace, 1960 to the Present," *Virginia Law Review* 96 (2010): 799–886; Jerry L. Mashaw, "Norms, Practices, and the Paradox of Deference: A Preliminary Inquiry into Agency Statutory Interpretation," *Administrative Law Review* 57 (2005): 501–542; Gillian E. Metzger, "Ordinary Administrative Law as Constitutional Common Law," *Columbia Law Review* 110 (2010): 479–536; Reuel E. Schiller, "The Administrative State, Front and Center: Studying Law and Administration in Postwar America," *Law and History Review* 26 (2008): 415–427; David A. Strauss, "Presidential Interpretation of the Constitution," *Cardozo Law Review* 15 (1993): 113–135.

30. Judson King (National Popular Government League) to Zechariah Chafee Jr., 30 July 1921, ZCP, reel 2.

31. ACLU, *Fight for Free Speech* (1921), 6; Proposed Reorganization of the Work for Civil Liberty, undated, ACLUR, reel 5, vol. 43 ("situation").

32. Proposed Reorganization of the Work for Civil Liberty, ACLUR, reel 5, vol. 44.

33. Walter Nelles, Suggestions for Reorganization of the National Civil Liberties Bureau, undated, ACLUR, reel 16, vol. 120; "American Conditions and Historical Review," *New York Legislative Documents*, vol. 18 (Albany, 1921), 1979–1980 (name change).

34. ACLU, *Fight for Free Speech* (1921), 16 ("right of workers"); "Civil Liberty: The Position of the American Civil Liberties Union on the Issues in the United States Today," undated, ACLUR, reel 16, vol. 120 ("at all times"); Proposed Reorganization of the Work for Civil Liberty, ACLUR, reel 5, vol. 44 ("issues of").

35. See, for example, ACLU, *The Record of the Fight for Free Speech in 1923: The Work of the American Civil Liberties Union January to December 1923* (New York, 1924), 21 (describing sponsorship of the Committee of Inquiry on Coal and Civil Liberties to influence the United States Coal Commission); Murphy, *Freedom of Speech*, 145–146 (describing appeals to Pennsylvania governor Gifford Pinchot); Roger Baldwin to William H. Jefferys, 22 December 1926, ACLUR, reel 46, vol. 303 (identifying "government agencies" as the chief antagonist). On the ACLU's turn away from grassroots organizing, see Emily Zackin, "Popular Constitutionalism's Hard when You're Not Very Popular: Why the ACLU Turned to Courts," *Law and Society Review* 42 (2008): 367–395; Laura Weinrib, "From Public Interest to Private Rights: Free Speech, Liberal Individualism, and the Making of Modern Tort Law," *Law and Social Inquiry* 34 (2009): 187–223.

36. "They Call It Socialism," *Texas Railway Journal* 13 (June 1919): 3; ACLU, *Fight for Free Speech* (1921), 4; Walter Nelles, Suggestions for Reorganization of the National Civil Liberties Bureau, undated, ACLUR, reel 16, vol. 120.

37. Albert DeSilver to Felix Frankfurter, 19 February 1921, ACLUR, reel 25, vol. 151. See, for example, Felix Frankfurter to Albert DeSilver, 17 February 1921, ACLUR, reel 25, vol. 151 (expressing concerns).

38. Walter Nelles, Suggestions for Reorganization of the National Civil Liberties Bureau, undated, ACLUR, reel 16, vol. 120.

39. Roger Baldwin to Duncan McDonald, 21 January 1920, ACLUR, reel 16, vol. 120; Roger Baldwin to William Foster, 18 February 1920, ACLUR, reel 16, vol. 120; Jane Addams to L. Hollingsworth Wood, 8 January 1920, ACLUR, reel 16, vol. 120. Chafee declined to join, reportedly due to the strong connection to the labor movement (he turned down a subsequent invitation on the basis that it would compromise his perceived objectivity). Letter from John Codman, 30 November 1920, ACLUR, reel 16, vol. 120; Zechariah Chafee Jr. to Roger Baldwin, 16 January 1929, ACLUR, reel 63, vol. 360.

40. Roger Baldwin to John A. Fitch, 15 January 1920, ACLUR, reel 16, vol. 120 (explaining that conservatives would not "subscribe to the doctrine of unlimited free speech and freedom of expulsion"); John Fitch to Albert DeSilver, 1 June 1920, ACLUR, reel 16, vol. 120; Scott Nearing to friends, 2 January 1920, ACLUR, reel 16, vol. 120; ACLU, *Fight for Free Speech* (1921), 15 ("orderly"); ACLU executive committee minutes, 12 July 1920, ACLUR, vol. 228 ("social value").

41. Roger Baldwin to Zona Gale, 23 August 1920, ACLUR, reel 16, vol. 120 ("political action"); Zona Gale to Roger Baldwin, 7 September 1920, ACLUR, reel 16, vol. 120 ("personal liberty"). Baldwin consistently emphasized that while he favored the right to advocate violence, he was a pacifist and did not himself endorse violence as a revolutionary strategy. For example, Roger Baldwin to editor, 20 May 1926, ACLUR, reel 46, vol. 303. Thomas thought that "direct incitement to violence" could justifiably be regulated. Norman Thomas to Zona Gale, 10 September 1920, ACLUR, reel 16, vol. 120.

42. Walter Nelles to Roger Baldwin, 11 December 1919, ACLUR, reel 16, vol. 120; ACLU, *Fight for Free Speech* (1921), 5–7.

43. ACLU, *Fight for Free Speech* (1921), 5, 18.

44. Walter Nelles, *Seeing Red: Civil Liberty and Law in the Period following the War* (New York, 1920) (pamphlet published by the ACLU).

45. ACLU to friends of civil liberty, 17 February 1920, ACLUS, box 1; Joseph Freeman, *An American Testament: A Narrative of Rebels and Romantics* (New York, 1936), 330. Freeman, reflecting back on the meetings from a period in which he belonged to the Communist Party, concluded that

police often continued to arrest strikers after victory was declared, though the organization did achieve some "useful" results. Ibid., 331.

46. Glaser, "Paterson 1924," 156. Insofar as the ACLU was pursuing affirmative legal remedies, including injunctions, it was moving into largely uncharted domain. See Chapter 6.

47. Transcript of testimony of Arthur Garfield Hays, ACLU v. Casey, ACLUR, reel 153, vol. 1051, 49–50 ("so-called"); Oswald Garrison Villard, review of *City Lawyer,* by Arthur Garfield Hays, *Harvard Law Review* 56 (1942): 333–336 ("intense sense"); ACLU, *A Year's Fight for Free Speech: The Work of the American Civil Liberties Union from Sept. 1921 to Jan. 1923* (New York, 1923), 27; Arthur Garfield Hays, *City Lawyer: The Autobiography of a Law Practice* (New York, 1942), 467.

48. On the ACLU's early tactics, see, for example, ACLU, *Fight for Free Speech* (1921), 8–9; "Hays Wins Indictments," *NYT,* June 10, 1922.

49. "Harding's Stand on Strikes," *NYT,* August 19, 1922 ("sustain"); Felix Frankfurter and Nathan Greene, *The Labor Injunction* (New York, 1930), 258; "Harding Approves Injunction," *Traffic World,* September 9, 1922, 541. The Wilkerson injunction is reprinted in Frankfurter and Greene, *Labor Injunction,* appendix 4, 253–259.

50. "Harding Approves Injunction," *Traffic World,* 542 (quoting Joseph Taylor Robinson); Great Northern Railway Co. v. Local Great Falls Lodge of International Assoc. of Mach., 283 F. 557 (1922); Great Northern Railway Company v. Brosseau, 286 F. 414 (1922); "The Federated Shop Crafts Injunction," *ABA Journal* 8 (1922): 624–625, 624. Amidon would become a member of the ACLU in 1929.

51. ACLU, *Sept. 1921 to Jan. 1923,* 20–21; Duplex Printing Press Co. v. Deering, 254 U.S. 443 (1921); Truax v. Corrigan, 257 U.S. 312 (1921); American Steel Foundries v. Tri-City Trade Council, 257 U.S. 184, 207 (1921) (picketing); United Mine Workers v. Coronado Coal Co., 259 U.S. 344 (1922) (Sherman Act damages); Chas. Wolff Packing Co. v. Court of Ind. Relations, 262 U.S. 522 (1923) (compulsory arbitration); Dorchy v. Kansas, 272 U.S. 306 (1926) (right to strike); ACLU, *Supreme Court vs. Civil Liberty.*

52. See Dubofsky, *State and Labor,* 84–99.

53. Albert DeSilver, "Freedom of Speech: A Review," review of *Freedom of Speech,* by Zechariah Chafee Jr., *World Tomorrow* 4 (1921): 56–57, 56 (indicating agreement with Chafee).

54. Ibid.; ACLU joint executive and national committee minutes, 6 December 1920, ACLUR, vol. 228 ("transfer"); Albert DeSilver and Roger Baldwin, on behalf of the ACLU, to ACLU members, September 1921, ACLUR, reel 7, vol. 69.

55. Glaser, "Paterson 1924," 157.

56. Keuffel and Esser v. International Association of Machinists, 116 A. 9, 15 (1922) (Minturn, J., dissenting). Minturn denounced the decision as "judicial legislation."

57. According to the ACLU, the closure was ordered in retaliation for criticism of local officials' complicity in suppressing strikers' rights, as well as general disaffection with the president and the judiciary. The vice-chancellor who made the injunction permanent was Vivian M. Lewis, a prominent New Jersey Republican who had lost the state's 1910 gubernatorial election to Woodrow Wilson. See Brief for Plaintiffs-in-Error, State v. Butterworth, New Jersey Supreme Court, 104 N.J.L. 43 (1927), ACLUR, reel 52, vol. 327 (hereafter Butterworth Supreme Court Brief).

58. See ACLU, *Paterson,* 1–11. At first, police officials rebuffed Baldwin at their headquarters and delayed him by telephone to avoid arresting him. When police chief John M. Tracey finally granted Baldwin an interview, he told Baldwin, "I am the law"—much like his better known counterpart, Jersey City mayor Frank Hague (discussed in Chapter 7), whose autocratic methods the ACLU would also eventually challenge. Ibid., 8.

59. Ibid., 9–11 (excerpting Baldwin's statement). The AFL declined to assist the ASW, which it claimed descended from the IWW. Glaser, "Paterson 1924," 162.

60. "Honors Roger N. Baldwin," *NYT,* April 15, 1925; "What Price Tolerance?," *Baltimore Sun,* April 11, 1925; "Strike Riot Cases Called," *NYT,* December 16, 1924; "A Great Opportunity to Do Something Worth While for the Workers of Paterson," *Paterson Evening News,* April 1, 1925; "Sees Liberty Going amid Indifference," *NYT,* May 16, 1925 (quoting Untermyer); Roger Baldwin, "Civil Liberties in the United States," 1926, ACLUR, reel 46, vol. 303. On the relationship between the decline of class consciousness and the emergence of consumerism, see, for example, Stuart Ewen, *Captains of Consciousness: Advertising and the Social Roots of the Consumer Culture* (New York, 1976); Daniel Horowitz, *The Morality of Spending: Attitudes Toward the Consumer Society in America, 1875–1940* (Baltimore, 1985). On welfare capitalism as a means of forestalling both worker militancy and government regulation, see Lizabeth Cohen, *Making a New Deal: Industrial Workers in Chicago, 1919–1939* (New York, 1990), ch. 4.

61. Golin, *Fragile Bridge,* 201; Freeman, *American Testament,* 330 ("distinguished"); ACLU, *1924,* 26 ("right").

62. Calvin Coolidge, "A Platform of Business Principles," *Nation's Business,* December 1924, 37 ("very citadel"); "Hughes Answers Critics of Party," *NYT,* October 5, 1924 (Hughes and free speech); Charles E. Hughes, "The Declaration of Independence," *ABA Journal* 11 (1925): 532.

63. Nelles, *Seeing Red;* ACLU, *1924,* 30. As the *New Republic* put it, the ACLU was "engaged in vindicating the civil and the political liberties of the American people against all attacks either from legislatures, executives or courts." "Scopes," *New Republic,* 331. On the La Follette effort, see Keith E. Whittington, "Preserving the 'Dignity and Influence of the Court': Political Supports for Judicial Review in the United States," in *Rethinking Political Institutions: The Art of the State,* ed. Ian Shapiro, Stephen Skowronek, and Daniel Galvin (New York, 2006), 283; Keith E. Whittington, *Political Foundations of Judicial Supremacy: The Presidency, the Supreme Court, and Constitutional Leadership in U.S. History* (Princeton, NJ, 2007), 265; William G. Ross, *A Muted Fury: Populists, Progressives, and Labor Unions Confront the Courts, 1890–1937* (Princeton, NJ, 1994), 282–283.

64. ACLU, *Free Speech 1925–1926: The Work of the American Civil Liberties Union* (New York, 1926), 3.

65. "Sees Liberty Going amid Indifference," *NYT,* May 16, 1925.

66. Samuel Untermyer to Roger Baldwin, 13 March 1926, ACLUR, reel 22, vol. 159A; Arthur Garfield Hays to Roger Baldwin, 19 January 1926, ACLUR, reel 22, vol. 159A; Felix Frankfurter to Samuel Smoleff, 26 January 1926, ACLUR, reel 22, vol. 159A.

67. Butterworth Supreme Court Brief, 47; Roger Baldwin to Walter Nelles, 20 January 1926, ACLUR, reel 22, vol. 159A; Walter Nelles to Roger Baldwin, 23 January 1926, ACLUR, reel 22, vol. 159A.

68. Butterworth Supreme Court Brief, 26–30; Reply Brief of Plaintiffs-in-Error, State v. Butterworth, New Jersey Supreme Court, 104 N.J.L. 43 (1927), ACLUR, reel 52, vol. 327; Roger Baldwin to Samuel Smoleff, 16 January 1928, ACLUR, reel 58, vol. 346 ("naive").

69. Walter Nelles to Roger Baldwin, 23 January 1926, ACLUR, reel 22, vol. 159A ("Constitutional"). In May 1925, one month before the Supreme Court issued its decision in *Gitlow v. New York,* 268 U.S. 652 (1925), suggesting that the Fourteenth Amendment incorporated the protections of the First Amendment, the ACLU issued a pamphlet on the Paterson case. It assumed that "no federal question is involved, and the issue is therefore confined to the state courts." ACLU, *Paterson,* 3. By the time the brief was drafted, *Gitlow* had been decided, and the authors cited the case for the presumptive applicability of the federal First Amendment. Discussion of the crowd's hostile reaction, for example, Walter Nelles to Roger Baldwin, 25 January 1926, ACLUR, reel 22, vol. 159A, anticipated the problem of the heckler's veto, discussed in Chapter 7.

70. *Gitlow,* 268 U.S. 652, and *Whitney v. California,* 274 U.S. 357 (1927), were argued by Nelles and Pollak.

71. Whitney, 274 U.S. at 373 (Brandeis, J., concurring); Gilbert v. Minnesota, 254 U.S. 325, 343 (1920) (Brandeis, J., dissenting).

72. Walter Nelles to Roger Baldwin, 23 January 1926, ACLUR, reel 22, vol. 159A.

73. Felix Frankfurter to Samuel Smoleff, 26 January 1926, ACLUR, reel 22, vol. 159A (*"cause"*); Felix Frankfurter to Walter Nelles, 25 January 1926, ACLUR, reel 22, vol. 159A ("Of course"); "Scopes," *New Republic*, 332. Frankfurter told Nelles that he should have suspended judicial efforts once Governor Al Smith was ready to pardon Gitlow. Felix Frankfurter to Walter Nelles, 25 January 1926, ACLUR, reel 22, vol. 159A.

74. Walter Nelles to Roger Baldwin, 23 January 1926, ACLUR, reel 22, vol. 159A.

75. State v. Butterworth, 104 N.J.L. 43 (1927).

76. Samuel D. Smoleff to Forrest Bailey, 1 November 1927, ACLUR, reel 52, vol. 327.

77. Samuel D. Smoleff to Roger Baldwin, 21 January 1928, ACLUR, reel 58, vol. 346 ("overawe"); Samuel D. Smoleff to Forrest Bailey, 25 November 1927, ACLUR, reel 52, vol. 327 (on Untermyer); Felix Frankfurter to Roger Baldwin, 24 January 1928, ACLUR, reel 58, vol. 346 (recommending Vanderbilt); Roger Baldwin to Felix Frankfurter, 2 February 1928, ACLUR, reel 58, vol. 346 ("perfect trump"); Roger Baldwin to Oswald Garrison Villard, 22 May 1928, ACLUR, reel 58, vol. 346 ("young chap"); Roger Baldwin to Samuel Untermyer, 2 February 1925, ACLUR, reel 58, vol. 346 (names). In addition, both Frankfurter and Vanderbilt advised against releasing a pamphlet or press statement until the appeal was decided, lest the judges perceive the publicity as an attempt to influence their decision. Arthur T. Vanderbilt to Forrest Bailey, 25 April 1928, ACLUR, reel 58, vol. 346; Felix Frankfurter to Samuel D. Smoleff, 2 March 1928, ACLUR, reel 58, vol. 346. Baldwin initially opposed the change in attorneys. Roger Baldwin to Samuel Untermyer, 16 January 1928, ACLUR, reel 58, vol. 346.

78. Arthur Vanderbilt to Roger Baldwin, 8 February 1928, ACLUR, reel 58, vol. 346.

79. ACLU bulletin 289, 9 February 1928, ACLUR, reel 58, vol. 346; Roger Baldwin to Samuel Untermyer, 8 November 1927, ACLUR, reel 52, vol. 327.

80. ACLU, *1927–1928*, 13–14.

81. ACLU bulletin 289, 9 February 1928, ACLUR, reel 58, vol. 346.

82. Brief for Plaintiffs-in-Error, New Jersey Court of Errors and Appeals, State of New Jersey v. Butterworth, 104 N.J.L. 579 (1928), ACLUR, reel 58, vol. 346, 25.

83. Ibid., 36.

84. ACLU, *The Victory in New Jersey* (New York, 1928), 3; Butterworth, 104 N.J.L. at 581 ("peaceful"); 104 N.J.L. at 587 ("reasonably"). According to Frankfurter, Kalisch believed that Vanderbilt's participation helped to persuade his colleagues. Felix Frankfurter to Roger Baldwin, 22 June 1928, ACLUR, reel 58, vol. 346.

85. Excerpts, "Fundamental Rights Sustained by Court," *Newark Evening News; New Republic;* "Free Speech Wins," *St. Louis Post-Dispatch;* "Baldwin Goes Free," *New York World,* reprinted in ACLU, *Victory in New Jersey,* 15, 20, 18, 16, ACLUR, reel 58, vol. 346; Samuel Smoleff to Roger Baldwin, 23 May 1928, ACLUR, reel 58, vol. 346; "Freedom of Speech Upheld," *Newark Sunday Call,* excerpt reprinted in ACLU, *Victory in New Jersey,* 15–16.

86. Gilbert E. Roe to Roger Baldwin, 29 May 1928, ACLUR, reel 58, vol. 346; Roger Baldwin to Gilbert E. Roe, 31 May 1928, ACLUR, reel 58, vol. 346; ACLU, *Victory in New Jersey,* 17; "There Are Judges in Trenton," *NYT,* May 16, 1928.

5. The New Battleground

1. Scopes v. Tennessee, 152 Tenn. 424 (1925). On the *Scopes* trial, see Edward J. Larson, *Summer for the Gods: The Scopes Trial and America's Continuing Debate over Science and Religion* (Cambridge, MA, 1997); Ray Ginger, *Six Days or Forever?: Tennessee v. John Thomas Scopes* (New York, 1958).

2. David E. Lilienthal, "Clarence Darrow," *Nation,* April 20, 1927, 417 (describing Scopes); William Jennings Bryan, *The Prince of Peace* (Chicago, 1909), 15; Clarence Darrow, *Absurdities of the Bible* (Girard, KS, undated); *Darrow-Case Debate: Has Religion Ceased to Function?* (Chicago, 1921), 8 ("cheaper").

3. "ACLU Statement on Civil Liberty Situation in America at Present," 29 August 1925, ACLUR, reel 41, vol. 285; letter from Roger Baldwin, undated, ACLUR, reel 38, vol. 274.

4. ACLU, *Free Speech 1925–1926: The Work of the American Civil Liberties Union* (New York, 1926), 3.

5. ACLU, *A Year's Fight for Free Speech: The Work of the American Civil Liberties Union from Sept. 1921 to Jan. 1923* (New York, 1923), 8; Brief for Plaintiffs-in-Error, State v. Butterworth, New Jersey Supreme Court, 104 N.J.L. 43 (1927), ACLUR, reel 52, vol. 327, 49. On the ACLU's activity in connection with early 1920s strikes, see Paul L. Murphy, *The Meaning of Freedom of Speech: First Amendment Freedoms from Wilson to FDR* (Westport, CT, 1972), 138–150.

6. G. W. Rappleyea to Forrest Bailey, 7 August 1925, ACLUR, reel 38, vol. 274.

7. ACLU, *1925–1926*, 3. On the labor movement during the 1920s, see Irving Bernstein, *The Lean Years: A History of the American Worker, 1920–1933* (Boston, 1960).

8. For the early history of academic freedom, see Richard Hofstadter, *Academic Freedom in the Age of the College* (New York, 1961); Walter. P. Metzger, *Academic Freedom in the Age of the University* (New York, 1964), 196; Robert C. Post and Matthew W. Finkin, *For the Common Good: Principles of American Academic Freedom* (New Haven, CT, 2009) (ch. 1).

9. John W. Boyer, *Academic Freedom and the Modern University: The Experience of the University of Chicago* (Chicago, 2002), 16, has noted some ambiguity in Edward W. Bemis's termination in light of his poor classroom performance.

10. "The Case of Professor Ross, of Stanford University," *Literary Digest,* December 1, 1900, 641; ibid. (excerpting *San Francisco Chronicle*).

11. AAUP, "1915 Declaration of Principles on Academic Freedom and Academic Tenure," reprinted in AAUP, *Policy Documents and Reports,* 11th ed. (Baltimore, 2015), 5; University of Pennsylvania alumni maga-zine, quoted in Daniel H. Pollitt and Jordan E. Kurland, "Entering the Academic Freedom Arena Running: The AAUP's First Year," *Academe,* July–August 1998, 45–52, 50.

12. AAUP, "1915 Declaration," 9, 11; "Teachers Must Be Left Free, Lowell Holds," *New York Call,* January 14, 1918. On the exclusion of outside activities, see J. Peter Byrne, "Academic Freedom: A 'Special Concern of the First Amendment,'" *Yale Law Journal* 99 (1989): 251–340. Academic freedom proved just as susceptible to popular pressures during the First World War as the broader progressive commitment to free speech. "Report of Committee on Academic Freedom in Wartime," *AAUP Bulletin* 4, no. 2–3 (1918): 8, 30. The association's Committee on Aca-demic Freedom in Wartime approved dismissal of any faculty member whose expression tended to impede the war effort or to undermine compliance with compulsory military service. It also recommended leniency for conscientious objectors on the faculty only if they were motivated by "sincere religious or ethical conviction[s]," and only as long they were circumspect about their views. Ibid., 36–41.

13. ACLU, *Sept. 1921 to Jan. 1923*, 8; Leon Whipple, "Free Speech and Jefferson's University," ACLUR, reel 5, vol. 37; ACLU, *Sept. 1921 to Jan. 1923*, 8. Nearing was also a leader of the People's Council of America for Democracy and Peace, which was closely associated with the radical wing of the AUAM.

14. "Quits Columbia; Assails Trustees," *NYT*, October 7, 1917. Other lecturers included Franklin H. Giddings, John Spargo, and James T. Shotwell.

15. "Opens Safe in New Rand School Raid," *NYT*, June 24, 1919 ("persons"); "Court Dismisses Rand School Case," *NYT*, July 31, 1919 (describing Untermyer's argument). The Lusk Committee simultaneously targeted the headquarters of the Left Wing Socialists and the local IWW offices, in a raid the *New York Times* called "the biggest of the kind in the history of the city." "Raid Rand School, 'Left Wing,' and I.W.W. Offices," *NYT*, June 22, 1919. The Rand School and the raid are described in People's Freedom Union, "The Truth about the Lusk Committee," March 1920, ACLUR, reel 16, vol. 115. See generally Todd J. Pfannestiel, *Rethinking the Red Scare: The Lusk Committee and New York's Crusade against Radicalism, 1919–1923* (New York, 2003). The committee was named for state senator Clayton R. Lusk.

16. NCLB, "Bolshevism and Cool Heads" (draft), 5 July 1919, ACLUR, reel 22, vol. 159A. The *New York Times* printed large excerpts of the statement. "Want Rand School Opened," *NYT*, July 19, 1919.

17. No. 1325, New York Legislative Record and Index (New York, 1920), 109 ("that organized government"); "Ask Legislature to End Rand School," *NYT*, March 18, 1920; "Gov. Smith Vetoes Six Bills Aimed at Socialist Party," *NYT*, May 20, 1920. Justice John V. McAvoy ordered that the case against the Rand School be brought by July 28, and he dismissed the case without prejudice when the deputy attorney general announced on July 30 that he was not ready to proceed with the case. "Court Dismisses Rand School Case," *NYT*.

18. "Governor Approves Two Loyalty Bills," *NYT*, May 10, 1921; Zechariah Chafee Jr., "The Rand School Case," *New Republic*, September 27, 1922, 118; Ives v. South Buffalo Railway Company, 201 N.Y. 271 (1911) (invalidating New York's workers' compensation statute); Matter of Jacobs, 98 N.Y. 98 (1885) (invalidating New York's prohibition on the manufacture of cigars in tenement houses); Lochner v. New York, 198 U.S. 45 (1905) (invalidating New York's maximum-hours law for bakers). See also Zechariah Chafee Jr., *The Inquiring Mind* (New York, 1928); People's Freedom Union, "The Truth about the Lusk Committee," March 1920, ACLUR, reel 16, vol. 115.

19. People v. American Socialist Soc., 202 A.D. 640, 649 (N.Y.A.D. 1922); Slaughterhouse Cases, 83 U.S. 36 (1873); Meyer v. Nebraska, 262 U.S. 390 (1923); "The Degradation of Teaching," *Nation*, December 7, 1921, 639; "Lusk Laws Repealed by Smith's Approval," *NYT*, May 26, 1923, 17. Contemporary commentators observed the inconsistency between the *Meyer* and the Rand School cases. See, for example, "Current Decisions:

Constitutional Law—Police Power—Statute Prohibiting Teaching Foreign Languages in School," *Yale Law Journal* 33 (1923): 215.

20. Pierce v. Society of Sisters, 268 U.S. 510, 535 (1925). On *Pierce,* see Paula Abrams, *Cross Purposes: Pierce v. Society of Sisters and the Struggle over Compulsory Public Education* (Ann Arbor, 2009).

21. William S. U'Ren to Roger Baldwin, 27 December 1922, ACLUR, reel 34, vol. 245 ("civil") ("every normal"); William S. U'Ren, 6 December 1922, ACLUR, reel 34, vol. 245 ("liberal").

22. Roger Baldwin to William S. U'Ren, 4 January 1923, ACLUR, reel 34, vol. 245 ("dictates"); Roger Baldwin to William S. U'Ren, 17 January 1923, ACLUR, reel 34, vol. 245 ("experimental"). The ACLU's involvement in the case was limited. Although the ACLU did not intend to "divert [its] energies" to the matter, given its commitments elsewhere, Baldwin reported that "there is some incidental legal work we can help them with, and we may also have something to say publicly when the proper time comes." Roger Baldwin to William S. U'Ren, 4 January 1923, ACLUR, reel 34, vol. 245.

23. ACLU, *Sept. 1921 to Jan. 1923,* 19; Roger Baldwin to A. W. Corbin, 1 May 1923, ACLUR, reel 34, vol. 245 ("to which").

24. ACLU, "Freedom of Speech in Schools and Colleges," June 1924, ACLUR, reel 35, vol. 248. The committee was chaired by Tufts professor Clarence R. Skinner.

25. Roger Baldwin to Ernst Freund, 27 August 1924, ACLUR, reel 35, vol. 248; ACLU, "Freedom of Speech in Schools and Colleges," June 1924, ACLUR, reel 35, vol. 248. The ACLU assured potential members of its own committee that the two organizations had different objectives and that the AAUP was fully aware and supportive of the ACLU's proposed work. For example, Roger Baldwin to Allyn A. Young, 29 August 1924, ACLUR, reel 35, vol. 248.

26. Roger Baldwin to Allyn A. Young, 29 August 1924, ACLUR, reel 35, vol. 248.

27. ACLU release, undated, ACLUR, reel 35, vol. 248.

28. ACLU, "Freedom of Speech in Schools and Colleges," June 1924, ACLUR, reel 35, vol. 248; ACLU, "The Tennessee Evolution Case," July 1925, ACLUR, reel 44, vol. 299.

29. See, for example, Walter Nelles to Arthur Garfield Hays, 10 September 1925, ACLUR, reel 38, vol. 274 (relaying Frankfurter's belief that Hughes was most likely to secure a victory in the case). Malone served as third assistant secretary of state during 1913; Bryan was secretary of state from 1913 until he resigned in 1915, concerned that President Wilson would involve the United States in the wold war.

30. Lilienthal, "Darrow," 417. By the same token, the state's attorney argued that instruction in evolution would "la[y] the foundation by which man can

be brought to accept the doctrine of communism and to the point where he believes it right to advocate murder." Quoted in Larson, *Summer,* 215.

31. William Jennings Bryan, "God and Evolution; Charge That American Teachers of Darwinism 'Make the Bible a Scrap of Paper,'" *NYT,* February 26, 1922; "The Subversion of Public Education," *New Republic,* February 1, 1922, 261 (Lusk); Brief to Supreme Court of Tennessee, John Thomas Scopes vs. State of Tennessee, No. 2. Rhea County Criminal Docket, September Term, 1925, 152 Tenn. 424 (1925), ACLUR, reel 38, vol. 274 (hereafter Scopes Supreme Court Brief), 78 (quoting Bryan). Although his views on biblical literalism helped to secure the bill's passage, Bryan advised a Tennessee senator not to include a penalty provision. Ginger, *Six Days,* 5–6.

32. Larson, *Summer,* 135 (quoting Bryan).

33. Lilienthal, "Darrow," 417.

34. "The Teaching of Evolution," *Federation Bulletin,* December 16, 1922, 80; Larson, *Summer,* 116.

35. Scopes Supreme Court Brief, 64. For example, Scopes's lawyers argued that "the Legislature might say that chemistry should not be taught, but if chemistry is to be taught, the Legislature could not make it a crime to teach that H_2O make water." Ibid. Article XI, Section 12 of the Tennessee constitution made it "the duty of the general assembly . . . to cherish literature and science."

36. Tenn. Code Ann. 27 (1925); *The World's Most Famous Court Trial: Tennessee Evolution Case: A Word-for-Word Report of the Famous Court Test of the Tennessee Anti-Evolution Act, at Dayton, July 10 to 21, 1925* (Cincinnati, 1925) (hereafter Scopes Trial Testimony), 300.

37. Scopes Trial Testimony, 304 ("fool religion"), 301 ("as good"); Arthur Garfield Hays, "The Strategy of the Scopes Defense," *Nation,* August 5, 1925, 332; "Final Scenes Dramatic," *NYT,* July 22, 1925.

38. Scopes Trial Testimony, 305 ("man descended"); "The Tennessee Case: Complete Text of the Last and Greatest Speech of William Jennings Bryan," ACLUR, reel 38, vol. 274.

39. "Final Scenes Dramatic," *NYT.*

40. Larson, *Summer,* 206–207, 125.

41. Arthur Garfield Hays, address to Rand School, 31 August 1925, AGHP, box 31, folder 7; Larson, *Summer,* 207.

42. "ACLU Statement on Civil Liberty Situation in America at Present," 29 August 1925, ACLUR, reel 41, vol. 285; Clarence Darrow to Forrest Bailey, 4 September 1925, ACLUR, reel 38, vol. 274.

43. Forrest Bailey to Charles H. Strong, 12 August 1925, ACLUR, reel 38, vol. 274 ("Darrow personality"); Forrest Bailey to George W. Rappleyea, 10 August 1925, ACLUR, reel 38, vol. 274 ("chills"); Forrest Bailey to

Arthur Garfield Hays, 6 January 1926, ACLUR, reel 44, vol. 299 (describing Frankfurter's preference for Tennessee lawyers); Walter Nelles to Arthur Garfield Hays, undated, ACLUR, reel 38, vol. 274 ("popular"); Forrest Bailey to Clarence Darrow, 14 September 1925, ACLUR, reel 38, vol. 274. Nelles declined to participate in *Scopes* because he was engaged in an "injunction job" for the American Fund for Public Service (see Chapter 6). Walter Nelles to Samuel Rosensohn, 18 June 1925, University of Minnesota Clarence Darrow Digital Collection, available at http:// darrow.law.umn.edu/documents/Walter_Nelles_ltr.pdf. In apparent confirmation of Frankfurter's concerns, the state's reply brief disparaged "the lawyers for Scopes who come out of New York." Reply Brief and Argument for the State of Tennessee, Scopes v. State, 152 Tenn. 424 (1925) (hereafter Scopes Reply Brief), 61.

44. Clarence Darrow to Forrest Bailey, 4 September 1925, ACLUR, reel 38, vol. 274 (on local counsel); letter to Felix Frankfurter, 10 November 1926, ACLUR, reel 44, vol. 299 (describing positions of various members of the ACLU leadership at October 1926 meeting to discuss potential appeal to Supreme Court); Ginger, *Six Days*, 198 ("I am not," quoting Hays). Ernst thought it would be a tactical error to force Darrow to withdraw, and Bailey agreed. By this time, Hays and Darrow were working closely together to defend Ossian Sweet against murder charges in Michigan.

45. John T. Scopes to Forrest Bailey, 23 October 1925, ACLUR, reel 38, vol. 274 (relaying speculation about delay); G. W. Rappleyea to Forrest Bailey, 7 August 1925, ACLUR, reel 38, vol. 274.

46. "Butler Denounces 'New Barbarians,'" *NYT,* June 4, 1925; "New Evolution Fights Brew: Teachers Band for Defense," Daily Science News Bulletin No. 203A, 3 January 1927, ACLUR, reel 44, vol. 299 (on AAUP); Blewett Lee, "Anti-Evolution Laws Unconstitutional," *ABA Journal* 11 (1925): 417. The ACLU-sponsored committee included Princeton president John Grier Hibben, Harvard's president emeritus Charles W. Eliot, and David Starr Jordan, who had delivered antiwar speeches for the AUAM during the world war. On Jordan and the AAUM, see Timothy Reese Cain, *Establishing Academic Freedom: Politics, Principles, and the Development of Core Values* (New York, 2012), 55.

47. Charles E. Hughes, "Liberty and Law," *ABA Journal* 11 (1925): 563–568, 564 (presidential address, September 2, 1925).

48. Ibid., 566; "Association Holds Memorable Meeting at Detroit," *ABA Journal* 11 (1925): 569–571, 573, 599–614, 569.

49. Bartels v. Iowa, 262 U.S. 404, 412 (1923) (Holmes, J., dissenting in *Meyer* as well as *Bartels*); Meyer v. Nebraska, 262 U.S. 390, 401 (1923); Pierce v. Society of Sisters, 268 U.S. 510, 534 (1925).

50. Pierce, 268 U.S. at 535.

51. George M. Marsden, *The Soul of the American University: From Protestant Establishment to Established Nonbelief* (New York, 1994), 327 (on Bryan and the Butler Act); Scopes Supreme Court Brief, 30 (quoting A. Thomas Stewart).

52. Scopes Supreme Court Brief, 69.

53. Ibid., 65, 66.

54. Argument of Arthur Garfield Hays in the Supreme Court of Tennessee, 31 May 1926, AGHP, box 31, folder 7, 12–14, 20; "The Conduct of the Scopes Trial," *New Republic*, August 19, 1925, 332–333.

55. Scopes Reply Brief, 80; Argument of Arthur Garfield Hays in the Supreme Court of Tennessee, 31 May 1926, AGHP, box 31, folder 7, 721, 21.

56. Scopes v. Tennessee, 154 Tenn. 105, 119 (1927). The plurality opinion was written by Chief Justice Grafton Green. Justice Alexander Chambliss concurred, though he would have confined the statute's prohibition to "materialistic" theories of evolution that explicitly denied any divine role. Ibid., 122 (Chambliss, J., concurring).

57. Ibid., 120.

58. Roger Baldwin, introduction to *American Civil Liberties Union Annual Reports,* vol. 1 (New York, 1970), xx. On the legacy of the trial, and its reimagining during the 1930s and after, see Larson, *Summer,* 222–224.

59. Forrest Bailey to Noah Cooper, 15 June 1925, ACLUR, reel 38, vol. 274. Representative ACLU assurances include telegram from ACLU to Noah W. Cooper, 11 June 1925, ACLUR, reel 38, vol. 274; "ACLU Statement on Civil Liberty Situation in America at Present," 29 August 1925, ACLUR, reel 41, vol. 285. See also Ginger, *Six Days,* 202.

60. "American Conditions and Historical Review," *New York Legislative Documents,* vol. 18 (Albany, 1921) (hereafter Lusk Committee Report), 1982; Roger Baldwin to John T. Scopes, 10 August 1926, ACLUR, reel 44, vol. 299; Clarence Darrow to Forrest Bailey, 9 June 1926, ACLUR, reel 44, vol. 299.

61. G. W. Rappleyea to A. M. Wickwire, president, Cumberland Coal and Iron Co., 14 August 1925, ACLUR, reel 38, vol. 274 (in response to *Iron Trade Review*); Brief for Plaintiffs-in-Error, New Jersey Court of Errors and Appeals, State of New Jersey v. Butterworth, 104 N.J.L. 579 (1928), ACLUR, reel 58, vol. 346, 36; ACLU, *The Fight for Civil Liberty, 1927–1928* (New York, 1928), 49.

62. Roger Baldwin to James P. Cannon, 26 May 1926, ACLUR, reel 46, vol. 303; Roger Baldwin, "Civil Liberties in the United States," fall 1926, ACLUR, reel 46, vol. 303 ("Libertarians"); ACLU, "The Tennessee Evolution Case," July 1925, ACLUR, reel 44, vol. 299; Roger Baldwin, "Civil Liberties in the United States" ("growth of intolerance").

63. ACLU press release, 16 May 1927, ACLUM, reel 1; Zechariah Chafee Jr., draft address to Old So. Church, 12 May 1925, ZCP, reel 26; Leon Whipple, *Our Ancient Liberties: The Story of the Origin and Meaning of Civil and Religious Liberty in the United States* (New York, 1927), 146.

64. Theodore Schroeder to Roger Baldwin, 27 November 1917, ACLUR, reel 1, vol. 3; Roger Baldwin to Theodore Schroeder, 7 December 1917, ACLUR, reel 1, vol. 3; Lusk Committee Report, 1982; "Civil Liberty and the Courts: Obscenity and Political Opinions," ACLU bulletin 63, November 1928, ACLUM, reel 2.

65. Oswald Garrison Villard, review of *City Lawyer,* by Arthur Garfield Hays, *Harvard Law Review* 56 (1942): 333–336, 336; Fred Rodell, "Morris Ernst: New York's Unlawyerlike Liberal Lawyer Is the Censor's Enemy, the President's Friend," *Life,* February 21, 1944, 97–98, 107; ACLU bulletin 325, 18 October 1928, ACLUM, reel 1; ACLU bulletin 391, 14 February 1930, ACLUM, reel 2.

66. Circular, "Is Liberalism a Menace," MWDP, reel 22, file 477 (arguing that "the solution of our economic problems must be accomplished by education and law, not by revolution"); John Haynes Holmes to Morris Ernst, 16 January 1940, MLEP, box 45, folder 3 ("squeamishness"). As was customary during this period, Robert Gordon, "The Legal Profession," in *Looking Back at Law's Century,* ed. Austin Sarat, Bryant Garth, and Robert A. Kagan (Ithaca, NY, 2002), 288–336, 319–320, both Hays and Ernst maintained private law practices in addition to their civil liberties work. As Jews, Ernst and Hays had reason to replace religious moralism with a secular worldview. See generally David A. Hollinger, *Science, Jews, and Secular Culture: Studies in Mid-Twentieth Century American Intellectual History* (Princeton, NJ, 1996).

67. Morris L. Ernst and William Seagle, *To the Pure . . . A Study of Obscenity and the Censor* (New York, 1928).

68. Arthur Garfield Hays to Mary Ware Dennett, 21 May 1926, MWDP, reel 21, file 441; Morris Ernst to Mary Ware Dennett, 30 August 1928, MWDP, reel 23, file 485; ACLU executive committee minutes, 29 April 1929, ACLUM, reel 2. The Comstock Act, 17 Stat. 598 (1873), also prohibited the circulation of contraceptives and abortifacients themselves. In 1908, it was amended to add materials "tending to incite arson, murder, or assassination." On the *Dennett* case, see John M. Craig, "'The Sex Side of Life': The Obscenity Trials of Mary Ware Dennett," *Frontiers* 15 (1995): 145–166; Laura M. Weinrib, "The Sex Side of Civil Liberties: *United States v. Dennett* and the Changing Face of Free Speech," *Law and History Review* 30 (2012): 325–386; Constance M. Chen, *The Sex Side of*

Life: Mary Ware Dennett's Pioneering Battle for Birth Control and Sex Education (New York, 1997).

69. Mary Ware Dennett to Rae Morris, 9 May 1929, MWDP, reel 21, file 449; memorandum in support of motion to quash indictment, United States v. Dennett, 39 F.2d 564 (2nd Cir. 1930), 4, Second Circuit case file 10712, record group 276, NARA NE, 4 ("complete"); Mary Ware Dennett to Florence Garvin, 17 August 1929, MWDP, reel 21, file 436 (retaliation); Brief for Appellant, United States v. Dennett, 39 F.2d 564 (2nd Cir. 1930), 59, Second Circuit case file 10712, record group 276, NARA NE (hereafter Dennett Brief), 59. On the social hygiene movement, see Kristin Luker, "Sex, Social Hygiene, and the State: The Double-Edged Sword of Social Reform," *Theory and Society* 27 (1998): 601–634.

70. Dennett Brief, 51–52; United States v. Dennett, 39 F.2d 564, 569 (2nd Cir. 1930); Roth v. United States, 354 U.S. 476, 489 (1957). The Supreme Court adopted the *Hicklin* test in *United States v. Bennett*, 16 Blatch. 338 (1879), upholding a conviction for mailing a pamphlet advocating the legalization of prostitution. Its name derived from *Regina v. Hicklin*, L. R. 3 Q. B. 360, 371, 8 Eng. Rul. Cas. 60 (1868).

71. ACLU press bulletin 339, 24 January 1929, ACLUM, reel 2 (announcing defense committee); ACLU press release, 14 November 1929, ACLUM, reel 2; Lewis Gannett, "Books and Other Things," *Tribune*, March 20, 1930. For an analysis of the press coverage, see Dolores Flamiano, "'The Sex Side of Life' in the News: Mary Ware Dennett's Obscenity Case, 1929–1930," *Journalism History* 25 (Summer 1999): 64–74.

72. ACLU, *The Prosecution of Mary Ware Dennett for "Obscenity": Who Determines Obscenity* (New York, June 1929), 8 ("whole method"); Forrest Bailey, letter to the editor, 23 May 1929, ACLUM, reel 2 ("sex subjects"); NCFC press release, 2 July 1931, ACLUM, reel 3 ("drive"). By the time the Dennett defense fund was depleted, censorship work was well established in the ACLU's program, and the board found alternative means of support. ACLU board minutes, 5 October 1931, ACLUM, reel 3. On the extension of activity, see executive committee to members of the national committee, 7 February 1929, ACLUR, reel 63, vol. 360; Roger Baldwin to the national committee, 5 April 1929, ACLUR, reel 63, vol. 360. The extension applied to books, plays, radio, and movies; rejected proposals are discussed in Chapter 6.

73. Dennett Brief, 61; ACLU bulletin 387, 16 January 1930, ACLUM, reel 2. Ernst and his associates would portray the materials at issue in the present case as comparatively unobjectionable. See, for example, Memorandum of Law Submitted on Behalf of the Defendants, People v. Brewer & Warren Inc. (N.Y. City Mag. Ct. 1930), MLEP, box 227, folder 5.

74. United States v. Schwimmer, 279 U.S. 644, 654–655 (1929) ("freedom"); "Mrs. Dennett Goes on Trial Today," *NYT,* March 6, 1929 ("sexual"); Mary Ware Dennett, "'Married Love' and Censorship," *Nation,* May 27, 1931, 579–580 ("varie[d]").

75. ACLU news release, 7 February 1929, ACLUM, reel 2; ACLU news release, 24 March 1931, ACLUM, reel 3 (describing Mastic Bill); ACLU news release, 29 March 1931, ACLUM, reel 3 (broader campaign).

76. See, for example, Motion to Set Aside Verdict, in Transcript of Record, 99, United States v. Dennett, 39 F.2d 564 (2nd Cir. 1930), Second Circuit Case File 10712, Record Group 276, NARA NE ("The mere ban of a bureaucrat in Washington is no token or indication of obscenity").

77. ACLU bulletin 396, 19 March 1930, ACLUM, reel 2. On the ACLU's role in the tariff bill debate, working with Senator Bronson Cutting, see Christopher M. Finan, *From the Palmer Raids to the Patriot Act: A History of the Fight for Free Speech in America* (Boston, 2007), 104.

78. Alexander Lindey to G. P. Putnam's Sons, 24 September 1930, MLEP, box 369, folder 2 ("public opinion"); Tariff Act of 1930, 46 Stat. 688 (1930); United States v. One Obscene Book, Entitled "Married Love," 48 F.2d 821 (S.D.N.Y. 1931); United States v. One Book Entitled "Contraception," 51 F.2d 525 (S.D.N.Y. 1931).

79. Gordon W. Moss to Arthur Garfield Hays, 18 August 1931, ACLUR, reel 86, vol. 503 ("take only"); Gordon W. Moss to Sidney J. Abelson, 7 April 1931, ACLUR, reel 86, vol. 503 ("old classics"). By 1935, a *Harvard Law Review* article cited Dennett for the conclusion that "under any 'test,' it seems clear that serious medico-scientific works are not within the obscenity ban." "Recent Cases: Obscenity, Test of Obscene Literature," *Harvard Law Review* 48 (January 1935): 519–520, 519.

80. United States v. One Book Called "Ulysses," 5 F. Supp. 182, 184 (S.D.N.Y 1933); Morris Ernst to Alexander Lindey, office memorandum, 12 August 1932, MLEP, box 366, folder 2 (on Woolsey); Statement by Morris L. Ernst upon the Handing Down of Judge Woolsey's Opinion in the Ulysses Case, undated, MLEP, box 366, folder 4 ("intolerance"). United States attorney George Medalie was sympathetic to the book but felt obligated to prosecute. On the relationship between the rise of the administrative state and the construction of individual rights in the Prohibition cases, see Robert Post, "Federalism, Positive Law, and the Emergence of the American Administrative State: Prohibition in the Taft Court Era," *William and Mary Law Review* 48 (2006): 1–182.

81. United States v. One Book Entitled Ulysses by James Joyce, 72 F.2d 705 (2d Cir. 1934); Roger Baldwin and Morris Ernst, "The New Deal and Civil Liberties" (radio debate over the Blue Network of NBC), 27 January

1934, ACLUR, reel 109, vol. 717; Leo M. Alpert, "Judicial Censorship of Obscene Literature," *Harvard Law Review* 52 (November 1938): 40–76, 41 ("New Deal").

82. Hazel C. Benjamin, "Lobbying for Birth Control," *Public Opinion Quarterly* 2 (January 1938): 48–60, 49; Leslie J. Reagan, *When Abortion Was a Crime: Women, Medicine, and Law in the United States, 1867–1973* (Berkeley, 1997), 132–136.

83. Morris Ernst, "Sex Wins in America," *Nation*, August 10, 1932, 123 ("nullification"); United States v. One Package, 86 F.2d 737 (2nd Cir. 1936); David J. Garrow, *Liberty and Sexuality: The Right to Privacy and the Making of Roe v. Wade* (New York, 1994), 42 (quoting Sanger). *United States v. One Package* was decided as a matter of statutory interpretation and applied only to the importation of contraceptives.

84. Samuel Walker, *In Defense of American Liberties: A History of the ACLU* (New York, 1990), 69 (lawyers), 81 (quoting Frankfurter); Walter Nelles, "Objections to Labor Injunctions," in *Civil Liberty*, ed. Edith M. Phelps (New York, 1927), 156 ("Judges"); ACLU, *1927–1928*, 6.

85. "Scopes," *New Republic*, 331; Larson, *Summer*, 122 (describing union responses).

86. Draft statement by the National Council on Freedom from Censorship, 16 July 1934, ACLUR, reel 105, vol. 678.

87. ACLU news release, April 1926, ACLUR, reel 46, vol. 303 ("Klan's," abstract of remarks by Baldwin); Roger Baldwin, "What Has Become of the Pre-war Radicals," 4 January 1926, ACLUR, reel 46, vol. 303 ("political"). Baldwin explained that the Russian Revolution had provoked the "propertied classes" to defend the status quo.

88. C. H. Scovell to Roger Baldwin, 20 October 1926, ACLUR, reel 46, vol. 303; Forrest Bailey to Robert Whitaker, 1 February 1926, ACLUR, reel 46, vol. 303.

89. Roger Baldwin to C. H. Scovell, 21 October 1926, ACLUR, reel 46, vol. 303; Roger Baldwin, draft speech, ACLUR, reel 46, vol. 303 (quoting *Gitlow v. New York*, 268 U.S. 652 [1925]).

90. Felix Frankfurter to Forrest Bailey, 10 January 1927, ACLUR, reel 50, vol. 319; ACLU, *The Fight for Civil Liberty: The Story of the Activities of the American Civil Liberties Union, 1928–1929* (New York, 1929), 3.

91. Harold Lord Varney, "The Civil Liberties Union," *American Mercury* 39 (December 1936): 385–399, 386 ("genuine"); Roger Baldwin to James P. Cannon (ILD), 26 May 1926, ACLUR, reel 46, vol. 303 ("not troubled").

6. Old Left, New Rights

1. ACLU press release, 21 May 1937, ACLUR, reel 143, vol. 978 ("how far"); Preliminary Report of the American Civil Liberties Union Temporary

Committee concerning the Supreme Court, ACLUR, reel 143, vol. 978 (hereafter Preliminary Report) ("widening").

2. ACLU, *The Fight for Civil Liberty, 1930–1931* (New York, 1931), 4 ("Negroes"); "The Worst Spots," *Civil Liberties Quarterly,* December 1931, 1 (decline in strikes and suppression); Stromberg v. California, 283 U.S. 359, 366 (1931) (quoting trial court); "In the Courts," *Civil Liberties Quarterly,* June 1931, 2. The ACLU handled the *Stromberg* case jointly with the ILD.

3. ACLU, *1930–1931,* 22.

4. Ibid. ("focused"); Felix Frankfurter and Nathan Greene, *The Labor Injunction* (New York, 1930); "Arguments Supporting the Draft of a Bill Declaring Public Policy to Labor and Abolishing 'Yellow Dog' Contracts," undated, PWP, folder "Committee on Labor Injunctions" ("liberty"); "Memorandum on the Proposed Injunction Bill," January 1932, ACLUR, reel 90, vol. 536 ("which involve"); "Monthly Bulletin for Action," January 1931, ACLUR, reel 79, vol. 444. On the Garland Fund's role in the early ACLU, NAACP, and radical causes, see Gloria Garrett Samson, *The American Fund for Public Service: Charles Garland and Radical Philanthropy, 1922–1941* (Westport, CT, 1996).

5. ACLU, *Sweet Land of Liberty, 1931–32* (New York, 1932), 16; William Green to Roger Baldwin, 29 December 1933, ACLUR, reel 99, vol. 615D.

6. Committee on Labor Injunctions, "The Federal Anti-injunction Bill," February 1932, ACLUR, reel 90, vol. 536.

7. Thomas J. Norton, "Further Light on Pending Anti-injunction Measure," *ABA Journal* 17 (1931): 59–62, 62 ("trial"), 59 ("so-called").

8. Morris Ernst, "Statement Prepared for Jerome Davis on the Labor Injunction," 19 January 1929, ACLUR, reel 63, vol. 360; ACLU, *The Fight for Civil Liberties: The Story of the Activities of the American Civil Liberties Union, 1928–1929* (New York, 1929), 18 ("most extensive").

9. Ibid., 19; Near v. Minnesota, 283 U.S. 697, 719 (1931). On the American Newspaper Publishers Association, see Sam Lebovic, *Free Speech and Unfree News: The Paradox of Press Freedom in America* (Cambridge, MA, 2016).

10. Near, 283 U.S. at 716, 721.

11. Ibid.

12. Ibid., 735 (Butler, J., dissenting). *Truax v. Corrigan,* 257 U.S. 312 (1921), held that the availability of injunctive relief was constitutionally mandated under the Equal Protection (rather than the Due Process) Clause of the Fourteenth Amendment. See Chapter 4.

13. John Ryan to Roger Baldwin, 15 December 1931, ACLUR, reel 80, vol. 451.

14. Roger Baldwin to Robert Whitaker, 6 April 1934, ACLUR, reel 105, vol. 678.

15. ACLU, *A Year's Fight for Free Speech: The Work of the American Civil Liberties Union from Sept. 1921 to Jan. 1923* (New York, 1923), 27 (Hays's use of injunction); ACLU executive committee minutes, 26 October 1925, ACLUR, reel 40, vol. 281 (describing study); Arthur Garfield Hays, Clement Wood, and McCalister Coleman, *Don't Tread on Me: A Study of Aggressive Legal Tactics for Labor* (New York, 1928). For a discussion of labor's use of injunctions, see William E. Forbath, *Law and the Shaping of the American Labor Movement* (Cambridge, MA, 1991), 118–127.

16. ACLU, *Legal Tactics for Labor's Rights* (New York, 1930), 8–9, 4–5.

17. Ibid., 17; "Injunctions to Protect Civil Liberties," ACLUR, reel 72, vol. 395 ("almost like"). See also Walter Nelles, "Objections to Labor Injunctions," in *Civil Liberty,* ed. Edith M. Phelps (New York, 1927), 156.

18. Roger Baldwin to William Pickens, 2 April 1934, ACLUR, reel 107, vol. 698.

19. Walter Nelles to Arthur Garfield Hays, 26 January 1926, ACLUR, reel 22, vol. 159A.

20. ACLU news release, 26 February 1926, ACLUM, reel 1 ("censorship"); ACLU news release, April 1926, ACLUR, reel 46, vol. 303 (abstract of remarks by Baldwin) ("State Department").

21. David J. Saposs, "The American Labor Movement since the War," *Quarterly Journal of Economics* 49 (1935): 236–254, 239. In his classic 1935 account, Saposs, who served as chief economist of the NLRB from 1935 to 1940, argued that labor had accomplished the most during "periods of widespread government intervention in industrial relations." Ibid.

22. James Gray Pope, "The Thirteenth Amendment versus the Commerce Clause: Labor and the Shaping of American Constitutional Law, 1921–1958," *Columbia Law Review* 102 (2002): 1–123, 1, 7–17, 61–65; Christopher Tomlins, *The State and the Unions: Labor Relations, Law, and the Organized Labor Movement in America, 1880–1960* (New York, 1985); ACLU, *Land of Pilgrim's Pride* (New York, 1933), 16; Cletus Daniel, *The ACLU and the Wagner Act: An Inquiry into the Depression-Era Crisis of American Liberalism* (Ithaca, NY, 1980), 34; David Montgomery, *The Fall of the House of Labor: The Workplace, the State, and American Labor Activism, 1865–1925* (New York, 1987), 357 (tracing the origins of exclusive bargaining to Woodrow Wilson's belief that "employers should be encouraged to negotiate with legitimate unions and to shun the IWW and other groups deemed 'outlaw' by the AFL").

23. ACLU, *1928–1929,* 27 ("objects," reporting assessment of Southern California Branch); Roger Baldwin to James P. Cannon, 26 May 1926, ACLUR, reel 46, vol. 303.

24. Jacob H. Rubin, "Russia Ended Socialism for Me," *Nation's Business,*
February 1924, 13; Roger Baldwin to George Hooker, 26 May 1926,
ACLUR, reel 46, vol. 303. On the AFL, free speech, and anti-
Communism, see Jennifer Luff, *Commonsense Anticommunism: Labor
and Civil Liberties between the World Wars* (Chapel Hill, NC, 2012).

25. William F. Dunne, editor, *Daily Worker,* to Roger Baldwin,
7 March 1925, ACLUR, reel 41, vol. 285; Earl Browder to Roger Baldwin,
12 March 1925, ACLUR, reel 58, vol. 346; statement, ACLUR, reel 10,
vol. 678 ("legalistic"); Roger Baldwin to William F. Dunne,
11 March 1925, ACLUR, reel 58, vol. 346; "How Liberalism United with
Assassins against the Soviet Union," *Daily Worker,* February 5, 1930.

26. On Gastonia, see ACLU, *Justice—North Carolina Style: The Record of
the Year's Struggle for Unions in Gastonia and Marion, April 1929 to
April 1930* (New York, 1930); ACLU, *The Story of Civil Liberty, 1929–
1930* (New York, 1930), 15. The Gastonia strikers were subject to brutal
vigilante violence. Hays, volunteering his services for the ILD, defended
the seven strikers at trial. Because the prosecution emphasized the
religious, political, and economic views of the defendants, the ACLU
agreed to assist on appeal. The bail fund is discussed in ACLU to friends,
November 1930, ACLUR, reel 71, vol. 384; ACLU, *1930–1931,* 5, 33;
Statement of the Civil Liberties Union concerning Bail in Communist
Cases, 9 October 1930, ACLUR, reel 78, vol. 432; William Foster to
Baldwin, 31 October 1930, ACLUR, reel 78, vol. 432.

27. ACLU, *1930–1931,* 39; Roger Baldwin to Alfred Wagenknecht, 24 January
1929, ACLUR, reel 63, vol. 360; ACLU, *1928–1929,* 15 ("hopeless");
ACLU, *1930–1931,* 39 ("class").

28. Executive committee to members of the national committee, 7 February
1929, ACLUR, reel 63, vol. 360; Felix Frankfurter to Roger Baldwin,
16 February 1929, ACLUR, reel 63, vol. 360; Roger Baldwin to William
Patterson, 10 January 1934, ACLUR, reel 105, vol. 678 ("negro"); Thomas
Hardwick to Roger Baldwin, 28 July 1930, ACLUR, reel 71, vol. 384
("political"); Roger Baldwin to Thomas Hardwick, 2 August 1930,
ACLUR, reel 71, vol. 384 ("no stand"). In 1929, the national committee
rejected involvement with the rights of criminal defendants, civil liberties
in areas under American military control, compulsory military training,
and the validity of the draft. Notably, the board did not propose greater
participation in Prohibition, "beyond protesting against illegal methods
which can only too readily be transferred to labor and radical cases."
Roger Baldwin to A. J. Muste, 20 February 1929, ACLUR, reel 63, vol.
360; Roger Baldwin to the national committee, 5 April 1929, ACLUR,
reel 63, vol. 360. Baldwin did, however, arrange for Walter Pollak and

Zechariah Chafee Jr. (along with Carl Stern) to draft Lawlessness in Law Enforcement for the Wickersham Commission, which was formed under Hoover in 1929.

29. "Ernst, Hays, Morris on NAACP Committee," *Afro American,* November 28, 1931, 10; Mark V. Tushnet, *Making Civil Rights Law: Thurgood Marshall and the Supreme Court, 1936–1961* (New York, 1994), 68 (Frankfurter); Roger Baldwin to Thomas Hardwick, 2 August 1930, ACLUR, reel 71, vol. 384 ("two"); ACLU board minutes, 13 July 1931, ACLUM, reel 3 (resignation); William Patterson to Roger Baldwin, 9 January 1934, ACLUR, reel 105, vol. 678 (ascribing position to Baldwin). On the NAACP's antilynching work, see Megan Ming Francis, *Civil Rights and the Making of the Modern American State* (New York, 2014).

30. *Guide to the Microfilm Edition of Papers of the NAACP,* part 6, *The Scottsboro Case, 1931–1950* (Frederick, MD, 1987), xii–xiii ("instruments"); Powell v. Alabama, 287 U.S. 45 (1932); Patterson v. Alabama, 294 U.S. 600 (1935). In addition, the ACLU dispatched an observer, Hollace Ransdell, to report on the case. Hollace Ransdell, "Report on the Scottsboro, Ala., Case," 27 May 1931, ILDP, reel 13. On Scottsboro, see James Goodman, *Stories of Scottsboro* (New York, 1994). On the accommodations and trade-offs adopted by radical black lawyers in the 1930s in the interest of a successful legal strategy, see Kenneth Mack, *Representing the Race: The Creation of the Civil Rights Lawyer* (Cambridge, MA, 2012).

31. Daniel, *ACLU,* 52 ("friends," quoting Baldwin); ACLU, "Proposals for Restoring or Protecting Civil Rights through Federal Action," 16 February 1933, ACLUR, reel 97, vol. 608 (proposals); Harry Ward, Helen Phelps Stokes, James Maurer, Arthur Garfield Hays, and Roger Baldwin to Franklin D. Roosevelt, 16 February 1933, ACLUR, reel 99, vol. 618 (proposals); Baldwin to Harold L. Ickes, 28 February 1933, ACLUR, reel 97, vol. 608 ("half a dozen").

32. Roger Baldwin and Morris Ernst, "The New Deal and Civil Liberties" (radio debate over the Blue Network of NBC), 27 January 1934, ACLUR, reel 109, vol. 717; Harry Ward and Arthur Garfield Hays to labor organizations, 14 July 1933, ACLUR, reel 99, vol. 618. See generally James A. Gross, *The Making of the National Labor Relations Board: A Study in Economics, Politics, and the Law* (Albany, 1974), 7–40.

33. Robert D. McFadden, "Corliss Lamont Dies at 93; Socialist Battled McCarthy," *NYT,* April 28, 1995; Baldwin and Ernst, "New Deal and Civil Liberties." William B. Spofford and Robert W. Dunn were also among the leftists.

34. Joseph Schlossberg to Roger Baldwin, 2 April 1934, ACLUR, reel 107, vol. 698 (referencing previous correspondence); Edward F. McGrady, address at U.S. Chamber of Commerce annual meeting, 27–29 April 1937,

CCUSR, box 31; Roger Baldwin to Paul Furnas, 12 January 1935, ACLUR, reel 115, vol. 772.

35. Baldwin and Ernst, "New Deal and Civil Liberties."

36. Roger Baldwin, address at ACLU annual meeting, 19 February 1934, ACLUR, reel 105, vol. 678 ("employers"); Roger Baldwin, "Coming Struggle for Freedom," 12 November 1934, ACLUR, reel 109, vol. 717 ("always an instrument"); Harry Ward to Franklin D. Roosevelt, 28 February 1934, FDRP, official file 2111 (company unions); Baldwin and Ernst, "New Deal and Civil Liberties" ("governmental").

37. Roger Baldwin, address at ACLU annual meeting, 19 February 1934, ACLUR, reel 105, vol. 678 ("against the extension"); Roger Baldwin, "Civil Liberties under the New Deal," 24 October 1934, ACLUR, reel 109, vol. 717 ("channels"); ACLU, *Liberty under the New Deal: The Record for 1933–34* (New York, 1934), 3.

38. Gross, *Making*, 41–72.

39. Harry Ward and Roger Baldwin, for the board of directors, to David I. Walsh, 20 March 1934, ACLUR, reel 107, vol. 698. Created in December 1933, the Committee on Workers' and Farmers' Rights sought to generate liberal opposition to New Deal labor policy. Roger Baldwin to friends, 2 December 1933, ACLUR, reel 96, vol. 598.

40. Gross, *Making*, 64–72; Charles J. Morris, *The Blue Eagle at Work: Reclaiming Democratic Rights in the American Workplace* (Ithaca, NY, 2005), 41–55; Harry Ward and Arthur Garfield Hays to senators, 5 June 1934, ACLUR, reel 107, vol. 698.

41. Statement of the Committee of Workers' Rights, 21 July 1934, ILDP, reel 19, box 21; United States v. Weirton Steel Corp., 10 F. Supp. 55 (D. Del. 1935); Peter H. Irons, *The New Deal Lawyers* (Princeton, NJ, 1982), 225 (quoting Biddle). *Schechter Poultry Corporation v. United States*, 295 U.S. 495 (1935), decided in May, thwarted an early effort by the Department of Justice to enforce an order issued under the NIRA. See Gross, *Making*, 33–40; Irons, *New Deal Lawyers*, 216–220. On labor militancy in the early New Deal, see Irving Bernstein, *Turbulent Years: A History of the American Worker, 1933–1941* (Boston, 1969).

42. Announcement of the Conference on Civil Liberties under the New Deal, 28 October 1934, ACLUR, reel 110, vol. 719 ("protect rights"); Program of the Conference on Civil Liberties under the New Deal, 8–9 December 1934, ACLUR, reel 110, vol. 721; ACLU press bulletin 641, 30 November 1934, ACLUR, reel 110, vol. 719.

43. Walter White to Roger Baldwin, 7 January 1935, ACLUR, reel 117, vol. 785 (antilynching legislation); "Memorandum of Bills Proposed for Discussion, Conference on Civil Liberties under the New Deal," ACLUR, reel 110, vol. 719; Louis G. Caldwell, "Excerpts from 'Freedom on the

Air,'" Conference on Civil Liberties and the New Deal, ACLUR, reel 110, vol. 721; ACLU press bulletin 643, 14 December 1934, ACLUR, reel 110, vol. 721 ("showed surprising").

44. "Memorandum of Bills Proposed for Discussion, Conference on Civil Liberties under the New Deal," ACLUR, reel 110, vol. 719; Daniel, *ACLU*, 94–95; minutes of the Conference on Civil Liberties under the New Deal, ACLUR, reel 110, vol. 721 ("vigorously").

45. Resolutions, Conference on Civil Liberties under the New Deal, 9 December 1934, ACLUR, reel 110, vol. 721 ("no illusions"); ACLU press bulletin 646, 11 January 1935, ACLUR, reel 117, vol. 784; ACLUR, reel 117, vol. 784 (responses to proposed legislation).

46. Robert Wagner to Roger Baldwin, 24 January 1935, ACLUR, reel 116, vol. 780. On the drafting and legislative history of the Wagner Act, see Irving Bernstein, *The New Deal Collective Bargaining Policy* (Berkeley, 1950); Gross, *Making*, 130–148.

47. Melvyn Dubofsky, *The State and Labor in Modern America* (Chapel Hill, NC, 1994), 130 (describing comments by Edward P. Costigan).

48. Daniel, *ACLU*, 97 ("fellow traveler," quoting Baldwin); Frankfurter and Greene, *Labor Injunction.*

49. Roger Baldwin to Robert Wagner, 1 April 1935, ACLUR, reel 116, vol. 780; Roger Baldwin to David I. Walsh, 30 March 1935, GJP, General Correspondence, box 3, folder "ACLU: Labor"; John W. Edelman to Roger Baldwin, ACLUR, reel 116, vol. 780 ("racial discrimination"); John P. Davis to Roger Baldwin, 25 January 1935, GJP, General Correspondence, box 3, folder "ACLU: Labor." On the exclusion of agricultural workers from New Deal labor policy, see Cletus E. Daniel, *Bitter Harvest: A History of California Farmworkers, 1870–1941* (Ithaca, NY, 1981), 173–178, 232–257. On race-based discrimination and the Wagner Act, see, for example, Paul Frymer, *Black and Blue: African Americans, the Labor Movement, and the Decline of the Democratic Party* (Princeton, NJ, 2008); Herbert Hill, *Black Labor and the American Legal System* (Washington, DC, 1977); Ira Katznelson, *Fear Itself: The New Deal and the Origins of Our Time* (New York, 2013); Sophia Z. Lee, *The Workplace Constitution from the New Deal to the New Right* (New York, 2014); Mark V. Tushnet, *The NAACP's Legal Strategy against Segregated Education, 1925–1950* (Chapel Hill, NC, 1987).

50. Robert F. Wagner to Roger Baldwin, 5 April 1935, ACLUR, reel 116, vol. 780.

51. Statement, ca. 1934, ACLUR, reel 10, vol. 678 ("that civil liberties"); Charles F. Amidon to Roger Baldwin, 27 April 1934, ACLUR, reel 105, vol. 678; Alexander Meiklejohn to Roger Baldwin, 20 May 1935, ACLUR, reel 116, vol. 780; letter from Arthur Garfield Hays, 7 May 1935, ACLUR,

reel 116, vol. 780. On the "problem of dependency" that plagued the "emancipatory project identified with constitutional rights consciousness" (that is, debate over "the appropriate quantity of protection that the federal government, as well as other structures of authority, ought to provide"), see Hendrik Hartog, "The Constitution of Aspiration and 'The Rights That Belong to Us All,'" *Journal of American History* 74 (1987): 1013–1034, 1019–1020.

52. Zechariah Chafee Jr., review of *Losing Liberty Judiciously,* by Thomas James Norton, *Nation,* December 26, 1928, 719; Leon Whipple, *Our Ancient Liberties: The Story of the Origin and Meaning of Civil and Religious Liberty in the United States* (New York, 1927), 139.

53. John Dewey, "Liberalism and Civil Liberties," *Social Frontier* (February 1936): 137–138, 138 ("social control"); John Dewey, "Authority and Social Change," in *Authority and the Individual* (Cambridge, MA, 1937), 184–190 (freedom); Francis Biddle to Roger Baldwin, 17 April 1935, ACLUR, reel 116, vol. 780.

54. Roger Baldwin, "Civil Liberties under the New Deal," 24 October 1934, ACLUR, reel 109, vol. 717 ("liberty"); Roger Baldwin, "The Main Issues of Civil Liberties under the New Deal," 8 December 1934, ACLUR, reel 110, vol. 721 ("human rights"); Roger Baldwin to Robert Wagner, 1 April 1935, ACLUR, reel 116, vol. 780 ("reactionary").

55. Francis Biddle to Roger Baldwin, 17 April 1935, ACLUR, reel 116, vol. 780 ("too damned"); Isadore Katz, John Edelman, and David Schlick to Roger Baldwin, 22 May 1935, ACLUR, reel 116, vol. 780 ("fight against").

56. Roger Baldwin to members of the national committee and local branches, 8 May 1935, ACLUR, reel 115, vol. 772; ACLU statement, 27 May 1935, ACLUR, reel 116, vol. 780; Robert Wagner to friends, 7 June 1935, ACLUR, reel 116, vol. 780.

57. Frymer, *Black and Blue,* 29 (NAACP). On Communists within the labor movement, see Bert Cochran, *Labor and Communism: The Conflict That Shaped American Unions* (Princeton, NJ, 1977). On the emergence of the CIO, see Melvyn Dubofsky and Warren Van Tyne, *John L. Lewis: A Biography* (New York, 1977); Robert H. Zieger, *The CIO: 1933–1955* (Chapel Hill, NC, 1997).

58. Senate Resolution 266, 74th Congress, June 6, 1936; Gardner Jackson to Roger Baldwin, 9 April 1936, GJP, box 42, folder "La Follette Civil Liberties" (conveying La Follette's surprise); Felix Frazer, investigator, to James A. Kinkead, 9 October 1936, "Violations of Free Speech and Rights of Labor," Sen 78A-F9, record group 46, NARA DC, box 4, folder "October 1936" ("the formation"). The resolution was motivated by the suppression of the Southern Tenant Farmers Union, an organization of

tenant farmers and sharecroppers in northeastern Arkansas. See generally Jerold Auerbach, *Labor and Liberty: The La Follette Committee and the New Deal* (Indianapolis, 1966).

59. Roger Baldwin to Robert La Follette Jr., 16 April 1936, ACLUR, reel 131, vol. 887; Auerbach, *Labor and Liberty,* 65 (quoting Madden). The ACLU initially urged the committee to investigate civil liberties abuses in other contexts as well, but the La Follette Committee limited its inquiry to labor relations. See, for example, Morris Ernst to Roger Baldwin, 9 April 1936, ACLUR, reel 131, vol. 887.

60. Felix Frazer to Byron Scott, 3 February 1937, "Violations of Free Speech and Rights of Labor," Sen 78A-F9, record group 46, NARA DC, box 5, folder "Feb. 1937"; Statement by Edwin S. Smith before Hearings of Subcommittee on Senate Resolution 266, 23 April 1936, ACLUR, reel 131, vol. 887.

61. Edwin S. Smith, "Civil Rights for Labor," address to Washington, DC, branch of ACLU, January 1938, ACLUR, reel 156, vol. 1078; Robert La Follette Jr., "Management, Too, Must Be Responsible," *National Lawyers Guild Quarterly* 1 (1937): 3–8, 4.

62. Roger Baldwin to Frederick Wright, 28 December 1937, ACLUR, reel 156, vol. 1078; J. Warren Madden, address to National Conference on Civil Liberties, 13 October 1939, GCP, box 86, folder 41.

63. "Professional Ethics Committee Rules Organization and Offer of National Lawyers Committee Not Unethical," *ABA Journal* 21 (1935): 776–778, 776, 778. On the American Liberty League, see Frederick Rudolph, "The American Liberty League, 1934–1940," *American Historical Review* 56 (October 1950): 19–33; George Wolfskill, *The Revolt of the Conservatives: A History of the American Liberty League* (Boston, 1962).

64. Carter v. Carter Coal Company, 298 U.S. 238 (1936); Gross, *Making,* 149–253; Irons, *New Deal Lawyers,* 201–271.

65. See generally Alan Brinkley, *End of Reform: New Deal Liberalism in Recession and War* (New York, 1995); Burt Solomon, *FDR v. the Constitution: The Court-Packing Fight and the Triumph of Democracy* (New York, 2009); Jeff Shesol, *Supreme Power: Franklin Roosevelt vs. the Supreme Court* (New York, 2010).

66. "Liberals Divided on Plan to Enlarge Supreme Court," *New York World-Telegram,* February 5, 1937; Robert M. La Follette Jr., radio address, 13 February 1937, ACLUR, reel 143, vol. 978; IJA, "Curbing the Courts," 1937, WGRP, box 19, folder 7. The guild distributed the IJA pamphlet in advance of a referendum on constitutional amendments at the first annual convention.

67. "Liberal Lawyers Form a New Guild," *NYT,* December 16, 1936; "Law Guild Is Seen in Clash with Bar," *NYT,* February 1, 1937 (committee); "The Bar Association Held Reactionary," *NYT,* December 23, 1936 (Ernst); National Lawyers Guild, "A Call to American Lawyers," ATVP, box 130, folder "National Lawyers Guild." On the National Lawyers Guild, see Ann Fagan Ginger and Eugene Tobin, eds., *The National Lawyers Guild: From Roosevelt through Reagan* (Philadelphia, 1988).

68. Victor S. Gettner to Lucille Milner, 30 March 1937, ACLUR, reel 142, vol. 969 ("dangerous"); National Lawyers Guild, resolutions adopted at the first annual convention, Washington, DC, 20–22 February 1937, GCP, box 80, folder 121.

69. De Jonge v. Oregon, 299 U.S. 353 (1937); "De Jonge Decision Upholds Free Speech," *Civil Liberties Quarterly,* March 1937, 1. Critics of the court thought that enthusiasm about *De Jonge* was misguided. For example, Louis Boudin to Osmond Fraenkel, 18 March 1937, ACLUR, reel 143, vol. 978.

70. "Talks—Special Supreme Court Edition Covering Broadcasts over the Columbia Network in February and March 1937," April 1937, Columbia Broadcasting System, Inc., New York, GCP, box 76, folder 36 (hereafter "Supreme Court Edition"), 142–146 (Holmes); Norman Thomas to Roger Baldwin, 25 February 1937, ACLUR, reel 142, vol. 969; "Supreme Court Edition," 162 ("a democracy").

71. "Supreme Court Edition," 162 ("the right"); Norman Thomas to Roger Baldwin, 25 February 1937, ACLUR, reel 142, vol. 969 ("flood"); William Fennell to Lucille Milner, 14 March 1937, ACLUR, reel 143, vol. 978 ("Have they").

72. Preliminary Report.

73. The Supreme Court's approach, articulated in *United States v. Carolene Products Company,* 304 U.S. 144, 152n4 (1938), is discussed in Chapter 7.

74. Preliminary Report (views of Walter Gellhorn); Edwin Borchard to Osmond Fraenkel, 4 February 1937, ACLUR, reel 143, vol. 978 ("expansion"); Morris L. Ernst, *The Ultimate Power* (Garden City, NY, 1937); Preliminary Report ("giving majorities"); Norman Thomas to Roger Baldwin, 25 February 1937, ACLUR, reel 142, vol. 969.

75. Osmond K. Fraenkel, *The Supreme Court and Civil Liberties: How the Court Has Protected the Bill of Rights* (New York, 1937); ACLU press release, 21 May 1937, ACLUR, reel 143, vol. 978; Preliminary Report ("so long").

76. For example, John Lord O'Brian, "The Menace of Administrative Law," 1929, ZCP, reel 25.

77. Archibald Stevenson, "Civil Liberty," radio talk over station WHN, 16 February 1935, ACLUR, reel 114, vol. 764; Rufus C. Harris, "What Next in American Law?" *American Law School Review* 8 (May 1936): 461–471, 471.

78. "Liberty of Expression in the Press, Radio, and Motion Pictures," Institute of Public Affairs, University of Virginia, 17 July 1936, GCP, series VIII, box 83, folder 53 (hereafter Panel Discussion), 31 ("You don't have"); annual meeting minutes, Chamber of Commerce of the United States, 2–4 May 1939, CCUSR, box 31, 395 ("American way"). For discussion of the American Newspaper Publishers Association and claims to press freedom, see Lebovic, *Unfree News.*

79. Panel Discussion, 27; Grosjean v. American Press Company, 297 U.S. 233 (1936). On the tax cases, see Jeremy K. Kessler, "The Early Years of First Amendment Lochnerism," *Columbia Law Review* 116 (forthcoming); Lebovic, *Unfree News.*

80. Panel Discussion, 36.

81. Merlin Hall Aylesworth, "The Listener Rules Broadcasting," *Nation's Business,* September 1929, 122 ("freedom of speech"); Louis G. Caldwell, "Excerpts from 'Freedom on the Air,'" Conference on Civil Liberties and the New Deal, ACLUR, reel 110, vol. 721; see also Louis G. Caldwell, "Freedom of Speech and Radio Broadcasting," *Annals of the American Academy of Political and Social Science* 177 (1935): 179–207. On Caldwell, see Daniel R. Ernst, *Tocqueville's Nightmare: The Administrative State Emerges in America, 1900–1940* (New York, 2014), 119.

82. Panel Discussion, 4. See also T. N. Carver, "What Liberties Shall We Fight For?," *Nation's Business,* March 1934, 13.

83. Albert Smith Faught, "Contempt of Federal Courts," *ABA Journal* 13 (1927): 636–637, 637 ("conservative members"); "Urges Citizens to Guard Rights from Congress," *Chicago Tribune,* April 16, 1936 ("one of"). On Black's role, see Gerald T. Dunne, *Hugo Black and the Judicial Revolution* (New York, 1977).

84. William Hard, "Looking On in Washington: Lobbyless Lawmaking," *Nation's Business,* February 1930, 78 ("propaganda"); "An Advertisement to the Business Man Who Wants to Know What the Chamber of Commerce of the U.S. Can Do for Him and His Firm," *Nation's Business,* December 1922, 53.

85. George Holden Tinkham, "Fear Helps Minorities Make Our Laws," *Nation's Business,* August 1931, 39 ("socialist"); "Meeting of Advisory Committee, NAM Committee on Public Relations," 17 March 1939, NAMP, box 112, folder "PR Advisory Committee 1939," 3 ("conservative viewpoint"); "De Propaganda Fide," *New York Herald-Tribune,* March 6, 1938 ("propaganda"); "Civil Liberty—For Whom?," *Cincinnati Times-Star,* March 3, 1938 ("interested").

86. Sherman Minton, address to American Press Society, 13 August 1938, GCP, box 80, folder 90 ("control[ling] thought"); open letter from Frank Gannett, ACLUR, reel 172, vol. 2100. In particular, Gannett objected to Section 606(c) of the Communications Act of 1934, as well as executive discretion to withhold renewal of radio licenses. Gannett's views on court-packing may have been influenced by the experiences of his father-in-law, William E. Werner, who incurred public outrage for his opinion striking down New York's workers' compensation statute in *Ives v. South Buffalo Railway Company*, 94 N.E. 431 (N.Y. 1911). That episode is discussed in John Fabian Witt, *The Accidental Republic: Crippled Workingmen, Destitute Widows, and the Remaking of American Law* (Cambridge, MA, 2004), 152–179.

87. James M. Beck, *The Duty of the Lawyer in the Present Crisis: Some Observations on the Attempt by New Deal Spokesmen to Curtail Freedom of Speech as Exercised by the National Lawyers Committee of the American Liberty League* (Washington, DC, 1935), 8 ("to defend"); James Beck to Arthur Garfield Hays, 28 October 1935, ACLUR, reel 114, vol. 764 ("sympathy"); annual meeting minutes, 28–30 April 1936, CCUSR, box 30, 188 (William L. Ransom on totalitarianism). A referendum taken in March 1937 (which was presented to the Senate) revealed that ABA members opposed the court-packing plan six to one. William L. Ransom, "Members of the American Bar Association Decide Its Policies as to the Federal Courts," *ABA Journal* 23 (1937): 271–274, 277.

88. Arthur Vanderbilt to Frank Grinnell, 18 March 1937, ATVP, box 113, folder "Correspondence 1937" ("best idea"); George Wharton Pepper, "Plain Speaking: The President's Case against the Supreme Court," *ABA Journal* 23 (1937): 247–251, 250 ("best friend"); Warren Olney Jr., "The President's Proposal to Add Six New Members to the Supreme Court," *ABA Journal* 23 (1937): 237–241, 264; William J. Donovan, "An Independent Supreme Court and the Protection of Minority Rights," *ABA Journal* 23 (1937): 254–260, 295–296, 254 ("question whether"). Among the minorities Donovan thought protected by the Supreme Court were white southerners in the post–Civil War cases.

89. "Reorganization of Federal Judiciary," addresses of Hon. Royal S. Copeland, Hon. David I. Walsh, and Hon. Edward R. Burke, 12 March 1937, GCP, box 76, folder 6; statement of Charles C. Burlingham to the Committee on the Judiciary of the U.S. Senate, 6 April 1937, GCP, box 76, folder 20.

90. West Coast Hotel Co. v. Parrish, 300 U.S. 379 (1937); NLRB v. Jones and Laughlin Steel, 301 U.S. 1 (1937).

91. Charles Evans Hughes, *Six Lectures on the Supreme Court of the United States: Its Foundations, Methods, and Achievements* (New York, 1928), 195. On the constitutional revolution, see Brinkley, *End of Reform;* Barry

Cushman, *Rethinking the New Deal Court: The Structure of a Constitutional Revolution* (New York, 1998); William E. Leuchtenburg, *The Supreme Court Reborn: The Constitutional Revolution in the Age of Roosevelt* (New York, 1995); Richard A. Maidment, *The Judicial Response to the New Deal: The United States Supreme Court and Economic Regulation, 1934–1936* (New York, 1991); "AHR Forum: The Debate over the Constitutional Revolution of 1937," *American Historical Review* 110 (2005): 1046–1115.

92. NLRB v. Jones and Laughlin Steel, 301 U.S. 1 (1937), 33. On the NLRB's decision not to claim a constitutional right to organize, see William E. Forbath, "Caste, Class, and Equal Citizenship," *Michigan Law Review* 98 (1999): 1–91. Andrew Furuseth promoted a Thirteenth Amendment justification for the right to organize. See Pope, "Thirteenth Amendment," 7.

93. Corrected draft of interview between Thomas Stix and Morris Ernst, 23 January 1935, MLEP, box 487, folder 5; Felix Frankfurter to Franklin D. Roosevelt, March 30, 1937, in *Roosevelt and Frankfurter: Their Correspondence, 1928–1945*, annotated by Max Freedman (Boston, 1968), 1932; Felix Frankfurter to Grenville Clark, 14 April 1937, GCP, box 65, folder 102. See also Felix Frankfurter to Charles C. Burlingham, 29 April 1937, GCP, box 71, folder 31 ("It will have been a very healthy education of the public mind to an understanding of what the Supreme Court really does when it decides constitutional controversies—and it will be a healthy thing for the Court to know that the people know it").

94. Morris Ernst to Heywood Broun, 21 May 1935, MLEP, box 401, folder 3.

95. Douglas Arant to Grenville Clark, 14 April 1938, GCP, box 70, folder 24 ("amazed"); Grenville Clark, "Memorandum for Messrs. Burlingham, Arant and Marbury," 31 August 1937, GCP, box 70, folder 114 ("possible").

96. Associated Press v. NLRB, 301 U.S. 103 (1937); Panel Discussion, 25.

97. Brief on Behalf of Petitioner the Associated Press, Associated Press v. NLRB, No. 365, 301 U.S. 103 (1937), 101 (U.S., filed February 5, 1937); Brief on Behalf of the American Newspaper Guild as Amicus Curiae, Associated Press v. NLRB, No. 365, 301 U.S. 103 (1937), 26–27 (U.S., filed January 22, 1937).

98. Associated Press, 301 U.S. at 132–133 ("no special"); ibid. at 135 (Sutherland, J. dissenting).

99. Brief for the Appellant, *Herndon v. Lowry,* Nos. 474, 475, 301 U.S. 242 (1937), 16 (U.S. filed January 21, 1937) ("young"); "Communist's Conviction Upheld in Georgia," *NYT,* June 14, 1936; Herndon v. Lowry, 301 U.S. 242 (1937). Whitney North Seymour argued the case.

100. "Herndon Set Free by Supreme Court," *NYT,* April 27, 1937; Herndon, 301 U.S. at 258 ("power"); ibid. at 276 (Van Devanter, J., dissenting).

101. Felix Frankfurter to Charles C. Burlingham, 29 April 1937, GCP, box 71, folder 31 ("You surprise me in being surprised by the 'Battalion of Death' in the *Herndon* case. Barring the Meyer, Pierce, and the De Jonge cases (The Huey Long tax case really does not count) that is the way those bunnies have substantially lined up since the war.").

102. "Through the Editor's Specs," *Nation's Business,* March 1937, 7; Walter J. Kohler, address to annual meeting of the Chamber of Commerce of the United States, 27–29 April 1937, CCUSR, box 31; H. W. Prentis, past president, NAM, "Safeguarding American Freedom," February 1945, NAMP, box 2, folder 100.

103. Senn v. Tile Layers Protecting Union, 201 U.S. 468, 478 (1937); Robert H. Jackson, "Labor's New Rights and Responsibilities," August 24, 1937, DOJR, box 6, folder Jackson.

104. Edward S. Corwin, "The Court Sees a New Light," *New Republic,* August 4, 1937, 354; "Reorganization of the Federal Judiciary," *Digest of Testimony at the Hearings before the Judiciary Committee of the United States Senate, Printed under the Auspices of the Special Committee on the Supreme Court Proposal of the American Bar Association* (Chicago, 1937).

105. Roger Baldwin to Mrs. John Rogers Jr., 28 December 1937, ACLUR, reel 142, vol. 967.

106. Roger Baldwin to Frederick Wright, 28 December 1937, ACLUR, reel 156, vol. 1078.

7. The Civil Liberties Consensus

1. ACLU, "Facts and Fancies," bulletin 4, undated, ACLUR, reel 165, vol. 2042.

2. David G. Wittels, "Hague Learned Red Scare Trick 18 Years Ago," *New York Post,* February 8, 1938 ("We took"). For a fuller account of Hague's speech and labor policies and the ACLU's activities in Jersey City, as well as the 1936 seamen's strike and associated legal proceedings, see Kenneth M. Casebeer, "Public . . . since Time Immemorial: The Labor History of *Hague v. CIO*," *Rutgers Law Review* 66 (2013): 1–32; Laura Weinrib, "The Liberal Compromise: Civil Liberties, Labor, and the Limits of State Power, 1917–1940" (PhD dissertation, Princeton University, 2011), 306–425; Timothy Zick, *Speech out of Doors: Preserving First Amendment Liberties in Public Places* (New York, 2009), ch. 6. The literature on *Hague v. CIO* includes John J. Gibbons, "*Hague v. CIO:* A Retrospective," *New York University Law Review* 52 (1977): 731–809; Abraham Isserman, "CIO v. Hague: The Battle of Jersey City," *Guild Practice* 36 (1979): 14–32; Benjamin Kaplan, "The Great Civil Rights Case of *Hague v. CIO:* Notes

of a Survivor," *Suffolk University Law Review* 25 (1991): 913–947. On Frank Hague, see Richard Connors, *A Cycle of Power: The Career of Jersey City Mayor Frank Hague* (Metuchen, NJ, 1971); James Fischer, *On the Irish Waterfront* (Ithaca, NY, 2009); Dayton David McKean, *The Boss: The Hague Machine in Action* (Boston, 1940); Matthew Raffety, "Political Ethics and Public Style in the Early Career of Jersey City's Frank Hague," *New Jersey History* 124 (2009): 29–56.

3. ACLU, *Civil Rights vs. Mayor Hague* (New York, 1938), 18.

4. Roger Baldwin and Morris Ernst, "The New Deal and Civil Liberties" (radio debate over the Blue Network of NBC), 27 January 1934, ACLUR, reel 109, vol. 717 ("the struggle"); Hague Injunction Proceedings, Transcript of Record, MLEP, box 275, folder 1 (hereafter Hague Trial Transcript), vol. 2, 1142–1143 (emphasizing ACLU impartiality).

5. "The Hague Injunction Proceedings," *Yale Law Journal* 48 (December 1938): 257–272, 257 ("real American," quoting Hague, January 12, 1938); Reinhold Niebuhr to Morris Ernst, 13 December 1937, MLEP, box 277, folder 4. In interviews, Hague insisted that his statement was taken out of context. "'Tyranny' Charges Resented by Hague," *NYT,* January 12, 1938.

6. Hague v. CIO, 307 U.S. 496 (1939).

7. See ACLU, "More Candid Views of Mayor Hague," bulletin 2, undated, ACLUR, reel 165, vol. 2042.

8. "The Constitution Re-enters Jersey City," *New York Herald-Tribune,* April 3, 1938; "Hague's Control Extends Even to Jury System," *New York Post,* May 24, 1938; "Just One Word in a Law Helped a Lot," *New York World-Telegram,* January 19, 1938. Alan Karcher has argued that the degree of corruption within the Hague administration has been exaggerated. Alan J. Karcher, *New Jersey's Multiple Municipal Madness* (New Brunswick, NJ, 1998), 185.

9. Harold F. Gosnell, *Machine Politics: Chicago Model* (Chicago, 1937), 7.

10. National Committee for the Defense of Political Prisoners, "Report on the Denial of Labor and Civil Rights in Hudson County," ACLUR, reel 153, vol. 1051; David G. Wittels, "Hague Always Labor's Friend—When It Paid," *New York Post,* February 2, 1938 ("friend"); Frank Hague to senator, 16 April 1936, ACLUR, reel 138, vol. 942 (anti-injunction bill); "Report of the Sub-Committee on Civil Rights of the Executive Council of the Junior Bar Conference of the American Bar Association," 26 July 1938, ATVP, box 127, folder "Civil Liberties 1939–1940," 16–17.

11. Robert Wohlforth to Felix Frazer and H. D. Cullen, 5 January 1937, "Violations of Free Speech and Rights of Labor," Sen 78A-F9, record group 46, NARA DC, 10.25, box 5, folder "January 1937"; "ACLU Report on Meeting concerning Jersey City Ban on Picketing," 23 December 1936, ACLUR, reel 153, vol. 1051.

12. Testimony of Arthur Garfield Hays, ACLU v. Casey, 5 March 1937, ACLUR, reel 153, vol. 1051 ("most ardent"). The Third Circuit issued its decision on December 13, 1938. Casey v. ACLU, 100 F.2d 354 (3rd Cir. 1938). During the 1936 presidential campaign, the ACLU had helped the Communist Party secure a court order allowing it to rent a hall in Jersey City.

13. Hague v. CIO, 101 F.2d 774, 778 (3rd Cir. 1939) ("invasion," quoting *Newark Evening News*); ACLU bulletin 793, 3 December 1937, ACLUR, reel 153, vol. 1051 ("go to").

14. Committee on Civil Rights in Jersey City, press release, 21 December 1937, ACLUR, reel 153, vol. 1051.

15. ACLU bulletin 795, 17 December 1937, ACLUR, reel 153, vol. 1051 ("siege"); clipping, *Hoboken (NJ) Observer,* 1 January 1938, ACLUR, reel 162, vol. 2020 ("leading Communist"). To minimize conflict in coordinating the multifaceted campaign, interested organizations ceded control to a joint committee headed by the CIO. ACLU board minutes, 20 December 1937, ACLUM, reel 7. Hague's fallback to anti-Communism conformed neatly to expected responses the ACLU had laid out in *Legal Tactics for Labor's Rights*, described in Chapter 6. See ACLU, *Tactics,* 14–15.

16. Clipping, *Hoboken (NJ) Observer,* January 1, 1938, ACLUR, reel 162, vol. 2020 ("Let us," quoting Frazer); Statement of William J. Carney, ACLUR, reel 167, vol. 2063; "Baldwin Denies Red or CIO Affiliation in Talk at Church," *Bayonne (NJ) Times,* 15 January 1938, ACLUR, reel 162, vol. 2020.

17. Baldwin to editor, *San Francisco Daily News,* 21 October 1935, ACLUR, reel 114, vol. 765 ("communism," defending statement); memorandum to Baldwin, 5 January 1938, ACLUR, reel 153, vol. 1051 ("any form"); telegram from Roger Baldwin to Frank Hague, 4 January 1938, ACLUR, reel 153, vol. 1051 ("high-handed").

18. William Carney to Roger Baldwin, 7 January 1938, ACLUR, reel 167, vol. 2063 ("tell"); Arthur Garfield Hays to Westbrook Pegler (*New York World-Telegram*), 4 January 1938, ACLUR, reel 167, vol. 2063; Committee on Civil Liberties in Jersey City, press release, 20 December 1937, ACLUR, reel 153, vol. 1051 ("front page"); letter from Morris Ernst, 13 December 1937, GJP, cont. 23, folder "Ernst, Morris" ("It does not").

19. Neil Brant to Morris Ernst, 7 January 1938, ACLUR, reel 167, vol. 2067; Jerome Britchey to Morris Ernst, 6 April 1938, ACLUR, reel 165, vol. 2040.

20. Morris Ernst to McAlister Coleman, 17 January 1938, MLEP, box 39, folder 2 ("bad tacticians"); Dorothy Thompson, "Who Loves Liberty?" *New York Tribune,* January 10, 1938; John Ryan to Roger Baldwin, 28 December 1937, ACLUR, reel 167, vol. 2063 (describing Lippmann's

position); "Memorandum on the Jersey City Work," 24 December 1937, ACLUR, reel 153, vol. 1051 (listing organizations).

21. Ernst received numerous antisemitic letters, including "A Loyal Patriotic American" to Morris Ernst, 21 June 1938, MLEP, box 39, folder 2. Many Jewish correspondents urged Ernst to withdraw from the matter lest he exacerbate antisemitic tendencies, for example, Otto Abraham to Morris Ernst, 18 June 1938, MLEP, box 39, folder 2.

22. Clipping, *New York Evening Post*, January 12, 1938, ACLUR, reel 162, vol. 2020; Arthur Garfield Hays to Frank Hague, 10 December 1937, ACLUR, reel 153, vol. 1051; Norman Thomas, *Hagueism Is Fascism* (New York, 1938), 4 (published by the Workers Defense League); "CIO Theatre Nite: 'Bring Democracy to Jersey City,'" 20 February 1938, ACLUR, reel 167, vol. 2063. Even the Jehovah's Witnesses, citing Hague's long history of persecuting Witnesses in Hudson County, offered "to cooperate in any way in bringing that dictator to time." O. R. Moyle to Harriet Pilpel, 18 December 1937, MLEP, box 277, folder 4.

23. Morris Ernst to McAlister Coleman, 17 January 1938, MLEP, box 39, folder 2 ("swell job"); "Jersey City's Mayor Hague: Last of the Bosses, Not First of the Dictators," *Life*, February 7, 1938, 45; "CIO Theatre Nite: 'Bring Democracy to Jersey City,'" 20 February 1938, ACLUR, reel 167, vol. 2063 ("progressive"); Liberal Ministers Club resolution, 10 January 1938, ACLUR, reel 167, vol. 2063; "Roosevelt Avoids Comment on Hague," *NYT*, May 11, 1938 (Newark diocese). On the influence of totalitarianism on subsequent interpretations of civil liberties, see Richard Primus, *The American Language of Rights* (New York, 1999); Owen Fiss, "The Idea of Political Freedom," in *Looking Back at Law's Century*, ed. Austin Sarat, Bryant Garth, and Robert A. Kagan (Ithaca, NY, 2002), 35–57; William Edward Nelson, *The Legalist Reformation: Law, Politics, and Ideology in New York, 1920–1980* (Chapel Hill, NC, 2001), 120–130.

24. "'End Hague's Terrorism,' Demands Aroused Public," *New York Post*, January 20, 1938; Morris Ernst to Roger Baldwin, 18 July 1938, ACLUR, reel 165, vol. 2041 ("people"); "How Does Hague Do It? Two Answers Are Given," *NYT*, June 12, 1938.

25. Clipping, *Jersey (City) Journal*, January 12, 1938, ACLUR, reel 162, vol. 2020 ("held"); Keith Sward to Governor A. Harry Moore, 13 January 1938, ACLUR, reel 167, vol. 2063 (resolution); "Hague Declines Senate Seat Because He 'Has to Fight Reds,'" *New York World-Telegram*, January 17, 1938 (revocation). Hague made calculated concessions to labor during 1938, including qualified support for a New Jersey "little Wagner act." "Hague Supports 'Little Labor Act,'" *New York Evening Post*, January 12, 1938.

26. "'Tyranny' Charges Resented by Hague," *NYT* ("any regard"); "700 Messages Praise Hague for His Talk," *Bayonne (NJ) Times,* January 8, 1938; Heywood Broun, "Shoot the Works," *New Republic,* January 19, 1938, 30; Fred Rodell, "Morris Ernst: New York's Unlawyerlike Liberal Lawyer Is the Censor's Enemy, the President's Friend," *Life,* February 21, 1944, 100 (describing friendship).

27. ACLU bulletin 806, 4 March 1938, ACLUR, reel 167, vol. 2063; telegram to Frank Hague, 20 March 1938, ACLUR, reel 167, vol. 2063; "Ruling of Corporation Counsel James A. Hammill on the Jersey City Ordinance Relating to the Distribution of Literature on the Streets," ACLUR, reel 165, vol. 2042; Lovell v. City of Griffin, 303 U.S. 444 (1938) (deeming ordinance overbroad).

28. "National Committee for People's Rights," 14 May 1938, ACLUR, reel 167, vol. 2063; Warren Hall, "Hague's Foes Fail 50,000 Awaiting Jersey City Battle," *New York Daily News,* May 8, 1938; "Jersey City Police Seize, Then 'Deport' O'Connell," *NYT,* May 28, 1938.

29. "Thomas Ejection Seen as Due for National Airing," *Christian Science Monitor,* May 3, 1938; "Ousting of Thomas Assailed by Landon," *Boston Globe,* May 2, 1938; "Landon and Sinclair—Both against Hague," *New York Post,* May 3, 1938. Thomas returned and was evicted by Hudson Tube.

30. "The Real Issue behind 'Hague Terror,'" *New York Post,* May 16, 1938; Arthur Vanderbilt to Reginald Heber Smith, 8 July 1937, ATVP, box 121. See also Arthur Vanderbilt to John H. Riordan, 7 December 1937, ATVP, box 130, folder "National Lawyers Guild" (reporting Ernst's opinion that Vanderbilt's nomination as ABA president had hurt National Lawyers Guild recruitment efforts).

31. Biographical note, 18 October 1937, ATVP, box 130, folder "1938"; "Vanderbilt Denies Hague 'Fee' Charge," *NYT,* December 25, 1938.

32. "Ban on Thomas Rally in Jersey City Upheld," *NYT,* October 19, 1938. In November 1939, the New Jersey Court of Errors and Appeals affirmed the state supreme court's refusal to grant a writ, claiming that the issue had become moot. On the heckler's veto, which the Supreme Court upheld in *Feiner v. New York,* 340 U.S. 315 (1951), but later implicitly repudiated, see Harry Kalven, *The Negro and the First Amendment* (Chicago, 1965).

33. "Mr. Cummings Uncovers a Law," *Pittsburgh Courier,* May 28, 1938 ("when colored"); Dean Dinwoodey, "Basic Law Is Examined in Light of Hague Ban," *NYT,* May 29, 1938. Section 52 originated in the Civil Rights Acts of 1866 and 1870; Section 51 in the Civil Rights Act of 1870. They are now codified at Sections 241 and 242 of Title 18 of the United States Code.

Thomas also pursued charges under the 1932 Lindbergh Law, Title 18, Section 408-A of the United States Code, which made it a federal crime to transport a kidnapping victim across state lines. That law, however, required ransom or torture, neither of which was involved in Thomas's ejection from New Jersey. For an analysis of why the Civil Rights Section eventually abandoned reliance on Section 51, see Risa Lauren Goluboff, *The Lost Promise of Civil Rights* (Cambridge, MA, 2007), 136–138.

34. "Case of Mary Helen," *Time,* May 30, 1938 ("coal barons"); ACLU, *"Sweet Land of Liberty" 1931–1932* (New York, 1932), 4; "69 Must Stand Trial," *NYT,* January 27, 1938. The cases narrowly interpreting Section 51 included *United States v. Wheeler,* 254 F. 611 (D. Ariz. 1918), affirmed, *United States v. Wheeler,* 254 U.S. 281 (1920), involving the perpetrators of the 1917 Bisbee deportation of IWW miners (see Chapter 3). The Harlan case never reached the court, because it was nolled as part of a negotiated settlement.

35. ACLU and New Jersey Civil Liberties Union, "Report to the Attorney General of the United States on Interference with Labor and Civil Rights in Hudson County, New Jersey," November 1938, ACLUR, reel 165, vol. 2041.

36. "'Free Speech' Test Trial Opens Today," *Jersey (City) Journal,* June 1, 1938 (describing call for Hague's appearance); Homer Cummings to Franklin D. Roosevelt, 18 May 1938, FDRP, official file 1581, folder "Civil Liberties 1933–1945"; guest log, FDRP; "Roosevelt Sees Hague Fight as 'Local Matter,'" *New York Herald-Tribune,* May 11, 1938 ("local"); ACLU bulletin 818, 28 May 1938, ACLUR, reel 167, vol. 2063 (Hague and the Democratic National Committee); "The President's Address," *NYT,* June 26, 1938.

37. Roger Baldwin to Robert La Follette Jr., 24 May 1938, ACLUR, reel 167, vol. 2063 (seeking assistance); Louis Colman, Assistant National Secretary, ILD, to Roger Baldwin, 24 January 1938, ACLU Papers, reel 167, vol. 2063 (explaining La Follette's hesitation); letter to Robert La Follette Jr., 13 September 1938, ACLUR, reel 165, vol. 2041 (expressing concern of sixty signers and requesting intervention).

38. Bill of Complaint, CIO v. Hague, 25 F. Supp. 127 (D.N.J. 1938), Equity 5685, record group 21, NARA NE, schedule D, 3. The complaint was filed by Spaulding Frazer in January 1938. The plaintiffs were the ACLU, the CIO, three New Jersey CIO unions, and six CIO organizers. Clark was appointed to the Third Circuit in the midst of the trial and had to obtain permission to sit as a district judge in order to finish hearing the case.

39. Hague Trial Transcript, vol. 2, 1255–1256.

40. Ibid., 2259.

41. Ibid., 1091 ("no desire"); ibid., 1149 ("suppress").

42. Russell B. Porter, "Hague Repudiates 'Red' Aid in Party," *NYT,* June 16, 1938 ("At times"); Russell B. Porter, "Hague Holds Reds Lack Civil Rights," *NYT,* June 17, 1938.

43. Porter, "Reds Lack Civil Rights" ("Americanism"); Hague Trial Transcript, vol. 2, 1091, 1150, 1255 (Communists); "Civil Liberties Hour: Civil Rights and Mayor Hague," WEVD broadcast, 27 November 1938, ACLUR, reel 161, vol. 2014 ("ten Communists"); Russell B. Porter, "Hague Urges Exile of 'Reds' to Alaska to Bar Revolution," *NYT,* June 15, 1938 (urging same solution for fascists).

44. "New Jersey Fascists," *Washington Post,* June 8, 1938; Workers Defense League news bulletin, May–June 1938, ATVP, box 127, folder "Civil Liberties," 1 ("man fighting"); press release, Council of United States Veterans, 4 January 1938, MLEP, box 272, folder 1.

45. ACLU bulletin 822, 24 June 1938, ACLUR, reel 167, vol. 2063; Morris Ernst to Roger Baldwin, 18 July 1938, ACLUR, reel 165, vol. 2041; ACLU press release, 8 August 1938, ACLUR, reel 165, vol. 2041.

46. "Hague Loses CIO Fight," *NYT,* October 28, 1938; Morris Ernst to Roger Baldwin, 18 July 1938, ACLUR, reel 165, vol. 2041; Hague Trial Transcript, vol. 2, 2173.

47. Zechariah Chafee Jr., "Freedom of Speech in War Time," *Harvard Law Review* 32 (1919): 932–973, 956; Hague v. CIO, 25 F. Supp. 127, 129 (D.N.J. 1938). On political science and pluralism, see Daniel T. Rodgers, *Contested Truths: Keywords in American Politics since Independence* (New York, 1987), 208–210. World War I had disrupted the "self-assurance about values that Progressives were able regularly to muster." Morton J. Horwitz, *The Transformation of American Law, 1870–1960: The Crisis of Legal Orthodoxy* (New York, 1992), 191; Vincent Blasi, "Holmes and the Marketplace of Ideas," *Supreme Court Review* 2004: 1–46.

48. Hague, 25 F. Supp. at 152, 129; William Clark to Grenville Clark, 20 January 1939, GCP, box 78, folder 26 ("events").

49. Morris Ernst to Roger Baldwin, 3 November 1938, ACLUR, reel 165, vol. 2041; Final Judgment and Decree, 7 November 1938, CIO v. Hague, Equity 5865, 25 F. Supp. 127 (D.N.J. 1938), record group 21, NARA NE (hereafter Final Judgment and Decree). The court did not consider the plaintiffs' claims under the Wagner Act in light of its decision on the same claims in the context of the 1937 injunction, which was still pending in the Third Circuit. That case was dismissed as moot in December 1938.

50. Final Judgment and Decree, 5; American Federation of Labor v. Bain, 106 P. 2d 544 (Or. 1940) (citing *Hague* in upholding a state statute prohibiting picketing in the proximity of employer property). On the failure of courts to require affirmative protection in subsequent decades,

see Owen Fiss, *Liberalism Divided: Freedom of Speech and the Many Uses of State Power* (Boulder, CO, 1996), 121–138. In practice, *Hague* did not settle the issue of the heckler's veto. The decision applied only to permit applications (a problem clearly implicating prior restraint), not to ongoing speeches at which violence was extant. Moreover, the issue was not resolved by the Supreme Court, which instructed the district court simply to declare the ordinance invalid, without providing guidance for future administration. On *Hague*'s application to "hostile audiences" problems, see Ruth McGaffey, "The Heckler's Veto: A Reexamination," *Marquette Law Review* 57 (1973): 39–64, 43–48.

51. ACLU bulletin 842, 12 November 1938, ACLUR, reel 165, vol. 2041; "Civil Liberties Win," *New York Post*, November 8, 1938; ACLU bulletin 842, 12 November 1938, ACLUR, reel 165, vol. 2041.

52. "Hague Foes Charge 'Packing' of Court," *NYT*, November 20, 1938; "A Brief for Free Speech," *NYT*, December 23, 1938.

53. Reginald Heber Smith to Arthur Vanderbilt, 15 February 1937, ATVP, box 115, folder "Legal Aid" ("devotes"); Arthur Vanderbilt to Reginald Heber Smith, 23 February 1937, ATVP, box 115, folder "Legal Aid"; Reginald Heber Smith to Arthur Vanderbilt, 9 July 1937, ATVP, box 115, folder "Legal Aid" ("fumble"). The creation of the National Lawyers Guild is described in Chapter 6.

54. John Devaney, "The Quarterly," *National Lawyers Guild Quarterly* 1 (December 1937): 1; "Report on the Conference on Public Relations," 8 January 1938, ATVP, box 369, folder "Supreme Court of the United States: Controversy of 1937"; George Morris to Arthur Vanderbilt, 9 December 1937, ATVP, box 369, folder "Supreme Court of the United States: Controversy of 1937" (recruitment). Hogan did recommend increasing the appropriation for legal aid work the following year. Frank J. Hogan, "Justice, Sure and Speedy, for All," address to the ABA annual meeting, 29 July 1938, GCP, box 83, folder 45.

55. Arthur Vanderbilt to Grenville Clark, 27 June 1938, GCP, box 235, folder 15 ("more conservative"); Grenville Clark to Maury Maverick, 16 January 1939, GCP, box 80, folder 77 ("broad"); telegram from Cloyd Laporte to Marion Smith, GCP, box 73, folder 47 ("independent"); Grenville Clark to Thomas H. Reed, Republican Program Committee, 13 July 1938, GCP, box 78, folder 78 (Republican childhood); Grenville Clark to Lloyd K. Garrison, 4 December 1936, GCP, box 65, folder 109. Persuaded, Garrison's revised version left "no doubt as to the applicability of the Bill of Rights." Lloyd Garrison to Grenville Clark, 29 January 1937, GCP, box 261, folder 3. On Clark, see Gerald T. Dunne, *Grenville Clark: Public Citizen* (New York, 1986); Nancy Peterson Hill, *A Very Private Public Citizen: The Life of Grenville Clark* (Columbia, MO, 2014).

56. Grenville Clark to Monte Lemann, 24 February 1937, GCP, box 71, folder 206 ("essentially"); Grenville Clark to Walter H. Pollak, 13 May 1937, GCP, box 72, folder 169; telegram from Roscoe Pound to Grenville Clark, 21 March 1937, GCP, box 72, folder 176; "Proposed Petition to Congress, National Committee for Independent Courts, as Adopted at Organization Meeting," 21–22 May 1937, GCP, box 74, folder 13; Grenville Clark, "Civil Liberties: Court Help or Self-Help," January 1938, GCP, box 235, folder 1 ("important"). See also Hill, *Clark*, 113.

57. Grenville Clark, "Conservatism and Civil Liberty," *ABA Journal* 24 (1938): 640–644, 640 ("reconciling"); Grenville Clark, "The Prospects for Civil Liberty," address to Chicago Bar Association, 15 September 1938, GCP, box 235, folder 22 ("reconcile").

58. Grenville Clark, "Conservatism," 640 ("gradually"), 641 ("active"); Grenville Clark, "The Bill of Rights, First Lecture," 13 January 1938, GCP, box 235, folder 4 ("purely"); Grenville Clark, "Conservatism," 641 ("public impression"). On the ACLU's change in reputation, see Ralph Easley to Grenville Clark, 13 June 1938, GCP, box 235, folder 15.

59. Grenville Clark, "Conservatism," 642.

60. Ibid., 643, 644.

61. Telegram from Earl Warren to Grenville Clark, 29 June 1938, GCP, box 235, folder 15; Walter Lippmann to Grenville Clark, 28 April 1938, GCP, box 65, folder 183; Arthur Vanderbilt to Grenville Clark, 27 June 1938, GCP, box 235, folder 15; Grenville Clark to Arthur Vanderbilt, 30 June 1938, ATVP, box 114, folder "Correspondence Re Committee, 1936–1938"; "Guild Secretary Points Bar's Way in Investigation," *Buffalo Daily Law Journal,* August 20, 1938.

62. Frank J. Hogan, "Justice, Sure and Speedy, for All," address to the ABA annual meeting, 29 July 1938, GCP, box 83, folder 45; Frank Hogan to Arthur Garfield Hays, 22 August 1938, ACLUR, reel 156, vol. 1079. Excerpts of Hogan's speech were reprinted in "The American Bar Association's Committee on the Bill of Rights," *Bill of Rights Review* 1 (Summer 1940): 63.

63. Frank J. Hogan, "Important Shifts in Constitutional Doctrines," *ABA Journal* 25 (1930): 629–638, 630 (1939) ("most devastating"); Frank Hogan to Robert Carey, 7 February 1939, GCP, box 79, folder 64 ("trampling"); Frank J. Hogan, "Justice, Sure and Speedy, for All," address to the ABA annual meeting, 29 July 1938, GCP, box 83, folder 45 ("Perhaps"); editorial comment, "The Bar Looks at Civil Rights" (from the *Norfolk Virginia-Pilot*), *ABA Journal* 24 (1938): 949–950 (skepticism). For a similar catalog of complaints, see Samuel B. Pettengill, address to annual meeting, minutes, Chamber of Commerce of the United States, 3–5 May 1938, CCUSR, box 31, 270. The Senate Committee on Ocean Mail and

Air Mail Contracts, which investigated MacCracken, was chaired by Hugo Black.

64. Frank Hogan to Grenville Clark, 12 August 1938, GCP, box 79, folder 64; Zechariah Chafee Jr. to Grenville Clark, 3 October 1938, GCP, box 78, folder 11; Grenville Clark to Douglas Arant, 13 August 1938, GCP, box 77, folder 8 (on Pressman). For a full list of members, see Edson R. Sunderland, *History of the American Bar Association and Its Work* (1953), 193–197. On Chafee's participation, see Donald L. Smith, *Zechariah Chafee Jr., Defender of Liberty and Law* (Cambridge, MA, 1986), ch. 9. The committee went through several name changes.

65. Zechariah Chafee Jr. to Grenville Clark, 28 September 1938, GCP, box 78, folder 11; ACLU board minutes, 8 August 1938, ACLUM, reel 7; Robert Carey to Grenville Clark, 30 December 1938, ATVP, box 123, folder "Correspondence September 1938–July 1939" (complaining about demands to integrate ABA). The National Lawyers Guild, too, lauded the ABA for its new undertaking and offered its cooperation. Edward Lamb to Grenville Clark, 12 November 1938, GCP, box 80, folder 2. Earlier, Clark had attempted to convene a conservative "Civil Liberties Group of Fifteen" to support the ACLU. Memorandum, 21 June 1938, GCP, box 65, folder 54. He declined an early invitation to join the organization. Arthur Garfield Hays to ACLU, 23 March 1938, ACLUR, reel 156, vol. 1080.

66. Roger Baldwin, memorandum on conference with Grenville Clark, 28 October 1938, ACLUR, reel 156, vol. 1079; Grenville Clark to Arthur Garfield Hays, 1 September 1938, ACLUR, reel 156, vol. 1079. By the summer of 1940, there were fifty-five state and local committees in operation. "The American Bar Association's Committee on the Bill of Rights," *Bill of Rights Review* 1: 63–69, 65.

67. Grenville Clark to Frederick Stinchfield, 20 March 1939, GCP, box 81, folder 137 ("had become"); "Committee," *Bill of Rights Review*, 65.

68. Grenville Clark to Jerome Britchey, 4 January 1939, ACLUR, reel 176, vol. 2133 (drafting roles); Grenville Clark to Harlan F. Stone, 4 August 1941, GCP, box 81, folder 141 ("conservative").

69. "Burkitt, Bail Denied, Wins Court Review," *NYT*, April 26, 1938; "Jersey Methodists Join Critics of Hague," *NYT*, April 26, 1938; "Severe Curb on Court Power to Void Legislative Acts Asked at Albany," *NYT*, April 26, 1938; "United States Supreme Court," *NYT*, April 26, 1938. The reference also indicated that Justice Stone had authored the opinion, in which Justice Black had concurred in part; that Justice Butler concurred in the result; and that Justice McReynolds had dissented. Burkitt was sentenced to six months in the county penitentiary when he attempted to speak publicly against Hague and on behalf of John Longo. The ILD initially

handled the case, but Burkitt subsequently turned to the ACLU. Claire Burkitt to Jerome Britchey, 28 September 1938, ACLUR, reel 165, vol. 2042.

70. United States v. Carolene Products Company, 304 U.S. 144, 152n4 (1938); Louis Lusky, "Footnote Redux: A 'Carolene Products' Reminiscence," *Columbia Law Review* 82 (1982): 1093–1109, 1098; Nelson, *Legalist Reformation,* 123–124 (on Nazism); Louis Lusky, *By What Right? A Commentary on the Supreme Court's Power to Revise the Constitution* (Charlottesville, VA, 1989). See also Felix Gilman, "The Famous Footnote Four: A History of the Carolene Products Footnote," *South Texas Law Review* 46 (2004): 163–243; Peter Linzer, "The *Carolene Products* Footnote and the Preferred Position of Individual Rights: Louis Lusky and John Hart Ely vs. Harlan Fiske Stone," *Constitutional Commentary* 12 (1995): 277–303.

71. Louis Lusky to Grenville Clark, 14 November 1938, GCP, box 80, folder 36. The definition he ultimately proposed was "rights protecting interests of such a nature that, despite their importance in the social scheme, general popular sentiment is often unlikely to be aroused by their abuse."

72. Ibid.

73. Brief of the Special Committee on the Bill of Rights of the American Bar Association as Friends of the Court (hereafter ABA Third Circuit Brief), 4, 38–39, in Transcript of Record, vol. 4, Hague v. CIO, Third Circuit case no. 6939, 101 F.2d 774, 808 (3rd Cir. 1939), NARA M-A, record group 276. The committee argued that *Davis v. Massachusetts,* 167 U.S. 43 (1897), was decided prior to the incorporation of the First Amendment into the Fourteenth Amendment and asserted a property rather than liberty interest in the use of the Boston Commons to deliver a speech. On *Davis,* see Chapter 1.

74. Wright v. Vinton Branch, 300 U.S. 440, 461 (1937); Morris Ernst to Grenville Clark, 25 February 1939, GCP, box 78, folder 100.

75. ABA Third Circuit Brief, 25; Louis Lusky, comments on the proposed draft of section on importance of the open-air meeting, 13 December 1938, GCP, box 80, folder 36. Other suggestions made by Lusky were also incorporated.

76. ABA Third Circuit Brief, 37, 19. The brief left open the possibility that denial of a permit might be constitutionally permissible on an "extreme state of facts," in which the police were demonstrably incapable of controlling public unrest. Ibid., 17.

77. Ibid., 30.

78. "Committee," *Bill of Rights Review,* 65 ("unanimous"); William Clark to Grenville Clark, 20 January 1939, GCP, box 78, folder 26; Felix Frank-

furter to Grenville Clark, 31 December 1938, GCP, box 78, folder 125; William Ransom to Grenville Clark, 28 December 1938, GCP, box 81, folder 45.

79. Hague v. CIO, 101 F.2d 774, 808 (3rd Cir. 1939) (Davis, J., dissenting in part).

80. Ibid., 786–787. Judge Albert Maris joined in Biggs's decision. Maris, also a Roosevelt appointee, wrote the majority decision in *Minersville School District v. Gobitis*, 108 F.2d 683 (3rd Cir. 1939), discussed in the Epilogue. The dissenting judge was John Warren Davis, a Wilson appointee, who was about to face federal charges for bribery.

81. Grenville Clark, "Current Events," *ABA Journal* 25 (1939): 1–2; Grenville Clark to Monte Lemann, 22 March 1939, GCP, box 80, folder 18 ("very nice"); Grenville Clark to Charles Edmundson, 8 February 1940, GCP, box 78, folder 93 ("influenced"). Robert Carey of New Jersey was vehemently against the committee's participation in the case. At the ABA's annual meeting in July 1939, he unsuccessfully proposed a resolution prohibiting the committee from participating in litigation. "Committee," *Bill of Rights Review*, 65.

82. Frank Hogan to Arthur Vanderbilt, 17 February 1939, ATVP, box 123, folder "Correspondence September 1938–June 1939"; Arthur Vanderbilt to Henry Armistead, 10 February 1939, ATVP, box 123, folder "Correspondence September 1938–June 1939"; Frank Hogan to members of the board of governors, 14 February 1939, ATVP, box 123, folder "Correspondence September 1938–June 1939."

83. William O. Douglas to Grenville Clark, 5 January 1939, GCP, box 78, folder 82; Charles A. Beardsley to Grenville Clark, 11 September 1939, GCP, box 77, folder 33 (quoting letter from Frankfurter); Frank Hogan to members of the board of governors, 14 February 1939, ATVP, box 123, folder "Correspondence September 1938–June 1939"; Frank Hogan to the board of governors, 8 June 1939, ATVP, box 123, folder "Correspondence September 1938–June 1939." On the grant, see Frank Hogan to the board of governors, 8 June 1939, ATVP, box 123, folder "Correspondence September 1938–June 1939" (reporting that the grant was $24,000, approximately equivalent to the operating budget of the ACLU). The purposes of the *Bill of Rights Review* are articulated in ABA, "A New Venture and Its Purposes," *Bill of Rights Review* 1 (Summer 1940): 3.

84. "The Association's Appreciation Is Expressed to Senator Byrnes," *ABA Journal* 25 (1939): 705.

85. "Murphy Appointed Attorney General," *NYT*, January 2, 1939 ("most enthusiastic"); "Statement of Honorable Frank Murphy," DOJR, box 5,

entry 132, folder "Murphy" ("honest"). On Murphy and the Civil Liberties Unit, see Sidney Fine, *Frank Murphy*, vol. 3, *The Washington Years* (Ann Arbor, 1984), 76–98.

86. Frank Murphy, "Civil Liberties," National Radio Forum, 27 March 1939, DOJR, box 5, entry 132, folder "Civil Liberties" ("social"); Frank Murphy, address to National Conference on Civil Liberties, 13 October 1939, GCP, box 80, folder 112 ("the idea").

87. Gordon Dean, memorandum, 27 January 1939, DOJR, box 5, entry 132, folder "Murphy" (guild); Frank Murphy to Roger Baldwin, 3 February 1939, ACLUR, reel 168, vol. 2070.

88. Order No. 3204, Office of the Attorney General, 3 February 1939, DOJR, box 22, entry 132, folder "Civil Liberties" ("civil rights"); Frank Murphy to Franklin D. Roosevelt, 7 July 1939, DOJR, box 5, entry 132, folder "Murphy: 6 Months Report" ("full weight").

89. ACLU bulletin 855, 11 February 1939, ACLUR, reel 176, vol. 2133; ACLU board to Frank Murphy, 6 February 1939, ACLUR, reel 168, vol. 2070.

90. "Murphy Tells Aides to Guard Civil Rights," *Washington Post*, April 20, 1939.

91. Frank Murphy, "Civil Liberties," National Radio Forum, 27 March 1939, DOJR, box 5, entry 132, folder "Civil Liberties."

92. Order No. 3204, Office of the Attorney General, 3 February 1939, DOJR, box 22, entry 132, folder "Civil Liberties" (describing research); Grenville Clark to Frank Murphy, 27 January 1939, GCP, box 80, folder 112 ("good deal"); memorandum for Mr. Dean, DOJR, box 22, entry 132, folder "Civil Liberties" ("somewhat difficult").

93. "F. S. P., Memorandum of Conference with Mr. Henry Schweinhaut, Chief of the Civil Liberties Unit of the Department of Justice," 3 October 1939, GCP, box 81, folder 90 ("violations"); "Labor Group Asks Hague Indictment," *NYT*, February 12, 1939.

94. The Civil Liberties Unit prepared a brief, but did not file it. Goluboff, *Lost Promise,* 118n14.

95. Brief on behalf of Petitioners, Hague v. CIO, 307 U.S. 532 (1939) (No. 651), 41.

96. Respondents' Brief, Hague v. CIO, 307 U.S. 532 (1939) (No. 651), 63.

97. "The Hague Case in the Supreme Court," *International Juridical Association Monthly Bulletin* 8 (July 1939), 1, ATVP, box 127, folder "Civil Liberties." On *Hague v. CIO* and the origins of public forum doctrine, see Robert C. Post, "Between Governance and Management: The History and Theory of the Public Forum," *UCLA Law Review* 34 (1987): 1721–1724; Geoffrey R. Stone, "Fora Americana: Speech in Public Places," *Supreme Court Review* 1974: 237–240.

98. Hughes agreed with Roberts "with respect to the merits." Hague, 307 U.S. at 531 (1939) (Hughes, J., concurring). He also approved Roberts's reasoning with respect to jurisdiction but believed that it was not adequately supported in the record. On that issue, he concurred in the opinion of Justice Stone.

99. Hague, 307 U.S. at 512–516.

100. Slaughter-House Cases, 83 U.S. 36 (1873); Hague, 307 U.S. at 520n1. The Department of Justice worried that Justice Roberts's opinion might be used to justify antialien measures that implicated civil liberties. O. John Rogge, address to National Conference on Civil Liberties, 14 October 1939, DOJR, box 22, entry 132, folder "Civil Rights."

101. Hague, 307 U.S. at 531–532.

102. Lewis Wood, "Hague Ban on C.I.O. Voided by the Supreme Court," *NYT*, June 6, 1939 (quoting Schweinhaut). On *United States v. Cruikshank*, 92 U.S. 542 (1875), see Pamela Brandwein, *Rethinking the Judicial Settlement of Reconstruction* (New York, 2011); Charles Lane, *The Day Freedom Died: The Colfax Massacre, the Supreme Court, and the Betrayal of Reconstruction* (New York, 2008).

103. "Civil Rights Conference," *Civil Liberties Quarterly*, September 1939, 1; O. John Rogge, address to National Conference on Civil Liberties, 14 October 1939, DOJR, box 22, entry 132, folder "Civil Rights."

104. O. John Rogge, address to National Conference on Civil Liberties, 14 October 1939, DOJR, box 22, entry 132, folder "Civil Rights" ("under"); Lewis Wood, "Hague Ban on CIO Voided by the Supreme Court," *NYT*, June 6, 1939 ("by violating," quoting Pressman). See also "Recent Development: Conspiracy to Coerce Employees into Union Activity Not Indictable under 18 U.S.C. 241," *Columbia Law Review* 55 (1955): 103–106; Tom C. Clark, "A Federal Prosecutor Looks at the Civil Rights Statutes," *Columbia Law Review* 47 (1947): 175–185; Goluboff, *Lost Promise*, 116–117.

105. "Murphy Acclaims Hague Case Ruling," *NYT*, June 8, 1939.

106. For example, "The Jersey City Case," *Washington Post*, June 6, 1939; "Affirming the Obvious," *Baltimore Sun*, June 7, 1939.

107. "Monster Public Meeting," ACLUR, reel 177, vol. 2134; ACLU press release, 7 June 1939, ACLUR, reel 176, vol. 2133 ("clear").

108. Jerome Britchey to Morris Ernst, 16 June 1939, ACLUR, reel 176, vol. 2133.

109. "Committee," *Bill of Rights Review*, 66; "The Rule of Law," *Washington Post*, June 14, 1939; "Jersey City Open to Free Assembly," *Civil Liberties Quarterly*, September 1939, 2.

110. Harry Graham Balter, "Recent Civil Rights Decision Discussed," *California State Bar Journal* 14 (June 1939): 200–204; McKean, *Boss*, 199 (quoting Carney).

111. "Hague City Hall Holds 'Open Door' for C.I.O.," *NYT*, August 1, 1939 ("always open"); "Hague Aids the C.I.O. in Jersey Labor Row," *NYT*, August 2, 1939; "Hague Is '100%' for Roosevelt Third Term," *NYT*, August 5, 1939; Frank R. Kent, "The Great Game of Politics," *Baltimore Sun*, August 11, 1939.

112. Arthur Krock, "In the Nation," *NYT*, January 19, 1940; "Murphy, Jackson Inducted Together," *NYT*, January 19, 1940 (quoting Ernst).

113. Hays repeatedly asked a police officer to arrest him, but the officer, after phoning headquarters, refused to do so. "CIO Seeking Truce with Hague, Based on Park for Free Speech," *New York World-Telegram*, May 20, 1938.

114. Hague Trial Transcript, vol. 2, 1077; William Callahan, address to Journal Square meeting, ACLUR, reel 177, vol. 2134.

115. ACLU press release, 22 June 1938, ACLUR, reel 167, vol. 2063 (emphasizing labor); letter to Roger Baldwin, 28 January 1938, ACLUR, reel 165, vol. 2040 ("I know"); Roger Baldwin, address to Journal Square meeting, 12 June 1939, ACLUR, reel 177, vol. 2134. The hearings of the Special Committee to Investigate Un-American Activities were convened on August 12, 1938, by Representative Martin Dies of Texas. On the relationship between the Dies Committee and civil liberties, see Jerold S. Auerbach, "The La Follette Committee: Labor and Civil Liberties in the New Deal," *Journal of American History* 51 (December 1964): 435–459, 450.

116. Morris Ernst to Roger Baldwin, 16 November 1938, ACLUR, reel 165, vol. 2041; Lee Pressman to Roger Baldwin, 21 February 1939, ACLUR, reel 176, vol. 2133.

117. "Hague Injunction," *Yale Law Journal*, 258.

118. "Committee," *Bill of Rights Review*, 69.

8. Free Speech or Fair Labor

1. "Limitations on Employer's Freedom of Expression," *NAM Law Digest* 3 (January 1940): 77–81, 77; "The Labor Board and Free Speech," *Bill of Rights Review* 1 (Summer 1940): 6.

2. Lucille Milner to Dorothea de Schweinitz, 1 August 1938, ACLUR, reel 160, vol. 2002.

3. See Sidney Fine, *Sit-Down: The General Motors Strike of 1936–1937* (Ann Arbor, 1969), 148–155, 231–311; J. Woodford Howard, *Mr. Justice Murphy: A Political Biography* (Princeton, NJ, 1968), 130–145; Nelson Lichtenstein, *Walter Reuther: The Most Dangerous Man in Detroit* (Urbana, IL, 1995), 75. On the creation of the Civil Liberties Unit, see Chapter 7.

4. "Talk by Maurice Sugar on the Legality and Ethics of the Sit-Down Strike," Cuyahoga County Bar Association, 14 April 1937, MSC, box 25, folder 25:3. Sugar was subsequently appointed chief legal counsel.

5. "Illegal Aspects of the 'Sit-Down' Strike," Law Department, National Association of Manufacturers, March 1937, NAMP, box 140, 27 ("direct precedent"); John D. Black (Winston, Strawn and Shaw), annual meeting minutes, 27–29 April 1937, CCUSR, box 31, 259 ("plainest principles"); Fine, *Sit-Down*, 239–331.

6. Melvyn Dubofsky, *The State and Labor in Modern America* (Chapel Hill, NC, 1994), 138; Fine, *Sit-Down*, 332–335; James T. Patterson, *Congressional Conservatism and the New Deal: The Growth of the Conservative Coalition in Congress, 1933–1939* (Lexington, 1967), 169. On "Roosevelt's Depression," see Richard Polenberg, *Reorganizing Roosevelt's Government: The Controversy over Executive Reorganization, 1936–1939* (Cambridge, MA, 1966), 149.

7. J. C. Pinkney to Robert La Follette Jr., 2 February 1937, "Violations of Free Speech and Rights of Labor," Sen 78A-F9, record group 46, NARA DC, 50.25, box 85 (blaming strikers); J. D. Fidler to Robert La Follette Jr., 25 February 1937, "Violations of Free Speech and Rights of Labor," Sen 78A-F9, record group 46, NARA DC, 50.25, box 85 (urging investigation).

8. "Statement on the Right of Picketing Adopted by the Board of Directors of the ACLU," 14 February 1938, ACLUR, reel, 156, vol. 1078 ("in any circumstances"); ACLU, "Civil Liberty: A Statement Defining the Position of the American Civil Liberties Union on the Chief Issues," December 1937, ACLUR, reel 156, vol. 1080.

9. "Statement on the Attitude of the American Civil Liberties Union to Current Issues of Civil Rights by the Board of Directors," March 1937, ACLUR, reel 142, vol. 969.

10. "Proposed Statement on So-Called Sit-Down and Stay-In Strikes Submitted to the National Committee of the American Civil Liberties Union by a Subcommittee Appointed by the Board of Directors," March 1937, ACLUR, reel 142, vol. 970; Morris Ernst to Roger Baldwin, 16 March 1936, ACLUR, reel 142, vol. 970; Arthur Garfield Hays to ACLU, 19 March 1937, ACLUR, reel 142, vol. 970; Arthur Garfield Hays to ACLU, 13 March 1937, ACLUR, reel 142, vol. 970 ("non-union").

11. John Codman to Roger Baldwin, 2 April 1937, ACLUR, reel 142, vol. 970 (trespassing); Edward D. Tittman to Roger Baldwin, 3 April 1937, ACLUR, reel 142, vol. 970 (trespassing); William Pickens to Roger Baldwin, 22 April 1937, ACLUR, reel 142, vol. 970 (dictatorship); Elizabeth Gurley Flynn to ACLU, 11 April 1937, ACLUR, reel 142, vol. 970; A. J. Muste to Roger Baldwin, 2 April 1937, ACLUR, reel 142, vol. 970 (American Liberty League); Herbert S. Bigelow to Roger Baldwin, 15 May

1937, ACLUR, reel 142, vol. 970 ("With the Labor"). The board submitted the statement to the national committee for an advisory referendum, but ultimately elected to retain its noncommittal course. "ACLU Statement on So-Called Sit-Down and Stay-In Strikes," April 1937, ACLUR, reel 142, vol. 970. A year later, the board revisited the issue of sit-down strikes, but after a long discussion and a request for revisions by its drafters, it made few significant changes. ACLU Committee on Labor's Rights, "Proposed Statement on Sit-Down Strikes," 9 February 1938, ACLUR, reel 156, vol. 1080. Edward D. Tittman eventually resigned over the issue of employer free speech. Edward D. Tittman to Roger Baldwin, 9 March 1938, ACLUR, reel 157, vol. 1081. Elizabeth Gurley Flynn returned to service on the board of directors during 1936–1937 and was listed in that year's annual report as a member of the national committee as well as the board. ACLU, *Let Freedom Ring! The Story of Civil Liberties, 1936–1937* (New York, 1937), 74, 90.

12. "Statement by the American Civil Liberties Union in Regard to Legisla-tion for Control of Trade Unions and Trade-Union Activities," April 1937, ACLUR, reel 142, vol. 969 (opposition to amendments); "Through the Editor's Specs," *Nation's Business*, November 1938, 7–9, 8–9 ("brutally," quoting Green). On the struggle between the AFL and CIO, see Melvyn Dubofsky and Warren Van Tyne, *John L. Lewis: A Biography* (New York, 1977), 307–309; Christopher Tomlins, *The State and the Unions: Labor Relations, Law, and the Organized Labor Movement in America, 1880–1960* (New York, 1985), 165–166.

13. John Codman to Roger Baldwin, 17 August 1938, ACLUR, reel 156, vol. 1078; "Statement by the ACLU on Violence in Strikes," 3 August 1937, ACLUR, reel 142, vol. 970.

14. "Committee Report on Legislative Proposals for Trade Union Control," 20 January 1938, ACLUR, reel 156, vol. 1078; "Draft of the Report of the Committee on Civil Rights in Labor Relations on Proposed Amendments to the National Labor Relations Act," 31 December 1938, ACLUR, reel 156, vol. 1078.

15. "Memorandum of the Special Committee to Consider Legislation to Curb Fascist Activities in the United States," 21 January 1938, ACLUR, reel 156, vol. 1080; O. R. McGuire to Jerome Britchey, 14 December 1939, ACLUR, reel 170, vol. 2081 (discussing Logan-Walter Bill and suggesting that "the enactment into law of the Administrative Law Bill is absolutely necessary for the protection of the civil liberties of the American people"). The debate over the Wagner Act, or NLRA, is described in Chapter 6.

16. William D. Scholle to Morris Ernst, 20 January 1938, ACLUR, reel 156, vol. 1078 ("no fault"); ACLU board minutes, 11 July 1938, ACLUM, reel 7; William Fennell, "What Shall the A.C.L.U. Do about Workers Discharged

for Failure to Join a Union in a 'Closed Shop,'" undated, ACLUR, reel 143, vol. 978. The notable exception is *Shelley v. Kraemer*, 334 U.S. 1 (1948). On the Wagner Act, state action, and the right to work, see Sophia Z. Lee, *The Workplace Constitution from the New Deal to the New Right* (New York, 2014).

17. "Resolution in Regard to Closed Shop Recommended by the Committee on Labor's Rights and Adopted by the Board of Directors at the Meeting on June 27, 1938," ACLUR, reel 156, vol. 1080.

18. "Newspaper Editor Questioned by NLRB, Says He Gave Information against Will," *NYT,* December 7, 1937 (describing interview with editor of St. Mary's Press regarding the Stackpole Carbon Company); "Barclay Ignores Subpoena by NLRB," *NYT,* December 7, 1937 (describing investigation of Weirton Steel and *Mill and Factory* magazine).

19. "Bridges Calls N.L.R.B. Peril to Free Press," *New York Herald-Tribune,* December 4, 1937 ("open attack[]," quoting Republican senator H. Styles Bridges); "NLRB Order Defied on Press Freedom," *NYT,* December 3, 1937; T. Henry Walnut to Roger Baldwin, 18 December 1937, ACLUR, reel 143, vol. 978 (requesting statement); Nathan Greene, "The National Labor Relations Board on Freedom of Press," ACLUR, reel 143, vol. 978; ACLU press release, 18 December 1937, ACLUR, reel 143, vol. 978. For the NLRB's position, see *Mansfield Mills Company,* 3 N.L.R.B. 901 (1937). On the "iron fist," see Roger Baldwin to *New York World-Telegram,* 30 December 1937, ACLUR, reel 143, vol. 978. The metaphor will be familiar to contemporary labor lawyers from *NLRB v. Exchange Parts,* 375 U.S. 405, 409 (1964).

20. See, for example, Roger Baldwin to Edward D. Tittman, 15 January 1938, ACLUR, reel 160, vol. 2002; Walter T. Fisher to Roger Baldwin, 5 October 1938, ACLUR, reel 156, vol. 1078; T. Henry Walnut to Roger Baldwin, 30 December 1937, ACLUR, reel 143, vol. 978.

21. Roger Baldwin to members of the national committee, 31 January 1938, ACLUR, reel 156, vol. 1078; "Proposed Statement on Employers' Rights in Industrial Conflict," 22 January 1938, ACLUR, reel 160, vol. 2002; "Majority Report, Committee on Labor's Rights Proposed Statement on Employers' Rights in Industrial Conflicts," 31 January 1938, ACLUR, reel 156, vol. 1078; R. W. Riis to Roger Baldwin, 7 January 1938, ACLU, reel 160, vol. 2002 ("free competition"); R. W. Riis, "Minority Report on the National Labor Relations Act and Free Speech," 31 January 1938, ACLUR, reel 156, vol. 1078 ("bring about").

22. Morris Ernst to Roger Baldwin, 5 February 1938, ACLUR, reel 157, vol. 1081; Lloyd Garrison to Roger Baldwin, 4 February 1938, ACLUR, reel 157, vol. 1081.

23. John Haynes Holmes to Roger Baldwin, 2 February 1938, ACLUR, reel 157, vol. 1081 ("most specious"); John Haynes Holmes to Harry Ward, 16 February 1938, ACLUR, reel 156, vol. 1080 ("excommunications"); John Haynes Holmes to Harry Ward, 11 February 1938, ACLUR, reel 156, vol. 1080 (means to end).

24. Harry Ward to John Haynes Holmes, 10 February 1938, ACLUR, reel 156, vol. 1080.

25. For example, "Shall We Defend Free Speech for Nazis in America?" ACLUR, reel 105, vol. 678. The most analogous issue was the ACLU's position on federal radio censorship, and in particular, licensing rules discouraging racial and religious animus in broadcasting by local stations. These stations, in many cases, were espousing hatred of racial minorities in localities where they were most vulnerable.

26. "Communist Cases Declined in 1937," *Civil Liberties Quarterly,* March 1938, 2. Of course, regulation of business speech to protect the *public,* in the context of advertising, disclosure rules, and competition, was commonplace.

27. Roger Baldwin to Dorothea de Schweinitz, 1 September 1938, ACLUR, reel 160, vol. 2002.

28. ACLU board minutes, 7 February 1938, ACLUM, reel 7; Felix Frankfurter to Roger Baldwin, 1 April 1937, ACLUR, reel 142, vol. 970.

29. There is very little literature on the *Ford* case, most likely because it was primarily an administrative case. For short descriptions, see William A. Donohue, *The Politics of the American Civil Liberties Union* (New Brunswick, NJ, 1985), 47–50; Ken I. Kersch, "How Conduct Became Speech and Speech Became Conduct: A Political Development Case Study in Labor Law and the Freedom of Speech," *University of Pennsylvania Journal of Constitutional Law* 8 (March 2006): 255–297. Laura Weinrib, "The Liberal Compromise: Civil Liberties, Labor, and the Limits of State Power, 1917–1940" (PhD dissertation, Princeton University, 2011), 423–514, provides a more detailed account of the litigation.

30. Stephen Harlan Norwood, *Strikebreaking and Intimidation: Mercenaries and Masculinity in Twentieth-Century America* (Chapel Hill, NC, 2002), 173.

31. Lichtenstein, *Reuther,* 74, 80; "200,000 Summoned to Aid Ford Drive," *NYT,* May 19, 1937.

32. National Citizens' Committee for the Protection of Civil Rights in the Automobile Industry, "The Trial That Shocked a Nation," RTFC, box 5, "UAW, 1933–1955, Battle of the Overpass."

33. Lichtenstein, *Reuther,* 83–86. The photographer was James Kilpatrick.

34. The Battle of the Overpass likely "boosted organization." J. T. C., "Memorandum for Mr. McCormack, Investigation of Smith Committee Exhibits," 2 January 1941, 5, FMCLP, acc. 897, box 2. See also Christopher H. Johnson, *Maurice Sugar: Law, Labor and the Left in Detroit, 1912–1950* (Detroit, 1988), 224.

35. National Citizens' Committee for the Protection of Civil Rights in the Automobile Industry, "The Trial That Shocked a Nation," RTFC, box 5, "UAW, 1933–1955, Battle of the Overpass." The NLRB trial examiner was John T. Lindsay.

36. Johnson, *Sugar*, 225; J. Warren Madden, address to United States Conference of Mayors, 16 November 1937, GCP, box 86, folder 35 ("employees").

37. J. T. C., "Memorandum for Mr. McCormack, Investigation of Smith Committee Exhibits," 2 January 1941, 6, FMCLP, acc. 897, box 2 (commenting on trial lawyers); E. F. B., "Memorandum for Mr. H. A. Moore," 28 August 1937, FMCLP, acc. 897, box 1, vol. 1 (ample evidence); Ford Motor Company (Highland Park and Dearborn, Mich.), 4 N.L.R.B. 621 (1937); H. D., "Memorandum for Mr. Wood," 26 December 1937, FMCLP, acc. 897, "Memoranda of Facts through Dec. 1938" ("were beaten"). E. F. B. was most likely E. Fontaine Broun, who would later serve as assistant general counsel of the navy. H. D. was likely Harmon Duncombe. In 1944, the firm was renamed Cravath, Swaine, and Moore.

38. Robert Taylor Swaine, *The Cravath Firm and Its Predecessors, 1819–1948* (New York, 1948), 328 (Frederick H. Wood), 565 (William D. Whitney; quoting Heywood Broun); "Memorandum for Mr. Whitney, Ford Labor Case," 28 December 1937, FMCLP, acc. 897, box 5, vol. 1 ("actual invasion"; describing Everett Moore).

39. H. D., "Memorandum for Mr. Whitney," 24 December 1937, FMCLP, acc. 897, box 1; F. A. E. S., "Memorandum for Mr. Wood," 10 June 1938, FMCLP, acc. 897, "Memoranda of Facts," vol. 1 ("by handing"). F. A. E. S. was likely Francis A. E. Spitzer.

40. "Suggested Recommendations to the Executive Committee and the Board of the National Association of Manufacturers from the Special Committee Appointed to Consider Ways and Means of Coordinating the Public Information Activities of the Association with Other Organizations," NAMP, box 112, folder "Committee—Public Relations Advisory Committee 1939"; W. D. W., "Memorandum for Mr. Wood," 11 January 1938, FMCLP, acc. 897, box 5, "Memoranda of Facts," vol. 1.

41. Ford Motor Company, 4 N.L.R.B. 621, 674 (December 22, 1937) ("ruthlessness"); "Paragraph 1(e) of the Board's order should be set aside," 23 May 1938, 18, FMCLP, acc. 897, box 4, vol. 2.

42. Exhibit A, Petition of Ford Motor Company to Vacate and Set Aside Decision and Order and for Rehearing before the NLRB, Sixth Circuit, 11 April 1938, FMCLP, acc. 51, box 4, 7919.

43. Luther K. Bell as told to Fred De Armond, "We Need One Big Union for Business," *Nation's Business,* August 1937, 22; "Why and How the Wagner Act Should Be Amended," NAM statement before the Committee on Education and Labor, June 1939, 23, NAMP, box 58. See also Herbert Corey, "Washington and Your Business," *Nation's Business,* November 1937, 56; "The Wagner Act 'Settles' a Strike," *Nation's Business,* October 1939, 15; "Washington and Your Business," *Nation's Business,* June 1940, 80.

44. "Memorandum in Regard to the Claim That the National Labor Relations Board Has Infringed the Employer's Constitutional Right of Free Speech," NLRB memorandum, GCP, box 86, folder 38 ("public press"); E. F. B., "Memorandum for Mr. H. A. Moore," 28 August 1937, FMCLP, acc. 897, box 1, "Memoranda of Law," vol. 1 ("fundamental right"); H. D., "Memorandum on Ford Labor Case," 15 January 1938, FMCLP, acc. 897, box 1 (summarizing cases). *Associated Press v. NLRB,* 301 U.S. 103 (1937), is discussed in Chapter 6.

45. Petition of Respondent, Ford Motor Company, for Leave to Adduce Additional Evidence, and Exhibit A Thereto, 4 April 1938, FMCLP, acc. 51, box 4; Ford Motor Company v. N.L.R.B., 305 U.S. 364 (1939). *Morgan v. United States,* 304 U.S. 1 (1938), was decided on April 28. On the influence of *Morgan* on the NLRB's procedures in the *Ford* case and others, see James A. Gross, *The Making of the National Labor Relations Board: A Study in Economics, Politics, and the Law* (Albany, 1974), 30–39.

46. 79 Congressional Record 10111 (1935) ("Nothing in this act shall abridge the freedom of speech or the press as guaranteed in the first amendment of the constitution"); 79 Congressional Record 7960 (1935) ("Indeed"). The proposed amendment was an effort to impede organizing by the Newspaper Guild. Irving Bernstein, *Turbulent Years: A History of the American Worker, 1933–1941* (Boston, 1969), 348.

47. "Paragraph 1(e) of the Board's order should be set aside," 23 May 1938, 18, FMCLP, acc. 897, box 4, vol. 2 ("workers should"); H. G. W. Jr., "Memorandum for Messrs. Wood and McCormack," 26 August 1938, FMCLP, acc. 897, box 5, vol. 1.

48. R. S. C. to George Alger, 11 March 1938, ACLUR, reel 156, vol. 1080 ("outwardly"). For ACLU criticism of New Dealers, see, for example, Special Committee to Investigate Lobbying Activities to Sherman Minton, 27 May 1938, ACLUR, reel 157, vol. 1078.

49. Johnson, *Sugar,* 116–124 (describing Ford Massacre; a fifth victim died months later of his injuries); Roger Baldwin to Frank Murphy,

30 March 1932, MSC, box 53, folder 53:12; Conference for the Protection of Civil Rights, "Support Right to Organize at Ford's," 15 July 1937, ACLUR, reel 152, vol. 1037; telegram to Harriet Chapman, 26 August 1937, ACLUR, reel 152, vol. 1037; National Citizens' Committee for the Protection of Civil Rights in the Automobile Industry, "The Trial That Shocked a Nation," RTFC, box 5, "UAW, 1933–1955, Battle of the Overpass." On the Conference for the Protection of Civil Rights, see Angela D. Dillard, *Faith in the City: Preaching Radical Social Change in Detroit* (Ann Arbor, 2007), 81.

50. Arthur Garfield Hays, "Proposed Statement on Ford," 21 February 1938, ACLUR, reel 156, vol. 1080; Nathan Greene, "Memorandum on Mr. Hays's Report," 14 February 1938, ACLUR, reel 156, vol. 1080; "Memorandum on the Ford Case by the Committee on Labor's Rights," 28 February 1938, ACLUR, reel 156, vol. 1078; "Memorandum on the Ford Case," ACLUR, reel 156, vol. 1078.

51. Minutes of special board meeting, 2 March 1938, ACLUR, reel 156, vol. 1078; Russell L. Greenman, "New Government Hurdles for Business," *Nation's Business*, October 1939, 19.

52. J. Warren Madden to Roger Baldwin, 11 March 1938, ACLUR, reel 164, vol. 2037 ("coercive per se"); J. Warren Madden, address to National Conference on Civil Liberties, 13 October 1939, GCP, box 86, folder 41; Coppage v. Kansas 236 U.S. 1, 27 (1915) (Holmes, J., dissenting); "N.L.R.B. and Free Speech," IJA Monthly, vol. 7, GCP, box 86, folder 35, 36 ("to establish"). See also Nathan Witt to Grenville Clark, 28 October 1938, GCP, box 82, folder 75 (stressing fair union elections in Mobile and New Orleans, where the NLRB had ensured "freedom of expression on the part of both negroes and whites").

53. Lucille Milner to Warren Madden, 15 March 1938, ACLUR, reel 164, vol. 2037; Roger Baldwin to Charles Fahy, 28 April 1938, ACLUR, reel 164, vol. 2037 (reporting that the ACLU was reaffirming its original position); Harry Ward, "Dissenting Opinion in the Ford Case," 17 June 1938, ACLUR, reel 156, vol. 1080; ACLU board minutes, 27 June 1938. William G. Fennell's persistent disagreement with the leftists on the Committee on Civil Rights in Labor Relations prompted the board to adopt a resolution prohibiting membership in policy subcommittees by nonmembers, thereby excluding him. ACLU board minutes, 8 August 1938, ACLUM, reel 7. Fennell decried the ousting as a "'liberal purge.'" William Fennell to Lucille B. Milner, 19 August 1938, ACLUR, reel 156, vol. 1078.

54. Muskin Shoe Company, 8 N.L.R.B. 1 (1938); Mock-Judson-Voehringer Company, 8 N.L.R.B. 133 (1938); "Employers' 'Free Speech' Not Curbed," *Civil Liberties Quarterly*, September 1938, 1.

55. NLRB v. Union Pacific Stages, 99 F.2d 153 (9th Cir. 1938); Roger Baldwin to Nathan Greene, 18 October 1938, ACLUR, reel 156, vol. 1078.

56. *Second Annual Report of the National Labor Relations Board* (Washington, DC, 1937), 4 ("no limitations"); *NLRA and Proposed Amendments: Hearings of the Committee on Education and Labor* (Washington, DC, 1939), 2128 (quoting Edwin Smith); NLRB release R-1082, Edwin S. Smith, address, 23 July 1938, ACLUR, reel 160, vol. 2002 ("working population").

57. ACLU, "Proceedings of the National Conference on Civil Liberties in the Present Emergency," New York City, 13–14 October 1939, GCP, box 77, folder 2, 17 (Frederick H. Wood).

58. See Sidney Fine, *Frank Murphy*, vol. 2, *The New Deal Years* (Ann Arbor, 1979), 481–516; James A. Gross, *The Reshaping of the National Labor Relations Board: National Labor Policy in Transition, 1937–1947* (Albany, 1981), 5–84. In November the CIO reorganized as the Congress of Industrial Organizations, an independent labor organization rather than a committee.

59. ACLU board minutes, 30 January 1939, ACLUM, reel 7; Arthur Garfield Hays to ACLU, 26 January 1939, ACLUR, reel 169, vol. 2080.

60. Testimony of J. Warren Madden, Hearings before the Senate Committee on Education and Labor, 19 April 1939, ACLUR, reel 169, vol. 2080.

61. John Haynes Holmes to Roger Baldwin, 20 April 1939, ACLUR, reel 169, vol. 2080 ("Brother"); Lee Pressman to Arthur Garfield Hays, 10 February 1939, ACLUR, reel 169, vol. 2080; CIO, "Why the Wagner Act Should NOT Be Amended," October 1938, ACLUR, reel 156, vol. 1078; resolution, annual meeting minutes, Chamber of Commerce of the United States, 2–4 May 1939, CCUSR, box 31, 395; Arthur Garfield Hays to ACLU, 14 February 1939, ACLUR, reel 169, vol. 2080 (arguing that the *Ford* case indicated that a free speech amendment was necessary); ACLU press release, 24 April 1939, ACLUR, reel 176, vol. 2130 ("either unnecessary").

62. Roger Baldwin to J. Warren Madden, 9 January 1939, ACLUR, reel 189, vol. 2233; Ford press release, quoted in "Memorandum for Mr. McCormack," 17 February 1939, FMCLP, acc. 897, box 4, vol. 2.

63. Jerome Britchey to Arthur Garfield Hays, 20 February 1939, ACLUR, reel 189, vol. 2233.

64. Arthur Garfield Hays to ACLU, 29 March 1939, ACLUR, reel 189, vol. 2233; Brief on Behalf of the ACLU, as Amicus Curiae, Ford Motor Company, No. C-199, 14 N.L.R.B. 346 (August 9, 1939), ACLUR, reel 189, vol. 2232 (signed by Walter Frank and Osmond Fraenkel); "Liberties Union Again Aids Ford," *NYT,* April 24, 1939; NLRA and Proposed Amendments, Hearings of the Committee on Education and Labor (Washington, DC, 1939), 2084. From the perspective of protecting labor

movement speech, the requirement of ongoing violence was an important qualification. Labor advocates had condemned courts for banning peaceful picketing by a labor union based on past violence. See, for example, "Recent Case: Prior Illegal Picketing as Ground for Enjoining All Picketing Despite Anti-injunction Act," *Harvard Law Review* 52 (1939): 1183–1184.

65. P. B., "Freedom of Speech and Corporations," 13 June 1939, FMCLP, box 3, vol. 3, "Memoranda of Law from Nov. 1, 1938 to Dec. 31, 1939." For example, *American Steel Foundries v. Tri-City Central Trades Council,* 257 U.S. 184 (1921) (holding mass picketing coercive).

66. P. B., "Memorandum: Ford Cases, Free Speech," 10 January 1939, FMCLP, acc. 897, box 3, vol. 3.

67. Ford Motor Company, 14 N.L.R.B. 346 (August 9, 1939) ("deliberately planned"); NLRB press release, 11 August 1939, ACLUR, reel 189, vol. 2233.

68. Nathan Greene to Jerome Britchey, 19 August 1939, ACLUR, reel 189, vol. 2233; Osmond Fraenkel to Jerome Britchey, 18 August 1939, ACLUR, reel 189, vol. 2233; "Report of Committee on Civil Rights in Labor Relations with Regard to the Ford Case, Adopted by the Board of Directors," 16 October 1939, ACLUR, reel 176, vol. 2130; ACLU press release, 22 October 1939, ACLUR, reel 176, vol. 2130.

69. Brief for Respondent, NLRB v. Ford Motor Company, 114 F.2d 905 (6th Cir. 1940), FMCLP, acc. 51, box 4, 46–48; Schneider v. New Jersey, 308 U.S. 147, 151 (1939) ("vital").

70. Brief for Respondent, NLRB v. Ford Motor Company, 114 F.2d 905 (6th Cir. 1940), FMCLP, acc. 51, box 4, 48.

71. "Statement for the Press by the ACLU to Accompany Announcement of Resolution Adopted on February 5, 1940," GJP, General Correspondence, cont. 3, box 3, folder "American Civil Liberties Union"; "Crisis in the Civil Liberties Union," ILDP, reel 19, box 21.

72. Norman Thomas, "Your World and Mine," *Call,* December 16, 1939; Gardner Jackson to Florence H. Luscomb, Civil Liberties Committee of Massachusetts, 21 December 1939, GJP, General Correspondence, cont. 3, box 3, folder "American Civil Liberties Union" ("pragmatic"). During the late 1930s, Ernst developed a close personal and political relationship with the president (as well as Eleanor Roosevelt, who joined the ACLU in 1950). See, for example, Franklin D. Roosevelt to Morris Ernst, 29 December 1940, FDRP, president's personal file 2841, "Ernest [*sic*], Morris L., 1935–1941."

73. "Resolution Adopted by the Board of Directors and National Committee," 5 February 1940, ACLUR, box 74, folder 6. The 1970 investigation by the ACLU concluded that the resolution was written by Ernst. Second Report, ACLUR, box 75, folder 11.

74. ACLU, "Statement to Members and Friends regarding the February 5th Resolution," May 1940, GJP, General Correspondence, cont. 3 (hereafter "Statement on February Resolution"), 9 ("create"); Harry Ward to national committee and board of directors, 4 March 1940, ACLUR, box 74, folder 4; I. F. Stone, press release, 18 March 1940, ACLUR, box 74, folder 4.

75. ACLU, "Statement on February Resolution," 14; B. W. Huebsch to fellow directors, 19 April 1940, ACLUR, box 74, folder 6. The ACLU in fact received a number of contributions from anti-Communists after the resolution. For example, Morrie Ryskind to Roger Baldwin, 4 March 1940, ACLUR, box 74, folder 14 (enclosing donation and promising to enlist "others who have been worried by the presence of the Commies").

76. "Reply of Elizabeth Gurley Flynn to Charges Filed by Dorothy Dunbar Bromley," ACLUR, box 75, folder 1. On the Flynn expulsion, see, for example, Corliss Lamont, ed., *The Trial of Elizabeth Gurley Flynn by the American Civil Liberties Union* (New York, 1968); Burt Neuborne, "Of Pragmatism and Principle: A Second Look at the Expulsion of Elizabeth Gurley Flynn from the ACLU's Board of Directors," *Tulsa Law Review* 41 (2006): 799–815; Samuel Walker, *In Defense of American Liberties: A History of the ACLU* (New York, 1990), 132–133; Judy Kutulas, *The American Civil Liberties Union and the Making of Modern Liberalism, 1930–1960* (Chapel Hill, NC, 2006), 75–81.

77. Elizabeth Gurley Flynn, "Why I Won't Resign from the ACLU," *New Masses,* March 19, 1940 ("steady"); "Reply of Elizabeth Gurley Flynn to Charges Filed by Dorothy Dunbar Bromley," ACLUR, box 75, folder 1 ("in a vacuum"). See also Elizabeth Gurley Flynn, "I Am Expelled from Civil Liberties!," *Daily Worker,* March 17, 1940.

78. ACLU, "Statement on February Resolution," 9; ACLU, "Summary of meeting of Board of Directors held on May 7, 1940 at the City Club," 166, ACLUR, box 74, folder 2 (votes). Thomas, who was not at the meeting, thought that the board should wait for Flynn to resign. Norman Thomas to John Haynes Holmes, 22 March 1940, ACLUR, box 74, folder 3. The national committee voted to approve Flynn's removal, twenty-seven to twelve. "Report of National Committee Returns," 10 August 1940, ACLUR, box 75, folder 4.

79. Abraham Isserman to the Board of Directors of the ACLU, 25 February 1941, ILDP, reel 19 box 21.

80. Roger Baldwin to Alexander Meiklejohn, 13 February 1940, AMP, box 4, folder 4; John Haynes Holmes to Alexander Meiklejohn, 23 February 1940, AMP, box 16, folder 37; John Haynes Holmes to Alexander Meiklejohn, 26 April 1940, AMP, box 16, folder 37. Meiklejohn contemplated resigning but did not want to harm the civil liberties cause. Alexander Meiklejohn to Roger Baldwin, 20 January 1942, AMP, box 1, folder 21.

81. See, for example, Kutulas, *Modern Liberalism,* 79 (recounting and echoing criticism by prior historians of the ACLU's purported departure from the principle of free speech for everyone). The ACLU was deliberate in its subsequent defenses of Communist speech. For example, ACLU, "Statement on Measures excluding Communists and German-American Bundists from Public and Private Employment," June 1940, ACLUR, reel 184, vol. 2199 (protesting exclusion of Communists and Nazis from the United States Civil Service and arguing that the "requirements of a private organization in selecting its personnel are wholly different from those of the public service").

82. ACLU, "Summary of meeting of Board of Directors held on May 7, 1940 at the City Club," 136, ACLUR, box 74, folder 2.

83. ACLU board minutes, 22 January 1940, ACLUM, reel 8 (describing decision involving the Adams Brothers Manifold Printing Company); Jerome Britchey to Charles Fahy, 28 January 1940, ACLUR, reel 189, vol. 2232; Ford Motor Company (Somerville, Mass.), 19 N.L.R.B. 732 (1940); "Memorandum on the NLRB Order in the Massachusetts Ford Motor Company Case," 26 January 1940, ACLUR, reel 189, vol. 2232; John Haynes Holmes to Roger Baldwin, 22 January 1940, ACLUR, reel 189, vol. 2232; Arthur Garfield Hays to NLRB, 2 February 1940, ACLUR, reel 189, vol. 2232; ACLU press release, 5 February 1940, ACLUR, reel 189, vol. 2232 ("strong").

84. ACLU press bulletin 923, 1 June 1940, ACLUR, reel 182, vol. 2177. The amendments, drafted at the instigation of Virginia representative Howard Smith, never made it out of committee.

85. Thornhill v. Alabama, 310 U.S. 88, 95 (1940); Carlson v. California, 310 U.S. 106, 113 (1940).

86. Lee Pressman to Arthur Garfield Hays, 10 February 1939, ACLUR, reel 169, vol. 2080. Despite his general antipathy toward a "legal approach to labor action," Pressman saw great potential in "the growing realization and acceptance of the fact that labor action is nothing more or less than the exercise of constitutional rights" to freedom of speech and assembly. Gilbert J. Gall, *Pursuing Justice: Lee Pressman, the New Deal, and the CIO* (Albany, 1990), 108 (quoting Pressman). On the ACLU's relationship with Murphy, see Fine, *Sit-Down,* 149–154.

87. Charles O. Gregory, "Peaceful Picketing and Freedom of Speech," *ABA Journal* 26 (1940): 709–715, 714.

88. Milk Wagon Drivers Union v. Meadowmoor Dairies, Inc., 312 U.S. 287, 293 (1941); H. D., "Memorandum for Messrs. Wood and McCormack," 13 February 1941, FMCLP, acc. 897, box 4, vol. 5; Gregory, "Peaceful Picketing," 715; Bethlehem Steel Co. v. NLRB, 120 F.2d 641, 688 (DC Cir. 1941).

89. NLRB v. Ford Motor Company, 114 F.2d 905 (6th Cir. 1940). Sit-down strikes were deemed outside the protection of the Wagner Act in *NLRB v. Fansteel Metallurgical Corp.*, 306 U.S. 240 (1939).

90. Ford, 114 F.2d at 912, 913; F. H. Wood, "Memorandum for Messrs. McCormack, Duncombe and Borie," 27 March 1940, FMCLP, acc. 897, box 4, vol. 2. The issue was no longer novel, and the Ninth Circuit's opinion in *Union Pacific Stages*, 99 F.2d 153 (9th Cir. 1938), indicated that courts would be receptive to a free speech claim. Although the Supreme Court had upheld NLRB orders prohibiting the circulation of antiunion statements, for example, *Consolidated Edison v. NLRB*, 305 U.S. 197 (1938), it had never addressed the issue squarely.

91. Ford, 114 F.2d at 914. A Ford memorandum made the same argument. P. B., "Memorandum: Ford Cases, Free Speech," 10 January 1939, FMCLP, acc. 897, box 3, vol. 3.

92. Ford, 114 F.2d at 914 (citing *Hague*).

93. NLRB press release, 20 June 1941, FMCLP, acc. 897, box 2, file "Press Releases"; F. H. W., "Memorandum for Mr. McCormack, NLRB v. Ford Motor Company," 13 October 1940, FMCLP, acc. 897, box 4, vol. 2.

94. "The Labor Board Goes Fascist," *New York Herald-Tribune*, December 4, 1937; "Denial of Free Speech and Fair Trial," *Chicago Daily Tribune*, February 9, 1940; "Muzzling the Employer," *New York Herald Tribune*, January 24, 1940; "Court Ruling on 'Free Speech' in the Ford Case," *NYT*, October 9, 1940; "Recent Case: NLRB Order Remanded to Correct Procedural Irregularity," *Harvard Law Review* 52 (1939): 680; "Employer Freedom of Speech under the Wagner Act," *Yale Law Journal* 48 (1938): 72–80; "ABC Union, Em One et al. v. Dorf Company, Supreme Court of Ames," FMCLP, acc. 897, box 4, vol. 5.

95. Grenville Clark to Pal Windels, 12 July 1938, GCP, box 82, folder 72; memorandum for members of the Special Committee of the Bill of Rights, 19 August 1939, GCP, box 78, folder 23; Grenville Clark to Charles A. Beardsley, 13 February 1940, GCP, box 77, folder 33.

96. Grenville Clark, memorandum for members of the Committee on the Bill of Rights, 23 January 1940, GCP, box 78, folder 23; report of the Committee on the Bill of Rights to the ABA House of Delegates, Chicago, 9 January 1940, Transcript of Proceedings, GCP, box 83, folder 2; Charles A. Beardsley to Grenville Clark, 23 January 1940, GCP, box 77, folder 33.

97. Frank Hogan to Grenville Clark, 4 January 1940, GCP, box 79, folder 64; "Report of Sub-Committee to the ABA Committee on the Bill of Rights, Re the Committee's Filing a Brief in the United States Supreme Court in NLRB vs. Ford Motor Company," undated, GCP, box 86, folder 35

("absolutely impartial"); Grenville Clark, memorandum for members of the Committee on the Bill of Rights, 23 January 1940, GCP, box 83, folder 11; Grenville Clark to George I. Haight, 25 January 1940, GCP, box 79, folder 32 ("vital issue"). Clark maintained, however, that "*on the whole* the governing authorities of the Association . . . ha[d] given excellent support" to the committee's activities. Grenville Clark to Charles Edmundson, *St. Louis Post-Dispatch,* 8 February 1940, GCP, box 78, folder 93.

98. "The Labor Board and Free Speech," *Bill of Rights Review* 1 (Summer 1940): 6; William L. Ransom, "Lawyers Can Help Meet Great Issues," *ABA Journal* 26 (1940): 561–565, 563 (address to Kansas bar).

99. Ford Motor Company v. NLRB, 312 U.S. 689 (1941); "Notes and Cases," *Bill of Rights Review* 1 (Winter 1941): 141–142.

100. ACLU, *A Report on American Democratic Liberties in War-Time* (New York, 1942), 39 (describing the Supreme Court's position as "substantially that taken by the Civil Liberties Union").

101. NLRB v. Virginia Electric and Power Company, 314 U.S. 469 (1941). Several post-*Ford* NLRB decisions had made similar findings. For example, Huch Leather Company, 11 N.L.R.B. 394 (1939) (violation of the Wagner Act to refer to the CIO as "a bunch of Bolsheviks"); Leitz Carpet Corporation, 27 N.L.R.B. 235 (1940) (coercive to refer to unions as "shyster outfits").

102. Herbert Corey, "He Beat a Path to Their Door," *Nation's Business,* August 1944, 32 (quoting William B. Barton). See, for example, Harry A. Millis and Emily Clark Brown, *From the Wagner Act to Taft-Hartley: A Study of National Labor Policy and Labor Relations* (Chicago, 1950), 174–189; W. Willard Wirtz, "The New National Labor Relations Board: Herein of 'Employer Persuasion,'" *Northwestern University Law Review* 49 (1954): 594–618.

103. For example, ACLU, *Civil Liberty: A Statement Defining the Position of the American Civil Liberties Union* (New York, 1945).

Epilogue

1. Frank Murphy, "In Defense of Democracy: Civil Liberties in Peace and War: Address to National Conference on Civil Liberties," October 1939, GCP, box 80, folder 112. See generally John W. Wertheimer, "A 'Switch in Time' beyond the Nine: Historical Memory and the Constitutional Revolution of the 1930s," *Studies in Law, Politics and Society* 53 (2010): 3–34.

2. Public Relations Advisory Group, October 23 (no year), NAMP, box 112, folder "Committee—Public Relations Advisory Committee 1939" ("link"); "Your Stake in Private Enterprise," NAM speakers bulletin, July 1940, NAMP, box 110, folder "Public Relations Speakers Bureau," 5–6 ("whole

structure"); ACLU, "Proceedings of the National Conference on Civil Liberties in the Present Emergency," New York City, 13–14 October 1939, GCP, box 77, folder 2 ("common"); ACLU press bulletin 1004, 22 December 1941, GCP, box 77, folder 2 ("Never"). See also "Summary of the Addresses of the Cleveland Executives Conference on Public Relations," NAMP, box 112, folder "Public Relations."

3. ACLU, *In the Shadow of War: The Story of Civil Liberty, 1939–1940* (New York, 1940), 17 (criticizing Murphy); Robert H. Jackson, "Mobilizing the Profession for Defense," *ABA Journal* 27 (1941): 350–353; Francis Biddle to all United States attorneys, Department of Justice Circular No. 3356, Supplement 2, 4 April 1942, FDRP, official file 1581, "Civil Liberties 1933–1945"; O. John Rogge, address to National Conference on Civil Liberties, 14 October 1939, DOJR, box 22, entry 132, folder "Civil Rights." On civil liberties during the Second World War, see, for example, Donna T. Haverty-Stacke, *Trotskyists on Trial: Free Speech and Political Persecution since the Age of FDR* (New York, 2016); Judy Kutulas, *The American Civil Liberties Union and the Making of Modern Liberalism, 1930–1960* (Chapel Hill, NC, 2006), 89–135; Richard Steele, *Free Speech in the Good War* (New York, 1999); Geoffrey R. Stone, *Perilous Times: Free Speech in Wartime from the Sedition Act of 1798 to the War on Terrorism* (New York, 2004), 235–310.

4. Bridges v. Wixon, 326 U.S. 135 (1945); Hartzel v. United States, 322 U.S. 680 (1944); Cramer v. United States, 325 U.S. 1 (1945); Korematsu v. United States, 323 U.S. 214, 216 (1944). On Japanese American internment, see Peter Irons, *Justice at War: The Story of the Japanese-American Internment Cases* (Berkeley, 1983); Greg Robinson, *By Order of the President: FDR and the Internment of Japanese Americans* (Cambridge, MA, 2001).

5. Bridges v. California, 314 U.S. 252, 263 (1941).

6. Franklin D. Roosevelt, Annual Message to Congress, January 6, 1941, available at http://www.archives.gov/historical-docs/todays-doc/?dod-date =106.

7. H. W. Prentis Jr., "Safeguarding American Freedom," February 1945, NAMP, acc. 1411, box 2, folder 100 ("free mind"; past president, NAM); IJA, "Civil Liberties and the NLRB," reprinted from address by Nathan Greene, 8 March 1940, MSC, folder 54:17, 5; Joseph Schlossberg, address to "Ford Workers' Mass Meeting," Fordson High School Auditorium, 13 February 1938, FMCLP, acc. 897, box 101, 44–46 ("the employers").

8. "Memorandum in Support of Proposal to Confine the National Labor Relations Board," FMCLP, box 3, vol. 3, 15 (quoting Edwin S. Smith, address to Carolina Political Union, 30 March 1938); "Statement of Attorney General Murphy before the Senate Committee of Education and Labor, re: Bill S. 1970," DOJR, box 6, entry 132. Jackson, Murphy's

successor as attorney general (and his future colleague on the Supreme Court), thought the prospect of government abuses outweighed the potential benefits of an affirmative prosecutorial program. Robert Jackson, "Message on the Launching of the 'Bill of Rights Review,'" *Bill of Rights Review* 1 (Summer 1940): 35. On debate over the La Follette Committee's bill, see Jerold S. Auerbach, "The La Follette Committee: Labor and Civil Liberties in the New Deal," *Journal of American History* 51 (December 1964): 435–459, 454.

9. Brief for Respondent, NLRB v. Ford Motor Company, 114 F.2d 905 (6th Cir. 1940), FMCLP, acc. 51, box 4, 54 ("liberty to emerge"; quoting J. Warren Madden, radio address, 29 January 1939); J. Warren Madden, address to National Conference on Civil Liberties, 13 October 1939, GCP, box 86, folder 41 ("new right"); J. Warren Madden, address over Columbia Broadcasting System, 29 August 1938, GCP, box 86, folder 35 ("backgrounds").

10. "Proceedings of the National Conference on Civil Liberties in the Present Emergency," New York City, 13–14 October 1939, 5, GCP, box 77, folder 2 (Wagner).

11. "Civil Liberties—A Field of Law," *Bill of Rights Review* 1 (Summer 1940): 7–9; Herbert Corey, "Defense Draws New Mark for Aliens to Toe," *Nation's Business,* October 1940: 21–23, 90–95, 95 ("such varied," quoting Henry Schweinhaut); John E. Mulder, "Democracy Must Introspect," *Bill of Rights Review* 1 (Summer 1941): 259–262, 259 (Bill of Rights week).

12. On the ABA and the origins of and precursors to the APA, see Joanna Grisinger, *The Unwieldy American State: Administrative Politics since the New Deal* (New York, 2012), 59–108; Daniel R. Ernst, *Tocqueville's Nightmare: The Administrative State Emerges in America, 1900–1940* (New York, 2014).

13. Grenville Clark to Monte Lemann, 8 March 1939, GCP, box 80, folder 18 ("fashionable"); Grenville Clark, "Perversions of Civil Liberties," *Bill of Rights Review* 1 (Summer 1941): 262 ("principle"; "independence"); Zechariah Chafee Jr. to Grenville Clark, 16 July 1941, GCP, box 78, folder 11.

14. Grenville Clark, "Perversions of Civil Liberties," *Bill of Rights Review* 1 (Summer 1941): 262; Gobitis v. Minersville School District, 24 F. Supp. 271 (E.D. Pa. 1938); Minersville School District v. Gobitis, 108 F.2d 685 (3d Cir. 1939); William Clark to Grenville Clark, 15 November 1939, GCP, box 78, folder 26; "The American Bar Association's Committee on the Bill of Rights," *Bill of Rights Review* 1 (Summer 1940): 66–68; Zechariah Chafee Jr. to George K. Gardner, 13 January 1939, GCP,

box 79, folder 5 ("obviously"). In April 1939, the ABA had filed a memorandum in support of jurisdiction in a separate flag salute case, *Johnson v.
Town of Deerfield*, 25 F. Supp. 918 (D. Mass. 1939); the Supreme Court
nonetheless affirmed in a per curiam opinion. As with all exercise of
government authority, Grenville Clark imagined a role for balancing
liberty against the legitimate needs of the state, but he denied that public
officials could compel participation in a ritual merely to enhance loyalty.
See Grenville Clark to Douglas Arant, 31 March 1939, GCP, box 77, folder
8 (listing as overriding government interests public health, internal safety
and order, public morals, and national service); Grenville Clark,
memorandum for members of the Committee on the Bill of Rights,
21 March 1940, GCP, box 78, folder 23. On the flag salute laws and
Gobitis, see Sarah Barringer Gordon, *The Spirit of the Law: Religious
Voices and the Constitution in Modern America* (Cambridge, MA, 2012),
27–47; Martha C. Nussbaum, *Liberty of Conscience: In Defense of
America's Tradition of Religious Equality* (New York, 2008), 199–214;
Shawn Francis Peters, *Judging Jehovah's Witnesses: Religious Persecution
and the Dawn of the Rights Revolution* (Lawrence, KS, 2000), 230–259;
Leah Weinryb-Grohsgal, *Reinventing Civil Liberties: Religious Groups,
Organized Litigation, and the Rights Revolution* (PhD dissertation,
Emory University, 2011). On the wartime expansion of the state, see
James Sparrow, *Warfare State: World War II Americans and the Age of
Big Government* (Oxford University Press, 2011). On Louis Lusky's
relationship to the ABA's Committee on the Bill of Rights, see Chapter 7.
15. Grenville Clark to George Gardner, 13 March 1940, GCP, box 79, folder 5
(on Lusky); Brief of the Committee on the Bill of Rights, of the American
Bar Association, as Friends of the Court, Minersville School District v.
Gobitis, No. 690, 310 U.S. 586 (1940), 18–19; Minersville School District
v. Gobitis, 310 U.S. 586 (1940); Brief for the American Civil Liberties
Union, Amicus Curiae, No. 690, 310 U.S. 586 (1940), West Virginia State
Board of Education v. Barnette, 319 U.S. 624 (1943); Brief of the Committee on the Bill of Rights of the American Bar Association as Friends of
the Court, West Virginia State Board of Education v. Barnette, No. 591,
319 U.S. 624 (1943), 10. Notably, Frankfurter left "personal freedom" to
the legislative process in *Gobitis* "[so] long as the remedial channels of the
democratic process remain open and unobstructed." Gobitis, 310 U.S. at
599. Lusky read Frankfurter as recognizing that legislative action
commanded deference least in the realm of expressive freedom, where
interference with democratic deliberation threatened to make laws
"self-perpetuating." Louis Lusky, "The Compulsory Flag Salute in the
Supreme Court," *Bull*, June 15, 1940, vol. 21, GCP, box 86, folder 4. On

Frankfurter's approach, see Melvin I. Urofsky, *Felix Frankfurter: Judicial Restraint and Individual Liberties* (Boston, 1991), 50–63.

16. Douglas Arant to Walter P. Armstrong, 26 July 1943, ZCP, reel 7 (choice of activities); Zechariah Chafee Jr., open letter, 22 January 1943, ZCP, reel 7.

17. "Draft of Interim Report of the Special Committee on the Bill of Rights," 24 February 1943, ZCP, reel 6; Esquire v. Walker, 55 F. Supp. 1015 (D.D.C. 1944). On the committee's later work, see Edson R. Sunderland, *History of the American Bar Association and Its Work* (1953), 193–197.

18. Robert M. Lichtman, *The Supreme Court and McCarthy-Era Repression* (Urbana, IL, 2012) (describing increasing willingness to challenge government policies after the appointment of Earl Warren as Chief Justice); 74 ABA Rep. 1949, 264–266 ("marked solicitude"); Grenville Clark to Osmer C. Fitts, 5 August 1958, GCP, box 78, folder 115 ("'perverted'"); Philip A. Graham, address to "A Publisher Looks at the Law," Association of the Bar of the City of New York, 15 November 1951, GCP, box 79, folder 22; "President's Letter on Rights and Security," *NYT*, September 19, 1951; Grenville Clark to Philip L. Graham, 12 March 1952, GCP, box 79, folder 22.

19. Felix Frankfurter, "Mr. Justice Roberts," *University of Pennsylvania Law Review* 104 (1955): 311–317, 315 (answering charges that Owen Roberts's "switch" was motivated by politics). See Mary Dudziak, *Cold War Civil Rights: Race and the Image of American Democracy* (Princeton, NJ, 2000); Christopher W. Schmidt, "The Civil Rights-Civil Liberties Divide," *Stanford Journal of Civil Rights and Civil Liberties* 12 (2016): 1–42.

20. Grenville Clark to Osmer C. Fitts, 5 August 1958, GCP, box 78, folder 115; Arthur Freund to Grenville Clark, 10 September 1959, GCP, box 78, folder 127; Irving Dilliard, "ABA Moves to Protect Individual's Rights," *Capital Times,* May 9, 1964. Answering Clark's concerns, Arthur Freund reported that when Attorney General William Pierce Rogers spoke in support of the "integration opinions of the Court," "he received the greatest ovation [Freund had] ever witnessed at an ABA meeting." Arthur Freund to Grenville Clark, 9 September 1958, GCP, box 78, folder 127.

21. This vast literature includes Derrick A. Bell Jr., "Serving Two Masters: Integration Ideals and Client Interests in School Desegregation Litigation," *Yale Law Journal* 85 (1976): 470–516; William E. Forbath, *Law and the Shaping of the American Labor Movement* (Cambridge, MA, 1991); Marc Galanter, "Why the 'Haves' Come Out Ahead: Speculations on the Limits of Legal Change," *Law and Society Review* 9 (1974): 95–160; Howard Gillman, *The Constitution Besieged: The Rise and Demise of Lochner Era Police Powers Jurisprudence* (Durham, NC, 1993); Robert W. Gordon, "Critical Legal Histories," *Stanford Law Review* 36 (1984):

57–125; Michael J. Klarman, *From Jim Crow to Civil Rights: The Supreme Court and the Struggle for Racial Equality* (New York, 2004); Michael W. McCann, *Rights at Work: Pay Equity Reform and the Politics of Legal Mobilization* (Chicago, 1994); Larry D. Kramer, *The People Themselves: Popular Constitutionalism and Judicial Review* (New York, 2004); Martha Nussbaum, "Foreword: Constitutions and Capabilities: 'Perception' against Lofty Formalism," *Harvard Law Review* 121 (2007): 4–97, 57; Gerald N. Rosenberg, *The Hollow Hope: Can Courts Bring About Social Change?* (Chicago, 1991); Robert Post and Reva Siegel, "Roe Rage: Democratic Constitutionalism and Backlash," *Harvard Civil Rights-Civil Liberties Law Review* 42 (2007): 373–434; Cass R. Sunstein, *One Case at a Time: Judicial Minimalism on the Supreme Court* (Cambridge, MA, 1999); Mark Tushnet, *Taking the Constitution Away from the Courts* (Cambridge, MA, 1999).

22. On uses of the First Amendment during the 1960s, see Risa Goluboff, *Vagrant Nation: Police Power, Constitutional Change, and the Making of the 1960s* (New York, 2016). Beginning in the 1980s, a growing body of scholarship identified and responded to this shift. See, for example, Owen Fiss, *Liberalism Divided: Freedom of Speech and the Many Uses of State Power* (Boulder, CO, 1996); Mark Graber, *Transforming Free Speech: The Ambiguous Legacy of Civil Libertarianism* (Berkeley, 1991); Morton Horwitz, "Foreword: The Constitution of Change: Legal Fundamentality without Fundamentalism," *Harvard Law Review* 30 (1993): 30–117, 109 ("Lochnerization of the First Amendment"); Cass R. Sunstein, *Democracy and the Problem of Free Speech* (New York, 1993).

23. "Symposium on Civil Liberties," AALS Annual Meeting, Chicago, December 27, 1940, *American Law School Review* 9 (April 1941): 881 ("major"); Cantwell v. Connecticut, 310 U.S. 296 (1940); Charles O. Gregory, "Peaceful Picketing and Freedom of Speech," *ABA Journal* 26 (1940): 709–715, 714–715. *Thornhill* and *Carlson* are discussed in Chapter 8.

24. Charles O. Gregory, "Peaceful Picketing and Freedom of Speech," *ABA Journal* 26 (1940): 709–715, 712 ("invest[ed] both"); Letter from Garvin Croonquist, "Are Peddlers a Nuisance?," *Nation's Business*, September 1940, 51; John Hosch Jr., Newspaper Publishers Committee, to Grenville Clark, 1 June 1941, GCP, box 79, folder 69; Samuel Pettengill, "What's Ahead for America?," *Nation's Business,* June 1941, 33; Albert W. Hawkes, "Rights and Duties of Business," 1 December 1941, CCUSR, box 12, 5 (address by president of the Chamber of Commerce of the United States).

25. Sherman Minton, address to American Press Society, 13 August 1938, GCP, box 80, folder 90; Respondents' Brief, Hague v. CIO, 307 U.S. 532 (1939) (No. 651), 151–152; Wendell Berge, address to John B. Stetson University College of Law, 3 May 1941, GCP, box 77, folder 41 (quoting

Robert H. Jackson, address to Council of State Governments, 21 January 1941) (attributing strength of American freedom to a "steady diet of propaganda—Republican propaganda, Democratic propaganda, Manufacturers' Association propaganda, labor propaganda, Communist propaganda, and Fascist-Nazi propaganda, to say nothing of high-powered advertising propaganda of every kind").

26. "Civil Liberties Union Condemns Labor Bill," *NYT,* June 16, 1947 ("direct," quoting ACLU); "Setback Reported for Civil Liberties," *NYT,* September 3, 1947 ("justified," quoting ACLU).

27. Labor-Management Relations Act, 61 Stat. 136 (1947); NLRB v. Gissel Packing, 395 U.S. 575, 617 (1969); "Revision in Labor Law Is Asked to End Political Spending Curb," *NYT,* July 12, 1947; Teamsters Union v. Vogt, 354 U.S. 284 (1957). On the rise of industrial pluralism and the corresponding preference for collective bargaining in place of the strike, see Christopher L. Tomlins, "The New Deal, Collective Bargaining, and the Triumph of Industrial Pluralism," *Industrial Labor Relations Review* 39 (1985): 19–34. The mature NLRB tolerated strikes primarily in response to employer interference with collective bargaining. Peter H. Irons, *The New Deal Lawyers* (Princeton, NJ, 1982), 295–296; Karl E. Klare, "Labor Law as Ideology: Toward a New Historiography of Collective Bargaining Law," *Berkeley Journal of Employment and Labor Law* 4 (1981): 450–482, 454–456.

28. Friedrichs v. California Teachers Association, No. 14-915, 2016 WL 1191684 (U.S. Mar. 29, 2016) (per curiam) (affirming by an equally divided court). Meanwhile, recent NLRB decisions have signaled concern for First Amendment principles in finding that new forms of labor protest are not "coercive" and thus do not violate restrictions on secondary activity under section 8(b)(4) of the NLRA. See Catherine Fisk and Jessica Rutter, "Labor Protest under the New First Amendment," *Berkeley Journal of Labor and Employment Law* 36 (2015): 277–329, 322.

29. Rose Feld, "Down with Censors! A Crusading Chronicle of Their Constant Threat to Books, Movies and Radio," *New York Herald-Tribune,* February 11, 1940.

30. ACLU board minutes, 16 October 1939, ACLUM, reel 7. On the crucial role of lawyers and legal advocacy groups, including compromise, in institutionalizing legal claims, see Jack M. Balkin, *Constitutional Redemption: Political Faith in an Unjust World* (Cambridge, MA, 2011); William N. Eskridge Jr., "Some Effects of Identity-Based Social Movements on Constitutional Law in the Twentieth Century," *Michigan Law Review* 100 (2002): 2062–2407; Marc Galanter, "Why the 'Haves' Come Out Ahead: Speculations on the Limits of Legal Change," *Law and*

Society Review 9 (1974): 95–160; Robert A. Kagan, *Adversarial Legalism: The American Way of Law* (Cambridge, MA, 2001).

31. ACLU, *Presenting the American Civil Liberties Union, Inc., November 1941* (New York, 1941), 3 ("battleground"); ACLU, *Presenting the American Civil Liberties Union, April 1947* (New York, 1947), 5 ("where decisions"); Roger Baldwin, introduction to *American Civil Liberties Union Annual Reports*, vol. 1 (New York, 1970) ("whole court"), xxii.

32. Alexander Crosby, "Baldwin Denies Civil Liberties Union Is Turning against Labor," 7 March 1940, GJP, General Correspondence, cont. 3; Merle D. Vincent to John Haynes Holmes, 9 May 1940, ACLUR, box 75, folder 8 ("large part"); Abraham Isserman to ACLU board 25 February 1941, ILDP, reel 19, box 21, 5 ("their right," quoting January 1940 ACLU policy statement), 6 ("autocratic," describing ACLU proposed study; "destructive," describing report on Dies Committee); ACLU, *A Report on American Democratic Liberties in War-Time* (New York, 1942), 22 ("democratic"); ACLU, *Civil Liberty: A Statement Defining the Position of the American Civil Liberties Union* (New York, 1945) ("not only of"); ACLU, *A Labor Union "Bill of Rights": Democracy in Labor Unions* (New York, 1958), 9 ("Unions should," reprint of a 1952 statement unanimously approved by the ACLU's board of directors). Ernst had also advocated an equivalent of the Securities and Exchange Commission for civil liberties, under which labor unions would be required to disclose their financial affairs and activities. Draft of proposal, MLEP, box 141, folder 13. On the ACLU's involvement in cases challenging segregated unions, see Sophia Z. Lee, *The Workplace Constitution from the New Deal to the New Right* (New York, 2014), 42–48. The ACLU did not endorse right-to-work laws. ACLU, *Democracy in Labor Unions*.

33. ACLU, *Liberty's National Emergency: The Story of Civil Liberty in the Crisis Year 1940–1941* (New York, 1941), 4 (right to organize); "Pickets Criticized by Liberties Union," *NYT*, January 21, 1946 ("keep").

34. ACLU, *Are You Free to See, Hear, Read?* (New York, 1947) ("sword"); ACLU, *Clearing the Main Channels* (New York, 1955), 101 ("fail[ed]"). On the perception that the department's new program would be less "radical" and more consistent with public opinion, see Risa Lauren Goluboff, *The Lost Promise of Civil Rights* (Cambridge, MA, 2007), 112. The Civil Rights Section pursued claims under the Thirteenth Amendment.

35. "Memorandum by Morris Ernst Prepared at the Request of the [ACLU] Board of Directors at the Special Meeting," 9 October 1941, LMP, box 11, folder "Morris Ernst" ("flow"); ACLU, *Liberty on the Home Front: In the Fourth Year of War* (New York, 1945), 60 ("traditional principles").

36. ACLU, *Radio Programs in the Public Interest* (New York, July 1946).

37. John Haynes Holmes to Alexander Meiklejohn, 27 January 1942, AMP, box 16, folder 37 ("public interest," quoting Meiklejohn; "first step"); "Memorandum by Morris Ernst Prepared at the Request of the [ACLU] Board of Directors at the Special Meeting," 9 October 1941, LMP, box 11, folder "Morris Ernst"; ACLU, *Are you Free,* 2 ("evils").

38. ACLU, *War-Time,* 17 (citing a commercial handbill decision); ACLU, "The ACLU and Citizens United," accessed March 22, 2016, https://www.aclu.org /aclu-and-citizens-united.

39. Roger Baldwin to Alexander Meiklejohn, 8 December 1941, AMP, box 4, folder 4.

40. IJA, "Civil Liberties and the NLRB," reprinted from address by Nathan Greene, 8 March 1940, MSC, folder 54:17, 5 (emphasis in original).

41. Constance L. Todd to Roger Baldwin, 7 May 1940, ACLUR, box 75, folder 11.

42. Roger Baldwin to John S. Codman, 7 July 1937, ACLUR, reel 142, vol. 969.

43. ACLU, *In Defense of Our Liberties: A Report of the American Civil Liberties Union in the Third Year of the War* (New York, 1944), 23 ("race relations"); ACLU, *Are you Free to See, Hear, Read?* (New York, June 1947), 8 ("isms"); ACLU, *Presenting* (1947), 2–3; Alexander Crosby, "Baldwin Denies Civil Liberties Union Is Turning against Labor," 7 March 1940, GJP, General Correspondence, cont. 3 (quoting Baldwin).

Acknowledgments

It is a great pleasure to thank the many individuals and institutions that have made this book possible. My acknowledgments begin where the book did, with Hendrik Hartog, who has advised the project since its inception. Dirk has immeasurably enriched countless drafts, and his extraordinary insight and unflagging encouragement have shaped every element of my trajectory as a scholar. I am immensely grateful for his friendship and guidance.

The roots of this project were laid in debates with the staff of the *Harvard Civil Rights-Civil Liberties Law Review*, with whom I explored the contradictions implicit in our journal's title. During the early stages of my research at Princeton University, Margot Canaday, Stanley Katz, Kevin Kruse, and Kim Lane Scheppele offered formative comments. Owen Fiss helped to refine the theoretical framework. Christine Stansell deeply influenced my approach to the materials and pushed me to write concisely and to think historically. Daniel Rodgers read my work with painstaking care; he broadened my perspective and sharpened my analysis.

Many others have offered crucial suggestions and clarifications along the way. For their myriad contributions, my sincere gratitude goes to Christopher Beauchamp, Debbie Becher, Richard Bernstein, Susanna Blumenthal, Erin Buzuvis, Jane Dailey, Deborah Dinner, Lauren Dubick, Daniel Ernst, William Forbath, Aurelie Gfeller, David Golove, Risa Goluboff, Robert Gordon, Alex Gourevitch, Sarah Barringer Gordon, Joanna Grisinger, Laura Kadetsky, Linda Kerber, Jeremy Kessler, Andrew Koppelman, Jedidiah Kroncke, Sam Lebovic, Jessica Lowe, Kenneth Mack, Deborah Malamud, Sara McDougall, Laura Mutterperl, Burt Neuborne, William Novak, Nicholas Parrillo, James Gray Pope, Intisar Rabb, David Rabban, Aziz Rana, Gautham Rao, Austin Sarat, Reuel Schiller, Christopher Schmidt, Louis Michael Seidman, Mitra Sharafi, David

Tanenhaus, Louisa Thomas, Mark Tushnet, Dov Weinryb Grohsgal, Leah Weinryb Grohsgal, Barbara Welke, Michael Wolraich, John Fabian Witt, Lawrence Zacharias, and Emily Zackin. As a Samuel I. Golieb Fellow at New York University School of Law, I benefited tremendously from the counsel of Daniel Hulsebosch, William Nelson, and John Phillip Reid. Members of two writing groups provided friendship and encouragement in addition to incisive criticism: Hannah Weiss Muller, Elena Schneider, and Jason Sharples; and Merlin Chowkwanyun, Sophia Lee, and Karen Tani. My colleagues at the University of Chicago have been enormously helpful in reading and improving portions or full drafts of the manuscript, especially Emily Buss, Mary Anne Case, Richard Epstein, Tom Ginsburg, Aziz Huq, Alison LaCroix, Genevieve Lakier, Martha Nussbaum, and David Strauss. Catherine Fisk and Geoffrey Stone, along with the anonymous readers for Harvard University Press, deserve special mention for their generosity in providing detailed feedback on the full manuscript during the final stages of revision. I am also very fortunate to have had the help of an outstanding research assistant, Evelyn Atkinson, in proofreading the book.

I deeply appreciate the questions and comments of participants at the workshops and conferences where I have presented chapters, including the annual meetings of the American Society for Legal History and of the Law and Society Association; the University of Pennsylvania Legal History Consortium; Princeton University's Center for Human Values, Program in Law and Public Affairs, and Modern America Workshop; the Cornell Law and Humanities Colloquium; the Brown University Watson Institute; the American Bar Foundation; the University of Virginia Legal History Workshop; the University of Minnesota Legal History Workshop; the Yale Legal History Forum; the NYU Law School Legal History Colloquium; the J. Willard Hurst Summer Institute in Legal History; and the University of Chicago Faculty Works in Progress workshop.

I am grateful to the many librarians and archivists who facilitated my research at the Benson Ford Research Center; the Georgetown University Special Collections; the Franklin D. Roosevelt Presidential Library; the Swarthmore College Peace Collection; the National Archives and Record Administration; the Wesleyan University Special Collections and Archives; the Walter P. Reuther Library of Labor and Urban Affairs at Wayne State University; the Cornell University Kheel Center; the Schlesinger Library; the Wisconsin Historical Society Archives; the Hagley Museum and Library; the Rauner Special Collection Library at Dartmouth College; and the Harry Ransom Humanities Research Center of the University of Texas at Austin. I appreciate the assistance of Shannon Hildenbrand in tracking down re-cataloged sources. Special thanks to Daniel Linke and Jarrett Drake at Princeton University's Seeley G. Mudd Manuscript Library and to the staff of the University of Chicago Law School library, including Sheri Lewis, Greg Nimmo, and Margaret Schilt, and especially Thomas

Drueke for his heroic undertaking in digitally processing my archival images and citation-checking the manuscript.

I have received generous financial assistance from the University of Chicago Law School, including the Legal History Fund and the Roger Levin Faculty Fund; Princeton University's Department of History and Center for Human Values; the New York University School of Law; the Harry Ransom Center at the University of Texas at Austin; the American Society for Legal History; and the William Nelson Cromwell Foundation.

My sincere thanks to Joyce Seltzer at Harvard University Press for trusting in the project and expertly shepherding it to completion. I am also grateful to Brian Distelberg and Kathleen Drummy for their assistance, to Derek Gottlieb for skillful indexing, and to Ashley Moore and Kimberly Giambattisto for excellent copyediting.

The longer path to this book began well before my graduate studies in history. I am indebted to Judge Thomas Ambro, John Benson, Beatrice Hanssen, Mike Herzig, and Martha Minow for fostering my intellectual and professional development and steering me toward historical scholarship.

Finally, I am profoundly grateful to my family. My brother, Oren, and my parents, Estee and Richard, have read innumerable drafts, carefully, astutely, and with enthusiastic encouragement. They are by my side whenever I need them, unhesitatingly and with love. My children, Simon and Eleanor, are a source of unceasing joy and inspiration. Above all, this book would not have been possible without my spouse and partner, David. He has patiently endured my many marathons. His emotional and intellectual support will sustain me well after the book is in print.

Index